2nd Workshop on Statistical Machine Translation 2007

(WMT 07)

Held in conjunction with ACL 2007

Prague, Czech Republic
23 June 2007

ISBN: 978-1-61738-518-6

Printed from e-media with permission by:

Curran Associates, Inc.
57 Morehouse Lane
Red Hook, NY 12571

Printed by Curran Associates, Inc. (2010)

Association for Computational Linguistics
209 N. Eighth Street
Stroudsburg, Pennsylvania 18360

Phone: 1-570-476-8006
Fax: 1-570-476-0860

acl@aclweb.org

Additional copies of this publication are available from:

Curran Associates, Inc.
57 Morehouse Lane
Red Hook, NY 12571 USA
Phone: 845-758-0400
Fax: 845-758-2634
Email: curran@proceedings.com
Web: www.proceedings.com

Preface

The ACL 2007 Workshop on Statistical Machine Translation (WMT-07) took place on Saturday, June 23 in Prague, Czech Republic, immediately preceding the annual meeting of the Association for Computational Linguistics, which was hosted by Charles University. This was the second time this workshop had been held, following the first workshop at the 2006 HLT-NAACL conference. But its ancestry can be traced back farther to the ACL 2005 Workshop on Building and Using Parallel Texts (when we started our evaluation campaign on European languages), and even the ACL 2001 Workshop on Data-Driven Machine Translation (which was the first ACL workshop mostly directed at statistical machine translation).

Over the last years, interest in statistical machine translation has been risen dramatically. We received an overwhelming number of full paper submission for a one-day workshop, 38 in total. Given our limited capacity, we were only able to accept 12 full papers for oral presentation and 9 papers for poster presentation, an acceptance rate of 55%. In a second poster session, 16 additional shared task papers were presented. The workshop also featured an invited talk by Jean Senellart of SYSTRAN Language Translation Technology, Paris.

Prior to the workshop, in addition to soliciting relevant papers for review and possible presentation we conducted a shared task that brought together machine translation systems for an evaluation on previously unseen data. This year's task resembled the shared tasks of previous years in many ways. Its focus was again the translation of European languages, using a relatively large training corpus. This year, we included a variety of manual evaluations of the MT systems' outputs, and a variety of automated evaluation metrics. Also, as a special challenge this year, we posed the problem of domain adaptation.

The results of the shared task were announced at the workshop, and these proceedings also include an overview paper for the shared task that summarizes the results, as well as provides information about the data used and any procedures that were followed in conducting or scoring the task. In addition, there are short papers from each participating team that describe their underlying system in some detail.

We would like to thank the members of the Program Committee for their timely reviews. We also would like to thank the participants of the shared task, the participants of the MT Marathon, which was organized by the University of Edinburgh in March this year, and all the other volunteers who helped with the manual evaluations. We also acknowledge financial support for the manual evaluation by the EuroMatrix project (funded by the European Commission under the Framework Programme 6).

Chris Callison-Burch, Philipp Koehn, Christof Monz, and Cameron Shaw Fordyce

Co-Organizers

Organizers

Chairs:

Chris Callison-Burch (Johns Hopkins University)
Philipp Koehn (University of Edinburgh)
Christof Monz (Queen Mary, University of London)
Cameron Shaw Fordyce (Center for the Evaluation of Language and Communication Technologies)

Invited Speaker:

Jean Senellart (SYSTRAN Language Translation Technology, Paris)

Program Committee:

Lars Ahrenberg (Linköping University)
Francisco Casacuberta (University of Valencia)
Colin Cherry (University of Alberta)
Stephen Clark (Oxford University)
Brooke Cowan (Massachusetts Institute of Technology)
Mona Diab (Columbia University)
Chris Dyer (University of Maryland)
Andreas Eisele (University Saarbrücken)
Marcello Federico (ITC-IRST)
George Foster (Canada National Research Council)
Alex Fraser (ISI/University of Southern California)
Ulrich Germann (University of Toronto)
Rebecca Hwa (University of Pittsburgh)
Kevin Knight (ISI/University of Southern California)
Philippe Langlais (University of Montreal)
Alon Lavie (Carnegie Melon University)
Lori Levin (Carnegie Mellon University)
Daniel Marcu (ISI/University of Southern California)
Bob Moore (Microsoft Research)
Miles Osborne (University of Edinburgh)
Michel Simard (Canada National Research Council)
Eiichiro Sumita (NICT/ATR)
Jörg Tiedemann (University of Groningen)
Christoph Tillmann (IBM Research)
Dan Tufiş (Romanian Academy)
Taro Watanabe (NTT)
Dekai Wu (HKUST)
Richard Zens (RWTH Aachen)

Additional Reviewers: Joshua Albrecht, Marine Carpuat, Hirofumi Yamamoto, and Keiji Yasuda.

Table of Contents

Using Dependency Order Templates to Improve Generality in Translation
Arul Menezes and Chris Quirk 1

CCG Supertags in Factored Statistical Machine Translation
Alexandra Birch, Miles Osborne and Philipp Koehn 9

Integration of an Arabic Transliteration Module into a Statistical Machine Translation System
Mehdi M. Kashani, Eric Joanis, Roland Kuhn, George Foster and Fred Popowich 17

Exploring Different Representational Units in English-to-Turkish Statistical Machine Translation
Kemal Oflazer and Ilknur Durgar El-Kahlout 25

Can We Translate Letters?
David Vilar, Jan-Thorsten Peter and Hermann Ney 33

A Dependency Treelet String Correspondence Model for Statistical Machine Translation
Deyi Xiong, Qun Liu and Shouxun Lin 40

Word Error Rates: Decomposition over POS classes and Applications for Error Analysis
Maja Popovic and Hermann Ney 48

Speech-Input Multi-Target Machine Translation
Alicia Pérez, M. Teresa González, M. Inés Torres and Francisco Casacuberta 56

Meta-Structure Transformation Model for Statistical Machine Translation
Jiadong Sun, Tiejun Zhao and Huashen Liang 64

Training Non-Parametric Features for Statistical Machine Translation
Patrick Nguyen, Milind Mahajan and Xiaodong He 72

Using Word-Dependent Transition Models in HMM-Based Word Alignment for Statistical Machine Translation
Xiaodong He 80

Efficient Handling of N-gram Language Models for Statistical Machine Translation
Marcello Federico and Mauro Cettolo 88

Human Evaluation of Machine Translation Through Binary System Comparisons
David Vilar, Gregor Leusch, Hermann Ney and Rafael E. Banchs 96

Labelled Dependencies in Machine Translation Evaluation
Karolina Owczarzak, Josef van Genabith and Andy Way 104

An Iteratively-Trained Segmentation-Free Phrase Translation Model for Statistical Machine Translation
Robert Moore and Chris Quirk 112

Using Paraphrases for Parameter Tuning in Statistical Machine Translation
Nitin Madnani, Necip Fazil Ayan, Philip Resnik and Bonnie Dorr 120

Mixture-Model Adaptation for SMT
George Foster and Roland Kuhn 128

(Meta-) Evaluation of Machine Translation
Chris Callison-Burch, Cameron Fordyce, Philipp Koehn, Christof Monz and Josh Schroeder . . . 136

Context-aware Discriminative Phrase Selection for Statistical Machine Translation
Jesús Giménez and Lluís Màrquez 159

Ngram-Based Statistical Machine Translation Enhanced with Multiple Weighted Reordering Hypotheses
Marta R. Costa-jussià, Josep M. Crego, Patrik Lambert, Maxim Khalilov, José A. R. Fonollosa, José B. Mario and Rafael E. Banchs 167

Analysis of Statistical and Morphological Classes to Generate Weigthed Reordering Hypotheses on a Statistical Machine Translation System
Marta R. Costa-jussià and José A. R. Fonollosa 171

Domain Adaptation in Statistical Machine Translation with Mixture Modelling
Jorge Civera and Alfons Juan 177

Getting to Know Moses: Initial Experiments on German-English Factored Translation
Maria Holmqvist, Sara Stymne and Lars Ahrenberg 181

NRC's PORTAGE System for WMT 2007
Nicola Ueffing, Michel Simard, Samuel Larkin and Howard Johnson 185

Building a Statistical Machine Translation System for French Using the Europarl Corpus
Holger Schwenk 189

Multi-Engine Machine Translation with an Open-Source SMT Decoder
Yu Chen, Andreas Eisele, Christian Federmann, Eva Hasler, Michael Jellinghaus and Silke Theison 193

The ISL Phrase-Based MT System for the 2007 ACL Workshop on Statistical Machine Translation
Matthias Paulik, Kay Rottmann, Jan Niehues, Silja Hildebrand and Stephan Vogel 197

Rule-Based Translation with Statistical Phrase-Based Post-Editing
Michel Simard, Nicola Ueffing, Pierre Isabelle and Roland Kuhn 203

The "Noisier Channel": Translation from Morphologically Complex Languages
Christopher J. Dyer 207

UCB System Description for the WMT 2007 Shared Task
Preslav Nakov and Marti Hearst 212

The Syntax Augmented MT (SAMT) System at the Shared Task for the 2007 ACL Workshop on Statistical Machine Translation
Andreas Zollmann, Ashish Venugopal, Matthias Paulik and Stephan Vogel 216

Statistical Post-Editing on SYSTRAN's Rule-Based Translation System
Loïc Dugast, Jean Senellart and Philipp Koehn 220

Experiments in Domain Adaptation for Statistical Machine Translation
Philipp Koehn and Josh Schroeder 224

METEOR: An Automatic Metric for MT Evaluation with High Levels of Correlation with Human Judgments
Alon Lavie and Abhaya Agarwal 228

English-to-Czech Factored Machine Translation
Ondřej Bojar 232

Sentence Level Machine Translation Evaluation as a Ranking
Yang Ye, Ming Zhou and Chin-Yew Lin 240

Localization of Difficult-to-Translate Phrases
Behrang Mohit and Rebecca Hwa 248

Linguistic Features for Automatic Evaluation of Heterogenous MT Systems
Jesús Giménez and Lluís Màrquez 256

Conference Program

Saturday, June 23, 2007

8:30–8:35 Opening Remarks

Full Paper Session 1

8:35–8:55 *Using Dependency Order Templates to Improve Generality in Translation*
Arul Menezes and Chris Quirk

8:55–9:15 *CCG Supertags in Factored Statistical Machine Translation*
Alexandra Birch, Miles Osborne and Philipp Koehn

9:15–9:35 *Integration of an Arabic Transliteration Module into a Statistical Machine Translation System*
Mehdi M. Kashani, Eric Joanis, Roland Kuhn, George Foster and Fred Popowich

9:35–9:55 *Exploring Different Representational Units in English-to-Turkish Statistical Machine Translation*
Kemal Oflazer and Ilknur Durgar El-Kahlout

9:55–10:15 *Can We Translate Letters?*
David Vilar, Jan-Thorsten Peter and Hermann Ney

Poster Session for Full Papers

10:15–10:45 Boaster session for full paper posters

10:45–11:45 Coffee break + full paper poster session

A Dependency Treelet String Correspondence Model for Statistical Machine Translation
Deyi Xiong, Qun Liu and Shouxun Lin

Word Error Rates: Decomposition over POS classes and Applications for Error Analysis
Maja Popovic and Hermann Ney

Speech-Input Multi-Target Machine Translation
Alicia Pérez, M. Teresa González, M. Inés Torres and Francisco Casacuberta

Saturday, June 23, 2007 (continued)

Meta-Structure Transformation Model for Statistical Machine Translation
Jiadong Sun, Tiejun Zhao and Huashen Liang

Training Non-Parametric Features for Statistical Machine Translation
Patrick Nguyen, Milind Mahajan and Xiaodong He

Using Word-Dependent Transition Models in HMM-Based Word Alignment for Statistical Machine Translation
Xiaodong He

Efficient Handling of N-gram Language Models for Statistical Machine Translation
Marcello Federico and Mauro Cettolo

Human Evaluation of Machine Translation Through Binary System Comparisons
David Vilar, Gregor Leusch, Hermann Ney and Rafael E. Banchs

Labelled Dependencies in Machine Translation Evaluation
Karolina Owczarzak, Josef van Genabith and Andy Way

Invited Talk

11:45–12:30 Invited Talk by Jean Senellart, Systran

Lunch

Full Paper Session 2

14:00–14:20 *An Iteratively-Trained Segmentation-Free Phrase Translation Model for Statistical Machine Translation*
Robert Moore and Chris Quirk

14:20–14:40 *Using Paraphrases for Parameter Tuning in Statistical Machine Translation*
Nitin Madnani, Necip Fazil Ayan, Philip Resnik and Bonnie Dorr

14:40–15:00 *Mixture-Model Adaptation for SMT*
George Foster and Roland Kuhn

Saturday, June 23, 2007 (continued)

Shared Task

15:00–15:15 *(Meta-) Evaluation of Machine Translation*
Chris Callison-Burch, Cameron Fordyce, Philipp Koehn, Christof Monz and Josh Schroeder

15:15–15:45 Boaster session for shared task posters

15:45–16:45 Coffee break + shared task poster session

Context-aware Discriminative Phrase Selection for Statistical Machine Translation
Jesús Giménez and Lluís Màrquez

Ngram-Based Statistical Machine Translation Enhanced with Multiple Weighted Reordering Hypotheses
Marta R. Costa-jussià, Josep M. Crego, Patrik Lambert, Maxim Khalilov, José A. R. Fonollosa, José B. Mario and Rafael E. Banchs

Analysis of Statistical and Morphological Classes to Generate Weigthed Reordering Hypotheses on a Statistical Machine Translation System
Marta R. Costa-jussià and José A. R. Fonollosa

Domain Adaptation in Statistical Machine Translation with Mixture Modelling
Jorge Civera and Alfons Juan

Getting to Know Moses: Initial Experiments on German-English Factored Translation
Maria Holmqvist, Sara Stymne and Lars Ahrenberg

NRC's PORTAGE System for WMT 2007
Nicola Ueffing, Michel Simard, Samuel Larkin and Howard Johnson

Building a Statistical Machine Translation System for French Using the Europarl Corpus
Holger Schwenk

Multi-Engine Machine Translation with an Open-Source SMT Decoder
Yu Chen, Andreas Eisele, Christian Federmann, Eva Hasler, Michael Jellinghaus and Silke Theison

The ISL Phrase-Based MT System for the 2007 ACL Workshop on Statistical Machine Translation
Matthias Paulik, Kay Rottmann, Jan Niehues, Silja Hildebrand and Stephan Vogel

Saturday, June 23, 2007 (continued)

Rule-Based Translation with Statistical Phrase-Based Post-Editing
Michel Simard, Nicola Ueffing, Pierre Isabelle and Roland Kuhn

The "Noisier Channel": Translation from Morphologically Complex Languages
Christopher J. Dyer

UCB System Description for the WMT 2007 Shared Task
Preslav Nakov and Marti Hearst

The Syntax Augmented MT (SAMT) System at the Shared Task for the 2007 ACL Workshop on Statistical Machine Translation
Andreas Zollmann, Ashish Venugopal, Matthias Paulik and Stephan Vogel

Statistical Post-Editing on SYSTRAN's Rule-Based Translation System
Loïc Dugast, Jean Senellart and Philipp Koehn

Experiments in Domain Adaptation for Statistical Machine Translation
Philipp Koehn and Josh Schroeder

METEOR: An Automatic Metric for MT Evaluation with High Levels of Correlation with Human Judgments
Alon Lavie and Abhaya Agarwal

Full Paper Session 4

16:45–17:05 *English-to-Czech Factored Machine Translation*
Ondřej Bojar

17:05–17:25 *Sentence Level Machine Translation Evaluation as a Ranking*
Yang Ye, Ming Zhou and Chin-Yew Lin

17:25–17:45 *Localization of Difficult-to-Translate Phrases*
Behrang Mohit and Rebecca Hwa

17:45–18:05 *Linguistic Features for Automatic Evaluation of Heterogenous MT Systems*
Jesús Giménez and Lluís Màrquez

Using Dependency Order Templates to Improve Generality in Translation

Arul Menezes and **Chris Quirk**
Microsoft Research
One Microsoft Way, Redmond, WA 98052, USA
{arulm, chrisq}@microsoft.com

Abstract

Today's statistical machine translation systems generalize poorly to new domains. Even small shifts can cause precipitous drops in translation quality. Phrasal systems rely heavily, for both reordering and contextual translation, on long phrases that simply fail to match out-of-domain text. Hierarchical systems attempt to generalize these phrases but their learned rules are subject to severe constraints. Syntactic systems can learn lexicalized and unlexicalized rules, but the joint modeling of lexical choice and reordering can narrow the applicability of learned rules. The treelet approach models reordering separately from lexical choice, using a discriminatively trained order model, which allows treelets to apply broadly, and has shown better generalization to new domains, but suffers a factorially large search space. We introduce a new reordering model based on *dependency order templates*, and show that it outperforms both phrasal and treelet systems on in-domain and out-of-domain text, while limiting the search space.

1 Introduction

Modern phrasal SMT systems such as (Koehn et al., 2003) derive much of their power from being able to memorize and use long phrases. Phrases allow for non-compositional translation, local reordering and contextual lexical choice. However the phrases are fully lexicalized, which means they generalize poorly to even slightly out-of-domain text. In an open competition (Koehn & Monz, 2006) systems trained on parliamentary proceedings were tested on text from 'news commentary' web sites, a very slightly different domain. The 9 phrasal systems in the English to Spanish track suffered an absolute drop in BLEU score of between 4.4% and 6.34% (14% to 27% relative). The treelet system of Menezes et al. (2006) fared somewhat better but still suffered an absolute drop of 3.61%.

Clearly there is a need for approaches with greater powers of generalization. There are multiple facets to this issue, including handling of unknown words, new senses of known words etc. In this work, we will focus on the issue of reordering, i.e. can we learn how to transform the sentence structure of one language into the sentence structure of another, in a way that is not tied to a specific domain or sub-domains, or indeed, sequences of individual words.

An early attempt at greater generality in a purely phrasal setting was the alignment template approach (Och & Ney 2004); newer approaches include formally syntactic (Chiang 2005), and linguistically syntactic approaches (Quirk et al. 2005), (Huang et al. 2006). In the next section, we examine these representative approaches to the reordering problem.

2 Related Work

Our discussion of related work will be grounded in the following tiny English to Spanish example, where the training set includes:

```
a very old book
un libro más  antiguo
a  book  very old[1]

the old man
el  hombre viejo
the man    old

it is very important
es muy  importante
is very important
```

[1] English gloss of Spanish sentences in italics.

Proceedings of the Second Workshop on Statistical Machine Translation, pages 1–8,
Prague, June 2007. ©2007 Association for Computational Linguistics

and the test sentence and reference translation are

```
a very old man
un hombre muy  viejo
a  man    very old
```

Note that while the first training pair has the correct structure for the test sentence, most of the contextually correct lexical choices come from the other two pairs.

2.1 Phrasal translation, Alignment templates

The relevant phrases (i.e. those that match the test sentence) extracted from these training pairs are shown in Table 2.1. Only phrases up to size 3 are shown. The ones in italics are 'correct' in that they can lead to the reference translation. Note that none of the multi-word phrases lead to the reference, so the local reordering often captured in the phrasal model is no help at all in ordering this sentence. The system is unable to learn the correct structure from the first sentence because the words are wrong, and from the second sentence even though the phrase *old man* has the right words in the right order, it does not lead to the reference translation because the translation of *very* cannot be inserted in the right place.

a	*un*
very	más
old	antiguo
very old	más antiguo
old	*viejo*
man	*hombre*
old man	hombre viejo
very	*muy*

Table 2.1: Relevant extracted phrases

Looking at this as a sparse data issue we might suspect that generalization could solve the problem. The alignment template approach (Och & Ney, 2004) uses word classes rather than lexical items to model phrase translation. Yet this approach loses the advantage of context-sensitive lexical selection: the word translation model depends only on the word classes to subcategorize for translations, which leads to less accurate lexical choice in practice (Zens & Ney, 2004).

2.2 Hierarchical translation

Hierarchical systems (Chiang, 2005) induce a context-free grammar with one non-terminal directly from the parallel corpus, with the advantage of not requiring any additional knowledge source or tools, such as a treebank or a parser. However this can lead to an explosion of rules. In order to make the problem tractable and avoid spurious ambiguity, Chiang restricts the learned rules in several ways. The most problematic of these is that every rule must have at least one pair of aligned words, and that adjacent non-terminals are not permitted on the source side. In Table 2.2 we show the additional hierarchical phrases that would be learned from our training pairs under these restrictions. Again only those applicable to the test sentence are shown and the 'correct' rules, i.e. those that lead to the reference, are italicized.

X1 old	X1 antiguo
very X1	más X1
very old X1	X1 más antiguo
X1 old X2	X2 X1 antiguo
very X1 X2	X2 más X1
X1 man	*hombre X1*
old X1	X1 viejo
X1 old man	X1 hombre viejo
X1 very	*X1 muy*
very X2	*muy X2*
X1 very X2	X1 muy X2

Table 2.2: Additional hierarchical phrases

Note that even though from the first pair, we learn several rules with the perfect reordering for the test sentence, they do not lead to the reference because they drag along the contextually incorrect lexical choices. From the second pair, we learn a rule (*X1 old man*) that has the right contextual word choice, but does not lead to the reference, because the paucity of the grammar's single non-terminal causes this rule to incorrectly imply that the translation of *very* be placed before *hombre.*

2.3 Constituency tree transduction

An alternate approach is to use linguistic information from a parser. Transduction rules between Spanish strings and English trees can be learned from a word-aligned parallel corpus with parse trees on one side (Graehl & Knight, 2004). Such rules can be used to translate from Spanish to English by searching for the best English language tree for a given Spanish language string (Marcu et al., 2006). Alternately English trees produced by a parser can be transduced to

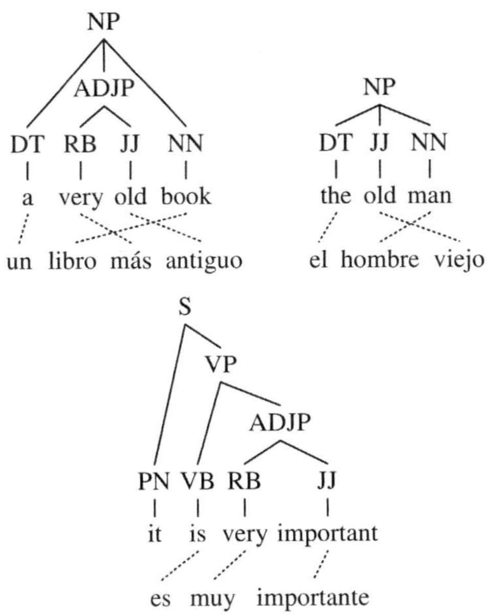

Figure 2.1: Constituency parses

Spanish strings using the same rules (Huang et al., 2006). Translation rules may reach beyond one level in the syntax tree; this extended domain of locality allows many phenomena including both lexicalized and unlexicalized rules. However reordering and translation are modeled jointly, which may exacerbate data sparsity. Furthermore it forces the system to pick between unlexicalized rules that capture reordering and lexicalized rules that model context-sensitive translation.

For instance, the following rules can be extracted from the first sentence of the corpus:

r_1: **un** x1 x2 → NP(DT(**a**) ADJP:x2 NN:x1)
r_2: x1 x2 → ADJP(RB:x1 JJ:x2)

Although together they capture the necessary reordering for our test sentence pair, they do not allow for context sensitive translations of the ambiguous terms *very* and *old*; each must be selected independently. Disappointingly, no single constituency tree transduction rule derived from this corpus translates *old man* as *hombre viejo* in a single step on the test sentence: the syntactic structures are slightly different, but the difference is sufficient to prevent matching.[2] Again we note that phrases provide utility by capturing both reordering and context. While xRS rules provide an elegant and powerful model of reordering, they come with a potential cost in context-sensitive translation.

2.4 Dependency treelet translation

We previously described (Quirk et al, 2005) a linguistically syntax-based system that parses the source language, uses word-based alignments to project a target dependency tree, and extracts paired dependency tree fragments (treelets) instead of surface phrases. In contrast to the xRS approach, ordering is very loosely coupled with translation via a separate discriminatively trained dependency tree-based order model. The switch to a dependency parse also changes the conditioning information available for translation: related lexical items are generally adjacent, rather than separated by a path of unlexicalized non-terminals. In effect, by using a looser matching requirement, treelets retain the context-sensitive lexical choice of phrases: treelets must only be a connected subgraph of the input sentence to be applicable; some children may remain uncovered.

Figure 2.2 shows source dependency parses and projected target dependencies for our training data; Figure 2.3 shows the treelet pairs that this system would extract that match the input

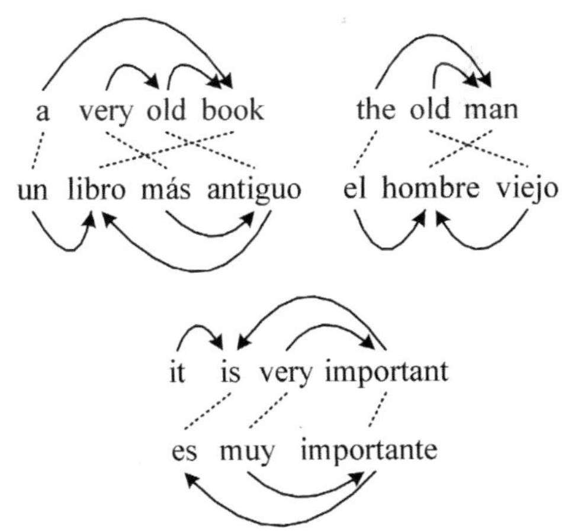

Figure 2.2: Dependency trees for training pairs

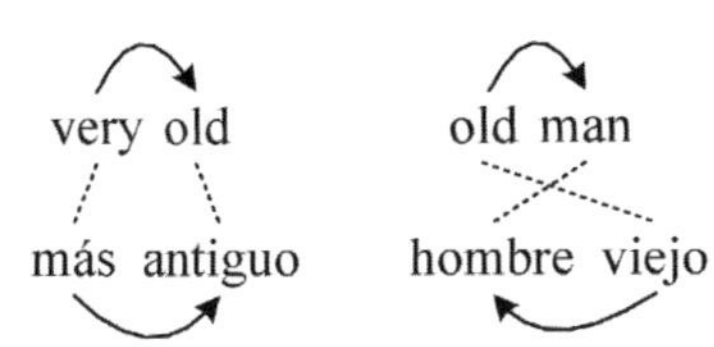

Figure 2.3: Relevant extracted treelets

[2] Marcu et al. (2006) and Zollmann et al. (2006) recognize this problem and attempt to alleviate it by grafting surface phrases into constituency trees by various methods.

sentence (treelets of size 1 are not shown). The second treelet supplies the order of *viejo* with respect to its head, and unlike the case with xRS rules, we can use this to make the correct contextual word choice. The difference is that because xRS rules provide *both* reordering and word choice, each rule must match all of the children at any given tree node. On the other hand, treelets are allowed to match more loosely. The translations of the unmatched children (*un* and *muy* in this case) are placed by exploring all possible orderings and scoring them with both order model and language model. Although this effectively decouples lexical selection from ordering, it comes at a huge cost in search space and translation quality may suffer due to search error. However, as mentioned in Section 1, this approach is able to generalize better to out-of-domain data than phrasal approaches. Koehn and Monz (2006) also include a human evaluation, in which this system ranked noticeably higher than one might have predicted from its BLEU score.

3 Dependency Order Templates

The Dependency Order Templates approach leverages the power of the xR rule formalism, while avoiding the problems mentioned in Section 2.3, by constructing the rules on the fly from two separately matched components: (a) Dependency treelet translation pairs described in Section 2.4 that capture contextual lexical translations but are underspecified with respect to ordering, and (b) Order templates, which are unlexicalized rules (over dependency, rather than constituency trees) that capture reordering phenomena.

Formally, an order template is an unlexicalized transduction rule mapping dependency trees containing only parts of speech to unlexicalized target language trees (see Figure 4.1b).

Given an input sentence, we combine relevant treelet translation pairs and order templates to construct lexicalized transduction rules for that sentence, and then decode using standard transduction approaches. By keeping lexical and ordering information orthogonal until runtime, we can produce novel transduction rules not seen in the training corpus. This allows greater generalization capabilities than the constituency tree transduction approaches of Section 2.3.

As compared to the treelet approach described in Section 2.4, the generalization capability is somewhat reduced. In the treelet system *all* reorderings are exhaustively evaluated, but the size of the search space necessitates tight pruning, leading to significant search error. By contrast, in the order template approach we consider only reorderings that are captured in some order template. The drastic reduction in search space leads to an overall improvement, not only in decoding speed, but also in translation quality due to reduced search error.

3.1 Extracting order templates

For each pair of parallel training sentences, we parse the source sentence, obtain a source dependency tree, and use GIZA++ word alignments to project a target dependency tree as described in Quirk et al. (2005).

Given this pair of aligned source and target dependency trees, we recursively extract one order template for each pair of aligned non-leaf source and target nodes. In the case of multi-word alignments, all contiguous [3] aligned nodes are added to the template. Next we recursively add child nodes as follows: For each node in the template, add all its children. For each such child, if it is aligned, stop recursing, if it is unaligned, recursively add its children.

On each template node we remove the lexical items; we retain the part of speech on the source nodes (we do not use target linguistic features). We also keep node alignment information[4]. The resulting aligned source and target sub-graphs comprise the order template. Figure 4.1b lists the order templates extracted from the training pairs in Figure 2.1 that capture all the patterns necessary to correctly reorder the test sentence.

4 Decoding

Decoding is treated as a problem of syntax-directed transduction. Input sentences are segmented into a token stream, annotated with part-of-speech information, and parsed into

[3] If a multi-word alignment is not contiguous in either source or target dependency tree no order template is extracted.
[4] If a source or target node aligns to a tree node outside the template, the template breaks phrasal cohesion and is currently discarded. We intend to address these 'structural divergence' patterns in future work.

unlabeled dependency trees. At each node in the input dependency tree we first find the set of matching treelet pairs: A pair matches if its source side corresponds to a connected subgraph of the input tree. Next we find matching order templates: order templates must also match a connected subgraph of the input tree, but in addition, for each input node, the template must match either all or none of its children [5]. Compatible combinations of treelets and order templates are merged to form xR rules. Finally, we search for the best transduction according to the constructed xR rules as scored by a log-linear combination of models (see Section 5).

4.1 Compatibility

A treelet and an order template are considered compatible if the following conditions are met: The treelet and the matching portions of the template must be structurally isomorphic. Every treelet node must match an order template node. Matching nodes must have the same part of speech. Unaligned treelet nodes must match an unaligned template node. Aligned treelet nodes must match aligned template nodes. Nodes that are aligned to each other in the treelet pair must match template nodes that are aligned to each other.

4.2 Creating transduction rules

Given a treelet, we can form a set of tree transduction rules as follows. We iterate over each source node *n* in the treelet pair; let *s* be the corresponding node in the input tree (identified during the matching). If, for all children of *s* there is a corresponding child of *n*, then this treelet specifies the placement of all children and no changes are necessary. Otherwise we pick a template that matched at *s* and is compatible with the treelet. The treelet and template are unified to produce an updated rule with variables on the source and target sides for each uncovered child of *s*. When all treelet nodes have been visited, we are left with a transduction rule that specifies the translation of all nodes in the treelet and contains variables that specify the placement of all

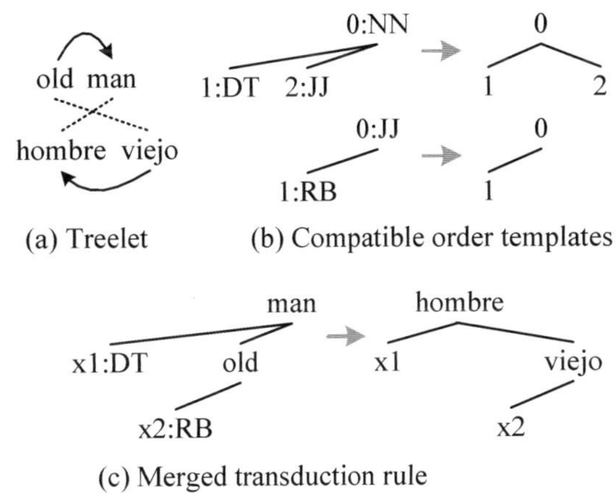

Figure 4.1: Merging templates and treelets

uncovered nodes. Due to the independence of ordering and lexical information, we may produce novel transduction rules not seen in the training corpus. Figure 4.1 shows this process as it applies to the test sentence in Section 2.

If, at any node *s*, we cannot find a matching template compatible with the current treelet, we create an artificial *source order template*, which simply preserves the source language order in the target translation. We add a feature function that counts the number of such templates and train its weight during minimum error rate training.

4.3 Transduction using xR rules

In the absence of a language model or other contextually dependent features, finding the highest scoring derivation would be a simple dynamic program (Huang et al. 2006) [6].However exact search using an n-gram language model leads to split states for each n-gram context. Instead we use an approximate beam search moving bottom-up in the tree, much like a CKY parser. Candidates in this search are derivations with respect to the transducer.

Each transduction rule r has a vector of variables $v_{r1}, \dots v_{rk}$. Each variable is associated with an input node $S(v)$. For each input node s, we keep a beam of derivations $b[s]$. Derivations are represented as a pair $\langle r, \mathbf{e} \rangle$ where r is a transduction rule and $\mathbf{e} \in \mathbb{N}^k$ is a vector with one integer for each of the k variables in r. The interpretation is that the complete candidate can be constructed by recursively substituting for each

[5] This is so the resulting rules fit within the xR formalism. At each node, a rule either fully specifies its ordering, or delegates the translation of the subtree to other rules.

[6] Like Chiang (2005) we only search for the yield of the most likely derivation, rather than the most likely yield.

GetTranslationBeam(s) // *memoized*
  $prioq \leftarrow \emptyset$
  $beam \leftarrow \emptyset$
  for $r \in \mathcal{R}(s)$
    Enqueue(*prioq*, $\langle r, \mathbf{1} \rangle$, EarlyScore($\langle r, \mathbf{1} \rangle$))
  while Size(*prioq*) > 0
    $\langle r, \mathbf{e} \rangle \leftarrow$ PopBest(*prioq*)
    AddToBeam(*beam*, $\langle r, \mathbf{e} \rangle$, TrueScore($\langle r, \mathbf{e} \rangle$))
    for i in $1..|\mathbf{e}|$
      Enqueue(*prioq*, $\langle r, \mathbf{e} + \mathbf{1}_i \rangle$,
        EarlyScore($\langle r, \mathbf{e} + \mathbf{1}_i \rangle$))
  return *beam*

EarlyScore($\langle r, \mathbf{e} \rangle$)
  $c \leftarrow$ RuleScore(r)
  for i in $1..|\mathbf{e}|$
    $s \leftarrow$ InputNode(GetVariable (r, i))
    beam $\leftarrow$ GetTranslationBeam(s)
    $c \leftarrow c$ +TrueScore(GetNthEntry(*beam*, e_i))
  return c

Figure 4.2: Beam tree transduction

$v_{ri} \in v_{r1} \dots v_{rk}$ the candidate constructed from the e_i^{th} entry in the beam $b[S(v_{ri})]$.

Figure 4.2 describes the transduction process. Since we approach decoding as xR transduction, the process is identical to that of constituency-based algorithms (e.g. Huang and Chiang, 2007). There are several free parameters to tune:

- Beam size – Maximum number of candidates per input node (in this paper we use 100)
- Beam threshold – maximum range of scores between top and bottom scoring candidate (we use a logprob difference of 30)
- Maximum combinations considered – To bound search time, we can stop after a specified number of elements are popped off the priority queue (we use 5000)

5 Models

We use all of the Treelet models we described in Quirk et al. (2005) namely:

- Treelet table with translation probabilities estimated using maximum likelihood, with absolute discounting.
- Discriminative tree-based order model.
- Forward and backward lexical weighting, using Model-1 translation probabilities.
- Trigram language model using modified Kneser-Ney smoothing.
- Word and phrase count feature functions.

In addition, we introduce the following:

- Order template table, with template probabilities estimated using maximum likelihood, with absolute discounting.
- A feature function that counts the number of artificial *source order templates* (see below) used in a candidate.

The models are combined in a log-linear framework, with weights trained using minimum error rate training to optimize the BLEU score.

6 Experiments

We evaluated the translation quality of the system using the BLEU metric (Papineni et al., 2002). We compared our system to Pharaoh, a leading phrasal SMT decoder (Koehn et al., 2003), and our treelet system. We report numbers for English to Spanish.

6.1 Data

We used the Europarl corpus provided by the NAACL 2006 Statistical Machine Translation workshop. The target language model was trained using only the target side of the parallel corpus. The larger monolingual corpus was not utilized. The corpus consists of European Parliament proceedings, 730,740 parallel sentence pairs of English-Spanish, amounting to about 15M words in each language. The test data consists of 2000 sentences each of development (*dev*), development-test (*devtest*) and test data (*test*) from the same domain. There is also a separate set of 1064 test sentences (*NC-test*) gathered from "news commentary" web sites.

6.2 Training

We parsed the source (English) side of the corpus using NLPWIN, a broad-coverage rule-based parser able to produce syntactic analyses at varying levels of depth (Heidorn, 2002). For the purposes of these experiments we used a dependency tree output with part-of-speech tags and unstemmed, case-normalized surface words. For word alignment we used GIZA++, under a training regimen of five iterations of Model 1, five iterations of HMM, and five iterations of Model 4, in both directions. The forward and backward alignments were symmetrized using a tree-based heuristic combination. The word alignments and English dependency tree were used to project a target tree. From the aligned tree pairs we extracted a treelet table and an order template table.

The comparison treelet system was identical except that no order template model was used.

The comparison phrasal system was constructed using the same GIZA++ alignments and the heuristic combination described in (Och & Ney, 2003). Except for the order models (Pharaoh uses a penalty on the deviance from monotone), the same models were used.

All systems used a treelet or phrase size of 7 and a trigram language model. Model weights were trained separately for all 3 systems using minimum error rate training to maximize BLEU (Och, 2003) on the development set *(dev)*. Some decoder pruning parameters were tuned on the development test *(devtest)*. The *test* and *NC-test* data sets were not used until final tests.

7 Results

We present the results of our system comparisons in Table 7.1 and Figure 7.1 using three different test sets: The in-domain development test data (*devtest*), the in-domain blind test data (*test*) and the out-of-domain news commentary test data (*NC-test*). All differences (except phrasal vs. template on *devtest*), are statistically significant at the p>=0.99 level under the bootstrap resampling test. Note that while the systems are quite comparable on the in-domain data, on the out-of-domain data the phrasal system's performance drops precipitously, whereas the performance of the treelet and order template systems drops much less, outperforming the phrasal system by 2.7% and 3.46% absolute BLEU.

	devtest	*test*	*NC-test*
Phrasal	0.2910	0.2935	0.2354
Treelet	0.2819	0.2981	0.2624
Template	0.2896	0.3045	0.2700

Table 7.1: System Comparisons across domains

Further insight may be had by comparing the recall[7] for different n-gram orders (Table 7.2). The phrasal system suffers a greater decline in the higher order n-grams than the treelet and template systems, indicating that latter show improved generality in reordering.

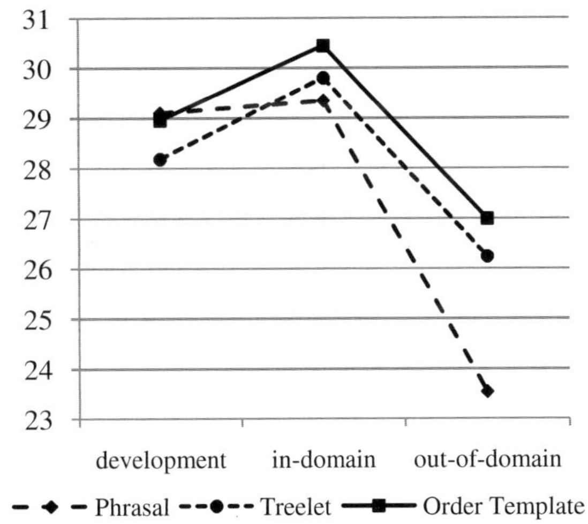

Figure 7.1: In-domain vs. Out-of-domain BLEU

		1gm	2gm	3gm	4gm
Test	Phrasal	0.61	0.35	0.23	0.15
	treelet	0.62	0.36	0.23	0.15
	template	0.62	0.36	0.24	0.16
NC-test	phrasal	0.58	0.30	0.17	0.10
	treelet	0.60	0.33	0.20	0.12
	template	0.61	0.34	0.20	0.13

Table 7.2: n-gram recall across domains

7.1 Treelet vs. Template systems

As described in Section 3.1, the order templates restrict the broad reordering space of the treelet system. Although in theory this might exclude reorderings necessary for some translations, Table 7.3 shows that in practice, the drastic search space reduction allows the decoder to explore a wider beam and more rules, leading to reduced search error *and* increased translation speed. (The *topK* parameter is the number of phrases explored for each span, or rules/treelets for each input node.)

	Devtest BLEU	Sents. per sec
Pharaoh, beam=100, topK=20	0.2910	0.94
Treelet, beam=12, topK=5	0.2819	0.21
Template, beam=100, topK=20	0.2896	0.56

Table 7.3: Performance comparisons

Besides the search space restriction, the other significant change in the template system is to include MLE template probabilities as an

[7] n-gram precision cannot be directly compared across output from different systems due to different levels of 'brevity'

additional feature function. Given that the template system operates over rules where the ordering is fully specified, and that most tree transduction systems use MLE rule probabilities to model both lexical selection and reordering, one might ask if the treelet system's discriminatively trained order model is now redundant. In Table 7.4 we see that this is not the case.[8] (Differences are significant at p>=0.99.)

	devtest	*test*	*NC-test*
MLE model only	0.2769	0.2922	0.2512
Discriminative and MLE models	0.2896	0.3045	0.2700

Table 7.4: Templates and discriminative order model

Finally we examine the role of frequency thresholds in gathering templates. In Table 7.5 it may be seen that discarding singletons reduces the table size by a factor of 5 and improves translation speed with negligible degradation in quality.

	devtest BLEU	Number of templates	Sentences per sec.
No threshold	0.2898	752,165	0.40
Threshold=1	0.2896	137,584	0.56

Table 7.5: Effect of template count cutoffs

8 Conclusions and Future Work

We introduced a new model of Dependency Order Templates that provides for separation of lexical choice and reordering knowledge, thus allowing for greater generality than the phrasal and xRS approaches, while drastically limiting the search space as compared to the treelet approach. We showed BLEU improvements over phrasal of over 1% in-domain and nearly 3.5% out-of-domain. As compared to the treelet approach we showed an improvement of about 0.5%, but a speedup of nearly 3x, despite loosening pruning parameters.

Extraposition and long distance movement still pose a serious challenge to syntax-based machine translation systems. Most of the today's search algorithms assume phrasal cohesion. Even if our search algorithms could accommodate such movement, we don't have appropriate models to account for such phenomena. Our system already extracts extraposition templates, which are a step in the right direction, but may prove too sparse and brittle to account for the range of phenomena.

[8] We speculate that other systems using transducers with MLE probabilities may also benefit from additional reordering models.

References

Chiang, David. A hierarchical phrase-based model for statistical machine translation. ACL 2005.

Galley, Michel, Mark Hopkins, Kevin Knight, and Daniel Marcu. What's in a translation rule? HLT-NAACL 2004.

Graehl, Jonathan and Kevin Knight. Training Tree Transducers. NAACL 2004.

Heidorn, George. "Intelligent writing assistance". In Dale et al. Handbook of Natural Language Processing, Marcel Dekker. (2000)

Huang, Liang, Kevin Knight, and Aravind Joshi. Statistical Syntax-Directed Translation with Extended Domain of Locality. AMTA 2006

Huang, Liang and David Chiang. Faster Algorithms for Decoding with Integrated Language Models. ACL 2007 (to appear)

Koehn, Philipp, Franz Josef Och, and Daniel Marcu. Statistical phrase based translation. NAACL 2003.

Koehn, Philipp and Christof Monz. Manual and automatic evaluation of machine translation between european languages. Workshop on Machine Translation, NAACL 2006.

Marcu, Daniel, Wei Wang, Abdessamad Echihabi, and Kevin Knight. SPMT: Statistical Machine Translation with Syntactified Target Language Phrases. EMNLP-2006.

Menezes, Arul, Kristina Toutanova and Chris Quirk. Microsoft Research Treelet translation system: NAACL 2006 Europarl evaluation. Workshop on Machine Translation, NAACL 2006

Och, Franz Josef and Hermann Ney. A systematic comparison of various statistical alignment models, Computational Linguistics, 29(1):19-51 (2003).

Och, Franz Josef. Minimum error rate training in statistical machine translation. ACL 2003.

Och, Franz Josef and Hermann Ney: The Alignment Template Approach to Statistical Machine Translation. Computational Linguistics 30 (4): 417-449 (2004)

Papineni, Kishore, Salim Roukos, Todd Ward, and Wei-Jing Zhu. BLEU: a method for automatic evaluation of machine translation. ACL 2002.

Quirk, Chris, Arul Menezes, and Colin Cherry. Dependency Tree Translation: Syntactically informed phrasal SMT. ACL 2005

Zens, Richard and Hermann Ney. Improvements in phrase-based statistical machine translation. HLT-NAACL 2004

CCG Supertags in Factored Statistical Machine Translation

Alexandra Birch a.c.birch-mayne@sms.ed.ac.uk
Miles Osborne miles@inf.ed.ac.uk
Philipp Koehn pkoehn@inf.ed.ac.uk
School of Informatics
University of Edinburgh
2 Buccleuch Place
Edinburgh, EH8 9LW, UK

Abstract

Combinatorial Categorial Grammar (CCG) supertags present phrase-based machine translation with an opportunity to access rich syntactic information at a word level. The challenge is incorporating this information into the translation process. Factored translation models allow the inclusion of supertags as a factor in the source or target language. We show that this results in an improvement in the quality of translation and that the value of syntactic supertags in flat structured phrase-based models is largely due to better local reorderings.

1 Introduction

In large-scale machine translation evaluations, phrase-based models generally outperform syntax-based models[1]. Phrase-based models are effective because they capture the lexical dependencies between languages. However, these models, which are equivalent to finite-state machines (Kumar and Byrne, 2003), are unable to model long range word order differences. Phrase-based models also lack the ability to incorporate the generalisations implicit in syntactic knowledge and they do not respect linguistic phrase boundaries. This makes it difficult to improve reordering in phrase-based models.

Syntax-based models can overcome some of the problems associated with phrase-based models because they are able to capture the long range structural mappings that occur in translation. Recently there have been a few syntax-based models that show performance comparable to the phrase-based models (Chiang, 2005; Marcu et al., 2006). However, reliably learning powerful rules from parallel data is very difficult and prone to problems with sparsity and noise in the data. These models also suffer from a large search space when decoding with an integrated language model, which can lead to search errors (Chiang, 2005).

In this paper we investigate the idea of incorporating syntax into phrase-based models, thereby leveraging the strengths of both the phrase-based models and syntactic structures. This is done using CCG supertags, which provide a rich source of syntactic information. CCG contains most of the structure of the grammar in the lexicon, which makes it possible to introduce CCG supertags as a factor in a factored translation model (Koehn et al., 2006). Factored models allow words to be vectors of features: one factor could be the surface form and other factors could contain linguistic information.

Factored models allow for the easy inclusion of supertags in different ways. The first approach is to generate CCG supertags as a factor in the target and then apply an n-gram model over them, increasing the probability of more frequently seen sequences of supertags. This is a simple way of including syntactic information in a phrase-based model, and has also been suggested by Hassan et al. (2007). For both Arabic-English (Hassan et al., 2007) and our experiments in Dutch-English, n-gram models over CCG supertags improve the quality of translation. By preferring more likely sequences of supertags, it is conceivable that the output of the decoder is

[1] www.nist.gov/speech/tests/mt/mt06eval_official_results.html

Proceedings of the Second Workshop on Statistical Machine Translation, pages 9–16,
Prague, June 2007.

more grammatical. However, its not clear exactly how syntactic information can benefit a flat structured model: the constraints contained within supertags are not enforced and relationships between supertags are not linear. We perform experiments to explore the nature and limits of the contribution of supertags, using different orders of n-gram models, reordering models and focussed manual evaluation. It seems that the benefit of using n-gram supertag sequence models is largely from improving reordering, as much of the gain is eroded by using a lexicalised reordering model. This is supported by the manual evaluation which shows a 44% improvement in reordering Dutch-English verb final sentences.

The second and novel way we use supertags is to direct the translation process. Supertags on the source sentence allows the decoder to make decisions based on the structure of the input. The subcategorisation of a verb, for instance, might help select the correct translation. Using multiple dependencies on factors in the source, we need a strategy for dealing with sparse data. We propose using a logarithmic opinion pool (Smith et al., 2005) to combine the more specific models (which depend on both words and supertags) with more general models (which only depends on words). This paper is the first to suggest this approach for combining multiple information sources in machine translation.

Although the addition of supertags to phrase-based translation does show some improvement, their overall impact is limited. Sequence models over supertags clearly result in some improvements in local reordering but syntactic information contains long distance dependencies which are simply not utilised in phrase-based models.

2 Factored Models

Inspired by work on factored language models, Koehn et al. (2006) extend phrase-based models to incorporate multiple levels of linguistic knowledge as factors. Phrase-based models are limited to sequences of words as their units with no access to additional linguistic knowledge. Factors allow for richer translation models, for example, the gender or tense of a word can be expressed. Factors also allow the model to generalise, for example, the lemma of a word could be used to generalise to unseen inflected forms.

The factored translation model combines features in a log-linear fashion (Och, 2003). The most likely target sentence $\hat{t}$ is calculated using the decision rule in Equation 1:

$$\hat{t} = \arg\max_{t} \left\{ \sum_{m=1}^{M} \lambda_m h_m(s_1^{F_s}, t_1^{F_t}) \right\} \quad (1)$$

$$\hat{t} \propto \sum_{m=1}^{M} \lambda_m h_m(s_1^{F_s}, t_1^{F_t}) \quad (2)$$

where M is the number of features, $h_m(s_1^{F_s}, t_1^{F_t})$ are the feature functions over the factors, and λ are the weights which combine the features which are optimised using minimum error rate training (Venugopal and Vogel, 2005). Each function depends on a vector $s_1^{F_s}$ of source factors and a vector $t_1^{F_t}$ of target factors. An example of a factored model used in upcoming experiments is:

$$\hat{t} \propto \sum_{m=1}^{M} \lambda_m h_m(s_w, t_{wc}) \quad (3)$$

where s_w means the model depends on (s)ource (w)ords, and t_{wc} means the model generates (t)arget (w)ords and (c)cg supertags. The model is shown graphically in Figure 1.

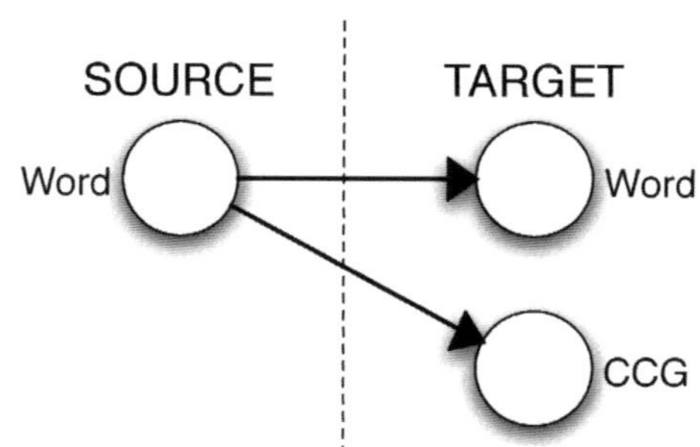

Figure 1. Factored translation with source words determining target words and CCG supertags

For our experiments we used the following features: the translation probabilities $Pr(s_1^{F_s}|t_1^{F_t})$ and $Pr(t_1^{F_t}|s_1^{F_s})$, the lexical weights (Koehn et al., 2003) $lex(s_1^{F_s}|t_1^{F_t})$ and $lex(t_1^{F_t}|s_1^{F_s})$, and a phrase penalty e, which allows the model to learn a preference for longer or shorter phrases. Added to these features is the word penalty e^{-1} which allows the model to learn a preference for longer or shorter sentences, the distortion model d that prefers monotone word order, and the language model probability $Pr(t)$. All these features are logged when combined in the log-linear model in order to retain the impact of very unlikely translations or sequences.

One of the strengths of the factored model is it allows for n-gram distributions over factors on the target. We call these distributions *sequence models*. By analogy with language models, for example, we can construct a bigram sequence model as follows:

$$p(f_1, f_2, \dots f_n) = p(f_1) \prod_{i=2}^{n} p(f_i | f_{(i-1)})$$

where f is a factor (eg. CCG supertags) and n is the length of the string. Sequence models over POS tags or supertags are smaller than language models because they have restricted lexicons. Higher order, more powerful sequence models can therefore be used.

Applying multiple factors in the source can lead to sparse data problems. One solution is to break down the translation into smaller steps and translate each factor separately like in the following model where source words are translated separately to the source supertags:

$$\hat{t} \propto \sum_{m=1}^{M} \lambda_m h_m(s_w, t_w) + \sum_{n=1}^{N} \lambda_n h_n(s_c, t_w)$$

However, in many cases multiple dependencies are desirable. For instance translating CCG supertags independently of words could introduce errors. Multiple dependencies require some form of backing off to simpler models in order to cover the cases where, for instance, the word has been seen in training, but not with that particular supertag. Different backoff paths are possible, and it would be interesting but prohibitively slow to apply a strategy similar to generalised parallel backoff (Bilmes and Kirchhoff, 2003) which is used in factored language models. Backoff in factored language models is made more difficult because there is no obvious backoff path. This is compounded for factored phrase-based translation models where one has to consider backoff in terms of factors and n-gram lengths in both source and target languages. Furthermore, the surface form of a word is probably the most valuable factor and so its contribution must always be taken into account. We therefore did not use backoff and chose to use a log-linear combination of features and models instead.

Our solution is to extract two translation models:

$$\hat{t} \propto \sum_{m=1}^{M} \lambda_m h_m(s_{wc}, t_w) + \sum_{n=1}^{N} \lambda_n h_n(s_w, t_w) \quad (4)$$

One model consists of more specific features m and would return log probabilities, for example $log_2 Pr(t_w|s_{wc})$, if the particular word and supertag had been seen before in training. Otherwise it returns $-C$, a negative constant emulating $log_2(0)$. The other model consist of more general features n and always returns log probabilities, for example $log_2 Pr(t_w|s_w)$.

3 CCG and Supertags

CCGs have syntactically rich lexicons and a small set of combinatory operators which assemble the parse-trees. Each word in the sentence is assigned a category from the lexicon. A category may either be atomic (**S**, **NP** etc.) or complex (**S\S**, **(S\NP)/NP** etc.). Complex categories have the general form α/β or $\alpha\backslash\beta$ where α and β are themselves categories. An example of a CCG parse is given:

Peter	eats	apples
NP	**(S\NP)/NP**	**NP**
	S\NP (>)	
S (<)		

where the derivation proceeds as follows: "eats" is combined with "apples" under the operation of forward application. "eats" can be thought of as a function that takes a **NP** to the right and returns a **S\NP**. Similarly the phrase "eats apples" can be thought of as a function which takes a noun phrase **NP** to the left and returns a sentence **S**. This operation is called backward application.

A sentence together with its CCG categories already contains most of the information present in a full parse. Because these categories are lexicalised, they can easily be included into factored phrase-based translation. CCG supertags are categories that have been provided by a supertagger. Supertags were introduced by Bangalore (1999) as a way of increasing parsing efficiency by reducing the number of structures assigned to each word. Clark (2002) developed a suppertagger for CCG which uses a conditional maximum entropy model to estimate the probability of words being assigned particular categories. Here is an example of a sentence that has been supertagged in the training corpus:

We	all	agree	on	that	.
NP	**NP\NP**	**(S[dcl]\NP)/PP**	**PP/NP**	**NP**	.

The verb "agree" has been assigned a complex supertag **(S[dcl]\NP)/PP** which determines the type and direction of its arguments. This information can be used to improve the quality of translation.

4 Experiments

The first set of experiments explores the effect of CCG supertags on the target, translating from Dutch into English. The last experiment shows the effect of CCG supertags on the source, translating from German into English. These language pairs present a considerable reordering challenge. For example, Dutch and German have SOV word order in subordinate clauses. This means that the verb often appears at the end of the clause, far from the position of the English verb.

4.1 Experimental Setup

The experiments were run using Moses[2], an open source factored statistical machine translation system. The SRILM language modelling toolkit (Stolcke, 2002) was used with modified Kneser-Ney discounting and interpolation. The CCG supertagger (Clark, 2002; Clark and Curran, 2004) was provided with the C&C Language Processing Tools[3]. The supertagger was trained on the CCGBank in English (Hockenmaier and Steedman, 2005) and in German (Hockenmaier, 2006).

The Dutch-English parallel training data comes from the Europarl corpus (Koehn, 2005) and excludes the proceedings from the last quarter of 2000. This consists of 855,677 sentences with a maximum of 50 words per sentence. 500 sentences of tuning data and the 2000 sentences of test data are taken from the ACL Workshop on Building and Using Parallel Texts[4].

The German-English experiments use data from the NAACL 2006 Workshop on Statistical Machine Translation[5]. The data consists of 751,088 sentences of training data, 500 sentences of tuning data and 3064 sentences of test data. The English and German training sets were POS tagged and supertagged before lowercasing. The language models and the sequence models were trained on the Europarl training data. Where not otherwise specified, the POS tag and supertag sequence models are 5-gram models and the language model is a 3-gram model.

4.2 Sequence Models Over Supertags

Our first Dutch-English experiment seeks to establish what effect sequence models have on machine translation. We show that supertags improve translation quality. Together with Shen et al. (2006) it is one of the first results to confirm the potential of the factored model.

Model	BLEU
s_w, t_w	23.97
s_w, t_{wp}	24.11
s_w, t_{wc}	24.42
s_w, t_{wpc}	**24.43**

Table 1. The effect of sequence models on Dutch-English BLEU score. Factors are (w)ords, (p)os tags, (c)cg supertags on the source s or the target t

Table 1 shows that sequence models over CCG supertags in the target (model s_w, t_{wc}) improves over the baseline (model s_w, t_w) which has no supertags. Supertag sequence models also outperform models which apply POS tag sequence models (s_w, t_{wp}) and, interestingly do just as well as models which apply both POS tag and supertag sequence models (s_w, t_{wps}). Supertags are more informative than POS tags as they contain the syntactic context of a word.

These experiments were run with the distortion limit set to 6. This means that at most 6 words in

[2]see http://www.statmt.org/moses/

[3]see http://svn.ask.it.usyd.edu.au/trac/candc/wiki

[4]see http://www.statmt.org/wpt05/

[5]see http://www.statmt.org/wpt06/

the source sentence can be skipped. We tried setting the distortion limit to 15 to see if allowing longer distance reorderings with CCG supertag sequence models could further improve performance, however it resulted in a decrease in performance to a BLEU score of 23.84.

4.3 Manual Analysis

The BLEU score improvement in Table 1 does not explain how the supertag sequence models affect the translation process. As suggested by Callison-Burch et al.(2006) we perform a focussed manual analysis of the output to see what changes have occurred.

From the test set, we randomly selected 100 sentences which required reordering of verbs: the Dutch sentences ended with a verb which had to be moved forward in the English translation. We record whether or not the verb was correctly translated and whether it was reordered to the correct position in the target sentence.

Model	Translated	Reordered
s_w, t_w	81	36
s_w, t_{wc}	87	52

Table 2. Analysis of % correct translation and reordering of verbs for Dutch-English translation

In Table 2 we can see that the addition of the CCG supertag sequence model improved both the translation of the verbs and their reordering. However, the improvement is much more pronounced for reordering. The difference in the reordering results is significant at $p < 0.05$ using the χ^2 significance test. This shows that the syntactic information in the CCG supertags is used by the model to prefer better word order for the target sentence.

In Figure 2 we can see two examples of Dutch-English translations that have improved with the application of CCG supertag sequence models. In the first example the verb "heeft" occurs at the end of the source sentence. The baseline model (s_w, t_w) does not manage to translate "heeft". The model with the CCG supertag sequence model (s_w, t_{wc}) translates it correctly as "has" and reorders it correctly 4 places to the left. The second example also shows the sequence model correctly translating the Dutch verb at the end of the sentence "nodig". One can see that it is still not entirely grammatical.

The improvements in reordering shown here are reorderings over a relatively short distance, two or three positions. This is well within the 5-gram order of the CCG supertag sequence model and we therefore consider this to be local reordering.

4.4 Order of the Sequence Model

The CCG supertags describe the syntactic context of the word they are attached to. Therefore they have an influence that is greater in scope than surface words or POS tags. Increasing the order of the CCG supertag sequence model should also increase the ability to perform longer distance reordering. However, at some point the reliability of the predictions of the sequence models is impaired due to sparse counts.

Model	None	1gram	3gram	5gram	7gram
s_w, t_{wc}	24.18	23.96	24.19	**24.42**	24.32
s_w, t_{wpc}	24.34	23.86	24.09	**24.43**	24.14

Table 3. BLUE scores for Dutch-English models which apply CCG supertag sequence models of varying orders

In Table 3 we can see that the optimal order for the CCG supertag sequence models is 5.

4.5 Language Model vs. Supertags

The language model makes a great contribution to the correct order of the words in the target sentence. In this experiment we investigate whether by using a stronger language model the contribution of the sequence model will no longer be relevant. The relative contribution of the language mode and different sequence models is investigated for different language model n-gram lengths.

Model	None	1gram	3gram	5gram	7gram
s_w, t_w	-	21.22	23.97	24.05	24.13
s_w, t_{wp}	21.87	21.83	24.11	24.25	24.06
s_w, t_{wc}	21.75	21.70	24.42	**24.67**	**24.60**
s_w, t_{wpc}	**21.99**	**22.07**	**24.43**	24.48	24.42

Table 4. BLEU scores for Dutch-English models which use language models of increasing n-gram length. Column None does not apply any language model. Model s_w, t_w does not apply any sequence models, and model s_w, t_{wpc} applies both POS tag and supertag sequence models.

In Table 4 we can see that if no language model is present(None), the system benefits slightly from

source:hij kan toch niet beweren dat hij daar geen exacte informatie over **heeft** !	
reference: how can he say he does not **have** any precise information ?	
s_w, t_w:he cannot say that he is not an exact information about .	
s_w, t_{wc}: he cannot say that he **has** no precise information on this !	
source: wij moeten hun verwachtingen niet beschamen . meer dan ooit hebben al die landen thans onze bijstand **nodig**	
reference: we must not disappoint them in their expectations , and now more than ever these countries **need** our help	
s_w, t_w:we must not fail to their expectations , more than ever to have all these countries now our assistance **necessary**	
s_w, t_{wc}: we must not fail to their expectations , more than ever , those countries now **need** our assistance	

Figure 2. Examples where the CCG supertag sequence model improves Dutch-English translation

having access to all the other sequence models. However, the language model contribution is very strong and in isolation contributes more to translation performance than any other sequence model. Even with a high order language model, applying the CCG supertag sequence model still seems to improve performance. This means that even if we use a more powerful language model, the structural information contained in the supertags continues to be beneficial.

4.6 Lexicalised Reordering vs. Supertags

In this experiment we investigate using a stronger reordering model to see how it compares to the contribution that CCG supertag sequence models make. Moses implements the lexicalised reordering model described by Tillman (2004), which learns whether phrases prefer monotone, inverse or disjoint orientations with regard to adjacent phrases. We apply this reordering models to the following experiments.

Model	None	Lex. Reord.
s_w, t_w	23.97	24.72
s_w, t_{wc}	24.42	24.78

Table 5. Dutch-English models with and without a lexicalised reordering model.

In Table 5 we can see that lexicalised reordering improves translation performance for both models. However, the improvement that was seen using CCG supertags without lexicalised reordering, almost disappears when using a stronger reordering model. This suggests that CCG supertags' contribution is similar to that of a reordering model. The lexicalised reordering model only learns the orientation of a phrase with relation to its adjacent phrase, so its influence is very limited in range. If it can replace CCG supertags, it suggests that supertags' influence is also within a local range.

4.7 CCG Supertags on Source

Sequence models over supertags improve the performance of phrase-based machine translation. However, this is a limited way of leveraging the rich syntactic information available in the CCG categories. We explore the potential of letting supertags direct translation by including them as a factor on the source. This is similar to syntax-directed translation originally proposed for compiling (Aho and Ullman, 1969), and also used in machine translation (Quirk et al., 2005; Huang et al., 2006). Information about the source words' syntactic function and subcategorisation can directly influence the hypotheses being searched in decoding. These experiments were performed on the German to English translation task, in contrast to the Dutch to English results given in previous experiments.

We use a model which combines more specific dependencies on source words and source CCG supertags, with a more general model which only has dependancies on the source word, see Equation 4. We explore two different ways of balancing the statistical evidence from these multiple sources. The first way to combine the general and specific sources of information is by considering features from both models as part of one large log-linear model. However, by including more and less informative features in one model, we may transfer too much explanatory power to the more specific features. To overcome this problem, Smith et al. (2006) demonstrated that using ensembles of separately trained models and combining them in a logarithmic opinion pool (LOP) leads to better parameter values. This approach was used as the second way in which we combined our models. An ensemble of log-linear models was combined using a multiplicative constant γ which we train manually using held out data.

$$\hat{t} \propto \sum_{m=1}^{M} \lambda_m h_m(s_{wc}, t_w) + \gamma \left(\sum_{n=1}^{N} \lambda_n h_n(s_w, t_w) \right)$$

Typically, the two models would need to be normalised before being combined, but here the multiplicative constant fulfils this rôle by balancing their separate contributions. This is the first work suggesting the application of LOPs to decoding in machine translation. In the future more sophisticated translation models and ensembles of models will need methods such as LOPs in order to balance statistical evidence from multiple sources.

Model	BLEU
s_w, t_w	23.30
s_{wc}, t_w	19.73
single	23.29
LOP	23.46

Table 6. German-English: CCG supertags are used as a factor on the source. The simple models are combined in two ways: either as a single log-linear model or as a LOP of log-linear models

Table 6 shows that the simple, general model (model s_w, t_w) performs considerably better than the simple specific model, where there are multiple dependencies on both words and CCG supertags (model s_{wc}, t_w). This is because there are words in the test sentence that have been seen before but not with the CCG supertag. Statistical evidence from multiple sources must be combined. The first way to combine them is to join them in one single log-linear model, which is trained over many features. This makes finding good weights difficult as the influence of the general model is greater, and its difficult for the more specific model to discover good weights. The second method for combining the information is to use the weights from the separately trained simple models and then combine them in a LOP. Held out data is used to set the multiplicative constant needed to balance the contribution of the two models. We can see that this second approach is more successful and this suggests that it is important to carefully consider the best ways of combining different sources of information when using ensembles of models. However, the results of this experiment are not very conclusive. There is no uncertainty in the source sentence and the value of modelling it using CCG supertags is still to be demonstrated.

5 Conclusion

The factored translation model allows for the inclusion of valuable sources of information in many different ways. We have shown that the syntactically rich CCG supertags do improve the translation process and we investigate the best way of including them in the factored model. Using CCG supertags over the target shows the most improvement, especially when using targeted manual evaluation. However, this effect seems to be largely due to improved local reordering. Reordering improvements can perhaps be more reliably made using better reordering models or larger, more powerful language models. A further consideration is that supertags will always be limited to the few languages for which there are treebanks.

Syntactic information represents embedded structures which are naturally incorporated into grammar-based models. The ability of a flat structured model to leverage this information seems to be limited. CCG supertags' ability to guide translation would be enhanced if the constraints encoded in the tags were to be enforced using combinatory operators.

6 Acknowledgements

We thank Hieu Hoang for assistance with Moses, Julia Hockenmaier for access to CCGbank lexicons in German and English, and Stephen Clark and James Curran for providing the supertagger. This work was supported in part under the GALE program of the Defense Advanced Research Projects Agency, Contract No. HR0011-06-C-0022 and in part under the EuroMatrix project funded by the European Commission (6th Framework Programme).

References

Alfred V. Aho and Jeffrey D. Ullman. 1969. Properties of syntax directed translations. *Journal of Computer and System Sciences*, 3(3):319–334.

Srinivas Bangalore and Aravind Joshi. 1999. Supertagging: An approach to almost parsing. *Computational Linguistics*, 25(2):237–265.

Jeff Bilmes and Katrin Kirchhoff. 2003. Factored language models and generalized parallel backoff. In *Proceedings of the North American Association for Computational Linguistics Conference*, Edmonton, Canada.

Chris Callison-Burch, Miles Osborne, and Philipp Koehn. 2006. Re-evaluating the role of Bleu in machine translation research. In *Proceedings of the European Chapter of the Association for Computational Linguistics*, Trento, Italy.

David Chiang. 2005. A hierarchical phrase-based model for statistical machine translation. In *Proceedings of the Association for Computational Linguistics*, pages 263–270, Ann Arbor, Michigan.

Stephen Clark and James R. Curran. 2004. Parsing the wsj using ccg and log-linear models. In *Proceedings of the Association for Computational Linguistics*, pages 103–110, Barcelona, Spain.

Stephen Clark. 2002. Supertagging for combinatory categorial grammar. In *Proceedings of the International Workshop on Tree Adjoining Grammars*, pages 19–24, Venice, Italy.

Hany Hassan, Khalil Sima'an, and Andy Way. 2007. Supertagged phrase-based statistical machine translation. In *Proceedings of the Association for Computational Linguistics*, Prague, Czech Republic. (to appear).

Julia Hockenmaier and Mark Steedman. 2005. Ccgbank manual. Technical Report MS-CIS-05-09, Department of Computer and Information Science, University of Pennsylvania.

Julia Hockenmaier. 2006. Creating a ccgbank and a wide-coverage ccg lexicon for german. In *Proceedings of the International Conference on Computational Linguistics and of the Association for Computational Linguistics*, Sydney, Australia.

Liang Huang, Kevin Knight, and Aravind Joshi. 2006. A syntax-directed translator with extended domain of locality. In *Proceedings of the Workshop on Computationally Hard Problems and Joint Inference in Speech and Language Processing*, pages 1–8, New York City, New York. Association for Computational Linguistics.

Philipp Koehn, Franz Och, and Daniel Marcu. 2003. Statistical phrase-based translation. In *Proceedings of the Human Language Technology and North American Association for Computational Linguistics Conference*, pages 127–133, Edmonton, Canada. Association for Computational Linguistics.

Philipp Koehn, Hieu Hoang, Chris Callison-Burch, Marcello Federico, Nicola Bertoldi, Richard Zens, Chris Dyer, Brooke Cowan, Wade Shen, Christine Moran, Ondrej Bojar, Alexandra Constantin, and Evan Herbst. 2006. Open source toolkit for statistical machine translation. In *Summer Workshop on Language Engineering, John Hopkins University Center for Language and Speech Processing*.

Philipp Koehn. 2005. Europarl: A parallel corpus for statistical machine translation. In *MT Summit*.

Shankar Kumar and William Byrne. 2003. A weighted finite state transducer implementation of the alignment template model for statistical machine translation. In *Proceedings of the Human Language Technology and North American Association for Computational Linguistics Conference*, pages 63–70, Edmonton, Canada.

Daniel Marcu, Wei Wang, Abdessamad Echihabi, and Kevin Knight. 2006. SPMT: Statistical machine translation with syntactified target language phrases. In *Proceedings of the Conference on Empirical Methods in Natural Language Processing*, pages 44–52, Sydney, Australia.

Franz Josef Och. 2003. Minimum error rate training in statistical machine translation. In *Proceedings of the Association for Computational Linguistics*, pages 160–167, Sapporo, Japan.

Chris Quirk, Arul Menezes, and Colin Cherry. 2005. Dependency treelet translation: Syntactically informed phrasal SMT. In *Proceedings of the Association for Computational Linguistics*, pages 271–279, Ann Arbor, Michigan.

Wade Shen, Richard Zens, Nicola Bertoldi, and Marcello Federico. 2006. The JHU workshop 2006 IWSLT system. In *Proceedings of the International Workshop on Spoken Language Translation (IWSLT)*, pages 59–63, Kyoto, Japan.

Andrew Smith and Miles Osborne. 2006. Using gazetteers in discriminative information extraction. In *The Conference on Natural Language Learning*, New York City, USA.

Andrew Smith, Trevor Cohn, and Miles Osborne. 2005. Logarithmic opinion pools for conditional random fields. In *Proceedings of the Association for Computational Linguistics*, pages 18–25, Ann Arbor, Michigan.

Andreas Stolcke. 2002. SRILM - an extensible language modeling toolkit. In *Proceedings of Spoken Language Processing*, pages 901–904.

Christoph Tillman. 2004. A unigram orientation model for statistical machine translation. In *Proceedings of the Human Language Technology and North American Association for Computational Linguistics Conference*, pages 101–104, Boston, USA. Association for Computational Linguistics.

Ashish Venugopal and Stephan Vogel. 2005. Considerations in MCE and MMI training for statistical machine translation. In *Proceedings of the European Association for Machine Translation*, Budapest, Hungary.

Integration of an Arabic Transliteration Module into a Statistical Machine Translation System

Mehdi M. Kashani[+], Eric Joanis[++], Roland Kuhn[++], George Foster[++], Fred Popowich[+]

[+] School of Computing Science
Simon Fraser University
8888 University Drive
Burnaby, BC V5A 1S6, Canada
mmostafa@sfu.ca
popowich@sfu.ca

[++] NRC Institute for Information Technology
101 St-Jean-Bosco Street
Gatineau, QC K1A 0R6, Canada
firstname.lastname@cnrc-nrc.gc.ca

Abstract

We provide an in-depth analysis of the integration of an Arabic-to-English transliteration system into a general-purpose phrase-based statistical machine translation system. We study the integration from different aspects and evaluate the improvement that can be attributed to the integration using the BLEU metric. Our experiments show that a transliteration module can help significantly in the situation where the test data is rich with previously unseen named entities. We obtain 70% and 53% of the theoretical maximum improvement we could achieve, as measured by an oracle on development and test sets respectively for OOV words (out of vocabulary source words not appearing in the phrase table).

1 Introduction

Transliteration is the practice of transcribing a word or text written in one writing system into another writing system. The most frequent candidates for transliteration are person names, locations, organizations and imported words. The lack of a fully comprehensive bilingual dictionary including the entries for all named entities (NEs) renders the task of transliteration necessary for certain natural language processing applications dealing with named entities. Two applications where transliteration can be particularly useful are machine translation (MT) and cross lingual information retrieval. While transliteration itself is a relatively well-studied problem, its effect on the aforementioned applications is still under investigation.

Transliteration as a self-contained task has its own challenges, but applying it to a real application introduces new challenges. In this paper we analyze the efficacy of integrating a transliteration module into a real MT system and evaluate the performance.

When working on a limited domain, given a sufficiently large amount of training data, almost all of the words in the unseen data (in the same domain) will have appeared in the training corpus. But this argument does not hold for NEs, because no matter how big the training corpus is, there will always be unseen names of people and locations. Current MT systems either leave such unknown names as they are in the final target text or remove them in order to obtain a better evaluation score. None of these methods can give the reader who is not familiar with the source language any information about those out-of-vocabulary (OOV) words, especially when the source and target languages use different scripts. If these words are not names, one can usually guess what they are, by using the partial information of other parts of speech. But, in the case of names, there is no way to determine the individual or location the sentence is talking about. So, to improve the usability of a translation, it is particularly important to handle NEs well.

The importance of NEs is not yet reflected in the evaluation methods used in the MT community, the most common of which is the BLEU metric. BLEU (Papineni et al, 2002) was devised to provide automatic evaluation of MT output. In this metric n-gram similarity of the MT output is computed with one or more references made by human

Proceedings of the Second Workshop on Statistical Machine Translation, pages 17–24,
Prague, June 2007.

translators. BLEU does not distinguish between different words and gives equal weight to all. In this paper, we base our evaluation on the BLEU metric and show that using transliteration has impact on it (and in some cases significant impact). However, we believe that such integration is more important for practical uses of MT than BLEU indicates.

Other than improving readability and raising the BLEU score, another advantage of using a transliteration system is that having the right translation for a name helps the language model select a better ordering for other words. For example, our phrase table[1] does not have any entry for "دالس" (Dulles) and when running MT system on the plain Arabic text we get

and this trip was cancelled [...] by the american authorities responsible for security ***at the airport*** **دالس .**

We ran our MT system twice, once by suggesting "dallas" and another time "dulles" as English equivalents for "دالس" and the decoder generated the following sentences, respectively:

and this trip was cancelled [...] by the american authorities responsible for security ***at the airport at dallas .***

and this trip was cancelled [...] by the american authorities responsible for security ***at dulles airport .***[2]

Every statistical MT (SMT) system assigns a probability distribution to the words that are seen in its parallel training data, including proper names. The richer the training data, the higher the chance for a given name in the test data to be found in the translation tables. In other words, an MT system with a relatively rich phrase table is able to translate many of the common names in the test data, with all the remaining words being rare and foreign. So unlike a self-contained transliteration module, which typically deals with a mix of 'easy' and 'hard' names, the primary use for a transliteration module embedded in an SMT system will be to deal with the 'hard' names left over after the phrase tables have provided translations for the 'easy' ones. That means that when measuring the performance improvements caused by embedding a transliteration module in an MT system, one must keep in mind that such improvements are difficult to attain: they are won mainly by correctly transliterating 'hard' names.

Another issue with OOV words is that some of them remained untranslated due to misspellings in the source text. For example, we encountered "هثيرو" ("Hthearow") instead of "هيثرو" ("Heathrow") or "بريزر" ("Brezer") instead of "بريمر" ("Bremer") in our development test set.

Also, evaluation by BLEU (or a similar automatic metric) is problematic. Almost all of the MT evaluations use one or more reference translations as the gold standard and, using some metrics, they give a score to the MT output. The problem with NEs is that they usually have more than a single equivalent in the target language (especially if they don't originally come from the target language) which may or may not have been captured in the gold standard. So even if the transliteration module comes up with a correct interpretation of a name it might not receive credit as far as the limited number of correct names in the references are concerned.

Our first impression was that having more interpretations for a name in the references would raise the transliteration module's chance to generate at least one of them, hence improving the performance. But, in practice, when references do not agree on a name's transliteration that is the sign of an ambiguity. In these cases, the transliteration module often suggests a correct transliteration that the decoder outputs correctly, but which fails to receive credit from the BLEU metric because this transliteration is not found in the references. As an example, for the name "سويريوس", four references came up with four different interpretations: swerios, swiriyus, severius, sweires. A quick query in Google showed us another four acceptable interpretations (severios, sewerios, sweirios, sawerios).

Machine transliteration has been an active research field for quite a while (Al-Onaizan and Knight, 2002; AbdulJaleel and Larkey, 2003; Klementiev and Roth, 2006; Sproat et al, 2006) but to

[1] A table where the conditional probabilities of target phrases given source phrases (and vice versa) is kept.

[2] Note that the language model can be trained on more text, and hence can know more NEs than the translation model does.

our knowledge there is little published work on evaluating transliteration within a real MT system.

The closest work to ours is described in (Hassan and Sorensen, 2005) where they have a list of names in Arabic and feed this list as the input text to their MT system. They evaluate their system in three different cases: as a word-based NE translation, phrase-based NE translation and in presence of a transliteration module. Then, they report the BLEU score on the final output. Since their text is comprised of only NEs, the BLEU increase is quite high. Combining all three models, they get a 24.9 BLEU point increase over the naïve baseline. The difference they report between their best method without transliteration and the one including transliteration is 8.12 BLEU points for person names (their best increase).

In section 2, we introduce different methods for incorporating a transliteration module into an MT system and justify our choice. In section 3, the transliteration module is briefly introduced and we explain how we prepared its output for use by the MT system. In section 4, an evaluation of the integration is provided. Finally, section 5 concludes the paper.

2 Our Approach

Before going into details of our approach, an overview of Portage (Sadat et al, 2005), the machine translation system that we used for our experiments and some of its properties should be provided.

Portage is a statistical phrase-based SMT system similar to Pharaoh (Koehn et al, 2003). Given a source sentence, it tries to find the target sentence that maximizes the joint probability of a target sentence and a phrase alignment according to a loglinear model. Features in the loglinear model consist of a phrase-based translation model with relative-frequency and lexical probability estimates; a 4-gram language model using Kneser-Ney smoothing, trained with the SRILM toolkit; a single-parameter distortion penalty on phrase reordering; and a word-length penalty. Weights on the loglinear features are set using Och's algorithm (Och, 2003) to maximize the system's BLEU score on a development corpus. To generate phrase pairs from a parallel corpus, we use the "diag-and" phrase induction algorithm described in (Koehn et al, 2003), with symmetrized word alignments generated using IBM model 2 (Brown et al, 1993).

Portage allows the use of SGML-like markup for arbitrary entities within the input text. The markup can be used to specify translations provided by external sources for the entities, such as rule-based translations of numbers and dates, or a transliteration module for OOVs in our work. Many SMT systems have this capability, so although the details given here pertain to Portage, the techniques described can be used in many different SMT systems.

As an example, suppose we already have two different transliterations with their probabilities for the Arabic name "محمد". We can replace every occurrence of the "محمد" in the Arabic input text with the following:

<NAME target="mohammed|mohamed"
prob=".7|.3"> محمد </NAME>

By running Portage on this marked up text, the decoder chooses between entries in its own phrase table and the marked-up text. One thing that is important for our task is that if the entry cannot be found in Portage's phrase tables, it is guaranteed that one of the candidates inside the markup will be chosen. Even if none of the candidates exist in the language model, the decoder still picks one of them, because the system assigns a small arbitrary probability (we typically use e^{-18}) as unigram probability of each unseen word.

We considered four different methods for incorporating the transliteration module into the MT system. The first and second methods need an NE tagger and the other two do not require any external tools.

Method 1: use an NE tagger to extract the names in the Arabic input text. Then, run the transliteration module on them and assign probabilities to top candidates. Use the markup capability of Portage and replace each name in the Arabic text with the SGML-like tag including different probabilities for different candidates. Feed the marked-up text to Portage to translate.

Method 2: similar to method 1 but instead of using the marked-up text, a new phrase table, only containing entries for the names in the Arabic input text is built and added to Portage's existing phrase tables. A weight is given to this phrase table and then the decoder uses this phrase table as well as its own phrase tables to decide which translation to choose when encountering the names in the text. The main difference between methods 1 and 2 is that in our system, method 2 allows for a bleu-optimal weight to be learned for the NE phrase table, whereas the weight on the rules for method 1 has to be set by hand.

Method 3: run Portage on the plain Arabic text. Extract all untranslated Arabic OOVs and run the transliteration module on them. Replace them with the top candidate.

Method 4: run Portage on the plain Arabic text. Extract all untranslated Arabic OOVs and run the transliteration module on them. Replace them with SGML-like tags including different probabilities for different candidates, as described previously. Feed the marked-up text to Portage to translate.

The first two methods need a powerful NE tagger with a high recall value. We computed the recall value on the development set OOVs using two different NE taggers, Tagger A and Tagger B (each from a different research group). Taggers A and B showed a recall of 33% and 53% respectively, both being low for our purposes. Another issue with these two methods is that for many of the names the transliteration module will compete with the internal phrase table. Our observations show that if a name exists in the phrase table, it is likely to be translated correctly. In general, observed parallel data (i.e. training data) should be a more reliable source of information than transliteration, encouraging us to use transliteration most appropriately as a 'back-off' method. In a few cases, the Arabic name is ambiguous with a common word and is mistakenly translated as such. For example, "هانی ابو نحل" is an Arabic name that should be transliterated as "Hani Abu Nahl" but since "نحل" also means "solve", the MT system outputs "Hani Abu Solve". The advantage of the first two methods is that they can deal with such cases. But considering the noise in the NE detectors, handling them increases the risk of losing already correct translations of other names.

The third method is simple and easy to use but not optimal: it does not take advantage of the decoder's internal features (notably the language models) and only picks up the highest scoring candidate from the transliteration module.

The fourth method only deals with those words that the MT system was unable to deal with and had to leave untranslated in the final text. Therefore whatever suggestions the transliteration module makes do not need to compete with the internal phrase tables, which is good because we expect the phrase tables to be a more reliable source of information. It is guaranteed that the translation quality will be improved (in the worst case, a bad transliteration is still more informative than the original word in Arabic script). Moreover, unlike the third method, we take advantage of all internal decoder features on the second pass. We adopt the fourth method for our experiment. The following example better illustrates how this approach works:

Example: Suppose we have the following sentence in the Arabic input text:

بلير يقبل تقرير هوتون بالكامل.

Portage is run on the Arabic plain text and yields the following output:

blair accepts هوتون *report in full .*

The Arabic word "هوتون" (Hutton) is extracted and fed to the transliteration module. The transliteration module comes up with some English candidates, each with different probabilities as estimated by the HMM. They are rescaled (as will be explained in section 3) and the following markup text will be generated to replace the untranslated "هوتون" in the first plain Arabic sentence:

<NAME target="hoton|hutton|authon" prob="0.1|0.00028|4.64e-05">هوتون</NAME>

Portage is then run on this newly marked up text (second pass). From now on, with the additional guidance of the language models, it is the decoder's task to decide between different markup suggestions. For the above example, the following output will be generated:

blair accepts hutton report in full .

3 Transliteration System

In this section we provide a brief overview of the embedded transliteration system we used for our experiment. For the full description refer to (Kashani et al, 2007).

3.1 Three Phase Transliteration

The transliteration module follows the noisy channel framework. The adapted spelling-based generative model is similar to (Al-Onaizan and Knight, 2002). It consists of three consecutive phases, the first two using HMMs and the Viterbi algorithm, and the third using a number of monolingual dictionaries to match the close entries or to filter out some invalid candidates from the first two phases.

Since in Arabic, the diacritics are usually omitted in writing, a name like "محمد" (Mohamed) would have an equivalent like "mhmd" if we only take into account the written letters. To address this issue, we run Viterbi in two different passes (each called a phase), using HMMs trained on data prepared in different ways.

In phase 1, the system tries to find the best transliterations of the written word, without caring about what the hidden diacritics would be (in our example, mhmd).

In phase 2, given the Arabic input and the output candidates from phase 1, the system fills in the possible blanks in between using the character-based language model (yielding "mohamed" as a possible output, among others).

To prepare the character-level translation model for both phases we adopted an approach similar to (AbdulJaleel and Larkey, 2003).

In phase 3, the Google unigram model (LDC2006T13 from the LDC catalog) is first used to filter out the noise (i.e. those candidates that do not exist in the Google unigram are removed from the candidate list). Then a combination of some monolingual dictionaries of person names is used to find close matches between their entries and the HMM output candidates based on the Levenshtein distance metric.

3.2 Task-specific Changes to the Module

Due to the nature of the task at hand and by observing the development test set and its references, the following major changes became necessary:

Removing Part of Phase Three: By observing the OOV words in the development test set, we realized that having the monolingual dictionary in the pipeline and using the Levensthtein distance as a metric for adding the closest dictionary entries to the final output, does not help much, mainly because OOVs are rarely in the dictionary. So, the dictionary part not only slows down the execution but would also add noise to the final output (by adding some entries that probably are not the desired outputs). However, we kept the Google unigram filtering in the pipeline.

Rescaling HMM Probabilities: Although the transliteration module outputs HMM probability score for each candidate, and the MT system also uses probability scores, in practice the transliteration scores have to be adjusted. For example, if three consecutive candidates have log probabilities -40, -42 and -50, the decoder should be given values with similar differences in scale, comparable with the typical differences in its internal features (eg. Language Models). Knowing that the entries in the internal features usually have exponential differences, we adopted the following conversion formula:

$$p'_i = 0.1*(p_i/p_{max})^{\alpha}$$

Equation 1

where $p_i = 10^{(\text{output of HMM for candidate } i)}$ and *max* is the best candidate.

We rescale the HMM probability so that the top candidate is (arbitrarily) given a probability of $p'_{max} = 0.1$. It immediately follows that the rescaled score would be $0.1 * p_i / p_{max}$. Since the decoder combines its models in a log-linear fashion, we apply an exponent α to the HMM probabilities before scaling them, as way to control the weight of those probabilities in decoding. This yields equation 1. Ideally, we would like the weight α to be optimized the same way other decoder weights are optimized, but our decoder does not support this yet, so for this work we arbitrarily set the weight to $\alpha = 0.2$, which seems to work well. For the above example, the distribution would be 0.1, 0.039 and 0.001.

Prefix Detachment: Arabic is a morphologically rich language. Even after performing tokenization, some words still remain untokenized. If the composite word is frequent, there is a chance that it exists in the phrase table but many times it does not, especially if the main part of that word is a named entity. We did not want to delve into the details of morphology: we only considered two frequent prefixes: "و" ("va" meaning "and") and "ال" ("al" determiner in Arabic). If a word starts with either of these two prefixes, we detach them and run the transliteration module once on the detached name and a second time on the whole word. The output candidates are merged automatically based on their scores, and the decoder decides which one to choose.

Keeping the Top 5 HMM Candidates: The transliteration module uses the Google unigram model to filter out the candidate words that do not appear above a certain threshold (200 times) on the Internet. This helps eliminate hundreds of unwanted sequences of letters. But, we decided to keep top-5 candidates on the output list, even if they are rejected by the Google unigram model because sometimes the transliteration module is unable to suggest the correct equivalent or in other cases the OOV should actually be translated rather than transliterated[3]. In these cases, the closest literal transliteration will still provide the end user more information about the entity than the word in Arabic script would.

4 Evaluation

Although there are metrics that directly address NE translation performance[4], we chose to use BLEU because our purpose is to assess NE translation within MT, and BLEU is currently the standard metric for MT.

4.1 Training Data

We used the data made available for the 2006 NIST Machine Translation Evaluation. Our bilingual training corpus consisted of 4M sentence pairs drawn mostly from newswire and UN domains. We trained one language model on the English half of this corpus (137M running words), and another on the English Gigaword corpus (2.3G running words). For tuning feature weights, we used LDC's "multiple translation part 1" corpus, which contains 1,043 sentence pairs.

4.2 Test Data

We used the NIST MT04 evaluation set and the NIST MT05 evaluation set as our development and blind test sets. The development test set consists of 1353 sentences, 233 of which contain OOVs. Among them 100 sentences have OOVs that are actually named entities. The blind test set consists of 1056 sentences, 189 of them having OOVs and 131 of them having OOV named entities. The number of sentences for each experiment is summarized in table 1.

	Whole Text	OOV Sentences	OOV-NE Sentences
Dev test set	1353	233	100
Blind test set	1056	189	131

Table 1: Distribution of sentences in test sets.

4.3 Results

As the baseline, we ran the Portage without the transliteration module on development and blind test sets. The second column of table 2 shows baseline BLEU scores. We applied method 4 as outlined in section 2 and computed the BLEU score, also in order to compare the results we implemented method 3 on the same test sets. The BLEU scores obtained from methods 3 and 4 are shown in columns 3 and 4 of table 2.

	baseline	Method 3	Method 4	Oracle
Dev	44.67	44.71	44.83	44.90
Blind	48.56	48.62	48.80	49.01

Table 2: BLEU score on different test sets.

Considering the fact that only a small portion of the test set has out-of-vocabulary named entities,

[3] This would happen especially for ancient names or some names that underwent sophisticated morphological transformations (For example, Abraham in English and ابراهيم (Ibrahim) in Arabic).

[4] NIST's NE translation task (http://www.nist.gov/speech/tests/ace/index.htm) is an example.

we computed the BLEU score on two different sub-portions of the test set: first, on the sentences with OOVs; second, only on the sentences containing OOV named entities. The BLEU increase on different portions of the test set is shown in table 3.

		baseline	Method 4
Dev	OOV sentences	39.17	40.02
	OOV-NE Sentences	44.56	46.31
blind	OOV sentences	43.93	45.07
	OOV-NE Sentences	42.32	44.87

Table 3: BLEU score on different portions of the test sets.

To set an upper bound on how much applying any transliteration module can contribute to the overall results, we developed an oracle-like dictionary for the OOVs in the test sets, which was then used to create a markup Arabic text. By feeding this markup input to the MT system we obtained the result shown in column 5 of table 2. This is the performance our system would achieve if it had perfect accuracy in transliteration, including correctly guessing what errors the human translators made in the references. Method 4 achieves 70% of this maximum gain on dev, and 53% on blind.

5 Conclusion

This paper has described the integration of a transliteration module into a state-of-the-art statistical machine translation (SMT) system for the Arabic to English task. The final version of the transliteration module operates in three phases. First, it generates English letter sequences corresponding to the Arabic letter sequence; for the typical case where the Arabic omits diacritics, this often means that the English letter sequence is incomplete (e.g., vowels are often missing). In the next phase, the module tries to guess the missing English letters. In the third phase, the module uses a huge collection of English unigrams to filter out improbable or impossible English words and names. We described four possible methods for integrating this module in an SMT system. Two of these methods require NE taggers of higher quality than those available to us, and were not explored experimentally. Method 3 inserts the top-scoring candidate from the transliteration module in the translation wherever there was an Arabic OOV in the source. Method 4 outputs multiple candidates from the transliteration module, each with a score; the SMT system combines these scores with language model scores to decide which candidate will be chosen. In our experiments, Method 4 consistently outperformed Model 3. Note that although we used BLEU as the metric for all experiments in this paper, BLEU greatly understates the importance of accurate transliteration for many practical SMT applications.

References

Nasreen AbdulJaleel and Leah S. Larkey, 2003. *Statistical Transliteration for English-Arabic Cross Language Information Retrieval*, Proceedings of the Twelfth International Conference on Information and Knowledge Management, New Orleans, LA

Yaser Al-Onaizan and Kevin Knight, 2002. *Machine Transliteration of Names in Arabic Text*, Proceedings of the ACL Workshop on Computational Approaches to Semitic Languages

Peter F. Brown, Vincent J. Della Pietra, Stephen A. Della Pietra, and Robert L. Mercer, 1993. *The Mathematics of Statistical Machine Translation: Parameter Estimation*, Computational Linguistics

Hany Hassan and Jeffrey Sorensen, 2005. *An Integrated Approach for Arabic-English Named Entity Translation*, Proceedings of the ACL Workshop on Computational Approaches to Semitic Languages (ACL), University of Michigan, Ann Arbor

Mehdi M. Kashani, Fred Popowich, and Anoop Sarkar, 2007. *Automatic Transliteration of Proper Nouns from Arabic to English*, Proceedings of the Second Workshop on Computational Approaches to Arabic Script-based Languages

Alexandre Klementiev and Dan Roth, 2006. *Named Entity Transliteration and Discovery from Multilingual Comparable Corpora*, COLING-ACL, Sidney, Australia

Philipp Koehn, Franz Josef Och, and Daniel Marcu, 2003. *Statistical Phrase-based Translation*, In Proceedings of HLT-NAACL, Edmonton, Canada

Franz Josef Och, 2003. *Minimum Error Rate Training for Statistical Machine Translation*, In Proceedings of the 41th Annual Meeting of the Association for Computation Linguistics, Sapporo

Kishore Papineni, Salim Roukos, Todd Ward, and Wei-Jing Zhu, 2002. *BLEU: a Method for Automatic Evaluation of Machine Translation*. In Proceedings of the 40th Annual Conference of the Association for Computational Linguistics (ACL), Philadelphia, PA

Fatiha Sadat, Howard Johnson, Akakpo Agbago, George Foster, Roland Kuhn, Aaron Tikuisis, 2005. *Portage: A Phrase-base Machine Translation System.* In Proceedings of the ACL Workshop on Building and Using Parallel Texts, Ann Arbor, Michigan

Richard Sproat, Tao Tao, and ChengXiang Zhai, 2006, *Named Entity Transliteration with Comparable Corpora*, COLING-ACL, Sidney, Australia

Exploring Different Representational Units in English-to-Turkish Statistical Machine Translation

Kemal Oflazer[†,‡]
[†]Language Technologies Institute
Carnegie Mellon University
Pittsburgh, PA, 15213, USA
oflazer@sabanciuniv.edu

İlknur Durgar El-Kahlout[‡]
[‡] Faculty of Engineering and Natural Sciences
Sabancı University
Istanbul, Tuzla, 34956, Turkey
ilknurdurgar@su.sabanciuniv.edu

Abstract

We investigate different representational granularities for sub-lexical representation in statistical machine translation work from English to Turkish. We find that (i) representing both Turkish and English at the morpheme-level but with some selective morpheme-grouping on the Turkish side of the training data, (ii) augmenting the training data with "sentences" comprising only the content words of the original training data to bias root word alignment, (iii) reranking the n-best morpheme-sequence outputs of the decoder with a word-based language model, and (iv) using model iteration all provide a non-trivial improvement over a fully word-based baseline. Despite our very limited training data, we improve from 20.22 BLEU points for our simplest model to 25.08 BLEU points for an improvement of 4.86 points or 24% relative.

1 Introduction

Statistical machine translation (SMT) from English-to-Turkish poses a number of difficulties. Typologically English and Turkish are rather distant languages: while English has very limited morphology and rather fixed SVO constituent order, Turkish is an agglutinative language with a very rich and productive derivational and inflectional morphology, and a very flexible (but SOV dominant) constituent order. Another issue of practical significance is the lack of large scale parallel text resources, with no substantial improvement expected in the near future.

In this paper, we investigate different representational granularities for sub-lexical representation of parallel data for English-to-Turkish phrase-based SMT and compare them with a word-based baseline. We also employ two-levels of language models: the decoder uses a morpheme based LM while it is generating an n-best list. The n-best lists are then rescored using a word-based LM.

The paper is structured as follows: We first briefly discuss issues in SMT and Turkish, and review related work. We then outline how we exploit morphology, and present results from our baseline and morphologically segmented models, followed by some sample outputs. We then describe discuss model iteration. Finally, we present a comprehensive discussion of our approach and results, and briefly discuss word-repair – fixing morphologicaly malformed words – and offer a few ideas about the adaptation of BLEU to morphologically complex languages like Turkish.

2 Turkish and SMT

Our previous experience with SMT into Turkish (Durgar El-Kahlout and Oflazer, 2006) hinted that exploiting sub-lexical structure would be a fruitful avenue to pursue. This was based on the observation that a Turkish word would have to align with a complete phrase on the English side, and that sometimes these phrases on the English side could be discontinuous. Figure 1 shows a pair of English and Turkish sentences that are aligned at the word (top) and morpheme (bottom) levels. At the morpheme level, we have split the Turkish words into their lexical morphemes while English words with overt morphemes have been stemmed, and such morphemes have been marked with a tag.

The productive morphology of Turkish implies potentially a very large vocabulary size. Thus, sparseness which is more acute when very modest

Proceedings of the Second Workshop on Statistical Machine Translation, pages 25–32,
Prague, June 2007.

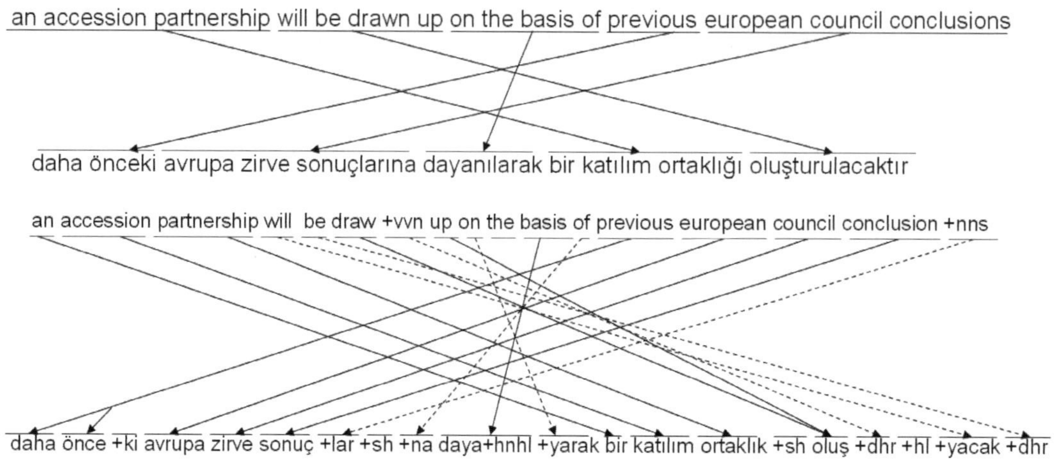

Figure 1: Word and morpheme alignments for a pair of English-Turkish sentences

parallel resources are available becomes an important issue. However, Turkish employs about 30,000 root words and about 150 distinct suffixes, so when morphemes are used as the units in the parallel texts, the sparseness problem can be alleviated to some extent.

Our approach in this paper is to represent Turkish words with their morphological segmentation. We use lexical morphemes instead of surface morphemes, as most surface distinctions are manifestations of word-internal phenomena such as vowel harmony, and morphotactics. With lexical morpheme representation, we can abstract away such word-internal details *and* conflate statistics for seemingly different suffixes, as at this level of representation words that look very different on the surface, look very similar.[1] For instance, although the words *evinde* 'in his house' and *masasında* 'on his table' look quite different, the lexical morphemes except for the root are the same: `ev+sH+ndA` vs. `masa+sH+ndA`.

We should however note that although employing a morpheme based representations dramatically reduces the vocabulary size on the Turkish side, it also runs the risk of overloading distortion mechanisms to account for *both* word-internal morpheme sequencing and sentence level word ordering.

The segmentation of a word in general is not unique. We first generate a representation that contains both the lexical segments and the morphological features encoded for all possible segmentations and interpretations of the word. For the word *emeli* for instance, our morphological analyzer generates the following with lexical morphemes bracketed with `(..)`:

`(em)em+Verb+Pos(+yAlH)^DB+Adverb+Since`
since (someone) sucked (something)
`(emel)emel+Noun+A3sg(+sH)+P3sg+Nom`
his/her ambition
`(emel)emel+Noun+A3sg+Pnon(+yH)+Acc`
ambition (as object of a transitive verb)

These analyses are then disambiguated with a statistical disambiguator (Yüret and Türe, 2006) which operates on the morphological features.[2] Finally, the morphological features are removed from each parse leaving the lexical morphemes.

Using morphology in SMT has been recently addressed by researchers translation from or into morphologically rich(er) languages. Niessen and Ney (2004) have used morphological decomposition to improve alignment quality. Yang and Kirchhoff (2006) use phrase-based backoff models to translate words that are unknown to the decoder, by morphologically decomposing the unknown source word. They particularly apply their method to translating *from* Finnish – another language with very similar structural characteristics to Turkish. Corston-Oliver and Gamon (2004) normalize inflectional morphology by stemming the word for German-English word alignment. Lee (2004) uses a morphologically analyzed and tagged parallel corpus for Arabic-English SMT. Zolmann et al. (2006) also exploit morphology in Arabic-English SMT. Popovic and Ney (2004) investigate improving translation qual-

[1] This is in a sense very similar to the more general problem of lexical redundancy addressed by Talbot and Osborne (2006) but our approach does not require the more sophisticated solution there.

[2] This disambiguator has about 94% accuracy.

ity from inflected languages by using stems, suffixes and part-of-speech tags. Goldwater and McClosky (2005) use morphological analysis on Czech text to get improvements in Czech to English SMT. Recently, Minkov et al. (2007) have used morphological postprocessing *on the output side* using structural information and information from the source side, to improve SMT quality.

3 Exploiting Morphology

Our parallel data consists mainly of documents in international relations and legal documents from sources such as the Turkish Ministry of Foreign Affairs, EU, etc. We process these as follows: (i) We segment the words in our Turkish corpus into lexical morphemes whereby differences in the surface representations of morphemes due to word-internal phenomena are abstracted out to improve statistics during alignment.[3] (ii) We tag the English side using TreeTagger (Schmid, 1994), which provides a *lemma* and a *part-of-speech* for each word. We then remove any tags which do not imply an explicit morpheme or an exceptional form. So for instance, if the word *book* gets tagged as *+NN*, we keep *book* in the text, but remove *+NN*. For *books* tagged as *+NNS* or *booking* tagged as *+VVG*, we keep *book* and *+NNS*, and *book* and *+VVG*. A word like *went* is replaced by *go +VVD*.[4] (iii) From these morphologically segmented corpora, we also extract for each sentence, the sequence of roots for open class content words (nouns, adjectives, adverbs, and verbs). For Turkish, this corresponds to removing *all* morphemes and any roots for closed classes. For English, this corresponds to removing all words tagged as closed class words along with the tags such as *+VVG* above that signal a morpheme on an open class content word. We use this to augment the training corpus and bias content word alignments, with the hope that such roots may get a chance to align without any additional "noise" from morphemes and other function words.

From such processed data, we compile the data sets whose statistics are listed in Table 1. One can note that Turkish has many more distinct word forms (about twice as many as English), but has much less

Turkish	**Sent.**	**Words (UNK)**	**Uniq. Words**
Train	45,709	557,530	52,897
Train-Content	56,609	436,762	13,767
Tune	200	3,258	1,442
Test	649	10,334 (545)	4,355
English			
Train	45,709	723,399	26,747
Train-Content	56,609	403,162	19,791
Test	649	13,484 (231)	3,220

Turkish	**Morph-emes**	**Uniq. Morp.**	**Morp./ Word**	**Uniq. Roots**	**Uniq. Suff.**
Train	1,005,045	15,081	1.80	14,976	105
Tune	6,240	859	1.92	810	49
Test	18,713	2,297	1.81	2,220	77

Table 1: Statistics on Turkish and English training and test data, and Turkish morphological structure

number of distinct content words than English.[5] For language models in decoding and n-best list rescoring, we use, in addition to the training data, a monolingual Turkish text of about 100,000 sentences (in a segmented and disambiguated form).

A typical sentence pair in our data looks like the following, where we have highlighted the content root words with bold font, coindexed them to show their alignments and bracketed the "words" that evaluation on test would consider.

- **T:** [**kat**$_1$ +hl +ma] [**ortaklık**$_2$ +sh +nhn] [**uygula**$_3$ +hn +ma +sh] [,] [**ortaklık**$_4$] [**anlaşma**$_5$ +sh] [**çerçeve**$_6$ +sh +nda] [**izle**$_7$ +hn +yacak +dhr] [.]
- **E:** the **implementation**$_3$ of the **accession**$_1$ **partnership**$_2$ will be **monitor**$_7$ +vvn in the **framework**$_6$ of the **association**$_4$ **agreement**$_5$.

Note that when the morphemes/tags (starting with a +) are concatenated, we get the "word-based" version of the corpus, since surface words are directly recoverable from the concatenated representation. We use this word-based representation also for word-based language models used for rescoring.

We employ the phrase-based SMT framework (Koehn et al., 2003), and use the Moses toolkit (Koehn et al., 2007), and the SRILM language modelling toolkit (Stolcke, 2002), and evaluate our decoded translations using the BLEU measure (Papineni et al., 2002), using a *single* reference translation.

[3]So for example, the surface plural morphemes *+ler* and *+lar* get conflated to *+lAr* and their statistics are hence combined.

[4]Ideally, it would have been very desirable to actually do derivational morphological analysis on the English side, so that one could for example analyze *accession* into *access* plus a marker indicating nominalization.

[5]The training set in the first row of 1 was limited to sentences on the Turkish side which had at most 90 tokens (roots and bound morphemes) in total in order to comply with requirements of the GIZA++ alignment tool. However when only the content words are included, we have more sentences to include since much less number of sentences violate the length restriction when morphemes/function word are removed.

Moses Dec. Parms.	BLEU	BLEU-c
Default	16.29	16.13
dl = -1, -weight-d = 0.1	20.16	19.77

Table 2: BLEU results for baseline experiments.
BLEU is for the model trained on the training set
BLEU-C is for the model trained on training set augmented with the content words.

3.1 The Baseline System

As a baseline system, we trained a model using default Moses parameters (e.g., maximum phrase length = 7), using the word-based training corpus. The English test set was decoded with both default decoder parameters and with the distortion limit (*-dl* in Moses) set to *unlimited* (-1 in Moses) and distortion weight (*-weight-d* in Moses) set to a very low value of 0.1 to allow for long distance distortions.[6] We also augmented the training set with the content word data and trained a second baseline model. Minimum error rate training with the tune set did not provide any tangible improvements.[7] Table 2 shows the BLEU results for baseline performance. It can be seen that adding the content word training data actually hampers the baseline performance.

3.2 Fully Morphologically Segmented Model

We now trained a model using the fully morphologically segmented training corpus *with* and *without content word parallel corpus augmentation*. For decoding, we used a 5-gram *morpheme-based* language model with the hope of capturing *local morphotactic ordering* constraints, and perhaps some sentence level ordering of words.[8] We then decoded and obtained 1000-best lists. The 1000-best sentences were then converted to "words" (by concatenating the morphemes) and then rescored with a 4-gram word-based language model with the hope of enforcing more distant *word sequencing* constraints. For this, we followed the following procedure: We tried various linear combinations of the word-based language model and the translation model scores on the *tune* corpus, and used the combination that performed best to evaluate the *test* corpus. We also experimented with both the default decoding parameters, and the modified parameters used in the baseline model decoding above.

The results in Table 3 indicate that the default decoding parameters used by the Moses decoder provide a very dismal results – much below the baseline scores. We can speculate that as the constituent orders of Turkish and English are very different, (root) words may have to be scrambled to rather long distances *along with* the translations of functions words and tags on the English side, to morphemes on the Turkish side. Thus limiting maximum distortion and penalizing distortions with the default higher weight, result in these low BLEU results. Allowing the decoder to consider longer range distortions and penalizing such distortions much less with the modified decoding parameters, seem to make an enormous difference in this case, providing close to almost 7 BLEU points improvement.[9]

We can also see that, contrary to the case with the baseline word-based experiments, using the additional content word corpus for training actually provides a tangible improvement (about 6.2% relative (w/o rescoring)), most likely due to slightly better alignments when content words are used.[10] Rescoring the 1000-best sentence output with a 4-gram word-based language model provides an additional 0.79 BLEU points (about 4% relative) – from 20.22 to 21.01 – for the model with the basic training set, and an additional 0.71 BLEU points (about 3% relative) – from 21.47 to 22.18– for the model with the augmented training set. The cumulative improvement is 1.96 BLEU points or about 9.4% relative.

3.3 Selectively Segmented Model

A systematic analysis of the alignment files produced by GIZA++ for a small subset of the training sentences showed that certain morphemes on the

[6]We arrived at this combination by experimenting with the decoder to avoid the almost monotonic translation we were getting with the default parameters.

[7]We ran MERT on the baseline model and the morphologically segmented models forcing *-weight-d* to range a very small around 0.1, but letting the other parameters range in their suggested ranges. Even though the procedure came back claiming that it achieved a better BLEU score on the tune set, running the new model on the test set did not show any improvement at all. This may have been due to the fact that the initial choice of *-weight-d* along with *-dl* set to 1 provides such a drastic improvement that perturbations in the other parameters do not have much impact.

[8]Given that on the average we have almost two bound morphemes per "word" (for inflecting word classes), a morpheme 5-gram would cover about 2 "words".

[9]The "morpheme" BLEU scores are much higher (34.43 on the test set) where we measure BLEU *using decoded morphemes* as tokens. This is just indicative and but correlates with word-level BLEU which we report in Table 3, and can be used to gauge relative improvements to the models.

[10]We also constructed phrase tables only from the actual training set (w/o the content word section) *after* the alignment phase. The resulting models fared slightly worse though we do not yet understand why.

Moses Dec. Parms.	BLEU	BLEU-c
Default	13.55	NA
dl = -1, -weight-d = 0.1	20.22	21.47
dl = -1, -weight-d = 0.1 **+ word-level LM rescoring**	21.01	22.18

Table 3: BLEU results for experiments with fully morphologically segmented training set

Turkish side were almost consistently never aligned with anything on the English side: e.g., the compound noun marker morpheme in Turkish (+sh) does not have a corresponding unit on the English side since English noun-noun compounds do not carry any overt markers. Such markers were never aligned to anything or were aligned almost randomly to tokens on the English side. Since we perform derivational morphological analysis on the Turkish side but not on the English side, we noted that most verbal nominalizations on the English side were just aligned to the verb roots on the Turkish side and the additional markers on the Turkish side indicating the nominalization and agreement markers etc., were mostly unaligned.

For just these cases, we selectively attached such morphemes (and in the case of verbs, the intervening morphemes) to the root, but otherwise kept other morphemes, especially any case morphemes, still by themselves, as they almost often align with prepositions on the English side quite accurately.[11]

This time, we trained a model on just the content-word augmented training corpus, with the better performing parameters for the decoder and again did 1000-best rescoring.[12] The results for this experiment are shown in Table 4. The resulting BLEU represents 2.43 points (11% relative) improvement over the best fully segmented model (and 4.39 points 21.7% compared to the very initial morphologically segmented model). This is a very encouraging result that indicates we should perhaps consider a much more detailed analysis of morpheme alignments to uncover additional morphemes with similar status. Table 5 provides additional details on the BLEU

[11]It should be noted that what to selectively attach to the root should be considered on a per-language basis; if Turkish were to be aligned with a language with similar morphological markers, this perhaps would not have been needed. Again one perhaps can use methods similar to those suggested by Talbot and Osborne (2006).

[12]Decoders for the fully-segmented model and selectively segmented model use different 5-gram language models, since the language model corpus should have the same selectively segmented units as those in the training set. However, the word-level language models used in rescoring are the same.

Moses Dec. Parms.	BLEU-c
dl = -1, -weight-d = 0.1 **+ word-level LM rescoring (Full Segmentation (from Table 3))**	22.18
dl = -1, -weight-d = 0.1	23.47
dl = -1, -weight-d = 0.1 **+ word-level LM rescoring**	**24.61**

Table 4: BLEU results for experiments with selectively segmented and content-word augmented training set

Range	Sent.	BLEU-c
1 - 10	172	44.36
1 - 15	276	34.63
5 - 15	**217**	**33.00**
1 - 20	369	28.84
1 - 30	517	27.88
1 - 40	589	24.90
All	649	24.61

Table 5: BLEU Scores for different ranges of (source) sentence length for the result in Table 4

scores for this model, for different ranges of (English source) sentence length.

4 Sample Rules and Translations

We have extracted some additional statistics from the translations produced from English test set. Of the 10,563 words in the decoded test set, a total of 957 words (9.0 %) were not seen in the training corpus. However, interestingly, of these 957 words, 432 (45%) were actually morphologically well-formed (some as complex as having 4-5 morphemes!) This indicates that the *phrase-based translation model is able to synthesize novel complex words.*[13] In fact, some phrase table entries seem to capture morphologically marked subcategorization patterns. An example is the phrase translation pair

```
after examine +vvg ⇒
        +acc incele+dhk +abl sonra
```

which very much resembles a typical structural transfer rule one would find in a symbolic machine translation system

$\texttt{PP(after examine +vvg NP}_{eng}\texttt{)} \Rightarrow$

$\texttt{PP(NP}_{turk}\texttt{+acc incele+dhk +abl sonra)}$

in that the accusative marker is tacked to the translation of the English NP.

Figure 2 shows how segments are translated to Turkish for a sample sentence. Figure 3 shows the translations of three sentences from the test data

[13]Though whether such words are actually correct in their context is not necessarily clear.

```
çocuk [[ child ]]
 hak+lar+sh +nhn [[ +nns +pos right ]]
 koru+hn+ma+sh [[ protection ]]
 +nhn [[ of ]]
 teşvik et+hl+ma+sh [[ promote ]]
 +loc [[ +nns in ]] ab [[ eu ]]
 ve ulus+lararasi standart +lar
    [[ and international standard +nns ]]
 +dat uygun [[ line with ]] +dhr .  [[ .]]
```

Figure 2: Phrasal translations selected for a sample sentence

Inp.: 1 . everyone's right to life shall be protected by law .
Trans.: 1 . herkesin yaşama hakkı kanunla korunur.
Lit.: everyone's living right is protected with law .
Ref.: 1 . herkesin yaşam hakkı yasanın koruması altındadır .
Lit.: everyone's life right is under the protection of the law.

Inp.: promote protection of children's rights in line with eu and international standards .
Trans.: çocuk haklarının korunmasının **ab ve uluslararası standartlar**a uygun şekilde geliştirilmesi.
Lit.: develop protection of children's rights in accordance with eu and international standards .
Ref.: **ab ve uluslararası standartlar** doğrultusunda çocuk haklarının korunmasının teşvik edilmesi.
Lit.: in line with eu and international standards promote/motivate protection of children's rights .

Inp.: as a key feature of such a strategy, an accession partnership will be drawn up on the basis of previous european council conclusions.
Trans.: bu stratejinin kilit unsuru bir katılım ortaklığı belgesi hazırlanacak kadarın temelinde , bir önceki avrupa konseyi sonuçlarıdır .
Lit.: as a key feature of this strategy, accession partnership document will be prepared ??? based are previous european council resolutions .
Ref.: bu stratejinin kilit unsuru olarak , daha önceki ab zirve sonuçlarına dayanılarak bir katılım ortaklığı oluşturulacaktır.
Lit.: as a key feature of this strategy an accession partnership based on earlier eu summit resolutions will be formed .

Figure 3: Some sample translations

along with the literal paraphrases of the translation and the reference versions. The first two are quite accurate and acceptable translations while the third clearly has missing and incorrect parts.

5 Model Iteration

We have also experimented with an iterative approach to use multiple models to see if further improvements are possible. This is akin to post-editing (though definitely not akin to the much more sophisticated approach in described in Simard et al. (2007)). We proceeded as follows: We used the selective segmentation based model above and decoded our English *training* data $\mathtt{E}_{Train}$ and English test data $\mathtt{E}_{Test}$ to obtain $\mathtt{T1}_{Train}$ and $\mathtt{T1}_{Test}$ respectively. We then trained the next model using $\mathtt{T1}_{Train}$ and $\mathtt{T}_{Train}$, to build a model that hopefully will improve upon the output of the previous model, $\mathtt{T1}_{Test}$, to bring it closer to $\mathtt{T}_{Test}$. This model when applied to $\mathtt{T1}_{Train}$ and $\mathtt{T1}_{Test}$ produce $\mathtt{T2}_{Train}$ and $\mathtt{T2}_{Test}$ respectively.

Step	BLEU
From Table 4	24.61
Iter. 1	24.77
Iter. 2	**25.08**

Table 6: BLEU results for two model iterations

We have not included the content word corpus in these experiments, as (i) our few very preliminary experiments indicated that using a morpheme-based models in subsequent iterations would perform worse than word-based models, and (ii) that for word-based models adding the content word training data was not helpful as our baseline experiments indicated. The models were tested by decoding the output of the previous model for original test data. For word-based decoding in the additional iterations we used a 3-gram word-based language model but reranked the 1000-best outputs using a 4-gram language model. Table 6 provides the BLEU results for these experiments corresponding to two additional model iterations.

The BLEU result for the second iteration, 25.08, represents a cumulative 4.86 points (24% relative) improvement over the initial fully morphologically segmented model using only the basic training set and no rescoring.

6 Discussion

Translation into Turkish seems to involve processes that are somewhat more complex than standard statistical translation models: sometimes words on the Turkish side are synthesized from the translations of two or more (SMT) phrases, and errors in any translated morpheme or its morphotactic position render the synthesized word incorrect, even though the rest of the word can be quite fine. If we just extract the root words (not just for content words but all words) in the decoded test set and the reference set, and compute *root word* BLEU, we obtain 30.62, [**64.6**/35.7/23.4/16.3]. The unigram precision score shows that we are getting almost 65% of the root words correct. However, the unigram precision score with full words is about 52% for our best model. Thus we are missing about 13% of the words *although we seem to be getting their roots* *correct*. With a tool that we have developed, *BLEU+* (Tantuğ et al., 2007), we have investigated such mismatches and have found that most of these are actually morphologically bogus, in that, although they have the root word right, the morphemes are either not the applicable ones or are in a morphotactically wrong position. These can easily be identified with the morphological generator that we have. In many cases, such morphologically bogus words are *one morpheme edit distance away* from the correct form in the reference file. Another avenue that *could* be pursued is the use of skip language models (supported by the SRILM toolkit) so that the content word order could directly be used by the decoder.[14]

At this point it is very hard to compare how our results fare in the grand scheme of things, since there is not much prior results for English to Turkish SMT. Koehn (2005) reports on translation from English to Finnish, another language that is morphologically as complex as Turkish, with the added complexity of compounding and stricter agreement between modifiers and head nouns. A standard phrase-based system trained with 941,890 pairs of sentences (about 20 times the data that we have!) gives a BLEU score of 13.00. However, in this study, nothing specific for Finnish was employed, and one can certainly employ techniques similar to presented here to improve upon this.

6.1 Word Repair

The fact that there are quite many erroneous words which are actually easy to fix suggests some ideas to improve unigram precision. One can utilize a morpheme level "spelling corrector" that operates on segmented representations, and corrects such forms to possible morphologically correct words in order to form a lattice which can again be rescored to select the contextually correct one.[15] With the *BLEU+* tool, we have done one experiment that shows that *if* we could recover all morphologically bogus words that are 1 and 2 morpheme edit distance from the correct form, the word BLEU score could rise to 29.86, [60.0/34.9/23.3/16.] and 30.48 [63.3/35.6/23.4/16.4] respectively. Obviously, these are upper-bound oracle scores, as subsequent candidate generation and lattice rescoring could make errors, but nevertheless they are very close to the root word BLEU scores above.

Another path to pursue in repairing words is to identify morphologically correct words which are either OOVs in the language model or for which the language model has low confidence. One can perhaps identify these using posterior probabilities (e.g., using techniques in Zens and Ney (2006)) and generate additional morphologically valid words that are "close" and construct a lattice that can be rescored.

6.2 Some Thoughts on BLEU

BLEU is particularly harsh for Turkish and the morpheme based-approach, because of the all-or-none nature of token comparison, as discussed above. There are also cases where words with different morphemes have very close morphosemantics, convey the relevant meaning and are almost interchangeable:

- *gel+hyor* (geliyor - he is coming) vs. *gel+makta* (gelmekte - he is (in a state of) coming) are essentially the same. On a scale of 0 to 1, one could rate these at about 0.95 in similarity.
- *gel+yacak* (gelecek - he will come) vs. *gel+yacak+dhr* (gelecektir - he *will* come) in a sentence final position. Such pairs could be rated perhaps at 0.90 in similarity.
- *gel+dh* (geldi - he came (past tense)) vs. *gel+mhs* (gelmiş - he came (hearsay past tense)). These essentially mark past tense but differ in how the speaker relates to the event and could be rated at perhaps 0.70 similarity.

Note that using stems and their synonyms as used in METEOR (Banerjee and Lavie, 2005) could also be considered for word similarity.

Again using the *BLEU+* tool and *a slightly different formulation of token similarity* in BLEU computation, we find that using morphological similarity our best score above, 25.08 BLEU increases to 25.14 BLEU, while using only root word synonymy and very close hypernymy from Wordnet, gives us 25.45 BLEU. The combination of rules and Wordnet match gives 25.46 BLEU. Note that these increases are much less than what can (potentially) be gained from solving the word-repair problem above.

7 Conclusions

We have presented results from our investigation into using different granularity of sub-lexical representations for English to Turkish SMT. We have found that employing a language-pair specific representation somewhere in between using full word-forms and fully morphologically segmented representations and using content words as additional

[14]This was suggested by one of the reviewers.

[15]It would however perhaps be much better if the decoder could be augmented with a filter that could be invoked at much earlier stages of sentence generation to check if certain generated segments violate *hard-constraints* (such as morphotactic constraints) regardless of what the statistics say.

data provide a significant boost in BLEU scores, in addition to contributions of word-level rescoring of 1000-best outputs and model iteration, to give a BLEU score of 25.08 points with very modest parallel text resources. Detailed analysis of the errors point at a few directions such as word-repair, to improve word accuracy. This also suggests perhaps hooking into the decoder, a mechanism for imposing hard constraints (such as morphotactic constraints) during decoding to avoid generating morphologically bogus words. Another direction is to introduce exploitation of limited structures such as bracketed noun phrases before considering full-fledged syntactic structure.

Acknowledgements

This work was supported by TÜBİTAK – The Turkish National Science and Technology Foundation under project grant 105E020. We thank the anonymous reviewer for some very useful comments and suggestions.

References

Satanjeev Banerjee and Alon Lavie. 2005. METEOR: An automatic metric for MT evaluation with improved correlation with human judgments. In *Proceedings of the ACL Workshop on Intrinsic and Extrinsic Evaluation Measures for Machine Translation and/or Summarization*, pages 65–72, Ann Arbor, Michigan, June.

Simon Corston-Oliver and Michael Gamon. 2004. Normalizing German and English inflectional morphology to improve statistical word alignment. In *Proceedings of AMTA*, pages 48–57.

İlknur Durgar El-Kahlout and Kemal Oflazer. 2006. Initial explorations in English to Turkish statistical machine translation. In *Proceedings on the Workshop on Statistical Machine Translation*, pages 7–14, New York City, June.

Sharon Goldwater and David McClosky. 2005. Improving statistical MT through morphological analysis. In *Proceedings of Human Language Technology Conference and Conference on Empirical Methods in Natural Language Processing*, pages 676–683, Vancouver, British Columbia, Canada, October.

Philipp Koehn, Franz J. Och, and Daniel Marcu. 2003. Statistical phrase-based translation. In *Proceedings of HLT/NAACL*.

Philipp Koehn, Hieu Hoang, Alexandra Birch, Chris Callison-Burch, Marcello Federico, Nicola Bertoldi, Brooke Cowan, Wade Shen, Christine Moran, Richard Zens, Chris Dyer, Ondrej Bojar, Alexandra Constantin, and Evan Herbst. 2007. Moses: Open source toolkit for statistical machine translation. In *Proceedings of the 45th Annual Meeting of the Association for Computational Linguistics (ACL'07) – Companion Volume*, June.

Philip Koehn. 2005. Europarl: A parallel corpus for statistical machine translation. In *MT Summit X*, Phuket, Thailand.

Young-Suk Lee. 2004. Morphological analysis for statistical machine translation. In *Proceedings of HLT-NAACL 2004 - Companion Volume*, pages 57–60.

Einat Minkov, Kristina Toutanova, and Hisami Suzuki. 2007. Generating complex morphology for machine translation. In *Proceedings of the 45th Annual Meeting of the Association for Computational Linguistics (ACL'07)*, Prague, Czech Republic, June.

Sonja Niessen and Hermann Ney. 2004. Statistical machine translation with scarce resources using morpho-syntatic information. *Computational Linguistics*, 30(2):181–204.

Kishore Papineni, Salim Roukos, Todd Ward, and Wei-Jing Zhu. 2002. Bleu: a method for automatic evaluation of machine translation. In *Proceedings of the 40th Annual Meeting of the Association for Computational Linguistics*, University of Pennsylvania.

Maja Popovic and Hermann Ney. 2004. Towards the use of word stems and suffixes for statistical machine translation. In *Proceedings of the 4th International Conference on Language Resources and Evaluation (LREC)*, pages 1585–1588, May.

Helmut Schmid. 1994. Probabilistic part-of-speech tagging using decision trees. In *Proceedings of International Conference on New Methods in Language Processing*.

Michel Simard, Cyril Goutte, and Pierre Isabelle. 2007. Statistical phrase-based post-editing. In *Proceedings of NAACL*, April.

Andreas Stolcke. 2002. SRILM – an extensible language modeling toolkit. In *Proceedings of the Intl. Conf. on Spoken Language Processing*.

David Talbot and Miles Osborne. 2006. Modelling lexical redundancy for machine translation. In *Proceedings of the 21st International Conference on Computational Linguistics and 44th Annual Meeting of the Association for Computational Linguistics*, pages 969–976, Sydney, Australia, July.

Cüneyd Tantuğ, Kemal Oflazer, and İlknur Durgar El-Kahlout. 2007. BLEU+: a tool for fine-grained BLEU computation. in preparation.

Mei Yang and Katrin Kirchhoff. 2006. Phrase-based backoff models for machine translation of highly inflected languages. In *Proceedings of EACL*, pages 41–48.

Deniz Yüret and Ferhan Türe. 2006. Learning morphological disambiguation rules for Turkish. In *Proceedings of the Human Language Technology Conference of the NAACL, Main Conference*, pages 328–334, New York City, USA, June.

Richard Zens and Hermann Ney. 2006. N-gram posterior probabilities for statistical machine translation. In *Proceedings on the Workshop on Statistical Machine Translation*, pages 72–77, New York City, June. Association for Computational Linguistics.

Andreas Zollmann, Ashish Venugopal, and Stephan Vogel. 2006. Bridging the inflection morphology gap for Arabic statistical machine translation. In *Proceedings of the Human Language Technology Conference of the NAACL, Companion Volume: Short Papers*, pages 201–204, New York City, USA, June.

Can We Translate Letters?

David Vilar, Jan-T. Peter and Hermann Ney
Lehrstuhl für Informatik 6
RWTH Aachen University
D-52056 Aachen, Germany
{vilar,peter,ney}@cs.rwth-aachen.de

Abstract

Current statistical machine translation systems handle the translation process as the transformation of a string of symbols into another string of symbols. Normally the symbols dealt with are the words in different languages, sometimes with some additional information included, like morphological data. In this work we try to push the approach to the limit, working not on the level of words, but treating both the source and target sentences as a string of letters. We try to find out if a nearly unmodified state-of-the-art translation system is able to cope with the problem and whether it is capable to further generalize translation rules, for example at the level of word suffixes and translation of unseen words. Experiments are carried out for the translation of Catalan to Spanish.

1 Introduction

Most current statistical machine translation systems handle the translation process as a "blind" transformation of a sequence of symbols, which represent the words in a source language, to another sequence of symbols, which represent words in a target language. This approach allows for a relative simplicity of the models, but also has drawbacks, as related word forms, like different verb tenses or plural-singular word pairs, are treated as completely different entities.

Some efforts have been made e.g. to integrate more information about the words in the form of Part Of Speech tags (Popović and Ney, 2005), using additional information about stems and suffixes (Popović and Ney, 2004) or to reduce the morphological variability of the words (de Gispert, 2006). State of the art decoders provide the ability of handling different word forms directly in what has been called factored translation models (Shen et al., 2006).

In this work, we try to go a step further and treat the words (and thus whole sentences) as sequences of letters, which have to be translated into a new sequence of letters. We try to find out if the translation models can generalize and generate correct words out of the stream of letters. For this approach to work we need to translate between two related languages, in which a correspondence between the structure of the words can be found.

For this experiment we chose a Catalan-Spanish corpus. Catalan is a romance language spoken in the north-east of Spain and Andorra and is considered by some authors as a transitional language between the Iberian Romance languages (e.g. Spanish) and Gallo-Romance languages (e.g. French). A common origin and geographic proximity result in a similarity between Spanish and Catalan, albeit with enough differences to be considered different languages. In particular, the sentence structure is quite similar in both languages and many times a nearly monotonical word to word correspondence between sentences can be found. An example of Catalan and Spanish sentences is given in Figure 1.

The structure of the paper is as follows: In Section 2 we review the statistical approach to machine translation and consider how the usual techniques can be adapted to the letter translation task. In Sec-

Proceedings of the Second Workshop on Statistical Machine Translation, pages 33–39,
Prague, June 2007.

Catalan	Perquè a mi m'agradaria estar-hi dues, una o dues setmanes, més o menys, depenent del preu i cada hotel.
Spanish	Porque a mí me gustaría quedarme dos, una o dos semanas, más o menos, dependiendo del precio y cada hotel.
English	Because I would like to be there two, one or two weeks, more or less, depending on the price of each hotel.

Catalan	Si baixa aquí tenim una guia de la ciutat que li podem facilitar en la que surt informació sobre els llocs més interessants de la ciutat.
Spanish	Si baja aquí tenemos una guía de la ciudad que le podemos facilitar en la que sale información sobre los sitios más interesantes de la ciudad.
English	If you come down here we have a guide book of the city that you can use, in there is information about the most interesting places in the city.

Figure 1: Example Spanish and Catalan sentences (the English translation is provided for clarity).

tion 3 we present the results of the letter-based translation and show how to use it for improving translation quality. Although the interest of this work is more academical, in Section 4 we discuss possible practical applications for this approach. The paper concludes in Section 5.

2 From Words To Letters

In the standard approach to statistical machine translation we are given a sentence (sequence of words) $f_1^J = f_1 \ldots f_J$ in a source language which is to be translated into a sentence $\hat{e}_1^I = \hat{e}_1 \ldots \hat{e}_I$ in a target language. Bayes decision rule states that we should choose the sentence which maximizes the posterior probability

$$\hat{e}_1^I = \operatorname*{argmax}_{e_1^I} p(e_1^I | f_1^J) , \quad (1)$$

where the argmax operator denotes the search process. In the original work (Brown et al., 1993) the posterior probability $p(e_1^I|f_1^J)$ is decomposed following a noisy-channel approach, but current state-of-the-art systems model the translation probability directly using a log-linear model(Och and Ney, 2002):

$$p(e_1^I|f_1^J) = \frac{\exp\left(\sum_{m=1}^M \lambda_m h_m(e_1^I, f_1^J)\right)}{\sum_{\tilde{e}_1^I} \exp\left(\sum_{m=1}^M \lambda_m h_m(\tilde{e}_1^I, f_1^J)\right)} , \quad (2)$$

with h_m different models, λ_m scaling factors and the denominator a normalization factor that can be ignored in the maximization process. The λ_m are usually chosen by optimizing a performance measure over a development corpus using a numerical optimization algorithm like the downhill simplex algorithm (Press et al., 2002).

The most widely used models in the log linear combination are phrase-based models in source-to-target and target-to-source directions, ibm1-like scores computed at phrase level, also in source-to-target and target-to-source directions, a target language model and different penalties, like phrase penalty and word penalty.

This same approach can be directly adapted to the letter-based translation framework. In this case we are given a sequence of letters $\mathcal{F}_1^{\mathcal{J}}$ corresponding to a source (word) string f_1^J, which is to be translated into a sequence of letters $\mathcal{E}_1^{\mathcal{I}}$ corresponding to a string e_1^I in a target language. Note that in this case whitespaces are also part of the vocabulary and have to be generated as any other letter. It is also important to remark that, without any further restrictions, the word sequences e_1^I corresponding to a generated letter sequence $\mathcal{E}_1^{\mathcal{I}}$ are not even composed of actual words.

2.1 Details of the Letter-Based System

The vocabulary of the letter-based translation system is some orders of magnitude smaller than the vocabulary of a full word-based translation system, at least for European languages. A typical vocabulary size for a letter-based system would be around 70, considering upper- and lowercase letter, digits, whitespace and punctuation marks, while the vocabulary size of a word-based system like the ones used in current evaluation campaigns is in the range of tens or hundreds of thousands words. In a normal situation there are no unknowns when carrying out the actual translation of a given test corpus. The situation can be very different if we consider languages like Chinese or Japanese.

This small vocabulary size allows us to deal with a larger context in the models used. For the phrase-based models we extract all phrases that can be used when translating a given test corpus, without any restriction on the length of the source or the target part[1]. For the language model we were able to use a high-order n-gram model. In fact in our experiments a 16-gram letter-based language model is used, while state-of-the-art translation systems normally use 3 or 4-grams (word-based).

In order to better try to generate "actual words" in the letter-based system, a new model was added in the log-linear combination, namely the count of words generated that have been seen in the training corpus, normalized with the length of the input sentence. Note however that this models enters as an additional feature function in the model and it does not constitute a restriction of the generalization capabilities the model can have in creating "new words". Somehow surprisingly, an additional word language model did not help.

While the vocabulary size is reduced, the average sentence length increases, as we consider each letter to be a unit by itself. This has a negative impact in the running time of the actual implementation of the algorithms, specially for the alignment process. In order to alleviate this, the alignment process was split into two passes. In the first part, a word alignment was computed (using the GIZA++ toolkit (Och and Ney, 2003)). Then the training sentences were split according to this alignment (in a similar way to the standard phrase extraction algorithm), so that the length of the source and target part is around thirty letters. Then, a letter-based alignment is computed.

2.2 Efficiency Issues

Somewhat counter-intuitively, the reduced vocabulary size does not necessarily imply a reduced memory footprint, at least not without a dedicated program optimization. As in a sensible implementations of nearly all natural language processing tools, the words are mapped to integers and handled as such. A typical implementation of a phrase table is then a prefix-tree, which is accessed through these word indices. In the case of the letter-based translation, the phrases extracted are much larger than the word-based ones, in terms of elements. Thus the total size of the phrase table increases.

The size of the search graph is also larger for the letter-based system. In most current systems the generation algorithm is a beam search algorithm with a "source synchronous" search organization. As the length of the source sentence is dramatically increased when considering letters instead of words, the total size of the search graph is also increased, as is the running time of the translation process.

The memory usage for the letter system can actually be optimized, in the sense that the letters can act as "indices" themselves for addressing the phrase table and the auxiliary mapping structure is not necessary any more. Furthermore the characters can be stored in only one byte, which provides a significant memory gain over the word based system where normally four bytes are used for storing the indices. These gains however are not expected to counteract the other issues presented in this section.

3 Experimental Results

The corpus used for our experiment was built in the framework of the LC-STAR project (Conejero et al., 2003). It consists of spontaneous dialogues in Spanish, Catalan and English[2] in the tourism and travelling domain. The test corpus (and an additional development corpus for parameter optimization) was randomly extracted, the rest of the sentences were used as training data. Statistics for the corpus can be seen in Table 1. Details of the translation system used can be found in (Mauser et al., 2006).

The results of the word-based and letter-based approaches can be seen in Table 2 (rows with label "Full Corpus"). The high BLEU scores (up to nearly 80%) denote that the quality of the translation is quite good for both systems. The word-

[1] For the word-based system this is also the case.

[2] The English part of the corpus was not used in our experiments.

		Spanish	Catalan
Training	Sentences	40 574	
	Running Words	482 290	485 514
	Vocabulary	14 327	12 772
	Singletons	6 743	5 930
Test	Sentences	972	
	Running Words	12 771	12 973
	OOVs [%]	1.4	1.3

Table 1: Corpus Statistics

based system outperforms the letter-based one, as expected, but the letter-based system also achieves quite a good translation quality. Example translations for both systems can be found in Figure 2. It can be observed that most of the words generated by the letter based system are correct words, and in many cases the "false" words that the system generates are very close to actual words (e.g. "elos" instead of "los" in the second example of Figure 2).

We also investigated the generalization capabilities of both systems under scarce training data conditions. It was expected that the greater flexibility of the letter-based system would provide an advantage of the approach when compared to the word-based approach. We randomly selected subsets of the training corpus of different sizes ranging from 1 000 sentences to 40 000 (i.e. the full corpus) and computed the translation quality on the same test corpus as before. Contrary to our hopes, however, the difference in BLEU score between the word-based and the letter-based system remained fairly constant, as can be seen in Figure 3, and Table 2 for representative training corpus sizes.

Nevertheless, the second example in Figure 2 provides an interesting insight into one of the possible practical applications of this approach. In the example translation of the word-based system, the word "centreamericans" was not known to the system (and has been explicitly marked as unknown in Figure 2). The letter-based system, however, was able to correctly learn the translation from "centre-" to "centro-" and that the ending "-ans" in Catalan is often translated as "-anos" in Spanish, and thus a correct translation has been found. We thus chose to combine both systems, the word-based system doing most of the translation work, but using the letter-based system for the translation of unknown words. The results of this combined approach can be found in Table 2 under the label "Combined System". The combination of both approaches leads to a 0.5% increase in BLEU using the full corpus as training material. This increase is not very big, but is it over a quite strong baseline and the percentage of out-of-vocabulary words in this corpus is around 1% of the total words (see Table 1). When the corpus size is reduced, the gain in BLEU score becomes more important, and for the small corpus size of 1 000 sentences the gain is 2.5% BLEU. Table 2 and Figure 3 show more details.

4 Practical Applications

The approach described in this paper is mainly of academical interest. We have shown that letter-based translation is in principle possible between similar languages, in our case between Catalan and Spanish, but can be applied to other closely related language pairs like Spanish and Portuguese or German and Dutch. The approach can be interesting for languages where very few parallel training data is available.

The idea of translating unknown words in a letter-based fashion can also have applications to state-of-the-art translation systems. Nowadays most automatic translation projects and evaluations deal with translation from Chinese or Arabic to English. For these language pairs the translation of named entities poses an additional problem, as many times they were not previously seen in the training data and they are actually one of the most informative words in the texts. The "translation" of these entities is in most cases actually a (more or less phonetic) transliteration, see for example (Al-Onaizan and Knight, 2002). Using the proposed approach for the translation of these words can provide a tighter integration in the translation process and hopefully increase the translation performance, in the same way as it helps for the case of the Catalan-Spanish translation for unseen words.

Somewhat related to this problem, we can find an additional application in the field of speech recognition. The task of grapheme-to-phoneme conversion aims at increasing the vocabulary an ASR system can recognize, without the need for additional

		BLEU	WER	PER
Word-Based System	Full Corpus	78.9	11.4	10.6
	10k	74.0	13.9	13.2
	1k	60.0	21.3	20.1
Letter-Based System	Full Corpus	72.9	14.7	13.5
	10k	69.8	16.5	15.1
	1k	55.8	24.3	22.8
Combined System	Full Corpus	79.4	11.2	10.4
	10k	75.2	13.4	12.6
	1k	62.5	20.2	19.0

Table 2: Translation results for selected corpus sizes. All measures are percentages.

Source (Cat)	Bé, en principi seria per a les vacances de Setmana Santa que són les següents que tenim ara, entrant a juliol.
Word-Based	Bueno, en principio sería para las vacaciones de Semana Santa que son las siguientes que tenemos ahora, entrando en julio.
Letter-Based	Bueno, en principio sería para las vacaciones de Semana Santa que son las siguientes que tenemos ahora, entrando bamos en julio .
Reference	Bueno, en principio sería para las vacaciones de Semana Santa que son las siguientes que tenemos ahora, entrando julio.

Source (Cat)	Jo li recomanaria per exemple que intentés apropar-se a algun país veí també com poden ser els països centreamericans, una mica més al nord Panamá.
Word-Based	Yo le recomendaría por ejemplo que intentase acercarse a algún país vecino también como pueden ser los países UNKNOWN_centreamericans, un poco más al norte Panamá.
Letter-Based	Yo le recomendaría por ejemplo que intentaseo acercarse a algún país veí también como pueden ser elos países centroamericanos, un poco más al norte Panamá.
Combined	Yo le recomendaría por ejemplo que intentase acercarse a algún país vecino también como pueden ser los países centroamericanos, un poco más al norte Panamá.
Reference	Yo le recomendaría por ejemplo que intentase acercarse a algún país vecino también como pueden ser los países centroamericanos, un poco más al norte Panamá.

Figure 2: Example translations of the different approaches. For the word-based system an unknown word has been explicitly marked.

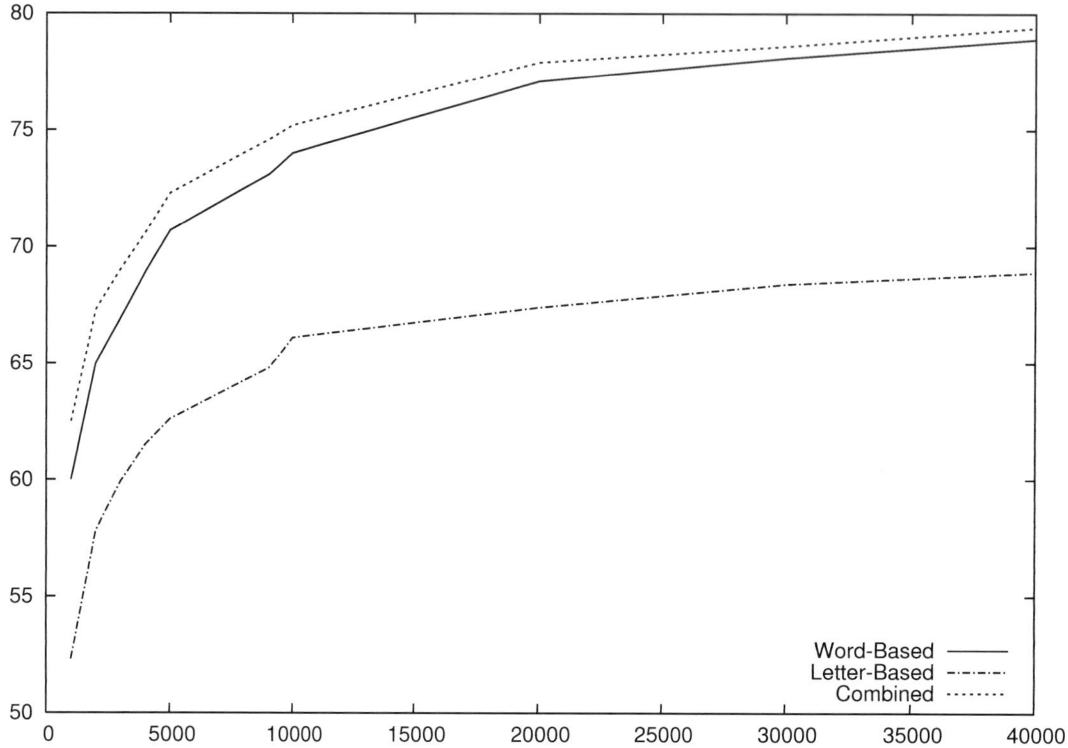

Figure 3: Translation quality depending of the corpus size.

acoustic data. The problem can be formulated as a translation from graphemes ("letters") to a sequence of graphones ("pronunciations"), see for example (Bisani and Ney, 2002). The proposed letter-based approach can also be adapted to this task.

Lastly, a combination of both, word-based and letter-based models, working in parallel and perhaps taking into account additional information like base forms, can be helpful when translating from or into rich inflexional languages, like for example Spanish.

5 Conclusions

We have investigated the possibility of building a letter-based system for translation between related languages. The performance of the approach is quite acceptable, although, as expected, the quality of the word-based approach is superior. The combination of both techniques, however, allows the system to translate words not seen in the training corpus and thus increase the translation quality. The gain is specially important when the training material is scarce.

While the experiments carried out in this work are more interesting from an academical point of view, several practical applications has been discussed and will be the object of future work.

Acknowledgements

This work was partly funded by the Deutsche Forschungsgemeinschaft (DFG) under the project "Statistische Textübersetzung" (NE 572/5-3).

References

Yaser Al-Onaizan and Kevin Knight. 2002. Machine transliteration of names in arabic text. In *Proceedings of the ACL-02 workshop on Computational approaches to semitic languages*, pages 1–13, Morristown, NJ, USA. Association for Computational Linguistics.

Max Bisani and Hermann Ney. 2002. Investigations on joint-multigram models for grapheme-to-phoneme conversion. In *Proceedings of the 7th International Conference on Spoken Language Processing*, volume 1, pages 105–108, Denver, CO, September.

Peter F. Brown, Stephen A. Della Pietra, Vincent J. Della Pietra, and Robert L. Mercer. 1993. The mathematics of statistical machine translation: Parameter estimation. *Computational Linguistics*, 19(2):263–311, June.

D. Conejero, J. Gimnez, V. Arranz, A. Bonafonte, N. Pascual, N. Castell, and A. Moreno. 2003. Lexica and corpora for speech-to-speech translation: A trilingual approach. In *European Conf. on Speech Communication and Technology*, pages 1593–1596, Geneva, Switzerland, September.

Adrià de Gispert. 2006. *Introducing Linguistic Knowledge into Statistical Machine Translation*. Ph.D. thesis, Universitat Politècnica de Catalunya, Barcelona, October.

Arne Mauser, Richard Zens, Evgeny Matusov, Saša Hasan, and Hermann Ney. 2006. The RWTH Statistical Machine Translation System for the IWSLT 2006 Evaluation. In *Proc. of the International Workshop on Spoken Language Translation*, pages 103–110, Kyoto, Japan.

Franz Josef Och and Hermann Ney. 2002. Discriminative training and maximum entropy models for statistical machine translation. In *Proc. of the 40th Annual Meeting of the Association for Computational Linguistics (ACL)*, pages 295–302, Philadelphia, PA, July.

Franz Josef Och and Hermann Ney. 2003. A systematic comparison of various statistical alignment models. *Computational Linguistics*, 29(1):19–51, March.

Maja Popović and Hermann Ney. 2004. Towards the Use of Word Stems and Suffixes for Statistical Machine Translation. In *4th International Conference on Language Resources and Evaluation (LREC)*, pages 1585–1588, Lisbon, Portugal, May.

Maja Popović and Hermann Ney. 2005. Exploiting Phrasal Lexica and Additional Morpho-syntactic Language Resources for Statistical Machine Translation with Scarce Training Data. In *10th Annual Conference of the European Association for Machine Translation (EAMT)*, pages 212–218, Budapest, Hungary, May.

William H. Press, Saul A. Teukolsky, William T. Vetterling, and Brian P. Flannery. 2002. *Numerical Recipes in C++*. Cambridge University Press, Cambridge, UK.

Wade Shen, Richard Zens, Nicola Bertoldi, and Marcello Federico. 2006. The JHU Workshop 2006 IWSLT System. In *Proc. of the International Workshop on Spoken Language Translation*, pages 59–63, Kyoto, Japan.

A Dependency Treelet String Correspondence Model for Statistical Machine Translation

Deyi Xiong, Qun Liu and Shouxun Lin
Key Laboratory of Intelligent Information Processing
Institute of Computing Technology
Chinese Academy of Sciences
Beijing, China, 100080
{dyxiong, liuqun, sxlin}@ict.ac.cn

Abstract

This paper describes a novel model using dependency structures on the source side for syntax-based statistical machine translation: Dependency Treelet String Correspondence Model (DTSC). The DTSC model maps source dependency structures to target strings. In this model translation pairs of source treelets and target strings with their word alignments are learned automatically from the parsed and aligned corpus. The DTSC model allows source treelets and target strings with variables so that the model can generalize to handle dependency structures with the same head word but with different modifiers and arguments. Additionally, target strings can be also discontinuous by using gaps which are corresponding to the uncovered nodes which are not included in the source treelets. A chart-style decoding algorithm with two basic operations–substituting and attaching–is designed for the DTSC model. We argue that the DTSC model proposed here is capable of lexicalization, generalization, and handling discontinuous phrases which are very desirable for machine translation. We finally evaluate our current implementation of a simplified version of DTSC for statistical machine translation.

1 Introduction

Over the last several years, various statistical syntax-based models were proposed to extend traditional word/phrase based models in statistical machine translation (SMT) (Lin, 2004; Chiang, 2005; Ding et al., 2005; Quirk et al., 2005; Marcu et al., 2006; Liu et al., 2006). It is believed that these models can improve the quality of SMT significantly. Compared with phrase-based models, syntax-based models lead to better reordering and higher flexibility by introducing hierarchical structures and variables which make syntax-based models capable of hierarchical reordering and generalization. Due to these advantages, syntax-based approaches are becoming an active area of research in machine translation.

In this paper, we propose a novel model based on dependency structures: Dependency Treelet String Correspondence Model (DTSC). The DTSC model maps source dependency structures to target strings. It just needs a source language parser. In contrast to the work by Lin (2004) and by Quirk et al. (2005), the DTSC model does not need to generate target language dependency structures using source structures and word alignments. On the source side, we extract treelets which are any connected subgraphs and consistent with word alignments. While on the target side, we allow the aligned target sequences to be generalized and discontinuous by introducing variables and gaps. The variables on the target side are aligned to the corresponding variables of treelets, while gaps between words or variables are corresponding to the uncovered nodes which are not included by treelets. To complete the translation process, we design two basic operations for the decoding: substituting and attaching. Substituting is used to replace variable nodes which have been already translated, while attaching is used to attach uncov-

Proceedings of the Second Workshop on Statistical Machine Translation, pages 40–47,
Prague, June 2007. ©2007 Association for Computational Linguistics

ered nodes to treelets.

In the remainder of the paper, we first define dependency treelet string correspondence in section 2 and describe an algorithm for extracting DTSCs from the parsed and word-aligned corpus in section 3. Then we build our model based on DTSC in section 4. The decoding algorithm and related pruning strategies are introduced in section 5. We also specify the strategy to integrate phrases into our model in section 6. In section 7 we evaluate our current implementation of a simplified version of DTSC for statistical machine translation. And finally, we discuss related work and conclude.

2 Dependency Treelet String Correspondence

A dependency treelet string correspondence π is a triple $< D, S, A >$ which describes a translation pair $< D, S >$ and their alignment A, where D is the dependency treelet on the source side and S is the translation string on the target side. $< D, S >$ must be consistent with the word alignment M of the corresponding sentence pair

$$\forall (i,j) \in M, i \in D \leftrightarrow j \in S$$

A **treelet** is defined to be any connected subgraph, which is similar to the definition in (Quirk et al., 2005). Treelet is more representatively flexible than subtree which is widely used in models based on phrase structures (Marcu et al., 2006; Liu et al., 2006). The most important distinction between the treelet in (Quirk et al., 2005) and ours is that we allow variables at positions of subnodes. In our definition, the root node must be lexicalized but the subnodes can be replaced with a wild card. The target counterpart of a wildcard node in S is also replaced with a wild card. The wildcards introduced in this way generalize DTSC to match dependency structures with the same head word but with different modifiers or arguments.

Another unique feature of our DTSC is that we allow target strings with gaps between words or wildcards. Since source treelets may not cover all subnodes, the uncovered subnodes will generate a gap as its counterpart on the target side. A sequence of continuous gaps will be merged to be one gap and gaps at the beginning and the end of S will be removed automatically.

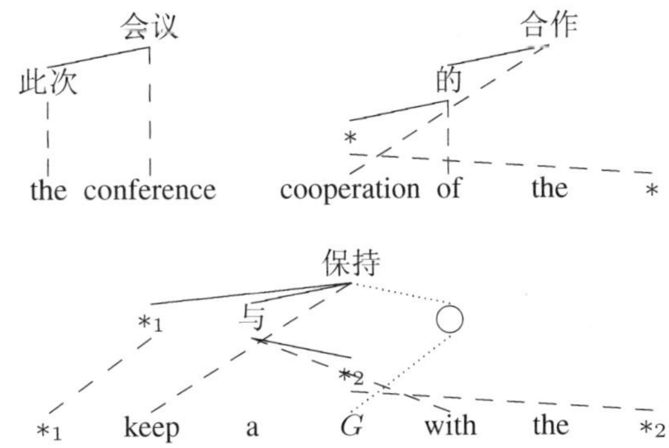

Figure 1: DTSC examples. Note that $*$ represents variable and G represents gap.

Gap can be considered as a special kind of variable whose counterpart on the source side is not present. This makes the model more flexible to match more partial dependency structures on the source side. If only variables can be used, the model has to match subtrees rather than treelets on the source side. Furthermore, the positions of variables on the target side are fixed so that some reorderings related with them can be recorded in DTSC. The positions of gaps on the target side, however, are not fixed until decoding. The presence of one gap and its position can not be finalized until attaching operation is performed. The introduction of gaps and the related attaching operation in decoding is the most important distinction between our model and the previous syntax-based models.

Figure 1 shows several different DTSCs automatically extracted from our training corpus. The top left DTSC is totally lexicalized, while the top right DTSC has one variable and the bottom has two variables and one gap. In the bottom DTSC, note that the node ◯ which is aligned to the gap G of the target string is an uncovered node and therefore not included in the treelet actually. Here we just want to show there is an uncovered node aligned with the gap G.

Each node at the source treelet has three attributes

1. The head word
2. The category, i.e. the part of speech of the head word
3. The node order which specifies the local order of the current node relative to its parent node.

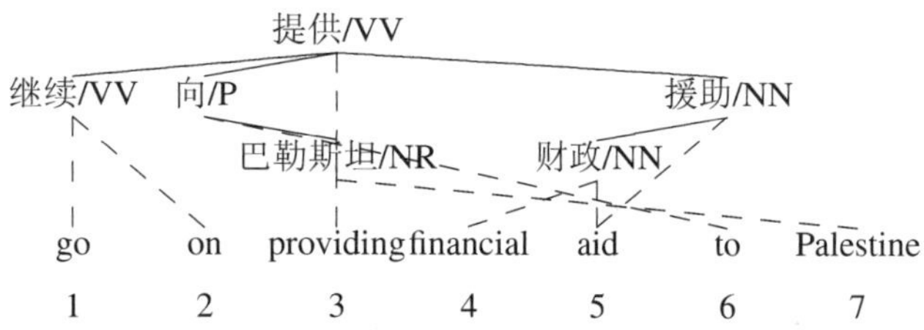

Figure 2: An example dependency tree and its alignments

Note that the node order is defined at the context of the extracted treelets but not the context of the original tree. For example, the attributes for the node 与 in the bottom DTSC of Figure 1 are {与, P, -1}. For two treelets, if and only if their structures are identical and each corresponding nodes share the same attributes, we say they are **matched**.

3 Extracting DTSCs

To extract DTSCs from the training corpus, firstly the corpus must be parsed on the source side and aligned at the word level. The source structures produced by the parser are unlabelled, ordered dependency trees with each word annotated with a part-of-speech. Figure 2 shows an example of dependency tree really used in our extractor.

When the source language dependency trees and word alignments between source and target languages are obtained, the DTSC extraction algorithm runs in two phases along the dependency trees and alignments. In the first step, the extractor annotates each node with specific attributes defined in section 3.1. These attributes are used in the second step which extracts all possible DTSCs rooted at each node recursively.

3.1 Node annotation

For each source dependency node n, we define three attributes: **word span**, **node span** and **crossed**. **Word span** is defined to be the target word sequence aligned with the head word of n, while **node span** is defined to be the closure of the union of node spans of all subnodes of n and its word span. These two attributes are similar to those introduced by Lin (Lin, 2004). The third attribute **crossed** is an indicator that has binary values. If the node span of n overlaps the word span of its parent node or the node span of its siblings, the **crossed** indicator of n is 1 and n is therefore a crossed node, otherwise the **crossed** indicator is 0 and n is a non-crossed node. Only non-crossed nodes can generate DTSCs because the target word sequence aligned with the whole subtree rooted at it does not overlap any other sequences and therefore can be extracted independently.

For the dependency tree and its alignments shown in Figure 2, only the node 财政 is a crossed node since its node span ([4,5]) overlaps the word span ([5,5]) of its parent node 援助.

3.2 DTSCs extraction

The DTSC extraction algorithm (shown in Figure 3) runs recursively. For each non-crossed node, the algorithm generates all possible DTSCs rooted at it by combining DTSCs from some subsets of its direct subnodes. If one subnode n selected in the combination is a crossed node, all other nodes whose word/node spans overlap the node span of n must be also selected in this combination. This kind of combination is defined to be consistent with the word alignment because the DTSC generated by this combination is consistent with the word alignment. All DTSCs generated in this way will be returned to the last call and outputted. For each crossed node, the algorithm generates pseudo DTSCs[1] using DTSCs from all of its subnodes. These pseudo DTSCs will be returned to the last call but not outputted.

During the combination of DTSCs from subnodes into larger DTSCs, there are two major tasks. One task is to generate the treelet using treelets from subnodes and the current node. This is a basic tree generation operation. It is worth mentioning that some non-crossed nodes are to be replaced with a wild card so the algorithm can learn generalized DTSCs described in section 2. Currently, we replace any non-crossed node alone or together with their sibling non-crossed nodes. The second task is to combine target strings. The word sequences aligned with uncovered nodes will be replaced with a gap. The word sequences aligned with wildcard nodes will be replaced with a wild card.

If a non-crossed node n has m direct subnodes, all 2^m combinations will be considered. This will generate a very large number of DTSCs, which is

[1]Some words in the target string are aligned with nodes which are not included in the source treelet.

```
DTSCExtractor(Dnode n)
ℜ := ∅ (DTSC container of n)
for each subnode k of n do
   R := DTSCExtractor(k)
   L := L ⋃ R
end for
if n.crossed! = 1 and there are no subnodes whose span
overlaps the word span of n then
   Create a DTSC π =< D, S, A > where the dependency
   treelet D only contains the node n (not including any chil-
   dren of it)
   output π
   for each combination c of n's subnodes do
      if c is consistent with the word alignment then
         Generate all DTSCs R by combining DTSCs (L)
         from the selected subnodes with the current node n
         ℜ := ℜ ⋃ R
      end if
   end for
   output ℜ
   return ℜ
else if n.crossed == 1 then
   Create pseudo DTSCs P by combining all DTSCs from
   n's all subnodes.
   ℜ := ℜ ⋃ P
   return ℜ
end if
```

Figure 3: DTSC Extraction Algorithm.

undesirable for training and decoding. Therefore we filter DTSCs according to the following restrictions

1. If the number of direct subnodes of node n is larger than 6, we only consider combining one single subnode with n each time because in this case reorderings of subnodes are always monotone.

2. On the source side, the number of direct subnodes of each node is limited to be no greater than *ary-limit*; the height of treelet D is limited to be no greater than *depth-limit*.

3. On the target side, the length of S (including gaps and variables) is limited to be no greater than *len-limit*; the number of gaps in S is limited to be no greater than *gap-limit*.

4. During DTSC combination, the DTSCs from each subnode are sorted by size (in descending order). Only the top *comb-limit* DTSCs will be selected to generate larger DTSCs.

As an example, for the dependency tree and its alignments in Figure 2, all DTSCs extracted by the algorithm with parameters { *ary-limit* = 2, *depth-limit* = 2, *len-limit* = 3, *gap-limit* = 1, *comb-limit* = 20 } are shown in the table 1.

Treelet	String
(继续/VV/0)	go on
(巴勒斯坦/NR/0)	Palestine
(向/P/0)	to
(向/P/0 (巴勒斯坦/NR/1))	to Palestine
(向/P/0 (∗/1))	to ∗
(援助/NN/0 (财政/NN/-1))	financial aid
(提供/VV/0)	providing
(提供/VV/0 (∗/1))	providing ∗
(提供/VV/0 (∗/-1))	providing G ∗
(提供/VV/0 (继续/VV/-1))	go on providing
(提供/VV/0 (∗/-1))	∗ providing
(提供/VV/0 ($*_1$/-1) ($*_2$/1))	providing $*_2$ $*_1$
(提供/VV/0 ($*_1$/-1) ($*_2$/1))	$*_1$ providing $*_2$

Table 1: Examples of DTSCs extracted from Figure 2. Alignments are not shown here because they are self-evident.

4 The Model

Given an input dependency tree, the decoder generates translations for each dependency node in bottom-up order. For each node, our algorithm will search all **matched** DTSCs automatically learned from the training corpus by the way mentioned in section 3. When the root node is traversed, the translating is finished. This complicated procedure involves a large number of sequences of applications of DTSC rules. Each sequence of applications of DTSC rules can derive a translation.

We define a derivation δ as a sequence of applications of DTSC rules, and let $c(\delta)$ and $e(\delta)$ be the source dependency tree and the target yield of δ, respectively. The score of δ is defined to be the product of the score of the DTSC rules used in the translation, and timed by other feature functions:

$$\S(\delta) = \prod_i \S(i) \cdot p_{lm}(e)^{\lambda}_{lm} \cdot exp(-\lambda_{ap} A(\delta)) \quad (1)$$

where $\S(i)$ is the score of the ith application of DTSC rules, $p_{lm}(e)$ is the language model score, and $exp(-\lambda_{ap} A(\delta))$ is the attachment penalty, where $A(\delta)$ calculates the total number of attachments occurring in the derivation δ. The attachment penalty gives some control over the selection of DTSC rules which makes the model prefer rules with more nodes covered and therefore less attaching operations involved.

For the score of DTSC rule π, we define it as follows:

$$\S(\pi) = \prod_j f_j(\pi)^{\lambda_j} \quad (2)$$

where the f_j are feature functions defined on DTSC rules. Currently, we used features proved to be effective in phrase-based SMT, which are:

1. The translation probability $p(D|S)$.
2. The inverse translation probability $p(S|D)$.
3. The lexical translation probability $p_{lex}(D|S)$ which is computed over the words that occur on the source and target sides of a DTSC rule by the IBM model 1.
4. The inverse lexical translation probability $p_{lex}(S|D)$ which is computed over the words that occur on the source and target sides of a DTSC rule by the IBM model 1.
5. The word penalty wp.
6. The DTSC penalty dp which allows the model to favor longer or shorter derivations.

It is worth mentioning how to integrate the N-gram language mode into our DTSC model. During decoding, we have to encounter many partial translations with gaps and variables. For these translations, firstly we only calculate the language model scores for word sequences in the translations. Later we update the scores when gaps are removed or specified by attachments or variables are substituted. Each updating involves merging two neighbor substrings s_l (left) and s_r (right) into one bigger string s. Let the sequence of $n-1$ (n is the order of N-gram language model used) rightmost words of s_l be s_l^r and the sequence of $n-1$ leftmost words of s_r be s_r^l. we have:

$$LM(s) = LM(s_l) + LM(s_r) + LM(s_l^r s_r^l) - LM(s_l^r) - LM(s_r^l) \quad (3)$$

where LM is the logarithm of the language model probability. We only need to compute the increment of the language model score:

$$\triangle_{LM} = LM(s_l^r s_r^l) - LM(s_l^r) - LM(s_r^l) \quad (4)$$

```
for each node n of the input tree T, in bottom-up order do
  Get all matched DTSCs rooted at n
  for each matched DTSC π do
    for each wildcard node n* in π do
      Substitute the corresponding wildcard on the target
      side with translations from the stack of n*
    end for
    for each uncovered node n@ by π do
      Attach the translations from the stack of n@ to the
      target side at the attaching point
    end for
  end for
end for
```

Figure 4: Chart-style Decoding Algorithm for the DTSC Model.

Melamed (2004) also used a similar way to integrate the language model.

5 Decoding

Our decoding algorithm is similar to the bottom-up chart parsing. The distinction is that the input is a tree rather than a string and therefore the chart is indexed by nodes of the tree rather than spans of the string. Also, several other tree-based decoding algorithms introduced by Eisner (2003), Quirk et al. (2005) and Liu et al. (2006) can be classified as the chart-style parsing algorithm too.

Our decoding algorithm is shown in Figure 4. Given an input dependency tree, firstly we generate the bottom-up order by postorder transversal. This order guarantees that any subnodes of node n have been translated before node n is done. For each node n in the bottom-up order, all **matched** DTSCs rooted at n are found, and a stack is also built for it to store the candidate translations. A DTSC π is said to **match** the input dependency subtree T rooted at n if and only if there is a treelet rooted at n that **matches** [2] the treelet of π on the source side.

For each matched DTSC π, two operations will be performed on it. The first one is **substituting** which replaces a wildcard node with the corresponding translated node. The second one is **attaching** which attaches an uncovered node to π. The two operations are shown in Figure 5. For each wildcard node n^*, translations from the stack of it will be selected to replace the corresponding wildcard on the

[2] The words, categories and orders of each corresponding nodes are matched. Please refer to the definition of **matched** in section 2.

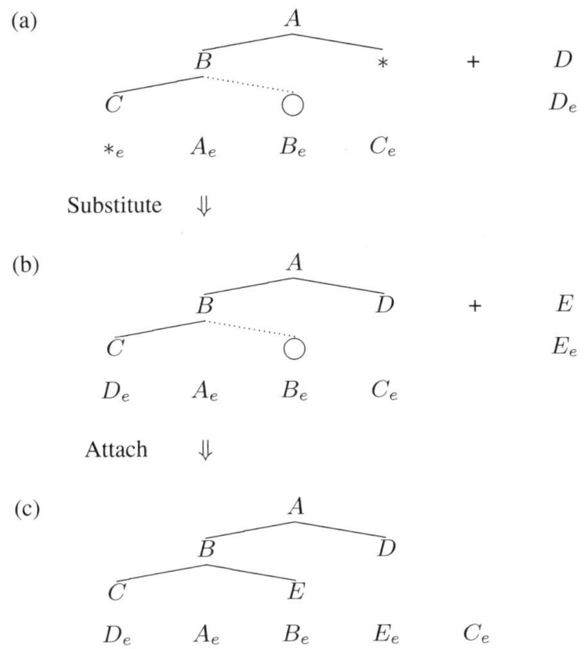

Figure 5: Substituting and attaching operations for decoding. X_e is the translation of X. Node that $*$ is a wildcard node to be substituted and node ◯ is an uncovered node to be attached.

target side and the scores of new translations will be calculated according to our model. For each uncovered node $n^@$, firstly we determine where translations from the stack of $n^@$ should be attached on the target side. There are several different mechanisms for choosing attaching points. Currently, we implement a heuristic way: on the source side, we find the node $n_p^@$ which is the nearest neighbor of $n^@$ from its parent and sibling nodes, then the attaching point is the left/right of the counterpart of $n_p^@$ on the target side according to their relative order. As an example, see the uncovered node ◯ in Figure 5. The nearest node to it is node B. Since node ◯ is at the right of node B, the attaching point is the right of B_e. One can search all possible points using an ordering model. And this ordering model can also use information from gaps on the target side. We believe this ordering model can improve the performance and let it be one of directions for our future research.

Note that the gaps on the target side are not necessarily attaching points in our current attaching mechanism. If they are not attaching point, they will be removed automatically.

The search space of the decoding algorithm is very large, therefore some pruning techniques have to be used. To speed up the decoder, the following pruning strategies are adopted.

1. **Stack pruning.** We use three pruning ways. The first one is recombination which converts the search to dynamic programming. When two translations in the same stack have the same w leftmost/rightmost words, where w depends on the order of the language model, they will be recombined by discarding the translation with lower score. The second one is the threshold pruning which discards translations that have a score worse than *stack-threshold* times the best score in the same stack. The last one is the histogram pruning which only keeps the top *stack-limit* best translations for each stack.

2. **Node pruning.** For each node, we only keep the top *node-limit* matched DTSCs rooted at that node, as ranked by the size of source treelets.

3. **Operation pruning.** For each operation, substituting and attaching, the decoding will generate a large number of partial translations[3] for the current node. We only keep the top *operation-limit* partial translations each time according to their scores.

6 Integrating Phrases

Although syntax-based models are good at dealing with hierarchical reordering, but at the local level, translating idioms and similar complicated expressions can be a problem. However, phrase-based models are good at dealing with these translations. Therefore, integrating phrases into the syntax-based models can improve the performance (Marcu et al., 2006; Liu et al., 2006). Since our DTSC model is based on dependency structures and lexicalized naturally, DTSCs are more similar to phrases than other translation units based on phrase structures. This means that phrases will be easier to be integrated into our model.

The way to integrate phrases is quite straightforward: if there is a treelet rooted at the current node,

[3]There are wildcard nodes or uncovered nodes to be handled.

of which the word sequence is continuous and identical to the source of some phrase, then a phrase-style DTSC will be generated which uses the target string of the phrase as its own target. The procedure is finished during decoding. In our experiments, integrating phrases improves the performance greatly.

7 Current Implementation

To test our idea, we implemented the dependency treelet string correspondence model in a Chinese-English machine translation system. The current implementation in this system is actually a simplified version of the DTSC model introduced above. In this version, we used a simple heuristic way for the operation of attaching rather than a sophisticated statistical model which can learn ordering information from the training corpus. Since dependency structures are more "flattened" compared with phrasal structures, there are many subnodes which will not be covered even by generalized matched DTSCs. This means the attaching operation is very common during decoding. Therefore better attaching model which calculates the best point for attaching , we believe, will improve the performance greatly and is a major goal for our future research.

To obtain the dependency structures of the source side, one can parse the source sentences with a dependency parser or parse them with a phrasal structure parser and then convert the phrasal structures into dependency structures. In our experiments we used a Chinese parser implemented by Xiong et al. (2005) which generates phrasal structures. The parser was trained on articles 1-270 of Penn Chinese Treebank version 1.0 and achieved 79.4% (F1 measure). We then converted the phrasal structure trees into dependency trees using the way introduced by Xia (1999).

To obtain the word alignments, we use the way of Koehn et al. (2005). After running GIZA++ (Och and Ney, 2000) in both directions, we apply the "grow-diag-final" refinement rule on the intersection alignments for each sentence pair.

The training corpus consists of 31, 149 sentence pairs with 823K Chinese words and 927K English words. For the language model, we used SRI Language Modeling Toolkit (Stolcke, 2002) to train a trigram model with modified Kneser-Ney smoothing on the 31, 149 English sentences. We selected 580 short sentences of length at most 50 characters from the 2002 NIST MT Evaluation test set as our development corpus and used it to tune λs by maximizing the BLEU score (Och, 2003), and used the 2005 NIST MT Evaluation test set as our test corpus.

Systems	BLEU-4
PB	20.88 ± 0.87
DTSC	20.20 ± 0.81
DTSC + phrases	21.46 ± 0.83

Table 2: BLEU-4 scores for our system and a phrase-based system.

From the training corpus, we learned 2, 729, 964 distinct DTSCs with the configuration { *ary-limit* = 4, *depth-limit* = 4, *len-limit* = 15, *gap-limit* = 2, *comb-limit* = 20 }. Among them, 160,694 DTSCs are used for the test set. To run our decoder on the development and test set, we set *stack-thrshold* = 0.0001, *stack-limit* = 100, *node-limit* = 100, *operation-limit* = 20.

We also ran a phrase-based system (PB) with a distortion reordering model (Xiong et al., 2006) on the same corpus. The results are shown in table 2. For all BLEU scores, we also show the 95% confidence intervals computed using Zhang's significant tester (Zhang et al., 2004) which was modified to conform to NIST's definition of the BLEU brevity penalty. The BLEU score of our current system with the DTSC model is lower than that of the phrase-based system. However, with phrases integrated, the performance is improved greatly, and the new BLEU score is higher than that of the phrase-based SMT. This difference is significant according to Zhang's tester. This result can be improved further using a better parser (Quirk et al., 2006) or using a statistical attaching model.

8 Related Work

The DTSC model is different from previous work based on dependency grammars by Eisner (2003), Lin (2004), Quirk et al. (2005), Ding et al. (2005) since they all deduce dependency structures on the target side. Among them, the most similar work is (Quirk et al., 2005). But there are still several major differences beyond the one mentioned above. Our treelets allow variables at any non-crossed nodes and target strings allow gaps, which are not available in (Quirk et al., 2005). Our language model is calculated during decoding while Quirk's language model is computed after decoding because of the complexity of their decoding.

The DTSC model is also quite distinct from previous tree-string models by Marcu et al. (2006) and Liu et al. (2006). Firstly, their models are based on phrase structure grammars. Secondly, subtrees instead of treelets are extracted in their models. Thirdly, it seems to be more difficult to integrate phrases into their models. And finally, our model allow gaps on the target side, which is an advantage shared by (Melamed, 2004) and (Simard, 2005).

9 Conclusions and Future Work

We presented a novel syntax-based model using dependency trees on the source side–dependency treelet string correspondence model–for statistical machine translation. We described an algorithm to learn DTSCs automatically from the training corpus and a chart-style algorithm for decoding.

Currently, we implemented a simple version of the DTSC model. We believe that our performance can be improved greatly using a more sophisticated mechanism for determining attaching points. Therefore the most important future work should be to design a better attaching model. Furthermore, we plan to use larger corpora for training and n-best dependency trees for decoding, which both are helpful for the improvement of translation quality.

Acknowledgements

This work was supported by National Natural Science Foundation of China, Contract No. 60603095 and 60573188.

References

David Chiang. 2005. A hierarchical phrase-based model for statistical machine translation. In *Proceedings of ACL*.

Yuan Ding and Martha Palmer. 2005. Machine Translation Using Probabilistic Synchronous Dependency Insertion Grammars. In *Proceedings of ACL*.

Jason Eisner. 2003. Learning non-isomorphic tree mappings for machine translation. In *Proceedings of ACL*.

Philipp Koehn, Amittai Axelrod, Alexandra Birch Mayne, Chris Callison-Burch, Miles Osborne and David Talbot. 2005. Edinburgh System Description for the 2005 IWSLT Speech Translation Evaluation. In *International Workshop on Spoken Language Translation*.

Daniel Marcu, Wei Wang, Abdessamad Echihabi, and Kevin Knight. 2006. SPMT: Statistical Machine Translation with Syntactified Target Language Phraases. In *Proceedings of EMNLP*.

I. Dan Melamed. 2004. Algorithms for Syntax-Aware Statistical Machine Translation. In *Proceedings of the Conference on Theoretical and Methodological Issues in Machine Translation (TMI)*, Baltimore, MD.

Dekang Lin. 2004. A path-based transfer model for machine translation. In *Proceedings of COLING*.

Yang Liu, Qun Liu, and Shouxun Lin. 2006. Tree-to-String Alignment Template for Statistical Machine Translation. In *Proceedings of ACL*.

Franz Josef Och. 2003. Minimum error rate training in statistical machine translation. In *Proceedings of ACL*.

Franz Josef Och and Hermann Ney. 2000. Improved statistical alignment models. In *Proceedings of ACL*.

Chris Quirk, Arul Menezes and Colin Cherry. 2005. Dependency Treelet Translation: Syntactically Informed Phrasal SMT. In *Proceedings of ACL*.

Chris Quirk and Simon Corston-Oliver. 2006. The impact of parse quality on syntactically-informed statistical machine translation. In *Proceedings of EMNLP*, Sydney, Australia.

Michel Simard, Nicola Cancedda, Bruno Cavestro, Marc Dymetman, Eric Gaussier, Cyril Goutte, Kenji Yamada. 2005. Translating with non-contiguous phrases. In *Proceedings of HLT-EMNLP*.

Andreas Stolcke. 2002. SRILM - an extensible language modeling toolkit. In *Proceedings of International Conference on Spoken Language Processing*, volume 2, pages 901-904.

Fei Xia. 1999. Automatic Grammar Generation from Two Different Perspectives. PhD thesis, University of Pennsylvania.

Deyi Xiong, Qun Liu, and Shouxun Lin. 2006. Maximum Entropy Based Phrase Reordering Model for Statistical Machine Translation. In *Proceedings of COLING-ACL*, Sydney, Australia.

Deyi Xiong, Shuanglong Li, Qun Liu, Shouxun Lin, Yueliang Qian. 2005. Parsing the Penn Chinese Treebank with Semantic Knowledge. In *Proceedings of IJCNLP*, Jeju Island, Korea.

Ying Zhang, Stephan Vogel, and Alex Waibel. 2004. Interpreting BLEU/NIST scores: How much improvement do we need to have a better system? In *Proceedings of LREC*, pages 2051 – 2054.

Word Error Rates: Decomposition over POS Classes and Applications for Error Analysis

Maja Popović
Lehrstuhl für Informatik 6
RWTH Aachen University
Aachen, Germany
popovic@cs.rwth-aachen.de

Hermann Ney
Lehrstuhl für Informatik 6
RWTH Aachen University
Aachen, Germany
ney@cs.rwth-aachen.de

Abstract

Evaluation and error analysis of machine translation output are important but difficult tasks. In this work, we propose a novel method for obtaining more details about actual translation errors in the generated output by introducing the decomposition of Word Error Rate (WER) and Position independent word Error Rate (PER) over different Part-of-Speech (POS) classes. Furthermore, we investigate two possible aspects of the use of these decompositions for automatic error analysis: estimation of inflectional errors and distribution of missing words over POS classes. The obtained results are shown to correspond to the results of a human error analysis. The results obtained on the European Parliament Plenary Session corpus in Spanish and English give a better overview of the nature of translation errors as well as ideas of where to put efforts for possible improvements of the translation system.

1 Introduction

Evaluation of machine translation output is a very important but difficult task. Human evaluation is expensive and time consuming. Therefore a variety of automatic evaluation measures have been studied over the last years. The most widely used are Word Error Rate (WER), Position independent word Error Rate (PER), the BLEU score (Papineni et al., 2002) and the NIST score (Doddington, 2002). These measures have shown to be valuable tools for comparing different systems as well as for evaluating improvements within one system. However, these measures do not give any details about the nature of translation errors. Therefore some more detailed analysis of the generated output is needed in order to identify the main problems and to focus the research efforts. A framework for human error analysis has been proposed in (Vilar et al., 2006), but as every human evaluation, this is also a time consuming task.

This article presents a framework for calculating the decomposition of WER and PER over different POS classes, i.e. for estimating the contribution of each POS class to the overall word error rate. Although this work focuses on POS classes, the method can be easily extended to other types of linguistic information. In addition, two methods for error analysis using the WER and PER decompositons together with base forms are proposed: estimation of inflectional errors and distribution of missing words over POS classes. The translation corpus used for our error analysis is built in the framework of the TC-STAR project (tcs, 2005) and contains the transcriptions of the European Parliament Plenary Sessions (EPPS) in Spanish and English. The translation system used is the phrase-based statistical machine translation system described in (Vilar et al., 2005; Matusov et al., 2006).

2 Related Work

Automatic evaluation measures for machine translation output are receiving more and more attention in the last years. The BLEU metric (Papineni et al., 2002) and the closely related NIST metric (Doddington, 2002) along with WER and PER

Proceedings of the Second Workshop on Statistical Machine Translation, pages 48–55,
Prague, June 2007. ©2007 Association for Computational Linguistics

have been widely used by many machine translation researchers. An extended version of BLEU which uses n-grams weighted according to their frequency estimated from a monolingual corpus is proposed in (Babych and Hartley, 2004). (Leusch et al., 2005) investigate preprocessing and normalisation methods for improving the evaluation using the standard measures WER, PER, BLEU and NIST. The same set of measures is examined in (Matusov et al., 2005) in combination with automatic sentence segmentation in order to enable evaluation of translation output without sentence boundaries (e.g. translation of speech recognition output). A new automatic metric METEOR (Banerjee and Lavie, 2005) uses stems and synonyms of the words. This measure counts the number of exact word matches between the output and the reference. In a second step, unmatched words are converted into stems or synonyms and then matched. The TER metric (Snover et al., 2006) measures the amount of editing that a human would have to perform to change the system output so that it exactly matches the reference. The CDER measure (Leusch et al., 2006) is based on edit distance, such as the well-known WER, but allows reordering of blocks. Nevertheless, none of these measures or extensions takes into account linguistic knowledge about actual translation errors, for example what is the contribution of verbs in the overall error rate, how many full forms are wrong whereas their base forms are correct, etc. A framework for human error analysis has been proposed in (Vilar et al., 2006) and a detailed analysis of the obtained results has been carried out. However, human error analysis, like any human evaluation, is a time consuming task.

Whereas the use of linguistic knowledge for improving the performance of a statistical machine translation system is investigated in many publications for various language pairs (like for example (Nießen and Ney, 2000), (Goldwater and McClosky, 2005)), its use for the analysis of translation errors is still a rather unexplored area. Some automatic methods for error analysis using base forms and POS tags are proposed in (Popović et al., 2006; Popović and Ney, 2006). These measures are based on differences between WER and PER which are calculated separately for each POS class using subsets extracted from the original texts. Standard overall WER and PER of the original texts are not at all taken into account. In this work, the standard WER and PER are decomposed and analysed.

3 Decomposition of WER and PER over POS classes

The standard procedure for evaluating machine translation output is done by comparing the hypothesis document hyp with given reference translations ref, each one consisting of K sentences (or segments). The reference document ref consists of R reference translations for each sentence. Let the length of the hypothesis sentence hyp_k be denoted as N_{hyp_k}, and the reference lengths of each sentence $N_{ref_{k,r}}$. Then, the total hypothesis length of the document is $N_{hyp} = \sum_k N_{hyp_k}$, and the total reference length is $N_{ref} = \sum_k N^*_{ref_k}$ where $N^*_{ref_k}$ is defined as the length of the reference sentence with the lowest sentence-level error rate as shown to be optimal in (Leusch et al., 2005).

3.1 Standard word error rates (overview)

The word error rate (WER) is based on the Levenshtein distance (Levenshtein, 1966) - the minimum number of substitutions, deletions and insertions that have to be performed to convert the generated text hyp into the reference text ref. A shortcoming of the WER is the fact that it does not allow reorderings of words, whereas the word order of the hypothesis can be different from word order of the reference even though it is correct translation. In order to overcome this problem, the position independent word error rate (PER) compares the words in the two sentences without taking the word order into account. The PER is always lower than or equal to the WER. On the other hand, shortcoming of the PER is the fact that the word order can be important in some cases. Therefore the best solution is to calculate both word error rates.

Calculation of WER: The WER of the hypothesis hyp with respect to the reference ref is calculated as:

$$\text{WER} = \frac{1}{N^*_{ref}} \sum_{k=1}^{K} \min_r d_L(ref_{k,r}, hyp_k)$$

where $d_L(ref_{k,r}, hyp_k)$ is the Levenshtein distance between the reference sentence $ref_{k,r}$ and the hypothesis sentence hyp_k. The calculation of WER is performed using a dynamic programming algorithm.

Calculation of PER: The PER can be calculated using the counts $n(e, hyp_k)$ and $n(e, ref_{k,r})$ of a word e in the hypothesis sentence hyp_k and the reference sentence $ref_{k,r}$ respectively:

$$\text{PER} = \frac{1}{N^*_{ref}} \sum_{k=1}^{K} \min_r d_{\text{PER}}(ref_{k,r}, hyp_k)$$

where

$$d_{\text{PER}}(ref_{k,r}, hyp_k) = \frac{1}{2}\Big(|N_{ref_{k,r}} - N_{hyp_k}| + \sum_e |n(e, ref_{k,r}) - n(e, hyp_k)| \Big)$$

3.2 WER decomposition over POS classes

The dynamic programming algorithm for WER enables a simple and straightforward identification of each erroneous word which actually contributes to WER. Let err_k denote the set of erroneous words in sentence k with respect to the best reference and p be a POS class. Then $n(p, err_k)$ is the number of errors in err_k produced by words with POS class p. It should be noted that for the substitution errors, the POS class of the involved reference word is taken into account. POS tags of the reference words are also used for the deletion errors, and for the insertion errors the POS class of the hypothesis word is taken. The WER for the word class p can be calculated as:

$$\text{WER}(p) = \frac{1}{N^*_{ref}} \sum_{k=1}^{K} n(p, err_k)$$

The sum over all classes is equal to the standard overall WER.

An example of a reference sentence and hypothesis sentence along with the corresponding POS tags is shown in Table 1. The WER errors, i.e. actual words participating in WER together with their POS classes can be seen in Table 2. The reference words involved in WER are denoted as reference errors, and hypothesis errors refer to the hypothesis words participating in WER.

Standard WER of the whole sentence is equal to $4/12 = 33.3\%$. The contribution of nouns is $\text{WER(N)} = 1/12 = 8.3\%$, of verbs $\text{WER(V)} = 2/12 = 16.7\%$ and of adverbs $\text{WER(ADV)} = 1/12 = 8.3\%$

reference: Mister#N Commissioner#N ,#PUN twenty-four#NUM hours#N sometimes#ADV can#V be#V too#ADV much#PRON time#N .#PUN
hypothesis: Mrs#N Commissioner#N ,#PUN twenty-four#NUM hours#N is#V sometimes#ADV too#ADV much#PRON time#N .#PUN

Table 1: Example for illustration of actual errors: a POS tagged reference sentence and a corresponding hypothesis sentence

reference errors	hypothesis errors	error type
Mister#N	Mrs#N	substitution
sometimes#ADV	is#V	substitution
can#V		deletion
be#V	sometimes#ADV	substitution

Table 2: WER errors: actual words which are participating in the word error rate and their corresponding POS classes

3.3 PER decomposition over POS classes

In contrast to WER, standard efficient algorithms for the calculation of PER do not give precise information about contributing words. However, it is possible to identify all words in the hypothesis which do not have a counterpart in the reference, and vice versa. These words will be referred to as PER errors.

reference errors	hypothesis errors
Mister#N	Mrs#N
be#V	is#V
can#V	

Table 3: PER errors: actual words which are participating in the position independent word error rate and their corresponding POS classes

An illustration of PER errors is given in Table 3.

The number of errors contributing to the standard PER according to the algorithm described in 3.1 is 3 - there are two substitutions and one deletion. The problem with standard PER is that it is not possible to detect which words are the deletion errors, which are the insertion errors, and which words are the substitution errors. Therefore we introduce an alternative PER based measure which corresponds to the F-measure. Let $herr_k$ refer to the set of words in the hypothesis sentence k which do not appear in the reference sentence k (referred to as hypothesis errors). Analogously, let $rerr_k$ denote the set of words in the reference sentence k which do not appear in the hypothesis sentence k (referred to as reference errors). Then the following measures can be calculated:

- reference PER (RPER) (similar to recall):

$$\text{RPER}(p) = \frac{1}{N^*_{ref}} \sum_{k=1}^{K} n(p, rerr_k)$$

- hypothesis PER (HPER) (similar to precision):

$$\text{HPER}(p) = \frac{1}{N_{hyp}} \sum_{k=1}^{K} n(p, herr_k)$$

- F-based PER (FPER):

$$\text{FPER}(p) = \frac{1}{N^*_{ref} + N_{hyp}} \cdot \sum_{k=1}^{K} (n(p, rerr_k) + n(p, herr_k))$$

Since we are basically interested in all words without a counterpart, both in the reference and in the hypothesis, this work will be focused on FPER. The sum of FPER over all POS classes is equal to the overall FPER, and the latter is always less or equal to the standard PER.

For the example sentence presented in Table 1, the number of hypothesis errors $n(e, herr_k)$ is 2 and the number of reference errors $n(e, rerr_k)$ is 3 where e denotes the word. The number of errors contributing to the standard PER is 3, since $|N_{ref} - N_{hyp}| = 1$ and $\sum_e |n(e, ref_k) - n(e, hyp_k)| = 5$. The standard PER is normalised over the reference length $N_{ref} = 12$ thus being equal to 25%. The FPER is the sum of hypothesis and reference errors divided by the sum of hypothesis and reference length: FPER $= (2+3)/(11+12) = 5/23 = 21.7\%$. The contribution of nouns is FPER(N) $= 2/23 = 8.7\%$ and the contribution of verbs is FPER(V) $= 3/23 = 13\%$.

4 Applications for error analysis

The decomposed error rates described in Section 3.2 and Section 3.3 contain more details than the standard error rates. However, for more precise information about certain phenomena some kind of further analysis is required. In this work, we investigate two possible aspects for error analysis:

- estimation of inflectional errors by the use of FPER errors and base forms
- extracting the distribution of missing words over POS classes using WER errors, FPER errors and base forms.

4.1 Inflectional errors

Inflectional errors can be estimated using FPER errors and base forms. From each reference-hypothesis sentence pair, only erroneous words which have the common base forms are taken into account. The inflectional error rate of each POS class is then calculated in the same way as FPER. For example, from the PER errors presented in Table 3, the words "is" and "be" are candidates for an inflectional error because they are sharing the same base form "be". Inflectional error rate in this example is present only for the verbs, and is calculated in the same way as FPER, i.e. IFPER(V) $= 2/23 = 8.7\%$.

4.2 Missing words

Distribution of missing words over POS classes can be extracted from the WER and FPER errors in the following way: the words considered as missing are those which occur as deletions in WER errors and at the same time occur only as reference PER errors without sharing the base form with any hypothesis error. The use of both WER and PER errors is much more reliable than using only the WER deletion erros because not all deletion errors are produced by missing words: a number of WER deletions appears due to reordering errors. The information about the base form is used in order to eliminate inflectional errors. The number of missing words is extracted for each word class and then normalised over the sum of all classes. For the example sentence pair presented in Table 1, from the WER errors in Table 2 and the PER errors in Table 3 the word "can" will be identified as missing.

5 Experimental settings

5.1 Translation System

The machine translation system used in this work is based on the statistical aproach. It is built as a log-linear combination of seven different statistical models: phrase based models in both directions, IBM1 models at the phrase level in both directions, as well as target language model, phrase penalty and length penalty are used. A detailed description of the system can be found in (Vilar et al., 2005; Matusov et al., 2006).

5.2 Task and corpus

The corpus analysed in this work is built in the framework of the TC-STAR project. The training corpus contains more than one million sentences and about 35 million running words of the European Parliament Plenary Sessions (EPPS) in Spanish and English. The test corpus contains about 1 000 sentences and 28 000 running words. The OOV rates are low, about 0.5% of the running words for Spanish and 0.2% for English. The corpus statistics can be seen in Table 4. More details about the EPPS data can be found in (Vilar et al., 2005).

TRAIN	Spanish	English
Sentences	1 167 627	
Running words	35 320 646	33 945 468
Vocabulary	159 080	110 636
TEST		
Sentences	894	1 117
Running words	28 591	28 492
OOVs	0.52%	0.25%

Table 4: Statistics of the training and test corpora of the TC-STAR EPPS Spanish-English task. Test corpus is provided with two references.

6 Error analysis

The translation is performed in both directions (Spanish to English and English to Spanish) and the error analysis is done on both the English and the Spanish output. Morpho-syntactic annotation of the English references and hypotheses is performed using the constraint grammar parser ENGCG (Voutilainen, 1995), and the Spanish texts are annotated using the FreeLing analyser (Carreras et al., 2004). In this way, all references and hypotheses are provided with POS tags and base forms. The decomposition of WER and FPER is done over the ten main POS classes: nouns (N), verbs (V), adjectives (A), adverbs (ADV), pronouns (PRON), determiners (DET), prepositions (PREP), conjunctions (CON), numerals (NUM) and punctuation marks (PUN). Inflectional error rates are also estimated for each POS class using FPER counts and base forms. Additionally, details about the verb tense and person inflections for both languages as well as about the adjective gender and person inflections for the Spanish output are extracted. Apart from that, the distribution of missing words over the ten POS classes is estimated using the WER and FPER errors.

6.1 WER and PER (FPER) decompositions

Figure 1 presents the decompositions of WER and FPER over the ten basic POS classes for both languages. The largest part of both word error rates comes from the two most important word classes, namely nouns and verbs, and that the least critical classes are punctuations, conjunctions and numbers.

Adjectives, determiners and prepositions are significantly worse in the Spanish output. This is partly due to the richer morphology of the Spanish language. Furthermore, the histograms indicate that the number of erroneus nouns and pronouns is higher in the English output. As for verbs, WER is higher for English and FPER for Spanish. This indicates that there are more problems with word order in the English output, and more problems with the correct verb or verb form in the Spanish output.

In addition, the decomposed error rates give an idea of where to put efforts for possible improvements of the system. For example, working on improvements of verb translations could reduce up to about 10% WER and 7% FPER, working on nouns

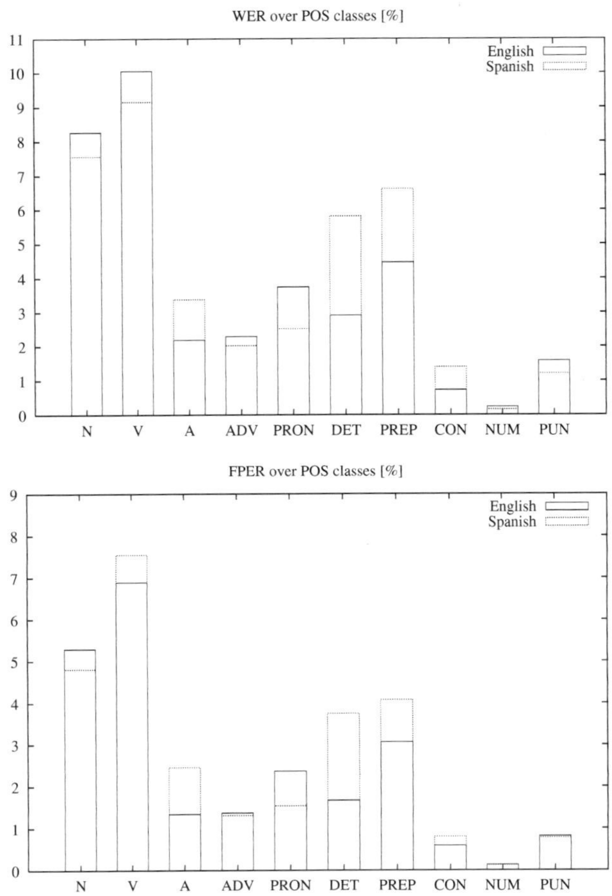

Figure 1: Decomposition of WER and FPER [%] over the ten basic POS classes for English and Spanish output

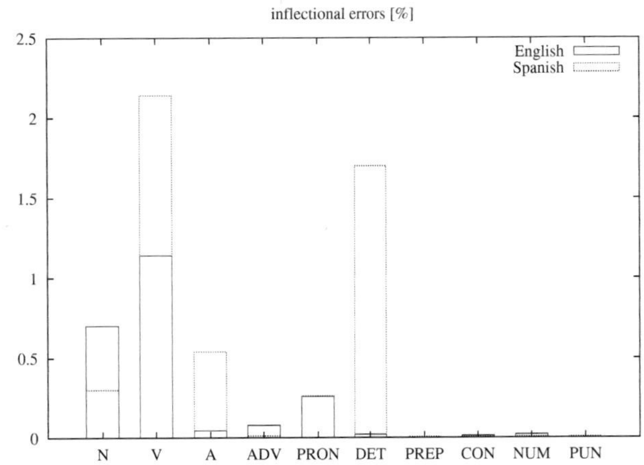

Figure 2: Inflectional error rates [%] for English and Spanish output

up to 8% WER and 5% FPER, whereas there is no reason to put too much efforts on e.g. adverbs since this could lead only to about 2% of WER and FPER reduction. [1]

6.2 Inflectional errors

Inflectional error rates for the ten POS classes are presented in Figure 2. For the English language, these errors are significant only for two POS classes: nouns and verbs. The verbs are the most problematic category in both languages, for Spanish having almost two times higher error rate than for English. This is due to the very rich morphology of Spanish verbs - one base form might have up to about fourty different inflections.

Nouns have a higher error rate for English than for Spanish. The reason for this difference is not clear, since the noun morphology of neither of the languages is particularly rich - there is only distinction between singular and plural. One possible explanation might be the numerous occurences of different variants of the same word, like for example "Mr" and "Mister".

In the Spanish output, two additional POS classes are showing significant error rate: determiners and adjectives. This is due to the gender and number inflections of those classes which do not exist in the English language - for each determiner or adjective, there are four variants in Spanish and only one in English. Working on inflections of Spanish verbs might reduce approximately 2% of FPER, on English verbs about 1%. Improvements of Spanish determiners could lead up to about 2% of improvements.

6.2.1 Comparison with human error analysis

The results obtained for inflectional errors are comparable with the results of a human error analysis carried out in (Vilar et al., 2006). Although it is difficult to compare all the numbers directly, the overall tendencies are the same: the largest number of translation errors are caused by Spanish verbs, and much less but still a large number of errors by English verbs. A much smaller but still significant number of errors is due to Spanish adjectives, and only a few errors of English adjectives are present.

Human analysis was done also for the tense and

[1] Reduction of FPER leads to a similar reduction of PER.

person of verbs, as well as for the number and gender of adjectives. We use more detailed POS tags in order to extract this additional information and calculate inflectional error rates for such tags. It should be noted that in contrast to all previous error rates, these error rates are not disjunct but overlapping: many words are contributing to both.

The results are shown in Figure 3, and the tendencies are again the same as those reported in (Vilar et al., 2006). As for verbs, tense errors are much more frequent than person errors for both languages. Adjective inflections cause certain amount of errors only in the Spanish output. Contributions of gender and of number are aproximately equal.

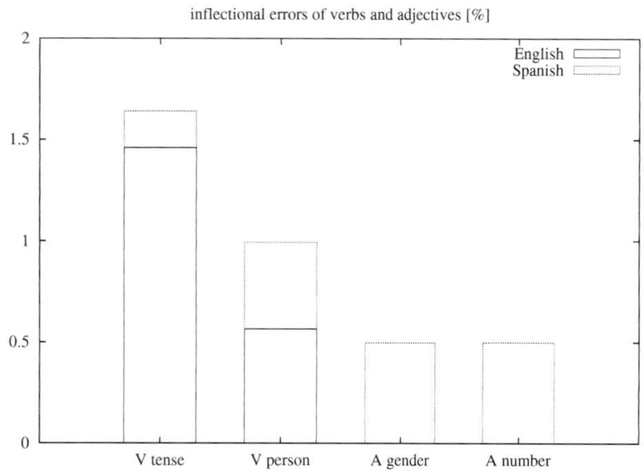

Figure 3: More details about inflections: verb tense and person error rates and adjective gender and number error rates [%]

6.3 Missing words

Figure 4 presents the distribution of missing words over POS classes. This distribution has a same behaviour as the one obtained by human error analysis. Most missing words for both languages are verbs. For English, the percentage of missing verbs is significantly higher than for Spanish. The same thing happens for pronouns. The probable reason for this is the nature of Spanish verbs. Since person and tense are contained in the suffix, Spanish pronouns are often omitted, and auxiliary verbs do not exist for all tenses. This could be problematic for a translation system, because it processes only one Spanish word which actually contains two (or more) English words.

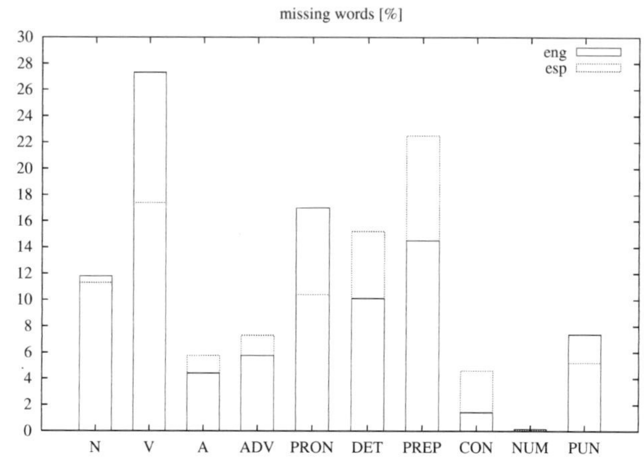

Figure 4: Distribution of missing words over POS classes [%] for English and Spanish output

Prepositions are more often missing in Spanish than in English, as well as determiners. A probable reason is the disproportion of the number of occurrences for those classes between two languages.

7 Conclusions

This work presents a framework for extraction of linguistic details from standard word error rates WER and PER and their use for an automatic error analysis. We presented a method for the decomposition of standard word error rates WER and PER over ten basic POS classes. We also carried out a detailed analysis of inflectional errors which has shown that the results obtained by our method correspond to those obtained by a human error analysis. In addition, we proposed a method for analysing missing word errors.

We plan to extend the proposed methods in order to carry out a more detailed error analysis, for example examining different types of verb inflections. We also plan to examine other types of translation errors like for example errors caused by word order.

Acknowledgements

This work was partly funded by the European Union under the integrated project TC-STAR– Technology and Corpora for Speech to Speech Translation (IST-2002-FP6-506738).

References

Bogdan Babych and Anthony Hartley. 2004. Extending BLEU MT Evaluation Method with Frequency Weighting. In *Proc. of the 42nd Annual Meeting of the Association for Computational Linguistics (ACL)*, Barcelona, Spain, July.

Satanjeev Banerjee and Alon Lavie. 2005. METEOR: An Automatic Metric for MT Evaluation with Improved Correlation with Human Judgements. In *43rd Annual Meeting of the Assoc. for Computational Linguistics: Proc. Workshop on Intrinsic and Extrinsic Evaluation Measures for MT and/or Summarization*, pages 65–72, Ann Arbor, MI, June.

Xavier Carreras, Isaac Chao, Lluís Padró, and Muntsa Padró. 2004. FreeLing: An Open-Source Suite of Language Analyzers. In *Proc. 4th Int. Conf. on Language Resources and Evaluation (LREC)*, pages 239–242, Lisbon, Portugal, May.

George Doddington. 2002. Automatic evaluation of machine translation quality using n-gram co-occurrence statistics. In *Proc. ARPA Workshop on Human Language Technology*, pages 128–132, San Diego.

Sharon Goldwater and David McClosky. 2005. Improving stastistical machine translation through morphological analysis. In *Proc. of the Conf. on Empirical Methods for Natural Language Processing (EMNLP)*, Vancouver, Canada, October.

Gregor Leusch, Nicola Ueffing, David Vilar, and Hermann Ney. 2005. Preprocessing and Normalization for Automatic Evaluation of Machine Translation. In *43rd Annual Meeting of the Assoc. for Computational Linguistics: Proc. Workshop on Intrinsic and Extrinsic Evaluation Measures for MT and/or Summarization*, pages 17–24, Ann Arbor, MI, June. Association for Computational Linguistics.

Gregor Leusch, Nicola Ueffing, and Hermann Ney. 2006. CDER: Efficient MT Evaluation Using Block Movements. In *EACL06*, pages 241–248, Trento, Italy, April.

Vladimir Iosifovich Levenshtein. 1966. Binary Codes Capable of Correcting Deletions, Insertions and Reversals. *Soviet Physics Doklady*, 10(8):707–710, February.

Evgeny Matusov, Gregor Leusch, Oliver Bender, and Hermann Ney. 2005. Evaluating Machine Translation Output with Automatic Sentence Segmentation. In *Proceedings of the International Workshop on Spoken Language Translation (IWSLT)*, pages 148–154, Pittsburgh, PA, October.

Evgeny Matusov, Richard Zens, David Vilar, Arne Mauser, Maja Popović, and Hermann Ney. 2006. The RWTH Machine Translation System. In *TC-Star Workshop on Speech-to-Speech Translation*, pages 31–36, Barcelona, Spain, June.

Sonja Nießen and Hermann Ney. 2000. Improving SMT quality with morpho-syntactic analysis. In *COLING '00: The 18th Int. Conf. on Computational Linguistics*, pages 1081–1085, Saarbrücken, Germany, July.

Kishore Papineni, Salim Roukos, Todd Ward, and Wie-Jing Zhu. 2002. BLEU: a method for automatic evaluation of machine translation. In *Proc. of the 40th Annual Meeting of the Association for Computational Linguistics (ACL)*, pages 311–318, Philadelphia, PA, July.

Maja Popović and Hermann Ney. 2006. Error Analysis of Verb Inflections in Spanish Translation Output. In *TC-Star Workshop on Speech-to-Speech Translation*, pages 99–103, Barcelona, Spain, June.

Maja Popović, Adrià de Gispert, Deepa Gupta, Patrik Lambert, Hermann Ney, José B. Mariño, Marcello Federico, and Rafael Banchs. 2006. Morpho-syntactic Information for Automatic Error Analysis of Statistical Machine Translation Output. In *Proc. of the HLT-NAACL Workshop on Statistical Machine Translation*, pages 1–6, New York, NY, June.

Matthew Snover, Bonnie Dorr, Richard Schwartz, Linnea Micciulla, and John Makhoul. 2006. A Study of Translation Error Rate with Targeted Human Annotation. In *Proc. of the 7th Conf. of the Association for Machine Translation in the Americas (AMTA 06)*, pages 223–231, Boston, MA.

2005. TC-STAR - technology and corpora for speech to speech translation. Integrated project TCSTAR (IST-2002-FP6-506738) funded by the European Commission. `http://www.tc-star.org/`.

David Vilar, Evgeny Matusov, Saša Hasan, Richard Zens, and Hermann Ney. 2005. Statistical Machine Translation of European Parliamentary Speeches. In *Proc. MT Summit X*, pages 259–266, Phuket, Thailand, September.

David Vilar, Jia Xu, Luis Fernando D'Haro, and Hermann Ney. 2006. Error Analysis of Statistical Machine Translation Output. In *Proc. of the Fifth Int. Conf. on Language Resources and Evaluation (LREC)*, pages 697–702, Genoa, Italy, May.

Atro Voutilainen. 1995. ENGCG - Constraint Grammar Parser of English. http://www2.lingsoft.fi/doc/engcg/intro/.

Speech-input multi-target machine translation

Alicia Pérez, M. Inés Torres
Dep. of Electricity and Electronics
University of the Basque Country
manes@we.lc.ehu.es

M. Teresa González, Francisco Casacuberta
Dep. of Information Systems and Computation
Technical University of Valencia
fcn@dsic.upv.es

Abstract

In order to simultaneously translate speech into multiple languages an extension of stochastic finite-state transducers is proposed. In this approach the speech translation model consists of a single network where acoustic models (in the input) and the multilingual model (in the output) are embedded.

The multi-target model has been evaluated in a practical situation, and the results have been compared with those obtained using several mono-target models. Experimental results show that the multi-target one requires less amount of memory. In addition, a single decoding is enough to get the speech translated into multiple languages.

1 Introduction

In this work we deal with finite-state models which constitute an important framework in syntactic pattern recognition for language and speech processing applications (Mohri et al., 2002; Pereira and Riley, 1997). One of their outstanding characteristics is the availability of efficient algorithms for both optimization and decoding purposes.

Specifically, stochastic finite-state transducers (SFSTs) have proved to be useful for machine translation tasks within restricted domains. There are several approaches implemented over SFSTs which range from word-based systems (Knight and Al-Onaizan, 1998) to phrase-based systems (Pérez et al., 2007). SFSTs usually offer high speed during the decoding step and they provide competitive results in terms of error rates. In addition, SFSTs have proved to be versatile models, which can be easily integrated with other finite-state models, such as a speech recognition system for speech-input translation purposes (Vidal, 1997). In fact, the integrated architecture has proved to work better than the decoupled one. Our main goal is, hence, to extend and assess these methodologies to accomplish spoken language multi-target translation.

As far as multilingual translation is concerned, there are two main trends in machine translation devoted to translate an input string simultaneously into m languages (Hutchins and Somers, 1992): *interlingua* and *parallel transfer*. The former has historically been a knowledge-based technique that requires a deep-analysis effort, and the latter consists on m decoupled translators in a parallel architecture. These translators can be either knowledge or example-based. On the other hand, in (González and Casacuberta, 2006) an example based technique consisting of a single SFST that cope with multiple target languages was presented. In that approach, when translating an input sentence, only one search through the multi-target SFST is required, instead of the m independent decoding processes required by the mono-target translators.

The classical layout for speech-input multi-target translation includes a speech recognition system in a serial architecture with m decoupled text-to-text translators. Thus, this architecture entails a decoding stage of the speech signal into the source language text, and m further decoding stages to translate the source text into each of the m target lan-

Proceedings of the Second Workshop on Statistical Machine Translation, pages 56–63,
Prague, June 2007.

guages. If we supplant the m translators with the multi-target SFST, the problem would be reduced to 2 searching stages. Nevertheless, in this paper we propose a natural way for acoustic models to be integrated in the multilingual network itself, in such a way that the input speech signal can be simultaneously decoded and translated into m target languages. As a result, due to the fact that there is just a single searching stage, this novel approach entails less computational cost.

The remainder of the present paper is structured as follows: section 2 describes both multi-target SFSTs and the inference algorithm from training examples; in section 3 a novel integrated architecture for speech-input multi-target translation is proposed; section 4 presents a practical application of these methods, including the experimental setup and the results they produced; finally, section 5 summarizes the main conclusions of this work.

2 Multi-target stochastic finite-state transducers

A multi-target SFST is a generalization of standard SFSTs, in such a way that every input string in the source language results in a tuple of output strings each being associated to a different target language.

2.1 Definition

A *multi-target stochastic finite-state transducer* is a tuple $\mathcal{T} = \langle \Sigma, \Delta_1 \ldots \Delta_m, Q, q_0, R, F, P \rangle$, where:

Σ is a finite set of input symbols (source vocabulary);

$\Delta_1 \ldots \Delta_m$ are m finite sets of output symbols (target vocabularies);

Q is a finite set of states;

$q_0 \in Q$ is the initial state;

$R \subseteq Q \times \Sigma \times \Delta_1^* \ldots \Delta_m^* \times Q$ is a set of transitions such as $(q, w, \tilde{p}_1, \ldots, \tilde{p}_m, q')$, which is a transition from the state q to the state q', with the source symbol w and producing the substrings $(\tilde{p}_1, \ldots, \tilde{p}_m)$;

$P : R \rightarrow [0, 1]$ is the transition probability distribution;

$F : Q \rightarrow [0, 1]$ is the final state probability distribution;

The probability distributions satisfy the stochastic constraint:

$$\forall q \in Q \qquad (1)$$
$$F(q) + \sum_{w, \tilde{p}_1, \ldots, \tilde{p}_m, q'} P(q, w, \tilde{p}_1, \ldots, \tilde{p}_m, q') = 1$$

2.2 Training the multilingual translation model

Both topology and parameters of an SFST can be learned fully automatically from bilingual examples making use of underlying alignment models (Casacuberta and Vidal, 2004). Furthermore, a multi-target SFST can be inferred from a multilingual set of samples (González and Casacuberta, 2006). Even though in realistic situations multilingual corpora are too scarce, recent works (Popović et al., 2005) show that bilingual corpora covering the same domain are sufficient to obtain generalized corpora based on which one can subsequently create the required collections of aligned tuples.

The inference algorithm, GIAMTI (*grammatical inference and alignments for multi-target transducer inference*), requires a multilingual corpus, that is, a finite set of multilingual samples $(\mathbf{s}, \mathbf{t_1}, \ldots, \mathbf{t_m}) \in \Sigma^* \times \Delta_1^* \times \cdots \times \Delta_m^*$, where $\mathbf{t_i}$ denotes the translation of the source sentence $\mathbf{s}$ into the i-th target language; Σ denotes the source language vocabulary, and Δ_i the i-th target language vocabulary; the algorithm can be outlined as follows:

1. Each multilingual sample is transformed into a single string from an *extended vocabulary* ($\Gamma \subseteq \Sigma \times \Delta_1^* \times \cdots \times \Delta_m^*$) using a *labeling function* ($\mathcal{L}^m$). This transformation searches an adequate monotonic segmentation for each of the m source-target language pairs on the basis of bilingual alignments such as those given by GIZA++ (Och, 2000). A monotonic segmentation copes with monotonic alignments, that is, $j < k \Rightarrow a_j < a_k$ following the notation of (Brown et al., 1993). Each source token, which can be either a word or a phrase (Pérez et al., 2007), is then joined with a target phrase of each language as the corresponding segmentation suggests. Each *extended symbol* consists of a token from the source language plus zero

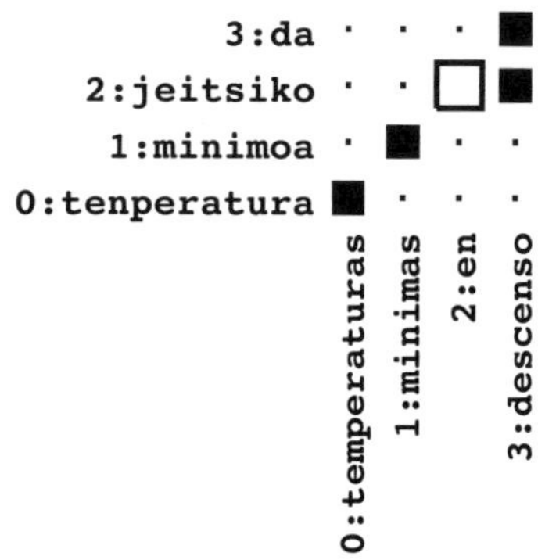

(a) *Spanish-Basque*

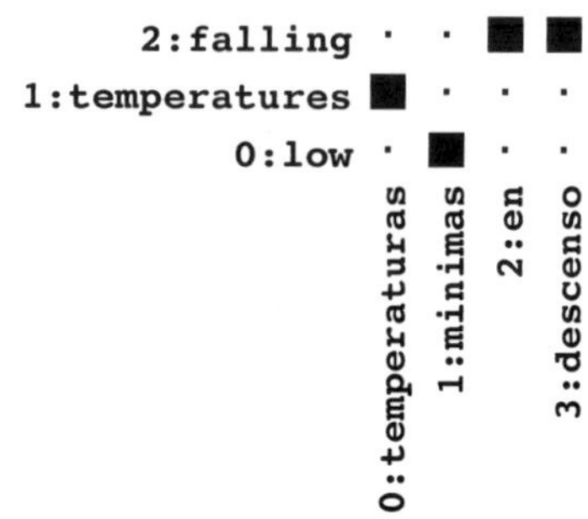

(b) *Spanish-English*

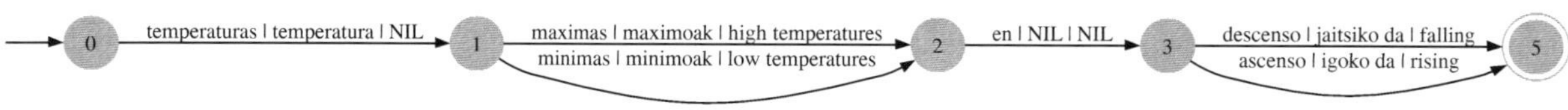

(c) *Multi-target SFST from Spanish into English and Basque.*

Figure 1: *Example of a trilingual alignment over a trilingual sentence extracted from the task under consideration;the related multi-target SFST (with Spanish as input, and English and Basque as output).*

or more words from each target language in their turn.

2. Once the set of multilingual samples has been converted into a set of single extended strings ($\mathbf{z} \in \Gamma^*$), a stochastic regular grammar can be inferred. Specifically, in this work we deal with k-testable in the string-sense grammars (García and Vidal, 1990), which are considered to be a syntactic approach of the n-gram models. In addition, they allow the integration of several order models in a single smoothed automaton (Torres and Varona, 2001).

3. The extended symbols associated with the transitions of the automaton are transformed into one input token and m output phrases ($w/\tilde{p}_1| \ldots |\tilde{p}_m$) by the inverse labeling function ($\mathcal{L}^{-m}$), leading to the required transducer.

Example An illustration of the inference of the multi-target SFST can be shown over a couple of simple trilingual sentences from the corpus (where "B" stands for Basque, "S" for Spanish and "E" for English):

1-B tenperatura maximoa jaitsiko da

1-S temperaturas máximas en descenso

1-E high temperatures falling

2-B tenperatura minimoa igoko da

2-S temperaturas mínimas en ascenso

2-E low temperatures rising

From the alignments, depicted in Figures 1(a) and 1(b), an input-language-synchronized monotonous segmentation can be built (bear in mind that we are considering Spanish as the input language). The corresponding extended strings with the following constituents for the first and second samples respectively are the following ones:

1 temperaturas|tenperatura|λ
mínimas|minimoa|low_temperatures
en|λ|λ
descenso|jaitsiko_da|falling

2 tempcraturas|tenperatura|λ
máximas|maximoa|high_temperatures
en|λ|λ
ascenso|igoko_da|rising

Finally, from this representation of the data, the multi-target SFST can be built as shown in Figure 1(c).

2.3 Decoding

Given an input string s (a sentence in the source language), the decoding module has to search the optimal m output strings $\mathbf{t}^m \in \Delta_1^* \times \cdots \times \Delta_m^*$ (a sentence in each of the target language) according to the underlying translation model ($\mathcal{T}$):

$$\widehat{\mathbf{t}^m} = \arg \max_{\mathbf{t}^m \in \Delta_1^* \times \cdots \times \Delta_m^*} P_{\mathcal{T}}(\mathbf{s}, \mathbf{t}^m) \qquad (2)$$

Solving equation (2) is a hard computational problem, however, it can be efficiently computed under the so called *maximum approach* as follows:

$$P_{\mathcal{T}}(\mathbf{s}, \mathbf{t}^m) \approx \max_{\phi(\mathbf{s}, \mathbf{t}^m)} P_{\mathcal{T}}(\phi(\mathbf{s}, \mathbf{t}^m)) \qquad (3)$$

where $\phi(\mathbf{s}, \mathbf{t}^m)$ is a *translation form*, that is, a sequence of transitions in the multi-target SFST compatible with both the input and the m output strings.

$$\phi(\mathbf{s}, \mathbf{t}^m) : (q_0, w_1, \tilde{p}_1^m, q_1) \cdots (q_{J-1}, w_J, \tilde{p}_J^m, q_J)$$

The input string (s) is a sequence of J input symbols, $\mathbf{s} = w_1^J$, and each of the m output strings consists of J phrases in its corresponding language $\mathbf{t}^m = (\mathbf{t}_1, \cdots, \mathbf{t}_m) = (\tilde{p_1})_1^J, \cdots, (\tilde{p_m})_1^J$. Thus, the probability supplied by the multi-target SFST to the translation form is given by:

$$P_{\mathcal{T}}(\phi(\mathbf{s}, \mathbf{t}^m)) = F(q_J) \prod_{j=1}^{J} P(q_{j-1}, w_j, \tilde{p}_j^m, q_j) \qquad (4)$$

In this context, the *Viterbi algorithm* can be used to obtain the optimal sequence of states through the multi-target SFST for a given input string. As a result, the established m translations are built concatenating the (J) output phrases for each language through the optimal path.

3 An embedded architecture for speech-input multi-target translation

3.1 Statistical framework

Given the acoustic representation ($\mathbf{x}$) of a speech signal, the goal of multi-target speech translation is to find the most likely m target strings ($\mathbf{t}^m$); that is, one string ($\mathbf{t}_i$) per target language involved ($i \in \{1, \ldots, m\}$). This approach is summarized in eq. (5), where the hidden variable s can be interpreted as the transcription of the speech signal:

$$\widehat{\mathbf{t}^m} = \arg \max_{\mathbf{t}^m} P(\mathbf{t}^m | \mathbf{x}) = \arg \max_{\mathbf{t}^m} \sum_{\mathbf{s}} P(\mathbf{t}^m, \mathbf{s} | \mathbf{x}) \qquad (5)$$

Making use of Bayes' rule, the former expression turns into:

$$\widehat{\mathbf{t}^m} = \arg \max_{\mathbf{t}^m} \sum_{s} P(\mathbf{t}^m, \mathbf{s}) P(\mathbf{x} | \mathbf{t}^m, \mathbf{s}) \qquad (6)$$

Empirically, there is no loss of generality if we assume that the acoustic signal representation depends only on the source string, i.e. $P(\mathbf{x}|\mathbf{t}^m, \mathbf{s})$ is independent of $\mathbf{t}^m$. In this sense, eq. (6) can be rewritten as:

$$\widehat{\mathbf{t}^m} = \arg \max_{\mathbf{t}^m} \sum_{s} P(\mathbf{t}^m, \mathbf{s}) P(\mathbf{x} | \mathbf{s}) \qquad (7)$$

Equation (7) combines a standard acoustic model, $P(\mathbf{x}|\mathbf{s})$, and a multi-target translation model, $P(\mathbf{t}^m, \mathbf{s})$, both of whom can be integrated on the fly during the searching routine as shown in Figure 2. That is, each acoustic sub-network is only expanded at decoding time when it is required.

The outer sum is computationally very expensive to search for the optimal tuple of target strings $\mathbf{t}^m$ in an effective way. Thus we make use of the so called Viterbi approximation, which finds the best path over the whole transducer.

3.2 Practical issues

The underlying recognizer used in this work is our own continuous-speech recognition system, which implements stochastic finite-state models at all levels: acoustic-phonetic, lexical and syntactic, and which allows to infer them based on samples.

The signal analysis was carried out in a standard way, based on the classical Mel-cepstrum parametrization. Each phone-like unit was modeled

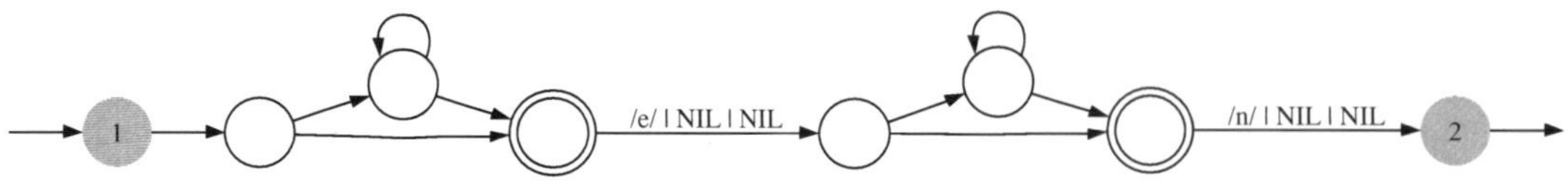

Figure 2: *Integration on the fly of acoustic models in one edge of the SFST shown in Figure 1(c)*

by a typical left to right hidden Markov model. A phonetically-balanced Spanish database, called Albayzin (Moreno et al., 1993), was used to train these models.

The lexical model consisted of the extended tokens of the multi-target SFST instead of running words. The acoustic transcription for each extended token was automatically obtained on the basis of the input projection of each unit, that is, the Spanish vocabulary in this case.

Instead of the usual language model, we make use of the multi-target SFST itself, which had the syntactic structure provided by a k-testable in the strict sense model, with k=3, and Witten-Bell smoothing. Note that the SFST implicitly involves both input and output language models.

4 Experimental results

4.1 Task and corpus

The described general methodology has been put into practice in a highly practical application that aims to translate on-line TV weather forecasts into several languages, taking the speech of the presenter as the input and producing as output text-strings, or sub-titles, in several languages. For this purpose, we used the corpus METEUS which consists of a set of trilingual sentences, in English, Spanish and Basque, as extracted from weather forecast reports that had been published on the Internet. Let us notice that it is a real trilingual corpus, which they are usually quite scarce.

Basque is a pre-Indoeuropean language of still unknown origin. It is a minority language, spoken in a small area of Europe and also within some small American communities (such as that in Reno, Nevada). In the Basque Country (located in the north of Spain) it has an official status along with Spanish. However, despite having coexisted for centuries in the same area, they differ greatly both in syntax and in semantics. Hence, efforts are being devoted nowadays to machine translation tools involving these two languages (Alegria et al., 2004), although they are still scarce. With regard to the order of the phrases within a sentence, the most common one in Basque is *Subject plus Objects plus Verb* (even though some alternative structures are also accepted), whereas in Spanish and English other constructions such as *Subject plus Verb plus Objects* are more frequent (see Figures 1(a) and 1(b)). Another difference between Basque and Spanish or English is that Basque is an extremely inflected language.

In this experiment we intend to translate Spanish speech simultaneously into both Basque and English. Just by having a look at the main features of the corpus in Table 1, we can realize that there are substantial differences among these three languages, in terms both of the size of the vocabulary and of the amount of running words. These figures reveal the agglutinant nature of the Basque language in comparison with English or Spanish.

		Spanish	Basque	English
Training	Total sentences	14,615		
	Different sentences	7,225	7,523	6,634
	Words	191,156	187,462	195,627
	Vocabulary	702	1,147	498
	Average Length	13.0	12.8	13.3
Test	Sentences	500		
	Words	8,706	8,274	9,150
	Average Length	17.4	16.5	18.3
	Perplexity (3grams)	4.8	6.7	5.8

Table 1: Main features of the METEUS corpus.

With regard to the speech test, the input consisted of the speech signal recorded by 36 speakers, each one reading out 50 sentences from the test-set in Table 1. That is, each sentence was read out by at least three speakers. The input speech resulted in approximately 3.50 hours of audio signal. Needless to say, the application that we envisage has to be speaker-independent if it is to be realistic.

4.2 System evaluation

The performance obtained by the acoustic integration has been experimentally tested for both multi-target and mono-target devices. As a matter of comparison, text-input translation results are also reported.

The multi-target SFST was learned from the training set described in Table 1 using the previously described GIAMTI algorithm. The 500 test sentences were then translated by the multi-target SFST. The translation provided by the system in each language was compared to the corresponding reference sentence. Additionally, two mono-target SFSTs were inferred with their outputs for the aforementioned test to be taken as baseline. The evaluation includes both computational cost and performance of the system.

4.2.1 Computational cost

The expected searching time and the amount of memory that needs to be allocated for a given model are two key parameters to bear in mind in speech-input machine translation applications. These values can be objectively measured in terms of the size and on the average branching factor of the model displayed in Table 2.

	multi-target	mono-target	
		S2B	S2E
Nodes	52,074	35,034	20,148
Edges	163,146	115,526	69,690
Branching factor	3.30	3.13	3.46

Table 2: Features of multi-target model and the two decoupled mono-target models (one for Spanish to Basque translation, referred to as S2B, and the second for Spanish to English, S2E).

Adding the edges up for the two mono-target SFSTs that take part in the decoupled architecture (see Table 2), we conclude that the decoupled model needs a total of $185,216$ edges to be allocated in memory, which represents an increment of 13% in memory-space with respect to the multi-target model.

On the other hand, the multi-target approach offers a slightly smaller branching factor than each mono-target approach. As a result, fewer paths have to be explored with the multi-target approach than with the decoupled one, which suggests that searching for a translation might be faster. As a matter of fact, experimental results in Table 3 show that the mono-target architecture works 11% more slowly than the multi-target one for speech-input machine translation and decoding, and 30% for text to text translation.

	Time (s)	
	multi-target	mono-target S2B+S2E
Text-input	0.36	0.47
Speech-input	16.9	18.9

Table 3: Average time needed to translate each input sentence into two languages.

Summarizing, in terms of computational cost (space and time), a multi-target SFST performs better than the mono-target decoupled system.

4.2.2 Performance

So far, the capability of the systems has been assessed in terms of time and spatial costs. However, the quality of the translations they provide is, doubtless, the most relevant evaluation criterion. In order to determine the performance of the system in a quantitative manner, the following evaluation parameters were computed for each scenario: *bilingual evaluation under study* (BLEU), *position independent error rate* (PER) and *word error rate* (WER). Both text and speech-input translation results provided by the multi-target and the mono-target models respectively are shown in Table 4.

As can be derived from the translation results, for text-input translation the classical approach performs slightly better than the multi-target one, but for speech-input translation from Spanish into English is the other way around. In any case, the differences in performance are marginal.

Comparing the text-input with the speech-input results we realize that, as could be expected, the process of speech signal decoding is itself introducing some errors. In an attempt to measure these errors, the text transcription of the recognized input signal was extracted and compared to the input reference in terms of WER as shown in the last row of the Table 4. Note that even though the input sentences are the same the three results differ due to the fact that we are making use of different SFST models that decode and translate at the same time.

		multi-target		mono-target	
		S2B	S2E	S2B	S2E
Text	**BLEU**	42.7	66.7	43.4	67.8
	PER	39.9	19.9	38.2	19.0
	WER	48.0	27.5	46.2	26.6
Speech	**BLEU**	39.5	59.0	39.2	61.1
	PER	42.2	25.3	41.5	23.6
	WER	51.5	33.9	50.5	31.9
	recognition WER	10.7		9.3	9.1

Table 4: Text-input and speech-input translation results for Spanish into Basque (S2B) and Spanish into English (S2E) using a multi-target SFST (columns on the left) or two mono-target SFSTs (columns on the right). The last row shows Spanish speech decoding results using each of the three devices.

In these series of experiments the same task has been compared with two extremely different language pairs under the same conditions. There is a noticeable difference in terms of quality between the English and the Basque translations. The underlying reason might be due to the fact that SFST models do not capture properly the rich morphology of the Basque as they have to face long-distance reordering issues. These differences in the performance of the system when translating into English or into Basque have been previously detected in other works (Ortiz et al., 2003). In our case, a manual review of the models and the obtained translations encourage us to make use of reordering models in future work, since they have proved to report good results in a similar framework (Kanthak et al., 2005).

5 Concluding remarks and further work

The main contribution of this paper is the proposal of a fully embedded architecture for multiple speech translation. Thus, acoustic models are integrated on the fly into a multi-target translation model. The most significant feature of this approach is its ability to carry out both the recognition and the translation into multiple languages integrated in a unique model. Due to the finite-state nature of this model, the speech translation engine is based on a Viterbi-like algorithm.

In contrast to the mono-target systems, multi-target SFSTs enable the translation from one source language simultaneously into several target languages with lower computational costs (in terms of space and time) and comparable qualitative results. Moreover, the integration of several languages and acoustic models is straightforward on means of finite-state devices.

Nevertheless, the integrated architecture needs more parameters to be estimated. In fact, as the amount of targets increase the data sparseness might become a difficult problem to cope with. In future work we intend to make a deeper study on the performance of the multi-target system with regard to the amount of parameters to be estimated. In addition, as the first step of the learning algorithm is decisive, we are planning to make use of reordering models in an attempt to face up to with long distance reordering and in order to homogenize all the languages involved.

Acknowledgments

This work has been partially supported by the University of the Basque Country and by Spanish CICYT under grants 9/UPV 00224.310-15900/2004, TIC2003-08681-C02-02, and CICYT es TIN2005-08660-C04-03 respectively.

References

Iñaki Alegria, Olatz Ansa, Xabier Artola, Nerea Ezeiza, Koldo Gojenola, and Ruben Urizar. 2004. Representation and treatment of multiword expressions in basque. In Takaaki Tanaka, Aline Villavicencio, Francis Bond, and Anna Korhonen, editors, *Second ACL Workshop on Multiword Expressions: Integrating Processing*, pages 48–55, Barcelona, Spain, July. Association for Computational Linguistics.

Peter F. Brown, Stephen A. Della Pietra, Vincent J. Della Pietra, and R. L. Mercer. 1993. The mathematics of statistical machine translation: Parameter estimation. *Computational Linguistics*, 19(2):263–311.

Francisco Casacuberta and Enrique Vidal. 2004. Machine translation with inferred stochastic finite-state transducers. *Computational Linguistics*, 30(2):205–225.

P. García and E. Vidal. 1990. Inference of k-testable languages in the strict sense and application to syntactic pattern recognition. *IEEE Transactions on Pattern Analysis and Machine Intelligence*, 12(9):920–925.

M.T. González and F. Casacuberta. 2006. Multi-Target Machine Translation using Finite-State Transducers. In *Proceedings of TC-Star Speech to Speech Translation Workshop*, pages 105–110.

John Hutchins and Harold L. Somers. 1992. *An Introduction to Machine Translation*. Academic Press, Cambridge, MA.

Stephan Kanthak, David Vilar, Evgeny Matusov, Richard Zens, and Hermann Ney. 2005. Novel reordering approaches in phrase-based statistical machine translation. In *Proceedings of the ACL Workshop on Building and Using Parallel Texts*, pages 167–174, Ann Arbor, Michigan, June. Association for Computational Linguistics.

K. Knight and Y. Al-Onaizan. 1998. Translation with finite-state devices. In *4th AMTA (Association for Machine Translation in the Americas)*.

Mehryar Mohri, Fernando Pereira, and Michael Riley. 2002. Weighted finite-state transducers in speech recognition. *Computer, Speech and Language*, 16(1):69–88, January.

A. Moreno, D. Poch, A. Bonafonte, E. Lleida, J. Llisterri, J. B. Mario, and C. Nadeu. 1993. Albayzin speech database: Design of the phonetic corpus. In *Proc. of the European Conference on Speech Communications and Technology (EUROSPEECH)*, Berlín, Germany.

Franz J. Och. 2000. GIZA++: Training of statistical translation models. `http://www.fjoch.com/GIZA++.html`.

Daniel Ortiz, Ismael García-Varea, Francisco Casacuberta, Antonio Lagarda, and Jorge González. 2003. On the use of statistical machine translation techniques within a memory-based translation system (AMETRA). In *Proc. of Machine Translation Summit IX*, pages 115–120, New Orleans, USA, September.

Fernando C.N. Pereira and Michael D. Riley. 1997. Speech Recognition by Composition of Weighted Finite Automata. In Emmanuel Roche and Yves Schabes, editors, *Finite-State Language Processing*, Language, Speech and Communication series, pages 431–453. The MIT Press, Cambridge, Massachusetts.

Alicia Pérez, M. Inés Torres, and Francisco Casacuberta. 2007. Speech translation with phrase based stochastic finite-state transducers. In *Proceedings of the 32nd International Conference on Acoustics, Speech, and Signal Processing (ICASSP 2007)*, Honolulu, Hawaii USA, April 15-20. IEEE.

Maja Popović, David Vilar, Hermann Ney, Slobodan Jovičić, and Zoran Šarić. 2005. Augmenting a small parallel text with morpho-syntactic language. In *Proceedings of the ACL Workshop on Building and Using Parallel Texts*, pages 41–48, Ann Arbor, Michigan, June. Association for Computational Linguistics.

M. Inés Torres and Amparo Varona. 2001. k-tss language models in speech recognition systems. *Computer Speech and Language*, 15(2):127–149.

Enrique Vidal. 1997. Finite-state speech-to-speech translation. In *Proc. IEEE International Conference on Acoustics, Speech, and Signal Processing*, volume 1, pages 111–114, Munich, Germany, April.

Meta-Structure Transformation Model for Statistical Machine Translation

Jiadong Sun, Tiejun, Zhao and **Huashen Liang**
MOE-MS Key Lab of National Language Processing and speech
Harbin Institute of Technology
No. 92, West Da-zhi Street ,Harbin Heilongjiang ,150001 ,China
jiadongsun@hit.edu.cn
{tjzhao, hsliang }@mtlab.hit.edu.cn

Abstract

We propose a novel syntax-based model for statistical machine translation in which meta-structure (**MS**) and meta-structure sequence (**SMS**) of a parse tree are defined. In this framework, a parse tree is decomposed into **SMS** to deal with the structure divergence and the alignment can be reconstructed at different levels of recombination of **MS** (**RM**). **RM** pairs extracted can perform the mapping between the substructures across languages. As a result, we have got not only the translation for the target language, but an **SMS** of its parse tree at the same time. Experiments with BLEU metric show that the model significantly outperforms Pharaoh, a state-art-the-art phrase-based system.

1 Introduction

The statistical approach has been widely used in machine translation, which use the noisy-channel-based model. A joint probability model, proposed by Marcu and Wong (2002), is a kind of phrase-based one. Och and Ney (2004) gave a framework of alignment templates for this kind of models. All of the phrase-based models outperformed the word-based models, by automatically learning word and phrase equivalents from bilingual corpus and reordering at the phrase level. But it has been found that phrases longer than three words have little improvement in the performance (Koehn, 2003). Above the phrase level, these models have a simple distortion model that reorders phrases independently, without consideration of their contents and syntactic information.

In recent years, applying different statistical learning methods to structured data has attracted various researchers. Syntax-based MT approaches began with Wu (1997), who introduced the Inversion Transduction Grammars. Utilizing syntactic structure as the channel input was introduced into MT by Yamada (2001). Syntax-based models have been presented in different grammar formalisms. The model based on Head-transducer was presented by Alshawi (2000). Daniel Gildea (2003) dealt with the problem of the parse tree isomorphism with a cloning operation to either tree-to-string or tree-to-tree alignment models. Ding and Palmer (2005) introduced a version of probabilistic extension of Synchronous Dependency Insertion Grammars (**SDIG**) to deal with the pervasive structure divergence. All these approaches don't model the translation process, but formalize a model that generates two languages at the same time, which can be considered as some kind of tree transducers. Graehl and Knight (2004) described the use of tree transducers for natural language processing and addressed the training problems for this kind of transducers.

In this paper, we define a model based on the **MS** decomposition of the parse trees for statistical machine translation, which can capture structural variations and has a proven generation capacity. During the translation process of our model, the parse tree of the source language is decomposed into different levels of **MS** and then transformed into the ones of the target language in the form of **RM**. The source language can be reordered according to the structure transformation. At last, the target translation string is generated in the scopes of **RM**. In the framework of this model,

Proceedings of the Second Workshop on Statistical Machine Translation, pages 64–71,
Prague, June 2007.

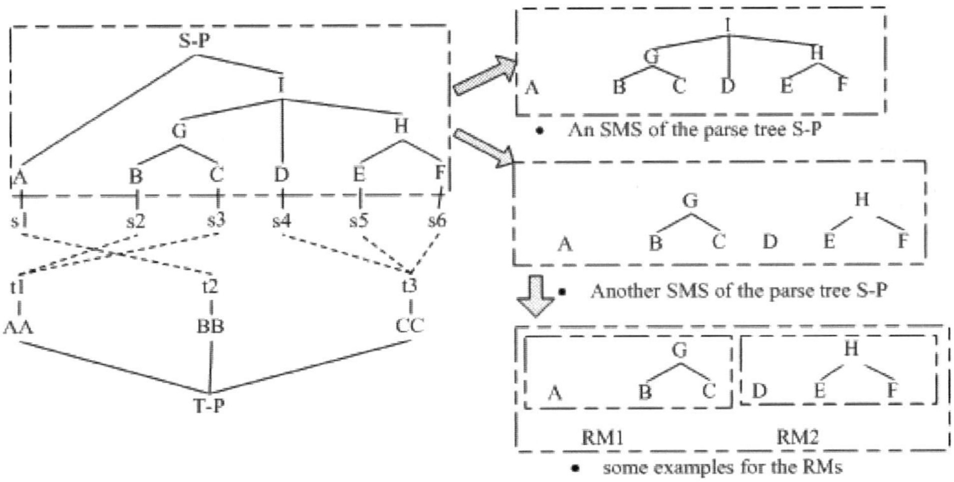

Figure 1: MS and the SMS and RM for a given parser tree

the **RM** transformation can be regarded as production rules and be extracted automatically from the bilingual corpus. The overall translation probability is thus decomposed.

In the rest of this paper, we first give the definitions for **MS**, **SMS**, **RM** and the decomposition of the parse tree in section 2.1, we give a detailed description of our model in section 2.2, section 3 describes the training details and section 4 describes the decoding algorithms, and then the experiment (section 5) proves that our model can outperform the baseline model, pharaoh, under the same condition.

2 The model

2.1 MS for a parse tree

A source language sentence (s1 s2 s3 s4 s5 s6), and its parse tree S-P, are given in Figure 1.We also give the translation of the sentence, which is illustrated as (t1 t2 t3).Its parse tree is T-P.

Definition 1

MS of a parse tree

We call a sub-tree a **MS** of a parse tree, if it satisfies the following constraints:

1. An **MS** should be a sub-tree of a parse tree
2. Its direct sons of the leaf nodes in the sub-tree are the words or punctuations of the sentence

For example, each of the sub-trees in the right-hand of Figure 1 is an **MS** for the parse tree of S-P. The sub-tree of [I [G, D, H]] of S-P is not an **MS**, because the direct sons of the leaf nodes, G, D, H, are not words in the sentence of `(s1 s2 s3 s4 s5 s6)`.

Definition 2 SMS and RM

A sequence of **MS** is called a **meta-structure sequence (SMS)** of a parse tree if and only if,

1. Its elements are **MS** of the parse tree
2. The parse tree can be reconstructed with the elements in the same order as in the sequence.

It is denoted as **SMS [T(S)]**.[1] Two examples for the concept of **SMS** can be found in Figure1.

RM(recombination of MS) is a sub-sequence of **SMS**. We can express an **SMS** as different $RM_1^k[T(S)]$ .The parse tree of S-P in Figure1 is decomposed into **SMS** and expressed in the framework of **RM**. The two RM, $RM_1^2[S-P]$, are used to express its parse tree in Figure1.It is noted that there is structure divergence between the two parse trees in Figure1. The corresponding node of Node **I** in the tree S-P cannot be found in the tree T-P. But under the conception of **RM**, the structure alignments can be achieved at the level of **RM**, which is illustrated in Figure2.

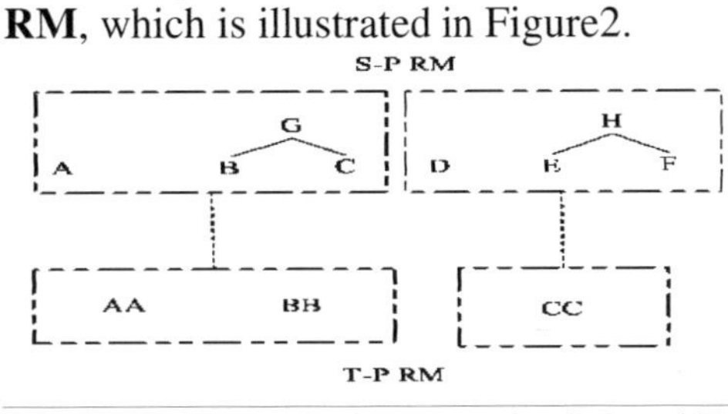

Figure2.The RM alignments for S-P and T-P

[1] **T[S]** denotes the parse tree of a given sentence
f and **e** denote the foreign and target sentences

In Figure2, both of the parse trees are decomposed and reconstructed in the forms of RM. The alignments based on RM are illustrated at the same time.

2.2 Description of the model

In the framework of Statistical machine translation, the task is to find the sentence **e** for the given foreign language **f**, which can be described in the following formulation.

$$\tilde{e} = \arg\max_{e}\{ P(e \mid f)\} \quad (1)$$

To make the model have the ability to model the structure transformation, some hidden variables are introduced into the probability equation. To make the equations simple to read, we take some denotations different from the above definitions. **SMS[T(S)]** is denoted as SM[T(S)].

The first variable is the **SM[T(S)]**, we induce the equation as follows,

$$P(e \mid f) = \sum_{SM(T(f))} P(e, SM[T(f)] \mid f)$$
$$= \sum_{SM[T(f)]} P(SM[T(f)] \mid f) P(e \mid SM[T(f)], f) \quad (2)$$

$$P(e \mid SM[T(f)], f) =$$
$$\sum_{SM[T(e)]} P(e, SM[T(e)] \mid SM[T(f)], f)$$
$$= \sum_{SM[T(e)]} P(SM[T(e)] \mid SM[T(f)], f) \times$$
$$P(e \mid SM[T(e)], SM[T(f)], f) \quad (3)$$

In order to simplify this model we have two assumptions:

An assumption is that the generation of **SMS** [T(e)] is only related with SMS[T(f)]:

$$P(SM[T(e)] \mid SM[T(f)], f)$$
$$\equiv P(SM[T(e)] \mid SM[T(f)]) \quad (4)$$

Here we do all segmentations for any **SMS** of **[T (f)]** to get different $RM_1^k[T(f)]$.

$$P(SM[T(e)] \mid SM[T(f)]) =$$
$$\sum_{RMT(f)]} \prod_{i=1}^{k} P(RM_i[T(e)] \mid RM_i[T(f)]) \quad (5)$$

The use of RM is to decompose bi-lingual parse trees and get the alignments in different hierarchical levels of the structure.

Now we have another assumption that all $P(SM[T(f)] \mid f)$ should have the same probability α. A simplified form for this model is derived:

$$P(e \mid f) =$$
$$\sum_{SM(T(f))} \sum_{SM(T(e))} \alpha \times$$
$$\sum_{RM[T(f)]} \prod_{i=1}^{k} P(RM_i[T(e)] \mid RM_i[T(f)])$$
$$\times P(e \mid RM_i[T(e)], RM_i[T(f)], f) \quad (6)$$

, Where $P(e \mid RM_i[T(e)], RM_i[T(f)], f)$ can be regarded as a lexical transformation process, which will be further decomposed.

In order to model the direct translation process better by extending the feature functions, the direct translation probability is obtained in the framework of maximum entropy model:

$$P(e \mid f) = \frac{\exp[\sum_{m=1}^{M} \lambda_m h_m(e, SM[T(e)], SM[T(f)], f)]}{\sum_{e, SM[T(e)], SM[T(f)]} \exp[\sum_{m=1}^{M} \lambda_m h_m(e, SM[T(e)], SM[T(f)], f)]} \quad (7)$$

We can achieve the translation according to the function below:

$$\tilde{e} = \arg\max\{\exp[\sum_{m=1}^{M} \lambda_m h_m(e, SM[T(e)], SM[T(f)], f)\} \quad (8)$$

A detailed list of the feature functions for the model and some explanations are given as below:

- Just as the derivation in the model, we take into consideration of the structure transformation when selecting the features. The **MS** are combined in the forms of RM and transformed as a whole structure.

$$h_1(e, f) = \log \prod_{i=1}^{k} P(RM_i[T(e)] \mid RM_i[T(f)]) \quad (9)$$

$$h_2(e, f) = \log \prod_{i=1}^{k} P(RM_i[T(f)] \mid RM_i[T(e)]) \quad (10)$$

- Features to model lexical transformation processes, and its inverted version, where the symbol **L** **(RM_i [T(S)])** denotes the words belonging to this sub-structure in the sentence. In Figure1, **L (RM_1)** denotes the words, s1 s2 s3, in the source language. This part of transformation happens in the scope of each RM, which means that all the words in any RM can be transformed into the target language words just in the way of phrase-based model, serving as another reordering factor at a different level:

$$h_3(e,f) = \log \prod_{i=1}^{k} P(L(RM_i[T(e)])) \mid L(RM_i[T(f)]) \quad (11)$$

$$h_4(e,f) = \log \prod_{i=1}^{k} P(L(RM_i[T(f)])) \mid L(RM_i[T(e)]) \quad (12)$$

- We define a 3-gram model for the RM of the target language, which is called a structure model according to the function of it in this model.

$$h_5(e,f) = \log \prod_{i=1}^{k} P(RM_i[T(e)] \mid RM_{i-2}[T(e)], RM_{i-1}[T(e)]) \quad (13)$$

This feature can model the recombination of the parse structure of the target sentences. For example in Figure3, $P(CC \mid AA, BB)$ is used to describe the probability of the RM sequence, (AA, BB) should be followed by RM (CC) in the translation process. This function can ensure that a more reasonable sub-tree can be generated for the target language. That would be explained further in section 3.

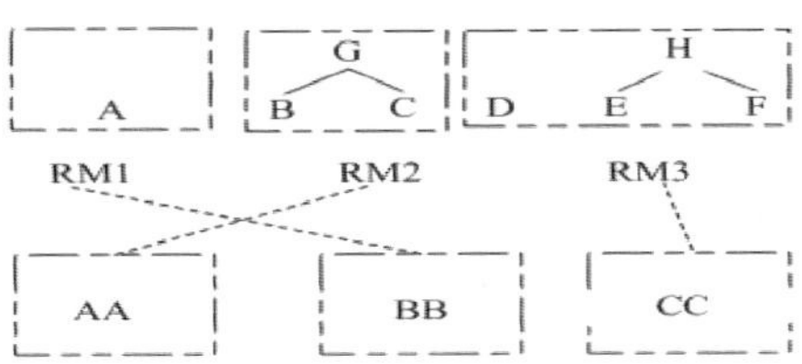

Figure3. The 3-gram structure model

- The 3-gram language model is also used

$$h_6(e,f) = \log P(e) \quad (14)$$

The phrase-based model (Koehn, 2003) is a special case of this framework, if we take the whole structure of the parse tree as the only MS of the parse tree of the sentence, and set some special feature weights to zero.

From the description above, we know the framework of this model. When transformed to target languages, the source language is reordered at the RM level first. In this process, only the knowledge of the structure is taken into consideration. It is obvious that a lot of sentences in the source language can have the same RM. So this model has better generative ability. At the same time, RM is a subsequence of **SMS**, which consists of different hierarchical MS. So RM is a structure, which can model the structure mapping across the sub-tree structure. By decomposing the source parse tree, the isomorphic between the parse trees can be obtained, at the level of RM.

When reordering at the RM level, this model just takes an RM as a symbol, and it can perform a long distance reordering job according to the knowledge of RM alignments.

3 Training

For training the model, a parallel tree corpus is needed. The methods and details are described as follows:

3.1 Decomposition of the parse tree

To reduce the amount of **MS** used in decoding and training, we take some constrains for the **MS**.

（1）.The height of the sub-tree shouldn't be greater than a fixed value α ;

（2）. $\frac{N(Leaf-nodes)}{N(height)} \geq \beta$

Given a parse tree, we get the initial **SMS** in such a top -down and left- to –right way.

Any node is deleted if the sub-tree can't satisfy the constrains (1), (2).

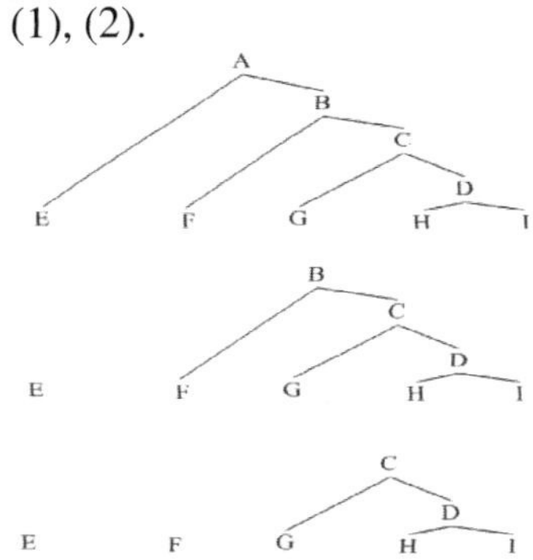

Figure3. Decomposition of a parse tree

RMS for Ch-Parse Tree	RMS for EN-Parse Tree	Pro for transformation
AP[AP[AP[a-a]-usde]-m]	NPB [DT-JJ-NN-PUNC.]	0.000155497
AP[AP[AP[r-a]-usde]-m]	NPB[PDT-DT-JJ-NN]	0.0151515
AP[AP[BMP[m-q]-a]-usde] wj	ADVP [RB-RB-PUNC.]	0.00344828
AP[AP[BMP[m-q]-a]-usde] wj	DT CD JJ NNS PUNC	0.0833333
AP[AP[BMP[m-q]-a]-usde] wj	DT JJ NN NNS PUNC.	0.015625

Table 1 some examples of the RM transformation

RM1	RM2	RM3	P(RM3|RM1,RM2)
IN	NP-A[NPB[PRP-NN]	IN	0.2479237
NPB	NP-A[NPB[PRP-NN]	VBZ	0.2479235
IN	NP-A[NPB[PRP-NN]	MD	0.6458637
<s>	NP-A[NPB[PRP-NN]	VBD	0.904308

Table 2 Examples for the 3-gram structure model of RM

Generate all of the **SMS** by deleting a node in any **Ms** to generate new **SMS**, applying the same operation to any **SMS**

3.2 Parallel SMS and Estimation of the parameters for RM transformations

We can get bi-lingual **SMS** by recombining all the possible **SMS** obtained from the parallel parse trees. $m * n$ Parallel **SMS** can be obtained if m is the number of **SMS** for a parse tree in the source language, n for the target one.

The alignments of the parallel **MS** and extraction can be performed in such a simple way. Given the parallel tree corpus, we first get the alignments based on the level of words, for which we used GIZA++ in both of the directions. According to the knowledge of the word alignments, we derived the alignments of leave nodes of the given parse trees, which are the direct root nodes of the words. Then all the knowledge of the words is discarded for the RM extraction. The next step for the extraction of the RM is based on the popular phrase-extraction algorithm of the phrase-based statistical machine translation model. The present alignment and phrase extraction methods can be applied to the extraction of the MS and RM [T(S)].

$$P(RM_{EI} \mid RM_{Fi}) = \frac{Count(RM_{Fi}, RM_{EI})}{\sum_{RM_{Ei}} Count(RM_{Fi}, RM_{Ei})}$$

$Count(A, B)$ is the expected number of times A is aligned with B in the training corpus.Table1 shows some parameters for this part in the model.

Training n-gram model for the monolingual structure model is based on the English RM of each parse tree, selected from the parallel tree corpus. The 3-gram structure model is defined as follows:

$$P(RM_I[T(e)] \mid RM_{i-2}[T(e)], RM_{i-1}[T(e)]) = \frac{Count(RM_{I-2}, RM_{I-1}, RM_I)}{\sum_j Count(RM_{I-2}, RM_{I-1}, RM_j)}$$

$Count(A, B, C)$ is the times of the situation, in which the RM is consecutive sub-trees of the parse trees in the training set. Some 3-gram parameters in the training task are given in Table2.

We didn't meet with the serious data sparseness problem in this part of work, because most of the MS structures have occurred enough times for parameters estimation. But we still set some fixed value for the unseen parameters in the training set.

4 Decoding

A beam search algorithm is applied to this model for decoding, which is based on the frame of the beam search for phrase-based statistical machine translation (Koehn et al, 03).

Here the process of the hypothesis generation is presented. Given a sentence and its parse tree, all the possible candidate **RM** are collected, which can cover a part of the parse tree at the bottom. With the candidates, the hypotheses can be formed and extended.

For example, all the parse tree's leaf nodes of a Chinese sentence in Figure4, are covered by **[r]**, **[pron]** and **VP[vg-BNP[pron-n]]** in the order of choosing candidate RM{ (1), (2), (3)}.

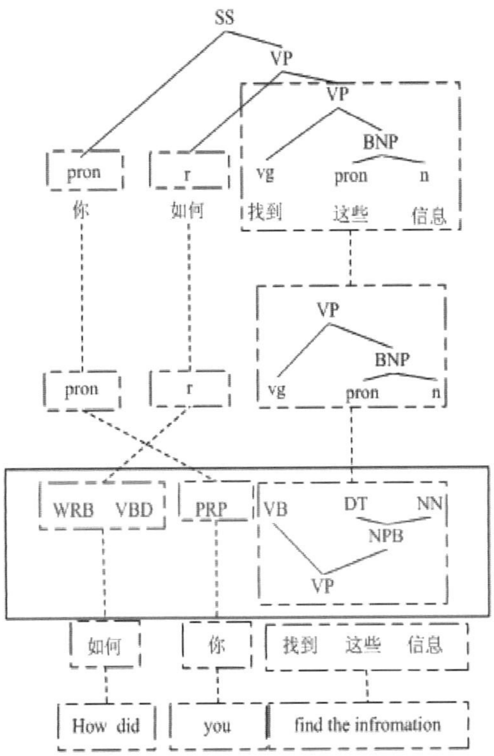

Figure4. Process of translation based on RM

$$(r, WRB \quad VBD) \qquad (1)$$

如何 → how did

$$(pron, PRP) \qquad (2)$$

你 → you

$$(VP[vg - BNP[pron - n]], \quad VP[VB - NPB[DT - NN]]) \qquad (3)$$

得到 这些 信息 → find the information

Before the next expansion of a hypothesis, the words in the scope of the present RM are translated into the target language and the corresponding $RM_i\,[T(e)]$ is generated. For example, when $(r, WRB \quad VBD)$, is used to expand the hypothesis , the words in the sub-tree are translated into the target language, 如何 → how did.

We also need to calculate the cost for the hypotheses according to the parameters in the model to perform the beam search. The task for the beam search is to find the hypothesis with the least cost. When the expansion of a hypothesis comes to the final state, the target language is generated. All of the leave nodes of the parse tree for the source language are covered. The parser for the target language isn't used for decoding. But a target **SMS** is generated during the process of decoding to achieve better reordering performance.

5 Experiments

The experiment was conducted for the task of Chinese-to-English translation. A corpus, which consists of 602,701 sentence pairs, was used as the training set. We took CLDC 863 test set as our test set (http://www.chineseldc.org/resourse.asp), which consists of 467 sentences with an average length of 14.287 Chinese words and 4 references. To evaluate the result of the translation, the BLEU metric (Papineni et al. 2002) was used.

5.1 The baseline

System used for comparison was Pharaoh (Koehn et al., 2003; Koehn, 2004), which uses a beam search algorithm for decoding. In its model, it takes the following features: language model, phrase translation probability in the two directions, distortion model, word penalty and phrase penalty, all of which can be achieved with the training toolkits distributed by Koehn. The training set and development set mentioned above were used to perform the training task and to tune the feature weights by the minimum error training algorithm. All the other settings were the same as the default ones. SRI Language Modeling Toolkit was used to train a 3-gram language model. After training, 164 MB language model were obtained.

5.2 Our model

All the common features shared with Pharaoh were trained with the same toolkits and the same corpus. Besides those features, we need to train the structure transformation model and the monolingual structure model for our model. First, 10,000 sentence pairs were selected to achieve the

System	BLEU-n	n-gram precisions							
	4	1	2	3	4	5	6	7	8
Pharaoh	0.2053	0.6449	0.4270	0.2919	0.2053	0.1480	0.1061	0.0752	0.0534
Ms system	0.2232	0.6917	0.4605	0.3160	0.2232	0.1615	0.1163	0.0826	0.0587

Table3. Comparison of Pharaoh and our system

		Features						
System	$P_{lm}(e)$	P(RT)	P(IRT)	$P_w(f\|e)$	$P_w(e\|f)$	Word	Phr	Ph(RM)
Pharaoh	0.151	----	------	0.08	0.14	-0.29	0.26	-----
MS system	0.157	0.16	0.23	0.06	0.11	-0.20	0.22	0.36

Table4.Feature weights obtained by minimum error rate training on development set

training set for this part of task. The Collins parser and a Chinese parser of our own lab were used. After processing this corpus, we get a parallel tree corpus. SRI Language Modeling Toolkits were used again to train this part of parameters. In this experiment, we set $\alpha = 3$,and $\beta = 1.5$. 149MB $RMS\ [T(s)]$ pairs and a 25 MB 3-gram monolingual structure model were obtained.

6. Conclusion and Future work

A framework for statistical machine translation is created in this paper. The results of the experiments show that this model gives better performance, compared with the baseline system.

This model can incorporate the syntactic information into the process of translation and model the sub-structure projections across the parallel parse trees.

The advantage of this frame work lies in that the reordering operations can be performed at the different levels according to the hierarchical RM of the parse tree.

But we should notice that some independent assumptions were made in the decomposition of the parse tree. In the future, a proper method should be introduced into this model to achieve the most possible decomposition of the parse tree. In fact, we can incorporate some other feature functions into the model to model the structure transformation more effectively.

Acknowledgement

Thanks to the reviewers for their reviews and comments on improving our presentation of this paper.

References

A.P.Dempster,N.M.Laird, and D.B.Rubin 1977.Maximum likelihood from imcomplete data via the EM algorithm. Journal of the Royal Statistical Society, 39(Ser B):1-38.

Christoph Tillman. *A projection extension algorithm for statistical machine translation.* Proceedings of the Conference on Empirical Methods in Natural Language Processing, Sapporo, Japan, June 30-July 4, 2003, 1-8.

Daniel Gildea.2003.*Loosely tree based alignment for machine translation.* In Proceedings of ACL-03

Daniel Marcu, William Wong. *A phrase-based, joint probability model for statistical machine translation.* Proceedings of the Conference on Empirical Methods in Natural Language Processing, Philadelphia, PA, USA, July 11-13, 2002, 133-139.

Dekai Wu. 1997. *Stochastic inversion transduction grammars and bilingual parsing of parallel corpora.* Computational Linguistics, 23(3):3-403.

F.Casacuberta, E. Vidal: *Machine Translation with Inferred Stochastic Finite-state Transducers.* Computational Linguistics, Vol. 30, No. 2, pp. 205-225, June 2004

Franz J. Och, C. Tillmann, Hermann Ney. *Improved alignment models for statistical machine translation.* Proceedings of the Joint SIGDAT Conference on Empirical Methods in Natural Language Processing and Very Large Corpora (EMNLP), College Park, MD, USA, June 21-22, 1999, 20-28.

Franz J. Och, Hermann Ney.2002 *Discriminative training and maximum entropy models.* In Proceedings of ACL-00, pages 440-447, Hong Kong, Octorber.

Hiyan Alshawi, Srinvas Bangalore, and Shona Douglas. 2000. *Learning dependency translation models as collections of finite state head transducers* Computational Linguistics, 26(1):45-60.

Ilya D. Melamed. *Automatic evaluation and uniform filter cascades for inducing n-best translation lexicons.* Proceedings of the Third Workshop on Very Large Corpora, Boston, USA, July 30, 1995, 197-211.

Jonathan Graehl Kevin Knight *Training Tree Transducers* In Proceedings of NAACL-HLT 2004, pages 105-112.

Kenji Yamada and Kevin Knight 2001. *A Syntax-based statistical translation model.* In Proceedings of the 39th Annual Meeting of the association for computational Linguists(ACL 01), Toulouse, France, July 6-11

Michael John Collins. 1999. *Head-driven statistical Models for Natural Language Parsing.* Ph.D. thesis,University of Pennsyvania,Philadelphia.

P. Koehn, Franz Josef Och, Daniel Marcu. *Statistical phrase-based translation.* Proceedings of the Conference on Human Language Technology, Edmonton, Canada, May 27-June 1, 2003, 127-133.

P. Koehn: Pharaoh: *a Beam Search Decoder for Phrase-based Statistical Machine Translation Models* . Meeting of the American Association for machine translation(AMTA), Washington DC, pp. 115-124 Sep./Oct. 2004

Peter F. Brown ,Stephen *A. Della Pietra,Vincent J.Della Pietra, and Robert Merrcer.1993. The mathematics of statistical machine translation:Parameter estimation.*Computational Linguistics,19(2).:263-311.

Quirk, Chris, Arul Menezes, and Colin Cherry. *Dependency Tree Translation.* Microsoft Research Technical Report: MSR-TR-2004-113.

Regina Barzilay and Lillian Lee. 2003. *Learning to paraphrase: An supervised approach using multiple-sequence alignment.* In Proceedings of HLT/NAACL

S. Nie β en , H. Ney: Statistical Machine Translation with Scarce Resources using Morpho-syntactic Information. Computational Linguistics, Vol. 30 No. 2, pp. 181-204, June 20

Yuan Ding and Martha Palmer. 2005. *Machine translation using probabilistic synchronous dependency insert grammars.* In Proceedings of 43rd Annual Meeting of the NAACL-HLT2004, pages 273-280..

Training Non-Parametric Features for Statistical Machine Translation

Patrick Nguyen, Milind Mahajan and Xiaodong He
Microsoft Corporation
1 Microsoft Way,
Redmond, WA 98052
{panguyen,milindm,xiaohe}@microsoft.com

Abstract

Modern statistical machine translation systems may be seen as using two components: feature extraction, that summarizes information about the translation, and a log-linear framework to combine features. In this paper, we propose to relax the linearity constraints on the combination, and hence relaxing constraints of monotonicity and independence of feature functions. We expand features into a non-parametric, non-linear, and high-dimensional space. We extend empirical Bayes reward training of model parameters to meta parameters of feature generation. In effect, this allows us to trade away some human expert feature design for data. Preliminary results on a standard task show an encouraging improvement.

1 Introduction

In recent years, statistical machine translation have experienced a quantum leap in quality thanks to automatic evaluation (Papineni et al., 2002) and error-based optimization (Och, 2003). The conditional log-linear feature combination framework (Berger, Della Pietra and Della Pietra, 1996) is remarkably simple and effective in practice. Therefore, recent efforts (Och et al., 2004) have concentrated on feature design – wherein more intelligent features may be added. Because of their simplicity, however, log-linear models impose some constraints on how new information may be inserted into the system to achieve the best results. In other words, new information needs to be *parameterized* carefully into one or more real valued feature functions. Therefore, that requires some human knowledge and understanding. When not readily available, this is typically replaced with painstaking experimentation. We propose to replace that step with automatic training of non-parametric agnostic features instead, hopefully relieving the burden of finding the optimal parameterization.

First, we define the model and the objective function training framework, then we describe our new non-parametric features.

2 Model

In this section, we describe the general log-linear model used for statistical machine translation, as well as a training objective function and algorithm.

The goal is to translate a French (source) sentence indexed by t, with surface string f_t. Among a set of K_t outcomes, we denote an English (target) a hypothesis with surface string $e_k^{(t)}$ indexed by k.

2.1 Log-linear Model

The prevalent translation model in modern systems is a conditional log-linear model (Och and Ney, 2002). From a hypothesis $e_k^{(t)}$, we extract features $\mathbf{h}_k^{(t)}$, abbreviated $\mathbf{h}_k$, as a function of $e_k^{(t)}$ and f_t. The conditional probability of a hypothesis $e_k^{(t)}$ given a source sentence f_t is:

$$p_k \triangleq p(e_k^{(t)}|f_t) \triangleq \frac{\exp[\lambda \cdot \mathbf{h}_k]}{Z_{f_t;\lambda}},$$

Proceedings of the Second Workshop on Statistical Machine Translation, pages 72–79,
Prague, June 2007.

where the *partition function* $Z_{f_t;\lambda}$ is given by:

$$Z_{f_t;\lambda} = \sum_j \exp[\lambda \cdot \mathbf{h}_j].$$

The vector of parameters of the model λ, gives a relative importance to each feature function component.

2.2 Training Criteria

In this section, we quickly review how to adjust λ to get better translation results. First, let us define the figure of merit used for evaluation of translation quality.

2.2.1 BLEU Evaluation

The BLEU score (Papineni et al., 2002) was defined to measure overlap between a hypothesized translation and a set of human references. n-gram overlap counts $\{c_n\}_{n=1}^4$ are computed over the test set sentences, and compared to the total counts of n-grams in the hypothesis:

$$c_k^{n,(t)} \triangleq \text{max. \# of matching } n\text{-grams for hyp. } e_k^{(t)},$$
$$a_k^{n,(t)} \triangleq \text{\# of } n\text{-grams in hypothesis } e_k^{(t)}.$$

Those quantities are abbreviated c_k and a_k to simplify the notation. The precision ratio P_n for an n-gram order n is:

$$P_n \triangleq \frac{\sum_t c_k^{n,(t)}}{\sum_t a_k^{n,(t)}}.$$

A *brevity penalty* BP is also taken into account, to avoid favoring overly short sentences:

$$\text{BP} \triangleq \min\{1; \exp(1 - \frac{r}{a})\},$$

where r is the average length of the shortest sentence[1], and a is the average length of hypotheses. The BLEU score the set of hypotheses $\{e_k^{(t)}\}$ is:

$$B(\{e_k^{(t)}\}) \triangleq \text{BP} \cdot \exp\left(\sum_{n=1}^{4} \frac{1}{4} \log P_n\right).$$

[1]As implemented by NIST `mteval-v11b.pl`.

Oracle BLEU hypothesis: There is no easy way to pick the set hypotheses from an n-best list that will maximize the overall BLEU score. Instead, to compute oracle BLEU hypotheses, we chose, for each sentence independently, the hypothesis with the highest BLEU score computed for a sentence itself. We believe that it is a relatively tight lower bound and equal for practical purposes to the true oracle BLEU.

2.2.2 Maximum Likelihood

Used in earlier models (Och and Ney, 2002), the likelihood criterion is defined as the likelihood of an oracle hypothesis $e_{k^*}^{(t)}$, typically a single reference translation, or alternatively the closest match which was decoded. When the model is correct and infinite amounts of data are available, this method will converge to the Bayes error (minimum achievable error), where we define a classification task of selecting k^* against all others.

2.2.3 Regularization Schemes

One can convert a maximum likelihood problem into maximum *a posteriori* using Bayes' rule:

$$\arg\max_\lambda \prod_t p(\lambda | \{e_k^{(t)}, f_t\}) = \arg\max_\lambda \prod_t p_k p_0(\lambda),$$

where $p_0(\cdot)$ is the prior distribution of λ. The most frequently used prior in practice is the normal prior (Chen and Rosenfeld, 2000):

$$\log p_0(\lambda) \triangleq -\frac{||\lambda||^2}{2\sigma^2} - \log |\sigma|,$$

where $\sigma^2 > 0$ is the variance. It can be thought of as the inverse of a Lagrange multiplier when working with constrained optimization on the Euclidean norm of λ. When not interpolated with the likelihood, the prior can be thought of as a penalty term. The entropy penalty may also be used:

$$H \triangleq -\frac{1}{T} \sum_{t=1}^{T} \sum_{k=1}^{K_t} p_k \log p_k.$$

Unlike the Gaussian prior, the entropy is independent of parameterization (i.e., it does not depend on how features are expressed).

2.2.4 Minimum Error Rate Training

A good way of training λ is to minimize empirical top-1 error on training data (Och, 2003). Compared to maximum-likelihood, we now give partial credit for sentences which are only partially correct. The criterion is:

$$\arg\max_{\lambda} \sum_t B(\{e_{\hat{k}}^{(t)}\}) : e_{\hat{k}}^{(t)} = \arg\max_{e_j^{(t)}} p_j.$$

We optimize the λ so that the BLEU score of the most likely hypotheses is improved. For that reason, we call this criterion *BLEU max*. This function is not convex and there is no known exact efficient optimization for it. However, there exists a linear-time algorithm for exact line search against that objective. The method is often used in conjunction with coordinate projection to great success.

2.2.5 Maximum Empirical Bayes Reward

The algorithm may be improved by giving partial credit for confidence p_k of the model to partially correct hypotheses outside of the most likely hypothesis (Smith and Eisner, 2006):

$$\frac{1}{T}\sum_{t=1}^{T}\sum_{k=1}^{K_t} p_k \log B(\{e_k(t)\}).$$

Instead of the BLEU score, we use its logrithm, because we think it is exponentially hard to improve BLEU. This model is equivalent to the previous model when p_k give all the probability mass to the top-1. That can be reached, for instance, when λ has a very large norm. There is no known method to train against this objective directly, however, efficient approximations have been developed. Again, it is not convex.

It is hoped that this criterion is better suited for high-dimensional feature spaces. That is our main motivation for using this objective function throughout this paper. With baseline features and on our data set, this criterion also seemed to lead to results similar to Minimum Error Rate Training.

We can normalize B to a probability measure $b(\{e_k^{(t)}\})$. The empirical Bayes reward also coincides with a divergence $D(p||b)$.

2.3 Training Algorithm

We train our model using a gradient ascent method over an approximation of the empirical Bayes reward function.

2.3.1 Approximation

Because the empirical Bayes reward is defined over a set of sentences, it may not be decomposed sentence by sentence. This is computationally burdensome. Its sufficient statistics are r, $\sum_t c_k$ and $\sum_t a_k$. The function may be reconstructed in a first-order approximation with respect to each of these statistics. In practice this has the effect of commuting the expectation inside of the functional, and for that reason we call this criterion *BLEU soft*. This approximation is called *linearization* (Smith and Eisner, 2006). We used a first-order approximation for speed, and ease of interpretation of the derivations. The new objective function is:

$$J \triangleq \log \bar{\mathrm{BP}} + \sum_{n=1}^{4} \frac{1}{4} \log \frac{\sum_t \mathbf{E} c_k^{n,(t)}}{\sum_t \mathbf{E} a_k^{n,(t)}},$$

where the average bleu penalty is:

$$\log \bar{\mathrm{BP}} \triangleq \min\{0; 1 - \frac{r}{\mathbf{E}_{k,t} a_k^{1,(t)}}\}.$$

The expectation is understood to be under the current estimate of our log-linear model. Because $\bar{\mathrm{BP}}$ is not differentiable, we replace the hard min function with a sigmoid, yielding:

$$\log \bar{\mathrm{BP}} \approx u(r - \mathbf{E}_{k,t} a_k^{1,(t)}) \left(1 - \frac{r}{\mathbf{E}_{k,t} a_k^{1,(t)}}\right),$$

with the sigmoid function $u(x)$ defines a soft step function:

$$u(x) \triangleq \frac{1}{1 + e^{-\tau x}},$$

with a parameter $\tau \gg 1$.

2.3.2 Gradients and Sufficient Statistics

We can obtain the gradients of the objective function using the chain rule by first differentiating with respect to the probability. First, let us decompose the log-precision of the expected counts:

$$\log \tilde{P}_n = \log \mathbf{E} c_k^{n,(t)} - \log \mathbf{E} a_k^{n,(t)}.$$

Each n-gram precision may be treated separately. For each n-gram order, let us define sufficient statistics ψ for the precision:

$$\psi_\lambda^c \triangleq \sum_{t,k} (\nabla_\lambda p_k) c_k; \quad \psi_\lambda^a \triangleq \sum_{t,k} (\nabla_\lambda p_k) a_k,$$

where the gradient of the probabilities is given by:

$$\nabla_\lambda p_k = p_k(\mathbf{h}_k - \bar{\mathbf{h}}),$$

with:

$$\bar{\mathbf{h}} \triangleq \sum_{j=1}^{K_t} p_j \mathbf{h}_j.$$

The derivative of the precision $\tilde{P}_n$ is:

$$\nabla_\lambda \log \tilde{P}_n = \frac{1}{T} \left[\frac{\psi_\lambda^c}{\mathbf{E}c_k} - \frac{\psi_\lambda^a}{\mathbf{E}a_k} \right]$$

For the length, the derivative of $\log \text{BP}$ is:

$$u(r - \mathbf{E}a) \left[(\frac{r}{a} - 1)[1 - u(r - \mathbf{E}a)]\tau + \frac{r}{(\mathbf{E}a)^2} \right] \psi_\lambda^{a_1},$$

where $\psi_\lambda^{a_1}$ is the 1-gram component of ψ_λ^a. Finally, the derivative of the entropy is:

$$\nabla_\lambda H = \sum_{k,t} (1 + \log p_k) \nabla_\lambda p_k.$$

2.3.3 RProp

For all our experiments, we chose RProp (Riedmiller and Braun, 1992) as the gradient ascent algorithm. Unlike other gradient algorithms, it is only based on the sign of the gradient components at each iteration. It is relatively robust to the objective function, requires little memory, does not require meta parameters to be tuned, and is simple to implement. On the other hand, it typically requires more iterations than stochastic gradient (Kushner and Yin, 1997) or L-BFGS (Nocedal and Wright, 1999).

Using fairly conservative stopping criteria, we observed that RProp was about 6 times faster than Minimum Error Rate Training.

3 Adding Features

The log-linear model is relatively simple, and is usually found to yield good performance in practice. With these considerations in mind, feature engineering is an active area of research (Och et al., 2004). Because the model is fairly simple, some of the intelligence must be shifted to feature design. After having decided what new information should go in the overall score, there is an extra effort involved in expressing or *parameterizing* features in a way which will be easiest for the model learn. Experimentation is usually required to find the best configuration.

By adding non-parametric features, we propose to mitigate the parameterization problem. We will not add new information, but rather, propose a way to insulate research from the parameterization. The system should perform equivalently invariant of any continuous invertible transformation of the original input.

3.1 Existing Features

The baseline system is a syntax based machine translation system as described in (Quirk, Menezes and Cherry, 2005). Our existing feature set includes 11 features, among which the following:

- Target hypothesis word count.
- Treelet count used to construct the candidate.
- Target language models, based on the Gigaword corpus (5-gram) and target side of parallel training data (3-gram).
- Order models, which assign a probability to the position of each target node relative to its head.
- Treelet translation model.
- Dependency-based bigram language models.

3.2 Re-ranking Framework

Our algorithm works in a re-ranking framework. In particular, we are adding features which are not causal or additive. Features for a hypothesis may not be accumulating by looking at the English (target) surface string words from the left to the right and adding a contribution per word. Word count, for instance, is causal and additive. This property is typically required for efficient first-pass decoding. Instead, we look at a hypothesis sentence as a whole. Furthermore, we assume that the K_t-best list provided to us contains the entire probability space.

In particular, the computation of the partition function is performed over all K_t-best hypotheses. This is clearly not correct, and is the subject of further study. We use the n-best generation scheme interleaved with λ optimization as described in (Och, 2003).

3.3 Issues with Parameterization

As alluded to earlier, when designing a new feature in the log-linear model, one has to be careful to find the best embodiment. In general, a set of features must satisfy the following properties, ranked from strict to lax:

- Linearity (warping)
- Monotonicity
- Independence (conjunction)

Firstly, a feature should be linearly correlated with performance. There should be no region were it matters less than other regions. For instance, instead of a word count, one might consider adding its logarithm instead. Secondly, the "goodness" of a hypothesis associated with a feature must be monotonic. For instance, using the signed difference between word count in the French (source) and English (target) does not satisfy this. (In that case, one would use the absolute value instead.) Lastly, there should be no inter-dependence between features. As an example, we can consider adding multiple language model scores. Whether we should consider ratios those of, globally linearly or log-linearly interpolating them, is open to debate. When features interact across dimensions, it becomes unclear what the best embodiment should be.

3.4 Non-parametric Features

A generic solution may be sought in non-parametric processing. Our method can be derived from a quantized Parzen estimate of the feature density function.

3.4.1 Parzen Window

The Parzen window is an early empirical kernel method (Duda and Hart, 1973). For an observation $\mathbf{h}_m$, we extrapolate probability mass around it with a smoothing window $\Phi(\cdot)$. The density function is:

$$p(\mathbf{h}) = \frac{1}{M} \sum_{m=1}^{K} \Phi(\mathbf{h} - \mathbf{h}_m),$$

assuming $\Phi(\cdot)$ is a density function. Parzen windows converge to the true density estimate, albeit slowly, under weak assumptions.

3.4.2 Bin Features

One popular way of using continuous features in log-linear models is to convert a single continuous feature into multiple "bin" features. Each bin feature is defined as the indicator function of whether the original continuous feature was in a certain range. The bins were selected so that each bin collects an equal share of the probability mass. This is equivalent to the maximum likelihood estimate of the density function subject to a fixed number of rectangular density kernels. Since that mapping is not differentiable with respect to the original features, one may use sigmoids to soften the boundaries.

Bin features are useful to relax the requirements of linearity and monotonicity. However, because they work on each feature individually, they do not address the problem of inter-dependence between features.

3.4.3 Gaussian Mixture Model Features

Bin features may be generalized to multi-dimensional kernels by using a Gaussian smoothing window instead of a rectangular window. The direct analogy is vector quantization. The idea is to weight specific regions of the feature space differently. Assuming that we have M Gaussians each with mean vector μ_m and diagonal covariance matrix C_m, and prior weight w_m. We will add m new features, each defined as the posterior in the mixture model:

$$h_m \triangleq \frac{w_m \mathcal{N}(\mathbf{h}; \mu_m, C_m)}{\sum_r w_r \mathcal{N}(\mathbf{h}; \mu_r, C_r)}.$$

It is believed that any reasonable choice of kernels will yield roughly equivalent results (Povey et al., 2004), if the amount of training data and the number of kernels are both sufficiently large. We show two methods for obtaining clusters. In contrast with bins, lossless representation becomes rapidly impossible.

ML kernels: The canonical way of obtaining cluster is to use the standard Gaussian mixture training. First, a single Gaussian is trained on the whole data set. Then, the Gaussian is split into two Gaussians, with each mean vector perturbed, and the Gaussians are retrained using maximum-likelihood in an expectation-maximization framework (Rabiner and Huang, 1993). The number of Gaussians is typically increased exponentially.

Perceptron kernels: We also experimented with another quicker way of obtaining kernels. We chose an equal prior and a global covariance matrix. Means were obtained as follows: for each sentence in the training set, if the top-1 candidate was different from the approximate maximum oracle BLEU hypothesis, both were inserted. It is a quick way to bootstrap and may reach the oracle BLEU score quickly.

In the limit, GMMs will converge to the oracle BLEU. In the next section, we show how to re-estimate these kernels if needed.

3.5 Re-estimation Formulæ

Features may also be trained using the same empirical maximum Bayes reward. Let θ be the hyper-parameter vector used to generate features. In the case of language models, for instance, this could be backoff weights. Let us further assume that the feature values are differentiable with respect to θ. Gradient ascent may be applied again but this time with respect to θ. Using the chain rule:

$$\nabla_\theta J = (\nabla_\theta \mathbf{h})(\nabla_{\mathbf{h}} p_k)(\nabla_{p_k} J),$$

with $\nabla_{\mathbf{h}} p_k = p_k(1 - p_k)\lambda$. Let us take the example of re-estimating the mean of a Gaussian kernel μ_m:

$$\nabla_{\mu_m} h_m = -w_m h_m (1 - h_m) C_m^{-1} (\mu_m - \mathbf{h}),$$

for its own feature, and for other posteriors $r \neq m$:

$$\nabla_{\mu_m} h_r = -w_r h_r h_m C_m^{-1} (\mu_m - \mathbf{h}),$$

which is typically close to zero if no two Gaussians fire simultaneously.

4 Experimental Results

For our experiments, we used the standard NIST MT-02 data set to evaluate our system.

4.1 NIST System

A relatively simple baseline was used for our experiments. The system is syntactically-driven (Quirk, Menezes and Cherry, 2005). The system was trained on 175k sentences which were selected from the NIST training data (NIST, 2006) to cover words in source language sentences of the MT02 development and evaluation sets. The 5-gram target language model was trained on the Gigaword monolingual data using absolute discounting smoothing. In a single decoding, the system generated 1000 hypotheses per sentence whenever possible.

4.2 Leave-one-out Training

In order to have enough data for training, we generated our n-best lists using 10-fold leave-one-out training: base feature extraction models were trained on $9/10^{\text{th}}$ of the data, then used for decoding the held-out set. The process was repeated for all 10 parts. A single λ was then optimized on the combined lists of all systems. That λ was used for another round of 10 decodings. The process was repeated until it reached convergence after 7 iterations. Each decoding generated about 100 hypotheses, and there was relatively little overlap across decodings. Therefore, there were about 1M hypotheses in total.

The combined list of all iterations was used for all subsequent experiments of feature expansion.

4.3 BLEU Training Results

We tried training systems under the empirical Bayes reward criterion, and appending either bin or GMM features. We will find that bin features are essentially ineffective while GMM features show a modest improvement. We did not retrain hyper-parameters.

4.3.1 Convexity of the Empirical Bayes Reward

The first question to ask is how many local optima does the cost surface have using the standard features. A complex cost surface indicates that some gain may be had with non-linear features, but it also shows that special care should be taken during optimization. Non-convexity is revealed by sensitivity to initialization points. Thus, we decided to initialize from all vertices of the unit hypercube, and since we had 11 features, we ran 2^{11} experiments. The histogram of BLEU scores on dev data after convergence is shown on Figure 1. We also plotted the histogram of an example dimension in Figure 2. The range of BLEU scores and lambdas is reasonably narrow. Even though λ seems to be bimodal, we see that this does not seriously affect the BLEU score. This is not definitive evidence but we provisionally pretend that the cost surface is almost convex for practical purposes.

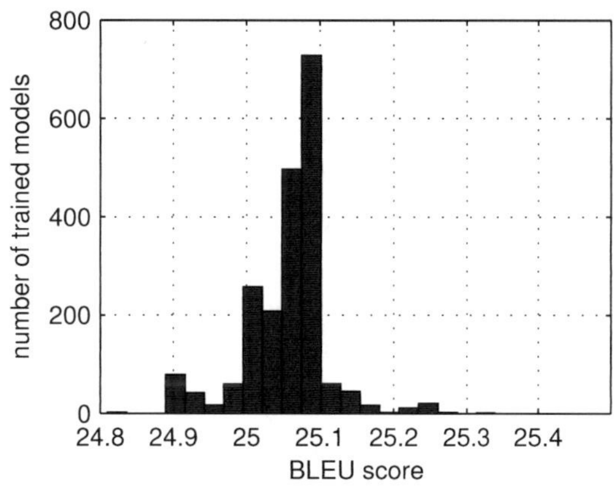

Figure 1: Histogram of BLEU scores after training from 2^{11} initializations.

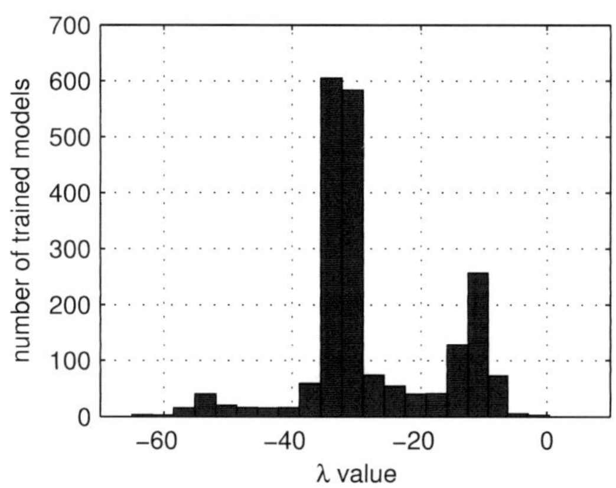

Figure 2: Histogram of one λ parameter after training from 2^{11} initializations.

4.3.2 Bin Features

A log-linear model can be converted into a bin feature model nearly exactly by setting λ values in such a way that scores will be equal. Equivalent weights (marked as 'original' in Figure 3) have the shape of an error function (erf): this is because the input feature is a cummulative random variable, which quickly converges to a Gaussian (by the central limit theorem). After training the λ weights for the log-linear model, weights may be converted into bins and re-trained. On Figure 3, we show that relaxing the monotonicity constraint leads to rough values for λ. Surprisingly, the BLEU score and objective on the *training* set only increases marginally. Starting from $\lambda = 0$, we obtained nearly exactly the same training objective value. By varying the number of bins (20-50), we observed similar behavior as well.

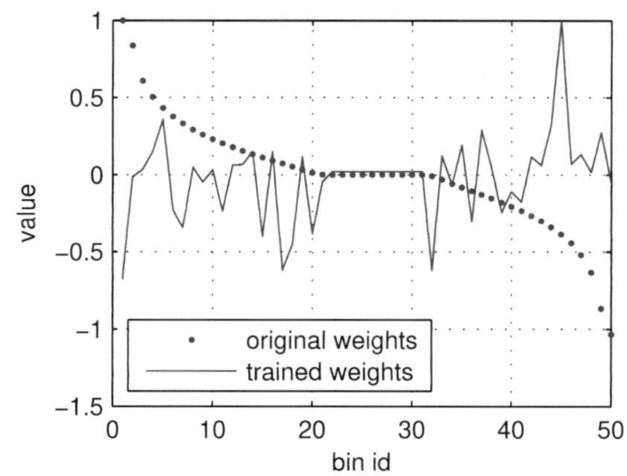

Figure 3: Values before and after training bin features. Monotonicity constraint has been relaxed. BLEU score is virtually unchanged.

4.3.3 GMM Features

Experiments were carried out with GMM features. The summary is shown on Table 1. The baseline was the log-linear model trained with the baseline features. The baseline features are included in all systems. We trained GMM models using the iterative mixture splitting interleaved with EM re-estimation, split up to 1024 and 16384 Gaussians, which we call GMM-ML-1k and GMM-ML-16k respectively. We also used the "perceptron" selection features on the training set to bootstrap quickly to 300k Gaussians (GMM-PCP-300k), and ran the same algorithm on the development set (GMM-PCP-2k). Therefore, GMM-PCP-300k had 300k features, and was trained on 175k sentences (each with about 700 hypotheses). For all experiments but "unreg" (unregularized), we chose a prior Gaussian prior with variance empirically by looking at the development set. For all but GMM-PCP-300k, regularization did not seem to have a noticeably positive effect on development BLEU scores. All systems were seeded with the baseline log-linear model, and all additional weights set to zero, and then trained with about 50 iterations, but convergence in BLEU score, empirical reward, and development BLEU score occurred after about 30 iterations. In that setting, we found that regularized empirical Bayes reward, BLEU score on training data, and BLEU score on development and evaluation to be well correlated. Cursory experiments revealed that using multiple initializations did not significantly alter the final BLEU score.

System	Train	Dev	Eval
Oracle	14.10	N/A	N/A
Baseline	10.95	35.15	25.95
GMM-ML-1k	10.95	35.15	25.95
GMM-ML-16k	11.09	35.25	25.89
GMM-PCP-2k	10.95	35.15	25.95
GMM-PCP-300k-unreg	13.00	N/A	N/A
GMM-PCP-300k	12.11	35.74	26.42

Table 1: BLEU scores for GMM features vs the linear baseline, using different selection methods and number of kernels.

Perceptron kernels based on the training set improved the baseline by 0.5 BLEU points. We measured significance with the Wilcoxon signed rank test, by batching 10 sentences at a time to produce an observation. The difference was found to be significant at a 0.9-confidence level. The improvement may be limited due to local optima or the fact that original feature are well-suited for log-linear models.

5 Conclusion

In this paper, we have introduced a non-parametric feature expansion, which guarantees invariance to the specific embodiment of the original features. Feature generation models, including feature expansion, may be trained using maximum regularized empirical Bayes reward. This may be used as an end-to-end framework to train all parameters of the machine translation system. Experimentally, we found that Gaussian mixture model (GMM) features yielded a 0.5 BLEU improvement.

Although this is an encouraging result, further study is required on hyper-parameter re-estimation, presence of local optima, use of complex original features to test the effectiveness of the parameterization invariance, and evaluation on a more competitive baseline.

References

K. Papineni, S. Roukos, T. Ward, W.-J. Zhu. 2002. *BLEU: a method for automatic evaluation of machine translation*. ACL'02.

A. Berger, S. Della Pietra, and V. Della Pietra. 1996. *A Maximum Entropy Approach to Natural Language Processing*. Computational Linguistics, vol 22:1, pp. 39–71.

S. Chen and R. Rosenfeld. 2000. *A survey of smoothing techniques for ME models*. IEEE Trans. on Speech and Audio Processing, vol 8:2, pp. 37–50.

R. O. Duda and P. E. Hart. 1973. *Pattern Classification and Scene Analysis*. Wiley & Sons, 1973.

H. J. Kushner and G. G. Yin. 1997. *Stochastic Approximation Algorithms and Applications*. Springer-Verlag, 1997.

National Institute of Standards and Technology. 2006. *The 2006 Machine Translation Evaluation Plan*.

J. Nocedal and S. J. Wright. 1999. *Numerical Optimization*. Springer-Verlag, 1999.

F. J. Och. 2003. *Minimum Error Rate Training in Statistical Machine Translation*. ACL'03.

F. J. Och, D. Gildea, S. Khudanpur, A. Sarkar, K. Yamada, A. Fraser, S. Kumar, L. Shen, D. Smith, K. Eng, V. Jain, Z. Jin, and D. Radev. 2004. *A Smorgasbord of Features for Statistical Machine Translation*. HLT/NAACL'04.

F. J. Och and H. Ney. 2002. *Discriminative Training and Maximum Entropy Models for Statistical Machine Translation*. ACL'02.

D. Povey, B. Kingsbury, L. Mangu, G. Saon, H. Soltau and G. Zweig. 2004. *fMPE: Discriminatively trained features for speech recognition*. RT'04 Meeting.

C. Quirk, A. Menezes and C. Cherry. 2005. *Dependency Tree Translation: Syntactically Informed Phrasal SMT*. ACL'05.

L. R. Rabiner and B.-H. Huang. 1993. *Fundamentals of Speech Recognition*. Prentice Hall.

M. Riedmiller and H. Braun. 1992. *RPROP: A Fast Adaptive Learning Algorithm*. Proc. of ISCIS VII.

D. A. Smith and J. Eisner. 2006. *Minimum-Risk Annealing for Training Log-Linear Models*. ACL-COLING'06.

Using Word Dependent Transition Models in HMM based Word Alignment for Statistical Machine Translation

Xiaodong He

Microsoft Research
One Microsoft Way
Redmond, WA 98052 USA
xiaohe@microsoft.com

Abstract

In this paper, we present a Bayesian Learning based method to train word dependent transition models for HMM based word alignment. We present word alignment results on the Canadian Hansards corpus as compared to the conventional HMM and IBM model 4. We show that this method gives consistent and significant alignment error rate (AER) reduction. We also conducted machine translation (MT) experiments on the Europarl corpus. MT results show that word alignment based on this method can be used in a phrase-based machine translation system to yield up to 1% absolute improvement in BLEU score, compared to a conventional HMM, and 0.8% compared to a IBM model 4 based word alignment.

1 Introduction

Word alignment is an important step of most modern approaches to statistical machine translation (Koehn et al., 2003). The classical approaches to word alignment are based on IBM models 1-5 (Brown et al., 1994) and the HMM based alignment model (Vogel et al., 1996) (Och and Ney, 2000a, 2000b), while recently discriminative approaches (Moore, 2006) and syntax based approaches (Zhang and Gildea, 2005) for word alignment are also studied. In this paper, we present improvements to the HMM based alignment model originally proposed by (Vogel et al., 1996, Och and Ney, 2000a).

Although HMM based word alignment approaches give good performance, one weakness of it is the coarse transition models. In the HMM based alignment model (Vogel et al., 1996), it is assumed that the HMM transition probabilities depend only on the jump width from the last state to the next state. Therefore, the knowledge of transition probabilities given a particular source word e is not sufficiently modeled.

In order to improve transition models in the HMM based alignment, Och and Ney (2000a) extended the transition models to be word-class dependent. In that approach, words of the source language are first clustered into a number of word classes, and then a set of transition parameters is estimated for each word class. In (2002), Toutanova et al. modeled self-transition (i.e., jump width is zero) probability separately from other transition probabilities. A word dependent self-transition model $\mathbf{P}(\mathbf{stay}|e)$ is introduced to decide whether to stay at the current source word e at the next step, or jump to a different word. It was also shown that with the assumption that a source word with fertility greater than one generates consecutive words in the target language, this probability approximates fertility modeling. Deng and Byrne in (2005) improved this idea. They proposed a word-to-phrase HMM in which a source word dependent phrase length model is used to model the approximate fertility, i.e., the length of consecutive target words generated by the source word. It provides more powerful modeling of approximate fertility than the single $\mathbf{P}(\mathbf{stay}|e)$ parameter.

However, these methods only model the probability of state occupancy rather than a full set of transition probabilities. Important knowledge of jumping from e to another position, e.g., jumping

Proceedings of the Second Workshop on Statistical Machine Translation, pages 80–87,
Prague, June 2007.

forward (monotonic alignment) or jumping backward (non-monotonic alignment), is not modeled.

In this paper, we present a method to further improve the transition models for HMM alignment model. For each source word *e*, we not only model its self-transition probability, but also the probability of jumping from word *e* to a different word. For this purpose, we estimate a full transition model for each source word.

A key problem for detailed word-dependent transition modeling is data sparsity. In (Toutanova et al., 2002), the word dependent self-transition probability **P(stay**|*e*) is interpolated with the global HMM self-transition probability to alleviate the data sparsity problem, where an interpolation weight is used for all words and that weight is tuned on a hold-out set. In the proposed word dependent transition model, because there are a large number of parameters to estimate, the data sparsity problem is even more severe. Moreover, since the sparsity of different words are very different, it is difficult to find a one-size-fits-all interpolation weight, and therefore simple linear interpolation is not optimal. In order to address this problem, we use Bayesian learning so that the transition model parameters are estimated by maximum *a posteriori* (MAP) training. With the help of the prior distribution of the model, the training is regularized and results in robust models.

In the next section we briefly review modeling of transition probabilities in a conventional HMM alignment model (Vogel et al., 1996, Och and Ney, 2000a). Then we describe the equations of MAP training for word dependent transition models. In section 5, we present word alignment results that show significant alignment error rate reductions compared to the baseline HMM and IBM model 4. We also conducted phrase-based machine translation experiments on the Europarl corpus, English – French track, and shown that the proposed method can lead to significant BLEU score improvement compared to the HMM and IBM model 4.

2 Baseline HMM alignment model

We briefly review the HMM based word alignment models (Vogel, 1996, Och and Ney, 2000a). Let's denote by $f_1^J = (f_1, ..., f_J)$ as the French sentence, $e_1^I = (e_1, ..., e_I)$ as the English sentence, and $a_1^J = (a_1, ..., a_J)$ as the alignment that specifies the position of the English word aligned to each French word. In the HMM based word alignment, a HMM is built at English side, i.e., each (*position*, *word*) pair, (a_j, e_{a_j}), is a HMM state, which emits the French word f_j. In order to mitigate the sparse data problem, it is assumed that the emission probability only depends on the English word, i.e., $p(f_j | a_j, e_{a_j}) = p(f_j | e_{a_j})$, and the transition probability only depends on the position of the last state and the length of the English sentence, i.e., $p(a_j | a_{j-1}, e_{a_{j-1}}, I) = p(a_j | a_{j-1}, I)$. Then, Vogel et al. (1996) give

$$p(f_1^J | e_1^I) = \sum_{a_1^J} \prod_{j=1}^{J} \left[p(a_j | a_{j-1}, I) p(f_j | e_{a_j}) \right] \quad (1)$$

In the HMM of (Vogel et al., 1996), it is further assumed these transition probabilities $p(a_j = i | a_{j-1} = i', I)$ depend only on the jump width $(i - i')$, i.e.,

$$p(i | i', I) = \frac{c(i - i')}{\sum_{l=1}^{I} c(l - i')} \quad (2)$$

Therefore, the transition probability $p(a_j | a_{j-1}, I)$ depends on a_{j-1} but only through the distortion set $\{c(i - i')\}$.

In (Och and Ney, 2000a), the word *null* is introduced to generate the French words that don't align to any English words. If we denote by *j_* the position of the last French word before *j* that aligns to a non-null English word, the transition probabilities $p(a_j = i | a_{j-1} = i', I)$ in (1) is computed as $p(a_j = i | a_{j\_} = i', I) = \tilde{p}(i | i', I)$, where

$$\tilde{p}(i | i', I) = \begin{cases} p_0 & \text{if } i = 0 \\ (1 - p_0) \cdot p(i | i', I) & \text{otherwise} \end{cases}$$

state i=0 denotes the state of a null word at the English side, and p_0 is the probability of jumping to state 0, which is estimated from hold-out data.

For convenience, we denote by $\Lambda = \{p(i | i', I), p(f_j | e_i)\}$ the HMM parameter set.

In the training stage, Λ are usually estimated through maximum likelihood (ML) training, i.e.,

$$\Lambda_{ML} = \arg\max_{\Lambda} p(f_1^J \mid e_1^I, \Lambda) \quad (3)$$

and the efficient Expectation-Maximization algorithm can be used to optimize Λ iteratively until convergence (Rabiner 1989).

For the interest of this paper, we elaborate transition parameter estimation with more details. These transition probabilities $\{p(i \mid i', I)\}$ is a multinomial distribution estimated according to (2), where at each iteration the distortion set $\{c(i - i')\}$ is the fractional count of transitions with jump width $d = i - i'$, i.e.,

$$c(d) = \sum_{j=1}^{J-1} \sum_{i=1}^{I} \Pr(a_j = i, a_{j+1} = i + d \mid f_1^J, e_1^I, \Lambda') \quad (4)$$

where Λ' is the model obtained from the immediate previous iteration and these terms in (4) can be efficiently computed by using the Forward-Backward algorithm (Rabiner 1989). In practice, we can bucket the distortion parameters $\{c(d)\}$ into a few buckets as implemented in (Liang et al., 2006). In our implementation, 15 buckets are used for $c(\leq -7)$, $c(-6)$, ... $c(0)$, ..., $c(\geq 7)$. The probability mass for transitions with jump width larger than 6 is uniformly divided. As suggested in (Liang et al., 2006), we also use two separate sets of distortion parameters for transitioning into the first state, and for transitioning out of the last state, respectively. Finally, we further smooth transition probabilities with a uniform distribution as described in (Och and Ney, 2000a),

$$p'(a_j \mid a_{j\_}, I) = \alpha \cdot \frac{1}{I} + (1 - \alpha) \cdot p(a_j \mid a_{j\_}, I).$$

After training, Viterbi decoding is used to find the best alignment sequence $\hat{a}_1^J$. i.e.,

$$\hat{a}_1^J = \arg\max_{a_1^J} \prod_{j=1}^{J} \left[p(a_j \mid a_{j\_}, I) p(f_j \mid e_{a_j}) \right].$$

3 Word-dependent transition models in HMM based alignment model

As discussed in the previous sections, conventional transition models that only depend on source word positions are not accurate enough. There are only limited distortion parameters to model the transition between HMM states for all English words, and the knowledge of transition probabilities given a particular source word is not represented. In order to improve the transition model in HMM, we extend the transition probabilities to be word dependent so that the probability of jumping from state $a_{j\_}$ to a_j not only depends on $a_{j\_}$, but also depends on the English word at position $a_{j\_}$. This gives

$$p(f_1^J \mid e_1^I) = \sum_{a_1^J} \prod_{j=1}^{J} \left[p(a_j \mid a_{j\_}, e_{a_{j\_}}, I) p(f_j \mid e_{a_j}) \right].$$

Compared to (1), we need to estimate the transition parameter $p(a_j \mid a_{j\_}, e_{a_{j\_}}, I)$ which is $e_{a_{j\_}}$ dependent. Correspondingly, the HMM parameters we need to estimate are $\Lambda = \{p(i \mid i', e_{i'}, I), p(f_j \mid e_i)\}$, which provides a much richer set of free parameters to model transition probabilities.

4 Bayesian Learning for word-dependent transition models

4.1 Maximum *a posteriori* training

Using ML training, we can obtain the estimation formula for word dependent transition probabilities $\{p(i \mid i', e, I)\}$ similar as (2), i.e.,

$$p_{ML}(i \mid i', e, I) = \frac{c(i - i'; e)}{\sum_{l=1}^{I} c(l - i'; e)} \quad (5)$$

where at each training iteration the word dependent distortion set $\{c(i - i'; e)\}$ is computed by

$$c(d; e) = \sum_{j=1}^{J-1} \sum_{i=1}^{I} \delta(e_{a_j} = e) \Pr(a_j = i, a_{j+1} = i + d \mid f_1^J, e_1^I, \Lambda') \quad (6)$$

where $d = i - i'$ is the jump width, and $\delta(e_{a_j} = e)$ is the Kronecker delta function that equals one if $e_{a_j} = e$, and zero otherwise.

However, for many non-frequent words, the data samples for $c(d;e)$ is very limited and therefore may lead to a biased model that severely overfits to the sparse data. In order to address this issue, maximum *a posteriori* (MAP) framework is applied (Gauvain and Lee, 1994). In MAP training, an appropriate prior distribution is used to incorporate prior knowledge into the model parameter estimation,

$$\Lambda_{MAP} = \arg\max_{\Lambda} p(f_1^J \mid e_1^I, \Lambda) g(\Lambda \mid e_1^I) \quad (7)$$

where the prior distribution $g(\Lambda \mid e_1^I)$ characterizes the distribution of the model parameter set Λ given the English sentence. The relation between ML and MAP estimation is through the Bayes' theorem where the posterior distribution $p(\Lambda \mid f_1^J, e_1^I) \propto p(f_1^J \mid e_1^I, \Lambda) g(\Lambda \mid e_1^I)$, and $p(f_1^J \mid e_1^I, \Lambda)$ is the likelihood function.

In transition model estimation, the transition model $\{p(i \mid i', e_{i'}, I)\}$ is a multinomial distribution. Its conjugate prior distribution is a Dirichlet distribution taking the following form (Bishop 2006),

$$g\left(p(i \mid i', e_{i'}, I) \mid e_1^I\right) \propto \prod_{i=1}^{I} p(i \mid i', e_{i'}, I)^{v_{i',i}-1} \quad (8)$$

where $\{v_{i',i}\}$ is the set of hyper-parameters of the prior distribution. Note that for mathematic tractability, $v_{i',i}$ needs to be greater than 1, which is usually the case in practice.

Substitute (8) into (7) and using EM algorithm, we can obtain the iterative MAP training formula for transition models (Gauvain and Lee, 1994)

$$p_{MAP}(i \mid i', e, I) = \frac{c(i-i'; e) + v_{i',i} - 1}{\sum_{l=1}^{I} c(l-i'; e) + \sum_{l=1}^{I} v_{i',l} - I} \quad (9)$$

4.2 Setting hyper-parameters for the prior distribution

In Bayesian learning, the hyper-parameter set $\{v_{i',i}\}$ of the prior distribution is assumed known based on a subjective knowledge about the model. In our method, we set the prior with word-independent transition probabilities.

$$v_{i',i} = \tau \cdot p(i \mid i', I) + 1 \quad (10)$$

where τ is a positive parameter that needs to tune on a hold-out data set. We will investigate the effect of τ with experimental results in later sections.

Substituting (10) into (9), the MAP based transition model training formula becomes

$$p_{MAP}(i \mid i', e, I) = \frac{c(i-i'; e) + \tau \cdot p(i \mid i', I)}{\sum_{l=1}^{I} c(l-i'; e) + \tau} \quad (11)$$

Note that for frequent words that have a large amount of data samples for *c*(*d*;*e*), the sum of $\sum_{l=1,\dots,I} c(l-i'; e)$ is large, so that $p_{MAP}(i \mid i', e, I)$ is dominated by the data distribution. For rare words that have low counts of *c*(*d*;*e*), $p_{MAP}(i \mid i', e, I)$ will approach to the word independent model. On the other hand, for the same word, when a small τ is used, a weak prior is applied, and the transition probability is more dependent on the training data of that word. When τ becomes larger and larger, a stronger prior knowledge is applied, and the word dependent transition model will approach to the word-independent transition model. Therefore, we can vary the parameter τ to control the contribution of prior distribution in model training and tune the word alignment performance.

5 Experimental Results

5.1 Word alignment on the Canadian Hansards English-French corpus

We evaluated our word dependent transition models for HMM based word alignment on the English-French Hansards corpus. Only a subset of 500K sentence pairs was used in our experiments including 447 test sentence-pairs. Tests sentence-pairs were manually aligned and were marked with both *sure* and *possible* alignments (Och and Ney 2000a). Using this annotation, we report the word alignment performance in terms of alignment error rate (AER) as defined by Och and Ney (2000a):

$$AER = 1 - \frac{|A \cap S| + |A \cap P|}{|A| + |S|} \quad (12)$$

where *S* denotes the set of *sure* gold alignments, *P* denotes the set of *possible* gold alignments, *A* denotes the set of alignments generated by the word alignment method under test.

We first trained the IBM model 1 and then a baseline HMM model as described in section 2 on the Hansards corpus. As the common practice, we initialized the translation probabilities of model 1 with uniform distribution over word pairs occur together in a same sentence pair. HMM was initialized with uniform transition probabilities and model 1 translation probabilities. Both model 1 and HMM were trained with 5 iterations. For the proposed word dependent transition model based HMM (WDHMM), we used the same settings as the HMM baseline except that the transition probability is computed according to (11). We also trained IBM model 4 using GIZA++ provided by Och and Ney (2000c), where 5 iterations of model 4 training was performed after 5 iterations of model 1 plus 5 iterations of HMM.

The effect of hyper-parameters in the prior distribution for WDHMM is shown in Figure 1. The horizontal dot line represents the AER given by the baseline HMM. The dash-line curve represents the AERs of WDHMM given different τ's. We vary the value of τ in the range from 0 to 1E5 and present that range in a log-scale in the figure. Since $\tau = 0$ is not a valid value in the log domain, we actually use the left-most point in the figure to represent the case of $\tau = 0$. From Fig. 1 it is shown that when τ is zero, we actually use the ML trained word-dependent transition model. Due to the sparse data problem, the model is poorly estimated and lead to a high AER. When increase τ to a larger value, a stronger prior is applied to give a more robust model. Then in a large range of $\tau \in [100, 2000]$, WDHMM outperforms baseline HMM significantly. When τ gets even larger, MAP model training becomes being over-dominated by the prior distribution, and that eventually results in a performance approaching to that of the baseline HMM. Fig. 1 only presents AER results that are calculated after combination of word alignments of both E→F and F→E directions based on a set of heuristics proposed by Och and Ney (2000b). We have observed the similar trend of AER change for the E→F and F→E alignment directions, respectively. However, due to the limit of the space, we didn't include them in this paper.

In table 1-3, we give a detailed comparison between baseline HMM, WDHMM (with $\tau = 1000$), and IBM model 4. Compared to the baseline HMM, the proposed WDHMM can reduce AER by more than 13%. It even outperforms IBM model 4 after two direction word alignment combination. Meanwhile we noticed that although IBM model 4 gives superior performance over the baseline HMM on both of the two alignment directions, its AER after combination is almost the same as that of the baseline HMM. We hypothesize that it may due to the modeling mechanism difference between HMM and model 4.

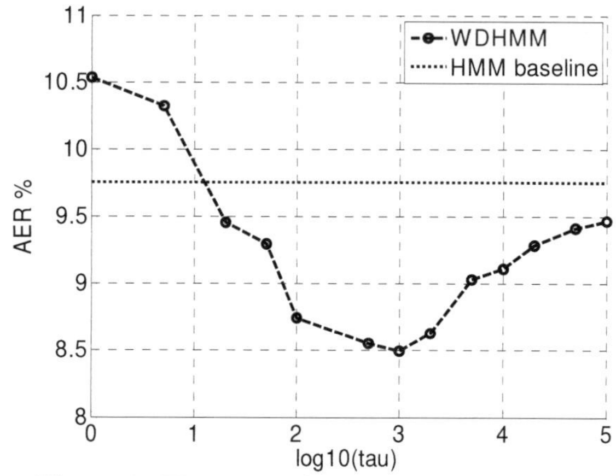

Figure 1: The AER of HMM baseline and the AER of WDHMM as the prior parameter τ is varied from 0 to 1E5. Note that the x axis is in log scale and we use the left-most point in the figure to represent the case of $\tau = 0$. These results are calculated after combination of word alignments of both E→F and F→E directions.

model	E → F	F → E	combined
baseline HMM	12.7	13.7	9.8
WDHMM ($\tau = 1000$)	11.6	12.7	8.5
IBM model 4 (GIZA++)	11.3	12.1	9.7

Table 1: Comparison of test set **AER** between various models trained on 500K sentence pairs. All numbers are in percentage.

model	E → F	F → E	combined
baseline HMM	85.2	83.1	91.7
WDHMM ($\tau = 1000$)	86.1	83.8	93.3
IBM model 4 (GIZA++)	87.2	86.2	91.6

Table 2: Comparison of test set **Precision** between various models trained on 500K sentence pairs. All numbers are in percentage.

model	E → F	F → E	combined
baseline HMM	90.6	91.4	88.3
WDHMM ($\tau = 1000$)	91.9	92.6	89.1
IBM model 4 (GIZA++)	91.1	90.8	88.4

Table 3: Comparison of test set **Recall** between various models trained on 500K sentence pairs. All numbers are in percentage.

5.2 Machine translation on Europarl corpus

We further tested our WDHMM on a phrase-based machine translation system to see whether our improvement on word alignment can also improve MT accuracy measured by BLEU score (Papineni et al., 2002). The machine translation experiment was conducted on the English-to-French track of NAACL 2006 Europarl evaluation workshop. The supplied training corpus contains 688K sentence pairs. Text data are already tokenized. In our experiment, we first lower-cased all text, then word clustering was performed to cluster words of English and French into 32 word classes respectively using the tool provided by (J. Goodman). Then word alignment was performed. Both baseline HMM and IBM model 4 use word-class based transition models, and in WDHMM the word-class based transition model was used for prior distribution. The IBM model 4 is trained by GIZA++ with a regimen of 5 iterations of Model 1, 5 iterations of HMM, and 5 iterations of Model 4. Alignments of both directions are generated and then are combined by heuristic rules described in (Och and Ney 2000b). Then phrase table was extracted from the word aligned bilingual texts. The maximum phrase length was set to 7. In the phrase-based MT system, there are four channel models. They are direct maximum likelihood estimate of the probability of target phrase given source phrase, and the same estimate of source given target; we also compute the lexicon weighting features for source given target and target given source, respectively. Other models include word count and phrase count, and a 3-gram language model provided by the workshop. These models are combined in a log-linear framework with different weights (Och and Ney, 2002). The model weight vector is trained on a dev set with 2000 English sentences, each of which has one French translation reference. In the experiment, only the first 500 sentences were used to train the log-linear model weight vector, where minimum error rate (MER) training was used (Och, 2003). After MER training, the weight vector that gives the best accuracy on the development set was selected. We then applied it to tests. There are 2000 sentences in the development-test set *devtest*, 2000 sentences in a test set *test*, and 1064 out-of-domain sentences called *nc-test*. The Pharaoh phrase-based decoder (Koehn 2004b) was used for decoding. The maximum re-ordering limit for decoding was set to 7. We used default settings for all other parameters.

We present BLEU scores of MT systems using different word alignments on all three test sets, where Fig 2 shows BLEU scores of the two in-domain tests, and Fig 3 shows MT results on the out-of-domain test set. In testing, the prior parameter τ of WDHMM was varied in the range of [20, 5000].

In Fig. 2, the horizontal dash line and the horizontal dot line represent BLEU scores of the baseline HMM on *devtest* set and *test* set, respectively. The dash-line curve and dot-line curve represent the BLEU scores of WDHMM on these two tests. It is shown in the figure that WDHMM can achieve the best BLEU scores on both *devtest* and *test* when the prior parameter τ is set to 100. Furthermore, WDHMM also gives considerable improvement on BLEU score over the baseline HMM in a broad range of τ from 50 to 1000, which indicates that WDHMM works pretty stable within a reasonable range of prior distributions.

In Fig. 3, the horizontal dash line represents the BLEU score of baseline HMM on *nc-test* set and the dash-line curve represents BLEU scores of WDHMM on the out-of-domain test. The best BLEU is obtained at $\tau = 500$. It is interesting to see that the best τ for the out-of-domain test is larger than that of an in-domain test. One possible explanation is that for out-of-domain data, we need more robust modeling for outliers other than more accurate (in-domain) modeling. However, since the difference between $\tau = 500$ and $\tau = 100$ are very small, further experiments are needed before we can draw a conclusion.

We gives a detailed BLEU-wise comparison between baseline HMM and WDHMM in Table 4, where for WDHMM, $\tau = 100$ is used since it gives the best performance on the development-test set *devtest*. In the same table, we also provide BLEU results of using IBM model 4. Compared to baseline HMM alignment model, WDHMM can improve the BLEU score nearly 1% on in-domain test sets, and the improvement reduces to about 0.5% on the out-of-domain test. When compared to IBM model 4, WDHMM still gives higher BLEU scores, and outperform model 4 by about 0.8% on the *test* set. However the gain is reduced to 0.3% on *devtest* and 0.5% on the out-of-domain *nc-test*.

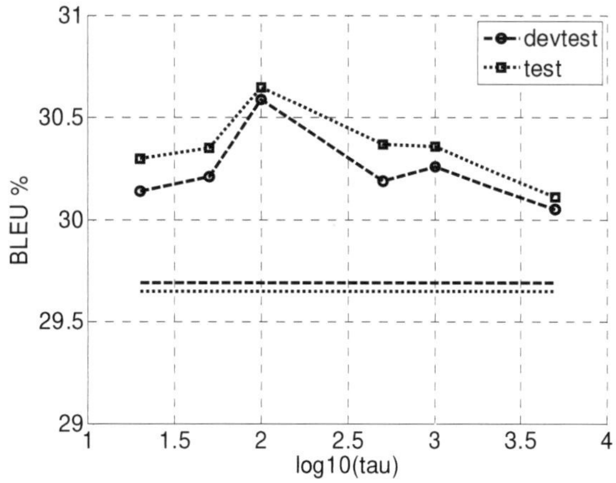

Figure 2: Machine translation results on Europarl, English to French track, devtest and test sets. The BLEU score of HMM baseline and the BLEU score of WDHMM as the prior parameter τ is varied from 20 to 5000. Note that the x axis is in log scale.

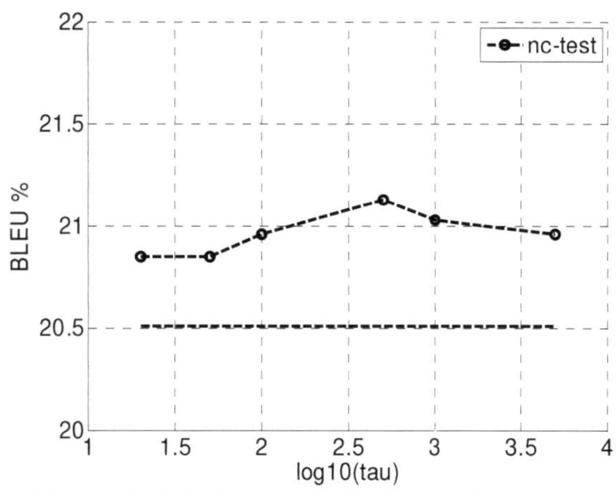

Figure 3: Machine translation results on Europarl, English to French track, out-of-domain test sets. The BLEU score of HMM baseline and the BLEU score of WDHMM as the prior parameter τ is varied from 20 to 5000. Note that the x axis is in log scale.

model	*devtest*	*test*	*nc-test*
baseline HMM	29.69	29.65	20.51
WDHMM (τ = 100)	30.59	30.65	20.96
IBM model 4	30.29	29.86	20.51

Table 4: Comparison of BLEU scores on devtest, test, and nc-test set between various word alignment models. All numbers are in percentage.

In order to verify whether these gains from WDHMM are statistically significant, we implemented paired bootstrap resampling method proposed by Koehn (2004b) to compute statistical significance of the above test results. In table 5, it is shown that BLEU gains of WDHMM over HMM and IBM-4 on different test sets, except the gain over IBM model 4 on the *devtest* set, are statistically significant with a significance level > 95%.

significance level	*devtest*	*test*	*nc-test*
WDHMM (τ=100) vs. HMM	99.9%	99.9%	99.5%
WDHMM (τ=100) vs. IBM model 4	93.7%	99.9%	99.3%

Table 5: Statistical significance test of the BLEU improvement of WDHMM (τ = 100) vs. HMM baseline, and WDHMM (τ = 100) vs. IBM model 4 on devtest, test, and nc-test sets.

5.3 Runtime performance of WDHMM

WDHMM runs as fast as a normal HMM, and the extra memory needed for the word dependent transition model is proportional to the vocabulary size of the source language given that the distortion sets of $\{c(d;e)\}$ are bucketed. Runtime speed of WDHMM and IBM-model 4 using GIZA++ is tabulated in table 6. The results are based on Europarl English to French alignment and these tests were conducted on a fast PC with 3.0GHz CPU and 16GB memory. In Table 6, WDHMM includes 5 iterations of model 1 training followed by 5 iterations of WDHMM, while "IBM model 4" includes 5 iterations for model 1, 5 iterations for HMM, and 5 iterations for model 4. It is shown in Table 6 that WDHMM is more than four times faster to produce the end-to-end word alignment.

model	runtime (min)
WDHMM	121
IBM model 4	537

Table 6: comparison of runtime performance bewteen WDHMM training and IBM model 4 training using GIZA++.

6 Discussion

Other works have been done to improve transition models in HMM based word alignment. Och and Ney (2000a) have suggested estimating word-class based transition models so as to provide more detailed transition probabilities. However, due to the sparse data problem, only a small number of word classes are usually used and the many words in the same class still have to share the same transition model. Toutanova et al. (2002) has proposed to estimate a word-dependent self-transition model **P(stay|**e**)** so that each word can have its own probability to decide whether to stay or jump to a different word. Later Deng and Byrne (2005) proposed a word dependent phrase length model to better model state occupancy. However, these model can only model the probability of self-jumping. Important knowledge of jumping from e to a different position should also be word dependent but is not modeled.

Another interesting comparison is between WDHMM and the fertility-based models, e.g., IBM model 3-5. Compared to these models, a major disadvantage of HMM is the absence of a model of source word fertility. However, as discussed in (Toutanova et al. 2002),the word dependent self-transition model can be viewed as an approximation of fertility model. i.e., it models the number of consecutive target words generated by the source word with a geometric distribution. Therefore, with a well estimated word dependent transition model, this weakness of HMM is alleviated.

In this work, we proposed estimating a full word-dependent transition models in HMM based word alignment, and with Bayesian learning we can achieve robust model estimation under the sparse data condition. We have conducted a series of experiments to evaluate this method on word alignment and machine translation tests, and show significant improvement over baseline HMM in terms of AER and BLEU. It also performs better than the much more complicated IBM model 4 based word alignment model on various word alignment and machine translation tasks.

Acknowledgments The author is grateful to Chris Quirk and Arul Menezes for assistance with the MT system and for the valuable suggestions and discussions.

References

C. M. Bishop, 2006. *Pattern Recognition and Machine Learning*. Springer.

P. Brown, S. D. Pietra, V. J. D. Pietra, and R. L. Mercer. 1994. The Mathematics of Statistical Machine Translation: Parameter Estimation. *Computational Linguistics*, 19:263–311.

Y. Deng and W. Byrne, 2005, HMM Word and Phrase Alignment For Statistical Machine Translation, in *Proceedings of HLT/EMNLP*.

J. Gauvain and C.-H. Lee, 1994, Maximum a Posteriori Estimation For Multivariate Gaussian Mixture Observations Of Markov Chains, *IEEE Trans on Speech and Audio Processing*.

J. Goodman, http://research.microsoft.com/~joshuago/

P. Koehn, F. J. Och, and D. Marcu. 2003. Statistical Phrase-Based Translation. In *Proceedings of HLT-NAACL*.

P. Koehn, 2004a, Statistical Significance Tests for Machine Translation Evaluation, in *Proceedings of EMNLP*.

P. Koehn. 2004b. Pharaoh: A Beam Search Decoder For Phrase Based Statistical Machine Translation Models. In *Proceedings of AMTA*.

P. Liang, B. Taskar, and D. Klein, 2006, Alignment by Agreement, in *Proceedings of NAACL*.

R. Moore, W. Yih and A. Bode, 2006, Improved Discriminative Bilingual Word Alignment, In *Proceedings of COLING/ACL*.

F. J. Och and H. Ney. 2000a. A comparison of Alignment Models for Statistical Machine Translation. In *Proceedings of COLING*.

F. J. Och and H. Ney. 2000b. Improved Statistical Alignment Models. In *Proceedings of ACL*.

F. J. Och and H. Ney. 2000c. Giza++: Training of statistical translation models. http://www-i6.informatik. rwthaachen.de/och/software/GIZA++.html.

F. J. Och and H. Ney. 2002. Discriminative training and Maximum Entropy Models for Statistical Machine Translation, In *Proceedings of ACL*.

F. J. Och, 2003, Minimum Error Rate Training in Statistical Machine Translation. In *Proceedings of ACL*.

K. A. Papineni, S. Roukos, T. Ward, and W.-J. Zhu. 2002. Bleu: A Method For Automatic Evaluation Of Machine Translation. in *Proceedings of ACL*.

L. R. Rabiner, 1989 A tutorial on hidden Markov models and selected applications in speech recognition. *Proceedings of the IEEE*.

K. Toutanova, H. T. Ilhan, and C. D. Manning. 2002. Extensions to HMM-based Statistical Word Alignment Models. In *Proceedings of EMNLP*.

S. Vogel, H. Ney, and C. Tillmann. 1996. HMM-based Word Alignment In Statistical Translation. In *Proceedings of COLING*.

H. Zhang and D. Gildea, 2005, Stochastic Lexicalized Inversion Transduction Grammar for Alignment, In *Proceedings of ACL*.

Efficient Handling of N-gram Language Models for Statistical Machine Translation

Marcello Federico
Fondazione Bruno Kessler - IRST
I-38050 Trento, Italy
federico@itc.it

Mauro Cettolo
Fondazione Bruno Kessler - IRST
I-38050 Trento, Italy
cettolo@itc.it

Abstract

Statistical machine translation, as well as other areas of human language processing, have recently pushed toward the use of large scale n-gram language models. This paper presents efficient algorithmic and architectural solutions which have been tested within the Moses decoder, an open source toolkit for statistical machine translation. Experiments are reported with a high performing baseline, trained on the Chinese-English NIST 2006 Evaluation task and running on a standard Linux 64-bit PC architecture. Comparative tests show that our representation halves the memory required by SRI LM Toolkit, at the cost of 44% slower translation speed. However, as it can take advantage of memory mapping on disk, the proposed implementation seems to scale-up much better to very large language models: decoding with a 289-million 5-gram language model runs in 2.1Gb of RAM.

1 Introduction

In recent years, we have seen an increasing interest toward the application of n-gram Language Models (LMs) in several areas of computational linguistics (Lapata and Keller, 2006), such as machine translation, word sense disambiguation, text tagging, named entity recognition, etc. The original framework of n-gram LMs was principally automatic speech recognition, under which most of the standard LM estimation techniques (Chen and Goodman, 1999) were developed. Nowadays, the availability of larger and larger text corpora is stressing the need for efficient data structures and algorithms to estimate, store and access LMs. Unfortunately, the rate of progress in computer technology seems for the moment below the space requirements of such huge LMs, at least by considering standard lab equipment.

Statistical machine translation (SMT) is today one of the research areas that, together with speech recognition, is pushing mostly toward the use of huge n-gram LMs. In the 2006 NIST Machine Translation Workshop (NIST, 2006), best performing systems employed 5-grams LMs estimated on at least 1.3 billion-word texts. In particular, Google Inc. presented SMT results with LMs trained on 8 trillion-word texts, and announced the availability of n-gram statistics extracted from one trillion of words. The n-gram Google collection is now publicly available through LDC, but their effective use requires either to significantly expand computer memory, in order to use existing tools (Stolcke, 2002), or to develop new ones.

This work presents novel algorithms and data structures suitable to estimate, store, and access very large LMs. The software has been integrated into a popular open source SMT decoder called Moses.[1] Experimental results are reported on the Chinese-English NIST task, starting from a quite well-performing baseline, that exploits a large 5-gram LM.

This paper is organized as follows. Section 2 presents techniques for the estimation and represen-

[1] http://www.statmt.org/moses/

Proceedings of the Second Workshop on Statistical Machine Translation, pages 88–95,
Prague, June 2007.

tation in memory of n-gram LMs that try to optimize space requirements. Section 3 describes methods implemented in order to efficiently access the LM at run time, namely by the `Moses` SMT decoder. Section 4 presents a list of experiments addressing specific questions on the presented implementation.

2 Language Model Estimation

LM estimation starts with the collection of n-grams and their frequency counters. Then, smoothing parameters are estimated (Chen and Goodman, 1999) for each n-gram level; infrequent n-grams are possibly pruned and, finally, a LM file is created containing n-grams with probabilities and back-off weights.

2.1 N-gram Collection

Clearly, a first bottleneck of the process might occur if all n-grams have to be loaded in memory. This problem is overcome by splitting the collection of n-grams statistics into independent steps and by making use of an efficient data-structure to collect and store n-grams. Hence, first the dictionary of the corpus is extracted and split into K word lists, balanced with respect to the frequency of the words. Then, for each list, only n-grams whose first word belongs to the list are extracted from the corpus. The value of K is determined empirically and should be sufficiently large to permit to fit the partial n-grams into memory. The collection of each subset of n-grams exploits a dynamic prefix-tree data structure shown in Figure 1. It features a table with all collected 1-grams, each of which points to its 2-gram successors, namely the 2-grams sharing the same 1-gram prefix. All 2-gram entries point to all their 3-gram successors, and so on. Successor lists are stored in memory blocks allocated on demand through a memory pool. Blocks might contain different number of entries and use 1 to 6 bytes to encode frequencies. In this way, a minimal encoding is used in order to represent the highest frequency entry of each block. This strategy permits to cope well with the high sparseness of n-grams and with the presence of relatively few highly-frequent n-grams, that require counters encoded with 6 bytes.

The proposed data structure differs from other implementations mainly in the use of dynamic allocation of memory required to store frequencies of n-

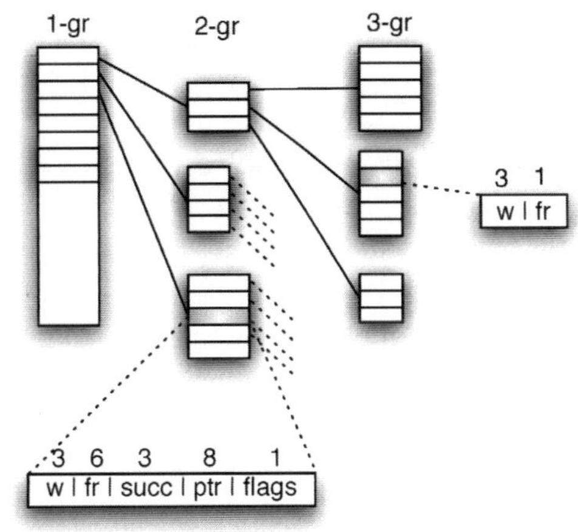

Figure 1: Dynamic data structure for storing n-grams. Blocks of successors are allocated on demand and might vary in the number of entries (depth) and bytes used to store counters (width). Size in bytes is shown to encode words (w), frequencies (fr), and number of (succ), pointer to (ptr) and table type of (flags) successors.

grams. In the structure proposed by (Wessel et al., 1997) counters of n-grams occurring more than once are stored into 4-byte integers, while singleton n-grams are stored in a special table with no counters. This solution permits to save memory at the cost of computational overhead during the collection of n-grams. Moreover, for historical reasons, this work ignores the issue with huge counts. In the SRILM toolkit (Stolcke, 2002), n-gram counts are accessed through a special class type. Counts are all represented as 4-byte integers by applying the following trick: counts below a given threshold are represented as unsigned integers, while those above the threshold, which are typically very sparse, correspond indeed to indexes of a table storing their actual value. To our opinion, this solution is ingenious but less general than ours, which does not make any assumption about the number of different high order counts.

2.2 LM Smoothing

For the estimation of the LM, a standard interpolation scheme (Chen and Goodman, 1999) is applied in combination with a well-established and simple smoothing technique, namely the Witten-Bell linear discounting method (Witten and Bell, 1991). Smoothing of probabilities up from 2-grams is performed separately on each subset of n-grams.

For example, smoothing statistics for a 5-gram (v, w, x, y, z) are computed by means of statistics that are local to the subset of n-grams starting with v. Namely, they are the counters $N(v, w, x, y, z)$, $N(v, w, x, y)$, and the number $D(v, w, x, y)$ of different words observed in context (v, w, x, y).

Finally, K LM files are created, by just reading through the n-gram files, which are indeed not loaded in memory. During this phase pruning of infrequent n-grams is also permitted. Finally, all LM files are joined, global 1-gram probabilities are computed and added, and a single large LM file, in the standard ARPA format (Stolcke, 2002), is generated.

We are well aware that the implemented smoothing method is below the state-of-the-art. However, from one side, experience tells that the gap in performance between simple and sophisticated smoothing techniques shrinks when very large corpora are used; from the other, the chosen smoothing method is very suited to the kind of decomposition we are applying to the n-gram statistics. In the future, we will nevertheless address the impact of more sophisticated LM smoothing on translation performance.

2.3 LM Compilation

The final textual LM can be compiled into a binary format to be efficiently loaded and accessed at runtime. Our implementation follows the one adopted by the CMU-Cambridge LM Toolkit (Clarkson and Rosenfeld, 1997) and well analyzed in (Whittaker and Raj, 2001). Briefly, n-grams are stored in a data structure which privileges memory saving rather than access time. In particular, single components of each n-gram are searched, via binary search, into blocks of successors stored contiguously (Figure 2). Further improvements in memory savings are obtained by quantizing both back-off weights and probabilities.

2.4 LM Quantization

Quantization provides an effective way of reducing the number of bits needed to store floating point variables. (Federico and Bertoldi, 2006) showed that best results were achieved with the so-called *binning method*. This method partitions data points into uniformly populated intervals or bins. Bins are filled in in a greedy manner, starting from the lowest value. The center of each bin corresponds to the mean value

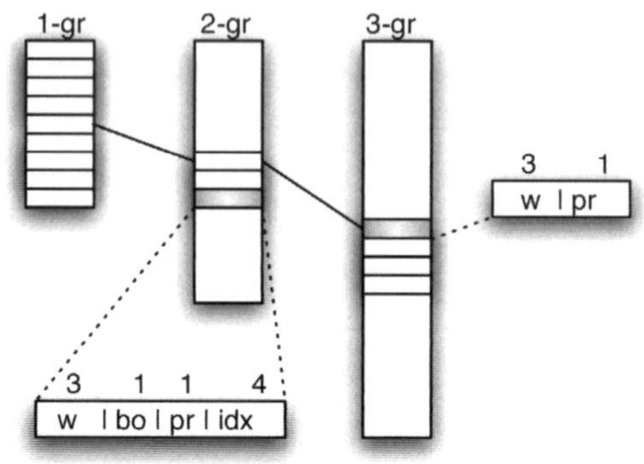

Figure 2: Static data structure for LMs. Number of bytes are shown used to encode single words (w), quantized back-off weights (bo) and probabilities (pr), and start index of successors (idx).

of all its points. Quantization is applied separately at each n-gram level and distinctly to probabilities or back-off weights. The chosen level of quantization is 8 bits (1 byte), that experimentally showed to introduce negligible loss in translation performance.

The quantization algorithm can be applied to any LM represented with the ARPA format. Quantized LMs can also be converted into a binary format that can be efficiently uploaded at decoding time.

3 Language Model Access

One motivation of this work is the assumption that efficiency, both in time and space, can be gained by exploiting peculiarities of the way the LM is used by the hosting program, i.e. the SMT decoder. An analysis of the interaction between the decoder and the LM was carried out, that revealed some important properties. The main result is shown in Figure 3, which plots all calls to a 3-gram LM by `Moses` during the translation from German to English of the following text, taken from the Europarl task:

```
ich bin kein christdemokrat und
glaube daher nicht an wunder .
doch ich möchte dem europäischen
parlament , so wie es gegenwürtig
beschaffen ist , für seinen
grossen beitrag zu diesen arbeiten
danken.
```

Translation of the above text requires about 1.7 million calls of LM probabilities, that however involve only 120,000 different 3-grams. The plot shows typical locality phenomena, that is the decoder tends to

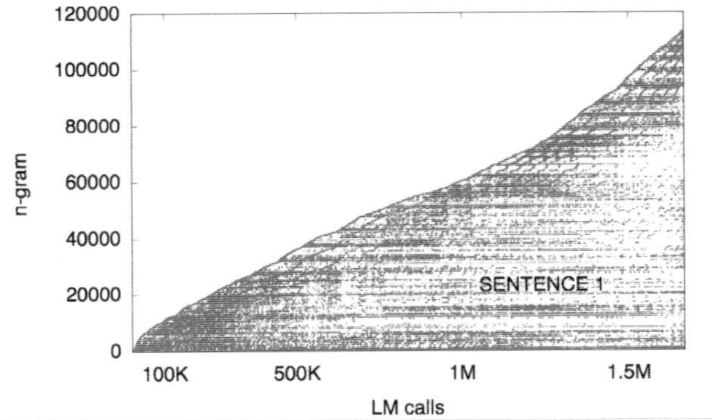

Figure 3: LM calls during translation of a German text: each point corresponds to a specific 3-gram.

access the LM n-grams in nonuniform, highly localized patterns. Locality is mainly temporal, namely the first call of an n-gram is easily followed by other calls of the same n-gram. This property suggests that gains in access speed can be achieved by exploiting a cache memory in which to store already called n-grams. Moreover, the relatively small amount of involved n-grams makes viable the access of the LM from disk on demand. Both techniques are briefly described.

3.1 Caching of probabilities

In order to speed-up access time of LM probabilities different cache memories have been implemented through the use of hash tables. Cache memories are used to store all final n-gram probabilities requested by the decoder, LM states used to recombine theories, as well as all partial n-gram statistics computed by accessing the LM structure. In this way, the need of performing binary searches, at every level of the LM tables, is reduced at a minimum.

All cache memories are reset before decoding each single input set.

3.2 Memory Mapping

Since a limited collection of all n-grams is needed to decode an input sentence, the LM is loaded on demand from disk. The data structure shown in Figure 2 permits indeed to efficiently exploit the so-called *memory mapped* file access.[2] Memory mapping basically permits to include a file in the address space of a process, whose access is managed as virtual memory (see Figure 4).

[2]POSIX-compliant operating systems and Windows support some form of memory-mapped file access.

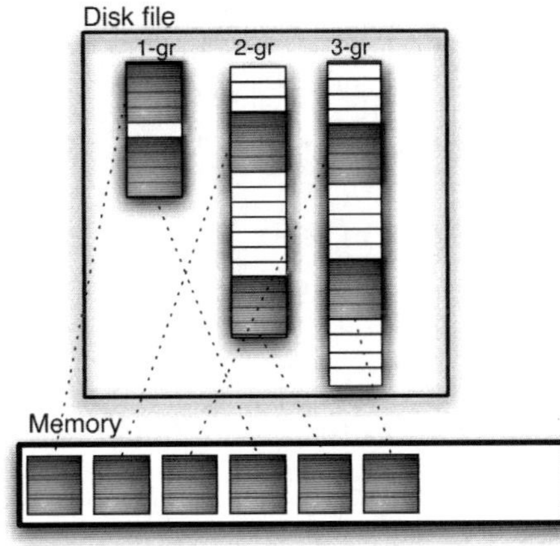

Figure 4: Memory mapping of the LM on disk. Only the memory pages (grey blocks) of the LM that are accessed while decoding the input sentence are loaded in memory.

During decoding of a sentence, only those n-grams, or better memory pages, of the LM that are actually accessed are loaded into memory, which results in a significant reduction of the resident memory space required by the process. Once the decoding of the input sentence is completed, all loaded pages are released, so that resident memory is available for the n-gram probabilities of the following sentence. A remarkable feature is that memory-mapping also permits to share the same address space among multiple processes, so that the same LM can be accessed by several decoding processes (running on the same machine).

4 Experiments

In order to assess the quality of our implementation, henceforth named IRSTLM, we have designed a suite of experiments with a twofold goal: from one side the comparison of IRSTLM against a popular LM library, namely the SRILM toolkit (Stolcke, 2002); from the other, to measure the actual impact of the implementation solution discussed in previous sections. Experiments were performed on a common statistical MT platform, namely `Moses`, in which both the IRSTLM and SRILM toolkits have been integrated.

The following subsection lists the questions

set	type	|W|	
		source	target
large	parallel	83.1M	87.6M
giga	monolingual	-	1.76G
NIST 02	dev	23.7K	26.4K
NIST 03	test	25.6K	28.5K
NIST 04	test	51.0K	58.9K
NIST 05	test	31.2K	34.6K
NIST 06 nw	test	18.5K	22.8K
NIST 06 ng	test	9.4K	11.1K
NIST 06 bn	test	12.0K	13.3K

Table 1: Statistics of training, dev. and test sets. Evaluation sets of NIST campaigns include 4 references: in table, average lenghts are provided.

which our experiments aim to answer.

Assessing Questions

1. Is LM estimation feasible for large amounts of data?
2. How does IRSTLM compare with SRILM w.r.t.:
   (a) decoding speed?
   (b) memory requirements?
   (c) translation performance?
3. How does LM quantization impact in terms of
   (a) memory consumption?
   (b) decoding speed?
   (c) translation performance?
   (d) tuning of decoding parameters?
4. What is the impact of caching on decoding speed?
5. What are the advantages of memory mapping?

Task and Experimental Setup

The task chosen for our experiments is the translation of news from Chinese to English, as proposed by the NIST MT Evaluation Workshop of 2006.[3] A translation system was trained according to the *large-data* condition. In particular, all the allowed bilingual corpora have been used for estimating the phrase-table. The target side of these texts was also employed for the estimation of three 5-gram LMs, henceforth named *large*. In particular, two LMs were estimated with the SRILM toolkit by pruning singletons events and by employing the Witten-Bell and the absolute discounting (Kneser and Ney, 1995) smoothing methods; the shorthand for these two LMs will be "lrg-sri-wb" and "lrg-sri-kn", respectively. Another large LM was estimated with the IRSTLM toolkit, by employing the only smoothing method available in the package (Witten-Bell) and by pruning singletons n-grams; its shorthand will be "lrg". An additional, much larger, 5-gram LM was instead trained with the IRSTLM toolkit on the so-called English Gigaword corpus, one of the allowed monolingual resources for this task.

Automatic translation was performed by means of `Moses` which, among other things, permits the contemporary use of more LMs, feature we exploited in our experiments as specified later.

Optimal interpolation weights for the log-linear model were estimated by running a minimum error training algorithm, available in the `Moses` toolkit, on the evaluation set of the NIST 2002 campaign. Tests were performed on the evaluation sets of the successive campaigns (2003 to 2006). Concerning the NIST 2006 evaluation set, results are given separately for three different types of texts, namely newswire (nw) and newsgroup (ng) texts, and broadcast news transcripts (bn).

Table 1 gives figures about training, development and test corpora, while Table 2 provides main statistics of the estimated LMs.

LM	millions of				
	1-gr	2-gr	3-gr	4-gr	5-gr
lrg-sri-kn	0.3	5.2	5.9	7.1	6.8
lrg-sri-wb	0.3	5.2	6.4	7.8	6.8
lrg	0.3	5.3	6.6	8.4	8.0
giga	4.5	64.4	127.5	228.8	288.6

Table 2: Statistics of LMs.

MT performance are provided in terms of case-insensitive BLEU and NIST scores, as computed with the NIST scoring tool. For time reasons, the decoder run with monotone search; preliminary experiments showed that this choice does not affect comparison of LMs. Reported decoding speed is the elapsed real time measured with the Linux/UNIX `time` command divided by the number of source words to be translated. dual Intel/Xeon

[3] `www.nist.gov/speech/tests/mt/`

CPU 3.20GHz with 8Gb RAM. Experiments run on dual Intel/Xeon CPUs 3.20GHz/8Gb RAM.

4.1 LM estimation

First of all, let us answer the question (number 1) on the feasibility of the procedure for the estimation of huge LMs. Given the amount of training data employed, it is worth to provide some details about the estimation process of the "giga" LM. According to the steps listed in Section 2.1, the whole dictionary was split into $K = 14$ frequency balanced lists. Then, 5-grams beginning with words from each list were extracted and stored. Table 3 shows some figures about these dictionaries and 5-gram collections. Note that the dictionary size increases with the list index: this means only that more frequent words were used first. This stage run in few hours with 1-2Gb parallel processes.

list index	dictionary size	number of 5-grams: observed	distinct	non-singletons
0	4	217M	44.9M	16.2M
1	11	164M	65.4M	20.7M
2	8	208M	85.1M	27.0M
3	44	191M	83.0M	26.0M
4	64	143M	56.6M	17.8M
5	137	142M	62.3M	19.1M
6	190	142M	64.0M	19.5M
7	548	142M	66.0M	20.1M
8	783	142M	63.3M	19.2M
9	1.3K	141M	67.4M	20.2M
10	2.5K	141M	69.7M	20.5M
11	6.1K	141M	71.8M	20.8M
12	25.4K	141M	74.5M	20.9M
13	4.51M	141M	77.4M	20.6M
total	4.55M	2.2G	951M	289M

Table 3: Estimation of the "giga" LM: dictionary and 5-gram statistics ($K = 14$).

The actual estimation of the LM was performed with the scheme presented in Section 2.2. For each collection of non-singletons 5-grams, a sub-LM was built by computing smoothed n-gram ($n = 1 \cdots 5$) probabilities and interpolation parameters. Again, by exploiting parallel processing, this phase took only few hours on standard HW resources. Finally, sub-LMs were joined in a single LM, which can be stored in two formats: (i) the standard textual ARPA format, and (ii) the binary format of Section 2.3. In addition, LM probabilities can be quantized according to the procedure of Section 2.4.

LM	format	quantization	file size
lrg-sri-kn	textual	n	893Mb
lrg-sri-wb	textual	n	952Mb
lrg	textual	n	1088Mb
		y	789Mb
	binary	n	368Mb
		y	220Mb
giga	textual	n	28.0Gb
		y	21.0Gb
	binary	n	8.5Gb
		y	5.1Gb

Table 4: Figures of LM files.

The estimation of the "lrg-sri" LMs, performed by means of the SRILM toolkit, took about 15 minutes requiring 5Gb of memory. The "lrg" LM was estimated as the "giga" LM in about half an hour demanding only few hundreds of Mb of memory.

Table 4 lists the size of files storing various versions of the "large" and "giga" LMs which differ in format and/or type.

4.2 LM run-time usage

Tables 5 and 6 shows BLEU and NIST scores, respectively, measured on test sets for each specific LM configuration. The first two rows of the two tables regards runs of `Moses` with the SRILM, that uses "lrg-sri" LMs. The other rows refer to runs of `Moses` with IRSTLM, either using LM "lrg" only, or both LMs, "lrg" and "giga". LM quantization is marked by a "q".

Finally, in Table 7 figures about the decoding processes are recorded. For each LM configuration, the process size, both virtual and resident, is provided together with the average time required for translating a source word with/without the activation of the caching mechanism described in Section 3.1. It is to worth noticing that the "giga" LM (both original and quantized) is loaded through the memory mapping service presented in Section 3.2.

Table 7 includes most of the answers to question number 2:

2.a Under the same conditions, `Moses` running with SRILM permits almost double faster

LM	NIST test set					
	03	04	05	06 nw	06 ng	06 bn
lrg-sri-kn	28.74	30.52	26.99	29.28	23.47	27.27
lrg-sri-wb	28.05	29.86	26.52	28.37	23.13	26.37
lrg	28.49	29.84	26.97	28.69	23.28	26.70
q-lrg	28.05	29.66	26.48	28.58	22.64	26.05
lrg+giga	30.77	31.93	29.09	29.74	24.39	28.50
q-lrg+q-giga	30.42	31.47	28.62	29.76	24.28	28.23

Table 5: BLEU scores on NIST evaluation sets for different LM configurations.

LM	NIST test set					
	03	04	05	06 nw	06 ng	06 bn
lrg-sri-kn	8.73	9.29	8.47	8.98	7.81	8.52
lrg-sri-wb	8.52	9.14	8.27	8.96	7.90	8.34
lrg	8.73	9.21	8.45	8.95	7.82	8.47
q-lrg	8.60	9.11	8.32	8.88	7.73	8.31
lrg+giga	9.08	9.49	8.80	8.92	7.86	8.66
q-lrg+q-giga	8.93	9.38	8.65	9.05	7.99	8.60

Table 6: NIST scores on NIST evaluation sets for different LM configurations.

translation than IRSTLM (13.33 vs. 6.80 words/s). Anyway, IRSTLM can be sped-up to 7.52 words/s by applying caching.

2.b IRSTLM requires about half memory than SRILM for storing an equivalent LM during decoding. If the LM is quantized, the gain is even larger. Concerning file sizes (Table 4), the size of IRSTLM binary files is about 30% of the corresponding textual versions. Quantization further reduces the size to 20% of the original textual format.

2.c Performance of IRSTLM and SRILM on the large LMs smoothed with the same method are comparable, as expected (see entries "lrg-sri-wb" and "lrg" of Tables 5 and 6). The small differences are due to different probability values assigned by the two libraries to out-of-vocabulary words.

Concerning quantization, gains in terms of memory space (question 3.a) have already been highlighted (see answer 2.b). For the remaining points:

3.b comparing "lrg" vs. "q-lrg" rows and "lrg+giga" vs. "q-lrg+q-giga" rows of Table 7, it results that quantization allows only a marginal decoding time reduction (1-3%)

3.c comparing the same rows of Tables 5 and 6, it can be claimed that quantization doesn't affect translation performance in a significant way

3.d no specific training of decoder weights is required since the original LM and its quantized version are equivalent. For example, by translating the NIST 05 test set with the weights estimated on the "lrg+giga" configuration, the following BLEU/NIST scores are got: 28.99/8.79 with the "q-lrg+q-giga" LMs, 29.09/8.80 with the "lrg+giga" LMs (the latter scores are also given in Tables 5 and 6). Employing weights estimated on "q-lrg+q-giga" scores are: 28.58/8.66 with "lrg+giga" LMs, 28.62/8.65 with "q-lrg+q-giga" LMs (again also in Tables 5 and 6). Also on other test sets differences are negligible.

LM	process size virtual	process size resident	caching	dec. speed (src w/s)
lrg-sri-kn/wb	1.2Gb	1.2Gb	-	13.33
lrg	750Mb	690Mb	n	6.80
			y	7.42
q-lrg	600Mb	540Mb	n	6.99
			y	7.52
lrg+giga	9.9Gb	2.1Gb	n	3.52
			y	4.28
q-lrg+q-giga	6.8Gb	2.1Gb	n	3.64
			y	4.35

Table 7: Process size and decoding speed with/wo caching for different LM configurations.

Table 7 answers the question number 4 on caching, by reporting the decoding speed-up due to this mechanism: a gain of 8-9% is observed on "lrg" and "q-lrg" configurations, of 20-21% in case also "giga/q-giga" LMs are employed.

The answer to the last question is that thanks to the memory mapping mechanism it is possible run `Moses` with huge LMs, which is expected to improve performance. Tables 5 and 6 provide quantitative support to the statement. In fact, a gain of 1-2 absolute BLEU was measured on different test sets when "giga" LM was employed in addition to

	NIST test set					
	03	04	05	06 nw	06 ng	06 bn
BLEU						
ci	33.62	35.04	31.92	32.74	26.18	32.43
cs	31.44	32.99	29.95	30.49	24.35	31.10
NIST						
ci	9.27	9.75	9.00	9.24	8.00	8.97
cs	8.88	9.40	8.64	8.82	7.69	8.77

Table 8: Case insensitive (ci) and sensitive (cs) scores of the best performing system.

"lrg" LM. The SRILM-based decoder would require a process of about 30Gb to load the "giga" LM; on the contrary, the virtual size of the IRSTLM-based decoder is 6.8Gb, while the actual resident memory is only 2.1Gb.

4.3 Best Performing System

Experimental results discussed so far are not the best we are able to get. In fact, the adopted setup fixed the monotone search and the use of no reordering model. Then, in order to allow a fair comparison of the IRSTLM-based `Moses` system with the ones participating to the NIST MT evaluation campaigns, we have (i) set the maximum reordering distance to 6 and (ii) estimated a lexicalized reordering model on the large parallel data by means of the training option "orientation-bidirectional-fe".

Table 8 shows BLEU/NIST scores measured on test sets by employing the IRSTLM-based `Moses` with this setting and employing "q-lrg+q-giga" LMs. It ranks at the top 5 systems (out of 24) with respect to the results of the NIST 06 evaluation campaign.

5 Conclusions

We have presented a method for efficiently estimating and handling large scale n-gram LMs for the sake of statistical machine translation. LM estimation is performed by splitting the task with respect to the initial word of the n-grams, and by merging the resulting sub-LMs. Estimated LMs can be quantized and compiled in a compact data structure. During the search, LM probabilities are cached and only the portion of effectively used LM n-grams is loaded in memory from disk. This method permits indeed to exploit locality phenomena shown by the search algorithm when accessing LM probabilities. Results show an halving of memory requirements, at the cost of 44% slower decoding speed. In addition, loading the LM on demand permits to keep the size of memory allocated to the decoder nicely under control.

Future work will investigate the way for including more sophisticated LM smoothing methods in our scheme and will compare IRSTLM and SRILM toolkits on increasing size training corpora.

6 Acknowledgments

This work has been funded by the European Union under the integrated project TC-STAR - Technology and Corpora for Speech-to-Speech Translation - (IST-2002-FP6-506738, http://www.tc-star.org).

References

S.F. Chen and J. Goodman. 1999. An empirical study of smoothing techniques for language modeling. *Computer Speech and Language*, 4(13):359–393.

P. Clarkson and R. Rosenfeld. 1997. Statistical language modeling using the CMU–cambridge toolkit. In *Proc. of Eurospeech*, pages 2707–2710, Rhodes, Greece.

M. Federico and N. Bertoldi. 2006. How many bits are needed to store probabilities for phrase-based translation? In *Proc. of the Workshop on Statistical Machine Translation*, pages 94–101, New York City, June. Association for Computational Linguistics.

R. Kneser and H. Ney. 1995. Improved backing-off for m-gram language modeling. In *Proc. of ICASSP*, volume 1, pages 181–184, Detroit, MI.

M. Lapata and F. Keller. 2006. Web-based models for natural language processing. *ACM Transactions on Speech and Language Processing*, 1(2):1–31.

NIST. 2006. Proc. of the NIST MT Workshop. Washington, DC. NIST.

A. Stolcke. 2002. SRILM - an extensible language modeling toolkit. In *Proc. of ICSLP*, Denver, Colorado.

F. Wessel, S. Ortmanns, and H. Ney. 1997. Implementation of word based statistical language models. In *Proc. SQEL Workshop on Multi-Lingual Information Retrieval Dialogs*, pages 55–59, Pilsen, Czech Republic.

E. W. D. Whittaker and B. Raj. 2001. Quantization-based Language Model Compression. In *Proc. of Eurospeech*, pages 33–36, Aalborg.

I. H. Witten and T. C. Bell. 1991. The zero-frequency problem: Estimating the probabilities of novel events in adaptive text compression. *IEEE Trans. Inform. Theory*, IT-37(4):1085–1094.

Human Evaluation of Machine Translation Through Binary System Comparisons

David Vilar, Gregor Leusch and Hermann Ney
Lehrstuhl für Informatik 6
RWTH Aachen University
D-52056 Aachen, Germany
{vilar,leusch,ney}@cs.rwth-aachen.de

Rafael E. Banchs
D. of Signal Theory and Communications
Universitat Politècnica de Catalunya
08034 Barcelona, Spain
rbanchs@gps.tsc.upc.edu

Abstract

We introduce a novel evaluation scheme for the human evaluation of different machine translation systems. Our method is based on direct comparison of two sentences at a time by human judges. These binary judgments are then used to decide between all possible rankings of the systems. The advantages of this new method are the lower dependency on extensive evaluation guidelines, and a tighter focus on a typical evaluation task, namely the ranking of systems. Furthermore we argue that machine translation evaluations should be regarded as statistical processes, both for human and automatic evaluation. We show how confidence ranges for state-of-the-art evaluation measures such as WER and TER can be computed accurately and efficiently without having to resort to Monte Carlo estimates. We give an example of our new evaluation scheme, as well as a comparison with classical automatic and human evaluation on data from a recent international evaluation campaign.

1 Introduction

Evaluation of machine translation (MT) output is a difficult and still open problem. As in other natural language processing tasks, automatic measures which try to asses the quality of the translation can be computed. The most widely known are the Word Error Rate (WER), the Position independent word Error Rate (PER), the NIST score (Doddington, 2002) and, especially in recent years, the BLEU score (Papineni et al., 2002) and the Translation Error Rate (TER) (Snover et al., 2005). All of theses measures compare the system output with one or more gold standard references and produce a numerical value (score or error rate) which measures the similarity between the machine translation and a human produced one. Once such reference translations are available, the evaluation can be carried out in a quick, efficient and reproducible manner.

However, automatic measures also have big disadvantages; (Callison-Burch et al., 2006) describes some of them. A major problem is that a given sentence in one language can have several correct translations in another language and thus, the measure of similarity with one or even a small amount of reference translations will never be flexible enough to truly reflect the wide range of correct possibilities of a translation. [1] This holds in particular for long sentences and wide- or open-domain tasks like the ones dealt with in current MT projects and evaluations.

If the actual quality of a translation in terms of usefulness for human users is to be evaluated, human evaluation needs to be carried out. This is however a costly and very time-consuming process. In this work we present a novel approach to human evaluation that simplifies the task for human judges. Instead of having to assign numerical scores to each sentence to be evaluated, as is done in current evaluation procedures, human judges choose the best one out of two candidate translations. We show how this method can be used to rank an arbitrary number of systems and present a detailed analysis of the statistical significance of the method.

[1] Compare this with speech recognition, where apart from orthographic variance there is only one correct reference.

Proceedings of the Second Workshop on Statistical Machine Translation, pages 96–103,
Prague, June 2007.

2 State-of-the-art

The standard procedure for carrying out a human evaluation of machine translation output is based on the manual scoring of each sentence with two numerical values between 1 and 5. The first one measures the *fluency* of the sentence, that is its readability and understandability. This is a monolingual feature which does not take the source sentence into account. The second one reflects the *adequacy*, that is whether the translated sentence is a correct translation of the original sentence in the sense that the meaning is transferred. Since humans will be the end users of the generated output,[2] it can be expected that these human-produced measures will reflect the usability and appropriateness of MT output better than any automatic measure.

This kind of human evaluation has however additional problems. It is much more time consuming than the automatic evaluation, and because it is subjective, results are not reproducible, even from the same group of evaluators. Furthermore, there can be biases among the human judges. Large amounts of sentences must therefore be evaluated and procedures like evaluation normalization must be carried out before significant conclusions from the evaluation can be drawn. Another important drawback, which is also one of the causes of the aforementioned problems, is that it is very difficult to define the meaning of the numerical scores precisely. Even if human judges have explicit evaluation guidelines at hand, they still find it difficult to assign a numerical value which represents the quality of the translation for many sentences (Koehn and Monz, 2006).

In this paper we present an alternative to this evaluation scheme. Our method starts from the observation that normally the final objective of a human evaluation is to find a "ranking" of different systems, and the absolute score for each system is not relevant (and it can even not be comparable between different evaluations). We focus on a method that aims to simplify the task of the judges and allows to rank the systems according to their translation quality.

3 Binary System Comparisons

The main idea of our method relies in the fact that a human evaluator, when presented two different translations of the same sentence, can normally choose the best one out of them in a more or less definite way. In social sciences, a similar method has been proposed by (Thurstone, 1927).

3.1 Comparison of Two Systems

For the comparison of two MT systems, a set of translated sentence pairs is selected. Each of these pairs consists of the translations of a particular source sentence from the two systems. The human judge is then asked to select the "best" translation of these two, or to mark the translations to be equally good. We are aware that the definition of "best" here is fuzzy. In our experiments, we made a point of not giving the evaluators explicit guidelines on how to decide between both translations. As a consequence, the judges were not to make a distinction between fluency and adequacy of the translation. This has a two-fold purpose: on the one hand it simplifies the decision procedure for the judges, as in most of the cases the decision is quite natural and they do not need to think explicitly in terms of fluency and adequacy. On the other hand, one should keep in mind that the final goal of an MT system is its usefulness for a human user, which is why we do not want to impose artificial constraints on the evaluation procedure. If only certain quality aspects of the systems are relevant for the ranking, for example if we want to focus on the fluency of the translations, explicit guidelines can be given to the judges. If the evaluators are bilingual they can use the original sentences to judge whether the information was preserved in the translation.

After our experiment, the human judges provided feedback on the evaluation process. We learned that the evaluators normally selected the translation which preserved most of the information from the original sentence. Thus, we expect to have a slight preference for adequacy over fluency in this evaluation process. Note however that adequacy and fluency have shown a high correlation[3] in previous experiments. This can be explained by noting that a low fluency renders the text incomprehensible and thus the adequacy score will also be low.

The difference in the amount of selected sentences of each system is an indicator of the difference in quality between the systems. Statistics can be carried out in order to decide whether this difference is statistically significant; we will describe this in more detail in Section 3.4.

[2]With the exception of cross-language information retrieval and similar tasks.

[3]At least for "sensible" translation systems. Academic counter-examples could easily be constructed.

3.2 Evaluation of Multiple Systems

We can generalize our method to find a ranking of several systems as follows: In this setting, we have a set of n systems. Furthermore, we have defined an order relationship "is better than" between pairs of these systems. Our goal now is to find an ordering of the systems, such that each system is better than its predecessor. In other words, this is just a sorting problem – as widely known in computer science.

Several efficient sorting algorithms can be found in the literature. Generally, the efficiency of sorting algorithms is measured in terms of the number of comparisons carried out. State-of-the-art sorting algorithms have a worst-case running time of $\mathcal{O}(n \log n)$, where n is the number of elements to sort. In our case, because such binary comparisons are very time consuming, we want to minimize the absolute number of comparisons needed. This minimization should be carried out in the strict sense, not just in an asymptotic manner.

(Knuth, 1973) discusses this issue in detail. It is relatively straightforward to show that, in the worst case, the minimum number of comparisons to be carried out to sort n elements is at least $\lceil \log n! \rceil$ (for which $n \log n$ is an approximation). It is not always possible to reach this minimum, however, as was proven e.g. for the case $n = 12$ in (Wells, 1971) and for $n = 13$ in (Peczarski, 2002). (Ford Jr and Johnson, 1959) propose an algorithm called *merge insertion* which comes very close to the theoretical limit. This algorithm is sketched in Figure 1. There are also algorithms with a better asymptotic runtime (Bui and Thanh, 1985), but they only take effect for values of n too large for our purposes (e.g., more than 100). Thus, using the algorithm from Figure 1 we can obtain the ordering of the systems with a (nearly) optimal number of comparisons.

3.3 Further Considerations

In Section 3.1 we described how to carry out the comparison between two systems when there is only one human judge carrying out this comparison. The comparison of systems is a very time consuming task. Therefore it is hardly possible for one judge to carry out the evaluation on a whole test corpus. Usually, subsets of these test corpora are selected for human evaluations instead. In order to obtain a better coverage of the test corpus, but also to try to alleviate the possible bias of a single evaluator, it is advantageous to have several evaluators carrying out the comparison between two systems. However, there are two points that must be considered.

The first one is the selection of sentences each human judge should evaluate. Assume that we have already decided the amount of sentences m each evaluator has to work with (in our case $m = 100$). One possibility is that all human judges evaluate the same set of sentences, which presumably will cancel possible biases of the evaluators. A second possibility is to give each judge a disjunct set of sentences. In this way we benefit from a higher coverage of the corpus, but do not have an explicit bias compensation.

In our experiments, we decided for a middle course: Each evaluator receives a randomly selected set of sentences. There are no restrictions on the selection process. This implicitly produces some overlap while at the same time allowing for a larger set of sentences to be evaluated. To maintain the same conditions for each comparison, we also decided that each human judge should evaluate the same set of sentences for each system pair.

The other point to consider is how the evaluation results of each of the human judges should be combined into a decision for the whole system. One possibility would be to take only a "majority vote" among the evaluators to decide which system is the best. By doing this, however, possible quantitative information on the quality difference of the systems is not taken into account. Consequently, the output is strongly influenced by statistical fluctuations of the data and/or of the selected set of sentences to evaluate. Thus, in order to combine the evaluations we just summed over all decisions to get a total count of sentences for each system.

3.4 Statistical Significance

The evaluation of MT systems by evaluating translations of test sentences – be it automatic evaluation or human evaluation – must always be regarded as a statistical process: Whereas the outcome, or score R, of an evaluation is considered to hold for "all" possible sentences from a given domain, a test corpus naturally consists of only a sample from all these sentences. Consequently, R depends on that sample of test sentences. Furthermore, both a human evaluation score and an automatic evaluation score for a hypothesis sentence are by itself noisy: Human evaluation is subjective, and as such is subject to "human noise", as described in Section 2. Each automatic score, on the other hand, depends heavily on the ambiguous selection of reference translations. Accordingly, evaluation scores underly a probability

1. Make pairwise comparisons of $\lfloor n/2 \rfloor$ disjoint pairs of elements. (If n is odd, leave one element out).
2. Sort the $\lfloor n/2 \rfloor$ larger elements found in step 1, recursively by merge insertion.
3. Name the $\lfloor n/2 \rfloor$ elements found in step 2 $a_1, a_2, \ldots, a_{\lfloor n/2 \rfloor}$ and the rest $b_1, b_2, \ldots, b_{\lceil n/2 \rceil}$, such that $a_1 \leq a_2 \leq \cdots \leq a_{\lfloor n/2 \rfloor}$ and $b_i \leq a_i$ for $1 \leq i \leq \lfloor n/2 \rfloor$. Call b_1 and the a's the "main chain".
4. Insert the remaining b's into the main chain, using binary insertion, in the following order (ignore the b_j such that $j > \lceil n/2 \rceil$): $b_3, b_2; b_5, b_4; b_{11}, \ldots, b_6; \ldots; b_{t_k}, \ldots, b_{t_{k-1}+1}; \ldots$ with $t_k = \frac{2^{k+1}+(-1)^k}{3}$.

Figure 1: The merge insertion algorithm as presented in (Knuth, 1973).

distribution, and each evaluation result we achieve must be considered as a sample from that distribution. Consequently, both human and automatic evaluation results must undergo statistical analysis before conclusions can be drawn from them.

A typical application of MT evaluation – for example in the method described in this paper – is to decide whether a given MT system X, represented by a set of translated sentences, is *significantly better* than another system Y with respect to a given evaluation measure. This outcome is traditionally called the *alternative hypothesis*. The opposite outcome, namely that the two systems are equal, is known as the *null hypothesis*. We say that certain values of R_X, R_Y confirm the *alternative hypothesis* if the *null hypothesis* can be rejected with a given level of certainty, e.g. 95%. In the case of comparing two MT systems, the null hypothesis would be "both systems are equal with regard to the evaluation measure; that is, both evaluation scores R, R' come from the same distribution R_0".

As R is randomly distributed, it has an expectation $E[R]$ and a standard error $se[R]$. Assuming a normal distribution for R, we can reject the null hypothesis with a confidence of 95% if the sampled score R is more than 1.96 times the standard error away from the null hypothesis expectation:

$$R \text{ significant} \Leftrightarrow |E[R_0] - R| > 1.96\, se[R_0] \quad (1)$$

The question we have to solve is: How can we estimate $E[R_0]$ and $se[R_0]$? The first step is that we consider R and R_0 to share the same standard error $se[R_0] = se[R]$. This value can then be estimated from the test data. In a second step, we give an estimate for $E[R_0]$, either inherent in the evaluation measure (see below), or from the estimate for the comparison system R'.

A universal estimation method is the *bootstrap estimate*: The core idea is to create replications of R by random sampling from the data set (Bisani and Ney, 2004). Bootstrapping is generally possible for all evaluation measures. With a high number of replicates, $se[R]$ and $E[R_0]$ can be estimated with satisfactory precision.

For a certain class of evaluation measures, these parameters can be estimated more accurately and efficiently from the evaluation data without resorting to Monte Carlo estimates. This is the class of errors based on the arithmetic mean over a sentence-wise score: In our binary comparison experiments, each judge was given hypothesis translations $e_{i,X}$, $e_{i,Y}$. She could then judge $e_{i,X}$ to be better than, equal to, or worse than $e_{i,Y}$. All these judgments were counted over the systems. We define a sentence score $r_{i,X,Y}$ for this evaluation method as follows:

$$r_{i,X,Y} := \begin{cases} +1 & e_{i,X} \text{ is better than } e_{i,Y} \\ 0 & e_{i,X} \text{ is equal to } e_{i,Y} \\ -1 & e_{i,X} \text{ is worse than } e_{i,Y} \end{cases} . \quad (2)$$

Then, the total evaluation score for a binary comparison of systems X and Y is

$$R_{X,Y} := \frac{1}{m} \sum_{i=1}^{m} r_{i,X,Y} , \quad (3)$$

with m the number of evaluated sentences.

For this case, namely R being an arithmetic mean, (Efron and Tibshirani, 1993) gives an explicit formula for the estimated standard error of the score $R_{X,Y}$. To simplify the notation, we will use R instead of $R_{X,Y}$ from now on, and r_i instead of $r_{i,X,Y}$.

$$se[R] = \frac{1}{m-1} \sqrt{\sum_{i=1}^{m} (r_i - R)^2} . \quad (4)$$

With x denoting the number of sentences where $r_i = 1$, and y denoting the number of sentences where $r_i = -1$,

$$R = \frac{x - y}{m} \tag{5}$$

and with basic algebra

$$se[R] = \frac{1}{m-1}\sqrt{x + y - \frac{(x-y)^2}{m}}. \tag{6}$$

Moreover, we can explicitly give an estimate for $E[R_0]$: The null hypothesis is that both systems are "equally good". Then, we should expect as many sentences where X is better than Y as vice versa, i.e. $x = y$. Thus, $E[R_0] = 0$.

Using Equation 4, we calculate $se[R]$ and thus a significance range for adequacy and fluency judgments. When comparing two systems X and Y, we assume for the null hypothesis that $se[R_0] = se[R_X]$ and $E[R_0] = E[R_Y]$ (or vice versa).

A very useful (and to our knowledge new) result for MT evaluation is that $se[R]$ can also be explicitly estimated for weighted means – such as WER, PER, and TER. These measures are defined as follows: Let $d_i, i = 1, \ldots, m$ denote the number of "errors" (edit operations) of the translation candidate e_i with regard to a reference translation with length l_i. Then, the total error rate will be computed as

$$R := \frac{1}{L}\sum_{i=1}^{m} d_i \tag{7}$$

where

$$L := \sum_{i=1}^{m} l_i \tag{8}$$

As a result, each sentence e_i affects the overall score with weight l_i – the effect of leaving out a sentence with length 40 is four times higher than that of leaving out one with length 10. Consequently, these weights must be considered when estimating the standard error of R:

$$se[R] = \sqrt{\frac{1}{(m-1)(L-1)}\sum_{i=1}^{m}\left(\frac{d_i}{l_i} - R\right)^2 \cdot l_i} \tag{9}$$

With this Equation, Monte-Carlo-estimates are no longer necessary for examining the significance of WER, PER, TER, etc. Unfortunately, we do not expect such a short explicit formula to exist for the standard BLEU score. Still, a confidence range for BLEU can be estimated by bootstrapping (Och, 2003; Zhang and Vogel, 2004).

		Spanish	English
Train	Sentences	1.2M	
	Words	32M	31M
	Vocabulary	159K	111K
	Singletons	63K	46K
Test	Sentences	1 117	
	Words	26K	
	OOV Words	72	

Table 1: Statistics of the EPPS Corpus.

4 Evaluation Setup

The evaluation procedure was carried out on the data generated in the second evaluation campaign of the TC-STAR project[4]. The goal of this project is to build a speech-to-speech translation system that can deal with real life data. Three translation directions are dealt with in the project: Spanish to English, English to Spanish and Chinese to English. For the system comparison we concentrated only in the English to Spanish direction.

The corpus for the Spanish–English language pair consists of the official version of the speeches held in the European Parliament Plenary Sessions (EPPS), as available on the web page of the European Parliament. A more detailed description of the EPPS data can be found in (Vilar et al., 2005). Table 1 shows the statistics of the corpus.

A total of 9 different MT systems participated in this condition in the evaluation campaign that took place in February 2006. We selected five representative systems for our study. Henceforth we shall refer to these systems as System A through System E. We restricted the number of systems in order to keep the evaluation effort manageable for a first experimental setup to test the feasibility of our method. The ranking of 5 systems can be carried out with as few as 7 comparisons, but the ranking of 9 systems requires 19 comparisons.

5 Evaluation Results

Seven human bilingual evaluators (6 native speakers and one near-native speaker of Spanish) carried out the evaluation. 100 sentences were randomly chosen and assigned to each of the evaluators for every system comparison, as discussed in Section 3.3. The results can be seen in Table 2 and Figure 2. Counts

[4] `http://www.tc-star.org/`

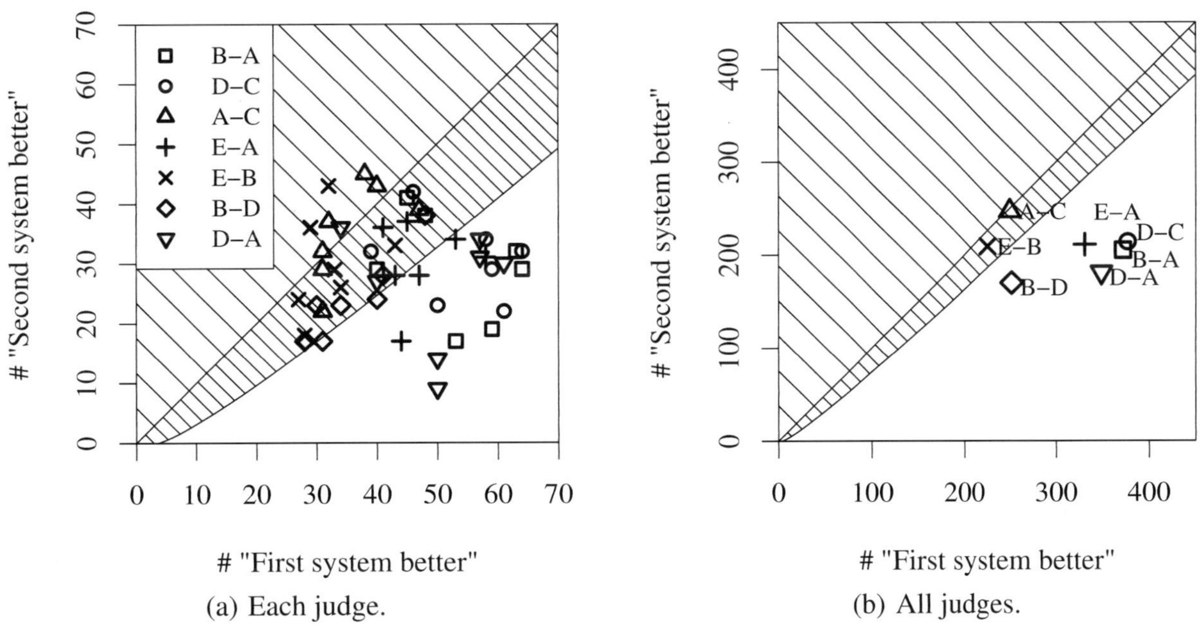

Figure 2: Results of the binary comparisons. Number of times the winning system was really judged "better" vs. number of times it was judged "worse". Results in hatched area can not reject null hypothesis, i.e. would be considered insignificant.

missing to 100 and 700 respectively denote "same quality" decisions.

As can be seen from the results, in most of the cases the judges clearly favor one of the systems. The most notable exception is found when comparing systems A and C, where a difference of only 3 sentences is clearly not enough to decide between the two. Thus, the two bottom positions in the final ranking could be swapped.

Figure 2(a) shows the outcome for the binary comparisons separately for each judge, together with an analysis of the statistical significance of the results. As can be seen, the number of samples (100) would have been too low to show significant results in many experiments (data points in the hatched area). In some cases, the evaluator even judged better the system which was scored to be worse by the majority of the other evaluators (data points above the bisector). As Figure 2(b) shows, "the only thing better than data is more data": When we summarize R over all judges, we see a significant difference (with a confidence of 95%) at all comparisons but two (A vs. C, and E vs. B). It is interesting to note that exactly these two pairs do not show a significant difference when using a majority vote strategy.

Table 3 shows also the standard evaluation metrics. Three BLEU scores are given in this table, the one computed on the whole corpus, the one computed on the set used for standard adequacy and fluency computations and the ones on the set we selected for this task[5]. It can be seen that the BLEU scores are consistent across all data subsets. In this case the ranking according to this automatic measure matches exactly the ranking found by our method. When comparing with the adequacy and fluency scores, however, the ranking of the systems changes considerably: B D E C A. However, the difference between the three top systems is quite small. This can be seen in Figure 3, which shows some automatic and human scores for the five systems in our experiments, along with the estimated 95% confidence range. The bigger difference is found when comparing the bottom systems, namely System A and System C. While our method produces nearly no difference the adequacy and fluency scores indicate System C as clearly superior to System A. It is worth noting that the both groups use quite different translation approaches (statistical vs. rule-based).

[5] Regretfully these two last sets were not the same. This is due to the fact that the "AF Test Set" was further used for evaluating Text-to-Speech systems, and thus a targeted subset of sentences was selected.

Sys	E1	E2	E3	E4	E5	E6	E7	$\sum$
A	29	19	38	17	32	29	41	205
B	**40**	**59**	**48**	**53**	**63**	**64**	**45**	**372**
C	32	22	29	23	32	34	42	214
D	**39**	**61**	**59**	**50**	**64**	**58**	**46**	**377**
A	32	**31**	31	**31**	**47**	38	40	**250**
C	**37**	29	**32**	22	39	**45**	**43**	247
A	36	28	17	28	34	37	31	211
E	**41**	**47**	**44**	**43**	**53**	**45**	**58**	**331**
B	26	29	18	24	**43**	**36**	33	209
E	**34**	**33**	**28**	**27**	32	29	**43**	**226**
B	**34**	**28**	**30**	**31**	**40**	**41**	**48**	**252**
D	23	17	23	17	24	28	38	170
A	**36**	14	27	9	31	30	34	181
D	34	**50**	**40**	**50**	**57**	**61**	**57**	**349**
Final ranking (best—worst): E B D A C								

Table 2: Result of the binary system comparison. Numbers of sentences for which each system was judged better by each evaluator (E1-E7).

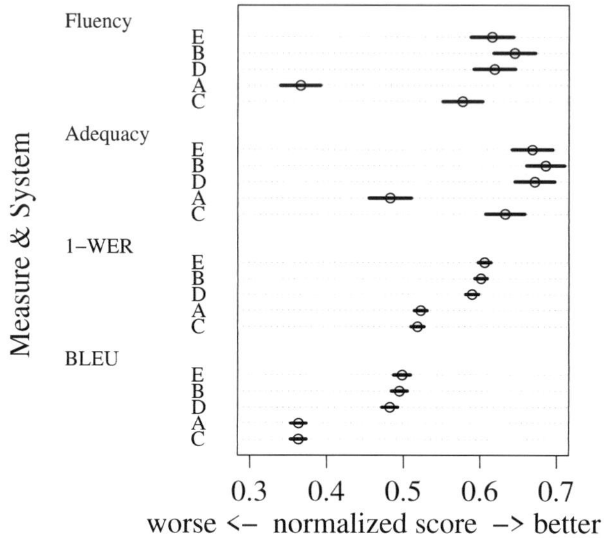

Figure 3: Normalized evaluation scores. Higher scores are better. Solid lines show the 95% confidence range. Automatic scores calculated on the whole test set, human scores on the A+F subset.

Subset:	Whole	A+F			Binary
Sys	BLEU	BLEU	A	F	BLEU
A	36.3	36.2	2.93	2.46	36.3
B	49.4	49.3	3.74	3.58	49.2
C	36.3	36.2	3.53	3.31	36.1
D	48.2	46.8	3.68	3.48	47.7
E	49.8	49.6	3.67	3.46	49.4

Table 3: BLEU scores and Adequacy and Fluency scores for the different systems and subsets of the whole test set. BLEU values in %, Adequacy (A) and Fluency (F) from 1 (worst) to 5 (best).

6 Discussion

In this section we will review the main drawbacks of the human evaluation listed in Section 2 and analyze how our approach deals with them. The first one was the use of explicit numerical scores, which are difficult to define exactly. Our system was mainly designed for the elimination of this issue.

Our evaluation continues to be time consuming. Even more, the number of individual comparisons needed is in the order of $\log(n!)$, in contrast with the standard adequacy-fluency evaluation which needs $2n$ individual evaluations (two evaluations per system, one for fluency, another one for adequacy). For n in the range of 1 up to 20 (a realistic number of systems for current evaluation campaigns) these two quantities are comparable. And actually each of our evaluations should be simpler than the standard adequacy and fluency ones. Therefore the time needed for both evaluation procedures is probably similar.

Reproducibility of the evaluation is also an important concern. We computed the number of "errors" in the evaluation process, i.e. the number of sentences evaluated by two or more evaluators where the evaluators' judgement was different. Only in 10% of the cases the evaluation was contradictory, in the sense that one evaluator chose one sentence as better than the other, while the other evaluator chose the other one. In 30% of the cases, however, one evaluator estimated both sentences to be of the same quality while the other judged one sentence as superior to the other one. As comparison, for the fluency-adequacy judgement nearly one third of the common evaluations have a difference in score greater or equal than two (where the maximum would be four), and another third a score difference of one point[6].

With respect to biases, we feel that it is almost impossible to eliminate them if humans are involved. If one of the judges prefers one kind of structure, there will a bias for a system producing such output, independently of the evaluation procedure. However, the suppression of explicit numerical scores eliminates an additional bias of evaluators. It has been observed that human judges often give scores within

[6]Note however that possible evaluator biases can have a great influence in these statistics.

a certain range (e.g. in the mid-range or only extreme values), which constitute an additional difficulty when carrying out the evaluation (Leusch et al., 2005). Our method suppresses this kind of bias.

Another advantage of our method is the possibility of assessing improvements within one system. With one evaluation we can decide if some modifications actually improve performance. This evaluation even gives us a confidence interval to weight the significance of an improvement. Carrying out a full adequacy-fluency analysis would require a lot more effort, without giving more useful results.

7 Conclusion

We presented a novel human evaluation technique that simplifies the task of the evaluators. Our method relies on two basic observations. The first one is that in most evaluations the final goal is to find a ranking of different systems, the absolute scores are usually not so relevant. Especially when considering human evaluation, the scores are not even comparable between two evaluation campaigns. The second one is the fact that a human judge can normally choose the best one out of two translations, and this is a much easier process than the assessment of numerical scores whose definition is not at all clear. Taking this into consideration we suggested a method that aims at finding a ranking of different MT systems based on the comparison of pairs of translation candidates for a set of sentences to be evaluated.

A detailed analysis of the statistical significance of the method is presented and also applied to some wide-spread automatic measures. The evaluation methodology was applied for the ranking of 5 systems that participated in the second evaluation campaign of the TC-STAR project and comparison with standard evaluation measures was performed.

8 Acknowledgements

We would like to thank the human judges who participated in the evaluation. This work has been funded by the integrated project TC-STAR– Technology and Corpora for Speech-to-Speech Translation – (IST-2002-FP6-506738).

References

M. Bisani and H. Ney. 2004. Bootstrap estimates for confidence intervals in ASR performance evaluationx. *IEEE ICASSP*, pages 409–412, Montreal, Canada, May.

T. Bui and M. Thanh. 1985. Significant improvements to the Ford-Johnson algorithm for sorting. *BIT Numerical Mathematics*, 25(1):70–75.

C. Callison-Burch, M. Osborne, and P. Koehn. 2006. Re-evaluating the role of BLEU in machine translation research. *Proceeding of the 11th Conference of the European Chapter of the ACL: EACL 2006*, pages 249–256, Trento, Italy, Apr.

G. Doddington. 2002. Automatic evaluation of machine translation quality using n-gram co-occurrence statistics. *Proc. ARPA Workshop on Human Language Technology*.

B. Efron and R. J. Tibshirani. 1993. *An Introduction to the Bootstrap*. Chapman & Hall, New York and London.

L. Ford Jr and S. Johnson. 1959. A Tournament Problem. *The American Mathematical Monthly*, 66(5):387–389.

D. E. Knuth. 1973. *The Art of Computer Programming*, volume 3. Addison-Wesley, 1st edition. Sorting and Searching.

P. Koehn and C. Monz. 2006. Manual and automatic evaluation of machine translation between european languages. *Proceedings of the Workshop on Statistical Machine Translation*, pages 102–121, New York City, Jun.

G. Leusch, N. Ueffing, D. Vilar, and H. Ney. 2005. Preprocessing and normalization for automatic evaluation of machine translation. *43rd ACL: Proc. Workshop on Intrinsic and Extrinsic Evaluation Measures for MT and/or Summarization*, pages 17–24, Ann Arbor, Michigan, Jun.

F. J. Och. 2003. Minimum error rate training in statistical machine translation. *Proc. of the 41st ACL*, pages 160–167, Sapporo, Japan, Jul.

K. Papineni, S. Roukos, T. Ward, and W.-J. Zhu. 2002. Bleu: a method for automatic evaluation of machine translation. *Proc. of the 40th ACL*, pages 311–318, Philadelphia, PA, Jul.

M. Peczarski. 2002. Sorting 13 elements requires 34 comparisons. *LNCS*, 2461/2002:785–794, Sep.

M. Snover, B. J. Dorr, R. Schwartz, J. Makhoul, L. Micciulla, and R. Weischedel. 2005. A study of translation error rate with targeted human annotation. Technical Report LAMP-TR-126, CS-TR-4755, UMIACS-TR-2005-58, University of Maryland, College Park, MD.

L. Thurstone. 1927. The method of paired comparisons for social values. *Journal of Abnormal and Social Psychology*, 21:384–400.

D. Vilar, E. Matusov, S. Hasan, R. Zens, and H. Ney. 2005. Statistical Machine Translation of European Parliamentary Speeches. *Proceedings of MT Summit X*, pages 259–266, Phuket, Thailand, Sep.

M. Wells. 1971. *Elements of combinatorial computing*. Pergamon Press.

Y. Zhang and S. Vogel. 2004. Measuring confidence intervals for the machine translation evaluation metrics. *Proceedings of the 10th International Conference on Theoretical and Methodological Issues in Machine Translation*, pages 4–6, Baltimore, MD.

Labelled Dependencies in Machine Translation Evaluation

Karolina Owczarzak **Josef van Genabith** **Andy Way**
National Centre for Language Technology
School of Computing, Dublin City University
Dublin 9, Ireland

{owczarzak,josef,away}@computing.dcu.ie

Abstract

We present a method for evaluating the quality of Machine Translation (MT) output, using labelled dependencies produced by a Lexical-Functional Grammar (LFG) parser. Our dependency-based method, in contrast to most popular string-based evaluation metrics, does not unfairly penalize perfectly valid syntactic variations in the translation, and the addition of WordNet provides a way to accommodate lexical variation. In comparison with other metrics on 16,800 sentences of Chinese-English newswire text, our method reaches high correlation with human scores.

1 Introduction

Since the creation of BLEU (Papineni et al., 2002) and NIST (Doddington, 2002), the subject of automatic evaluation metrics for MT has been given quite a lot of attention. Although widely popular thanks to their speed and efficiency, both BLEU and NIST have been criticized for inadequate accuracy of evaluation at the segment level (Callison-Burch et al., 2006). As string based-metrics, they are limited to superficial comparison of word sequences between a translated sentence and one or more reference sentences, and are unable to accommodate any legitimate grammatical variation when it comes to lexical choices or syntactic structure of the translation, beyond what can be found in the multiple references. A natural next step in the field of evaluation was to introduce metrics that would better reflect our human judgement by accepting synonyms in the translated sentence or evaluating the translation on the basis of what syntactic features it shares with the reference.

Our method follows and substantially extends the earlier work of Liu and Gildea (2005), who use syntactic features and unlabelled dependencies to evaluate MT quality, outperforming BLEU on segment-level correlation with human judgement. Dependencies abstract away from the particulars of the surface string (and syntactic tree) realization and provide a "normalized" representation of (some) syntactic variants of a given sentence.

While Liu and Gildea (2005) calculate n-gram matches on non-labelled head-modifier sequences derived by head-extraction rules from syntactic trees, we automatically evaluate the quality of translation by calculating an f-score on labelled dependency structures produced by a Lexical-Functional Grammar (LFG) parser. These dependencies differ from those used by Liu and Gildea (2005), in that they are extracted according to the rules of the LFG grammar and they are labelled with a type of grammatical relation that connects the head and the modifier, such as *subject*, *determiner*, etc. The presence of grammatical relation labels adds another layer of important linguistic information into the comparison and allows us to account for partial matches, for example when a lexical item finds itself in a correct relation but with an incorrect partner. Moreover, we use a number of best parses for the translation and the reference, which serves to decrease the amount of noise that can be introduced by the process of parsing and extracting dependency information.

The translation and reference files are analyzed by a treebank-based, probabilistic LFG parser (Cahill et al., 2004), which produces a set of dependency triples for each input. The translation set is compared to the reference set, and the number of matches is calculated, giving the

Proceedings of the Second Workshop on Statistical Machine Translation, pages 104–111,
Prague, June 2007. ©2007 Association for Computational Linguistics

precision, recall, and f-score for each particular translation.

In addition, to allow for the possibility of valid lexical differences between the translation and the references, we follow Kauchak and Barzilay (2006) in adding a number of synonyms in the process of evaluation to raise the number of matches between the translation and the reference, leading to a higher score.

In an experiment on 16,800 sentences of Chinese-English newswire text with segment-level human evaluation from the Linguistic Data Consortium's (LDC) Multiple Translation project, we compare the LFG-based evaluation method with other popular metrics like BLEU, NIST, General Text Matcher (GTM) (Turian et al., 2003), Translation Error Rate (TER) (Snover et al., 2006)[1], and METEOR (Banerjee and Lavie, 2005), and we show that combining dependency representations with synonyms leads to a more accurate evaluation that correlates better with human judgment. Although evaluated on a different test set, our method also outperforms the correlation with human scores reported in Liu and Gildea (2005).

The remainder of this paper is organized as follows: Section 2 gives a basic introduction to LFG; Section 3 describes related work; Section 4 describes our method and gives results of the experiment on the Multiple Translation data; Section 5 discusses ongoing work; Section 6 concludes.

2 Lexical-Functional Grammar

In Lexical-Functional Grammar (Kaplan and Bresnan, 1982; Bresnan, 2001) sentence structure is represented in terms of c(onstituent)-structure and f(unctional)-structure. C-structure represents the word order of the surface string and the hierarchical organisation of phrases in terms of CFG trees. F-structures are recursive feature (or attribute-value) structures, representing abstract grammatical relations, such as *subj*(ect), *obj*(ect), *obl*(ique), *adj*(unct), etc., approximating to predicate-argument structure or simple logical forms. C-structure and f-structure are related in terms of functional annotations (attribute-value structure equations) in c-structure trees, describing f-structures.

While c-structure is sensitive to surface rearrangement of constituents, f-structure abstracts away from the particulars of the surface realization. The sentences *John resigned yesterday* and *Yesterday, John resigned* will receive different tree representations, but identical f-structures, shown in (1).

(1) *C-structure:* *F-structure:*

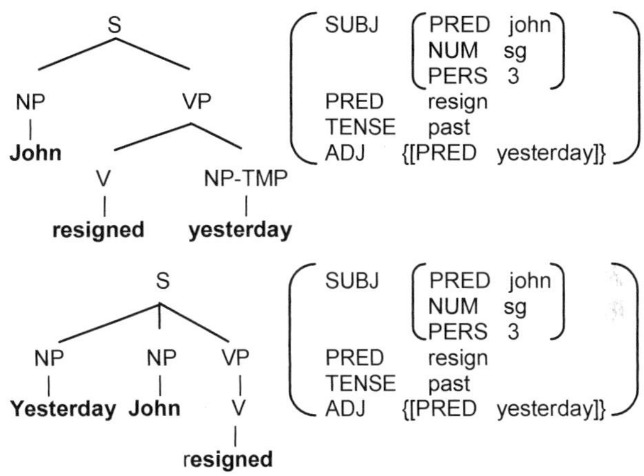

Note that if these sentences were a translation-reference pair, they would receive a less-than-perfect score from string-based metrics. For example, BLEU with add-one smoothing[2] gives this pair a score of barely 0.3781. This is because, although all three unigrams from the "translation" (*John*; *resigned*; *yesterday*) are present in the reference, which contains four items including the comma (*Yesterday*; ,; *John*; *resigned*), the "translation" contains only one bigram (*John resigned*) that matches the "reference" (*Yesterday ,*; *, John*; *John resigned*), and no matching trigrams.

The f-structure can also be described in terms of a flat set of triples. In triples format, the f-structure in (1) is represented as follows: {*subj*(resign, john), *pers*(john, 3), *num*(john, sg), *tense*(resign, past), *adj*(resign, yesterday), *pers*(yesterday, 3), *num*(yesterday, sg)}.

[1] We omit HTER (Human-Targeted Translation Error Rate), as it is not fully automatic and requires human input.

[2] We use smoothing because the original BLEU metric gives zero points to sentences with fewer than one four-gram.

Cahill et al. (2004) presents a set of Penn-II Treebank-based LFG parsing resources. Their approach distinguishes 32 types of dependencies, including grammatical functions and morphological information. This set can be divided into two major groups: a group of predicate-only dependencies and non-predicate dependencies. Predicate-only dependencies are those whose path ends in a predicate-value pair, describing grammatical relations. For example, for the f-structure in (1), predicate-only dependencies would include: {*subj*(resign, john), *adj*(resign, yesterday)}.

Other predicate-only dependencies include: *apposition*, *complement*, *open complement*, *coordination*, *determiner*, *object*, *second object*, *oblique*, *second oblique*, *oblique agent*, *possessive*, *quantifier*, *relative clause*, *topic*, and *relative clause pronoun*. The remaining non-predicate dependencies are: *adjectival degree*, *coordination surface form*, *focus*, complementizer forms: *if*, *whether*, and *that*, *modal*, *number*, *verbal particle*, *participle*, *passive*, *person*, *pronoun surface form*, *tense*, and *infinitival clause*.

In parser evaluation, the quality of the f-structures produced automatically can be checked against a set of gold standard sentences annotated with f-structures by a linguist. The evaluation is conducted by calculating the precision and recall between the set of dependencies produced by the parser, and the set of dependencies derived from the human-created f-structure. Usually, two versions of f-score are calculated: one for all the dependencies for a given input, and a separate one for the subset of predicate-only dependencies.

In this paper, we use the parser developed by Cahill et al. (2004), which automatically annotates input text with c-structure trees and f-structure dependencies, obtaining high precision and recall rates.[3]

3 Related work

3.1 String-based metrics

The insensitivity of BLEU and NIST to perfectly legitimate syntactic and lexical variation has been raised, among others, in Callison-Burch et al. (2006), but the criticism is widespread. Even the creators of BLEU point out that it may not correlate particularly well with human judgment at the sentence level (Papineni et al., 2002).

Recently a number of attempts to remedy these shortcomings have led to the development of other automatic MT evaluation metrics. Some of them concentrate mainly on word order, like General Text Matcher (Turian et al., 2003), which calculates precision and recall for translation-reference pairs, weighting contiguous matches more than non-sequential matches, or Translation Error Rate (Snover et al., 2006), which computes the number of substitutions, insertions, deletions, and shifts necessary to transform the translation text to match the reference. Others try to accommodate both syntactic and lexical differences between the candidate translation and the reference, like CDER (Leusch et al., 2006), which employs a version of edit distance for word substitution and reordering; or METEOR (Banerjee and Lavie, 2005), which uses stemming and WordNet synonymy. Kauchak and Barzilay (2006) and Owczarzak et al. (2006) use paraphrases during BLEU and NIST evaluation to increase the number of matches between the translation and the reference; the paraphrases are either taken from WordNet[4] in Kauchak and Barzilay (2006) or derived from the test set itself through automatic word and phrase alignment in Owczarzak et al. (2006). Another metric making use of synonyms is the linear regression model developed by Russo-Lassner et al. (2005), which makes use of stemming, WordNet synonymy, verb class synonymy, matching noun phrase heads, and proper name matching. Kulesza and Shieber (2004), on the other hand, train a Support Vector Machine using features such as proportion of *n*-gram matches and word error rate to judge a given translation's distance from human-level quality.

3.2 Dependency-based metric

The metrics described above use only string-based comparisons, even while taking into consideration reordering. By contrast, Liu and Gildea (2005) present three metrics that use syntactic and unlabelled dependency information. Two of these metrics are based on matching syntactic subtrees between the translation and the reference, and one

[3] A demo of the parser can be found at http://lfg-demo.computing.dcu.ie/lfgparser.html

[4] http://wordnet.princeton.edu/

is based on matching headword chains, i.e. sequences of words that correspond to a path in the unlabelled dependency tree of the sentence. Dependency trees are created by extracting a headword for each node of the syntactic tree, according to the rules used by the parser of Collins (1999), where every subtree represents the modifier information for its root headword. The dependency trees for the translation and the reference are converted into flat headword chains, and the number of overlapping *n*-grams between the translation and the reference chains is calculated. Our method, extending this line of research with the use of labelled LFG dependencies, partial matching, and *n*-best parses, allows us to considerably outperform Liu and Gildea's (2005) highest correlations with human judgement (they report 0.144 for the correlation with human fluency judgement, 0.202 for the correlation with human overall judgement), although it has to be kept in mind that such comparison is only tentative, as their correlation is calculated on a different test set.

4 LFG f-structure in MT evaluation

LFG-based automatic MT evaluation reflects the same process that underlies the evaluation of parser-produced f-structure quality against a gold standard: we parse the translation and the reference, and then, for each sentence, we check the set of labelled translation dependencies against the set of labelled reference dependencies, counting the number of matches. As a result, we obtain the precision and recall scores for the translation, and we calculate the f-score for the given pair.

4.1 Determining parser noise

Because we are comparing two outputs that were produced automatically, there is a possibility that the result will not be noise-free, even if the parser fails to provide a parse only in 0.1% of cases.

To assess the amount of noise that the parser introduces, Owczarzak et al. (2006) conducted an experiment where 100 English sentences were hand-modified so that the position of adjuncts was changed, but the sentence remained grammatical and the meaning was not influenced. This way, an ideal parser should give both the source and the modified sentence the same f-structure, similarly to the example presented in (1). The modified sentences were treated like a translation file, and the original sentences played the part of the reference. Each set was run through the parser, and the dependency triples obtained from the "translation" were compared against the dependency triples for the "reference", calculating the f-score. Additionally, the same "translation-reference" set was scored with other metrics (TER, METEOR, BLEU, NIST, and GTM). The results, including the distinction between f-scores for all dependencies and predicate-only dependencies, appear in Table 1.

	baseline	**modified**
TER	0.0	6.417
METEOR	1.0	0.9970
BLEU	1.0000	0.8725
NIST	11.5232	11.1704 (96.94%)
GTM	100	99.18
dep f-score	100	96.56
dep_preds f-score	100	94.13

Table 1. Scores for sentences with reordered adjuncts

The baseline column shows the upper bound for a given metric: the score which a perfect translation, word-for-word identical to the reference, would obtain.[5] The other column lists the scores that the metrics gave to the "translation" containing reordered adjunct. As can be seen, the dependency and predicate-only dependency scores are lower than the perfect 100, reflecting the noise introduced by the parser.

We propose that the problem of parser noise can be alleviated by introducing a number of best parses into the comparison between the translation and the reference. Table 2 shows how increasing the number of parses available for comparison brings our method closer to an ideal noise-free parser.

[5] Two things have to be noted here: (1) in the case of NIST the perfect score differs from text to text, which is why the percentage points are provided along the numerical score, and (2) in the case of TER the lower the score, the better the translation, so the perfect translation will receive 0, and there is no upper bound on the score, which makes this particular metric extremely difficult to directly compare with others.

	dependency f-score
1 best	96.56
2 best	97.31
5 best	97.90
10 best	98.31
20 best	98.59
30 best	98.74
50 best	98.79
baseline	100

Table 2. Dependency f-scores for sentences with reordered adjuncts with n-best parses available

It has to be noted, however, that increasing the number of parses beyond a certain threshold does little to further improve results, and at the same time it considerably decreases the efficiency of the method, so it is important to find the right balance between these two factors. In our opinion, the optimal value would be 10-best parses.

4.2 Correlation with human judgement – MultiTrans

4.2.1 Experimental design

To evaluate the correlation with human assessment, we used the data from the Linguistic Data Consortium Multiple Translation Chinese (MTC) Parts 2 and 4, which consists of multiple translations of Chinese newswire text, four human-produced references, and segment-level human scores for a subset of the translation-reference pairs. Although a single translated segment was always evaluated by more than one judge, the judges used a different reference every time, which is why we treated each translation-reference-human score triple as a separate segment. In effect, the test set created from this data contained 16,800 segments. As in the previous experiment, the translation was scored using BLEU, NIST, GTM, TER, METEOR, and our labelled dependency-based method.

4.2.2 Labelled dependency-based method

We examined a number of modifications of the dependency-based method in order to find out which one gives the highest correlation with human scores. The correlation differences between immediate neighbours in the ranking were often too small to be statistically significant; however, there is a clear overall trend towards improvement.

Besides the plain version of the dependency f-score, we also looked at the f-score calculated on predicate dependencies only (ignoring "atomic" features such as *person*, *number*, *tense*, etc.), which turned out not to correlate well with human judgements.

Another addition was the use of 2-, 10-, or 50-best parses of the translation and reference sentences, which partially neutralized parser noise and resulted in increased correlations.

We also created a version where predicate dependencies of the type *subj*(resign,John) are split into two parts, each time replacing one of the elements participating in the relation with a variable, giving in effect *subj*(resign,x) and *subj*(y,John). This lets us score partial matches, where one correct lexical object happens to find itself in the correct relation, but with an incorrect "partner".

Lastly, we added WordNet synonyms into the matching process to accommodate lexical variation, and to compare our WordNet-enhanced method with the WordNet-enhanced version of METEOR.

4.2.3 Results

We calculated Pearson's correlation coefficient for segment-level scores that were given by each metric and by human judges. The results of the correlation are shown in Table 3. Note that the correlation for TER is negative, because in TER zero is the perfect score, in contrast to other metrics where zero is the worst possible score; however, this time the absolute values can be easily compared to each other. Rows are ordered by the highest value of the (absolute) correlation with the human score.

First, it seems like none of the metrics is very good at reflecting human fluency judgments; the correlation values in the first column are significantly lower than the correlation with accuracy. This finding has been previously reported, among others, in Liu and Gildea (2005). However, the dependency-based method in almost all its versions has decidedly the highest correlation in this area. This can be explained by the method's sensitivity to the grammatical structure of the sentence: a more grammatical translation is also a translation that is more fluent.

As to the correlation with human evaluation of translation accuracy, our method currently falls short of METEOR. This is caused by the fact that METEOR assign relatively little importance to the position of a specific word in a sentence, therefore rewarding the translation for content rather than linguistic form. Interestingly, while METEOR, with or without WordNet, considerably outperforms all other metrics when it comes to the correlation with human judgements of translation accuracy, it falls well behind most versions of our dependency-based method in correlation with human scores of translation fluency.

Surprisingly, adding partial matching to the dependency-based method resulted in the greatest increase in correlation levels, to the extent that the partial-match versions consistently outperformed versions with a larger number of parses available but without the partial match. The most interesting effect was that the partial-match versions (even those with just a single parse) offered results comparable to or higher than the addition of WordNet to the matching process when it comes to accuracy and overall judgement.

5 Current and future work

Fluency and accuracy are two very different aspects of translation quality, each with its own set of conditions along which the input is evaluated. Therefore, it seems unfair to expect a single automatic metric to correlate highly with human judgements of both at the same time. This pattern is very noticeable in Table 3: if a metric is (relatively) good at correlating with fluency, its accuracy correlation suffers (GTM might serve as an example here), and the opposite holds as well (see METEOR's scores). It does not mean that any improvement that increases the method's correlation with one aspect will result in a decrease in the correlation with the other aspect; but it does suggest that a possible way of development would be to target these correlations separately, if we want our automated metrics to reflect human scores better. At the same time, string-based metrics might have already exhausted their potential when it comes to increasing their correlation with human evaluation; as has been pointed out before, these metrics can only tell us that two strings differ, but they cannot distinguish legitimate grammatical variance from ungrammatical variance. As the quality of MT improves, the community will need metrics that are more sensitive in this respect. After all, the true quality of MT depends on producing grammatical output which describes the same concept as the source utterance, and the string identity with a reference is only a very selective approximation of this goal.

fluency		**accuracy**		**average**	
d_50+WN	0.177	**M+WN**	0.294	**M+WN**	0.255
d+WN	0.175	**M**	0.278	**d_50_var**	0.252
d_50_var	0.174	**d_50_var**	0.273	**d_50+WN**	0.250
GTM	0.172	**NIST**	0.273	**d_10_var**	0.250
d_10_var	0.172	**d_10_var**	0.273	**d_2_var**	0.247
d_50	0.171	**d_2_var**	0.270	**d+WN**	0.244
d_2_var	0.168	**d_50+WN**	0.269	**d_50**	0.243
d_10	0.168	**d_var**	0.266	**d_var**	0.243
d_var	0.165	**d_50**	0.262	**M**	0.242
d_2	0.164	**d_10**	0.262	**d_10**	0.242
d	0.161	**d+WN**	0.260	**NIST**	0.238
BLEU	0.155	**d_2**	0.257	**d_2**	0.237
M+WN	0.153	**d**	0.256	**d**	0.235
M	0.149	**d_pr**	0.240	**d_pr**	0.216
NIST	0.146	**GTM**	0.203	**GTM**	0.208
d_pr	0.143	**BLEU**	0.199	**BLEU**	0.197
TER	-0.133	**TER**	-0.192	**TER**	-0.182

Table 3. Pearson's correlation between human scores and evaluation metrics. Legend: d = dependency f-score, _pr = predicate-only f-score, 2, 10, 50 = n-best parses; var = partial-match version; M = METEOR, WN = WordNet[6]

[6] In general terms, an increase of 0.022 or more between any two scores in the same column is significant with a 95% confidence interval. The statistical significance of correlation differences was calculated using Fisher's z' transformation and the general formula for confidence interval.

In order to maximize the correlation with human scores of fluency, we plan to look more closely at the parser output, and implement some basic transformations which would allow an even deeper logical analysis of input (e.g. passive to active voice transformation).

Additionally, we want to take advantage of the fact that the score produced by the dependency-based method is the proportional average of matches for a group of up to 32 (but usually far fewer) different dependency types. We plan to implement a set of weights, one for each dependency type, trained in such a way as to maximize the correlation of the final dependency f-score with human evaluation. In a preliminary experiment, for example, assigning a low weight to the *topic* dependency increases our correlations slightly (this particular case can also be seen as a transformation into a more basic logical form by removing non-elementary dependency types).

In a similar direction, we want to experiment more with the f-score calculations. Initial check shows that assigning a higher weight to recall than to precision improves results.

To improve the correlation with accuracy judgements, we would like to experiment using a paraphrase set derived from a large parallel corpus, as described in Owczarzak et al. (2006). While retaining the advantage of having a similar size to a corresponding set of WordNet synonyms, this set will also capture low-level syntactic variations, which can increase the number of matches.

6 Conclusions

In this paper we present a linguistically-motivated method for automatically evaluating the output of Machine Translation. Most currently used popular metrics rely on comparing translation and reference on a string level. Even given reordering, stemming, and synonyms for individual words, current methods are still far from reaching human ability to assess the quality of translation, and there exists a need in the community to develop more dependable metrics. Our method explores one such direction of development, comparing the sentences on the level of their grammatical structure, as exemplified by their f-structure labelled dependency triples produced by an LFG parser. In our experiments we showed that the dependency-based method correlates higher than any other metric with human evaluation of translation fluency, and shows high correlation with the average human score. The use of dependencies in MT evaluation has not been extensively researched before (one exception here would be Liu and Gildea (2005)), and requires more research to improve it, but the method shows potential to become an accurate evaluation metric.

Acknowledgements

This work was partly funded by Microsoft Ireland PhD studentship 2006-8 for the first author of the paper. We would also like to thank our reviewers and Dan Melamed for their insightful comments. All remaining errors are our own.

References

Satanjeev Banerjee and Alon Lavie. 2005. METEOR: An Automatic Metric for MT Evaluation with Improved Correlation with Human Judgments. *Proceedings of the Workshop on Intrinsic and Extrinsic Evaluation Measures for MT and/or Summarization at the Association for Computational Linguistics Conference 2005*: 65-73. Ann Arbor, Michigan.

Joan Bresnan. 2001. *Lexical-Functional Syntax*, Blackwell, Oxford.

Aoife Cahill, Michael Burke, Ruth O'Donovan, Josef van Genabith, and Andy Way. 2004. Long-Distance Dependency Resolution in Automatically Acquired Wide-Coverage PCFG-Based LFG Approximations, In *Proceedings of Association for Computational Linguistics 2004*: 320-327. Barcelona, Spain.

Chris Callison-Burch, Miles Osborne and Philipp Koehn. 2006. Re-evaluating the role of BLEU in Machine Translation Research. *Proceedings of the European Chapter of the Association for Computational Linguistics 2006*: 249-256. Oslo, Norway.

Michael J. Collins. 1999. Head-driven Statistical Models for Natural Language Parsing. Ph.D. thesis, University of Pennsylvania, Philadelphia.

George Doddington. 2002. Automatic Evaluation of MT Quality using N-gram Co-occurrence Statistics. *Proceedings of Human Language Technology Conference 2002*: 138-145. San Diego, California.

Kaplan, R. M., and J. Bresnan. 1982. *Lexical-functional Grammar: A Formal System for Grammatical*

Representation. In J. Bresnan (ed.), The Mental Representation of Grammatical Relations. MIT Press, Cambridge.

David Kauchak and Regina Barzilay. 2006. Paraphrasing for Automatic Evaluation. *Proceedings of Human Language Technology – North American Chapter of the Association for Computational Linguistics Conference 2006*: 45-462. New York, New York.

Philipp Koehn. 2004. Pharaoh: a beam search decoder for phrase-based statistical machine translation models. *Proceedings of the Workshop on Machine Translation: From real users to research at the Association for Machine Translation in the Americas Conference 2004*: 115-124. Washington, DC.

Philipp Koehn. 2005. Europarl: A Parallel Corpus for Statistical Machine Translation. *Proceedings of MT Summit 2005*: 79-86. Phuket, Thailand.

Alex Kulesza and Stuart M. Shieber. 2004. A learning approach to improving sentence-level MT evaluation. In *Proceedings of* the *Conference on Theoretical and Methodological Issues in Machine Translation 2004*: 75-84. Baltimore, Maryland.

Gregor Leusch, Nicola Ueffing and Hermann Ney. 2006. CDER: Efficient MT Evaluation Using Block Movements. *Proceedings of European Chapter of the Association for Computational Linguistics Conference 2006*: 241-248. Trento, Italy.

Ding Liu and Daniel Gildea. 2005. Syntactic Features for Evaluation of Machine Translation. In *Proceedings of the Workshop on Intrinsic and Extrinsic Evaluation Measures for Machine Translation and/or Summarization at the Association for Computational Linguistics Conference 2005*. Ann Arbor, Michigan.

Franz Josef Och and Hermann Ney. 2003. A Systematic Comparison of Various Statistical Alignment Modes. *Computational Linguistics*, 29:19-51.

Karolina Owczarzak, Declan Groves, Josef van Genabith, and Andy Way. 2006. Contextual Bitext-Derived Paraphrases in Automatic MT Evaluation. *Proceedings of the Workshop on Statistical Machine Translation at the Human Language Technology – North American Chapter of the Association for Computational Linguistics Conference 2006*: 86-93. New York, New York.

Kishore Papineni, Salim Roukos, Todd Ward, and WeiJing Zhu. 2002. BLEU: a method for automatic evaluation of machine translation. In *Proceedings of Association for Computational Linguistics Conference 2002*: 311-318. Philadelphia, Pennsylvania.

Grazia Russo-Lassner, Jimmy Lin, and Philip Resnik. 2005. A Paraphrase-based Approach to Machine Translation Evaluation. Technical Report LAMP-TR-125/CS-TR-4754/UMIACS-TR-2005-57, University of Maryland, College Park, Maryland.

Mathew Snover, Bonnie Dorr, Richard Schwartz, John Makhoul, Linnea Micciula. 2006. A Study of Translation Error Rate with Targeted Human Annotation. *Proceedings of the Association for Machine Translation in the Americas Conference 2006*: 223-231. Boston, Massachusetts.

Joseph P. Turian, Luke Shen, and I. Dan Melamed. 2003. Evaluation of Machine Translation and Its Evaluation. *Proceedings of MT Summit 2003*: 386-393. New Orleans, Luisiana.

Ying Zhang and Stephan Vogel. 2004. Measuring confidence intervals for the machine translation evaluation metrics. *Proceedings of Conference on Theoretical and Methodological Issues in Machine Translation 2004*: 85-94. Baltimore, Maryland.

An Iteratively-Trained Segmentation-Free Phrase Translation Model for Statistical Machine Translation

Robert C. Moore **Chris Quirk**
Microsoft Research
Redmond, WA 98052, USA
{bobmoore,chrisq}@microsoft.com

Abstract

Attempts to estimate phrase translation probablities for statistical machine translation using iteratively-trained models have repeatedly failed to produce translations as good as those obtained by estimating phrase translation probablities from surface statistics of bilingual word alignments as described by Koehn, et al. (2003). We propose a new iteratively-trained phrase translation model that produces translations of quality equal to or better than those produced by Koehn, et al.'s model. Moreover, with the new model, translation quality degrades much more slowly as pruning is tightend to reduce translation time.

1 Introduction

Estimates of conditional phrase translation probabilities provide a major source of translation knowledge in phrase-based statistical machine translation (SMT) systems. The most widely used method for estimating these probabilities is that of Koehn, et al. (2003), in which phrase pairs are extracted from word-aligned bilingual sentence pairs, and their translation probabilities estimated heuristically from surface statistics of the extracted phrase pairs. We will refer to this approach as "the standard model".

There have been several attempts to estimate phrase translation probabilities directly, using generative models trained iteratively on a parallel corpus using the Expectation Maximization (EM) algorithm. The first of these models, that of Marcu and Wong (2002), was found by Koehn, et al. (2003), to produce translations not quite as good as their method. Recently, Birch et al. (2006) tried the Marcu and Wong model constrained by a word alignment and also found that Koehn, et al.'s model worked better, with the advantage of the standard model increasing as more features were added to the overall translation model. DeNero et al. (2006) tried a different generative phrase translation model analogous to IBM word-translation Model 3 (Brown et al., 1993), and again found that the standard model outperformed their generative model.

DeNero et al. (2006) attribute the inferiority of their model and the Marcu and Wong model to a hidden segmentation variable, which enables the EM algorithm to maximize the probability of the training data without really improving the quality of the model. We propose an iteratively-trained phrase translation model that does not require different segmentations to compete against one another, and we show that this produces translations of quality equal to or better than those produced by the standard model. We find, moreover, that with the new model, translation quality degrades much more slowly as pruning is tightend to reduce translation time.

Decoding efficiency is usually considered only in the design and implementation of decoding algorithms, or the choice of model structures to support faster decoding algorithms. We are not aware of any attention previously having been paid to the effect of different methods of parameter estimation on translation efficiency for a given model structure.

The time required for decoding is of great importance in the practical application of SMT tech-

Proceedings of the Second Workshop on Statistical Machine Translation, pages 112–119,
Prague, June 2007.

nology. One of the criticisms of SMT often made by adherents of rule-based machine translation is that SMT is too slow for practical application. The rapidly falling price of computer hardware has ameliorated this problem to a great extent, but the fact remains that every factor of 2 improvement in translation efficiency means a factor of 2 decrease in hardware cost for intensive applications of SMT, such as a web-based translation service ("Translate this page"). SMT surely needs all the help in can get in this regard.

2 Previous Approaches

Koehn, et al.'s (2003) method of estimating phrase-translation probabilities is very simple. They start with an automatically word-aligned corpus of bilingual sentence pairs, in which certain words are linked, indicating that they are translations of each other, or that they are parts of phrases that are translations of each other. They extract every possible phrase pair (up to a given length limit) that (a) contains at least one pair of linked words, and (b) does not contain any words that have links to other words not included in the phrase pair.[1] In other words, word alignment links cannot cross phrase pair boundaries. Phrase translation probabilities are estimated simply by marginalizing the counts of phrase instances:

$$p(x|y) = \frac{C(x,y)}{\sum_{x'} C(x',y)}$$

This method is used to estimate the conditional probabilities of both target phrases give source phrases and source phrases given target phrases.

In contrast to the standard model, DeNero, et al. (2006) estimate phrase translation probabilities according to the following generative model:

1. Begin with a source sentence a.
2. Stochastically segment a into some number of phrases.
3. For each selected phrase in a, stochastically choose a phrase position in the target sentence b that is being generated.
4. For each selected phrase in a and the corresponding phrase position in b, stochastically choose a target phrase.
5. Read off the target sentence b from the sequence of target phrases.

DeNero et al.'s analysis of why their model performs relatively poorly hinges on the fact that the segmentation probabilities used in step 2 are, in fact, not trained, but simply assumed to be uniform. Given complete freedom to select whatever segmentation maximizes the likelihood of any given sentence pair, EM tends to favor segmentations that yield source phrases with as few occurrences as possible, since more of the associated conditional probability mass can be concentrated on the target phrase alignments that are possible in the sentence at hand. Thus EM tends to maximize the probability of the training data by concentrating probability mass on the rarest source phrases it can construct to cover the training data. The resulting probability estimates thus have less generalizability to unseen data than if probability mass were concentrated on more frequently occurring source phrases.

3 A Segmentation-Free Model

To avoid the problem identified by DeNero et al., we propose an iteratively-trained model that does not assume a segmentation of the training data into non-overlapping phrase pairs. We refer to our model as "iteratively-trained" rather than "generative" because we have not proved any of the mathematical properties usually associated with generative models; e.g., that the training procedure maximizes the likelihood of the training data. We will motivate the model, however, with a generative story as to how phrase alignments are produced, given a pair of source and target sentences. Our model extends to phrase alignment the concept of a sentence pair generating a word alignment developed by Cherry and Lin (2003).

Our model is defined in terms of two stochastic processes, *selection* and *alignment*, as follows:

1. For each word-aligned sentence pair, we identify all the possible phrase pair instances according to the criteria used by Koehn et al.

[1] This method of phrase pair extraction was originally described by Och et al. (1999).

2. Each source phrase instance that is included in any of the possible phrase pair instances independently selects one of the target phrase instances that it forms a possible phrase pair instance with.

3. Each target phrase instance that is included in any of the possible phrase pair instances independently selects one of the source phrase instances that it forms a possible phrase pair instance with.

4. A source phrase instance is aligned to a target phrase instance, if and only if each selects the other.

Given a set of selection probability distributions and a word-aligned parallel corpus, we can easily compute the expected number of alignment instances for a given phrase pair type. The probability of a pair of phrase instances x and y being aligned is simply $p_s(x|y) \times p_s(y|x)$, where p_s is the applicable selection probability distribution. The expected number of instances of alignment, $E(x, y)$, for the pair of phrases x and y, is just the sum of the alignment probabilities of all the possible instances of that phrase pair type.

From the expected number of alignments and the total number of occurrences of each source and target phrase type in the corpus (whether or not they particpate in possible phrase pairs), we estimate the conditional phrase translation probabilities as

$$p_t(y|x) = \frac{E(x,y)}{C(x)}, \quad p_t(x|y) = \frac{E(x,y)}{C(y)},$$

where E denotes expected counts, and C denotes observed counts.

The use of the total observed counts of particular source and target phrases (instead of marginalized expected joint counts) in estimating the conditional phrase translation probabilities, together with the multiplication of selection probabilities in computing the alignment probability of particular phrase pair instances, causes the conditional phrase translation probability distributions generally to sum to less than 1.0. We interpret the missing probability mass as the probability that a given word sequence does not translate as any contiguous word sequence in the other language.

We have seen how to derive phrase translation probabilities from the selection probabilities, but where do the latter come from? We answer this question by adding the following constraint to the model:

> The probabilty of a phrase y selecting a phrase x is proportional to the probability of x translating as y, normalized over the possible non-null choices for x presented by the word-aligned sentence pair.

Symbolically, we can express this as

$$p_s(x|y) = \frac{p_t(y|x)}{\sum_{x'} p_t(y|x')}$$

where p_s denotes selection probability, p_t denotes translation probability, and x' ranges over the phrase instances that could possibly align to y. We are, in effect, inverting and renormalizing translation probabilities to get selection probabilities. The reason for the inversion may not be immediately apparent, but it in fact simply generalizes the e-step formula in the EM training for IBM Model 1 from words to phrases.

This model immediately suggests (and, in fact, was designed to suggest) the following EM-like training procedure:

1. Initialize the translation probability distributions to be uniform. (It doesn't matter at this point whether the possibility of no translation is included or not.)

2. E step: Compute the expected phrase alignment counts according to the model, deriving the selection probabilities from the current estimates of the translation probabilities as described.

3. M step: Re-estimate the phrase translation probabilities according to the expected phrase alignment counts as described.

4. Repeat the E and M steps, until the desired degree of convergence is obtained.

We view this training procedure as iteratively trying to find a set of phrase translation probabilities that satisfies all the constraints of the model, although we have not proved that this training procedure always converges. We also have not proved that the procedure maximizes the likelihood of anything, although we find empirically that each iteration decreases the conditional entropy of the phrase translation model. In any case, the training procedure seems to work well in practice. It is also very similar to the joint training procedure for HMM word-alignment models in both directions described by Liang et al. (2006), which was the original inspiration for our training procedure.

4 Experimental Set-Up and Data

We evaluated our phrase translation model compared to the standard model of Koehn et al. in the context of a fairly typical end-to-end phrase-based SMT system. The overall translation model score consists of a weighted sum of the following eight aggregated feature values for each translation hypothesis:

- the sum of the log probabilities of each source phrase in the hypothesis given the corresponding target phrase, computed either by our model or the standard model,
- the sum of the log probabilities of each target phrase in the hypothesis given the corresponding source phrase, computed either by our model or the standard model,
- the sum of lexical scores for each source phrase given the corresponding target phrase,
- the sum of lexical scores for each target phrase given the corresponding source phrase,
- the log of the target language model probability for the sequence of target phrases in the hypothesis,
- the total number of words in the target phrases in the hypothesis,
- the total number of source/target phrase pairs composing the hypothesis,
- the distortion penalty as implemented in the Pharaoh decoder (Koehn, 2003).

The lexical scores are computed as the (unnormalized) log probability of the Viterbi alignment for a phrase pair under IBM word-translation Model 1 (Brown et al., 1993). The feature weights for the overall translation models were trained using Och's (2003) minimum-error-rate training procedure. The weights were optimized separately for our model and for the standard phrase translation model. Our decoder is a reimplementation in Perl of the algorithm used by the Pharaoh decoder as described by Koehn (2003).[2]

The data we used comes from an English-French bilingual corpus of Canadian Hansards parliamentary proceedings supplied for the bilingual word alignment workshop held at HLT-NAACL 2003 (Mihalcea and Pedersen, 2003). Automatic sentence alignment of this data was provided by Ulrich Germann. We used 500,000 sentences pairs from this corpus for training both the phrase translation models and IBM Model 1 lexical scores. These 500,000 sentence pairs were word-aligned using a state-of-the-art word-alignment method (Moore et al., 2006). A separate set of 500 sentence pairs was used to train the translation model weights, and two additional held-out sets of 2000 sentence pairs each were used as test data.

The two phrase translation models were trained using the same set of possible phrase pairs extracted from the word-aligned 500,000 sentence pair corpus, finding all possible phrase pairs permitted by the criteria followed by Koehn et al., up to a phrase length of seven words. This produced approximately 69 million distinct phrase pair types. No pruning of the set of possible phrase pairs was done during or before training the phrase translation models. Our phrase translation model and IBM Model 1 were both trained for five iterations. The training procedure for our phrase translation model trains models in both directions simultaneously, but for IBM Model 1, models were trained separately in each direction. The models were then pruned to include only phrase pairs that matched the source sides of the small training and test sets.

5 Entropy Measurements

To verify that our iterative training procedure was behaving as expected, after each training iteration

[2]Since Perl is a byte-code interpreted language, absolute decoding times will be slower than with the standard machine-language-compiled implementation of Pharaoh, but relative times between models should be comparable.

we measured the conditional entropy of the model in predicting English phrases given French phrases, according to the formula

$$H(E|F) = \sum_f p(f) \sum_e p_t(e|f) \log_2 p_t(e|f),$$

where e and f range over the English and French phrases that occur in the extracted phrase pairs, and $p(f)$ was estimated according to the relative frequency of these French phrases in a 2000 sentence sample of the French sentences from the 500,000 word-aligned sentence pairs. Over the five training iterations, we obtained a monotonically decreasing sequence of entropy measurements in bits per phrase: 1.329, 1.177, 1.146, 1.140, 1.136.

We also compared the conditional entropy of the standard model to the final iteration of our model, estimating $p(f)$ using the first of our 2000 sentence pair test sets. For this data, our model measured 1.38 bits per phrase, and the standard model measured 4.30 bits per phrase. DeNero et al. obtained corresponding measurements of 1.55 bits per phrase and 3.76 bits per phrase, for their model and the standard model, using a different data set and a slightly different estimation method.

6 Translation Experiments

We wanted to look at the trade-off between decoding time and translation quality for our new phrase translation model compared to the standard model. Since this trade-off is also affected by the settings of various pruning parameters, we compared decoding time and translation quality, as measured by BLEU score (Papineni et al, 2002), for the two models on our first test set over a broad range of settings for the decoder pruning parameters.

The Pharaoh decoding algorithm, has five pruning parameters that affect decoding time:

- Distortion limit
- Translation table limit
- Translation table threshold
- Beam limit
- Beam threshold

The distortion limit is the maximum distance allowed between two source phrases that produce adjacent target phrases in the decoder output. The distortion limit can be viewed as a model parameter, as well as a pruning paramter, because setting it to an optimum value usually improves translation quality over leaving it unrestricted. We carried out experiments with the distortion limit set to 1, which seemed to produce the highest BLEU scores on our data set with the standard model, and also set to 5, which is perhaps a more typical value for phrase-based SMT systems. Translation model weights were trained separately for these two settings, because the greater the distortion limit, the higher the distortion penalty weight needed for optimal translation quality.

The translation table limit and translation table threshold are applied statically to the phrase translation table, which combines all components of the overall translation model score that can be computed for each phrase pair in isolation. This includes all information except the distortion penalty score and the part of the language model score that looks at n-grams that cross target phrase boundaries. The translation table limit is the maximum number of translations allowed in the table for any given source phrase. The translation table threshold is the maximum difference in combined translation table score allowed between the highest scoring translation and lowest scoring translation for any given source phrase. The beam limit and beam threshold are defined similarly, but they apply dynamically to the sets of competing partial hypotheses that cover the same number of source words in the beam search for the highest scoring translation.

For each of the two distortion limits we tried, we carried out a systematic search for combinations of settings of the other four pruning parameters that gave the best trade-offs between decoding time and BLEU score. Starting at a setting of 0.5 for the threshold parameters[3] and 5 for the limit parameters we performed a hill-climbing search over step-wise relaxations of all combinations of the four parame-

[3]We use difference in weighted linear scores directly for our pruning thresholds, whereas the standard implementation of Pharaoh expresses these as probability ratios. Hence the specific values for these parameters are not comparable to published descriptions of experiments using Pharaoh, although the effects of pruning are exactly the same.

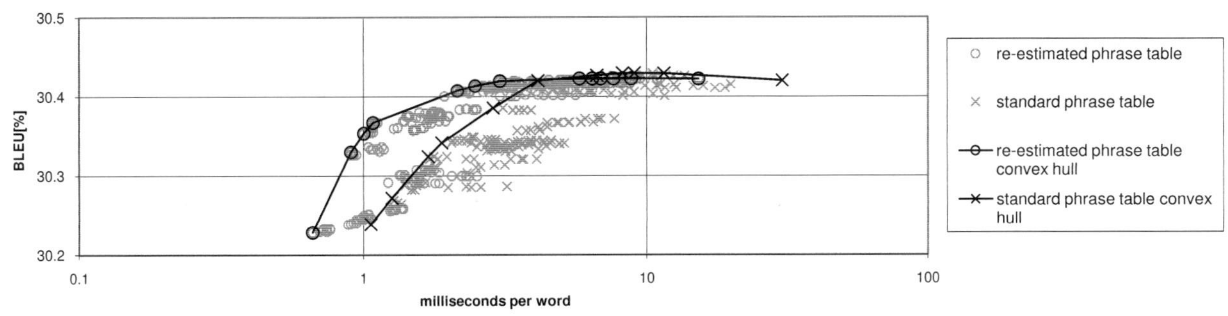

Figure 1: BLEU vs Decoding Time (DL = 1)

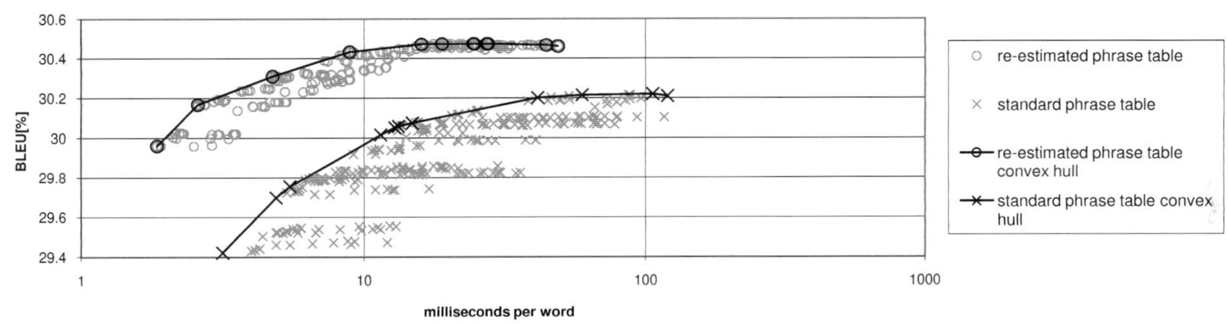

Figure 2: BLEU vs Decoding Time (DL = 5)

ters, incrementing the threshold parameters by 0.5 and the limit parameters by 5 at each step. For each resulting point that provided the best BLEU score yet seen for the amount of decoding time used, we iterated the search.

The resulting possible combinations of BLEU score and decoding time for the two phrase translation models are displayed in Figure 1, for a distortion limit of 1, and Figure 2, for a distortion limit of 5. BLEU score is reported on a scale of 1–100 (BLEU[%]), and decoding time is measured in milliseconds per word. Note that the decoding time axis is presented on a log scale.

The points that represent pruning parameter settings one might consider using in a practical system are those on or near the upper convex hull of the set of points for each model. These upper-convex-hull points are highlighted in the figures. Points far from these boundaries represent settings of one or more of the parameters that are too restrictive to obtain good translation quality, together with settings of other parameters that are too permissive to obtain good translation time.

Examining the results for a distortion limit of 1, we found that the BLEU score obtained with the loosest pruning parameter settings (2.5 for both threshold paramters, and 25 for both limit parameters) were essentially identical for the two models: 30.42 BLEU[%]. As the pruning parameters are tightened to reduce decoding time, however, the new model performs much better. At a decoding time almost 6 times faster than for the settings that produced the highest BLEU score, the change in score was only -0.07 BLEU[%] with the new model. To obtain a slightly worse[4] BLEU score (-0.08 BLEU[%]) using the standard model took 90% more decoding time.

It does appear, however, that the best BLEU score for the standard model is slightly better than the best BLEU score for the new model: 30.43 vs. 30.42. It is in fact currious that there seem to be numerous points where the standard model gets a slightly

[4] Points on the convex hulls with exactly comparable BLEU scores do not often occur.

better BLEU score than it does with with the loosest pruning settings, which should have the lowest search error.

We conjectured that this might be an artifact of our test procedure. If a model is at all reasonable, most search errors will reduce the ultimate objective function, in our case the BLEU score, but occasionally a search error will increase the objective function just by chance. The smaller the number of search errors in a particular test, the greater the likelihood that, by chance, more search errors will increase the objective function than decrease it. Since we are sampling a fairly large number of combinations of pruning parameter settings (179 for the standard model with a distortion limit of 1), it is possible that a small number of these have more "good" search errors than "bad" search errors simply by chance, and that this accounts for the small number of points (13) at which the BLEU score exceeds that of the point which should have the fewest search errors. This effect may be more pronounced with the standard model than with the new model, simply because there is more noise in the standard model.

To test the hypothesis that the BLEU scores greater than the score for the loosest pruning settings simply represent noise in the data, we collected all the pruning settings that produced BLEU scores greater than or equal to the the one for the loosest pruning settings, and evaluated the standard model at those settings on our second held-out test set. We then looked at the correlation between the BLEU scores for these settings on the two test sets, and found that it was very small and negative, with $r = -0.099$. The standard F-test for the significance of a correlation yielded $p = 0.74$; in other words, completely insignificant. This strongly suggests that the apparent improvement in BLEU score for certain tighter pruning settings is illusory.

As a sanity check, we tested the BLEU score correlation between the two test sets for the points on the upper convex hull of the plot for the standard model, between the point with the fastest decoding time and the point with the highest BLEU score. That correlation was very high, with $r = 0.94$, which was significant at the level $p = 0.0004$ according to the F-test. Thus the BLEU score differences along most of the upper convex hull seem to reflect reality, but not in the region where they equal or exceed the score for the loosest pruning settings.

At a distortion limit of 5, there seems no question that the new model performs better than the standard model. The difference BLEU scores for the upper-convex-hull points ranges from about 0.8 to 0.2 BLEU[%] for comparable decoding times. Again, the advantage of the new model is greater at shorter decoding times. Compared to the results with a distortion limit of 1, the standard model loses translation quality, with a change of about -0.2 BLEU[%] for the loosest pruning settings, while the new model gains very slightly ($+0.04$ BLEU[%]).

7 Conclusions

This study seems to confirm DeNero et al.'s diagnosis that the main reason for poor performance of previous iteratively-trained phrase translation models, compared to Koehn et al.'s model, is the effect of the hidden segmentation variable in these models. We have developed an iteratively-trained phrase translation model that is segmentation free, and shown that, at a minimum, it eliminates the shortfall in BLEU score compared to the standard model. With a larger distortion limit, the new model produced translations with a noticably better BLEU score.

From a practical point of view, the main result is probably that BLEU score degrades much more slowly with our model than with the standard model, when the decoding search is tuned for speed. For some settings that appear reasonable, this difference is close to a factor of 2, even if there is no difference in the translation quality obtainable when pruning is loosened. For high-demand applications like web page translation, roughly half of the investment in translation servers could be saved while providing this level of translation quality with the same response time.

Acknowledgement

The authors would like to thank Mark Johnson for many valuable discussions of how to analyze and present the results obtained in this study.

References

Alexandra Birch, Chris Callison-Burch, Miles Osborne, and Philipp Koehn. 2006. Constraining the Phrase-Based, Joint Probability Statistical Translation Model. In *Proceedings of the HLT-NAACL 06 Workshop, Statistical Machine Translation*, pp. 154–157, New York City, New York, USA.

Peter F. Brown, Stephen A. Della Pietra, Vincent J. Della Pietra, and Robert L. Mercer. 1993. The Mathematics of Statistical Machine Translation: Parameter Estimation. *Computational Linguistics*, 19(2):263–311.

Colin Cherry and Dekang Lin. 2003. A Probability Model to Improve Word Alignment. In *Proceedings of the 41st Annual Meeting of the ACL*, pp. 88–95, Sapporo, Japan.

John DeNero, Dan Gillick, James Zhang, and Dan Klein. 2006. Why Generative Phrase Models Underperform Surface Heuristics. In *Proceedings of the HLT-NAACL 06 Workshop, Statistical Machine Translation*, pp. 31–38, New York City, New York, USA.

Philipp Koehn. 2003. Noun Phrase Translation. PhD Dissertation, Computer Science, University of Southern California, Los Angeles, California, USA.

Philipp Koehn, Franz Joseph Och, and Daniel Marcu. 2003. Statistical Phrase-Based Translation. In *Proceedings of the Human Language Technology Conference of the North American Chapter of the Association for Computational Linguistics*, pp. 127–133, Edmonton, Alberta, Canada.

Percy Liang, Ben Taskar, and Dan Klein. 2006. Alignment by Agreement. In *Proceedings of the Human Language Technology Conference of the North American Chapter of the Association for Computational Linguistics*, pp. 104–111, New York City, New York, USA.

Daniel Marcu and William Wong. 2002. A Phrase-Based, Joint Probability Model for Statistical Machine Translation. In *Proceedings of the 2002 Conference on Empirical Methods in Natural Language Processing*, pp. 133–139, Philadelphia, Pennsylvania, USA.

Rada Mihalcea and Ted Pedersen. 2003. An Evaluation Exercise for Word Alignment. In *Proceedings of the HLT-NAACL 2003 Workshop, Building and Using Parallel Texts: Data Driven Machine Translation and Beyond*, pp. 1–6, Edmonton, Alberta, Canada.

Robert C. Moore, Wen-tau Yih, and Andreas Bode. 2006. Improved Discriminative Bilingual Word Alignment. In *Proceedings of the 21st International Conference on Computational Linguistics and 44th Annual Meeting of the Association for Computational Linguistics*, pp. 513-520, Sydney, Australia.

Franz Joseph Och, Christoff Tillmann, and Hermann Ney. 1999. Improved Alignment Models for Statistical Machine Translation. In *Proceedings of the 1999 Joint SIGDAT Conference on Empirical Methods in Natural Language Processing and Very Large Corpora*, pp. 20–28, College Park, Maryland, USA.

Franz Joseph Och. 2003. Minimum Error Rate Training in Statistical Machine Translation. In *Proceedings of the 41st Annual Meeting of the ACL*, pp. 160–167, Sapporo, Japan.

Kishore Papineni, Salim Roukos, Todd Ward, and Wei-Jing Zhu. 2002. BLEU: a Method for Automatic Evaluation of Machine Translation. In *Proceedings of the 40th Annual Meeting of the Association for Computational Linguistics*, pp. 311–318, Philadelphia, Pennsylvania, USA.

Using Paraphrases for Parameter Tuning in Statistical Machine Translation

Nitin Madnani, Necip Fazil Ayan, Philip Resnik & Bonnie J. Dorr
Institute for Advanced Computer Studies
University of Maryland
College Park, MD, 20742
{nmadnani,nfa,resnik,bonnie}@umiacs.umd.edu

Abstract

Most state-of-the-art statistical machine translation systems use log-linear models, which are defined in terms of hypothesis features and weights for those features. It is standard to tune the feature weights in order to maximize a translation quality metric, using held-out test sentences and their corresponding reference translations. However, obtaining reference translations is expensive. In this paper, we introduce a new full-sentence paraphrase technique, based on English-to-English decoding with an MT system, and we demonstrate that the resulting paraphrases can be used to drastically reduce the number of human reference translations needed for parameter tuning, without a significant decrease in translation quality.

1 Introduction

Viewed at a very high level, statistical machine translation involves four phases: language and translation model training, parameter tuning, decoding, and evaluation (Lopez, 2007; Koehn et al., 2003). Since their introduction in statistical MT by Och and Ney (2002), log-linear models have been a standard way to combine sub-models in MT systems. Typically such a model takes the form

$$\sum_i \lambda_i \phi_i(\bar{f}, \bar{e}) \qquad (1)$$

where ϕ_i are features of the hypothesis e and λ_i are weights associated with those features.

Selecting appropriate weights λ_i is essential in order to obtain good translation performance. Och (2003) introduced minimum error rate training (MERT), a technique for optimizing log-linear model parameters relative to a measure of translation quality. This has become much more standard than optimizing the conditional probability of the training data given the model (i.e., a maximum likelihood criterion), as was common previously. Och showed that system performance is best when parameters are optimized using the same objective function that will be used for evaluation; BLEU (Papineni et al., 2002) remains common for both purposes and is often retained for parameter optimization even when alternative evaluation measures are used, e.g., (Banerjee and Lavie, 2005; Snover et al., 2006).

Minimum error rate training—and more generally, optimization of parameters relative to a translation quality measure—relies on data sets in which source language sentences are paired with (sets of) reference translations. It is widely agreed that, at least for the widely used BLEU criterion, which is based on n-gram overlap between hypotheses and reference translations, the criterion is most accurate when computed with as many distinct reference translations as possible. Intuitively this makes sense: if there are alternative ways to phrase the meaning of the source sentence in the target language, then the translation quality criterion should take as many of those variations into account as possible. To do otherwise is to risk the possibility that the criterion might judge good translations to be poor when they fail to match the exact wording within the reference translations that have been provided.

This reliance on multiple reference translations creates a problem, because reference translations are labor intensive and expensive to obtain. A common source of translated data for MT research is the Linguistic Data Consortium (LDC), where an elaborate process is undertaken that involves translation agencies, detailed translation guidelines, and quality control processes (Strassel et al., 2006). Some

Proceedings of the Second Workshop on Statistical Machine Translation, pages 120–127,
Prague, June 2007.

efforts have been made to develop alternative processes for eliciting translations, e.g., from users on the Web (Oard, 2003) or from informants in low-density languages (Probst et al., 2002). However, reference translations for parameter tuning and evaluation remain a severe data bottleneck for such approaches.

Note, however, one crucial property of reference translations: they are paraphrases, i.e., multiple expressions of the same meaning. Automatic techniques exist for generating paraphrases. Although one would clearly like to retain human translations as the benchmark for *evaluation* of translation, might it be possible to usefully increase the number of reference translations for *tuning* by using automatic paraphrase techniques?

In this paper, we demonstrate that it is, in fact, possible to do so. Section 2 briefly describes our translation framework. Section 3 lays out a novel technique for paraphrasing, designed with the application to parameter tuning in mind. Section 4 presents evaluation results using a state of the art statistical MT system, demonstrating that half the human reference translations in a standard 4-reference tuning set can be replaced with automatically generated paraphrases, with no significant decrease in MT system performance. In Section 5 we discuss related work, and in Section 6 we summarize the results and discuss plans for future research.

2 Translation Framework

The work described in this paper makes use of the Hiero statistical MT framework (Chiang, 2007). Hiero is formally based on a weighted synchronous context-free grammar (CFG), containing synchronous rules of the form

$$X \rightarrow \langle \bar{e}, \bar{f}, \phi_1^k(\bar{f}, \bar{e}, X) \rangle \tag{2}$$

where X is a symbol from the nonterminal alphabet, and $\bar{e}$ and $\bar{f}$ can contain both words (terminals) and variables (nonterminals) that serve as placeholders for other phrases. In the context of statistical MT, where phrase-based models are frequently used, these synchronous rules can be interpreted as pairs of *hierarchical phrases*. The underlying strength of a hierarchical phrase is that it allows for effective learning of not only the lexical re-orderings, but phrasal re-orderings, as well. Each $\phi(\bar{e}, \bar{f}, X)$ denotes a feature function defined on the pair of hierarchical phrases.[1] Feature functions represent conditional and joint co-occurrence probabilities over the hierarchical paraphrase pair.

The Hiero framework includes methods to learn grammars and feature values from unannotated parallel corpora, without requiring syntactic annotation of the data. Briefly, training a Hiero model proceeds as follows:

- GIZA++ (Och and Ney, 2000) is run on the parallel corpus in both directions, followed by an alignment refinement heuristic that yields a many-to-many alignment for each parallel sentence.
- Initial phrase pairs are identified following the procedure typically employed in phrase based systems (Koehn et al., 2003; Och and Ney, 2004).
- Grammar rules in the form of equation (2) are induced by "subtracting" out hierarchical phrase pairs from these initial phrase pairs.
- Fractional counts are assigned to each produced rule:

$$c(X \rightarrow \langle \bar{e}, \bar{f} \rangle) = \sum_{j=1}^{m} \frac{1}{n_{jr}} \tag{3}$$

  where m is the number of initial phrase pairs that give rise to this grammar rule and n_{jr} is the number of grammar rules produced by the jth initial phrase pair.
- Feature functions $\phi_1^k(\bar{f}, \bar{e}, X)$ are calculated for each rule using the accumulated counts.

Once training has taken place, minimum error rate training (Och, 2003) is used to tune the parameters λ_i.

Finally, decoding in Hiero takes place using a CKY synchronous parser with beam search, augmented to permit efficient incorporation of language model scores (Chiang, 2007). Given a source language sentence *f*, the decoder parses the source language sentence using the grammar it has learned

[1]Currently only one nonterminal symbol is used in Hiero productions.

during training, with parser search guided by the model; a target-language hypothesis is generated simultaneously via the synchronous rules, and the yield of that hypothesized analysis represents the hypothesized string e in the target language.

3 Generating Paraphrases

As discussed in Section 1, our goal is to make it possible to accomplish the parameter-tuning phase using fewer human reference translations. We accomplish this by beginning with a small set of human reference translations for each sentence in the development set, and expanding that set by automatically paraphrasing each member of the set rather than by acquiring more human translations.

Most previous work on paraphrase has focused on high quality rather than coverage (Barzilay and Lee, 2003; Quirk et al., 2004), but generating artificial references for MT parameter tuning in our setting has two unique properties compared to other paraphrase applications. First, we would like to obtain 100% coverage, in order to avoid modifications to our minimum error rate training infrastructure.[2] Second, we prefer that paraphrases be as distinct as possible from the original sentences, while retaining as much of the original meaning as possible.

In order to satisfy these two properties, we approach sentence-level paraphrase for English as a problem of English-to-English translation, constructing the model using English-F translation, for a second language F, as a pivot. Following Bannard and Callison-Burch (2005), we first identify English-to-F correspondences, then map from English to English by following translation units from English to F and back. Then, generalizing their approach, we use those mappings to create a well defined English-to-English translation model. The parameters of this model are tuned using MERT, and then the model is used in an the (unmodified) statistical MT system, yielding sentence-level English paraphrases by means of decoding input English sentences. The remainder of this section presents this process in detail.

[2]Strictly speaking, this was not a requirement of the approach, but rather a concession to practical considerations.

3.1 Mapping and Backmapping

We employ the following strategy for the induction of the required monolingual grammar. First, we train the Hiero system in standard fashion on a bilingual English-F training corpus. Then, for each existing production in the resulting Hiero grammar, we create multiple new English-to-English productions by pivoting on the foreign hierarchical phrase in the rule. For example, assume that we have the following toy grammar for English-F, as produced by Hiero:

$$X \rightarrow \langle \bar{e1}, \bar{f1} \rangle$$
$$X \rightarrow \langle \bar{e3}, \bar{f1} \rangle$$
$$X \rightarrow \langle \bar{e1}, \bar{f2} \rangle$$
$$X \rightarrow \langle \bar{e2}, \bar{f2} \rangle$$
$$X \rightarrow \langle \bar{e4}, \bar{f2} \rangle$$

If we use the foreign phrase $\bar{f1}$ as a pivot and backmap, we can extract the two English-to-English rules: $X \rightarrow \langle \bar{e1}, \bar{e3} \rangle$ and $X \rightarrow \langle \bar{e3}, \bar{e1} \rangle$. Backmapping using both $\bar{f1}$ and $\bar{f2}$ produces the following new rules (ignoring duplicates and rules that map any English phrase to itself):

$$X \rightarrow \langle \bar{e1}, \bar{e2} \rangle$$
$$X \rightarrow \langle \bar{e1}, \bar{e3} \rangle$$
$$X \rightarrow \langle \bar{e1}, \bar{e4} \rangle$$
$$X \rightarrow \langle \bar{e2}, \bar{e1} \rangle$$
$$X \rightarrow \langle \bar{e2}, \bar{e4} \rangle$$

3.2 Feature values

Each rule production in a Hiero grammar is weighted by several feature values defined on the rule themselves. In order to perform accurate backmapping, we must recompute these feature functions for the newly created English-to-English grammar. Rather than computing approximations based on feature values already existing in the bilingual Hiero grammar, we calculate these features in a more principled manner, by computing maximum likelihood estimates directly from the fractional counts that Hiero accumulates in the penultimate training step.

We use the following features in our induced English-to-English grammar:[3]

[3]Hiero also uses lexical weights (Koehn et al., 2003) in both

- The joint probability of the two English hierarchical paraphrases, conditioned on the nonterminal symbol, as defined by this formula:

$$p(\bar{e_1}, \bar{e_2}|x) = \frac{c(X \rightarrow \langle \bar{e_1}, \bar{e_2} \rangle)}{\sum_{\bar{e_1}', \bar{e_2}'} c(X \rightarrow \langle \bar{e_1}', \bar{e_2}' \rangle)} = \frac{c(X \rightarrow \langle \bar{e_1}, \bar{e_2} \rangle)}{c(X)} \quad (4)$$

where the numerator is the fractional count of the rule under consideration and the denominator represents the marginal count over all the English hierarchical phrase pairs.

- The conditionals $p(\bar{e_1}, x|\bar{e_2})$ and $p(\bar{e_2}, x|\bar{e_1})$ defined as follows:

$$p(\bar{e_1}, x|\bar{e_2}) = \frac{c(X \rightarrow \langle \bar{e_1}, \bar{e_2} \rangle)}{\sum_{\bar{e_1}'} c(X \rightarrow \langle \bar{e_1}', \bar{e_2} \rangle)} \quad (5)$$

$$p(\bar{e_2}, x|\bar{e_1}) = \frac{c(X \rightarrow \langle \bar{e_1}, \bar{e_2} \rangle)}{\sum_{\bar{e_2}'} c(X \rightarrow \langle \bar{e_1}, \bar{e_2}' \rangle)} \quad (6)$$

Finally, for all induced rules, we calculate a word penalty $exp(-T(\bar{e_2}))$, where $T(\bar{e_2})$ just counts the number of terminal symbols in $\bar{e_2}$. This feature allows the model to learn whether it should produce shorter or longer paraphrases.

In addition to the features above that are estimated from the training data, we also use a trigram language model. Since we are decoding to produce English sentences, we can use the same language model employed in a standard statistical MT setting.

Calculating the proposed features is complicated by the fact that we don't actually have the counts for English-to-English rules because there is no English-to-English parallel corpus. This is where the counts provided by Hiero come into the picture. We estimate the counts that we need as follows:

$$c(X \rightarrow \langle \bar{e_1}, \bar{e_2} \rangle) = \sum_{\bar{f}} c(X \rightarrow \langle \bar{e_1}, \bar{f} \rangle) c(X \rightarrow \langle \bar{e_2}, \bar{f} \rangle) \quad (7)$$

An intuitive way to think about the formula above is by using an example at the corpus level. Assume that, in the given bilingual parallel corpus, there are m sentences in which the English phrase $\bar{e_1}$ co-occurs with the foreign phrase $\bar{f}$ and n sentences in which the same foreign phrase $\bar{f}$ co-occurs with the English phrase $\bar{e_2}$. The problem can then be thought of as defining a function $g(m, n)$ which computes the number of sentences in a hypothetical English-to-English parallel corpus wherein the phrases $\bar{e_1}$ and $\bar{e_1}$ co-occur. For this paper, we define $g(m, n)$ to be the upper bound mn.

Tables 1 and 2 show some examples of paraphrases generated by our system across a range of paraphrase quality for two different pivot languages.

3.3 Tuning Model Parameters

Although the goal of the paraphrasing approach is to make it less data-intensive to tune log-linear model parameters for translation, our paraphrasing approach, since it is based on an English-to-English log-linear model, also requires its own parameter tuning. This, however, is straightforward: regardless of how the paraphrasing model will be used in statistical MT, e.g., irrespective of source language, it is possible to use any existing set of English paraphrases as the tuning set for English-to-English translation. We used the 2002 NIST MT evaluation test set reference translations. For every item in the set, we randomly chose one sentence as the source sentence, and the remainder as the "reference translations" for purposes of minimum error rate training.

4 Evaluation

Having developed a paraphrasing approach based on English-to-English translation, we evaluated its use in improving minimum error rate training for translation from a second language into English.

Generating paraphrases via English-to-English translation makes use of a parallel corpus, from which a weighted synchronous grammar is automatically acquired. Although nothing about our approach requires that the paraphrase system's training bitext be the same one used in the translation experiments (see Section 6), doing so is not precluded, either, and it is a particularly convenient choice when the paraphrasing is being done in support of MT.[4] The training bitext comprised of Chinese-English

directions as features but we don't use them for our grammar.

[4]The choice of the foreign language used as the pivot should not really matter but it is worth exploring this using other language pairs as our bitext.

O:	we must bear in mind the community as a whole .
P:	we must remember the wider community .
O:	thirdly , the implications of enlargement for the union 's regional policy cannot be overlooked .
P:	finally , the impact of enlargement for eu regional policy cannot be ignored .
O:	how this works in practice will become clear when the authority has to act .
P:	how this operate in practice will emerge when the government has to play .
O:	this is an ill-advised policy .
P:	this is an unwelcome in europe .

Table 1: Example paraphrases with French as the pivot language. **O** = Original Sentence, **P** = Paraphrase.

O:	alcatel added that the company's whole year earnings would be announced on february 4 .
P:	alcatel said that the company's total annual revenues would be released on february 4 .
O:	he was now preparing a speech concerning the us policy for the upcoming world economic forum .
P:	he was now ready to talk with regard to the us policies for the forthcoming international economic forum .
O:	tibet has entered an excellent phase of political stability, ethnic unity and people living in peace .
P:	tibetans have come to cordial political stability, national unity and lived in harmony .
O:	its ocean and blue-sky scenery and the mediterranean climate make it world's famous scenic spot .
P:	its harbour and blue-sky appearance and the border situation decided it world's renowned tourist attraction .

Table 2: Example paraphrases with Chinese as the pivot language. **O** = Original Sentence, **P** = Paraphrase.

Corpus	# Sentences	# Words
HK News	542540	11171933
FBIS	240996	9121210
Xinhua	54022	1497562
News1	9916	314121
Treebank	3963	125848
Total	851437	22230674

Table 3: Chinese-English corpora used as training bitext both for paraphrasing and for evaluation.

parallel corpora containing 850,000 sentence pairs – approx. 22 million words (details shown in Table 3).

As the source of development data for minimum error rate training, we used the 919 source sentences and human reference translations from the 2003 NIST Chinese-English MT evaluation exercise. As raw material for experimentation, we generated a paraphrase for each reference sentence via 1-best decoding using the English-to-English translation approach of Section 3.

As our test data, we used the 1082 source sentences and human reference translations from the 2005 NIST Chinese-English MT evaluation.

Our core experiment involved three conditions where the only difference was the set of references for the development set used for tuning feature weights. For each condition, once the weights were tuned, they were used to decode the test set. Note that for all the conditions, the decoded test set was always scored against the *same* four high-quality human reference translations included with the set.

The three experimental conditions were designed around the constraint that our development set contains a total of four human reference translations per sentence, and therefore a maximum of four human references with which to compute an upper bound:

- **Baseline (2H):** For each item in the development set, we randomly chose two of the four human-constructed reference translations as references for minimum error rate training.
- **Expanded (2H + 2P):** For each of the two human references in the baseline tuning set, we automatically generated a corresponding paraphrase using (1-best) English-to-English translation, decoding using the model developed in Section 3. This condition represents the critical case in which you have a limited number of hu-

man references (two, in this case) and augment them with artificially generated reference translations. This yields a set of four references for minimum error rate training (two human, two paraphrased), which permits a direct comparison against the upper bound of four human-generated reference translations.

- **Upper bound: 4H**: We performed minimum error rate training using the four human references from the development set.

In addition to these core experimental conditions, we added a fourth condition to assess the effect on performance when all four human reference translations are used in expanding the reference set via paraphrase:

- **Expanded (4H + 4P):** This is the same as Condition 2, but using all four human references.

Note that since we have only four human references per item, this fourth condition does not permit comparison with an upper bound of eight human references.

Table 4 shows BLEU and TER scores on the test set for all four conditions.[5] If only two human references were available (simulated by using only two of the available four), expanding to four using paraphrases would yield a clear improvement. Using bootstrap resampling to compute confidence intervals (Koehn, 2004), we find that the improvement in BLEU score is statistically significant at $p < .01$.

Equally interesting, expanding the number of reference translations from two to four using paraphrases yields performance that approaches the upper bound obtained by doing MERT using all four human reference translations. The difference in BLEU between conditions 2 and 3 is *not* significant.

Finally, our fourth condition asks whether it is possible to improve MT performance given the typical four human reference translations used for MERT in most statistical MT systems, by adding a paraphrase to each one for a total eight references per translation. There is indeed further improvement, although the difference in BLEU score does not reach significance.

[5]We plan to include METEOR scores in future experiments.

Condition	References used	BLEU	TER
1	2 H	30.43	59.82
2	2 H + 2 P	31.10	58.79
3	4 H	31.26	58.66
4	4 H + 4 P	31.68	58.24

Table 4: BLEU and TER scores showing utility of paraphrased reference translations. **H** = human references, **P** = paraphrased references.

We also evaluated our test set using TER (Snover et al., 2006) and observed that the TER scores follow the same trend as the BLEU scores. Specifically, the TER scores demonstrate that using paraphrases to artificially expand the reference set is better than using only 2 human reference translations and as good as using 4 human reference translations.[6]

5 Related Work

The approach we have taken here arises from a typical situation in NLP systems: the lack of sufficient data to accurately estimate a model based on supervised training data. In a structured prediction problem such as MT, we have an example input and a single labeled, correct output. However, this output is chosen from a space in which the number of possible outputs is exponential in the input size, and in which there are many good outputs in this space (although they are vastly outnumbered by the bad outputs). Various discriminative learning methods have attempted to deal with the first of these issues, often by restricting the space of examples. For instance, some max-margin methods restrict their computations to a set of examples from a "feasible set," where they are expected to be maximally discriminative (Tillmann and Zhang, 2006). The present approach deals with the second issue: in a learning problem where the use of a single positive example is likely to be highly biased, how can we produce a set of positive examples that is more representative of the space of correct outcomes? Our method exploits alternative sources of information to produce new positive examples that are, we hope, reasonably likely to represent a consensus of good examples.

Quite a bit of work has been done on paraphrase,

[6]We anticipate doing significance tests for differences in TER in future work.

some clearly related to our technique, although in general previous work has been focused on human readability rather than high coverage, noisy paraphrases for use downstream in an automatic process.

At the sentence level, (Barzilay and Lee, 2003) employed an unsupervised learning approach to cluster sentences and extract *lattice pairs* from comparable monolingual corpora. Their technique produces a paraphrase *only* if the input sentence matches any of the extracted lattice pairs, leading to a bias strongly favoring quality over coverage. They were able to generate paraphrases for 59 sentences (12%) out of a 484-sentence test set, generating no paraphrases at all for the remainder.

Quirk et al. (2004) also generate sentential paraphrases using a monolingual corpus. They use IBM Model-1 scores as the only feature, and employ a monotone decoder (i.e., one that cannot produce phrase-level reordering). This approach emphasizes very simple "substitutions of words and short phrases," and, in fact, almost a third of their best sentential "paraphrases" are identical to the input sentence.

A number of other approaches rely on parallel monolingual data and, additionally, require parsing of the training sentences (Ibrahim et al., 2003; Pang et al., 2003). Lin and Pantel (2001) use a non-parallel corpus and employ a dependency parser and computation of distributional similarity to learn paraphrases.

There has also been recent work on using paraphrases to improve statistical machine translation. Callison-Burch et al. (2006) extract phrase-level paraphrases by mapping input phrases into a phrase table and then mapping back to the source language. However, they do not generate paraphrases of entire sentences, but instead employ paraphrases to add entries to an existing phrase table solely for the purpose of increasing source-language coverage.

Other work has incorporated paraphrases into MT evaluation: Russo-Lassner et al. (2005) use a combination of paraphrase-based features to evaluate translation output; Zhou et al. (2006) propose a new metric that extends n-gram matching to include synonyms and paraphrases; and Lavie's METEOR metric (Banerjee and Lavie, 2005) can be used with additional knowledge such as WordNet in order to support inexact lexical matches.

6 Conclusions and Future Work

We introduced an automatic paraphrasing technique based on English-to-English translation of full sentences using a statistical MT system, and demonstrated that, using this technique, it is possible to cut in half the usual number of reference translations used for minimum error rate training with no significant loss in translation quality. Our method enables the generation of paraphrases for thousands of sentences in a very short amount of time (much shorter than creating other low-cost human references). This might prove beneficial for various discriminative training methods (Tillmann and Zhang, 2006).

This has important implications for data acquisition strategies For example, it suggests that rather than obtaining four reference translations per sentence for development sets, it may be more worthwhile to obtain fewer translations for a wider range of sentences, e.g., expanding into new topics and genres. In addition, this approach can significantly increase the utility of datasets which include only a single reference translation.

A number of future research directions are possible. First, since we have already demonstrated that noisy paraphrases can nonetheless add value, it would be straightforward to explore the quantity/quality tradeoff by expanding the MERT reference translations with n-best paraphrases for $n > 1$.

We also plan to conduct an intrinsic evaluation of the quality of paraphrases that our technique generates. It is important to note that a different tradeoff ratio may lead to even better results, e.g, using *only* the paraphrased references when they pass some goodness threshold, as used in Ueffing's (2006) self-training MT approach.

We have also observed that named entities are usually paraphrased incorrectly if there is a genre mismatch between the training and the test data. The Hiero decoder allows spans of source text to be annotated with inline translations using XML. We plan to identify and annotate named entities in the English source so that they are left unchanged.

Also, since the language F for English-F pivoting is arbitrary, we plan to investigate using English-to-English grammars created using *multiple* English-F grammars based on different languages, both individually and in combination, in order to improve paraphrase quality.

We also plan to explore a wider range of paraphrase-creation techniques, ranging from simple word substitutions (e.g., based on WordNet) to using the pivot technique with other translations systems.

7 Acknowledgments

We are indebted to David Chiang, Adam Lopez and Smaranda Muresan for insights and comments. This work has been supported under the GALE program of the Defense Advaned Research Projects Agency, Contract No. HR0011-06-2-001. Any opinions, findings, conclusions or recommendations expressed in this paper are those of the authors and do not necessarily reflect the view of DARPA.

References

S. Banerjee and A. Lavie. 2005. Meteor: An automatic metric for mt evaluation with improved correlation with human judgments. In *Proceedings of Workshop on Intrinsic and Extrinsic Evaluation Measures for MT and/or Summarization at ACL*.

Colin Bannard and Chris Callison-Burch. 2005. Paraphrasing with bilingual parallel corpora. In *Proceedings of ACL*.

Regina Barzilay and Lillian Lee. 2003. Learning to paraphrase: An unsupervised approach using multiple-sequence alignment. In *Proceedings of HLT-NAACL*.

Chris Callison-Burch, Philipp Koehn, and Miles Osborne. 2006. Improved statistical machine translation using paraphrases. In *Proceedings of HLT-NAACL*.

David Chiang. 2007. Hierarchical phrase-based translation. *Computational Linguistics*, 33(2).

A. Ibrahim, B. Katz, and J. Lin. 2003. Extracting structural paraphrases from aligned monolingual corpora. In *Proceedings the Second International Workshop on Paraphrasing (ACL 2003)*.

Philipp Koehn, Franz Och, and Daniel Marcu. 2003. Statistical phrase-based translation. In *Proceedings of HLT-NAACL*.

Philipp Koehn. 2004. Statistical significance tests for machine translation evaluation. In *Proceedings of EMNLP*.

Dekang Lin and Patrick Pantel. 2001. DIRT - discovery of inference rules from text. In *Proceedings of ACM SIGKDD Conference on Knowledge Discovery and Data Mining*.

A. Lopez. 2007. A survey of statistical machine translation. Technical Report 2006-47, University of Maryland, College Park.

D. W. Oard. 2003. The surprise langauge exercises. *ACM Transactions on Asian Language Information Processing*, 2(3).

Franz J. Och and Hermann Ney. 2000. Improved statistical alignment models. In *Proceedings of ACL*.

Franz J. Och and Hermann Ney. 2002. Discriminative training and maximum entropy models for statistical machine translation. In *Proceedings of ACL*.

Franz Och and Hermann Ney. 2004. The alignment template approach to statistical machine translation. *Computational Linguistics*, 30(4).

Franz Josef Och. 2003. Minimum error rate training in statistical machine translation. In *Proceedings of ACL*.

Bo Pang, Kevin Knight, and Daniel Marcu. 2003. Syntax-based alignment of multiple translations: Extracting paraphrases and generating new sentences. In *Proceedings of HLT/NAACL*.

K. Papineni, S. Roukos, T. Ward, and W.-J. Zhu. 2002. Bleu: a method for automatic evaluation of machine translation. In *Proceedings of ACL*.

K. Probst, L. Levin, E. Peterson, A. Lavie, and J. Carbonell. 2002. Mt for minority languages using elicitation-based learning of syntactic transfer rules. *Machine Translation*, 17(4).

Chris Quirk, Chris Brockett, and William Dolan. 2004. Monolingual machine translation for paraphrase generation. In *Proceedings of EMNLP 2004*.

Grazia Russo-Lassner, Jimmy Lin, and Philip Resnik. 2005. A paraphrase-based approach to machine translation evaluation. Technical Report UMIACS-TR-2005-57, University of Maryland, College Park.

M. Snover, B. Dorr, R. Schwartz, L. Micciulla, and J. Makhoul. 2006. A study of translation edit rate with targeted human annotation. In *Proceedings of AMTA*.

S. Strassel, C. Cieri, A. Cole, D. DiPersio, M. Liberman, X. Ma, M. Maamouri, and K. Maeda. 2006. Integrated linguistic resources for language exploitation technologies. In *Proceedings of LREC*.

Christoph Tillmann and Tong Zhang. 2006. A discriminative global training algorithm for statistical MT. In *Proceedings of ACL*.

Nicola Ueffing. 2006. Using monolingual source-language data to improve MT performance. In *Proceedings of IWSLT*.

L. Zhou, C.-Y. Lin, D. Muntenau, and E. Hovy. 2006. ParaEval: Using paraphrases to evaluate summaries automatically. In *Proceedings of HLT-NAACL*.

Mixture-Model Adaptation for SMT

George Foster and **Roland Kuhn**
National Research Council Canada
first.last@nrc.gc.ca

Abstract

We describe a mixture-model approach to adapting a Statistical Machine Translation System for new domains, using weights that depend on text distances to mixture components. We investigate a number of variants on this approach, including cross-domain versus dynamic adaptation; linear versus loglinear mixtures; language and translation model adaptation; different methods of assigning weights; and granularity of the source unit being adapted to. The best methods achieve gains of approximately one BLEU percentage point over a state-of-the art non-adapted baseline system.

1 Introduction

Language varies significantly across different genres, topics, styles, etc. This affects empirical models: a model trained on a corpus of car-repair manuals, for instance, will not be well suited to an application in the field of tourism. Ideally, models should be trained on text that is representative of the area in which they will be used, but such text is not always available. This is especially the case for bilingual applications, because parallel training corpora are relatively rare and tend to be drawn from specific domains such as parliamentary proceedings.

In this paper we address the problem of adapting a statistical machine translation system by adjusting its parameters based on some information about a test domain. We assume two basic settings. In *cross-domain* adaptation, a small sample of parallel in-domain text is available, and it is used to optimize for translating future texts drawn from the same domain. In *dynamic* adaptation, no domain information is available ahead of time, and adaptation is based on the current source text under translation. Approaches developed for the two settings can be complementary: an in-domain development corpus can be used to make broad adjustments, which can then be fine tuned for individual source texts.

Our method is based on the classical technique of mixture modeling (Hastie et al., 2001). This involves dividing the training corpus into different components, training a model on each part, then weighting each model appropriately for the current context. Mixture modeling is a simple framework that encompasses many different variants, as described below. It is naturally fairly low dimensional, because as the number of sub-models increases, the amount of text available to train each, and therefore its reliability, decreases. This makes it suitable for discriminative SMT training, which is still a challenge for large parameter sets (Tillmann and Zhang, 2006; Liang et al., 2006).

Techniques for assigning mixture weights depend on the setting. In cross-domain adaptation, knowledge of both source and target texts in the in-domain sample can be used to optimize weights directly. In dynamic adaptation, training poses a problem because no reference text is available. Our solution is to construct a multi-domain development sample for learning parameter settings that are intended to generalize to new domains (ones not represented in the sample). We do not learn mixture weights directly with this method, because there is little hope

Proceedings of the Second Workshop on Statistical Machine Translation, pages 128–135,
Prague, June 2007.

that these would be well suited to new domains. Instead we attempt to learn how weights should be set as a function of distance. To our knowledge, this approach to dynamic adaptation for SMT is novel, and it is one of the main contributions of the paper.

A second contribution is a fairly broad investigation of the large space of alternatives defined by the mixture-modeling framework, using a simple genre-based corpus decomposition. We experimented with the following choices: cross-domain versus dynamic adaptation; linear versus loglinear mixtures; language and translation model adaptation; various text distance metrics; different ways of converting distance metrics into weights; and granularity of the source unit being adapted to.

The remainder of the paper is structured follows: section 2 briefly describes our phrase-based SMT system; section 3 describes mixture-model adaptation; section 4 gives experimental results; section 5 summarizes previous work; and section 6 concludes.

2 Phrase-based Statistical MT

Our baseline is a standard phrase-based SMT system (Koehn et al., 2003). Given a source sentence s, this tries to find the target sentence $\hat{\mathbf{t}}$ that is the most likely translation of s, using the Viterbi approximation:

$$\hat{\mathbf{t}} = \operatorname*{argmax}_{\mathbf{t}} p(\mathbf{t}|\mathbf{s}) \approx \operatorname*{argmax}_{\mathbf{t},\mathbf{a}} p(\mathbf{t},\mathbf{a}|\mathbf{s}),$$

where alignment $\mathbf{a} = (\tilde{s}_1, \tilde{t}_1, j_1), ..., (\tilde{s}_K, \tilde{t}_K, j_K)$; $\tilde{t}_k$ are target phrases such that $\mathbf{t} = \tilde{t}_1 \dots \tilde{t}_K$; $\tilde{s}_k$ are source phrases such that $\mathbf{s} = \tilde{s}_{j_1} \dots \tilde{s}_{j_K}$; and $\tilde{s}_k$ is the translation of the kth target phrase $\tilde{t}_k$.

To model $p(\mathbf{t},\mathbf{a}|\mathbf{s})$, we use a standard loglinear approach:

$$p(\mathbf{t},\mathbf{a}|\mathbf{s}) \propto \exp\left[\sum_i \alpha_i f_i(\mathbf{s},\mathbf{t},\mathbf{a})\right] \qquad (1)$$

where each $f_i(\mathbf{s},\mathbf{t},\mathbf{a})$ is a feature function, and weights α_i are set using Och's algorithm (Och, 2003) to maximize the system's BLEU score (Papineni et al., 2001) on a development corpus. The features used in this study are: the length of $\mathbf{t}$; a single-parameter distortion penalty on phrase reordering in $\mathbf{a}$, as described in (Koehn et al., 2003); phrase translation model probabilities; and 4-gram language model probabilities $\log p(\mathbf{t})$, using Kneser-Ney smoothing as implemented in the SRILM toolkit.

Phrase translation model probabilities are features of the form: $\log p(\mathbf{s}|\mathbf{t},\mathbf{a}) \approx \sum_{k=1}^{K} \log p(\tilde{s}_k|\tilde{t}_k)$. We use two different estimates for the conditional probabilities $p(\tilde{t}|\tilde{s})$ and $p(\tilde{s}|\tilde{t})$: relative frequencies and "lexical" probabilities as described in (Zens and Ney, 2004). In both cases, the "forward" phrase probabilities $p(\tilde{t}|\tilde{s})$ are not used as features, but only as a filter on the set of possible translations: for each source phrase $\tilde{s}$ that matches some ngram in s, only the 30 top-ranked translations $\tilde{t}$ according to $p(\tilde{t}|\tilde{s})$ are retained.

To derive the joint counts $c(\tilde{s},\tilde{t})$ from which $p(\tilde{s}|\tilde{t})$ and $p(\tilde{t}|\tilde{s})$ are estimated, we use the phrase induction algorithm described in (Koehn et al., 2003), with symmetrized word alignments generated using IBM model 2 (Brown et al., 1993).

3 Mixture-Model Adaptation

Our approach to mixture-model adaptation can be summarized by the following general algorithm:

1. Split the corpus into different components, according to some criterion.
2. Train a model on each corpus component.
3. Weight each model according to its fit with the test domain:
    - For cross-domain adaptation, set parameters using a development corpus drawn from the test domain, and use for all future documents.
    - For dynamic adaptation, set global parameters using a development corpus drawn from several different domains. Set mixture weights as a function of the distances from corpus components to the current source text.
4. Combine weighted component models into a single global model, and use it to translate as described in the previous section.

We now describe each aspect of this algorithm in more detail.

3.1 Corpus Decomposition

We partition the corpus into different genres, defined as being roughly identical to corpus source. This is the simplest way to exploit heterogeneous training material for adaptation. An alternative, which we have not explored, would be to cluster the corpus automatically according to topic.

3.2 Component Models

We adapt both language and translation model features within the overall loglinear combination (1).

To train translation models on each corpus component, we used a global IBM2 model for word alignment (in order to avoid degradation in alignment quality due to smaller training corpora), then extracted component-specific relative frequencies for phrase pairs. Lexical probabilities were also derived from the global IBM2 model, and were not adapted.

The procedure for training component-specific language models on the target halves of each corpus component is identical to the procedure for the global model described in section 2. In addition to the component models, we also used a large static global model.

3.3 Combining Framework

The most commonly-used framework for mixture models is a linear one:

$$p(x|h) = \sum_c \lambda_c p_c(x|h) \qquad (2)$$

where $p(x|h)$ is either a language or translation model; $p_c(x|h)$ is a model trained on component c, and λ_c is the corresponding weight. An alternative, suggested by the form of the global model, is a loglinear combination:

$$p(x|h) = \prod_c p_c(x|h)^{\alpha_c}$$

where we write α_c to emphasize that in this case the mixing parameters are global weights, like the weights on the other features within the loglinear model. This is in contrast to linear mixing, where the combined model $p(x|h)$ receives a loglinear weight, but the weights on the components do not participate in the global loglinear combination. One consequence is that it is more difficult to set linear weights using standard minimum-error training techniques, which assume only a "flat" loglinear model.

3.4 Distance Metrics

We used four standard distance metrics to capture the relation between the current source or target text q and each corpus component.[1] All are monolingual—they are applied only to source text or only to target text.

The *tf/idf* metric commonly used in information retrieval is defined as $\cos(\mathbf{v}_c, \mathbf{v}_q)$, where $\mathbf{v_c}$ and $\mathbf{v_q}$ are vectors derived from component c and document q, each consisting of elements of the form: $-\tilde{p}(w)\log \tilde{p}_{doc}(w)$, where $\tilde{p}(w)$ is the relative frequency of word w within the component or document, and $p_{doc}(w)$ is the proportion of components it appears in.

Latent Semantic Analysis (LSA) (Deerwester et al., 1990) is a technique for implicitly capturing the semantic properties of texts, based on the use of Singular Value Decomposition to produce a rank-reduced approximation of an original matrix of word and document frequencies. We applied this technique to all documents in the training corpus (as opposed to components), reduced the rank to 100, then calculated the projections of the component and document vectors described in the previous paragraph into the reduced space.

Perplexity (Jelinek, 1997) is a standard way of evaluating the quality of a language model on a test text. We define a perplexity-based distance metric $p_c(q)^{1/|q|}$, where $p_c(q)$ is the probability assigned to q by an ngram language model trained on component c.

The final distance metric, which we call *EM*, is based on expressing the probability of q as a word-level mixture model: $p(q) = \prod_{i=1}^{|q|} \sum_c d_c p_c(w_i|h_i)$, where $q = w_1 \dots w_{|q|}$, and $p_c(w|h)$ is the ngram probability of w following word sequence h in component c. It is straighforward to use the EM algorithm to find the set of weights $\hat{d}_c, \forall c$ that maximizes the likelihood of q. The weight $\hat{d}_c$ is defined as the distance to component c. For all experiments described below, we used a probability difference threshold of 0.001 as the EM convergence criterion.

[1]Although we refer to these metrics as distances, most are in fact proximities, and we use the convention throughout that higher values mean closer.

3.5 Learning Adaptive Parameters

Our focus in this paper is on adaptation via mixture weights. However, we note that the usual loglinear parameter tuning described in section 2 can also be considered adaptation in the cross-domain setting, because learned preferences for word penalty, relative LM/TM weighting, etc, will reflect the target domain. This is not the case for dynamic adaptation, where, in the absence of an in-domain development corpus, the only information we can hope to glean are the weights on adapted models compared to other features of the system.

The method used for adapting mixture weights depends on both the combining framework (loglinear versus linear), and the adaptive setting (cross-domain versus dynamic), as described below.

3.5.1 Setting Loglinear Mixture Weights

When using a loglinear combining framework as described in section 3.3, mixture weights are set in the same way as the other loglinear parameters when performing cross-domain adaptation. Loglinear mixture models were not used for dynamic adaptation.

3.5.2 Setting Linear Mixture Weights

For both adaptive settings, linear mixture weights were set as a function of the distance metrics described in section 3.4. Given a set of metrics $\{D_1, \ldots, D_m\}$, let $d_{i,c}$ be the distance from the current text to component c according to metric D_i. A simple approach to weighting is to choose a single metric D_i, and set the weights in (2) to be proportional to the corresponding distances:

$$\lambda_c = d_{i,c} / \sum_{c'} d_{i,c'}. \quad (3)$$

Because different distance metrics may capture complementary information, and because optimal weights might be a non-linear function of distance, we also experimented with a linear combination of metrics transformed using a sigmoid function:

$$\lambda_c = \sum_{i=1}^{m} \frac{\beta_i}{1 + exp(a_i(b_i - d_{i,c}))} \quad (4)$$

where β_i reflects the relative predictive power of D_i, and the sigmoid parametes a_i and b_i can be set to selectively suppress contributions from components that are far away. Here we assume that β_i absorbs a normalization constant, so that the λ_c's sum to 1. In this approach, there are three parameters per distance metric to learn: β_i, a_i, and b_i. In general, these parameters are also specific to the particular model being adapted, ie the LM or the TM.

To optimize these parameters, we fixed global loglinear weights at values obtained with Och's algorithm using representative adapted models based on a single distance metric in (3), then used the Downhill Simplex algorithm (Press et al., 2002) to maximize BLEU score on the development corpus. For tractability, we followed standard practice with this technique and considered only monotonic alignments when decoding (Zens and Ney, 2004).

The two approaches just described avoid conditioning λ_c explicitly on c. This is necessary for dynamic adaptation, since any genre preferences learned from the development corpus cannot be expected to generalize. However, it is not necessary for cross-domain adaptation, where the genre of the development corpus is assumed to represent the test domain. Therefore, we also experimented with using Downhill Simplex optimization to *directly* learn the set of linear weights λ_c that yield maximum BLEU score on the development corpus.

A final variant on setting linear mixture weights is a hybrid between cross-domain and dynamic adaptation. In this approach, both the global loglinear weights and, if they are being used, the mixture parameters β_i, a_i, b_i are set to characterize the test domain as in cross-domain adaptation. When translating, however, distances to the current source text are used in (3) or (4) instead of distances to the in-domain development corpus. This obviously limits the metrics used to ones that depend only on source text.

4 Experiments

All experiments were run on the NIST MT evaluation 2006 Chinese data set. Table 1 summarizes the corpora used. The training corpus was divided into seven components according to genre; in all cases these were identical to LDC corpora, with the exception of the *Newswire* component, which was amalgamated from several smaller corpora. The target genre for cross-domain adaptation was newswire, for which high-quality training material is available. The cross-domain development set *NIST04-nw* is the newswire subset of the NIST 2004 evaluation set, and the dynamic adaptation development set *NIST04-mix* is a balanced mixed-genre subset of NIST 2004. The NIST 2005 evaluation set was used for testing cross-domain adaptation, and the NIST 2006 evaluation set (both the "GALE" and "NIST" parts) was used to test dynamic adaptation.

Because different development corpora are used for cross-domain and dynamic adaptation, we trained one static baseline model for each of these adaptation settings, on the corresponding development set.

All results given in this section are BLEU scores.

role	corpus	genres	sent
train	FBIS04	nw	182k
	HK Hans	proceedings	1,375k
	HK Laws	legal	475k
	HK News	press release	740k
	Newswire	nw	26k
	Sinorama	news mag	366k
	UN	proceedings	4,979k
dev	NIST04-nw	nw	901
	NIST04-mix	nw, sp, ed	889
test	NIST05	nw	1,082
	NIST06-GALE	nw, ng, bn, bc	2,276
	NIST06-NIST	nw, ng, bn	1,664

Table 1: Corpora. In the *genres* column: nw = newswire, sp = speeches, ed = editorial, ng = newsgroup, bn = broadcast news, and bc = broadcast conversation.

4.1 Linear versus Loglinear Combination

Table 2 shows a comparison between linear and loglinear mixing frameworks, with uniform weights used in the linear mixture. Both types of mixture model are better than the baseline, but the linear mixture is slightly better than the loglinear mixture. This is quite surprising, because these results are on the *development* set: the loglinear model tunes its component weights on this set, whereas the linear model only adjusts global LM and TM weights. We speculated that this may have been due to non-smooth component models, and tried various smoothing schemes, including Kneser-Ney phrase table smoothing similar to that described in (Foster et al., 2006), and binary features to indicate phrase-pair presence within different components. None helped, however, and we conclude that the problem is most likely that Och's algorithm is unable to find a good maximimum in this setting. Due to this result, all experiments we describe below involve linear mixtures only.

combination	adapted model		
	LM	TM	LM+TM
baseline	30.2	30.2	30.2
loglinear mixture	30.9	31.2	31.4
uniform linear mixture	31.2	31.1	31.8

Table 2: Linear versus loglinear combinations on NIST04-nw.

4.2 Distance Metrics for Weighting

Table 3 compares the performance of all distance metrics described in section 3.4 when used on their own as defined in (3). The difference between them is fairly small, but appears to be consistent across LM and TM adaptation and (for the LM metrics) across source and target side matching. In general, LM metrics seem to have a slight advantage over the vector space metrics, with EM being the best overall. We focus on this metric for most of the experiments that follow.

metric	source text		target text	
	LM	TM	LM	TM
tf/idf	31.3	31.3	31.1	31.1
LSA	31.5	31.6		
perplexity	31.6	31.3	31.7	31.5
EM	31.7	31.6	32.1	31.3

Table 3: Distance metrics for linear combination on the NIST04-nw development set. (Entries in the top right corner are missing due to lack of time.)

Table 4 shows the performance of the parameterized weighting function described by (4), with source-side EM and LSA metrics as inputs. This is compared to direct weight optimization, as both these techniques use Downhill Simplex for parameter tuning. Unfortunately, neither is able to beat the performance of the normalized source-side EM metric on its own (reproduced on the first line from table 3). In additional tests we verified that this also holds for the test corpus. We speculate that this disappointing result is due to compromises made in order to run Downhill Simplex efficiently, including holding global weights fixed, using only a single starting point, and running with monotone decoding.

weighting	LM	TM
EM-src, direct	31.7	31.6
EM-src + LSA-src, parameterized	31.0	30.0
direct optimization	31.7	30.2

Table 4: Weighting techniques for linear combination on the NIST04-nw development set.

4.3 Cross-Domain versus Dynamic Adaptation

Table 5 shows results for cross-domain adaptation, using the source-side EM metric for linear weighting. Both LM and TM adaptation are effective, with test-set improvements of approximately 1 BLEU point over the baseline for LM adaptation and somewhat less for TM adaptation. Performance also improves on the NIST06 out-of-domain test set (although this set includes a newswire portion as well). However, combined LM and TM adaptation is not better than LM adaptation on its own, indicating that the individual adapted models may be capturing the same information.

model	dev	test	
	nist04-nw	nist05	nist06-nist
baseline	30.2	30.3	26.5
EM-src LM	31.7	31.2	27.8
EM-src TM	31.6	30.9	27.3
EM-src LM+TM	32.5	31.2	27.7

Table 5: Cross-Domain adaptation results.

Table 6 contains results for dynamic adaptation, using the source-side EM metric for linear weighting. In this setting, TM adaptation is much less effective, not significantly better than the baseline; performance of combined LM and TM adaptation is also lower. However, LM adaptation improves over the baseline by up to a BLEU point. The performance of cross domain adaptation (reproduced from table 5 on the second line) is slightly better for the in-domain test set (NIST05), but worse than dynamic adaptation on the two mixed-domain sets.

model	dev	test		
	nist04-mix	nist05	nist06-nist	nist06-gale
baseline	31.9	30.4	27.6	12.9
cross LM	n/a	31.2	27.8	12.5
LM	32.8	30.8	28.6	13.4
TM	32.4	30.7	27.6	12.8
LM+TM	33.4	30.8	28.5	13.0

Table 6: Dynamic adaptation results, using src-side EM distances.

model	NIST05
baseline	30.3
cross EM-src LM	31.2
cross EM-src TM	30.9
hybrid EM-src LM	30.9
hybrid EM-src TM	30.7

Table 7: Hybrid adaptation results.

Table 7 shows results for the hybrid approach described at the end of section 3.5.2: global weights are learned on NIST04-nw, but linear weights are derived dynamically from the current test file. Performance drops slightly compared to pure cross-domain adaptation, indicating that it may be important to have a good fit between global and mixture weights.

4.4 Source Granularity

The results of the final experiment, to determine the effects of source granularity on dynamic adaptation, are shown in table 8. Source-side EM distances are applied to the whole test set, to genres within the set, and to each document individually. Global weights were tuned specifically for each of these conditions. There appears to be little difference among these approaches, although genre-based adaptation perhaps has a slight advantage.

granularity	dev	test		
	nist04-mix	nist05	nist06-nist	nist06-gale
baseline	31.9	30.4	27.6	12.9
file	32.4	30.8	28.6	13.4
genre	32.5	31.1	28.9	13.2
document	32.9	30.9	28.6	13.4

Table 8: The effects of source granularity on dynamic adaptation.

5 Related Work

Mixture modeling is a standard technique in machine learning (Hastie et al., 2001). It has been widely used to adapt language models for speech recognition and other applications, for instance using cross-domain topic mixtures, (Iyer and Ostendorf, 1999), dynamic topic mixtures (Kneser and Steinbiss, 1993), hierachical mixtures (Florian and Yarowsky, 1999), and cache mixtures (Kuhn and De Mori, 1990).

Most previous work on adaptive SMT focuses on the use of IR techniques to identify a relevant subset of the training corpus from which an adapted model can be learned. Byrne et al (2003) use cosine distance from the current source document to find relevant parallel texts for training an adapted translation model, with background information for smoothing alignments. Hildebrand et al (1995) describe a similar approach, but apply it at the sentence level, and use it for language model as well as translation model adaptation. They rely on a perplexity heuristic to determine an optimal size for the relevant subset. Zhao et al (2004) apply a slightly different sentence-level strategy to language model adaptation, first generating an nbest list with a baseline system, then finding similar sentences in a monolingual target-language corpus. This approach has the advantage of not limiting LM adaptation to a parallel corpus, but the disadvantage of requiring two translation passes (one to generate the nbest lists, and another to translate with the adapted model).

Ueffing (2006) describes a *self-training* approach that also uses a two-pass algorithm. A baseline system generates translations that, after confidence filtering, are used to construct a parallel corpus based on the test set. Standard phrase-extraction techniques are then applied to extract an adapted phrase table from the system's own output.

Finally, Zhang et al (2006) cluster the parallel training corpus using an algorithm that heuristically minimizes the average entropy of source-side and target-side language models over a fixed number of clusters. Each source sentence is then decoded using the language model trained on the cluster that assigns highest likelihood to that sentence.

The work we present here is complementary to both the IR approaches and Ueffing's method because it provides a way of exploiting a pre-established corpus division. This has the potential to allow sentences having little surface similarity to the current source text to contribute statistics that may be relevant to its translation, for instance by raising the probability of rare but pertinent words. Our work can also be seen as extending all previous approaches in that it assigns weights to components depending on their degree of relevance, rather than assuming a binary distinction between relevant and non-relevant components.

6 Conclusion and Future Work

We have investigated a number of approaches to mixture-based adaptation using genres for Chinese to English translation. The most successful is to weight component models in proportion to maximum-likelihood (EM) weights for the current text given an ngram language model mixture trained on corpus components. This resulted in gains of around one BLEU point. A more sophisticated approach that attempts to transform and combine multiple distance metrics did not yield positive results, probably due to an unsucessful optmization procedure.

Other conclusions are: linear mixtures are more tractable than loglinear ones; LM-based metrics are better than VS-based ones; LM adaptation works well, and adding an adapted TM yields no improvement; cross-domain adaptation is optimal, but dynamic adaptation is a good fallback strategy; and source granularity at the genre level is better than the document or test-set level.

In future work, we plan to improve the optimization procedure for parameterized weight functions. We will also look at bilingual metrics for cross-domain adaptation, and investigate better combinations of cross-domain and dynamic adaptation.

References

Peter F. Brown, Stephen A. Della Pietra, Vincent Della J. Pietra, and Robert L. Mercer. 1993. The mathematics of Machine Translation: Parameter estimation. *Computational Linguistics*, 19(2):263–312, June.

W. Byrne, S. Khudanpur, W. Kim, S. Kumar, P. Pecina, P. Virga, P. Xu, and D. Yarowsky. 2003. The JHU 2003 Chinese-English Machine Translation System. In *MT Summit IX*, New Orleans, September.

S. Deerwester, S. T. Dumais, G. W. Furnas, T. K. Landauer, and R. Harshman. 1990. Indexing by latent semantic analysis. *JASIS*, 41(6):391–407.

Radu Florian and David Yarowsky. 1999. Dynamic nonlocal language modeling via hierarchical topic-based adaptation. In *ACL 1999*, pages 167–174, College Park, Maryland, June.

George Foster, Roland Kuhn, and Howard Johnson. 2006. Phrasetable smoothing for statistical machine translation. In *EMNLP 2006*, Sydney, Australia.

Trevor Hastie, Robert Tibshirani, and Jerome Friedman. 2001. *The Elements of Statistical Learning*. Springer.

Almut Silja Hildebrand, Matthias Eck, Stephan Vogel, and Alex Waibel. 1995. Adaptation of the translation model for statistical machine translation based on information retrieval. In *EAMT 1995*, Budapest, May.

R. Iyer and M. Ostendorf. 1999. Modeling long distance dependence in language: Topic mixtures vs. dynamic cache models. In *IEEE Trans on Speech and Language Processing, 1999*.

Frederick Jelinek. 1997. *Statistical Methods for Speech Recognition*. MIT Press.

Reinhard Kneser and Volker Steinbiss. 1993. On the dynamic adaptation of stochastic language models. In *ICASSP 1993*, pages 586–589, Minneapolis, Minnesota. IEEE.

Philipp Koehn, Franz Josef Och, and Daniel Marcu. 2003. Statistical phrase-based translation. In *NAACL 2003*, pages 127–133.

Roland Kuhn and Renato De Mori. 1990. A cache-based natural language model for speech recognition. *IEEE Trans on PAMI*, 12(6):570–583, June.

Percy Liang, Alexandre Bouchard-Côté, Dan Klein, and Ben Taskar. 2006. An end-to-end discriminative approach to machine translation. In *ACL 2006*

Franz Josef Och. 2003. Minimum error rate training for statistical machine translation. In *ACL 2003*, Sapporo, July.

Kishore Papineni, Salim Roukos, Todd Ward, and Wei-Jing Zhu. 2001. BLEU: A method for automatic evaluation of Machine Translation. Technical Report RC22176, IBM, September.

William H. Press, Saul A. Teukolsky, William T. Vetterling, and Brian P. Flannery. 2002. *Numerical Recipes in C++*. Cambridge University Press, Cambridge, UK.

Christoph Tillmann and Tong Zhang. 2006. A discriminative global training algorithm for statistical MT. In *ACL 2006*.

Nicola Ueffing. 2006. Self-training for machine translation. In *NIPS 2006 Workshop on MLIA*, Whistler, B.C., December.

Richard Zens and Hermann Ney. 2004. Improvements in phrase-based statistical machine translation. In *HLT/NAACL 2004*, Boston, May.

R. Zhang, H. Yamamoto, M. Paul, H. Okuma, K. Yasuda, Y. Lepage, E. Denoual, D. Mochihashi, A. Finch, and E. Sumita. 2006. The NiCT-ATR statistical machine translation system for the IWSLT 2006 evaluation. In *IWSLT 2006*.

Bing Zhao, Matthias Eck, and Stephan Vogel. 2004. Language model adaptation for statistical machine translation with structured query models. In *COLING 2004*, Geneva, August.

(Meta-) Evaluation of Machine Translation

Chris Callison-Burch
Johns Hopkins University
ccb@clsp.jhu.edu

Cameron Fordyce
CELCT
fordyce@celct.it

Philipp Koehn
University of Edinburgh
pkoehn@inf.ed.ac.uk

Christof Monz
Queen Mary, University of London
christof@dcs.qmul.ac.uk

Josh Schroeder
University of Edinburgh
j.schroeder@ed.ac.uk

Abstract

This paper evaluates the translation quality of machine translation systems for 8 language pairs: translating French, German, Spanish, and Czech to English and back. We carried out an extensive human evaluation which allowed us not only to rank the different MT systems, but also to perform higher-level analysis of the evaluation process. We measured timing and intra- and inter-annotator agreement for three types of subjective evaluation. We measured the correlation of automatic evaluation metrics with human judgments. This meta-evaluation reveals surprising facts about the most commonly used methodologies.

1 Introduction

This paper presents the results for the shared translation task of the 2007 ACL Workshop on Statistical Machine Translation. The goals of this paper are twofold: First, we evaluate the shared task entries in order to determine which systems produce translations with the highest quality. Second, we analyze the evaluation measures themselves in order to try to determine "best practices" when evaluating machine translation research.

Previous ACL Workshops on Machine Translation were more limited in scope (Koehn and Monz, 2005; Koehn and Monz, 2006). The 2005 workshop evaluated translation quality only in terms of Bleu score. The 2006 workshop additionally included a limited manual evaluation in the style of NIST machine translation evaluation workshop. Here we apply eleven different automatic evaluation metrics, and conduct three different types of manual evaluation.

Beyond examining the quality of translations produced by various systems, we were interested in examining the following questions about evaluation methodologies: How consistent are people when they judge translation quality? To what extent do they agree with other annotators? Can we improve human evaluation? Which automatic evaluation metrics correlate most strongly with human judgments of translation quality?

This paper is organized as follows:

- Section 2 gives an overview of the shared task. It describes the training and test data, reviews the baseline system, and lists the groups that participated in the task.
- Section 3 describes the manual evaluation. We performed three types of evaluation: scoring with five point scales, relative ranking of translations of sentences, and ranking of translations of phrases.
- Section 4 lists the eleven different automatic evaluation metrics which were also used to score the shared task submissions.
- Section 5 presents the results of the shared task, giving scores for each of the systems in each of the different conditions.
- Section 6 provides an evaluation of the different types of evaluation, giving intra- and

Proceedings of the Second Workshop on Statistical Machine Translation, pages 136–158,
Prague, June 2007.

inter-annotator agreement figures for the manual evaluation, and correlation numbers for the automatic metrics.

2 Shared task overview

This year's shared task changed in some aspects from last year's:

- We gave preference to the manual evaluation of system output in the ranking of systems. Manual evaluation was done by the volunteers from participating groups and others. Additionally, there were three modalities of manual evaluation.

- Automatic metrics were also used to rank the systems. In total eleven metrics were applied, and their correlation with the manual scores was measured.

- As in 2006, translation was *from* English, and *into* English. English was again paired with German, French, and Spanish. We additionally included Czech (which was fitting given the location of the WS).

Similar to the IWSLT International Workshop on Spoken Language Translation (Eck and Hori, 2005; Paul, 2006), and the NIST Machine Translation Evaluation Workshop (Lee, 2006) we provide the shared task participants with a common set of training and test data for all language pairs. The major part of data comes from current and upcoming full releases of the Europarl data set (Koehn, 2005).

2.1 Description of the Data

The data used in this year's shared task was similar to the data used in last year's shared task. This year's data included training and development sets for the News Commentary data, which was the surprise out-of-domain test set last year.

The majority of the training data for the Spanish, French, and German tasks was drawn from a new version of the Europarl multilingual corpus. Additional training data was taken from the News Commentary corpus. Czech language resources were drawn from the News Commentary data. Additional resources for Czech came from the CzEng Parallel Corpus (Bojar and Žabokrtský, 2006). Overall, there are over 30 million words of training data per language from the Europarl corpus and 1 million words from the News Commentary corpus. Figure 1 provides some statistics about the corpora used this year.

2.2 Baseline system

To lower the barrier of entrance to the competition, we provided a complete baseline MT system, along with data resources. To summarize, we provided:

- sentence-aligned training corpora
- development and dev-test sets
- language models trained for each language
- an open source decoder for phrase-based SMT called Moses (Koehn et al., 2006), which replaces the Pharaoh decoder (Koehn, 2004)
- a training script to build models for Moses

The performance of this baseline system is similar to the best submissions in last year's shared task.

2.3 Test Data

The test data was again drawn from a segment of the Europarl corpus from the fourth quarter of 2000, which is excluded from the training data. Participants were also provided with three sets of parallel text to be used for system development and tuning.

In addition to the Europarl test set, we also collected editorials from the Project Syndicate website[1], which are published in all the five languages of the shared task. We aligned the texts at a sentence level across all five languages, resulting in 2,007 sentences per language. For statistics on this test set, refer to Figure 1.

The News Commentary test set differs from the Europarl data in various ways. The text type are editorials instead of speech transcripts. The domain is general politics, economics and science. However, it is also mostly political content (even if not focused on the internal workings of the European Union) and opinion.

2.4 Participants

We received submissions from 15 groups from 14 institutions, as listed in Table 1. This is a slight

[1] `http://www.project-syndicate.com/`

Europarl Training corpus

	Spanish ↔ English	French ↔ English	German ↔ English
Sentences	1,259,914	1,288,901	1,264,825
Foreign words	33,159,337	33,176,243	29,582,157
English words	31,813,692	32,615,285	31,929,435
Distinct foreign words	345,944	344,287	510,544
Distinct English words	266,976	268,718	250,295

News Commentary Training corpus

	Spanish ↔ English	French ↔ English	German ↔ English	Czech ↔ English
Sentences	51,613	43,194	59,975	57797
Foreign words	1,263,067	1,028,672	1,297,673	1,083,122
English words	1,076,273	906,593	1,238,274	1,188,006
Distinct foreign words	84,303	68,214	115,589	142,146
Distinct English words	70,755	63,568	76,419	74,042

Language model data

	English	Spanish	French	German
Sentence	1,407,285	1,431,614	1,435,027	1,478,428
Words	34,539,822	36,426,542	35,595,199	32,356,475
Distinct words	280,546	385,796	361,205	558,377

Europarl test set

	English	Spanish	French	German
Sentences	2,000			
Words	53,531	55,380	53,981	49,259
Distinct words	8,558	10,451	10,186	11,106

News Commentary test set

	English	Spanish	French	German	Czech
Sentences	2,007				
Words	43,767	50,771	49,820	45,075	39,002
Distinct words	10,002	10,948	11,244	12,322	15,245

Figure 1: Properties of the training and test sets used in the shared task. The training data is drawn from the Europarl corpus and from the Project Syndicate, a web site which collects political commentary in multiple languages.

ID	Participant
cmu-uka	Carnegie Mellon University, USA (Paulik et al., 2007)
cmu-syntax	Carnegie Mellon University, USA (Zollmann et al., 2007)
cu	Charles University, Czech Republic (Bojar, 2007)
limsi	LIMSI-CNRS, France (Schwenk, 2007)
liu	University of Linköping, Sweden(Holmqvist et al., 2007)
nrc	National Research Council, Canada (Ueffing et al., 2007)
pct	a commercial MT provider from the Czech Republic
saar	Saarland University & DFKI, Germany (Chen et al., 2007)
systran	SYSTRAN, France & U. Edinburgh, UK (Dugast et al., 2007)
systran-nrc	National Research Council, Canada (Simard et al., 2007)
ucb	University of California at Berkeley, USA (Nakov and Hearst, 2007)
uedin	University of Edinburgh, UK (Koehn and Schroeder, 2007)
umd	University of Maryland, USA (Dyer, 2007)
upc	University of Catalonia, Spain (Costa-Jussà and Fonollosa, 2007)
upv	University of Valencia, Spain (Civera and Juan, 2007)

Table 1: Participants in the shared task. Not all groups participated in all translation directions.

increase over last year's shared task where submissions were received from 14 groups from 11 institutions. Of the 11 groups that participated in last year's shared task, 6 groups returned this year.

This year, most of these groups follow a phrase-based statistical approach to machine translation. However, several groups submitted results from systems that followed a hybrid approach.

While building a machine translation system is a serious undertaking we hope to attract more newcomers to the field by keeping the barrier of entry as low as possible. The creation of parallel corpora such as the Europarl, the CzEng, and the News Commentary corpora should help in this direction by providing freely available language resources for building systems. The creation of an open source baseline system should also go a long way towards achieving this goal.

For more on the participating systems, please refer to the respective system description in the proceedings of the workshop.

3 Human evaluation

We evaluated the shared task submissions using both manual evaluation and automatic metrics. While automatic measures are an invaluable tool for the day-to-day development of machine translation systems, they are an imperfect substitute for human assessment of translation quality. Manual evaluation is time consuming and expensive to perform, so comprehensive comparisons of multiple systems are rare. For our manual evaluation we distributed the workload across a number of people, including participants in the shared task, interested volunteers, and a small number of paid annotators. More than 100 people participated in the manual evaluation, with 75 of those people putting in at least an hour's worth of effort. A total of 330 hours of labor was invested, nearly doubling last year's all-volunteer effort which yielded 180 hours of effort.

Beyond simply ranking the shared task submissions, we had a number of scientific goals for the manual evaluation. Firstly, we wanted to collect data which could be used to assess how well automatic metrics correlate with human judgments. Secondly, we wanted to examine different types of manual evaluation and assess which was the best. A number of criteria could be adopted for choosing among different types of manual evaluation: the ease with which people are able to perform the task, their agreement with other annotators, their reliability when asked to repeat judgments, or the number of judgments which can be collected in a fixed time period.

There are a range of possibilities for how human

evaluation of machine translation can be done. For instance, it can be evaluated with reading comprehension tests (Jones et al., 2005), or by assigning subjective scores to the translations of individual sentences (LDC, 2005). We examined three different ways of manually evaluating machine translation quality:

- Assigning scores based on five point adequacy and fluency scales
- Ranking translated sentences relative to each other
- Ranking the translations of syntactic constituents drawn from the source sentence

3.1 Fluency and adequacy

The most widely used methodology when manually evaluating MT is to assign values from two five point scales representing *fluency* and *adequacy*. These scales were developed for the annual NIST Machine Translation Evaluation Workshop by the Linguistics Data Consortium (LDC, 2005).

The five point scale for adequacy indicates how much of the meaning expressed in the reference translation is also expressed in a hypothesis translation:

5 = All
4 = Most
3 = Much
2 = Little
1 = None

The second five point scale indicates how fluent the translation is. When translating into English the values correspond to:

5 = Flawless English
4 = Good English
3 = Non-native English
2 = Disfluent English
1 = Incomprehensible

Separate scales for fluency and adequacy were developed under the assumption that a translation might be disfluent but contain all the information from the source. However, in principle it seems that people have a hard time separating these two aspects of translation. The high correlation between people's fluency and adequacy scores (given in Tables 17 and 18) indicate that the distinction might be false.

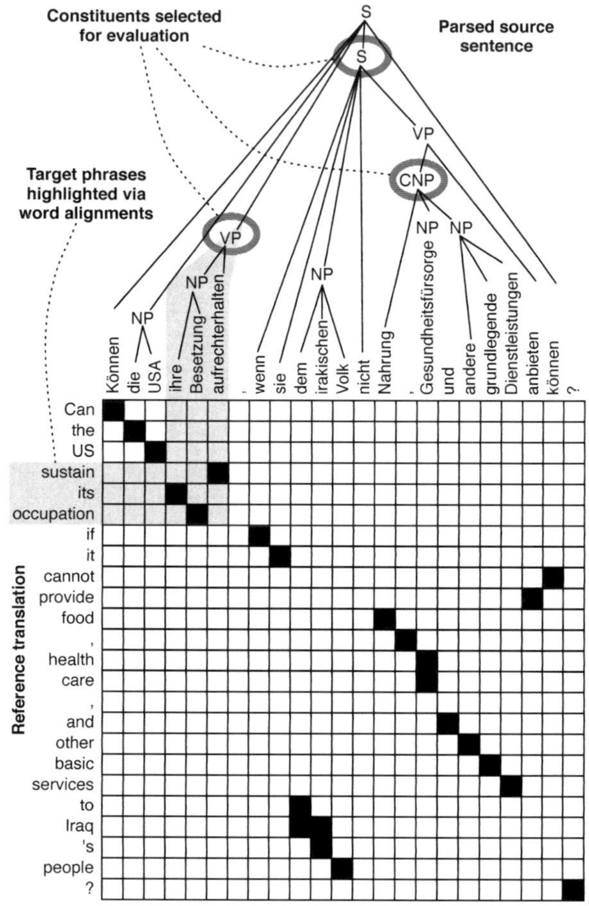

Figure 2: In constituent-based evaluation, the source sentence was parsed, and automatically aligned with the reference translation and systems' translations

Another problem with the scores is that there are no clear guidelines on how to assign values to translations. No instructions are given to evaluators in terms of how to quantify meaning, or how many grammatical errors (or what sort) separates the different levels of fluency. Because of this many judges either develop their own rules of thumb, or use the scales as relative rather than absolute. These are borne out in our analysis of inter-annotator agreement in Section 6.

3.2 Ranking translations of sentences

Because fluency and adequacy were seemingly difficult things for judges to agree on, and because many people from last year's workshop seemed to be using them as a way of ranking translations, we decided to try a separate evaluation where people were simply asked to rank translations. The instructions for this task were:

> Rank each whole sentence translation from Best to Worst relative to the other choices (ties are allowed).

These instructions were just as minimal as for fluency and adequacy, but the task was considerably simplified. Rather than having to assign each translation a value along an arbitrary scale, people simply had to compare different translations of a single sentence and rank them.

3.3 Ranking translations of syntactic constituents

In addition to having judges rank the translations of whole sentences, we also conducted a pilot study of a new type of evaluation methodology, which we call *constituent-based evaluation*. In our constituent-based evaluation we parsed the source language sentence, selected constituents from the tree, and had people judge the translations of those syntactic phrases. In order to draw judges' attention to these regions, we highlighted the selected source phrases and the corresponding phrases in the translations. The corresponding phrases in the translations were located via automatic word alignments.

Figure 2 illustrates the constituent based evaluation when applied to a German source sentence. The German source sentence is parsed, and various phrases are selected for evaluation. Word alignments are created between the source sentence and the reference translation (shown), and the source sentence and each of the system translations (not shown). We parsed the test sentences for each of the languages aside from Czech. We used Cowan and Collins (2005)'s parser for Spanish, Arun and Keller (2005)'s for French, Dubey (2005)'s for German, and Bikel (2002)'s for English.

The word alignments were created with Giza++ (Och and Ney, 2003) applied to a parallel corpus containing 200,000 sentence pairs of the training data, plus sets of 4,007 sentence pairs created by pairing the test sentences with the reference translations, and the test sentences paired with each of the system translations. The phrases in the translations were located using techniques from phrase-based statistical machine translation which extract phrase pairs from word alignments (Koehn et al., 2003; Och and Ney, 2004). Because the word-alignments were created automatically, and because the phrase extraction is heuristic, the phrases that were selected may not exactly correspond to the translations of the selected source phrase. We noted this in the instructions to judges:

> Rank each constituent translation from Best to Worst relative to the other choices (ties are allowed). Grade **only the highlighted part** of each translation.
>
> *Please note that segments are selected automatically, and they should be taken as an approximate guide. They might include extra words that are not in the actual alignment, or miss words on either end.*

The criteria that we used to select which constituents were to be evaluated were:

- The constituent could not be the whole source sentence
- The constituent had to be longer three words, and be no longer than 15 words
- The constituent had to have a corresponding phrase with a consistent word alignment in each of the translations

The final criterion helped reduce the number of alignment errors.

3.4 Collecting judgments

We collected judgments using a web-based tool. Shared task participants were each asked to judge 200 sets of sentences. The sets consisted of 5 system outputs, as shown in Figure 3. The judges were presented with batches of each type of evaluation. We presented them with five screens of adequacy/fluency scores, five screens of sentence rankings, and ten screens of constituent rankings. The order of the types of evaluation were randomized.

In order to measure intra-annotator agreement 10% of the items were repeated and evaluated twice by each judge. In order to measure inter-annotator agreement 40% of the items were randomly drawn from a common pool that was shared across all

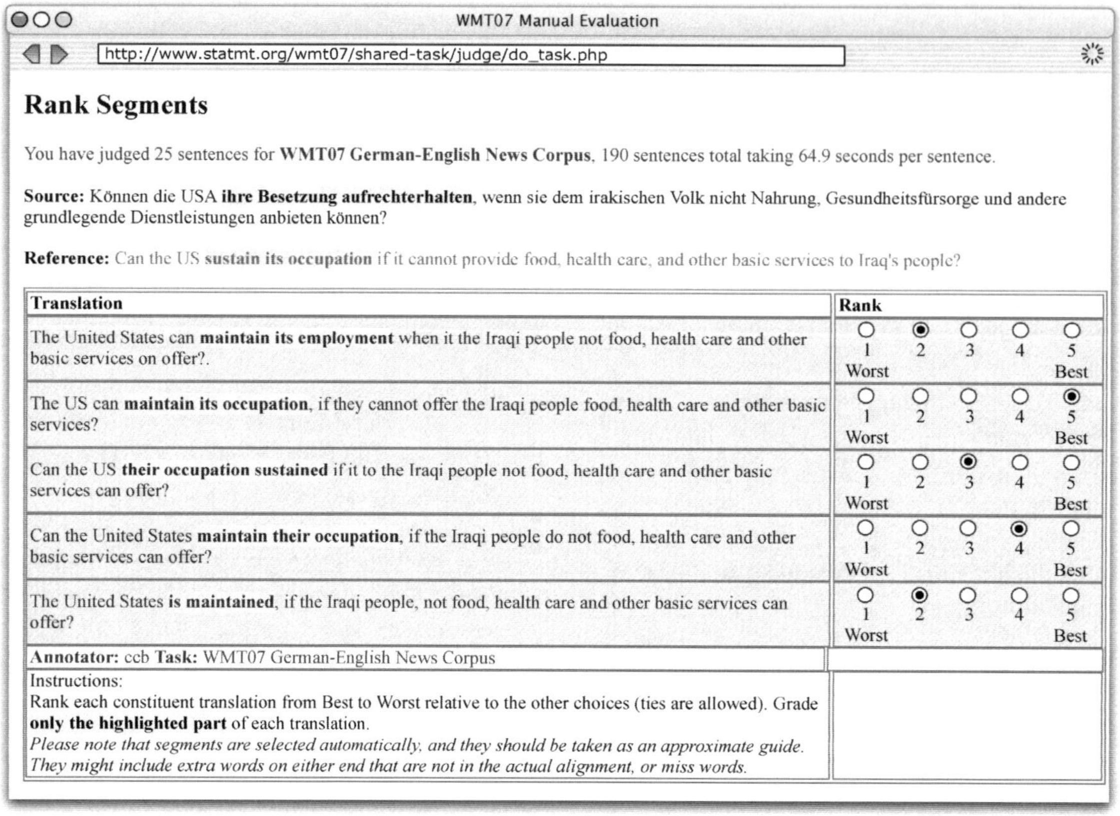

Figure 3: For each of the types of evaluation, judges were shown screens containing up to five different system translations, along with the source sentence and reference translation.

annotators so that we would have items that were judged by multiple annotators.

Judges were allowed to select whichever data set they wanted, and to evaluate translations into whatever languages they were proficient in. Shared task participants were excluded from judging their own systems.

Table 2 gives a summary of the number of judgments that we collected for translations of individual sentences. Since we had 14 translation tasks and four different types of scores, there were 55 different conditions.[2] In total we collected over 81,000 judgments. Despite the large number of conditions we managed to collect more than 1,000 judgments for most of them. This provides a rich source of data for analyzing the quality of translations produced by different systems, the different types of human evaluation, and the correlation of automatic metrics with human judgments.[3]

[2]We did not perform a constituent-based evaluation for Czech to English because we did not have a syntactic parser for Czech. We considered adapting our method to use Bojar (2004)'s dependency parser for Czech, but did not have the time.

[3]The judgment data along with all system translations are available at `http://www.statmt.org/wmt07/`

4 Automatic evaluation

The past two ACL workshops on machine translation used Bleu as the sole automatic measure of translation quality. Bleu was used exclusively since it is the most widely used metric in the field and has been shown to correlate with human judgments of translation quality in many instances (Doddington, 2002; Coughlin, 2003; Przybocki, 2004). However, recent work suggests that Bleu's correlation with human judgments may not be as strong as previously thought (Callison-Burch et al., 2006). The results of last year's workshop further suggested that Bleu systematically underestimated the quality of rule-based machine translation systems (Koehn and Monz, 2006).

We used the manual evaluation data as a means of testing the correlation of a range of automatic metrics in addition to Bleu. In total we used eleven different automatic evaluation measures to rank the shared task submissions. They are:

- Meteor (Banerjee and Lavie, 2005)—Meteor measures precision and recall of unigrams when comparing a hypothesis translation

Language Pair	Test Set	Adequacy	Fluency	Rank	Constituent
English-German	Europarl	1,416	1,418	1,419	2,626
	News Commentary	1,412	1,413	1,412	2,755
German-English	Europarl	1,525	1,521	1,514	2,999
	News Commentary	1,626	1,620	1,601	3,084
English-Spanish	Europarl	1,000	1,003	1,064	1,001
	News Commentary	1,272	1,272	1,238	1,595
Spanish-English	Europarl	1,174	1,175	1,224	1,898
	News Commentary	947	949	922	1,339
English-French	Europarl	773	772	769	1,456
	News Commentary	729	735	728	1,313
French-English	Europarl	834	833	830	1,641
	News Commentary	1,041	1,045	1,035	2,036
English-Czech	News Commentary	2,303	2,304	2,331	3,968
Czech-English	News Commentary	1,711	1,711	1,733	0
	Totals	**17,763**	**17,771**	**17,820**	**27,711**

Table 2: The number of items that were judged for each task during the manual evaluation

against a reference. It flexibly matches words using stemming and WordNet synonyms. Its flexible matching was extended to French, Spanish, German and Czech for this workshop (Lavie and Agarwal, 2007).

- Bleu (Papineni et al., 2002)—Bleu is currently the *de facto* standard in machine translation evaluation. It calculates n-gram precision and a brevity penalty, and can make use of multiple reference translations as a way of capturing some of the allowable variation in translation. We use a single reference translation in our experiments.

- GTM (Melamed et al., 2003)—GTM generalizes precision, recall, and F-measure to measure overlap between strings, rather than overlap between bags of items. An "exponent" parameter which controls the relative importance of word order. A value of 1.0 reduces GTM to ordinary unigram overlap, with higher values emphasizing order.[4]

- Translation Error Rate (Snover et al., 2006)—TER calculates the number of edits required to change a hypothesis translation into a reference translation. The possible edits in TER include insertion, deletion, and substitution of single words, and an edit which moves sequences of contiguous words.

- ParaEval precision and ParaEval recall (Zhou et al., 2006)–ParaEval matches hypothesis and reference translations using paraphrases that are extracted from parallel corpora in an unsupervised fashion (Bannard and Callison-Burch, 2005). It calculates precision and recall using a unigram counting strategy.

- Dependency overlap (Amigó et al., 2006)—This metric uses dependency trees for the hypothesis and reference translations, by computing the average overlap between words in the two trees which are dominated by grammatical relationships of the same type.

- Semantic role overlap (Giménez and Màrquez, 2007)—This metric calculates the lexical overlap between semantic roles (i.e., semantic arguments or adjuncts) of the same type in the the hypothesis and reference translations. It uniformly averages lexical overlap over all semantic role types.

[4]The GTM scores presented here are an F-measure with a weight of 0.1, which counts recall at 10x the level of precision. The exponent is set at 1.2, which puts a mild preference towards items with words in the correct order. These parameters could be optimized empirically for better results.

- Word Error Rate over verbs (Popovic and Ney, 2007)—WER' creates a new reference and a new hypothesis for each POS class by extracting all words belonging to this class, and then to calculate the standard WER. We show results for this metric over verbs.

- Maximum correlation training on adequacy and on fluency (Liu and Gildea, 2007)—a linear combination of different evaluation metrics (Bleu, Meteor, Rouge, WER, and stochastic iterative alignment) with weights set to maximize Pearson's correlation with adequacy and fluency judgments. Weights were trained on WMT-06 data.

The scores produced by these are given in the tables at the end of the paper, and described in Section 5. We measured the correlation of the automatic evaluation metrics with the different types of human judgments on 12 data conditions, and report these in Section 6.

5 Shared task results

The results of the human evaluation are given in Tables 9, 10, 11 and 12. Each of those tables present four scores:

- FLUENCY and ADEQUACY are normalized versions of the five point scores described in Section 3.1. The tables report an average of the normalized scores.[5]

- RANK is the average number of times that a system was judged to be better than any other system in the sentence ranking evaluation described in Section 3.2.

- CONSTITUENT is the average number of times that a system was judged to be better than any other system in the constituent-based evaluation described in Section 3.3.

There was reasonably strong agreement between these four measures at which of the entries was the best in each data condition. There was complete agreement between them in 5 of the 14 conditions, and agreement between at least three of them in 10 of the 14 cases.

[5]Since different annotators can vary widely in how they assign fluency and adequacy scores, we normalized these scores on a per-judge basis using the method suggested by Blatz et al. (2003) in Chapter 5, page 97.

SYSTRAN (systran)	32%
University of Edinburgh (uedin)	20%
University of Catalonia (upc)	15%
LIMSI-CNRS (limsi)	13%
University of Maryland (umd)	5%
National Research Council of Canada's joint entry with SYSTRAN (systran-nrc)	5%
Commercial Czech-English system (pct)	5%
University of Valencia (upv)	2%
Charles University (cu)	2%

Table 3: The proportion of time that participants' entries were top-ranked in the human evaluation

University of Edinburgh (uedin)	41%
University of Catalonia (upc)	12%
LIMSI-CNRS (limsi)	12%
University of Maryland (umd)	9%
Charles University (cu)	4%
Carnegie Mellon University (cmu-syntax)	4%
Carnegie Mellon University (cmu-uka)	4%
University of California at Berkeley (ucb)	3%
National Research Council's joint entry with SYSTRAN (systran-nrc)	2%
SYSTRAN (systran)	2%
Saarland University (saar)	0.8%

Table 4: The proportion of time that participants' entries were top-ranked by the automatic evaluation metrics

Table 3 gives a summary of how often different participants' entries were ranked #1 by any of the four human evaluation measures. SYSTRAN's entries were ranked the best most often, followed by University of Edinburgh, University of Catalonia and LIMSI-CNRS.

The following systems were the best performing for the different language pairs: SYSTRAN was ranked the highest in German-English, University of Catalonia was ranked the highest in Spanish-English, LIMSI-CNRS was ranked highest in French-English, and the University of Maryland and a commercial system were the highest for

Evaluation type	$P(A)$	$P(E)$	K
Fluency (absolute)	.400	.2	.250
Adequacy (absolute)	.380	.2	.226
Fluency (relative)	.520	.333	.281
Adequacy (relative)	.538	.333	.307
Sentence ranking	.582	.333	.373
Constituent ranking	.693	.333	.540
Constituent ranking (w/identical constituents)	.712	.333	.566

Table 5: Kappa coefficient values representing the inter-annotator agreement for the different types of manual evaluation

Evaluation type	$P(A)$	$P(E)$	K
Fluency (absolute)	.630	.2	.537
Adequacy (absolute)	.574	.2	.468
Fluency (relative)	.690	.333	.535
Adequacy (relative)	.696	.333	.544
Sentence ranking	.749	.333	.623
Constituent ranking	.825	.333	.738
Constituent ranking (w/identical constituents)	.842	.333	.762

Table 6: Kappa coefficient values for intra-annotator agreement for the different types of manual evaluation

Czech-English.

While we consider the human evaluation to be primary, it is also interesting to see how the entries were ranked by the various automatic evaluation metrics. The complete set of results for the automatic evaluation are presented in Tables 13, 14, 15, and 16. An aggregate summary is provided in Table 4. The automatic evaluation metrics strongly favor the University of Edinburgh, which garners 41% of the top-ranked entries (which is partially due to the fact it was entered in every language pair). Significantly, the automatic metrics disprefer SYSTRAN, which was strongly favored in the human evaluation.

6 Meta-evaluation

In addition to evaluating the translation quality of the shared task entries, we also performed a "meta-evaluation" of our evaluation methodologies.

6.1 Inter- and Intra-annotator agreement

We measured pairwise agreement among annotators using the kappa coefficient (K) which is widely used in computational linguistics for measuring agreement in category judgments (Carletta, 1996). It is defined as

$$K = \frac{P(A) - P(E)}{1 - P(E)}$$

where $P(A)$ is the proportion of times that the annotators agree, and $P(E)$ is the proportion of time that they would agree by chance. We define chance agreement for fluency and adequacy as $\frac{1}{5}$, since they are based on five point scales, and for ranking as $\frac{1}{3}$ since there are three possible out comes when ranking the output of a pair of systems: $A > B$, $A = B$, $A < B$.

For inter-annotator agreement we calculated $P(A)$ for fluency and adequacy by examining all items that were annotated by two or more annotators, and calculating the proportion of time they assigned identical scores to the same items. For the ranking tasks we calculated $P(A)$ by examining all pairs of systems which had been judged by two or more judges, and calculated the proportion of time that they agreed that $A > B$, $A = B$, or $A < B$. For intra-annotator agreement we did similarly, but gathered items that were annotated on multiple occasions by a single annotator.

Table 5 gives K values for inter-annotator agreement, and Table 6 gives K values for intra-annoator agreement. These give an indication of how often different judges agree, and how often single judges are consistent for repeated judgments, respectively. The interpretation of Kappa varies, but according to Landis and Koch (1977) $0 - -.2$ is slight, $.21 - -.4$ is fair, $.41 - -.6$ is moderate, $.61 - -.8$ is substantial and the rest almost perfect.

The K values for fluency and adequacy should give us pause about using these metrics in the future. When we analyzed them as they are intended to be—scores classifying the translations of sentences into different types—the inter-annotator agreement was barely considered *fair*, and the intra-annotator agreement was only *moderate*. Even when we reassessed fluency and adequacy as relative ranks the agreements increased only minimally.

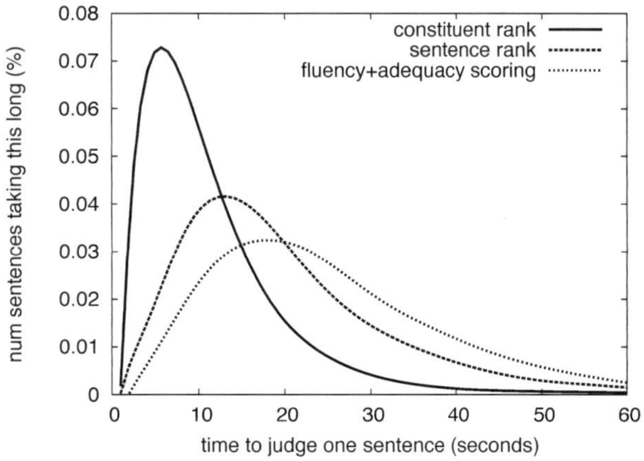

Figure 4: Distributions of the amount of time it took to judge single sentences for the three types of manual evaluation

The agreement on the other two types of manual evaluation that we introduced were considerably better. The both the sentence and constituent ranking had *moderate* inter-annotator agreement and *substantial* intra-annotator agreement. Because the constituent ranking examined the translations of short phrases, often times all systems produced the same translations. Since these trivially increased agreement (since they would always be equally ranked) we also evaluated the inter- and intra-annotator agreement when those items were excluded. The agreement remained very high for constituent-based evaluation.

6.2 Timing

We used the web interface to collect timing information. The server recorded the time when a set of sentences was given to a judge and the time when the judge returned the sentences. We divided the time that it took to do a set by the number of sentences in the set. The average amount of time that it took to assign fluency and adequacy to a single sentence was 26 seconds.[6] The average amount of time it took to rank a sentence in a set was 20 seconds. The average amount of time it took to rank a highlighted constituent was 11 seconds. Figure 4 shows the distribution of times for these tasks.

[6]Sets which took longer than 5 minutes were excluded from these calculations, because there was a strong chance that annotators were interrupted while completing the task.

These timing figures are promising because they indicate that the tasks which the annotators were the most reliable on (constituent ranking and sentence ranking) were also much quicker to complete than the ones that they were unreliable on (assigning fluency and adequacy scores). This suggests that fluency and adequacy should be replaced with ranking tasks in future evaluation exercises.

6.3 Correlation between automatic metrics and human judgments

To measure the correlation of the automatic metrics with the human judgments of translation quality we used Spearman's rank correlation coefficient ρ. We opted for Spearman rather than Pearson because it makes fewer assumptions about the data. Importantly, it can be applied to ordinal data (such as the fluency and adequacy scales). Spearman's rank correlation coefficient is equivalent to Pearson correlation on ranks.

After the raw scores that were assigned to systems by an automatic metric and by one of our manual evaluation techniques have been converted to ranks, we can calculate ρ using the simplified equation:

$$\rho = 1 - \frac{6 \sum d_i^2}{n(n^2 - 1)}$$

where d_i is the difference between the rank for system$_i$ and n is the number of systems. The possible values of ρ range between 1 (where all systems are ranked in the same order) and -1 (where the systems are ranked in the reverse order). Thus an automatic evaluation metric with a higher value for ρ is making predictions that are more similar to the human judgments than an automatic evaluation metric with a lower ρ.

Table 17 reports ρ for the metrics which were used to evaluate translations into English.[7]. Table 7 summarizes the results by averaging the correlation numbers by equally weighting each of the data conditions. The table ranks the automatic evaluation metrics based on how well they correlated with human judgments. While these are based on a relatively few number of items, and while we have not performed any tests to determine whether the differences in ρ are statistically significant, the results

[7]The Czech-English conditions were excluded since there were so few systems

are nevertheless interesting, since three metrics have higher correlation than Bleu:

- Semantic role overlap (Giménez and Màrquez, 2007), which makes its debut in the proceedings of this workshop
- ParaEval measuring recall (Zhou et al., 2006), which has a model of allowable variation in translation that uses automatically generated paraphrases (Callison-Burch, 2007)
- Meteor (Banerjee and Lavie, 2005) which also allows variation by introducing synonyms and by flexibly matches words using stemming.

Tables 18 and 8 report ρ for the six metrics which were used to evaluate translations into the other languages. Here we find that Bleu and TER are the closest to human judgments, but that overall the correlations are much lower than for translations into English.

7 Conclusions

Similar to last year's workshop we carried out an extensive manual and automatic evaluation of machine translation performance for translating from four European languages into English, and vice versa. This year we substantially increased the number of automatic evaluation metrics and were also able to nearly double the efforts of producing the human judgments.

There were substantial differences in the results results of the human and automatic evaluations. We take the human judgments to be authoritative, and used them to evaluate the automatic metrics. We measured correlation using Spearman's coefficient and found that three less frequently used metrics were stronger predictors of human judgments than Bleu. They were: semantic role overlap (newly introduced in this workshop) ParaEval-recall and Meteor.

Although we do not claim that our observations are indisputably conclusive, they again indicate that the choice of automatic metric can have a significant impact on comparing systems. Understanding the exact causes of those differences still remains an important issue for future research.

metric	ADEQUACY	FLUENCY	RANK	CONSTITUENT	OVERALL
Semantic role overlap	.774	.839	.803	.741	.789
ParaEval-Recall	.712	.742	.768	.798	.755
Meteor	.701	.719	.745	.669	.709
Bleu	.690	.722	.672	.602	.671
1-TER	.607	.538	.520	.514	.644
Max adequ-correlation	.651	.657	.659	.534	.626
Max fluency correlation	.644	.653	.656	.512	.616
GTM	.655	.674	.616	.495	.610
Dependency overlap	.639	.644	.601	.512	.599
ParaEval-Precision	.639	.654	.610	.491	.598
1-WER of verbs	.378	.422	.431	.297	.382

Table 7: Average corrections for the different automatic metrics when they are used to evaluate translations into English

metric	ADEQUACY	FLUENCY	RANK	CONSTITUENT	OVERALL
Bleu	.657	.445	.352	.409	.466
1-TER	.589	.419	.361	.380	.437
Max fluency correlation	.534	.419	.368	.400	.430
Max adequ-correlation	.498	.414	.385	.409	.426
Meteor	.490	.356	.279	.304	.357
1-WER of verbs	.371	.304	.359	.359	.348

Table 8: Average corrections for the different automatic metrics when they are used to evaluate translations into the other languages

This year's evaluation also measured the agreement between human assessors by computing the Kappa coefficient. One striking observation is that inter-annotator agreement for fluency and adequacy can be called 'fair' at best. On the other hand, comparing systems by ranking them manually (constituents or entire sentences), resulted in much higher inter-annotator agreement.

Acknowledgments

This work was supported in part by the EuroMatrix project funded by the European Commission (6th Framework Programme), and in part by the GALE program of the US Defense Advanced Research Projects Agency, Contract No. HR0011-06-C-0022.

We are grateful to Jesús Giménez, Dan Melamed, Maja Popvic, Ding Liu, Liang Zhou, and Abhaya Agarwal for scoring the entries with their automatic evaluation metrics. Thanks to Brooke Cowan for parsing the Spanish test sentences, to Josh Albrecht for his script for normalizing fluency and adequacy on a per judge basis, and to Dan Melamed, Rebecca Hwa, Alon Lavie, Colin Bannard and Mirella Lapata for their advice about statistical tests.

References

Enrique Amigó, Jesús Giménez, Julio Gonzalo, and Lluís Màrquez. 2006. MT Evaluation: Human-Like vs. Human Acceptable. In *Proceedings of COLING-ACL06*.

Abhishek Arun and Frank Keller. 2005. Lexicalization in crosslinguistic probabilistic parsing: The case of French. In *Proceedings of ACL*.

Satanjeev Banerjee and Alon Lavie. 2005. Meteor: An automatic metric for MT evaluation with improved correlation with human judgments. In *Workshop on Intrinsic and Extrinsic Evaluation Measures for MT and/or Summarization*, Ann Arbor, Michigan.

Colin Bannard and Chris Callison-Burch. 2005. Paraphrasing with bilingual parallel corpora. In *ACL-2005*.

Dan Bikel. 2002. Design of a multi-lingual, parallel-processing statistical parsing engine. In *Proceedings of HLT*.

John Blatz, Erin Fitzgerald, George Foster, Simona Gandrabur, Cyril Goutte, Alex Kulesza, Alberto Sanchis, and Nicola Ueffing. 2003. Confidence estimation for machine translation. CLSP Summer Workshop Final Report WS2003, Johns Hopkins University.

Ondřej Bojar and Zdeněk Žabokrtský. 2006. CzEng: Czech-English Parallel Corpus, Release version 0.5. *Prague Bulletin of Mathematical Linguistics*, 86.

Ondřej Bojar. 2004. Problems of inducing large coverage constraint-based dependency grammar for Czech. In *Constraint Solving and Language Processing, CSLP 2004*, volume LNAI 3438. Springer.

Ondřej Bojar. 2007. English-to-Czech factored machine translation. In *Proceedings of the ACL-2007 Workshop on Statistical Machine Translation (WMT-07)*, Prague.

Chris Callison-Burch, Miles Osborne, and Philipp Koehn. 2006. Re-evaluating the role of Bleu in machine translation research. In *Proceedings of EACL*.

Chris Callison-Burch. 2007. *Paraphrasing and Translation*. Ph.D. thesis, University of Edinburgh, Scotland.

Jean Carletta. 1996. Assessing agreement on classification tasks: The kappa statistic. *Computational Linguistics*, 22(2):249–254.

Yu Chen, Andreas Eisele, Christian Federmann, Eva Hasler, Michael Jellinghaus, and Silke Theison. 2007. Multi-engine machine translation with an open-source decoder for statistical machine translation. In *Proceedings of the ACL-2007 Workshop on Statistical Machine Translation (WMT-07)*, Prague.

Jorge Civera and Alfons Juan. 2007. Domain adaptation in statistical machine translation with mixture modelling. In *Proceedings of the ACL-2007 Workshop on Statistical Machine Translation (WMT-07)*, Prague.

Marta R. Costa-Jussà and José A.R. Fonollosa. 2007. Analysis of statistical and morphological classes to generate weighted reordering hypotheses on a statistical machine translation system. In *Proceedings of the ACL-2007 Workshop on Statistical Machine Translation (WMT-07)*, Prague.

Deborah Coughlin. 2003. Correlating automated and human assessments of machine translation quality. In *Proceedings of MT Summit IX*.

Brooke Cowan and Michael Collins. 2005. Morphology and reranking for the statistical parsing of Spanish. In *Proceedings of EMNLP 2005*.

George Doddington. 2002. Automatic evaluation of machine translation quality using n-gram co-occurrence statistics. In *Human Language Technology: Notebook Proceedings*, pages 128–132, San Diego.

Amit Dubey. 2005. What to do when lexicalization fails: parsing German with suffix analysis and smoothing. In *Proceedings of ACL*.

Loïc Dugast, Jean Senellart, and Philipp Koehn. 2007. Statistical post-editing on SYSTRAN's rule-based translation system. In *Proceedings of the ACL-2007 Workshop on Statistical Machine Translation (WMT-07)*, Prague.

Christopher J. Dyer. 2007. The 'noisier channel': translation from morphologically complex languages. In *Proceedings of the ACL-2007 Workshop on Statistical Machine Translation (WMT-07)*, Prague.

Matthias Eck and Chiori Hori. 2005. Overview of the IWSLT 2005 evaluation campaign. In *Proceedings of International Workshop on Spoken Language Translation*.

Jesús Giménez and Lluís Màrquez. 2007. Linguistic features for automatic evaluation of heterogenous mt systems. In *Proceedings of ACL Workshop on Statistical Machine Translation*.

Maria Holmqvist, Sara Stymne, and Lars Ahrenberg. 2007. Getting to know Moses: Initial experiments on German-English factored translation. In *Proceedings of the ACL-2007 Workshop on Statistical Machine Translation (WMT-07)*, Prague.

Douglas Jones, Wade Shen, Neil Granoien, Martha Herzog, and Clifford Weinstein. 2005. Measuring translation quality by testing english speakers with a new defense language proficiency test for arabic. In *Proceedings of the 2005 International Conference on Intelligence Analysis*.

Philipp Koehn and Christof Monz. 2005. Shared task: Statistical machine translation between European languages. In *Proceedings of ACL 2005 Workshop on Parallel Text Translation*.

Philipp Koehn and Christof Monz. 2006. Manual and automatic evaluation of machine translation between European languages. In *Proceedings of NAACL 2006 Workshop on Statistical Machine Translation*.

Philipp Koehn and Josh Schroeder. 2007. Experiments in domain adaptation for statistical machine translation. In *Proceedings of the ACL-2007 Workshop on Statistical Machine Translation (WMT-07)*, Prague.

Philipp Koehn, Franz Josef Och, and Daniel Marcu. 2003. Statistical phrase-based translation. In *Proceedings of HLT/NAACL*.

Philipp Koehn, Nicola Bertoldi, Ondrej Bojar, Chris Callison-Burch, Alexandra Constantin, Brooke Cowan, Chris Dyer, Marcello Federico, Evan Herbst, Hieu Hoang, Christine Moran, Wade Shen, and Richard Zens. 2006. Factored translation models. CLSP Summer Workshop Final Report WS-2006, Johns Hopkins University.

Philipp Koehn. 2004. Pharaoh: A beam search decoder for phrase-based statistical machine translation models. In *Proceedings of AMTA*.

Philipp Koehn. 2005. A parallel corpus for statistical machine translation. In *Proceedings of MT-Summit*.

J. R. Landis and G. G. Koch. 1977. The measurement of observer agreement for categorical data. *Biometrics*, 33:159–174.

Alon Lavie and Abhaya Agarwal. 2007. METEOR: An automatic metric for MT evaluation with high levels of correlation with human judgments. In *Proceedings of the Workshop on Statistical Machine Translation*, Prague, June. Association for Computational Linguistics.

LDC. 2005. Linguistic data annotation specification: Assessment of fluency and adequacy in translations. Revision 1.5.

Audrey Lee. 2006. NIST 2006 machine translation evaluation official results. Official release of automatic evaluation scores for all submissions, November.

Ding Liu and Daniel Gildea. 2007. Source-language features and maximum correlation training for machine translation evaluation. In *Proceedings of NAACL*.

Dan Melamed, Ryan Green, and Jospeh P. Turian. 2003. Precision and recall of machine translation. In *Proceedings of HLT/NAACL*.

Preslav Nakov and Marti Hearst. 2007. UCB system description for the WMT 2007 shared task. In *Proceedings of the ACL-2007 Workshop on Statistical Machine Translation (WMT-07)*, Prague.

Franz Josef Och and Hermann Ney. 2003. A systematic comparison of various statistical alignment models. *Computational Linguistics*, 29(1):19–51, March.

Franz Josef Och and Hermann Ney. 2004. The alignment template approach to statistical machine translation. *Computational Linguistics*.

Kishore Papineni, Salim Roukos, Todd Ward, and Wei-Jing Zhu. 2002. Bleu: A method for automatic evaluation of machine translation. In *Proceedings of ACL*.

Michael Paul. 2006. Overview of the IWSLT 2006 evaluation campaign. In *Proceedings of International Workshop on Spoken Language Translation*.

Matthias Paulik, Kay Rottmann, Jan Niehues, Silja Hildebrand, and Stephan Vogel. 2007. The ISL phrase-based MT system for the 2007 ACL Workshop on Statistical Machine Translation. In *Proceedings of the ACL-2007 Workshop on Statistical Machine Translation (WMT-07)*, Prague.

Maja Popovic and Hermann Ney. 2007. Word error rates: Decomposition over POS classes and applications for error analysis. In *Proceedings of ACL Workshop on Statistical Machine Translation.*

Mark Przybocki. 2004. NIST 2004 machine translation evaluation results. Confidential e-mail to workshop participants, May.

Holger Schwenk. 2007. Building a statistical machine translation system for French using the Europarl corpus. In *Proceedings of the ACL-2007 Workshop on Statistical Machine Translation (WMT-07)*, Prague.

Michel Simard, Nicola Ueffing, Pierre Isabelle, and Roland Kuhn. 2007. Rule-based translation with statistical phrase-based post-editing. In *Proceedings of the ACL-2007 Workshop on Statistical Machine Translation (WMT-07)*, Prague.

Matthew Snover, Bonnie Dorr, Richard Schwartz, Linnea Micciulla, and John Makhoul. 2006. A study of translation edit rate with targeted human annotation. In *Proceedings of Association for Statistical Machine Translation in the Americas.*

Nicola Ueffing, Michel Simard, Samuel Larkin, and Howard Johnson. 2007. NRC's PORTAGE system for WMT 2007. In *Proceedings of the ACL-2007 Workshop on Statistical Machine Translation (WMT-07)*, Prague.

Liang Zhou, Chin-Yew Lin, and Eduard Hovy. 2006. Reevaluating machine translation results with paraphrase support. In *Proceedings of EMNLP.*

Andreas Zollmann, Ashish Venugopal, Matthias Paulik, and Stephan Vogel. 2007. The syntax augmented MT (SAMT) system for the shared task in the 2007 ACL Workshop on Statistical Machine Translation. In *Proceedings of the ACL-2007 Workshop on Statistical Machine Translation (WMT-07)*, Prague.

system	ADEQUACY	FLUENCY	RANK	CONSTITUENT
German-English Europarl				
cmu-uka	0.511	0.496	0.395	0.206
liu	0.541	0.55	0.415	0.234
nrc	0.474	0.459	0.354	0.214
saar	0.334	0.404	0.119	0.104
systran	**0.562**	**0.594**	**0.530**	**0.302**
uedin	0.53	0.554	0.43	0.187
upc	0.534	0.533	0.384	0.214
German-English News Corpus				
nrc	0.459	0.429	0.325	0.245
saar	0.278	0.341	0.108	0.125
systran	**0.552**	**0.56**	**0.563**	**0.344**
uedin	0.508	0.536	0.485	0.332
upc	0.536	0.512	0.476	0.330
English-German Europarl				
cmu-uka	0.557	0.508	0.416	0.333
nrc	0.534	0.511	0.328	0.321
saar	0.369	0.383	0.172	0.196
systran	0.543	0.525	**0.511**	0.295
uedin	**0.569**	**0.576**	0.389	**0.350**
upc	0.565	0.522	0.438	0.3
English-German News Corpus				
nrc	0.453	0.4	0.437	0.340
saar	0.186	0.273	0.108	0.121
systran	**0.542**	**0.556**	**0.582**	**0.351**
ucb	0.415	0.403	0.332	0.289
uedin	0.472	0.445	0.455	0.303
upc	0.505	0.475	0.377	0.349

Table 9: Human evaluation for German-English submissions

system	ADEQUACY	FLUENCY	RANK	CONSTITUENT
Spanish-English Europarl				
cmu-syntax	0.552	0.568	0.478	0.152
cmu-uka	0.557	0.564	0.392	0.139
nrc	0.477	0.489	0.382	0.143
saar	0.328	0.336	0.126	0.075
systran	0.525	0.566	0.453	0.156
uedin	**0.593**	**0.610**	0.419	0.14
upc	0.587	0.604	**0.5**	**0.188**
upv	0.562	0.573	0.326	0.154
Spanish-English News Corpus				
cmu-uka	0.522	0.495	0.41	0.213
nrc	0.479	0.464	0.334	0.243
saar	0.446	0.46	0.246	0.198
systran	0.525	0.503	0.453	0.22
uedin	0.546	0.534	0.48	0.268
upc	**0.566**	**0.543**	**0.537**	**0.312**
upv	0.435	0.459	0.295	0.151
English-Spanish Europarl				
cmu-uka	0.563	0.581	0.391	0.23
nrc	0.546	0.548	0.323	0.22
systran	0.495	0.482	0.329	0.224
uedin	**0.586**	**0.638**	**0.468**	0.225
upc	0.584	0.578	0.444	0.239
upv	0.573	0.587	0.406	**0.246**
English-Spanish News Corpus				
cmu-uka	0.51	0.492	0.45	0.277
nrc	0.408	0.392	0.367	0.224
systran	0.501	**0.507**	**0.481**	**0.352**
ucb	0.449	0.414	0.390	0.307
uedin	0.429	0.419	0.389	0.266
upc	**0.51**	0.488	0.404	0.311
upv	0.405	0.418	0.250	0.217

Table 10: Human evaluation for Spanish-English submissions

system	ADEQUACY	FLUENCY	RANK	CONSTITUENT
French-English Europarl				
limsi	**0.634**	0.618	0.458	**0.290**
nrc	0.553	0.551	0.404	0.253
saar	0.384	0.447	0.176	0.157
systran	0.494	0.484	0.286	0.202
systran-nrc	0.604	0.6	0.503	0.267
uedin	0.616	**0.635**	**0.514**	0.283
upc	0.616	0.619	0.448	0.267
French-English News Corpus				
limsi	0.575	**0.596**	**0.494**	**0.312**
nrc	0.472	0.442	0.306	0.241
saar	0.280	0.372	0.183	0.159
systran	0.553	0.534	0.469	0.288
systran-nrc	0.513	0.49	0.464	0.290
uedin	0.556	0.586	0.493	0.306
upc	**0.576**	0.587	0.493	0.291
English-French Europarl				
limsi	**0.635**	**0.627**	0.505	0.259
nrc	0.517	0.518	0.359	0.206
saar	0.398	0.448	0.155	0.139
systran	0.574	0.526	0.353	0.179
systran-nrc	0.575	0.58	**0.512**	0.225
uedin	0.620	0.608	0.485	**0.273**
upc	0.599	0.566	0.45	0.256
English-French News Corpus				
limsi	0.537	0.495	0.44	0.363
nrc	0.481	0.484	0.372	0.324
saar	0.243	0.276	0.086	0.121
systran	0.536	0.546	**0.634**	**0.440**
systran-nrc	**0.557**	**0.572**	0.485	0.287
ucb	0.401	0.391	0.316	0.245
uedin	0.466	0.447	0.485	0.375
upc	0.509	0.469	0.437	0.326

Table 11: Human evaluation for French-English submissions

system	ADEQUACY	FLUENCY	RANK	CONSTITUENT
Czech-English News Corpus				
cu	0.468	0.478	0.362	—
pct	0.418	0.388	0.220	—
uedin	0.458	0.471	0.353	—
umd	**0.550**	**0.592**	**0.627**	—
English-Czech News Corpus				
cu	0.523	0.510	0.405	**0.440**
pct	**0.542**	**0.541**	**0.499**	0.381
uedin	0.449	0.433	0.249	0.258

Table 12: Human evaluation for Czech-English submissions

system	METEOR	BLEU	1-TER	GTM	PARAEVAL-RECALL	PARAEVAL-PRECISION	DEPENDENCY-OVERLAP	SEMANTIC-ROLE-OVERLAP	1-WER-OF-VERBS	MAX-CORR-FLUENCY	MAX-CORR-ADEQUACY
German-English Europarl											
cmu-uka	0.559	0.247	0.326	0.455	0.528	0.531	0.259	0.182	0.848	1.91	1.910
liu	0.559	0.263	0.329	0.460	0.537	0.535	0.276	0.197	0.846	1.91	1.910
nrc	0.551	0.253	0.324	0.454	0.528	0.532	0.263	0.185	0.848	1.88	1.88
saar	0.477	0.198	0.313	0.447	0.44	0.527	0.228	0.157	0.846	1.76	1.710
systran	**0.560**	0.268	0.342	0.463	**0.543**	0.541	0.261	0.21	0.849	1.91	1.91
systran-2	0.501	0.154	0.238	0.376	0.462	0.448	0.237	0.154	—	1.71	1.73
uedin	0.56	**0.277**	0.319	**0.480**	0.536	**0.562**	**0.298**	**0.217**	**0.855**	**1.96**	**1.940**
upc	0.541	0.250	**0.343**	0.470	0.506	0.551	0.27	0.193	0.846	1.89	1.88
German-English News Corpus											
nrc	0.563	0.221	0.333	0.454	0.514	0.514	0.246	0.157	0.868	1.920	1.91
saar	0.454	0.159	0.288	0.413	0.405	0.467	0.193	0.120	0.86	1.700	1.64
systran	0.570	0.200	0.275	0.418	0.531	0.472	0.274	0.18	0.858	1.910	1.93
systran-2	0.556	0.169	0.238	0.397	0.511	0.446	0.258	0.163	—	1.86	1.88
uedin	**0.577**	**0.242**	**0.339**	**0.459**	**0.534**	**0.524**	**0.287**	**0.181**	**0.871**	**1.98**	**1.970**
upc	0.575	0.233	**0.339**	0.455	0.527	0.516	0.265	0.171	0.865	1.96	1.96
English-German Europarl											
cmu-uka	0.268	0.189	0.251	—	—	—	—	—	0.884	1.66	1.63
nrc	0.272	0.185	0.221	—	—	—	—	—	0.882	1.660	1.630
saar	0.239	0.174	0.237	—	—	—	—	—	0.881	1.61	1.56
systran	0.198	0.123	0.178	—	—	—	—	—	0.866	1.46	1.42
uedin	**0.277**	**0.201**	**0.273**	—	—	—	—	—	**0.889**	**1.690**	**1.66**
upc	0.266	0.177	0.195	—	—	—	—	—	0.88	1.640	1.62
English-German News Corpus											
nrc	0.257	0.157	0.25	—	—	—	—	—	**0.891**	1.590	1.560
saar	0.162	0.098	0.212	—	—	—	—	—	0.881	1.400	1.310
systran	0.223	0.143	0.266	—	—	—	—	—	0.887	1.55	1.500
ucb	0.256	0.156	0.249	—	—	—	—	—	0.889	1.59	1.56
ucb-2	0.252	0.152	0.229	—	—	—	—	—	—	1.57	1.55
uedin	**0.266**	0.166	**0.266**	—	—	—	—	—	**0.891**	**1.600**	**1.58**
upc	0.256	**0.167**	**0.266**	—	—	—	—	—	0.89	1.590	1.56

Table 13: Automatic evaluation scores for German-English submissions

system	METEOR	BLEU	1-TER	GTM	PARAEVAL-REC	PARAEVAL-PREC	DEPENDENCY	SEMANTIC-ROLE	1-WER-OF-VERBS	MAX-CORR-FLU	MAX-CORR-ADEQ
Spanish-English Europarl											
cmu-syntax	0.602	0.323	0.414	0.499	0.59	0.588	0.338	**0.254**	0.866	**2.10**	**2.090**
cmu-syntax-2	**0.603**	0.321	0.408	0.494	**0.593**	0.584	0.336	0.249	—	2.09	2.09
cmu-uka	0.597	0.32	**0.42**	**0.501**	0.581	**0.595**	0.336	0.247	0.867	2.09	2.080
nrc	0.596	0.313	0.402	0.484	0.581	0.581	0.321	0.227	0.867	2.04	2.04
saar	0.542	0.245	0.32	0.432	0.531	0.511	0.272	0.198	0.854	1.870	1.870
systran	0.593	0.290	0.364	0.469	0.586	0.550	0.321	0.238	0.858	2.02	2.03
systran-2	0.535	0.202	0.288	0.406	0.524	0.49	0.263	0.187	—	1.81	1.84
uedin	0.6	**0.324**	0.414	0.499	0.584	0.589	**0.339**	0.252	**0.868**	2.09	2.080
upc	0.600	0.322	0.407	0.492	0.593	0.583	0.334	0.253	0.865	2.08	2.08
upv	0.594	0.315	0.400	0.493	0.582	0.581	0.329	0.249	0.865	2.060	2.06
Spanish-English News Corpus											
cmu-uka	0.64	0.299	0.428	0.497	0.617	0.575	0.339	0.246	0.89	2.17	2.17
cmu-uka-2	0.64	0.297	0.427	0.496	0.616	0.574	0.339	0.246	—	2.17	2.17
nrc	0.641	0.299	0.434	0.499	0.615	0.584	0.329	0.238	0.892	2.160	2.160
saar	0.607	0.244	0.338	0.447	0.587	0.512	0.303	0.208	0.879	2.04	2.05
systran	0.628	0.259	0.35	0.453	0.611	0.523	0.325	0.221	0.877	2.08	2.10
systran-2	0.61	0.233	0.321	0.438	0.602	0.506	0.311	0.209	—	2.020	2.050
uedin	**0.661**	0.327	0.457	0.512	**0.634**	0.595	**0.363**	0.264	0.893	**2.25**	**2.24**
upc	0.654	**0.346**	**0.480**	**0.528**	0.629	**0.616**	**0.363**	**0.265**	**0.895**	2.240	2.23
upv	0.638	0.283	0.403	0.485	0.614	0.562	0.334	0.234	0.887	2.15	2.140
English-Spanish Europarl											
cmu-uka	**0.333**	0.311	0.389	—	—	—	—	—	0.889	1.98	**2.00**
nrc	0.322	0.299	0.376	—	—	—	—	—	0.886	1.92	1.940
systran	0.269	0.212	0.301	—	—	—	—	—	0.878	1.730	1.760
uedin	0.33	**0.316**	**0.399**	—	—	—	—	—	**0.891**	**1.980**	1.990
upc	0.327	0.312	0.393	—	—	—	—	—	0.89	1.960	1.98
upv	0.323	0.304	0.379	—	—	—	—	—	0.887	1.95	1.97
English-Spanish News Corpus											
cmu-uka	0.368	0.327	0.469	—	—	—	—	—	0.903	2.070	2.090
cmu-uka-2	0.355	0.306	0.461	—	—	—	—	—	—	2.04	2.060
nrc	0.362	0.311	0.448	—	—	—	—	—	0.904	2.04	2.060
systran	0.335	0.281	0.439	—	—	—	—	—	0.906	1.970	2.010
ucb	0.374	**0.331**	0.464	—	—	—	—	—	—	**2.09**	2.11
ucb-2	**0.375**	0.325	0.456	—	—	—	—	—	—	**2.09**	**2.110**
ucb-3	0.372	0.324	0.457	—	—	—	—	—	—	2.08	2.10
uedin	0.361	0.322	**0.479**	—	—	—	—	—	**0.907**	2.08	2.09
upc	0.361	0.328	0.467	—	—	—	—	—	0.902	2.06	2.08
upv	0.337	0.285	0.432	—	—	—	—	—	0.900	1.98	2.000

Table 14: Automatic evaluation scores for Spanish-English submissions

system	METEOR	BLEU	1-TER	GTM	PARAEVAL-REC	PARAEVAL-PREC	DEPENDENCY	SEMANTIC-ROLE	1-WER-OF-VERBS	MAX-CORR-FLU	MAX-CORR-ADEQ
French-English Europarl											
limsi	**0.604**	**0.332**	0.418	0.504	**0.589**	0.591	**0.344**	**0.259**	**0.865**	**2.100**	**2.10**
limsi-2	0.602	0.33	0.417	0.504	0.587	0.592	0.302	0.257	—	2.05	2.05
nrc	0.594	0.312	0.403	0.488	0.578	0.58	0.324	0.244	0.861	2.05	2.050
saar	0.534	0.249	0.354	0.459	0.512	0.546	0.279	0.202	0.856	1.880	1.88
systran	0.549	0.211	0.308	0.417	0.525	0.501	0.277	0.201	0.849	1.850	1.890
systran-nrc	0.594	0.313	0.404	0.492	0.578	0.580	0.330	0.248	0.862	2.06	2.060
uedin	0.595	0.318	**0.424**	**0.505**	0.574	**0.599**	0.338	0.254	**0.865**	2.08	2.08
upc	0.6	0.319	0.409	0.495	0.588	0.583	0.337	0.255	0.861	2.08	2.080
French-English News Corpus											
limsi	0.595	**0.279**	**0.405**	**0.478**	0.563	**0.555**	0.289	**0.235**	0.875	2.030	2.020
nrc	0.587	0.257	0.389	0.470	0.557	0.546	0.301	0.22	**0.876**	2.020	2.020
saar	0.503	0.206	0.301	0.418	0.475	0.476	0.245	0.169	0.864	1.80	1.78
systran	0.568	0.202	0.28	0.415	0.554	0.472	0.292	0.198	0.866	1.930	1.96
systran-nrc	0.591	0.269	0.398	0.475	0.558	0.547	0.323	0.226	0.875	2.050	2.06
uedin	**0.602**	0.27	0.392	0.471	**0.569**	0.545	**0.326**	0.233	0.875	**2.07**	**2.07**
upc	0.596	0.275	0.400	0.476	0.567	0.552	0.322	0.233	**0.876**	2.06	2.06
English-French Europarl											
limsi	**0.226**	**0.306**	0.366	—	—	—	—	—	0.891	**1.940**	1.96
nrc	0.218	0.294	0.354	—	—	—	—	—	0.888	1.930	1.96
saar	0.190	0.262	0.333	—	—	—	—	—	**0.892**	1.86	1.87
systran	0.179	0.233	0.313	—	—	—	—	—	0.885	1.79	1.83
systran-nrc	0.220	0.301	0.365	—	—	—	—	—	**0.892**	**1.940**	**1.960**
uedin	0.207	0.262	0.301	—	—	—	—	—	0.886	1.930	1.950
upc	0.22	0.299	**0.379**	—	—	—	—	—	**0.892**	**1.940**	**1.960**
English-French News Corpus											
limsi	0.206	0.255	0.354	—	—	—	—	—	0.897	1.84	1.87
nrc	0.208	0.257	0.369	—	—	—	—	—	0.9	1.87	1.900
saar	0.151	0.188	0.308	—	—	—	—	—	0.896	1.65	1.65
systran	0.199	0.243	0.378	—	—	—	—	—	0.901	1.860	1.90
systran-nrc	**0.23**	**0.290**	**0.408**	—	—	—	—	—	**0.903**	**1.940**	**1.98**
ucb	0.201	0.237	0.366	—	—	—	—	—	0.897	1.830	1.860
uedin	0.197	0.234	0.340	—	—	—	—	—	0.899	1.87	1.890
upc	0.212	0.263	0.391	—	—	—	—	—	0.900	1.87	1.90

Table 15: Automatic evaluation scores for French-English submissions

system	METEOR	BLEU	1-TER	GTM	PARAEVAL-REC	PARAEVAL-PREC	DEPENDENCY	SEMANTIC-ROLE	1-WER-OF-VERBS	MAX-CORR-FLU	MAX-CORR-ADEQ
Czech-English News Corpus											
cu	0.545	0.215	0.334	0.441	0.502	0.504	0.245	0.165	0.867	1.87	1.88
cu-2	0.558	0.223	0.344	0.447	0.510	0.514	0.254	0.17	—	1.90	1.910
uedin	0.54	0.217	0.340	0.445	0.497	0.51	0.243	0.160	0.865	1.860	1.870
umd	**0.581**	**0.241**	**0.355**	**0.460**	**0.531**	**0.526**	**0.273**	**0.184**	**0.868**	**1.96**	**1.97**
English-Czech News Corpus											
cu	0.429	**0.134**	**0.231**	—	—	—	—	—	—	**1.580**	**1.53**
cu-2	**0.430**	0.132	0.219	—	—	—	—	—	—	1.58	1.520
uedin	0.42	0.119	0.211	—	—	—	—	—	—	1.550	1.49

Table 16: Automatic evaluation scores for Czech-English submissions

	ADEQUACY	FLUENCY	RANK	CONSTITUENT	METEOR	BLEU	1-TER	GTM	PARAEVAL-REC	PARAEVAL-PREC	DEPENDENCY	SEMANTIC-ROLE	1-WER-OF-VS	MAX-CORR-FLU	MAX-CORR-ADEQ
German-English News Corpus															
adequacy	1	0.900	0.900	0.900	0.600	0.300	-0.025	0.300	**0.700**	0.300	**0.700**	**0.700**	-0.300	0.300	0.600
fluency	—	1	1.000	1.000	0.700	0.400	-0.025	0.400	**0.900**	0.400	**0.900**	**0.900**	-0.100	0.400	0.700
rank	—	—	1	1.000	0.700	0.400	-0.025	0.400	**0.900**	0.400	**0.900**	**0.900**	-0.100	0.400	0.700
constituent	—	—	—	1	0.700	0.400	-0.025	0.400	**0.900**	0.400	**0.900**	**0.900**	-0.100	0.400	0.700
German-English Europarl															
adequacy	1	0.893	0.821	0.750	0.599	0.643	**0.787**	0.68	0.750	0.643	0.464	0.750	0.206	0.608	0.447
fluency	—	1	0.964	0.537	0.778	0.858	0.500	0.821	0.821	0.787	0.571	**0.93**	0.562	0.821	0.661
rank	—	—	1	0.500	**0.902**	0.821	0.393	0.714	0.858	0.643	0.464	0.858	0.652	0.893	0.769
constituent	—	—	—	1	0.456	0.464	0.714	0.18	**0.750**	0.250	0.214	0.43	0.117	0.214	0.126
Spanish-English News Corpus															
adequacy	1	1.000	0.964	0.893	0.643	0.68	0.68	0.68	0.68	0.68	0.634	**0.714**	0.571	0.68	0.68
fluency	—	1	0.964	0.893	0.643	0.68	0.68	0.68	0.68	0.68	0.634	**0.714**	0.571	0.68	0.68
rank	—	—	1	0.858	0.714	0.750	0.750	0.750	0.750	0.750	0.741	**0.787**	0.608	0.750	0.750
constituent	—	—	—	1	0.787	**0.821**	**0.821**	**0.821**	0.714	**0.821**	0.599	0.750	0.750	0.714	0.714
Spanish-English Europarl															
adequacy	1	0.93	0.452	0.333	0.596	**0.810**	0.62	0.690	0.542	0.714	0.762	0.739	0.489	0.638	0.638
fluency	—	1	0.571	0.524	0.596	0.787	0.43	0.500	0.732	0.524	0.690	**0.810**	0.346	0.566	0.566
rank	—	—	1	0.643	0.739	0.596	0.43	0.262	**0.923**	0.406	0.500	0.739	0.168	0.542	0.542
constituent	—	—	—	1	0.262	0.143	-0.143	-0.143	**0.816**	-0.094	0.000	0.477	-0.226	0.042	0.042
French-English News Corpus															
adequacy	1	0.964	0.964	0.858	**0.787**	0.750	0.68	0.68	**0.787**	0.571	0.321	**0.787**	0.456	0.68	0.554
fluency	—	1	1.000	0.93	0.750	0.787	0.714	0.714	0.750	0.608	0.214	**0.858**	0.367	0.608	0.482
rank	—	—	1	0.93	0.750	0.787	0.714	0.714	0.750	0.608	0.214	**0.858**	0.367	0.608	0.482
constituent	—	—	—	1	0.858	0.858	0.787	0.787	0.858	0.643	0.393	**0.964**	0.349	0.750	0.661
French-English Europarl															
adequacy	1	0.884	0.778	0.991	0.982	0.956	0.902	0.902	0.812	0.902	0.956	0.956	0.849	0.964	**0.991**
fluency	—	1	0.858	0.893	0.849	0.821	**0.93**	**0.93**	0.571	**0.93**	0.858	0.821	0.787	0.849	0.858
rank	—	—	1	0.821	0.670	0.68	0.858	0.858	0.43	0.858	0.787	0.68	**0.893**	0.741	0.714
constituent	—	—	—	1	0.956	0.93	0.93	0.93	0.750	0.93	**0.964**	0.93	0.893	0.956	**0.964**

Table 17: Correlation of the automatic evaluation metrics with the human judgments when translating into English

	ADEQUACY	FLUENCY	RANK	CONSTITUENT	METEOR	BLEU	1-TER	1-WER-OF-VS	MAX-CORR-FLU	MAX-CORR-ADEQ
English-German News Corpus										
adequacy	1	0.943	0.83	0.943	0.187	0.43	**0.814**	0.243	0.33	0.187
fluency	—	1	0.714	0.83	0.100	0.371	**0.758**	0.100	0.243	0.100
rank	—	—	1	0.771	0.414	0.258	**0.671**	0.414	0.414	0.414
constituent	—	—	—	1	0.13	0.371	**0.671**	0.243	0.243	0.13
English-German Europarl										
adequacy	1	0.714	0.487	0.714	0.487	**0.600**	0.314	0.371	0.487	0.487
fluency	—	1	0.543	0.43	**0.258**	0.200	-0.085	0.03	**0.258**	**0.258**
rank	—	—	1	0.03	-0.37	-0.256	-0.543	-0.485	-0.37	-0.37
constituent	—	—	—	1	0.887	**0.943**	0.658	0.83	0.887	0.887
English-Spanish News Corpus										
adequacy	1	0.714	0.771	0.83	0.314	**0.658**	0.487	0.03	0.314	0.600
fluency	—	1	0.943	0.887	-0.200	0.03	0.143	0.200	-0.085	**0.258**
rank	—	—	1	0.943	-0.029	0.087	0.258	**0.371**	-0.029	**0.371**
constituent	—	—	—	1	-0.143	0.143	0.200	**0.314**	-0.085	0.258
English-Spanish Europarl										
adequacy	1	0.83	0.943	0.543	0.658	**0.943**	**0.943**	**0.943**	0.83	0.658
fluency	—	1	0.771	0.543	0.714	0.771	0.771	0.771	**0.83**	0.714
rank	—	—	1	0.600	0.600	**0.887**	**0.887**	**0.887**	0.771	0.600
constituent	—	—	—	1	**0.43**	**0.43**	**0.43**	**0.43**	0.371	**0.43**
English-French News Corpus										
adequacy	1	0.952	0.762	0.452	0.690	**0.787**	0.690	0.709	0.596	0.686
fluency	—	1	0.810	0.477	0.62	0.739	0.714	**0.792**	0.62	0.780
rank	—	—	1	0.762	0.239	0.381	0.500	**0.757**	0.596	0.601
constituent	—	—	—	1	-0.048	0.096	0.143	**0.411**	0.333	0.304
English-French Europarl										
adequacy	1	0.964	0.750	0.93	0.608	0.528	0.287	-0.07	**0.652**	0.376
fluency	—	1	0.858	0.893	0.643	0.562	0.214	-0.07	**0.652**	0.376
rank	—	—	1	0.750	0.821	0.76	0.393	0.214	**0.830**	0.697
constituent	—	—	—	1	0.571	0.473	0.18	-0.07	**0.652**	0.447

Table 18: Correlation of the automatic evaluation metrics with the human judgments when translating out of English

Context-aware Discriminative Phrase Selection for Statistical Machine Translation

Jesús Giménez and **Lluís Màrquez**
TALP Research Center, LSI Department
Universitat Politècnica de Catalunya
Jordi Girona Salgado 1–3, E-08034, Barcelona
{jgimenez,lluism}@lsi.upc.edu

Abstract

In this work we revise the application of discriminative learning to the problem of phrase selection in Statistical Machine Translation. Inspired by common techniques used in Word Sense Disambiguation, we train classifiers based on local context to predict possible phrase translations. Our work extends that of Vickrey et al. (2005) in two main aspects. First, we move from word translation to phrase translation. Second, we move from the *'blank-filling'* task to the *'full translation'* task. We report results on a set of highly frequent source phrases, obtaining a significant improvement, specially with respect to adequacy, according to a rigorous process of manual evaluation.

1 Introduction

Translations tables in Phrase-based Statistical Machine Translation (SMT) are often built on the basis of Maximum-likelihood Estimation (MLE), being one of the major limitations of this approach that the source sentence context in which phrases occur is completely ignored (Koehn et al., 2003).

In this work, inspired by state-of-the-art Word Sense Disambiguation (WSD) techniques, we suggest using Discriminative Phrase Translation (DPT) models which take into account a wider feature context. Following the approach by Vickrey et al. (2005), we deal with the *'phrase translation'* problem as a classification problem. We use Support Vector Machines (SVMs) to predict phrase translations in the context of the whole source sentence. We extend the work by Vickrey et al. (2005) in two main aspects. First, we move from *'word translation'* to *'phrase translation'*. Second, we move from the *'blank-filling'* task to the *'full translation'* task.

Our approach is fully described in Section 2. We apply it to the Spanish-to-English translation of European Parliament Proceedings. In Section 3, prior to considering the 'full translation' task, we analyze the impact of using DPT models for the isolated 'phrase translation' task. In spite of working on a very specific domain, a large room for improvement, coherent with WSD performance, and results by Vickrey et al. (2005), is predicted. Then, in Section 4, we tackle the full translation task. DPT models are integrated in a 'soft' manner, by making them available to the decoder so they can fully interact with other models. Results using a reduced set of highly frequent source phrases show a significant improvement, according to several automatic evaluation metrics. Interestingly, the BLEU metric (Papineni et al., 2001) is not able to reflect this improvement. Through a rigorous process of manual evaluation we have verified the gain. We have also observed that it is mainly related to adequacy. These results confirm that better phrase translation probabilities may be helpful for the full translation task. However, the fact that no gain in fluency is reported indicates that the integration of these probabilities into the statistical framework requires further study.

2 Discriminative Phrase Translation

In this section we describe the phrase-based SMT baseline system and how DPT models are built and integrated into this system in a 'soft' manner.

Proceedings of the Second Workshop on Statistical Machine Translation, pages 159–166,
Prague, June 2007.

2.1 Baseline System

The baseline system is a phrase-based SMT system (Koehn et al., 2003), built almost entirely using freely available components. We use the *SRI Language Modeling Toolkit* (Stolcke, 2002) for language modeling. We build trigram language models applying linear interpolation and Kneser-Ney discounting for smoothing. Translation models are built on top of word-aligned parallel corpora linguistically annotated at the level of shallow syntax (i.e., lemma, part-of-speech, and base phrase chunks) as described by Giménez and Màrquez (2005). Text is automatically annotated, using the *SVMTool* (Giménez and Màrquez, 2004), *Freeling* (Carreras et al., 2004), and *Phreco* (Carreras et al., 2005) packages. We used the *GIZA++ SMT Toolkit*[1] (Och and Ney, 2003) to generate word alignments. We apply the phrase-extract algorithm, as described by Och (2002), on the Viterbi alignments output by GIZA++ following the *'global phrase extraction'* strategy described by Giménez and Màrquez (2005) (i.e., a single phrase translation table is built on top of the union of alignments corresponding to different linguistic data views). We work with the union of source-to-target and target-to-source alignments, with no heuristic refinement. Phrases up to length five are considered. Also, phrase pairs appearing only once are discarded, and phrase pairs in which the source/target phrase is more than three times longer than the target/source phrase are ignored. Phrase pairs are scored on the basis of unsmoothed relative frequency (i.e., MLE). Regarding the argmax search, we used the *Pharaoh* beam search decoder (Koehn, 2004), which naturally fits with the previous tools.

2.2 DPT for SMT

Instead of relying on MLE estimation to score the phrase pairs (f_i, e_j) in the translation table, we suggest considering the translation of every source phrase f_i as a multi-class classification problem, where every possible translation of f_i is a class.

We use *local linear SVMs* [2]. Since SVMs are binary classifiers, the problem must be binarized. We have applied a simple *one-vs-all* binarization, i.e., a SVM is trained for every possible translation candidate e_j. Training examples are extracted from the same training data as in the case of MLE models, i.e., an aligned parallel corpus, obtained as described in Section 2.1. We use each sentence pair in which the source phrase f_i occurs to generate a positive example for the classifier corresponding to the actual translation of f_i in that sentence, according to the automatic alignment. This will be as well a negative example for the classifiers corresponding to the rest of possible translations of f_i.

2.2.1 Feature Set

We consider different kinds of information, always from the source sentence, based on standard WSD methods (Yarowsky et al., 2001). As to the local context, inside the source phrase to disambiguate, and 5 tokens to the left and to the right, we use n-grams ($n \in \{1, 2, 3\}$) of: words, parts-of-speech, lemmas and base phrase chunking IOB labels. As to the global context, we collect topical information by considering the source sentence as a bag of lemmas.

2.2.2 Decoding. A Trick.

At translation time, we consider every instance of f_i as a separate case. In each case, for all possible translations of f_i, we collect the SVM score, according to the SVM classification rule. We are in fact modeling $P(e_j|f_i)$. However, these scores are not probabilities. We transform them into probabilities by applying the *softmax function* described by Bishop (1995). We do not constrain the decoder to use the translation e_j with highest probability. Instead, we make all predictions available and let the decoder choose. We have avoided implementing a new decoder by pre-computing all the SVM predictions for all possible translations for all source phrases appearing in the test set. We input this information onto the decoder by replicating the entries in the translation table. In other words, each distinct occurrence of every single source phrase has a distinct list of phrase translation candidates with their corresponding scores. Accordingly, the source sentence is transformed into a sequence of identifiers,

[1] `http://www.fjoch.com/GIZA++.html`

[2] We use the SVM^{light} package, which is freely available at `http://svmlight.joachims.org` (Joachims, 1999).

in our case a sequence of (w, i) pairs[3], which allow us to uniquely identify every distinct instance of every word in the test set during decoding, and to retrieve DPT predictions in the translation table. For that purpose, source phrases in the translation table must comply with the same format.

This imaginative trick[4] saved us in the short run a gigantic amount of work. However, it imposes a severe limitation on the kind of features which the DPT system may use. In particular, features from the target sentence under construction and from the correspondence between source and target (i.e., alignments) can not be used.

3 Phrase Translation

Analogously to the *'word translation'* definition by Vickrey et al. (2005), rather than predicting the sense of a word according to a given sense inventory, in *'phrase translation'*, the goal is to predict the correct translation of a *phrase*, for a given target language, in the context of a sentence. This task is simpler than the 'full translation' task, but provides an insight to the gain prospectives.

We used the data from the *Openlab 2006* Initiative[5] promoted by the TC-STAR Consortium[6]. This test suite is entirely based on European Parliament Proceedings. We have focused on the Spanish-to-English task. The training set consists of 1,281,427 parallel sentences. Performing phrase extraction over the training data, as described in Section 2.1, we obtained translation candidates for 1,729,191 source phrases. We built classifiers for *all* the source phrases with more than one possible translation and more than 10 occurrences. 241,234 source phrases fulfilled this requirement. For each source phrase, we used 80% of the instances for training, 10% for development, and 10% for test.

Table 1 shows "phrase translation" results over the test set. We compare the performance, in terms of accuracy, of DPT models and the "most frequent translation" baseline ('MFT'). The MFT baseline is equivalent to selecting the translation candidate with highest probability according to MLE. The 'macro' column shows macro-averaged results over all phrases, i.e., the accuracy for each phrase counts equally towards the average. The 'micro' column shows micro-averaged accuracy, where each test example counts equally. The 'all' set includes results for the 241,234 phrases, whereas the 'frequent' set includes results for a selection of 41 very frequent phrases ocurring more than 50,000 times.

phrase set	model	macro	micro
all	MFT	0.66	0.70
	DPT	0.68	0.76
frequent	MFT	0.76	0.75
	DPT	0.86	0.86

Table 1: "Phrase Translation" Accuracy (test set).

A priori, DPT models seem to offer a significant room for potential improvement. Although phrase translation differs from WSD in a number of aspects, the increase with respect to the MFT baseline is comparable. Results are also coherent with those attained by Vickrey et al. (2005).

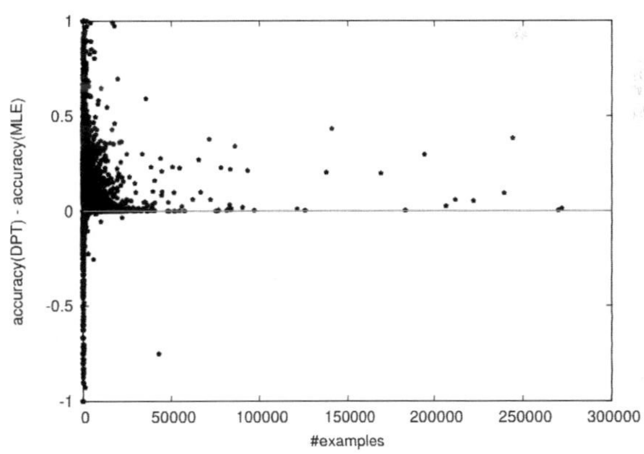

Figure 1: Analysis of "Phrase Translation" Results on the development set (Spanish-to-English).

Figure 1 shows the relationship between the accuracy[7] gain and the number of training examples. In general, with a sufficient number of examples (over 10,000), DPT outperforms the MFT baseline.

[3] w is a word and i corresponds to the number of instances of word w seen in the test set before the current instance.

[4] We have checked that results following this type of decoding when translation tables are estimated on the basis of MLE are identical to regular decoding results.

[5] `http://tc-star.itc.it/openlab2006/`

[6] `http://www.tc-star.org/`

[7] We focus on micro-averaged accuracy.

4 Full Translation

In the "phrase translation" task the predicted phrase does not interact with the rest of the target sentence. In this section we analyze the impact of DPT models when the goal is to translate the whole sentence.

For evaluation purposes we count on a set of 1,008 sentences. Three human references per sentence are available. We randomly split this set in two halves, and use them for development and test, respectively.

4.1 Evaluation

Evaluating the effects of using DPT predictions, directed towards a better word selection, in the full translation task presents two serious difficulties.

In first place, the actual room for improvement caused by a better translation modeling is smaller than estimated in Section 3. This is mainly due to the SMT architecture itself which relies on a search over a probability space in which several models cooperate. For instance, in many cases errors caused by a poor translation modeling may be corrected by the language model. In a recent study, Vilar et al. (2006) found that only around 25% of the errors are related to word selection. In half of these cases errors are caused by a wrong word sense disambiguation, and in the other half the word sense is correct but the lexical choice is wrong.

In second place, most conventional automatic evaluation metrics have not been designed for this purpose. For instance, metrics such as BLEU (Papineni et al., 2001) tend to favour longer n-gram matchings, and are, thus, biased towards word ordering. We might find better suited metrics, such as METEOR (Banerjee and Lavie, 2005), which is oriented towards word selection[8]. However, a new problem arises. Because different metrics are biased towards different aspects of quality, scores conferred by different metrics are often controversial.

In order to cope with evaluation difficulties we have applied several complementary actions:

1. Based on the results from Section 3, we focus on a reduced set of 41 very promising phrases trained on more than 50,000 examples. This set covers 25.8% of the words in the test set, and exhibits a potential absolute accuracy gain around 11% (See Table 1).
2. With the purpose of evaluating the changes related only to this small set of very promising phrases, we introduce a new measure, $\mathbf{A}_{pt}$, which computes "phrase translation" accuracy for a given list of source phrases. For every test case, A_{pt} counts the proportion of phrases from the list appearing in the source sentence which have a valid[9] translation both in the target sentence and in any of the reference translations. In fact, because in general source-to-target alignments are not known, A_{pt} calculates an approximate[10] solution.
3. We evaluate overall MT quality on the basis of 'Human Likeness'. In particular, we use the QUEEN[11] meta-measure from the QARLA Framework (Amigó et al., 2005). QUEEN operates under the assumption that a good translation must be similar to all human references according to all metrics. Given a set of automatic translations A, a set of similarity metrics X, and a set of human references R, QUEEN is defined as the probability, over $R \times R \times R$, that for every metric in X the automatic translation a is more similar to a reference r than two other references r' and r'' to each other. Formally:

$$\mathrm{QUEEN}_{X,R}(a) = Prob(\forall x \in X : x(a,r) \geq x(r',r''))$$

QUEEN captures the features that are common to all human references, rewarding those automatic translations which share them, and penalizing those which do not. Thus, QUEEN provides a robust means of combining several metrics into a single measure of quality. Following the methodology described by Giménez and Amigó (2006), we compute the QUEEN measure over the metric combination with highest KING, i.e., discriminative power. We have considered all the lexical metrics[12] provided by

[8]METEOR works at the unigram level, may consider word stemming and, for the case of English is also able to perform a lookup for synonymy in WordNet (Fellbaum, 1998).

[9]Valid translations are provided by the translation table.

[10]Current A_{pt} implementation searches phrases from left to right in decreasing length order.

[11]QUEEN is available inside the IQMT package for MT Evaluation based on 'Human Likeness' (Giménez and Amigó, 2006). `http://www.lsi.upc.edu/~nlp/IQMT`

[12]Consult the IQMT Technical Manual v1.3 for a detailed description of the metric set. `http://www.lsi.upc.edu/~nlp/IQMT/IQMT.v1.3.pdf`

	QUEEN	A_{pt}	BLEU	METEOR	ROUGE
$P(e) + P_{MLE}(f\|e)$	0.43	0.86	0.59	0.77	0.42
$P(e) + P_{MLE}(e\|f)$	0.45	0.87	0.62	0.77	0.43
$P(e) + P_{DPT}(e\|f)$	**0.47**	**0.89**	0.62	0.78	0.44

Table 2: Automatic evaluation of the 'full translation' results on the test set.

IQ$_{\text{MT}}$. The optimal set is:

{ METEOR$_{wnsyn}$, ROUGE$_{w_1.2}$ }

which includes variants of METEOR, and ROUGE (Lin and Och, 2004).

4.2 Adjustment of Parameters

Models are combined in a log-linear fashion:

$$logP(e|f) \propto \lambda_{lm} logP(e) + \lambda_g logP_{MLE}(f|e) + \lambda_d logP_{MLE}(e|f) + \lambda_{DPT} logP_{DPT}(e|f)$$

$P(e)$ is the language model probability. $P_{MLE}(f|e)$ corresponds to the MLE-based generative translation model, whereas $P_{MLE}(e|f)$ corresponds to the analogous discriminative model. $P_{DPT}(e|f)$ corresponds to the DPT model which uses SVM-based predictions in a wider feature context. In order to perform fair comparisons, model weights must be adjusted.

Because we have focused on a reduced set of frequent phrases, in order to translate the whole test set we must provide alternative translation probabilities for all the source phrases in the vocabulary which do not have a DPT prediction. We have used MLE predictions to complete the model. However, interaction between DPT and MLE models is problematic. Problems arise when, for a given source phrase, f_i, DPT predictions must compete with MLE predictions for larger phrases f_j overlapping with or containing f_i (See Section 4.3). We have alleviated these problems by splitting DPT tables in 3 subtables: (1) phrases with DPT prediction, (2) phrases with DPT prediction only for subphrases of it, and (3) phrases with no DPT prediction for any subphrase; and separately adjusting their weights.

Counting on a reliable automatic measure of quality is a crucial issue for system development. Optimal configurations may vary very significantly depending on the metric governing the optimization process. We optimize the system parameters over the QUEEN measure, which has proved to lead to more robust system configurations than BLEU (Lambert et al., 2006). We exhaustively try all possible parameter configurations, at a resolution of 0.1, over the development set and select the best one. In order to keep the optimization process feasible, in terms of time, the search space is pruned[13] during decoding.

4.3 Results

We compare the systems using the generative and discriminative MLE-based translation models to the discriminative translation model which uses DPT predictions for the set of 41 very 'frequent' source phrases. Table 2 shows automatic evaluation results on the test set, according to several metrics. Phrase translation accuracy (over the 'frequent' set of phrases) and MT quality are evaluated by means of the A_{pt} and QUEEN measures, respectively. For the sake of informativeness, BLEU, METEOR$_{wnsyn}$ and ROUGE$_{w_1.2}$ scores are provided as well.

Interestingly, discriminative models outperform the (noisy-channel) default generative model. Improvement in A_{pt} measure also reveals that DPT predictions provide a better translation for the set of 'frequent' phrases than the MLE models. This improvement remains when measuring overall translation quality via QUEEN. If we take into account that DPT predictions are available for only 25% of the words in the test set, we can say that the gain reported by the QUEEN and A_{pt} measures is consistent with the accuracy prospectives predicted in Table 1. METEOR$_{wnsyn}$ and ROUGE$_{w_1.2}$ reflect a slight improvement as well. However, according to BLEU there is no difference between both systems. We suspect that BLEU is unable to accurately reflect the possible gains attained by a better 'phrase selection' over a small set of phrases because of its tendency

[13]For each phrase only the 30 top-scoring translations are used. At all times, only the 100 top-scoring solutions are kept. We also disabled distortion and word penalty models. Therefore, translations are monotonic, and source and target tend to have the same number of words (that is not mandatory).

to reward long n-gram matchings. In order to clarify this scenario a rigorous process of manual evaluation has been conducted. We have selected a subset of sentences based on the following criteria:

- sentence length between 10 and 30 words.
- at least 5 words have a DPT prediction.
- DPT and MLE outputs differ.

A total of 114 sentences fulfill these requirements. In each translation case, assessors must judge whether the output by the discriminative 'MLE' system is better, equal to or worse than the output by the 'DPT' system, with respect to adequacy, fluency, and overall quality. In order to avoid any bias in the evaluation, we have randomized the respective position in the display of the sentences corresponding to each system. Four judges participated in the evaluation. Each judge evaluated only half of the cases. Each case was evaluated by two different judges. Therefore, we count on 228 human assessments.

Table 3 shows the results of the manual system comparison. Statistical significance has been determined using the sign-test (Siegel, 1956). According to human assessors, the 'DPT' system outperforms the 'MLE' system very significantly with respect to adequacy, whereas for fluency there is a slight advantage in favor of the 'MLE' system. Overall, there is a slight but significant advantage in favor of the 'DPT' system. Manual evaluation confirms our suspicion that the BLEU metric is less sensitive than QUEEN to improvements related to adequacy.

Error Analysis

Guided by the QUEEN measure, we carefully inspect particular cases. We start, in Table 4, by showing a positive case. The three phrases highlighted in the source sentence (*'tiene'*, *'señora'* and *'una cuestión'*) find a better translation with the help of the DPT models: *'tiene'* translates into *'has'* instead of *'i give'*, *'señora'* into *'mrs'* instead of *'lady'*, and *'una cuestión'* into *'a point'* instead of *'a ... motion'*.

In contrast, Table 5 shows a negative case. The translation of the Spanish word *'señora'* as *'mrs'* is acceptable. However, it influences very negatively the translation of the following word *'diputada'*, whereas the 'MLE' system translates the phrase *'señora diputada'*, which does not have a DPT prediction, as a whole. Similarly, the translation of *'cuestión'* as *'matter'*, although acceptable, is breaking the phrase *'cuestión de orden'* of high cohesion, which is commonly translated as *'point of order'*. The cause underlying these problems is that DPT predictions are available only for a subset of phrases. Thus, during decoding, for these cases our DPT models may be in disadvantage.

	Adequacy	Fluency	Overall
MLE > DPT	39	**84**	83
MLE = DPT	100	76	46
MLE < DPT	**89**	68	**99**

Table 3: Manual evaluation of the 'full translation' results on the test set. Counts on the number of translation cases for which the 'MLE' system is better than (>), equal to (=), or worse than (<) the 'DPT' system, with respect to adequacy, fluency, and overall MT quality, are presented.

5 Related Work

Recently, there is a growing interest in the application of WSD technology to MT. For instance, Carpuat and Wu (2005b) suggested integrating WSD predictions into a SMT system in a *'hard'* manner, either for decoding, by constraining the set of acceptable translation candidates for each given source word, or for post-processing the SMT system output, by directly replacing the translation of each selected word with the WSD system prediction. They did not manage to improve MT quality. They encountered several problems inherent to the SMT architecture. In particular, they described what they called the *"language model effect"* in SMT: *"The lexical choices are made in a way that heavily prefers phrasal cohesion in the output target sentence, as scored by the language model."*. This problem is a direct consequence of the 'hard' interaction between their WSD and SMT systems. WSD predictions cannot adapt to the surrounding target context. In a later work, Carpuat and Wu (2005a) analyzed the converse question, i.e. they measured the WSD performance of SMT models. They showed that dedicated WSD models significantly outperform current state-of-the-art SMT models. Consequently, SMT should benefit from WSD predictions.

Simultaneously, Vickrey et al. (2005) studied the

Source	**tiene** la palabra la **señora** mussolini para **una cuestión** de orden .
Ref 1	**mrs** mussolini **has** the floor for **a point** of order .
Ref 2	you have the floor , **missus** mussolini , for **a question** of order .
Ref 3	**ms** mussolini **has** now the floor for **a point** of order .
$P(e) + P_{MLE}(e\|f)$	**i give** the floor to the **lady** mussolini for **a procedural motion** .
$P(e) + P_{DPT}(e\|f)$	**has** the floor the **mrs** mussolini on **a point** of order .

Table 4: Case of Analysis of sentence #422. DPT models help.

Source	**señora** diputada , ésta **no es una cuestión** de orden .
Ref 1	**mrs mussolini** , that is **not a point** of order .
Ref 2	**honourable member** , this is **not a question** of order .
Ref 3	**my honourable friend** , this is **not a point** of order .
$P(e) + P_{MLE}(e\|f)$	**honourable member** , this is **not a point** of order .
$P(e) + P_{DPT}(e\|f)$	**mrs karamanou** , this is **not a matter** of order .

Table 5: Case of Analysis of sentence #434. DPT models fail.

application of discriminative models based on WSD technology to the *"blank-filling"* task, a simplified version of the translation task, in which the target context surrounding the word translation is available. They did not encounter the "language model effect" because they approached the task in a *'soft'* way, i.e., allowing their WSD models to interact with other models during decoding. Similarly, our DPT models are, as described in Section 2.2, *softly* integrated in the decoding step, and thus do not suffer from the detrimental "language model effect" either, in the context of the "full translation" task. Besides, DPT models enforce phrasal cohesion by considering disambiguation at the level of phrases.

6 Conclusions and Further Work

Despite the fact that measuring improvements in word selection is a very delicate issue, we have showed that dedicated discriminative translation models considering a wider feature context provide a useful mechanism in order to improve the quality of current phrase-based SMT systems, specially with regard to adequacy. However, the fact that no gain in fluency is reported indicates that the integration of these probabilities into the statistical framework requires further study.

Moreover, there are several open issues. First, for practical reasons, we have limited to a reduced set of 'frequent' phrases, and we have disabled reordering and word penalty models. We are currently studying the impact of a larger set of phrases, covering over 99% of the words in the test set. Experiments with enabled reordering and word penalty models should be conducted as well. Second, automatic evaluation of the results revealed a low agreement between BLEU and other metrics. For system comparison, we solved this through a process of manual evaluation. However, this is impractical for the adjustment of parameters, where hundreds of different configurations are tried. In this work we have relied on automatic evaluation based on 'Human Likeness' which allows for metric combinations and provides a stable and robust criterion for the metric set selection. Other alternatives could be tried. The crucial issue, in our opinion, is that the metric guiding the optimization is able to capture the changes.

Finally, we argue that, if DPT models considered features from the target side, and from the correspondence between source and target, results could further improve. However, at the short term, the incorporation of these type of features will force us to either build a new decoder or extend an existing one, or to move to a new MT architecture, for instance, in the fashion of the architectures suggested by Tillmann and Zhang (2006) or Liang et al. (2006).

Acknowledgements

This research has been funded by the Spanish Ministry of Education and Science, projects OpenMT (TIN2006-15307-C03-02) and TRAN-

GRAM (TIN2004-07925-C03-02). We are recognized as a Quality Research Group (2005 SGR-00130) by DURSI, the Research Department of the Catalan Government. Authors are thankful to the TC-STAR Consortium for providing such very valuable data sets.

References

Enrique Amigó, Julio Gonzalo, Anselmo Peñas, and Felisa Verdejo. 2005. QARLA: a Framework for the Evaluation of Automatic Sumarization. In *Proceedings of the 43th Annual Meeting of the Association for Computational Linguistics*.

Satanjeev Banerjee and Alon Lavie. 2005. METEOR: An Automatic Metric for MT Evaluation with Improved Correlation with Human Judgments. In *Proceedings of ACL Workshop on Intrinsic and Extrinsic Evaluation Measures for MT and/or Summarization*.

Christopher M. Bishop. 1995. 6.4: Modeling conditional distributions. In *Neural Networks for Pattern Recognition*, page 215. Oxford University Press.

Marine Carpuat and Dekai Wu. 2005a. Evaluating the Word Sense Disambiguation Performance of Statistical Machine Translation. In *Proceedings of IJCNLP*.

Marine Carpuat and Dekai Wu. 2005b. Word Sense Disambiguation vs. Statistical Machine Translation. In *Proceedings of ACL*.

Xavier Carreras, Isaac Chao, Lluís Padró, and Muntsa Padró. 2004. FreeLing: An Open-Source Suite of Language Analyzers. In *Proceedings of the 4th LREC*.

Xavier Carreras, Lluís Márquez, and Jorge Castro. 2005. Filtering-ranking perceptron learning for partial parsing. *Machine Learning*, 59:1–31.

C. Fellbaum, editor. 1998. *WordNet. An Electronic Lexical Database*. The MIT Press.

Jesús Giménez and Enrique Amigó. 2006. IQMT: A Framework for Automatic Machine Translation Evaluation. In *Proceedings of the 5th LREC*.

Jesús Giménez and Lluís Màrquez. 2004. SVMTool: A general POS tagger generator based on Support Vector Machines. In *Proceedings of 4th LREC*.

Jesús Giménez and Lluís Màrquez. 2005. Combining Linguistic Data Views for Phrase-based SMT. In *Proceedings of the Workshop on Building and Using Parallel Texts, ACL*.

T. Joachims. 1999. Making large-Scale SVM Learning Practical. In B. Schölkopf, C. Burges, and A. Smola, editors, *Advances in Kernel Methods - Support Vector Learning*. The MIT Press.

Philipp Koehn, Franz Josef Och, and Daniel Marcu. 2003. Statistical Phrase-Based Translation. In *Proceedings of HLT/NAACL*.

Philipp Koehn. 2004. Pharaoh: a Beam Search Decoder for Phrase-Based Statistical Machine Translation Models. In *Proceedings of AMTA*.

Patrik Lambert, Jesús Giménez, Marta R. Costa-jussá, Enrique Amigó, Rafael E. Banchs, Lluís Márquez, and J.A. R. Fonollosa. 2006. Machine Translation System Development based on Human Likeness. In *Proceedings of IEEE/ACL 2006 Workshop on Spoken Language Technology*.

Percy Liang, Alexandre Bouchard-Côté, Dan Klein, , and Ben Taskar. 2006. An End-to-End Discriminative Approach to Machine Translation. In *Proceedings of COLING-ACL06*.

Chin-Yew Lin and Franz Josef Och. 2004. Automatic Evaluation of Machine Translation Quality Using Longest Common Subsequence and Skip-Bigram Statics. In *Proceedings of ACL*.

Franz Josef Och and Hermann Ney. 2003. A Systematic Comparison of Various Statistical Alignment Models. *Computational Linguistics*, 29(1):19–51.

Franz Josef Och. 2002. *Statistical Machine Translation: From Single-Word Models to Alignment Templates*. Ph.D. thesis, RWTH Aachen, Germany.

Kishore Papineni, Salim Roukos, Todd Ward, and Wei-Jing Zhu. 2001. Bleu: a method for automatic evaluation of machine translation, rc22176. Technical report, IBM T.J. Watson Research Center.

Sidney Siegel. 1956. *Nonparametric Statistics for the Behavioral Sciences*. McGraw-Hill.

Andreas Stolcke. 2002. SRILM - An Extensible Language Modeling Toolkit. In *Proceedings of ICSLP*.

Christoph Tillmann and Tong Zhang. 2006. A Discriminative Global Training Algorithm for Statistical MT. In *Proceedings of COLING-ACL06*.

D. Vickrey, L. Biewald, M. Teyssier, and D. Koller. 2005. Word-Sense Disambiguation for Machine Translation. In *Proceedings of HLT/EMNLP*.

David Vilar, Jia Xu, Luis Fernando D'Haro, and Hermann Ney. 2006. Error Analysis of Machine Translation Output. In *Proceedings of the 5th LREC*.

David Yarowsky, Silviu Cucerzan, Radu Florian, Charles Schafer, and Richard Wicentowski. 2001. The Johns Hopkins Senseval2 System Descriptions. In *Proceedings of Senseval-2: Second International Workshop on Evaluating Word Sense Disambiguation Systems*.

Ngram-based statistical machine translation enhanced with multiple weighted reordering hypotheses

Marta R. Costa-jussà, Josep M. Crego, Patrik Lambert, Maxim Khalilov
José A. R. Fonollosa, José B. Mariño and **Rafael E. Banchs**
Department of Signal Theory and Communications
TALP Research Center (UPC)
Barcelona 08034, Spain
(mruiz,jmcrego,lambert,khalilov,adrian,canton,rbanchs)@gps.tsc.upc.edu

Abstract

This paper describes the 2007 Ngram-based statistical machine translation system developed at the TALP Research Center of the UPC (Universitat Politècnica de Catalunya) in Barcelona. Emphasis is put on improvements and extensions of the previous years system, being highlighted and empirically compared. Mainly, these include a novel word ordering strategy based on: (1) statistically monotonizing the training source corpus and (2) a novel reordering approach based on weighted reordering graphs. In addition, this system introduces a target language model based on statistical classes, a feature for out-of-domain units and an improved optimization procedure.

The paper provides details of this system participation in the ACL 2007 SECOND WORKSHOP ON STATISTICAL MACHINE TRANSLATION. Results on three pairs of languages are reported, namely from Spanish, French and German into English (and the other way round) for both the in-domain and out-of-domain tasks.

1 Introduction

Based on estimating a joint-probability model between the source and the target languages, Ngram-based SMT has proved to be a very competitive alternatively to phrase-based and other state-of-the-art systems in previous evaluation campaigns, as shown in (Koehn and Monz, 2005; Koehn and Monz, 2006).

Given the challenge of domain adaptation, efforts have been focused on improving strategies for Ngram-based SMT which could generalize better. Specifically, a novel reordering strategy is explored. It is based on extending the search by using precomputed statistical information. Results are promising while keeping computational expenses at a similar level as monotonic search. Additionally, a bonus for tuples from the out-of-domain corpus is introduced, as well as a target language model based on statistical classes. One of the advantages of working with statistical classes is that they can easily be used for any pair of languages.

This paper is organized as follows. Section 2 briefly reviews last year's system, including tuple definition and extraction, translation model and feature functions, decoding tool and optimization criterion. Section 3 delves into the word ordering problem, by contrasting last year strategy with the novel weighted reordering input graph. Section 4 focuses on new features: both tuple-domain bonus and target language model based on classes. Later on, Section 5 reports on all experiments carried out for WMT 2007. Finally, Section 6 sums up the main conclusions from the paper and discusses future research lines.

2 Baseline N-gram-based SMT System

The translation model is based on bilingual n-grams. It actually constitutes a language model of bilingual units, referred to as tuples, which approximates the joint probability between source and target languages by using bilingual n-grams.

Tuples are extracted from a word-to-word aligned corpus according to the following two constraints: first, tuple extraction should produce a monotonic segmentation of bilingual sentence pairs; and second, no smaller tuples can be extracted without violating the previous constraint.

For all experiments presented here, the translation model consisted of a 4-gram language model of tuples. In addition to this bilingual n-gram translation model, the baseline system implements a log linear combination of four feature functions. These four additional models are: a **target language model** (a 5-gram model of words); a **word bonus**; a **source-to-target lexicon model** and a **target-to-source lexicon model**, both features provide a complementary probability for each tuple in the translation table.

The decoder (called MARIE) for this translation sys-

Proceedings of the Second Workshop on Statistical Machine Translation, pages 167–170,
Prague, June 2007.

tem is based on a beam search [1].

This baseline system is actually the same system used for the first shared task *"Exploiting Parallel Texts for Statistical Machine Translation"* of the ACL 2005 Workshop on Building and Using Parallel Texts: Data-Driven Machine Translation and Beyond. A more detailed description of the system can be found in (Mariño et al., 2006).

3 Baseline System Enhanced with a Weighted Reordering Input Graph

This section briefly describes the statistical machine reordering (SMR) technique. Further details on the architecture of SMR system can be found on (Costa-jussà and Fonollosa, 2006).

3.1 Concept

The SMR system can be seen as a SMT system which translates from an original source language (*S*) to a reordered source language (*S'*), given a target language (*T*). The SMR technique works with statistical word classes (Och, 1999) instead of words themselves (particularly, we have used 200 classes in all experiments).

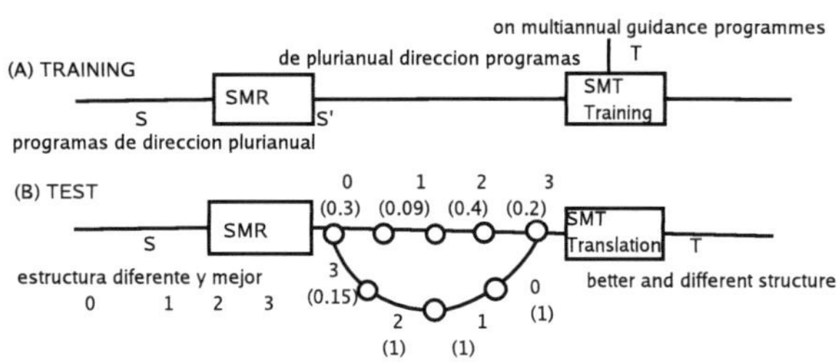

Figure 1: *SMR approach in the (A) training step (B) in the test step (the weight of each arch is in brackets).*

3.2 Using SMR technique to improve SMT training

The original source corpus *S* is translated into the reordered source corpus *S'* with the SMR system. Figure 1 (A) shows the corresponding block diagram. The reordered training source corpus and the original training target corpus are used to build the SMT system.

The main difference here is that the training is computed with the *S'2T* task instead of the *S2T* original task. Figure 2 (A) shows an example of the alignment computed on the original training corpus. Figure 2 (B) shows the same links but with the source training corpus in a different order (this training corpus comes from the SMR output). Although, the quality in alignment is the same, the tuples that can be extracted change (notice that the tuple extraction is monotonic). We are able to extract smaller tuples which reduces the translation vocabulary sparseness. These new tuples are used to build the SMT system.

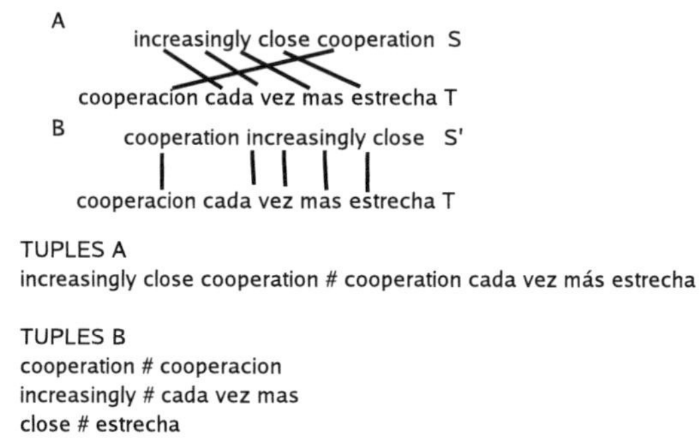

Figure 2: *Alignment and tuple extraction (A) original training source corpus (B) reordered training source corpus.*

3.3 Using SMR technique to generate multiple weighted reordering hypotheses

The SMR system, having its own search, can generate either an output 1-best or an output graph. In decoding, the SMR technique generates an output graph which is used as an input graph by the SMT system. Figure 1 (B) shows the corresponding block diagram in decoding: the SMR output graph is given as an input graph to the SMT system. Hereinafter, this either SMR output graph or SMT input graph will be referred to as (weighted) reordering graph. The monotonic search in the SMT system is extended with reorderings following this reordering graph. This reordering graph has multiple paths and each path has its own weight. This weight is added as a feature function in the log-linear framework. Figure 3 shows the weighted reordering graph.

The main difference with the reordering technique for WMT06 (Crego et al., 2006) lies in (1) the tuples are extracted from the word alignment between the reordered source training corpus and the given target training corpus and (2) the graph structure: the SMR graph provides weights for each reordering path.

4 Other features and functionalities

In addition to the novel reordering strategy, we consider two new features functions.

4.1 Target Language Model based on Statistical Classes

This feature implements a 5-gram language model of target statistical classes (Och, 1999). This model is trained by considering statistical classes, instead of words, for

[1] http://gps-tsc.upc.es/veu/soft/soft/marie/

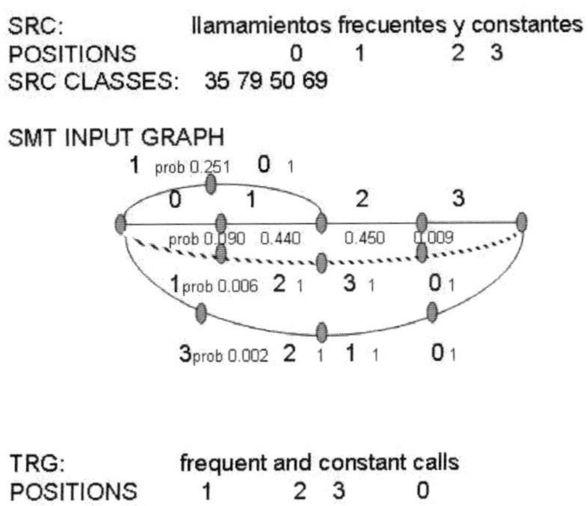

Figure 3: *Weighted reordering input graph for SMT system.*

the target side of the training corpus. Accordingly, the tuple translation unit is redefined in terms of a triplet which includes: a source string containing the source side of the tuple, a target string containing the target side of the tuple, and a class string containing the statistical classes corresponding to the words in the target strings.

4.2 Bonus for out-of-domain tuples

This feature adds a bonus to those tuples which comes from the training of the out-of-domain task. This feature is added when optimizing with the development of the out-of-domain task.

4.3 Optimization

Finally, a n-best re-ranking strategy is implemented which is used for optimization purposes just as proposed in *http://www.statmt.org/jhuws/*. This procedure allows for a faster and more efficient adjustment of model weights by means of a double-loop optimization, which provides significant reduction of the number of translations that should be carried out. The current optimization procedure uses the Simplex algorithm.

5 Shared Task Framework

5.1 Data

The data provided for this shared task corresponds to a subset of the official transcriptions of the European Parliament Plenary Sessions [2]. Additionally, there was available a smaller corpus called News-Commentary. For all tasks and domains, our training corpus was the catenation of both.

[2]http://www.statmt.org/wmt07/shared-task/

5.2 Processing details

Word Alignment. The word alignment is automatically computed by using GIZA++ [3] in both directions, which are symmetrized by using the union operation. Instead of aligning words themselves, stems are used for aligning. Afterwards case sensitive words are recovered.

Spanish Morphology Reduction. We implemented a morphology reduction of the Spanish language as a preprocessing step. As a consequence, training data sparseness due to Spanish morphology was reduced improving the performance of the overall translation system. In particular, the pronouns attached to the verb were separated and contractions as *del* or *al* are splited into *de el* or *a el*. As a post-processing, in the En2Es direction we used a POS target language model as a feature (instead of the target language model based on classes) that allowed to recover the segmentations (de Gispert, 2006).

Language Model Interpolation. In other to better adapt the system to the out-of-domain condition, the target language model feature was built by combining two 5-gram target language models (using SRILM [4]). One was trained from the EuroParl training data set, and the other from the available, but much smaller, news-commentary data set. The combination weights for the EuroParl and news-commentary language models were empirically adjusted by following a minimum perplexity criterion. A relative perplexity reduction around 10-15% respect to original EuroParl language model was achieved in all the tasks.

5.3 Experiments and Results

The main difference between this year's and last year's systems are: the amount of data provided; the word alignment; the Spanish morphology reduction; the reordering technique; the extra target language model based on statistical classes (except for the En2Es); and the bonus for the out-of-domain task (only for the En2Es task).

Among them, the most important is the reordering technique. That is why we provide a fair comparison between the reordering patterns (Crego and Mariño, 2006) technique and the SMR reordering technique. Table 1 shows the system described above using either reordering patterns or the SMR technique. The BLEU calculation was case insensitive and sensitive to tokenization.

Table 2 presents the *BLEU* score obtained for the 2006 test data set comparing last year's and this year's systems. The computed *BLEU* scores are case insensitive, sensitive to tokenization and uses one translation reference. The improvement in BLEU results shown from *UPC-jm*

[3]http://www.fjoch.com/GIZA++.html

[4]http://www.speech.sri.com/projects/srilm/

Task	Reordering patterns	SMR technique
es2en	31.21	33.34
en2es	31.67	32.33

Table 1: *BLEU comparison: reordering patterns vs. SMR technique.*

Task	UPC-jm 2006		UPC 2007	
	in-d	out-d	in-d	out-d
es2en	31.01	27.92	33.34	32.85
en2es	30.44	25.59	32.33	33.07
fr2en	30.42	21.79	32.44	26.93
en2fr	31.75	23.30	32.30	27.03
de2en	24.43	17.57	26.54	21.63
en2de	17.73	10.96	19.74	15.06

Table 2: *BLEU scores for each of the six translation directions considered (computed over 2006 test set) comparing last year's and this year's system results (in-domain and out-domain).*

2006 Table 2 and *reordering patterns* Table 1 in the English/Spanish in-domain task comes from the combination of: the additional corpora, the word alignment, the Spanish morphology reduction and the extra target language model based on classes (only in the Es2En direction).

6 Conclusions and Further Work

This paper describes the UPC system for the WMT07 Evaluation. In the framework of Ngram-based system, a novel reordering strategy which can be used for any pair of languages has been presented and it has been showed to significantly improve translation performance. Additionally two features has been added to the log-lineal scheme: the target language model based on classes and the bonus for out-of-domain translation units.

7 Acknowledgments

This work has been funded by the European Union under the TC-STAR project (IST-2002-FP6-506738) and the Spanish Government under grant TEC2006-13964-C03 (AVIVAVOZ project).

References

M.R. Costa-jussà and J.A.R. Fonollosa. 2006. Statistical machine reordering. In *EMNLP*, pages 71–77, Sydney, July. ACL.

J.M. Crego and J.B. Mariño. 2006. Reordering experiments for n-gram-based smt. In *SLT*, pages 242–245, Aruba.

Josep M. Crego, Adrià de Gispert, Patrik Lambert, Marta R. Costa-jussà, Maxim Khalilov, Rafael Banchs, José B. Mariño, and José A. R. Fonollosa. 2006. N-gram-based smt system enhanced with reordering patterns. In *WMT*, pages 162–165, New York City, June. ACL.

Adrià de Gispert. 2006. *Introducing Linguistic Knowledge in Statistical Machine Translation*. Ph.D. thesis, Universitat Politècnica de Catalunya, December.

Philipp Koehn and Christof Monz. 2005. Shared task: Statistical machine translation between european languages. In *WMT*, pages 119–124, Michigan, June. ACL.

Philipp Koehn and Christof Monz. 2006. Manual and automatic evaluation of machine translation between european languages. In *WMT*, pages 102–121, New York City, June. ACL.

J.B. Mariño, R.E. Banchs, J.M. Crego, A. de Gispert, P. Lambert, J.A.R. Fonollosa, and M.R. Costa-jussà. 2006. N-gram based machine translation. *Computational Linguistics*, 32(4):527–549, December.

F.J. Och. 1999. An efficient method for determining bilingual word classes. In *EACL*, pages 71–76, Bergen, Norway, June.

Analysis of statistical and morphological classes to generate weighted reordering hypotheses on a Statistical Machine Translation system

Marta R. Costa-jussà and **José A. R. Fonollosa**
Department of Signal Theory and Communications
TALP Research Center (UPC)
Barcelona 08034, Spain
(mruiz,adrian)@gps.tsc.upc.edu

Abstract

One main challenge of statistical machine translation (SMT) is dealing with word order. The main idea of the statistical machine reordering (SMR) approach is to use the powerful techniques of SMT systems to generate a weighted reordering graph for SMT systems. This technique supplies reordering constraints to an SMT system, using statistical criteria.

In this paper, we experiment with different graph pruning which guarantees the translation quality improvement due to reordering at a very low increase of computational cost.

The SMR approach is capable of generalizing reorderings, which have been learned during training, by using word classes instead of words themselves. We experiment with statistical and morphological classes in order to choose those which capture the most probable reorderings.

Satisfactory results are reported in the WMT07 Es/En task. Our system outperforms in terms of BLEU the WMT07 Official baseline system.

1 Introduction

Nowadays, statistical machine translation is mainly based on phrases (Koehn et al., 2003). In parallel to this phrase-based approach, the use of bilingual n-grams gives comparable results, as shown by Crego et al. (2005). Two basic issues differentiate the n-gram-based system from the phrase-based: training data is monotonically segmented into bilingual units; and, the model considers n-gram probabilities rather than relative frequencies. The n-gram-based system follows a maximum entropy approach, in which a log-linear combination of multiple models is implemented (Mariño et al., 2006), as an alternative to the source-channel approach.

Introducing reordering capabilities is important in both systems. Recently, new reordering strategies have been proposed such as the reordering of each source sentence to match the word order in the corresponding target sentence, see Kanthak et al. (2005) and Mariño et al. (2006). These approaches are applied in the training set and they lack of reordering generalization.

Applied both in the training and decoding step, Collins et al. (2005) describe a method for introducing syntactic information for reordering in SMT. This approach is applied as a pre-processing step.

Differently, Crego et al. (2006) presents a reordering approach based on reordering patterns which is coupled with decoding. The reordering patterns are learned directly from word alignment and all reorderings have the same probability.

In our previous work (Costa-jussà and Fonollosa, 2006) we presented the SMR approach which is based on using the powerful SMT techniques to generate a reordered source input for an SMT system both in training and decoding steps. One step further, (Costa-jussà et al., 2007) shows how the SMR system can generate a weighted reordering graph, allowing the SMT system to make the final reordering decision.

In this paper, the SMR approach is used to train the SMT system and to generate a weighted reordering graph for the decoding step. The SMR system uses word classes instead of words themselves and we analyze both statistical and morphological classes. Moreover, we present experiments regarding the reordering graph efficiency: we analyze different graph pruning and we show the very low increase in computational cost (compared to a monotonic translation). Finally, we compare the performance our system in terms of BLEU with the WMT07 baseline system.

This paper is organized as follows. The first two sections explain the SMT and the SMR baseline systems, respectively. Section 4 reports the study of statistical and

Proceedings of the Second Workshop on Statistical Machine Translation, pages 171–176,
Prague, June 2007.

morphological classes. Section 5 describes the experimental framework and discusses the results. Finally, Section 6 presents the conclusions and some further work.

2 Ngram-based SMT System

This section briefly describes the Ngram-based SMT (for further details see (Mariño et al., 2006)). The Ngram-based SMT system uses a translation model based on bilingual n-grams. It is actually a language model of bilingual units, referred to as tuples, which approximates the joint probability between source and target languages by using bilingual n-grams. Tuples are extracted from any word alignment according to the following constraints:

1. a monotonic segmentation of each bilingual sentence pairs is produced,
2. no word inside the tuple is aligned to words outside the tuple, and
3. no smaller tuples can be extracted without violating the previous constraints.

As a result of these constraints, only one segmentation is possible for a given sentence pair.

In addition to the bilingual n-gram translation model, the baseline system implements a log-linear combination of feature functions, which are described as follows:

- A **target language model**. This feature consists of a 4-gram model of words, which is trained from the target side of the bilingual corpus.
- A **class target language model**. This feature consists of a 5-gram model of words classes, which is trained from the target side of the bilingual corpus using the statistical classes from (Och, 1999).
- A **word bonus function**. This feature introduces a bonus based on the number of target words contained in the partial-translation hypothesis. It is used to compensate for the system's preference for short output sentences.
- A **source-to-target lexicon model**. This feature, which is based on the lexical parameters of the IBM Model 1 (Brown et al., 1993), provides a complementary probability for each tuple in the translation table. These lexicon parameters are obtained from the source-to-target alignments.
- A **target-to-source lexicon model**. Similarly to the previous feature, this feature is based on the lexical parameters of the IBM Model 1 but, in this case, these parameters are obtained from target-to-source alignments.

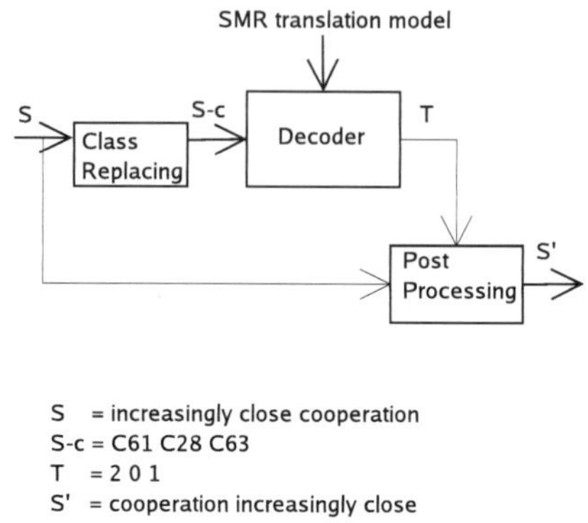

Figure 1: *SMR block diagram.*

3 SMR Baseline System

As mentioned in the introduction, SMR and SMT are based on the same principles.

3.1 Concept

The aim of SMR consists in using an SMT system to deal with reordering problems. Therefore, the SMR system can be seen as an SMT system which translates from an original source language (*S*) to a reordered source language (*S'*), given a target language (*T*).

3.2 Description

Figure 1 shows the SMR block diagram and an example of the input and output of each block inside the SMR system. The input is the initial source sentence (*S*) and the output is the reordered source sentence (*S'*). There are three blocks inside SMR: (1) the class replacing block; (2) the decoder, which requires an Ngram model containing the reordering information; and, (3) the post-processing block which either reorders the source sentence given the indexes of the decoder output 1-best (training step) or transforms the decoder output graph to an input graph for the SMT system (decoding step).

The decoder in Figure 1 requires a *translation* model which is an Ngram model. Given a training parallel corpus this model has been built following the next steps:

1. Select source and target word classes.
2. Align parallel training sentences at the word level in both translation directions. Compute the union of the two alignments to obtain a symmetrized many-to-many word alignment.
3. Use the IBM1 Model to obtain a many-to-one word alignment from the many-to-many word alignment.
4. Extract translation units from the computed many-to-one alignment. Replace source words by their

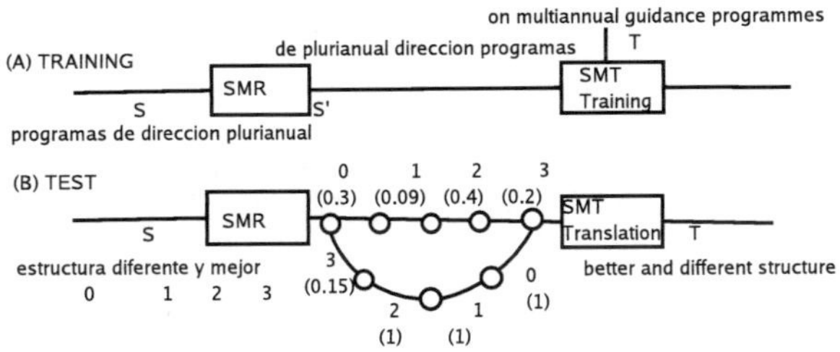

Figure 2: *SMR approach in the (A) training step (B) in the test step (the weight of each arch is in brackets).*

classes and target words by the index of the linked source word. An example of a translation unit here is: *C61 C28 C63#2 0 1*, where # divides source (word classes) and target (positions).

5. Compute the sequence of the above units and learn the language model

For further information about the SMR training procedure see (Costa-jussà and Fonollosa, 2006).

3.3 Improving SMT training

Figure 2 (A) shows the corresponding block diagram for the training corpus: first, the given training corpus *S* is translated into the reordered training source corpus *S'* with the SMR system. Then, this reordered training source corpus *S'* and the given training target corpus *T* are used to build the SMT system

The main difference here is that the training is computed with the *S'2T* task instead of the *S2T* given task. Figure 3 (A) shows an example of the word alignment computed on the given training parallel corpus *S2T*. Figure 3 (B) shows the same links but with the reordered source training corpus *S'*. Although the quality in alignment is the same, the tuples that can be extracted change (notice that tuple extraction is monotonic). We now are able to extract smaller tuples which reduce the translation vocabulary sparseness. These new tuples are used to build the SMT system.

3.4 Generation of multiple weighted reordering hypotheses

The SMR system, having its own search, can generate either an output 1-best or an output graph. In decoding, the SMR technique generates an output graph which is used as an input graph by the SMT system. Figure 2 (B) shows the corresponding block diagram in decoding: the SMR output graph is given as an input graph to the SMT system. Hereinafter, this either SMR output graph or SMT input graph will be referred to as (weighted) reordering graph. The monotonic search in the SMT system is extended with reorderings following this reordering graph.

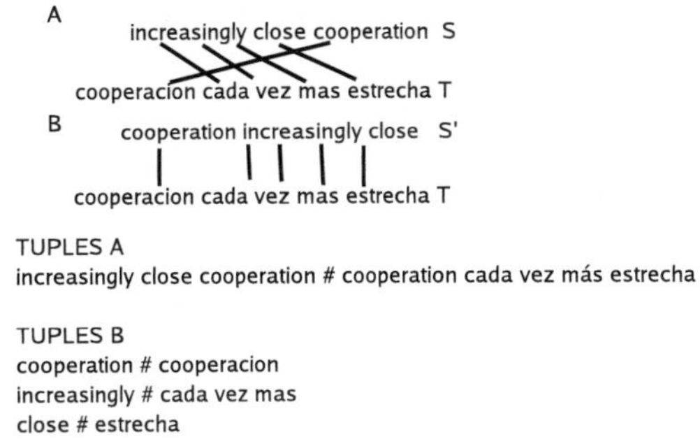

Figure 3: *Alignment and tuple extraction (A) original training source corpus (B) reordered training source corpus.*

This reordering graph has multiple paths and each path has its own weight. This weight is added as a feature function in the log-linear model.

4 Morphological vs Statistical Classes

Previous SMR studies (Costa-jussà and Fonollosa, 2006) (Costa-jussà et al., 2007) considered only statistical classes. On the one hand, these statistical classes performed fairly well and had the advantage of being suitable for any language. On the other hand, it should be taken into account the fact of training them in the training set allows for unknown words in the development or in the test set. Additionally, they do not have any reordering information because they are trained on a monolingual set.

The first problem, unknown words which appear in the development or in the test set, may be solved by using a disambiguation technique. Unknown words can be assigned to one class by taking into account their own context. The second problem, incorporating information about order, might be solved by training classes in the reordered training source corpus. In other words, we monotonized the training corpus with the alignment information (i.e. reorder the source corpus in the way that matches the target corpus under the alignment links criterion). After that, we train the statistical classes, hereinafter, called statistical reordered classes.

In some pair of languages, as for example English/Spanish, the reordering that may be performed is related to word's morphology (i.e. *TAGS*). Some *TAGS* rules (with some lexical exceptions) can be extracted as in (Popovic and Ney, 2006) where they were applied with reordering purposes as a preprocessing step. Another approach that has related *TAGS* and reordering was presented in (Crego and Mariño, 2006) where instead of rules, they learned reordering patterns based on *TAGS* as named in this paper's introduction. Hence, the SMR tech-

		Spanish	English
Train	Sentences	1,3M	
	Words	37,9M	35,5M
	Vocabulary	138,9k	133k
Dev	Sentences	2 000	2 000
	Words	60.5k	58.7k
	Vocabulary	8.1k	6.5k
Test	Sentences	2 000	2 000
	Words	60,2k	58k
	Vocabulary	8,2k	6,5k

Table 1: *Corpus Statistics.*

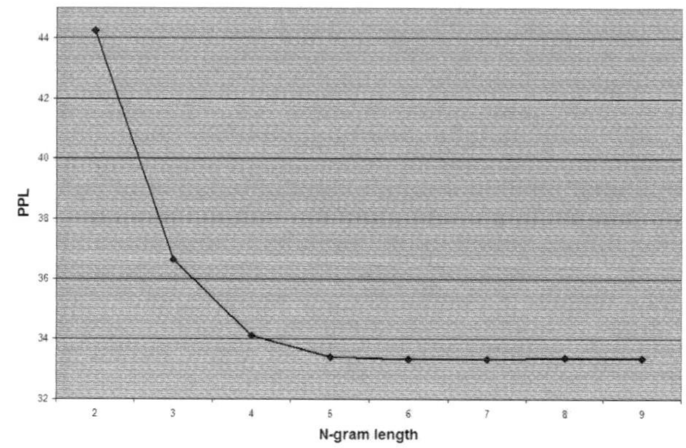

Figure 5: *Perplexity over the manually aligned test set given the SMR Ngram length.*

nique may take advantage of the morphological information. Notice that an advantage is that there is a *TAG* for each word, hence there are not unknown words.

5 Evaluation Framework

5.1 Corpus Statistics

Experiments were carried out using the data in the second evaluation campaign of the WMT07 [1].

This corpus consists in the official version of the speeches held in the European Parliament Plenary Sessions (EPPS), as available on the web page of the European Parliament. Additionally, there was available a smaller corpus (News-Commentary). Our training corpus was the catenation of both. Table 1 shows the corpus statistics.

5.2 Tools and preprocessing

The system was built similarly to (Costa-jussà et al., 2007). The SMT baseline system uses the Ngram-based approach, which has been explained in Section 2. Tools used are defined as follows: word alignments were computed using GIZA++ [2]; language model was estimated using SRILM [3]; decoding was carried out with MARIE[4]; an n-best re-ranking strategy is implemented which is used for optimization purposes just as proposed in *http://www.statmt.org/jhuws/* using the simplex method (Nelder and Mead, 1965) and BLEU as a loss function.

The SMT system we use a 4gram translation language model, a 5gram target language model and a 5gram class target language model.

Spanish data have been processed so that the pronouns which are attached to verbs are split up. Additionally, several article and prepositions words are separated (i.e. *del* goes into *de el*). This preprocessing was performed using Freeling software (Atserias et al., 2006). Training and evaluation were both true-case.

5.3 Classes and Ngram length Study for the SMR-Graph generation

This section evaluates several types of classes and n-gram lengths in the SMR model in order to choose the SMR configuration which provides the best results in translation in terms of quality. To accomplish this evaluation, we have designed the following experiment. Given 500 manually aligned parallel sentences of the EPPS corpora (Lambert et al., 2006), we order the source test in the way that better matches the target set. This ordered source set is considered our reference as it is based on manual alignments. On the other hand, the 500 sentences set is translated using the SMR configurations to be tested. Finally, the *Word Error Rate (WER)* is used as quality measure.

Figure 4 shows the WER behavior given different types of classes. As statistical classes *(cl50,cl100,cl200)* we used the Och monolingual classes (Och, 1999), which can be performed using 'mkcls' (a tool available with GIZA). Also we used the statistical reordered classes *(cl100mono)* which were explained in Section 4. Both statistical and statistical reordered classes used the *disamb* tool of SRILM in order to classify unknown words. As morphological classes we used the *TAGS* provided by Freeling. Clearly, statistical classes perform better than *TAGS* and best results can be achieved with 100 and 200 classes and an n-gram length of 5.

For the sake of completeness, we have evaluated the perplexity of the SMR Ngram model over the aligned test set above and choosing 200 classes. Figure 5 is coherent with the WER results above and it shows that perplexity is not reduced for an n-gram length greater than 5.

[1] http://www.statmt.org/wmt07/

[2] http://www.fjoch.com/GIZA++.html

[3] http://www.speech.sri.com/projects/srilm/

[4] http://gps-tsc.upc.es/veu/soft/soft/marie/

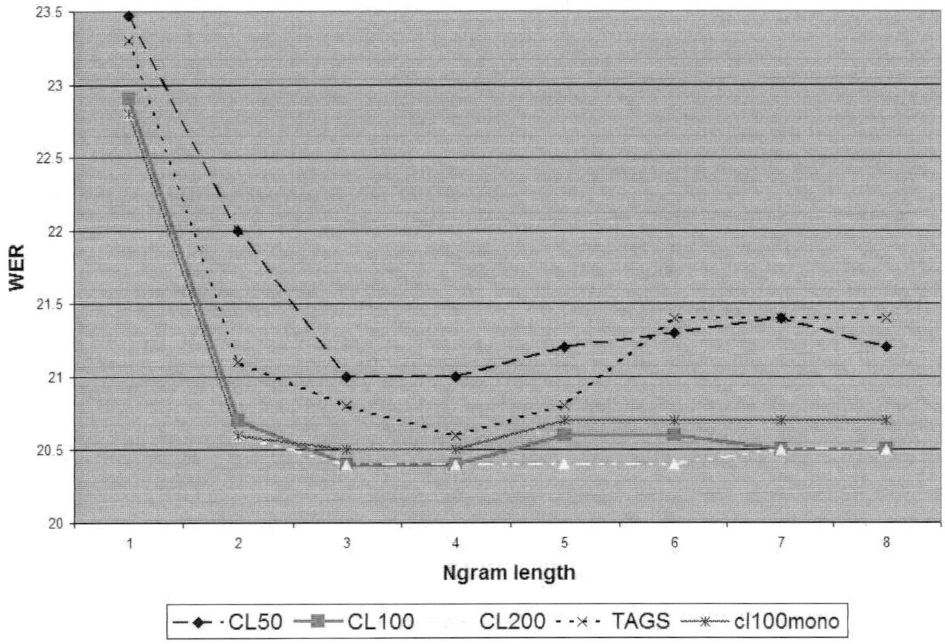

Figure 4: *WER over the reference given various sets of classes and Ngram lengths.*

5.4 Graph pruning

The more complex is the reordering graph, the less efficient is the decoding. That is why, in this section, we experiment with several ways of graph pruning. Additionally, for each pruning we see the influence of considering the graph weights (i.e. reordering feature importance).

Given that the reordering graph is the output of a beam search decoder, we can consider pruning the reordering graph by limiting the SMR beam, i.e. limiting the size of hypothesis stacks.

Given a reordering graph, another option is to prune states and arches only used in paths s times worse than the best path.

Table 2 gives the results of the proposed pruning. Note that computational time is given in terms of the monotonic translation time (and it is the same for both directions). It is shown that graph pruning guarantees the efficiency of the system and even increases the translation's quality. Similar results are obtained in terms of BLEU for both types of pruning. In this task and for both translation directions, it seems more appropriate to limit directly the beam search in the SMR step to 5.

As expected, the influence of the reordering feature, which takes into account the graph weights, tends to be more important as pruning decreases (i.e. when the graph has more paths).

Pruning	W_r	$BLEU_{En2Es}$	$BLEU_{Es2En}$	TIME
b5	yes	31.32	32.64	$2.4T_m$
b5	no	31.25	31.82	$2.5T_m$
b50	yes	30.95	32.28	$5.3T_m$
b50	no	30.90	27.44	$4.8T_m$
b50 s10	yes	31.19	32.20	$1.5T_m$
b50 s10	no	31.07	32.41	$1.4T_m$

Table 2: Performance in BLEU in the test set of different graph pruning (b stands for beam and s for states); the use of reordering feature function (W_r indicates its use); and the time increase related to T_m (monotonic translation time).

5.5 Results and discussion

Table 3 shows the performance of our Ngram-based system using the SMR technique. First row is the WMT07 baseline system which can be reproduced following the instructions in *http://www.statmt.org/wmt07/baseline.html.* This baseline system uses a non-monotonic search. Second row shows the results of the Ngram-based system presented in section 2 using the weighted reordering graph trained with the best configuration found in the above section (200 statistical classes and an Ngram of length 5).

System	$BLEU_{es2en}$	$BLEU_{en2es}$
WMT07 Of. Baseline	31.21	30.74
Ngram-based	32.64	31.32

Table 3: *BLEU Results.*

6 Conclusions and further work

The proposed SMR technique can be used both in training and test steps in a SMT system. Applying the SMR technique in the training step reduces the sparseness in the translation vocabulary. Applying SMR technique in the test step allows to generate a weighted reordering graph for SMT system.

The use of classes plays an important role in the SMR technique, and experiments have shown that statistical classes are better than morphological ones.

Moreover, we have experimented with different graph pruning showing that best translation results can be achieved at a very low increase of computational cost when comparing to the monotonic translation computational cost.

Finally, we have shown that our translation system using the SMR technique outperforms the WMT07 Official baseline system (which uses a non-monotonic search) in terms of BLEU.

As further work, we want to introduce the SMR technique in a state-of-the-art phrase-based system.

7 Acknowledgments

This work has been funded by the European Union under the TC-STAR project (IST- 2002-FP6-506738) and the Spanish Government under grant TEC2006-13964-C03 (AVIVAVOZ project).

References

J. Atserias, B. Casas, E. Comelles, M. González, L. Padró, and M. Padró. 2006. Freeling 1.3: Syntactic and semantic services in an open-source nlp library. In *5th Int. Conf. on Language Resource and Evaluation (LREC)*, pages 184–187.

P. Brown, S. Della Pietra, V. Della Pietra, and R. Mercer. 1993. The mathematics of statistical machine translation. *Computational Linguistics*, 19(2):263–311.

M. Collins, P. Koehn, and I. Kucerová. 2005. Clause restructuring for statistical machine translation. In *43st Annual Meeting of the Association for Computational Linguistics (ACL'05)*, pages 531 – 540, Michigan.

M.R. Costa-jussà and J.A.R. Fonollosa. 2006. Statistical machine reordering. In *Empirical Methods in Natural Language Processing (EMNLP)*, pages 71–77, Sydney.

M. R. Costa-jussà, P. Lambert, J.M. Crego, M. Khalilov, J.A.R. Fonollosa, J.B. Mariño, and R. Banchs. 2007. Ngram-based statistical machine translation enhanced with multiple weighted reordering hypotheses. In *ACL: Workshop of Statistical Machine Translation (WMT07)*, Prague.

J.M. Crego and J.B. Mariño. 2006. Reordering experiments for n-gram-based smt. *Ist IEEE/ACL International Workshop on Spoken Language Technology (SLT'06)*, pages 242–245.

J. M. Crego, M. R. Costa-jussà, J. Mariño, and J. A. Fonollosa. 2005. Ngram-based versus phrase-based statistical machine translation. In *Proc. of the Int. Workshop on Spoken Language Translation, IWSLT'05*, pages 177–184, Pittsburgh, October.

S. Kanthak, D. Vilar, E. Matusov, R. Zens, and H. Ney. 2005. Novel reordering approaches in phrase-based statistical machine translation. In *Proceedings of the ACL Workshop on Building and Using Parallel Texts: Data-Driven Machine Translation and Beyond*, pages 167–174, Ann Arbor, MI, June.

P. Koehn, F.J. Och, and D. Marcu. 2003. Statistical phrase-based translation. In *Proc. of the Human Language Technology Conference, HLT-NAACL'2003*, pages 48 – 54, Edmonton, Canada, May.

P. Lambert, A. de Gispert, R. Banchs, and J. Mariño. 2006. Guidelines for word alignment and manual alignment. *Language Resources and Evaluation*, 39(4):267–285.

J.B. Mariño, R.E. Banchs, J.M. Crego, A. de Gispert, P. Lambert, J.A.R. Fonollosa, and M.R. Costa-jussà. 2006. N-gram based machine translation. *Computational Linguistics*, 32(4):527–549.

J.A. Nelder and R. Mead. 1965. A simplex method for function minimization. *The Computer Journal*, 7:308–313.

F.J. Och. 1999. An efficient method for determining bilingual word classes. In *9th Conf. of the European Chapter of the Association for Computational Linguistics (EACL)*, pages 71–76, June.

M. Popovic and H. Ney. 2006. Pos-based word reorderings for statistical machine translation. In *5th International Conference on Language Resources and Evaluation (LREC)*, pages 1278–1283, Genova, May.

Domain Adaptation in Statistical Machine Translation with Mixture Modelling *

Jorge Civera and **Alfons Juan**
Universidad Politécnica de Valencia
Camino de Vera s/n
46022 Valencia, Spain
{jorcisai,ajuan}@iti.upv.es

Abstract

Mixture modelling is a standard technique for density estimation, but its use in statistical machine translation (SMT) has just started to be explored. One of the main advantages of this technique is its capability to learn specific probability distributions that better fit subsets of the training dataset. This feature is even more important in SMT given the difficulties to translate polysemic terms whose semantic depends on the context in which that term appears. In this paper, we describe a mixture extension of the HMM alignment model and the derivation of Viterbi alignments to feed a state-of-the-art phrase-based system. Experiments carried out on the Europarl and News Commentary corpora show the potential interest and limitations of mixture modelling.

1 Introduction

Mixture modelling is a popular approach for density estimation in many scientific areas (G. J. McLachlan and D. Peel, 2000). One of the most interesting properties of mixture modelling is its capability to model multimodal datasets by defining soft partitions on these datasets, and learning specific probability distributions for each partition, that better explains the general data generation process.

* Work supported by the EC (FEDER) and the Spanish MEC under grant TIN2006-15694-CO2-01, the *Conselleria d'Empresa, Universitat i Ciència - Generalitat Valenciana* under contract GV06/252, the *Universidad Politécnica de Valencia* with ILETA project and Ministerio de Educación y Ciencia.

In Machine Translation (MT), it is common to encounter large parallel corpora devoted to heterogeneous topics. These topics usually define sets of topic-specific lexicons that need to be translated taking into the semantic context in which they are found. This semantic dependency problem could be overcome by learning topic-dependent translation models that capture together the semantic context and the translation process.

However, there have not been until very recently that the application of mixture modelling in SMT has received increasing attention. In (Zhao and Xing, 2006), three fairly sophisticated bayesian topical translation models, taking IBM Model 1 as a baseline model, were presented under the bilingual topic admixture model formalism. These models capture latent topics at the document level in order to reduce semantic ambiguity and improve translation coherence. The models proposed provide in some cases better word alignment and translation quality than HMM and IBM models on an English-Chinese task. In (Civera and Juan, 2006), a mixture extension of IBM model 2 along with a specific dynamic-programming decoding algorithm were proposed. This IBM-2 mixture model offers a significant gain in translation quality over the conventional IBM model 2 on a semi-synthetic task.

In this work, we present a mixture extension of the well-known HMM alignment model first proposed in (Vogel and others, 1996) and refined in (Och and Ney, 2003). This model possesses appealing properties among which are worth mentioning, the simplicity of the first-order word alignment distribution that can be made independent of absolute positions while

Proceedings of the Second Workshop on Statistical Machine Translation, pages 177–180,
Prague, June 2007. ©2007 Association for Computational Linguistics

taking advantage of the localization phenomenon of word alignment in European languages, and the efficient and exact computation of the E-step and Viterbi alignment by using a dynamic-programming approach. These properties have made this model suitable for extensions (Toutanova et al., 2002) and integration in a phrase-based model (Deng and Byrne, 2005) in the past.

2 HMM alignment model

Given a bilingual pair (x, y), where x and y are mutual translation, we incorporate the hidden variable $a = a_1 a_2 \cdots a_{|x|}$ to reveal, for each source word position j, the target word position $a_j \in \{0, 1, \ldots, |y|\}$ to which it is connected. Thus,

$$p(x \mid y) = \sum_{a \in \mathcal{A}(x,y)} p(x, a \mid y) \tag{1}$$

where $\mathcal{A}(x, y)$ denotes the set of all possible alignments between x and y. The *alignment-completed* probability $P(x, a \mid y)$ can be decomposed in terms of source position-dependent probabilities as:

$$p(x, a \mid y) = \prod_{j=1}^{|x|} p(a_j \mid a_1^{j-1}, x_1^{j-1}, y)\, p(x_j \mid a_1^j, x_1^{j-1}, y) \tag{2}$$

The original formulation of the HMM alignment model assumes that each source word is *connected to exactly one* target word. This connection depends on the target position to which was aligned the previous source word and the length of the target sentence. Here, we drop both dependencies in order to simplify to a jump width alignment probability distribution:

$$p(a_j \mid a_1^{j-1}, x_1^{j-1}, y) \approx \begin{cases} p(a_j) & j = 1 \\ p(a_j - a_{j-1}) & j > 1 \end{cases} \tag{3}$$

$$p(x_j \mid a_1^j, x_1^{j-1}, y) \approx p(x_j \mid y_{a_j}) \tag{4}$$

Furthermore, the treatment of the NULL word is the same as that presented in (Och and Ney, 2003).

Finally, the HMM alignment model is defined as:

$$p(x \mid y) = \sum_{a \in \mathcal{A}(x,y)} p(a_1) \prod_{j=2}^{|x|} p(a_j - a_{j-1}) \prod_{j=1}^{|x|} p(x_j | y_{a_j}) \tag{5}$$

3 Mixture of HMM alignment models

Let us suppose that $p(x \mid y)$ has been generated using a T-component mixture of HMM alignment models:

$$\begin{aligned} p(x \mid y) &= \sum_{t=1}^{T} p(t \mid y)\, p(x \mid y, t) \\ &= \sum_{t=1}^{T} p(t \mid y) \sum_{a \in \mathcal{A}(x,y)} p(x, a \mid y, t) \end{aligned} \tag{6}$$

In Eq. 6, we introduce mixture coefficients $p(t \mid y)$ to weight the contribution of each HMM alignment model in the mixture. While the term $p(x, a \mid y, t)$ is decomposed as in the original HMM model.

The assumptions of the constituent HMM models are the same than those of the previous section, but we obtain topic-dependent statistical dictionaries and word alignments. Apropos of the mixture coefficients, we simplify these terms dropping its dependency on y, leaving as future work its inclusion in the model. Formally, the assumptions are:

$$p(t \mid y) \approx p(t) \tag{7}$$

$$p(a_j \mid a_1^{j-1}, x_1^{j-1}, y, t) \approx \begin{cases} p(a_j \mid t) & j = 1 \\ p(a_j - a_{j-1} \mid t) & j > 1 \end{cases} \tag{8}$$

$$p(x_j \mid a_1^j, x_1^{j-1}, y, t) \approx p(x_j \mid y_{a_j}, t) \tag{9}$$

Replacing the assumptions in Eq. 6, we obtain the (incomplete) HMM mixture model as follows:

$$\begin{aligned} p(x \mid y) = \sum_{t=1}^{T} p(t) &\sum_{a \in \mathcal{A}(x,y)} p(a_1 \mid t) \times \\ &\times \prod_{j=2}^{|x|} p(a_j - a_{j-1} \mid t) \prod_{j=1}^{|x|} p(x_j | y_{a_j}, t) \end{aligned} \tag{10}$$

and the set of unknown parameters comprises:

$$\vec{\Theta} = \begin{cases} p(t) & t = 1 \ldots T \\ p(i \mid t) & j = 1 \\ p(i - i' \mid t) & j > 1 \\ p(u \mid v, t) & \forall u \in \mathcal{X} \text{ and } v \in \mathcal{Y} \end{cases} \tag{11}$$

$\mathcal{X}$ and $\mathcal{Y}$, being the source and target vocabularies.

The estimation of the unknown parameters in Eq. 10 is troublesome, since topic and alignment data are missing. Here, we revert to the EM optimisation algoritm to compute these parameters.

In order to do that, we define the complete version of Eq. 10 incorporating the indicator variables z_t and z_a, uncovering, the until now hidden variables. The variable z_t is a T-dimensional bit vector with 1 in the position corresponding to the component generating (x, y) and zeros elsewhere, while the variable $z_a = z_{a_1} \dots z_{a_{|x|}}$ where z_{a_j} is a $|y|$-dimensional bit vector with 1 in the position corresponding to the target position to which position j is aligned and zeros elsewhere. Then, the complete model is:

$$p(x, z_t, z_a \,|\, y) \approx \prod_{t=1}^{T} p(t)^{z_t} \prod_{i=1}^{|y|} p(i \,|\, t)^{z_{a_{1i}} z_t} \times \\ \times \prod_{j=1}^{|x|} \prod_{i=1}^{|y|} p(x_j \,|\, y_i, t)^{z_{a_{ji}} z_t} \prod_{i'=1}^{|y|} p(i - i' \,|\, t)^{z_{a_{j-1i'}} z_{a_{ji}} z_t} \tag{12}$$

Given the complete model, the EM algorithm works in two basic steps in each iteration: the E(xpectation) step and the M(aximisation) step. At iteration k, the E step computes the expected value of the hidden variables given the observed data (x, y) and the estimate of the parameters $\vec{\Theta}^{(k)}$.

The E step reduces to the computation of the expected value of z_t, $z_{a_{ji}} z_t$ and $z_{a_{j-1i'}} z_{a_{ji}} z_t$ for each sample n:

$$z_t \propto p(t) \sum_{i=1}^{|y|} \alpha_{|x|it} \tag{13}$$

$$z_{a_{ji}} z_t = z_{a_{jit}} \, z_t \tag{14}$$

$$z_{a_{j-1i'}} z_{a_{ji}} z_t = (z_{a_{j-1i'}} z_{a_{ji}})_t \, z_t \tag{15}$$

where

$$z_{a_{jit}} \propto \sum_{k=1}^{|y|} \alpha_{jkt} \beta_{jkt}$$

$$(z_{a_{j-1i'}} z_{a_{ji}})_t \propto \alpha_{j-1it} \, p(i - i' \,|\, t) \, p(x_j | y_i, t) \, \beta_{jit}$$

and the recursive functions α and β defined as:

$$\alpha_{jit} = \begin{cases} p(i \,|\, t) \, p(x_j \,|\, y_i, t) & j = 1 \\ \sum_{k=1}^{|y|} \alpha_{j-1kt} \, p(i - k \,|\, t) \, p(x_j \,|\, y_i, t) & j > 1 \end{cases}$$

$$\beta_{jit} = \begin{cases} 1 & j = |x| \\ \sum_{k=1}^{|y|} p(k - i \,|\, t) \, p(x_{j+1} \,|\, y_k, t) \beta_{j+1kt} & j < |x| \end{cases}$$

The M step finds a new estimate of $\vec{\Theta}$, by maximising Eq. 12, using the expected value of the missing data from Eqs. 13,14 and 15 over all sample n:

$$p(t) = \frac{1}{N} \sum_{n=1}^{N} z_{nt}$$

$$p(i \,|\, t) \propto \sum_{n=1}^{N} z_{na_{1i}t}$$

$$p(i - i' \,|\, t) \propto \sum_{n=1}^{N} \sum_{j=1}^{|x_n|} (z_{na_{j-1i'}} z_{na_{ji}})_t$$

$$p(u \,|\, v, t) \propto \sum_{n=1}^{N} \sum_{j=1}^{|x_n|} \sum_{i=1}^{|y_n|} z_{na_{jit}} \, \delta(x_{nj}, u) \delta(y_{ni}, v)$$

3.1 Word alignment extraction

The HMM mixture model described in the previous section was used to generate Viterbi alignments on the training dataset. These optimal alignments are the basis for phrase-based systems.

In the original HMM model, the Viterbi alignment can be efficiently computed by a dynamic-programming algorithm with a complexity $O(|x| \cdot |y|^2)$. In the mixture HMM model, we approximate the Viterbi alignment by maximising over the components of the mixture:

$$\hat{a} \approx \arg\max_a \max_t p(t) \, p(x, a \,|\, y, t)$$

So we have that the complexity of the computation of the Viterbi alignment in a T-component HMM mixture model is $O(T \cdot |x| \cdot |y|^2)$.

4 Experimental results

The data that was employed in the experiments to train the HMM mixture model corresponds to the concatenation of the Spanish-English partitions of the Europarl and the News Commentary corpora. The idea behind this decision was to let the mixture model distinguish which bilingual pairs should contribute to learn a given HMM component in the mixture. Both corpora were preprocessed as suggested for the baseline system by tokenizing, filtering sentences longer than 40 words and lowercasing.

Regarding the components of the translation system, 5-gram language models were trained on the monolingual version of the corpora for English(En) and Spanish(Es), while phrase-based models with lexicalized reordering model were trained using the Moses toolkit (P. Koehn and others, 2007), but replacing the Viterbi alignments, usually provided by GIZA++ (Och and Ney, 2003), by those of the HMM mixture model with training scheme $mix\,1^5H^5$. This configuration was used to translate both test development sets, Europarl and News Commentary.

Concerning the weights of the different models, we tuned those weights by minimum error rate training and we employed the same weighting scheme for all the experiments in the same language pair. Therefore, the same weighting scheme was used over different number of components.

BLEU scores are reported in Tables 1 and 2 as a function of the number of components in the HMM mixture model on the preprocessed development test sets of the Europarl and News Commentary corpora.

Table 1: BLEU scores on the Europarl development test data

T	1	2	3	4
En-Es	31.27	31.08	31.12	31.11
Es-En	31.74	31.70	31.80	31.71

Table 2: BLEU scores on the News-Commentary development test data

T	1	2	3	4
En-Es	29.62	30.01	30.17	29.95
Es-En	29.15	29.22	29.11	29.02

As observed in Table 1, if we compare the BLEU scores of the conventional single-component HMM model to those of the HMM mixture model, it seems that there is little or no gain from incorporating more topics into the mixture for the Europarl corpus. However, in Table 2, the BLEU scores on the English-Spanish pair significantly increase as the number of components is incremented. We believe that this is due to the fact that the News Commentary corpus seems to have greater influence on the mixture model than on the single-component model, specializing Viterbi alignments to favour this corpus.

5 Conclusions and future work

In this work, a novel mixture version of the HMM alignment model was introduced. This model was employed to generate topic-dependent Viterbi alignments that were input into a state-of-the-art phrase-based system. The preliminary results reported on the English-Spanish partitions of the Europarl and News-Commentary corpora may raise some doubts about the applicability of mixture modelling to SMT, nonetheless in the advent of larger open-domain corpora, the idea behind topic-specific translation models seem to be more than appropriate, necessary. On the other hand, we are fully aware that indirectly assessing the quality of a model through a phrase-based system is a difficult task because of the different factors involved (Ayan and Dorr, 2006).

Finally, the main problem in mixture modelling is the linear growth of the set of parameters as the number of components increases. In the HMM, and also in IBM models, this problem is aggravated because of the use of statistical dictionary entailing a large number of parameters. A possible solution is the implementation of interpolation techniques to smooth sharp distributions estimated on few events (Och and Ney, 2003; Zhao and Xing, 2006).

References

N. F. Ayan and B. J. Dorr. 2006. Going beyond AER: an extensive analysis of word alignments and their impact on MT. In *Proc. of ACL'06*, pages 9–16.

J. Civera and A. Juan. 2006. Mixtures of IBM Model 2. In *Proc. of EAMT'06*, pages 159–167.

Y. Deng and W. Byrne. 2005. HMM word and phrase alignment for statistical machine translation. In *Proc. of HLT-EMNLP'05*, pages 169–176.

G. J. McLachlan and D. Peel. 2000. *Finite Mixture Models*. Wiley.

F. J. Och and H. Ney. 2003. A systematic comparison of various statistical alignment models. *Computational Linguistics*, 29(1):19–51.

P. Koehn and others. 2007. Moses: Open Source Toolkit for Statistical Machine Translation. In *Proc. of ACL'07 Demo Session*, page To be published.

K. Toutanova, H. T. Ilhan, and C. D. Manning. 2002. Extensions to HMM-based statistical word alignment models. In *Proc. of EMNLP '02*, pages 87–94.

S. Vogel et al. 1996. HMM-based word alignment in statistical translation. In *Proc. of CL*, pages 836–841.

B. Zhao and E. P. Xing. 2006. BiTAM: Bilingual Topic AdMixture Models for Word Alignment. In *Proc. of COLING/ACL'06*.

Getting to know Moses: Initial experiments on German–English factored translation

Maria Holmqvist, Sara Stymne, and Lars Ahrenberg
Department of Computer and Information Science
Linköpings universitet, Sweden
{marho,sarst,lah}@ida.liu.se

Abstract

We present results and experiences from our experiments with phrase-based statistical machine translation using Moses. The paper is based on the idea of using an off-the-shelf parser to supply linguistic information to a factored translation model and compare the results of German–English translation to the shared task baseline system based on word form. We report partial results for this model and results for two simplified setups. Our best setup takes advantage of the parser's lemmatization and decompounding. A qualitative analysis of compound translation shows that decompounding improves translation quality.

1 Introduction

One of the stated goals for the shared task of this workshop is "to offer newcomers a smooth start with hands-on experience in state-of-the-art statistical machine translation methods". As our previous research in machine translation has been mainly concerned with rule-based methods, we jumped at this offer.

We chose to work on German-to-English translation for two reasons. Our primary practical interest lies with translation between Swedish and English, and of the languages offered for the shared task, German is the one closest in structure to Swedish. While there are differences in word order and morphology between Swedish and German, there are also similarities, e.g., that both languages represent nominal compounds as single orthographic words. We chose the direction from German to English because our knowledge of English is better than our knowledge of German, making it easier to judge the quality of translation output. Experiments were performed on the Europarl data.

With factored statistical machine translation, different levels of linguistic information can be taken into account during training of a statistical translation system and decoding. In our experiments we combined syntactic and morphological factors from an off-the-shelf parser with the factored translation framework in Moses (Moses, 2007). We wanted to test the following hypotheses:

- Translation models based on lemmas will improve translation quality (Popovič and Ney, 2004)
- Decompounding German nominal compounds will improve translation quality (Koehn and Knight, 2003)
- Re-ordering models based on word forms and parts-of-speech will improve translation quality (Zens and Ney, 2006).

2 The parser

The parser, *Machinese Syntax*, is a commercially available dependency parser from Connexor Oy [1]. It provides each word with lemma, part-of-speech, morphological features and dependency relations (see Figure 1). In addition, the lemmas of compounds are marked by a '#' separating the two parts of the compound. For the shared task we only used shallow linguistic information: lemma, part-of-speech and morphology. The compound boundary identification was used to split noun com-

[1] Connexor Oy, http://www.connexor.com.

Proceedings of the Second Workshop on Statistical Machine Translation, pages 181–184,
Prague, June 2007.

pounds to make the German input more similar to English text.

```
1 Mit   mit   pm>2      @PREMARK PREP
2 Blick blick advl>10 @NH N MSC SG DAT
3 auf   auf   pm>5      @PREMARK PREP
```

Figure 1. Example of parser output

We used the parser's tokenization as given. Some common multiword units, such as 'at all' and 'von heute', are treated as single words by the parser (cf. Niessen and Ney, 2004). The German parser also splits contracted prepositions and determiners like 'zum' – 'zu dem' ("to the").

3 System description

For our experiments with Moses we basically followed the shared task baseline system setup to train our factored translation models. After training a statistical model, minimum error-rate tuning was performed to tune the model parameters. All experiments were performed on an AMD 64 Athlon 4000+ processor with 4 Gb of RAM and 32 bit Linux (Ubuntu).

Since time as well as computer resources were limited we designed a model that we hoped would make the best use of all available factors. This model turned out to be too complex for our machine and in later experiments we abandoned it for a simpler model.

3.1 Pre-processing

In the pre-processing step we used the standard pre-processing of the shared task baseline system, parsed the German and English texts and processed the output to obtain four factors: word form, lemma, part-of-speech and morphology. Missing values for lemma, part-of-speech and morphology were replaced with default values.

Noun compounds are very frequent in German, 2.9% of all tokens in the tuning corpus were identified by the parser as noun compounds. Compounds tend to lead to sparse data problems and splitting them has been shown to improve German-English translation (Koehn and Knight, 2003). Thus we decided to decompund German noun compounds identified as such by our parser.

We used a simple strategy to remove fillers and to correct some obvious mistakes. We removed the filler '-s' that appear before a marked split unless it was one of '-ss', '-urs', '-eis' or '-us'. This applied to 35% of the noun compounds in the tuning corpus. The fillers were removed both in the word form and the lemma (see Figure 2).

There were some mistakes made by the parser, for instance on compounds containing the word 'nahmen' which was incorrectly split as 'stellungn#ahmen' instead of 'stellung#nahmen' ("statement"). These splits were corrected by moving the 'n' to the right side of the split.

We then split noun-lemmas on hyphens unless there were numbers on either side of it and on the places marked by '#'. Word forms were split in the corresponding places as the lemmas.

The part-of-speech and morphology of the last word in the compound is the same as for the whole compound. For the other parts we hypothesized that part-of-speech is Noun and the morphology is unknown, marked by the tag *UNK*.

```
Parser output:
unionsländer unions#land N NEU PL ACC

Factored output:
union|union|N|UNK
länder|land|N|NEU_PL_ACC
```

Figure 2. Compound splitting for 'unionsländer' ("countries in the union")

These strategies are quite crude and could be further refined by studying the parser output thoroughly to pinpoint more problems.

3.2 Training translation models with linguistic factors

After pre-processing, the German–English Europarl training data contains four factors: 0: word form, 1: lemma, 2: part-of-speech, 3: morphology. As a first step in training our translation models we performed word alignment on lemmas as this could potentially improve word alignment.

3.2.1 First setup

Factored translation requires a number of decoding steps, which are either *mapping* steps mapping a source factor to a target factor or *generation* steps generating a target factor from other target factors. Our first setup contained three mapping steps, T0–T2, and one generation step, G0.

T0: 0-0 (word – word)
T1: 1-1 (lemma – lemma)
T2: 2,3-2,3 (pos+morph – pos+morph)
G0: 1,2,3-0 (lemma+pos+morph – word)

With the generation step, word forms that did not appear in the training data may still get translated if the lemma, part-of-speech and morphology can be translated separately and the target word form can be generated from these factors.

Word order varies a great deal between German and English. This is especially true for the placement of verbs. To model word order changes we included part-of-speech information and created two reordering models, one based on word form (0), the other on part-of-speech (2):

0-0.msd-bidirectional-fe
2-2.msd-bidirectional-fe

The decoding times for this setup turned out to be unmanageable. In the first iteration of parameter tuning, decoding times were approx. 6 min/sentence. In the second iteration decoding time increased to approx. 30 min/sentence. Removing one of the reordering models did not result in a significant change in decoding time. Just translating the 2000 sentences of test data with untuned parameters would take several days. We interrupted the tuning and abandoned this setup.

3.2.2 Second setup

Because of the excessive decoding times of the first factored setup we resorted to a simpler system that only used the word form factor for the translation and reordering models. This setup differs from the shared task baseline in the following ways: First, it uses the tokenization provided by the parser. Second, alignment was performed on the lemma factor. Third, German compounds were split using the method described above. To speed up tuning and decoding, we only used the first 200 sentences of development data (dev2006) for tuning and reduced stack size to 50.

T0: 0-0 (word – word)
R: 0-0.msd-bidirectional-fe

3.2.3 Third setup

To test our hypothesis that word reordering would benefit from part-of-speech information we created another simpler model. This setup has two mapping steps, T0 and T1, and a reordering model based on part-of-speech.

T0: 0-0 (word – word)
T1: 2,3-2,3 (pos+morph – pos+morph)
R: 2-2.msd-bidirectional-fe

4 Results

We compared our systems to a baseline system with the same setup as the WMT2007 shared task baseline system but tuned with our system's simplified tuning settings (200 instead of 2000 tuning sentences, stack size 50). Table 1 shows the Bleu improvement on the 200 sentences development data from the first and last iteration of tuning.

System	Dev2006 (200)	
	1st iteration	Last iteration
Baseline	19.56	27.07
First	21.68	-
Second	20.43	27.16
Third	20.72	24.72

Table 1. Bleu scores on 200 sentences of tuning data before and after tuning

The final test of our systems was performed on the development test corpus (devtest2006) using stack size 50. The results are shown in Table 2. The low Bleu score for the third setup implies that reordering on part-of-speech is not enough on its own. The second setup performed best with a slightly higher Bleu score than the baseline. We used the second setup to translate test data for our submission to the shared task.

System	Devtest2006 (NIST/Bleu)
Baseline	6.7415 / 25.94
First	-
Second	6.8036 / 26.04
Third	6.5504 / 24.57

Table 2. NIST and Bleu scores on development test data

4.1 Decompounding

We have evaluated the decompounding strategy by analyzing how the first 75 identified noun compounds of the devtest corpus were translated by our second setup compared to the baseline. The sample excluded doubles and compounds that had no clear translation in the reference corpus.

Out of these 75 compounds 74 were nouns that were correctly split and 1 was an adjective that was split incorrectly: 'allumfass#ende'. Despite that it was incorrectly identified and split it was translated satisfyingly to 'comprehensive'.

The translations were grouped into the categories shown in Table 3. The 75 compounds were classified into these categories for our second system and the baseline system, as shown in Table 4. As can be seen the compounds were handled better by our system, which had 62 acceptable translations (C or V) compared to 48 for the baseline and did not leave any noun compounds untranslated.

Category	Example
C-correct	Regelungsentwurf Draft regulation Ref: Draft regulation
V-variant	Schlachthöfen Abattoirs Ref: Slaughter houses
P-partly correct	Anpassungsdruck Pressure Ref: Pressure for adaption
F-wrong form	Länderberichte Country report Ref: Country reports
W-wrong	Erbonkel Uncle dna Ref: Sugar daddy
U-untranslated	Schlussentwurf Schlussentwurf Ref: Final draft

Table 3. Classification scheme with examples for compound translations

		Baseline system						
		C	V	P	W	U	F	Tot
Second system	C	36	1	3		3	1	44
	V	1	9	2	1	5		18
	P			3		2		5
	W				1	2		3
	U							0
	F	1					4	5
	Tot	38	10	8	2	12	5	75

Table 4. Classification of 75 compounds from our second system and the baseline system

Decompounding of nouns reduced the number of untranslated words, but there were still some left. Among these were cases that can be handled such as separable prefix verbs like 'aufzeigten' ("pointed out") (Niessen and Ney, 2000) or adjective compounds such as 'multidimensionale' ("multi dimensional"). There were also some noun compounds left which indicates that we might need a better decompounding strategy than the one used by the parser (see e.g. Koehn and Knight, 2003).

4.2 Experiences and future plans

With the computer equipment at our disposal, training of the models and tuning of the parameters turned out to be a very time-consuming task. For this reason, the number of system setups we could test was small, and much fewer than we had hoped for. Thus it is too early to draw any conclusions as regards our hypotheses, but we plan to perform more tests in the future, also on Swedish–English data. The parser's ability to identify compounds that can be split before training seems to give a definite improvement, however, and is a feature that can likely be exploited also for Swedish-to-English translation with Moses.

References

Koehn, Philipp and Kevin Knight, 2003. Empirical methods for compound splitting. In *Proceedings of EACL 2003*, 187-194. Budapest, Hungary.

Moses – a factored phrase-based beam-search decoder for machine translation. 13 April 2007, URL: http://www.statmt.org/moses/ .

Niessen, Sonja and Hermann Ney, 2004. Statistical machine translation with scarce resources using morpho-syntactic information. *Computational Linguistics*, 181-204 .

Niessen, Sonja and Hermann Ney, 2000. Improving SMT Quality with Morpho-syntactic Analysis. In *Proceedings of Coling 2000.* 1081-1085. Saarbrücken, Germany.

Popovič, Maja and Hermann Ney, 2004. Improving Word Alignment Quality using Morpho-Syntactic Information. In *Proceedings of Coling 2004,* 310-314, Geneva, Switzerland.

Zens, Richard and Hermann Ney, 2006. Discriminative Reordering Models for Statistical Machine Translation. In *HLT-NAACL: Proceedings of the Workshop on Statistical Machine Translation*, 55-63, New York City, NY.

NRC's PORTAGE system for WMT 2007

Nicola Ueffing, Michel Simard, Samuel Larkin
Interactive Language Technologies Group
National Research Council Canada
Gatineau, Québec, Canada
firstname.lastname@nrc.gc.ca

Howard Johnson
Interactive Information Group
National Research Council Canada
Ottawa, Ontario, Canada
Howard.Johnson@nrc.gc.ca

Abstract

We present the PORTAGE statistical machine translation system which participated in the shared task of the ACL 2007 Second Workshop on Statistical Machine Translation. The focus of this description is on improvements which were incorporated into the system over the last year. These include adapted language models, phrase table pruning, an IBM1-based decoder feature, and rescoring with posterior probabilities.

1 Introduction

The statistical machine translation (SMT) system PORTAGE was developed at the National Research Council Canada and has recently been made available to Canadian universities and research institutions. It is a state-of-the-art phrase-based SMT system. We will shortly describe its basics in this paper and then highlight the new methods which we incorporated since our participation in the WMT 2006 shared task. These include new scoring methods for phrase pairs, pruning of phrase tables based on significance, a higher-order language model, adapted language models, and several new decoder and rescoring models. PORTAGE was also used in a joint system developed in cooperation with Systran. The interested reader is referred to (Simard et al., 2007).

Throughout this paper, let $s_1^J := s_1 \ldots s_J$ denote a source sentence of length J, $t_1^I := t_1 \ldots t_I$ a target sentence of length I, and $\tilde{s}$ and $\tilde{t}$ phrases in source and target language, respectively.

2 Baseline

As baseline for our experiments, we used a version of PORTAGE corresponding to its state at the time of the WMT 2006 shared task. We provide a basic description of this system here; for more details see (Johnson et al., 2006).

PORTAGE implements a two-stage translation process: First, the decoder generates N-best lists, using a basic set of models which are then rescored with additional models in a second step. In the baseline system, the decoder uses the following models (or feature functions):

- one or several phrase table(s), which model the translation direction $p(\tilde{s} \mid \tilde{t})$. They are generated from the training corpus via the "diag-and" method (Koehn et al., 2003) and smoothed using Kneser-Ney smoothing (Foster et al., 2006),
- one or several n-gram language model(s) trained with the SRILM toolkit (Stolcke, 2002); in the baseline experiments reported here, we used a trigram model,
- a distortion model which assigns a penalty based on the number of source words which are skipped when generating a new target phrase,
- a word penalty.

These different models are combined loglinearly. Their weights are optimized w.r.t. BLEU score using the algorithm described in (Och, 2003). This is done on the provided development corpus. The search algorithm implemented in the decoder is a dynamic-programming beam-search algorithm.

Proceedings of the Second Workshop on Statistical Machine Translation, pages 185–188,
Prague, June 2007.

After the decoding step, rescoring with additional models is performed. The baseline system generates a 1,000-best list of alternative translations for each source sentence. These lists are rescored with the different models described above, a character penalty, and three different features based on IBM Models 1 and 2 (Brown et al., 1993) calculated in both translation directions. The weights of these additional models and of the decoder models are again optimized to maximize BLEU score.

Note that we did not use the decision-tree-based distortion models described in (Johnson et al., 2006) here because they did not improve translation quality.

In the following subsections, we will describe the new models added to the system for our WMT 2007 submissions.

3 Improvements in PORTAGE

3.1 Phrase translation models

Whereas the phrase tables used in the baseline system contain only one score for each phrase pair, namely conditional probabilities calculated using Kneser-Ney smoothing, our current system combines seven different phrase scores.

First, we used several types of phrase table smoothing in the WMT 2007 system because this proved helpful on other translation tasks: relative frequency estimates, Kneser-Ney- and Zens-Ney-smoothed probabilities (Foster et al., 2006). Furthermore, we added normalized joint probability estimates to the phrase translation model. The other three scores will be explained at the end of this subsection.

We pruned the generated phrase tables following the method introduced in (Johnson et al., 2007). This approach considers all phrase pairs $(\tilde{s}, \tilde{t})$ in the phrase table. The count $C(\tilde{s}, \tilde{t})$ of all sentence pairs containing $(\tilde{s}, \tilde{t})$ is determined, as well as the count of all source/target sentences containing $\tilde{s}/\tilde{t}$. Using these counts, Fisher's exact test is carried out to calculate the significance of the phrase pair. The phrase tables are then pruned based on the p-value. Phrase pairs with low significance, i.e. which are only weakly supported by the training data, are pruned. This reduces the size of the phrase tables to 8-16% on the different language pairs. See (Johnson et al., 2007) for details.

Three additional phrase scores were derived from information on which this pruning is based:

- the significance level (or p-value),
- the number $C(\tilde{s}, \tilde{t})$ of sentence pairs containing the phrase pair, normalized by the number of source sentences containing $\tilde{s}$,
- $C(\tilde{s}, \tilde{t})$, normalized by the number of target sentences containing $\tilde{t}$.

For our submissions, we used the last three phrase scores only when translating the EuroParl data. Initial experiments showed that they do not improve translation quality on the News Commentary data. Apart from this, the systems for both domains are identical.

3.2 Adapted language models

Concerning the language models, we made two changes to our system since WMT 2006. First, we replaced the trigram language model by a 4-gram model trained on the WMT 2007 data. We also investigated the use of a 5-gram, but that did not improve translation quality. Second, we included adapted language models which are specific to the development and test corpora. For each development or test corpus, we built this language model using information retrieval[1] to find relevant sentences in the training data. To this end, we merged the training corpora for EuroParl and News Commentary. The source sentences from the development or test corpus served as individual queries to find relevant training sentence pairs. For each source sentence, we retrieved 10 sentence pairs from the training data and used their target sides as language model training data. On this small corpus, we trained a trigram language model, again using the SRILM toolkit. The feature function weights in the decoder and the rescoring model were optimized using the adapted language model for the development corpus. When translating the test corpus, we kept these weights, but replaced the adapted

[1] We used the lemur toolkit for querying, see http://www.lemurproject.org/

language model by that specific to the test corpus.

3.3 New decoder and rescoring features

We integrated several new decoder and rescoring features into PORTAGE. During decoding, the system now makes use of a feature based on IBM Model 1. This feature calculates the probability of the (partial) translation over the source sentence, using an IBM1 translation model in the direction $p(t_1^I \mid s_1^J)$.

In the rescoring process, we additionally included several types of posterior probabilities. One is the posterior probability of the sentence length over the N-best list for this source sentence. The others are determined on the level of words, phrases, and n-grams, and then combined into a value for the whole sentence. All posterior probabilities are calculated over the N-best list, using the sentence probabilities which the baseline system assigns to the translation hypotheses. For details on the posterior probabilities, see (Ueffing and Ney, 2007; Zens and Ney, 2006). This year, we increased the length of the N-best lists from 1,000 to 5,000.

3.4 Post-processing

For truecasing the translation output, we used the model described in (Agbago et al., 2005). This model uses a combination of statistical components, including an n-gram language model, a case mapping model, and a specialized language model for unknown words. The language model is a 5-gram model trained on the WMT 2007 data. The detokenizer which we used is the one provided for WMT 2007.

4 Experimental results

We submitted results for six of the translation directions of the shared task: French $\leftrightarrow$ English, German $\leftrightarrow$ English, and Spanish $\leftrightarrow$ English.

Table 1 shows the improvements resulting from incorporating new techniques into PORTAGE on the Spanish $\rightarrow$ English EuroParl task. The baseline system is the one described in section 2. Trained on the 2007 training corpora, this yields a BLEU score of 30.48. Adding the new phrase scores introduced in section 3.1 yields a slight improvement in translation quality. This improvement by itself is not significant, but we observed it consistently across all evaluation metrics and across the different development and test corpora. Increasing the order of the language model and adding an adapted language model specific to the translation input (see section 3.2) improves the BLEU score by 0.6 points. This is the biggest gain we observe from introducing a new method. The incorporation of the IBM1-based decoder feature causes a slight drop in translation quality. This surprised us because we found this feature to be very helpful on the NIST Chinese $\rightarrow$ English translation task. Adding the posterior probabilities presented in section 3.3 in rescoring and increasing the length of the N-best lists yielded a small, but consistent gain in translation quality. The overall improvement compared to last year's system is around 1 BLEU point. The gain achieved from introducing the new methods by themselves are relatively small, but they add up.

Table 2 shows results on all six language pairs we translated for the shared task. The translation quality achieved on the 2007 test set is similar to that on the 2006 test set. The system clearly performs better on the EuroParl domain than on News Commentary.

Table 2: *Translation quality in terms of BLEU[%] and NIST score on all tasks. Truecased and detokenized translation output.*

		test2006		test2007	
task		BLEU	NIST	BLEU	NIST
Eu	D→E	25.27	6.82	26.02	6.91
	E→D	19.36	5.86	18.94	5.71
	S→E	31.54	7.55	32.09	7.67
	E→S	30.94	7.39	30.92	7.41
	F→E	30.90	7.51	31.90	7.68
	E→F	30.08	7.26	30.06	7.26
NC	D→E	20.23	6.19	23.17	7.10
	E→D	13.84	5.38	16.30	5.95
	S→E	31.07	7.68	31.08	8.11
	E→S	30.79	7.73	32.56	8.25
	F→E	24.97	6.78	26.84	7.47
	E→F	24.91	6.79	26.60	7.24

Table 1: *Effect of integrating new models and methods into the PORTAGE system. Translation quality in terms of BLEU and NIST score, WER and PER on the EuroParl Spanish–English 2006 test set. True-cased and detokenized translation output. Best results printed in boldface.*

system	BLEU[%]	NIST	WER[%]	PER[%]
baseline	30.48	7.44	58.62	42.74
+ new phrase table features	30.66	7.48	58.25	42.46
+ 4-gram LM + adapted LM	31.26	7.53	57.93	42.26
+ IBM1-based decoder feature	31.18	7.51	58.13	42.53
+ refined rescoring	**31.54**	**7.55**	**57.81**	**42.24**

5 Conclusion

We presented the PORTAGE system with which we translated six language pairs in the WMT 2007 shared task. Starting from the state of the system during the WMT 2006 evaluation, we analyzed the contribution of new methods which were incorporated over the last year in detail. Our experiments showed that most of these changes result in (small) improvements in translation quality. In total, we gain about 1 BLEU point compared to last year's system.

6 Acknowledgments

Our thanks go to the PORTAGE team at NRC for their contributions and valuable feedback.

References

A. Agbago, R. Kuhn, and G. Foster. 2005. Truecasing for the Portage system. In *Recent Advances in Natural Language Processing*, pages 21–24, Borovets, Bulgaria, September.

P. F. Brown, S. A. Della Pietra, V. J. Della Pietra, and R. L. Mercer. 1993. The mathematics of statistical machine translation: Parameter estimation. *Computational Linguistics*, 19(2):263–311, June.

G. Foster, R. Kuhn, and J. H. Johnson. 2006. Phrasetable smoothing for statistical machine translation. In *Proc. of the Conf. on Empirical Methods for Natural Language Processing (EMNLP)*, pages 53–61, Sydney, Australia, July.

J. H. Johnson, F. Sadat, G. Foster, R. Kuhn, M. Simard, E. Joanis, and S. Larkin. 2006. Portage: with smoothed phrase tables and segment choice models. In *Proc. HLT/NAACL Workshop on Statistical Machine Translation (WMT)*, pages 134–137, New York, NY, June.

H. Johnson, J. Martin, G. Foster, and R. Kuhn. 2007. Improving translation quality by discarding most of the phrasetable. In *Proc. of the Conf. on Empirical Methods for Natural Language Processing and Conf. on Computational Natural Language Learning (EMNLP-CoNLL)*, to appear, Prague, Czech Republic, June.

P. Koehn, F. J. Och, and D. Marcu. 2003. Statistical phrase-based translation. In *Proc. of the Human Language Technology Conf. (HLT-NAACL)*, pages 127–133, Edmonton, Canada, May/June.

F. J. Och. 2003. Minimum error rate training in statistical machine translation. In *Proc. of the 41st Annual Meeting of the Association for Computational Linguistics (ACL)*, pages 160–167, Sapporo, Japan, July.

M. Simard, J. Senellart, P. Isabelle, R. Kuhn, J. Stephan, and N. Ueffing. 2007. Knowledge-based translation with statistical phrase-based post-editing. In *Proc. ACL Second Workshop on Statistical Machine Translation (WMT)*, to appear, Prague, Czech Republic, June.

A. Stolcke. 2002. SRILM – an extensible language modeling toolkit. In *Proc. Int. Conf. on Spoken Language Processing (ICSLP)*, volume 2, pages 901–904, Denver, CO.

N. Ueffing and H. Ney. 2007. Word-level confidence estimation for machine translation. *Computational Linguistics*, 33(1):9–40, March.

R. Zens and H. Ney. 2006. N-gram posterior probabilities for statistical machine translation. In *Proc. HLT/NAACL Workshop on Statistical Machine Translation (WMT)*, pages 72–77, New York, NY, June.

Building a Statistical Machine Translation System for French using the Europarl Corpus

Holger Schwenk

LIMSI-CNRS, bat 508, BP 133
91403 Orsay cedex, FRANCE
schwenk@limsi.fr

Abstract

This paper describes the development of a statistical machine translation system based on the Moses decoder for the 2007 WMT shared tasks. Several different translation strategies were explored. We also use a statistical language model that is based on a continuous representation of the words in the vocabulary. By these means we expect to take better advantage of the limited amount of training data. Finally, we have investigated the usefulness of a second reference translation of the development data.

1 Introduction

This paper describes the development of a statistical machine translation system based on the Moses decoder (Koehn et al., 2007) for the 2007 WMT shared tasks. Due to time constraints, we only considered the translation between French and English. A system with a similar architecture was successfully applied to the translation between Spanish and English in the framework of the 2007 TC-STAR evaluation.[1] For the 2007 WMT shared task a recipe is provided to build a baseline translation system using the Moses decoder. Our system differs in several aspects from this base-line: 1) the training data is not lower-cased; 2) Giza alignments are calculated on sentences of up to 90 words; 3) a two pass-decoding was used; and 4) a so called continuous space language model is used in order to take better advantage of the limited amount of training data.

[1] A paper on this work is submitted to MT Sumit 2007.

This architecture is motivated and detailed in the following sections.

2 Architecture of the system

The goal of statistical machine translation (SMT) is to produce a target sentence $\mathbf{e}$ from a source sentence $\mathbf{f}$. It is today common practice to use phrases as translation units (Koehn et al., 2003; Och and Ney, 2003) and a log linear framework in order to introduce several models explaining the translation process:

$$\begin{aligned} \mathbf{e}^* &= \arg\max p(\mathbf{e}|\mathbf{f}) \\ &= \arg\max_e \{exp(\sum_i \lambda_i h_i(\mathbf{e},\mathbf{f}))\} \end{aligned} \quad (1)$$

The feature functions h_i are the system models and the λ_i weights are typically optimized to maximize a scoring function on a development set (Och and Ney, 2002). In our system fourteen features functions were used, namely phrase and lexical translation probabilities in both directions, seven features for the lexicalized distortion model, a word and a phrase penalty and a target language model (LM).

The system is constructed as follows. First, Giza++ is used to perform word alignments in both directions. Second, phrases and lexical reorderings are extracted using the default settings of the Moses SMT toolkit. A target LM is then constructed as detailed in section 2.1. The translation itself is performed in two passes: first, Moses in run and a 1000-best list is generated for each sentence. When generating n-best lists it may happen that the same target sentence is generated multiple times, for instance using different segmentations of the source sentence

Proceedings of the Second Workshop on Statistical Machine Translation, pages 189–192,
Prague, June 2007. ©2007 Association for Computational Linguistics

or a different set of phrases. We enforced all the hypothesis in an n-best list to be lexically different since our purpose was to rescore them with a LM. The parameters of Moses are tuned on devtest2006 for the Europarl task and nc-dev2007 for the news commentary task, using the cmert tool.

These 1000-best lists are then rescored with different language models, either using a longer context or performing the probability estimation in the continuous space. After rescoring, the weights of the feature functions are optimized again using the numerical optimization toolkit Condor (Berghen and Bersini, 2005). Note that this step operates only on the 1000-best lists, no re-decoding is performed. In general, this results in an increased weight for the LM. Comparative results are provided in the result section whether it seems to be better to use higher order language models already during decoding, or to generate first rich n-best lists and to use the improved LMs during rescoring.

2.1 Language modeling

The monolingual part of the Europarl (38.3M English and 43.1 French words) and the news commentary corpus (1.8M/1.2M words) were used. Separate LMs were build on each data source and then linearly interpolated, optimizing the coefficients with an EM procedure. This usually gives better results than building an LM on the pooled data. Note that we build two sets of LMs: a first set tuned on devtest2006, and a second one on nc-dev2007. It is not surprising to see that the interpolation coefficients differ significantly: 0.97/0.03 for devtest2006 and 0.42/0.58 for nc-dev2007. The perplexities of the interpolated LMs are given in Table 1.

2.2 Continuous space language model

Overall, there are roughly 40 million words of texts available to train the target language models. This is a quite limited amount in comparison to tasks like the NIST machine translation evaluations for which several billion words of newspaper texts are available. Therefore, new techniques must be deployed to take the best advantage of the limited resources.

Here, we propose to use the so-called continuous space LM. The basic idea of this approach is to project the word indices onto a continuous space and to use a probability estimator operating on this space

	French		English	
	Eparl	News	Eparl	News
Back-off LM:				
3-gram	47.0	91.6	57.2	160.1
4-gram	41.5	85.2	51.6	152.4
Continuous space LM:				
4-gram	35.8	73.9	44.5	133.4
5-gram	33.9	71.2	-	-
6-gram	33.1	70.1	41.2	127.0

Table 1: Perplexities on devtest2006 (Europarl) and nc-dev2007 (news commentary) for various LMs.

(Bengio et al., 2003). Since the resulting probability functions are smooth functions of the word representation, better generalization to unknown n-grams can be expected. A neural network can be used to simultaneously learn the projection of the words onto the continuous space and to estimate the n-gram probabilities. This is still a n-gram approach, but the LM probabilities are "interpolated" for any possible context of length n-1 instead of backing-off to shorter contexts.

This approach was successfully used in large vocabulary continuous speech recognition (Schwenk, 2007) and in a phrase-based system for a small task (Schwenk et al., 2006). Here, it is the first time applied in conjunction with a lexicalized reordering model. A 4-gram continuous space LM achieves a perplexity reduction of about 13% relative with respect to a 4-gram back-off LM (see Table 1). Additional improvements can be obtained by using a longer context. Note that this is difficult for back-off LMs due to insufficient training data.

3 Experimental Evaluation

The system was trained on the Europarl parallel texts only (approx. 1.3M words). The news commentary parallel texts were not used. We applied the tokenization proposed by the Moses SMT toolkit and the case was preserved. While case sensitivity may hurt the alignment process, we believe that true case is beneficial for language modeling, in particular in future versions of our system in which we plan to use POS information. Experiences with alternative tokenizations are undergoing.

The parameters of the system were tuned on

	DevTest2006		Test2006	
Decode:	3-gram	4-gram	3-gram	4-gram
Back-off LM:				
decode	30.88	-	30.82	-
4-gram	31.65	31.43	31.35	30.86
Continuous space LM:				
4-gram	31.96	31.75	32.03	31.59
5-gram	31.97	31.86	31.90	31.50
6-gram	**32.00**	31.93	**31.89**	31.64
Lex. diff.	904.2	797.6	900.6	795.8
Oracle	37.82	37.64	-	-

Table 2: Comparison of different translation strategies (BLEU scores for English to French): 3- or 4-gram decoding (columns) and n-best list rescoring with various language models (lines).

	DevTest2006		Test2006	
Decode:	3-gram	4-gram	3-gram	4-gram
Back-off LM:				
decode	32.21	-	31.50	-
4-gram	32.46	32.34	32.07	32.12
Continuous space LM:				
4-gram	32.87	32.90	30.51	32.47
6-gram	32.85	**32.98**	32.46	**32.50**
Lex. diff.	791.3	822.7	802.5	827.8
Oracle	38.80	39.69	-	-

Table 3: Comparison of different translation strategies (BLEU scores for French to English).

devtest2006 and nc-dev2007 respectively. The generalization performance was estimated on the test2006 and nc-devtest2007 corpora respectively.

3.1 Comparison of decoding strategies

Two different decoding strategies were compared in order to find out whether it is necessary to already use higher-order LMs during decoding or whether the incorporation of this knowledge can be postponed to the n-best list rescoring. Tri- or 4-gram back-off language models were used during decoding. In both cases the generated n-best lists were rescored with higher order back-off or the continuous space language model. A beam of 0.6 was used in all our experiments.

The oracle BLEU scores of the generated n-best lists were estimated by rescoring the n-best lists with a cheating LM trained on the development data. We also provide the average number of lexically different hypothesis in the n-best lists. The results are summarized in Table 2 and 3. The numbers in bold indicate the systems that were used in the evaluation.

These results are somehow contradictory : while running Moses with a trigram LM seems to be better when translating from English to French, a 4-gram LM achieves better results when translating to English. An analysis after the evaluation seems to indicate that the pruning was too aggressive for a 4-gram LM, at least for a morphologically rich language like French. Using a beam of 0.4 and a faster implementation of lexical reordering in the Moses decoder, it is apparently better to use a 4-gram LM during decoding. The oracle scores of the n-best lists and the average number of lexically different hypothesis seem to correlate well with the BLEU scores: in all cases it is better to use the system that produced n-best lists with more variety and a higher oracle BLEU score.

The continuous space language model achieved improvements in the BLEU by about 0.4 on the development data. It is interesting to note that this approach showed a very good generalization behavior: the improvements obtained on the test data are as good or even exceed those observed on the Dev data.

3.2 Multiple reference translations

Only one reference translation is provided for all tasks in the WMT'07 evaluation. This may be problematic since systems that do not use the official jargon or different word order may get "incorrectly" a low BLEU score. We have also noticed that the reference translations are not always real translations of the input, but they rely on document wide context information. Therefore, we have produced a second set of sentence based reference translations.[2]

The improvements brought by the continuous space LM are much higher using the new reference translations. Using both reference translations together leads to an important increase of the BLEU score and confirms the improvements obtained by the continuous space LM. These results are in line

[2]The second reference translations can be downloaded from `http://instar.limsi.fr/en/data.html`

Ref. transl.:	official	addtl.	both	retuned
Back-off	31.64	32.91	47.62	47.95
CSLM	32.00	33.81	48.66	49.02

Table 4: Impact of additional human reference translations (devtest2006, English to French)

with our experiences when translating from English to Spanish in the framework of the TC-STAR project (gain of about 1 point BLEU). The BLEU scores can be further improved by rerunning the whole tuning process using two reference translations (last column of Table 4).

Second reference translations for the test data are not yet available. Therefore the devtest data was split into two parts: the back-off and the CSLM achieve BLEU scores of 47.98 and 48.66 respectively on the first half used for tuning, and of 47.95 and 49.02 on the second half used for testing.

3.3 Adaptation to the news commentary task

We only performed a limited domain adaptation: the LMs and the coefficients of the log-linear combination of the feature functions were optimized on nc-dev2007. We had no time to add the news commentary parallel texts which may result in missing translations for some news specific words. The BLEU scores on the development and development test data are summarized in Table 5. A trigram was used to generate 1000-best lists that were then rescored with various language models.

Language modeling seems to be difficult when translating from English to French: the use of a 4-gram has only a minor impact. The continuous space LM achieves an improvement of 0.3 on nc-dev and 0.5 BLEU on nc-devtest. There is no benefit for using longer span LMs. The BLEU score is even 0.5 worse on nc-devtest due to a brevity penalty of 0.95. The continuous space LM also achieves interesting improvements in the BLEU score when translating from French to English.

	English/French		French/English	
	dev	devtest	dev	devtest
Back-off LM:				
decode	27.11	25.31	27.57	26.21
4-gram	27.35	25.53	27.56	26.55
Continuous space LM:				
4-gram	**27.63**	**26.01**	28.25	26.87
6-gram	27.60	25.64	**28.38**	**27.26**

Table 5: BLEU scores for news commentary task.

4 Acknowledgments

This work has been partially funded by the European Union under the integrated project TC-STAR and by the French Government under the project INSTAR (ANR JCJC06_143038). The author would like to recognize the contributions of A. Allauzen for his help with the creation of the second reference translations.

References

Yoshua Bengio, Rejean Ducharme, Pascal Vincent, and Christian Jauvin. 2003. A neural probabilistic language model. *Journal of Machine Learning Research*, 3(2):1137–1155.

Frank Vanden Berghen and Hugues Bersini. 2005. CONDOR, a new parallel, constrained extension of powell's UOBYQA algorithm: Experimental results and comparison with the DFO algorithm. *Journal of Computational and Applied Mathematics*, 181:157–175.

Philipp Koehn, Franz Josef Och, and Daniel Marcu. 2003. Statistical phrased-based machine translation. In *HLT/NACL*, pages 127–133.

Philipp Koehn, Hieu Hoang, Alexandra Birch, Chris Callison-Burch, Marcello Federico, Nicola Bertoldi, Brooke Cowan, Wade Shen, Christine Moran, Richard Zens, Chris Dyer, Ondrej Bojar, Alexandra Constantin, and Evan Herbst. 2007. Moses: Open source toolkit for statistical machine translation. In *Proceedings of ACL, demonstation session*.

Franz Josef Och and Hermann Ney. 2002. Discriminative training and maximum entropy models for statistical machine translation. In *ACL*, pages 295–302.

Franz Josef Och and Hermann Ney. 2003. A systematic comparison of various statistical alignement models. *Computational Linguistics*, 29(1):19–51.

Holger Schwenk, Marta R. Costa-jussà, and José A. R. Fonollosa. 2006. Continuous space language models for the IWSLT 2006 task. In *IWSLT*, pages 166–173, November.

Holger Schwenk. 2007. Continuous space language models. *Computer Speech and Language*, 21:492–518.

Multi-Engine Machine Translation with an Open-Source Decoder for Statistical Machine Translation

Yu Chen[1], Andreas Eisele[1,2], Christian Federmann[2], Eva Hasler[3], Michael Jellinghaus[1], Silke Theison[1]

(authors listed in alphabetical order)

1: Saarland University, Saarbrücken, Germany

2: DFKI GmbH, Saarbrücken, Germany

3: University of Cologne, Germany

Abstract

We describe an architecture that allows to combine statistical machine translation (SMT) with rule-based machine translation (RBMT) in a multi-engine setup. We use a variant of standard SMT technology to align translations from one or more RBMT systems with the source text. We incorporate phrases extracted from these alignments into the phrase table of the SMT system and use the open-source decoder Moses to find good combinations of phrases from SMT training data with the phrases derived from RBMT. First experiments based on this hybrid architecture achieve promising results.

1 Introduction

Recent work on statistical machine translation has led to significant progress in coverage and quality of translation technology, but so far, most of this work focuses on translation into English, where relatively simple morphological structure and abundance of monolingual training data helped to compensate for the relative lack of linguistic sophistication of the underlying models. As SMT systems are trained on massive amounts of data, they are typically quite good at capturing implicit knowledge contained in co-occurrence statistics, which can serve as a shallow replacement for the world knowledge that would be required for the resolution of ambiguities and the insertion of information that happens to be missing in the source text but is required to generate well-formed text in the target language.

Already before, decades of work went into the implementation of MT systems (typically rule-based) for frequently used language pairs[1], and these systems quite often contain a wealth of linguistic knowledge about the languages involved, such as fairly complete mechanisms for morphological and syntactic analysis and generation, as well as a large number of bilingual lexical entries spanning many application domains.

It is an interesting challenge to combine the different types of knowledge into integrated systems that could then exploit both explicit linguistic knowledge contained in the rules of one or several conventional MT system(s) and implicit knowledge that can be extracted from large amounts of text.

The recently started EuroMatrix[2] project will explore this integration of rule-based and statistical knowledge sources, and one of the approaches to be investigated is the combination of existing rule-based MT systems into a multi-engine architecture. The work described in this paper is one of the first incarnations of such a multi-engine architecture within the project, and a careful analysis of the results will guide us in the choice of further steps within the project.

2 Architectures for multi-engine MT

Combinations of MT systems into multi-engine architectures have a long tradition, starting perhaps with (Frederking and Nirenburg, 1994). Multi-engine systems can be roughly divided into simple

[1] See (Hutchins et al., 2006) for a list of commercial MT systems

[2] See http://www.euromatrix.net

Proceedings of the Second Workshop on Statistical Machine Translation, pages 193–196, Prague, June 2007.

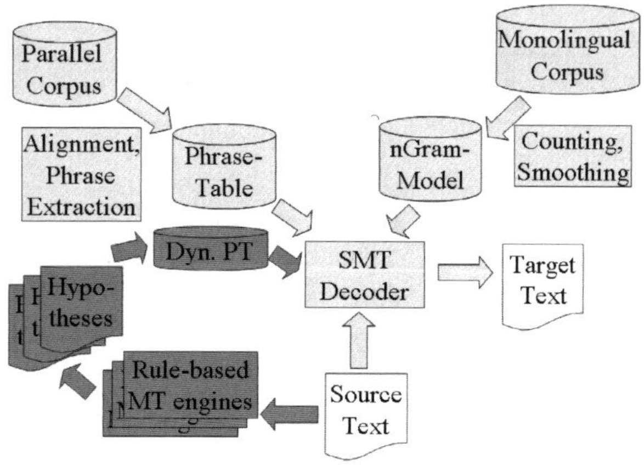

Figure 1: Architecture for multi-engine MT driven by a SMT decoder

architectures that try to select the best output from a number of systems, but leave the individual hypotheses as is (Tidhar and Küssner, 2000; Akiba et al., 2001; Callison-Burch and Flournoy, 2001; Akiba et al., 2002; Nomoto, 2004; Eisele, 2005) and more sophisticated setups that try to recombine the best parts from multiple hypotheses into a new utterance that can be better than the best of the given candidates, as described in (Rayner and Carter, 1997; Hogan and Frederking, 1998; Bangalore et al., 2001; Jayaraman and Lavie, 2005; Matusov et al., 2006; Rosti et al., 2007).

Recombining multiple MT results requires finding the correspondences between alternative renderings of a source-language expression proposed by different MT systems. This is generally not straightforward, as different word order and errors in the output can make it hard to identify the alignment. Still, we assume that a good way to combine the various MT outcomes will need to involve word alignment between the MT output and the given source text, and hence a specialized module for word alignment is a central component of our setup.

Additionally, a recombination system needs a way to pick the best combination of alternative building blocks; and when judging the quality of a particular configuration, both the plausibility of the building blocks as such and their relation to the context need to be taken into account. The required optimization process is very similar to the search in a SMT decoder that looks for naturally sounding combinations of highly probable partial translations. Instead of implementing a special-purpose search procedure from scratch, we transform the information contained in the MT output into a form that is suitable as input for an existing SMT decoder. This has the additional advantage that resources used in standard phrase-based SMT can be flexibly combined with the material extracted from the rule-based MT results; the optimal combination can essentially be reduced to the task of finding good relative weights for the various phrase table entries.

A sketch of the overall architecture is given in Fig. 1, where the blue (light) parts represent the modules and data sets used in purely statistical MT, and the red (dark) parts are the additional modules and data sets derived from the rule-based engines. It should be noted that this is by far not the only way to combine systems. In particular, as this proposed setup gives the last word to the SMT decoder, we risk that linguistically well-formed constructs from one of the rule-based engines will be deteriorated in the final decoding step. Alternative architectures are under exploration and will be described elsewhere.

3 MT systems and other knowledge sources

For the experiments, we used a set of six rule-based MT engines that are partly available via web interfaces and partly installed locally. The web based systems are provided by Google (based on Systran for the relevant language pairs), SDL, and ProMT which all deliver significantly different output. Locally installed systems are OpenLogos, Lucy (a recent offspring of METAL), and translate pro by lingenio (only for German ↔ English). In addition to these engines, we also used the scripts included in the Moses toolkit (Koehn et al., 2006)[3] to generate phrase tables from the training data. We enhanced the phrase tables with information on whether a given pair of phrases can also be derived via a third, intermediate language. We assume that this can be useful to distinguish different degrees of reliability, but due to lack of time for fine-tuning we could not yet show that it indeed helps in increasing the overall quality of the output.

[3]see http://www.statmt.org/moses/

4 Implementation Details

4.1 Alignment of MT output

The input text and the output text of the MT systems was aligned by means of GIZA++ (Och and Ney, 2003), a tool with which statistical models for alignment of parallel texts can be trained. Since training new models on merely short texts does not yield very accurate results, we applied a method where text can be aligned based on existing models that have been trained on the Europarl Corpus (Koehn, 2005) beforehand. This was achieved by using a modified version of GIZA++ that is able to load given models.

The modified version of GIZA++ is embedded into a client-server setup. The user can send two corresponding files to the server, and specify two models for both translation directions from which alignments should be generated. After generating alignments in both directions (by running GIZA++ twice), the system also delivers a combination of these alignments which then serves as input to the following steps described below.

4.2 Phrase tables from MT output

We then concatenated the phrase tables from the SMT baseline system and the phrase tables obtained from the rule-based MT systems and augmented them by additional columns, one for each system used. With this additional information it is clear which of the MT systems a phrase pair stems from, enabling us to assign relative weights to the contributions of the different systems. The optimal weights for the different columns can then be assigned with the help of minimum error rate training (Och, 2003).

5 Results

We compared the hybrid system to a purely statistical baseline system as well as two rule-based systems. The only differences between the baseline system and our hybrid system are the phrase table – the hybrid system includes more lexical entries than the baseline – and the weights obtained from minimum error rate training.

For a statistical system, lexical coverage becomes an obstacle – especially when the bilingual lexical entries are trained on documents from different domains. However, due to the distinct mechanisms used to generate these entries, rule-based systems and statistical systems usually differ in coverage. Our system managed to utilize lexical entries from various sources by integrating the phrase tables derived from rule-based systems into the phrase table trained on a large parallel corpus. Table 1 shows

Systems	Token #
Ref.	2091 (4.21%)
R-I	3886 (7.02%)
R-II	3508 (6.30%)
SMT	3976 (7.91%)
Hybrid	2425 (5.59%)

Table 1: Untranslated tokens (excl. numbers and punctuations) in output for news commentary task (de-en) from different systems

a rough estimation of the number of untranslated words in the respective output of different systems. The estimation was done by counting "words" (i.e. tokens excluding numbers and punctuations) that appear in both the source document and the outputs. Note that, as we are investigating translations from German to English, where the languages share a lot of vocabulary, e.g. named entities such as "USA", there are around 4.21% of words that should stay the same throughout the translation process. In the hybrid system, 5.59% of the words remain unchanged, which is is the lowest percentage among all systems. Our baseline system (SMT in Table 1), not comprising additional phrase tables, was the one to produce the highest number of such untranslated words.

	Baseline	Hybrid
test	18.07	21.39
nc-test	21.17	22.86

Table 2: Performance comparison (BLEU scores) between baseline and hybrid systems, on in-domain (test) and out-of-domain (nc-test) test data

Higher lexical coverage leads to better performance as can be seen in Table 2, which compares BLEU scores of the baseline and hybrid systems, both measured on in-domain and out-of-domain test data. Due to time constraints these numbers reflect results from using a single RBMT system (Lucy); using more systems would potentially further improve results.

6 Outlook

Due to lack of time for fine-tuning the parameters and technical difficulties in the last days before delivery, the results submitted for the shared task do not yet show the full potential of our architecture.

The architecture described here places a strong emphasis on the statistical models and can be seen as a variant of SMT where lexical information from rule-based engines is used to increase lexical coverage. We are currently also exploring setups where statistical alignments are fed into a rule-based system, which has the advantage that well-formed syntactic structures generated via linguistic rules cannot be broken apart by the SMT components. But as rule-based systems typically lack mechanisms for ruling out implausible results, they cannot easily cope with errors that creep into the lexicon due to misalignments and similar problems.

7 Acknowledgements

This research has been supported by the European Commission in the FP6-IST project EuroMatrix. We also want to thank Teresa Herrmann for helping us with the Lucy system.

References

Yasuhiro Akiba, Kenji Imamura, and Eiichiro Sumita. 2001. Using multiple edit distances to automatically rank machine translation output. In *Proceedings of MT Summit VIII*, Santiago de Compostela, Spain.

Yasuhiro Akiba, Taro Watanabe, and Eiichiro Sumita. 2002. Using language and translation models to select the best among outputs from multiple mt systems. In *COLING*.

Srinivas Bangalore, German Bordel, and Giuseppe Riccardi. 2001. Computing consensus translation from multiple machine translation systems. In *ASRU*, Italy.

Chris Callison-Burch and Raymond S. Flournoy. 2001. A program for automatically selecting the best output from multiple machine translation engines. In *Proc. of MT Summit VIII*, Santiago de Compostela, Spain.

Andreas Eisele. 2005. First steps towards multi-engine machine translation. In *Proceedings of the ACL Workshop on Building and Using Parallel Texts*, June.

Robert E. Frederking and Sergei Nirenburg. 1994. Three heads are better than one. In *ANLP*, pages 95–100.

Christopher Hogan and Robert E. Frederking. 1998. An evaluation of the multi-engine MT architecture. In *Proceedings of AMTA*, pages 113–123.

John Hutchins, Walter Hartmann, and Etsuo Ito. 2006. IAMT compendium of translation software. Twelfth Edition, January.

Shyamsundar Jayaraman and Alon Lavie. 2005. Multi-engine machine translation guided by explicit word matching. In *Proc. of EAMT*, Budapest, Hungary.

P. Koehn, M. Federico, W. Shen, N. Bertoldi, O. Bojar, C. Callison-Burch, B. Cowan, C. Dyer, H. Hoang, R. Zens, A. Constantin, C. C. Moran, and E. Herbst. 2006. Open source toolkit for statistical machine translation: Factored translation models and confusion network decoding. Final Report of the 2006 JHU Summer Workshop.

Philipp Koehn. 2005. Europarl: A parallel corpus for statistical machine translation. In *Proceedings of the MT Summit*.

Evgeny Matusov, Nicola Ueffing, and Hermann Ney. 2006. Computing consensus translation from multiple machine translation systems using enhanced hypotheses alignment. In *In Proc. EACL*, pages 33–40.

Tadashi Nomoto. 2004. Multi-engine machine translation with voted language model. In *Proc. of ACL*.

Franz Josef Och and Hermann Ney. 2003. A systematic comparison of various statistical alignment models. *Computational Linguistics*, 29(1):19–51, March.

Franz Josef Och. 2003. Minimum error rate training for statistical machine translation. In *Proceedings of ACL*, Sapporo, Japan, July.

Manny Rayner and David M. Carter. 1997. Hybrid language processing in the spoken language translator. In *Proc. ICASSP '97*, pages 107–110, Munich, Germany.

Antti-Veikko Rosti, Necip Fazil Ayan, Bing Xiang, Spyros Matsoukas, Richard Schwartz, and Bonnie J. Dorr. 2007. Combining translations from multiple machine translation systems. In *Proceedings of the Conference on Human Language Technology and North American chapter of the Association for Computational Linguistics Annual Meeting (HLT-NAACL'2007)*, pages 228–235, Rochester, NY, April 22-27.

Dan Tidhar and Uwe Küssner. 2000. Learning to select a good translation. In *COLING*, pages 843–849.

The ISL Phrase-Based MT System for the 2007 ACL Workshop on Statistical Machine Translation

M. Paulik[1,2], K. Rottmann[2], J. Niehues[2], S. Hildebrand [1,2] and S. Vogel[1]
[1]Interactive Systems Laboratories, Carnegie Mellon University, Pittsburgh, PA, USA
[2]Institut für Theoretische Informatik, Universität Karlsruhe (TH), Karlsruhe, Germany
{paulik|silja|vogel}@cs.cmu.edu ; {jniehues|rottmann}@ira.uka.de

Abstract

In this paper we describe the Interactive Systems Laboratories (ISL) phrase-based machine translation system used in the shared task "Machine Translation for European Languages" of the ACL 2007 Workshop on Statistical Machine Translation. We present results for a system combination of the ISL syntax-augmented MT system and the ISL phrase-based system by combining and rescoring the n-best lists of the two systems. We also investigate the combination of two of our phrase-based systems translating from different source languages, namely Spanish and German, into their common target language, English.

1 Introduction

The shared task of the ACL 2007 Workshop on Statistical Machine Translation focuses on the automatic translation of European language pairs. The workshop provides common training sets for translation model training and language model training to allow for easy comparison of results between the participants.

Interactive Systems Laboratories participated in the English ↔ Spanish Europarl and News Commentary task as well as in the English ↔ German Europarl task. This paper describes the phrase-based machine translation (MT) system that was applied to these tasks. We also investigate the feasibility of combining the ISL syntax-augmented MT system (Zollmann et al., 2007) with our phrase-based system by combining and rescoring the n-best lists produced by both systems for the Spanish → English Europarl task. Furthermore, we apply the same combination technique to combine two of our phrase-based systems that operate on different source languages (Spanish and German), but share the same target language (English).

The paper is organized as follows. In section 2 we give a general description of our phrase-based statistical machine translation system. Section 3 gives an overview of the data and of the final systems used for the English ↔ Spanish Europarl and News Commentary tasks, along with corresponding performance numbers. Section 4 shows the data, final systems and results for the English ↔ German Europarl task. In Section 5, we present our experiments involving a combination of the syntax-augmented MT system with the phrase-based MT system and a combination of the Spanish → English and German → English phrase-based systems.

2 The ISL Phrase-Based MT System

2.1 Word and Phrase Alignment

Phrase-to-phrase translation pairs are extracted by training IBM Model-4 word alignments in both directions, using the GIZA++ toolkit (Och and Ney, 2000), and then extracting phrase pair candidates which are consistent with these alignments, starting from the intersection of both alignments. This is done with the help of phrase model training code provided by University of Edinburgh during the NAACL 2006 Workshop on Statistical Machine Translation (Koehn and Monz, 2006). The raw rel-

Proceedings of the Second Workshop on Statistical Machine Translation, pages 197–202,
Prague, June 2007.

ative frequency estimates found in the phrase translation tables are then smoothed by applying modified Kneser-Ney discounting as explained in (Foster et al., 2006). The resulting phrase translation tables are pruned by using the combined translation model score as determined by Minimum Error Rate (MER) optimization on the development set.

2.2 Word Reordering

We apply a part-of-speech (POS) based reordering scheme (J. M. Crego et al., 2006) to the POS-tagged source sentences before decoding. For this, we use the GIZA++ alignments and the POS-tagged source side of the training corpus to learn reordering rules that achieve a (locally) monotone alignment. Figure 1 shows an example in which three reordering rules are extracted from the POS tags of an English source sentence and its corresponding Spanish GIZA++ alignment. Before translation, we construct lattices for every source sentence. The lattices include the original source sentence along with all the reorderings that are consistent with the learned rules. All incoming edges of the lattice are annotated with distortion model scores. Figure 2 gives an example of such a lattice. In the subsequent lattice decoding step, we apply either monotone decoding or decoding with a reduced local reordering window, typically of size 2.

2.3 Decoder and MER Training

The ISL beam search decoder (Vogel, 2003) combines all the different model scores to find the best translation. Here, the following models were used:

- The translation model, i.e. the phrase-to-phrase translations extracted from the bilingual corpus, annoted with four translation model scores. These four scores are the smoothed forward and backward phrase translation probabilities and the forward and backward lexical weights.
- A 4-gram language model. The SRI language model toolkit was used to train the language model and we applied modified Kneser-Ney smoothing.
- An internal word reordering model in addition to the already described POS-based reordering.

  This internal reordering model assigns higher costs to longer distance reordering.
- Simple word and phrase count models. The former is essentially used to compensate for the tendency of the language model to prefer shorter translations, while the latter can give preference to longer phrases, potentially improving fluency.

```
We all agree on that
PRP DT VB IN DT
En {4} esto {5} estamos {1} todos {2} de {} acuerdo {3}
⇒ PRP DT VB IN DT : 4 - 5 - 1 - 2 - 3
⇒ PRP DT VB: 2 - 3 - 1
⇒ PRP DT VB IN: 3 - 4 - 1 - 2
```

Figure 1: Rule extraction for the POS-based reordering scheme.

The ISL SMT decoder is capable of loading several language models (LMs) at the same time, namely n-gram SRI language models with n up to 4 and suffix array language models (Zhang and Vogel, 2006) of arbitrary length. While we typically see gains in performance for using suffix array LMs with longer histories, we restricted ourselves here to one 4-gram SRI LM only, due to a limited amount of available LM training data. The decoding process itself is organized in two stages. First, all available word and phrase translations are found and inserted into a so-called translation lattice. Then the best combination of these partial translations is found by doing a best path search through the translation lattice, where we also allow for word reorderings within a predefined local reordering window.

To optimize the system towards a maximal BLEU or NIST score, we use Minimum Error Rate (MER) Training as described in (Och, 2003). For each model weight, MER applies a multi-linear search on the development set n-best list produced by the system. Due to the limited numbers of translations in the n-best list, these new model weights are suboptimal. To compensate for this, a new full translation is done. The resulting new n-best list is then merged with the old n-best list and the optimization process is repeated. Typically, the translation quality converges after three iterations.

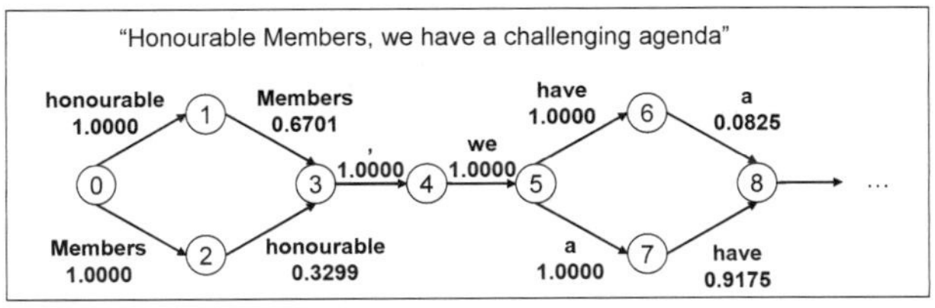

Figure 2: Example for a source sentence lattice from the POS-based reordering scheme.

	English	Spanish
sentence pairs	1259914	
unique sent. pairs	1240151	
sentence length	25.3	26.3
words	31.84 M	33.16 M
vocabulary	266.9 K	346.3 K

Table 1: Corpus statistics for the English/Spanish Europarl corpus.

3 Spanish ↔ English Europarl and News Commentary Task

3.1 Data and Translation Tasks

The systems for the English ↔ Spanish translation tasks were trained on the sentence-aligned Europarl corpus (Koehn, 2005). Detailed corpus statistics can be found in Table 1. The available parallel News Commentary training data of approximately 1 million running words for both languages was only used as additional language model training data, to adapt our in-domain (Europarl) system to the out-of-domain (News Commentary) task.

The development sets consist of 2000 Europarl sentences (dev-EU) and 1057 News Commentary sentences (dev-NC). The available development-test data consists of 2 x 2000 Europarl sentences (devtest-EU and test06-EU) and 1064 News Commentary sentences (test06-NC). All development and development-test sets have only one reference translation per sentence.

3.2 Data Normalization

The ACL shared task is very close in form and content to the Final Text Editions (FTE) task of the TC-STAR (TC-STAR, 2004) evaluation. For this reason, we decided to apply a similar normalization scheme to the training data as was applied in our TC-STAR verbatim SMT system. Although trained on "verbatimized" data that did not contain any numbers, but rather had all numbers and dates spelled out, it yielded consistently better results than our TC-STAR FTE SMT system. When translating FTE content, the verbatim system treated all numbers as unknown words, i.e. they were left unchanged during translation. To compensate for this, we applied extended postprocessing to the translations that conducts the necessary conversions between Spanish and English numbers, e.g. the conversion of decimal comma in Spanish to decimal point in English. Other key points which we adopted from this normalization scheme were the tokenization of punctuation marks, the true-casing of the first word of each sentence, as well as extended cleaning of the training data. The latter mainly consisted of the removal of sections with a highly unbalanced source to target words ratio and the removal of unusual string combinations and document references, like for example "B5-0918/2000", "(COM(2000) 335 - C5-0386/2000 - 2000/0143(CNS))", etc.

Based on this normalization scheme, we trained and optimized a baseline in-domain system on accordingly normalized source and reference sentences. For optimization, we combined the available development sets for the Europarl task and the News Commentary task. In order to further improve the applied normalization scheme, we experimented with replacing all numbers with the string "NMBR", rather than spelling them out and by replacing all document identifiers with the string "DCMNT", rather than deleting them. This was first done for the language model training data only, and then for all data, i.e. for the bilingual training data and for the development set source and reference sentences. In the latter case, the respective tags were again replaced by the correct numbers and document identifiers during postprocessing. Table 2 shows the case sensitive BLEU scores for the three normalization approaches on the English ↔ Spanish Europarl and News Commentary development sets. These scores were computed with the official NIST scoring script against the original (not normalized) references.

3.3 In-domain System

As mentioned above, we combined the Europarl and News Commentary development sets when optimizing the in-domain system. This resulted in only one

Task	baseline	LM only	all data
Europarl	30.94	31.20	31.26
News Com.	31.28	31.39	31.73

Table 2: Case sensitive BLEU scores on the in-domain and out-of-domain development sets for the three different normalization schemes.

Task	Eng → Spa	Spa → Eng
dev-EU	31.29	31.77
dev-NC	31.81	31.12
devtest-EU	31.01	31.40
test06-EU	31.87	31.76
test06-NC	30.23	29.22

Table 3: Case sensitive BLEU scores for the final English ↔ Spanish in-domain systems.

set of scaling factors, i.e. the in-domain system applies the same scaling factors for translating in-domain data as for translating out-of-domain data. Our baseline system applied only monotone lattice decoding. For our final in-domain system, we used a local reordering window of length 2, which accounts for the slightly higher scores when compared to the baseline system. The BLEU scores for both translation directions on the different development and development-test sets can be found in Table 3.

3.4 Out-of-domain System

In order to adapt our in-domain system towards the out-of-domain News Commentary task, we considered two approaches based on language model adaptation. First, we interpolated the in-domain LM with an out-of-domain LM computed on the available News Commentary training data. The interpolation weights were chosen such as to achieve a minimal LM perplexity on the out-of-domain development set. For both languages, the interpolation weights were approximately 0.5. Our second approach was to simply load the out-of-domain LM as an additional LM into our decoder. In both cases, we optimized the translation system on the out-of-domain development data only. For the second approach, MER optimization assigned three to four times higher scaling factors to the considerably smaller out-domain LM than to the original in-domain LM. Table 4 shows the results in BLEU on the out-of-domain development and development-test sets for both translation directions. While loading a second LM gives similar or slightly better results on the development set during MER optimization, we see consistently worse results on the unseen development-test set. This, in the context of the relatively small amount of development data, can be explained by stronger overfitting during optimization.

Task	Eng → Spa		Spa → Eng	
	interp	2 LMs	interp	2 LMs
dev-NC	33.31	33.28	32.61	32.70
test06-NC	32.55	32.15	30.73	30.55

Table 4: Case sensitive BLEU scores for the final English ↔ Spanish out-of-domain systems.

4 English ↔ German Europarl Task

The systems for the English ↔ German translation tasks were trained on the sentence-aligned Europarl corpus only. The complete corpus consists of approximately 32 million English and 30 million German words.

We applied a similar normalization scheme to the training data as for the English ↔ Spanish system. The main difference was that we did not replace numbers and that we removed all document references. In the translation process, the document references were treated as unknown words and therefore left unchanged. As above, we trained and optimized a first baseline system on the normalized source and reference sentences. However, we used only the Europarl task development set during optimization. To achieve further improvements on the German → English task, we applied a compound splitting technique. The compound splitting was based on (Koehn and Knight, 2003) and was applied on the lowercased source sentences. The words generated by the compound splitting were afterwards true-cased. Instead of replacing a compound by its separate parts, we added a parallel path into the source sentence lattices used for translation. The source sentence lattices were augmented with scores on their edges indicating whether each edge represents a word of the original text or if it was generated during compound splitting.

Table 5 shows the case-sensitive BLEU scores for the final German ↔ English systems. In contrast to the English ↔ Spanish systems, we used only monotonous decoding on the lattices containing the

task	Eng → Ger	Ger → Eng
dev-EU	18.58	23.85
devtest-EU	18.50	23.87
test06-EU	18.39	23.88

Table 5: Case sensitive BLEU scores for the final English ↔ German in-domain systems.

task	PHRA	SYNT	COMB
dev-EU	31.77	32.48	32.77
test06-EU	31.76	32.15	32.27

Table 6: Results for combining the syntax-augmented system (SYNT) with the phrase-based system (PHRA).

syntactical reorderings.

5 System Combination via n-best List Combination and Rescoring

5.1 N-best List Rescoring

For n-best list rescoring we used unique 500-best lists, which may have less than 500 entries for some sentences. In this evaluation, we used several features computed from different information sources such as features from the translation system, additional language models, IBM-1 word lexica and the n-best list itself. We calculated 4 features from the IBM-1 word lexica: the word probability sum as well as the maximum word probability in both language directions. From the n-best list itself, we calculated three different sets of scores. A position-dependent word agreement score as described in (Ueffing and Ney, 2005) with a position window instead of the Levenshtein alignment, the n-best list n-gram probability as described in (Zens and Ney, 2006) and a position-independent n-gram agreement, which is a variation on the first two. To tune the feature combination weights, we used MER optimization.

Rescoring the n-best lists from our individual systems did not give significant improvements on the available unseen development-test data. For this reason, we did not apply n-best list rescoring to the individual systems. However, we investigated the feasibility of combining two different systems by rescoring the joint n-best lists of both systems. The corresponding results are described in the following sections.

5.2 Combining Syntax-Augmented MT and Phrase-Based MT

On the Spanish → English in-domain task, we participated not only with the ISL phrase-based SMT system as described in this paper, but also with the ISL syntax-augmented system. The syntax-augmented system was trained on the same normalized data as the phrase-based system. However, it was optimized on the in-domain development set only. More details on the syntax-augmented system can be found in (Zollmann et al., 2007). Table 6 lists the respective BLEU scores of both systems as well as the BLEU score achieved by combining and rescoring the individual 500-best lists.

5.3 Combining MT Systems with Different Source Languages

(Och and Ney, 2001) describes methods for translating text given in multiple source languages into a single target language. The ultimate goal is to improve the translation quality when translating from one source language, for example English into multiple target languages, such as Spanish and German. This can be done by first translating the English document into German and then using the translation as an additional source, when translating to Spanish. Another scenario where a multi-source translation becomes desirable was described in (Paulik et al., 2005). The goal was to improve the quality of automatic speech recognition (ASR) systems by employing human-provided simultaneous translations. By using automatic speech translation systems to translate the speech of the human interpreters back into the source language, it is possible to bias the source language ASR system with the additional knowledge. Having these two frameworks in mind, we investigated the possibility of combining our in-domain German → English and Spanish → English translation systems using n-best list rescoring. Table 7 shows the corresponding results. Even though the German → English translation performance was approximately 8 BLEU below the translation performance of the Spanish → English system, we were able to improve the final translation performance by up to 1 BLEU.

task	Spa → Eng	Ger → Eng	Comb.
dev-EU	31.77	23.85	32.76
devtest-EU	31.40	23.87	32.41
test06-EU	31.76	23.88	32.51

Table 7: Results for combining the Spanish → English and German → English phrase-based systems on the in-domain tasks.

6 Conclusion

We described the ISL phrase-based statistical machine translation systems that were used for the 2007 ACL Workshop on Statistical Machine Translation. Using the available out-of-domain News Commentary task training data for language model adaptation, we were able to significantly increase the performance on the out-of-domain task by 2.3 BLEU for English → Spanish and by 1.3 BLEU for Spanish → English. We also showed the feasibility of combining different MT systems by combining and rescoring their respective n-best lists. In particular, we focused on the combination of our phrase-based and syntax-augmented systems and the combination of two phrase-based systems operating on different source languages. While we saw only a minimal improvement of 0.1 BLEU for the phrase-based and syntax-augmented combination, we gained up to 1 BLEU, in case of the multi-source translation.

References

G. Foster, R. Kuhn, and H. Johnson. 2006. Phrasetable Smoothing for Statistical Machine Translation. In *Proc. of Empirical Methods in Natural Language Processing*, Sydney, Australia.

J. M. Crego et al. 2006. N-gram-based SMT System Enhanced with Reordering Patterns. In *Proc. of the Workshop on Statistical Machine Translation*, pages 162–165, New York, USA.

P. Koehn and K. Knight. 2003. Empirical Methods for Compound Splitting. In *Proc. of the tenth conference on European chapter of the Association for Computational Linguistics*, pages 187–193, Budapest, Hungary.

P. Koehn and C. Monz. 2006. Manual and Automatic Evaluation of Machine Translation between European Langauges. In *Proc. of the Workshop on Statistical Machine Translation*, pages 102–121, New York, USA.

P. Koehn. 2005. Europarl: A Parallel Corpus for Statistical Machine Translation. In *Proc. of Machine Translation Summit*.

F.J. Och and H. Ney. 2000. Improved Statistical Alignment Models. In *Proc. of the 38th Annual Meeting of the Association for Computational Linguistics*, Hongkong, China.

F. J. Och and H. Ney. 2001. Statistical Multi-Source Translation. In *Proc. of Machine Translation Summit*, pages 253–258, Santiago de Compostela, Spain.

F. J. Och. 2003. Minimum Error Rate Training in Statistical Machine Translation. In *Proc. of the 41st Annual Meeting of the Association for Computational Linguistics*, pages 160 – 167, Sapporo, Japan.

M. Paulik, S. Stueker, C. Fuegen, T. Schultz, T. Schaaf, and A. Waibel. 2005. Speech Translation Enhanced Automatic Speech Recognition. In *Proc. of the Workshop on Automatic Speech Recognition and Understanding*, San Juan, Puerto Rico.

TC-STAR. 2004. Technology and Corpora for Speech to Speech Translation. *http://www.tc-star.org.*

N. Ueffing and H. Ney. 2005. Word-Level Confidence Estimation for Machine Translation using Phrase-Based Translation Models. In *Proc. of HLT and EMNLP*, pages 763–770, Vancouver, British Columbia, Canada.

S. Vogel. 2003. SMT Decoder Dissected: Word Reordering. In *Proc. of Int. Conf. on Natural Language Processing and Knowledge Engineering*, Beijing, China.

R. Zens and H. Ney. 2006. N-gram Posterior Probabilities for Statistical Machine Translation. In *Proc. of the Workshop on Statistical Machine Translation*, pages 72–77, New York, USA.

Y. Zhang and S. Vogel. 2006. Suffix Array and its Applications in Empirical Natural Language Processing. In *the Technical Report CMU-LTI-06-010*, Pittsburgh, USA.

A. Zollmann, A. Venugopal, M. Paulik, and S. Vogel. 2007. The Syntax Augmented MT (SAMT) system at the Shared Task for the 2007 ACL Workshop on Statistical Machine Translation. In *Proc. of ACL 2007 Workshop on Statistical MachineTranslation*, Prague, Czech Republic.

Rule-based Translation With Statistical Phrase-based Post-editing

Michel Simard, Nicola Ueffing, Pierre Isabelle and **Roland Kuhn**
Interactive Language Technologies Group
National Research Council of Canada
Gatineau, Canada, K1A 0R6
firstname.lastname@nrc-cnrc.gc.ca

Abstract

This article describes a machine translation system based on an *automatic post-editing* strategy: initially translate the input text into the target-language using a rule-based MT system, then automatically post-edit the output using a statistical phrase-based system. An implementation of this approach based on the SYSTRAN and PORTAGE MT systems was used in the shared task of the Second Workshop on Statistical Machine Translation. Experimental results on the test data of the previous campaign are presented.

1 Introduction

Simard et al. (2007) have recently shown how a statistical phrase-based machine translation system can be used as an *automatic post-editing* (APE) layer, on top of a rule-based machine translation system. The motivation for their work is the repetitive nature of the errors typically made by rule-based systems. Given appropriate training material, a statistical MT system can be trained to correct these systematic errors, therefore reducing the post-editing effort. The statistical system views the output of the rule-based system as the source language, and reference human translations as the target language. Because the training material for the APE layer will typically be domain-specific, this process can be viewed as a way of *automatically adapting* a rule-based system to a specific application domain.

This approach has been shown experimentally to produce large improvements in performance not only over the baseline rule-based system that it corrects, but also over a similar statistical phrase-based MT system used in standalone mode, i.e. translating the "real" source text directly: Simard et al. report a reduction in post-editing effort of up to a third when compared to the input rule-based translation, and as much as 5 BLEU points improvement over the direct SMT approach.

These impressive results, however, were obtained in a very specific and somewhat unusual context: the training and test corpora were extracted from a collection of manually post-edited machine translations. The two corpora (one English-to-French, one French-to-English) each contained three parallel "views" of the same data: 1) the source language text, 2) a machine translation of that text into the target language, as produced by a commercial rule-based MT system, and 3) the final target-language version of the text, produced by manually post-editing the machine translation. Furthermore, the corpus was very small, at least by SMT standards: 500K words of source-language data in the French-to-English direction, 350K words in the English-to-French. Because of this, the authors were left with two important questions: 1) how would the results scale up to much larger quantities of training data? and 2) are the results related to the dependent nature of the translations, i.e. is the automatic post-editing approach still effective when the machine and human translations are produced independently of one another?

With these two questions in mind, we participated in the shared task of the Second Workshop on Statistical Machine Translation with an automatic post-editing strategy: initially translate the input text into the target-language using a rule-based system, namely SYSTRAN, and automatically post-edit the output using a statistical phrase-based system, namely PORTAGE. We describe our system in more detail in Section 2, and present some experimental results in Section 3.

Proceedings of the Second Workshop on Statistical Machine Translation, pages 203–206,
Prague, June 2007.

2 System description

Our system is composed of two main components: a rule-based MT system, which handles the initial translation into the target language, and a statistical phrase-based post-editing system, which performs domain-specific corrections and adaptations to the output. We describe each component separately below.

2.1 Rule-based Translation

The initial source-to-target language translation is performed using the SYSTRAN machine translation system, version 6. A detailed overview of SYSTRAN systems can be found in Dugast et al. (2007). For this shared task, we used the French-to-English and English-to-French configurations of the system. Although it is possible to provide the system with specialized lexica, we did not rely on this feature, and used the system in its basic "out-of-the-box" configuration.

2.2 Statistical Phrase-based Post-Editing

The output of the rule-based MT system described above is fed into a post-editing layer that performs domain-specific corrections and adaptation. This operation is conceptually not very different from a "target-to-target" translation; for this task, we used the PORTAGE system, a state-of-the-art statistical phrase-based machine translation system developed at the National Research Council of Canada (NRC).[1] A general description of PORTAGE can be found in (Sadat et al., 2005).

For our participation in this shared task, we decided to configure and train the PORTAGE system for post-editing in a manner as much as possible similar to the corresponding translation system, the details of which can be found in (Ueffing et al., 2007). The main features of this configuration are:

- The use of two distinct phrase tables, containing phrase pairs extracted from the Europarl and the News Commentary training corpora respectively.

- Multiple phrase-probability feature functions in the log-linear models, including a joint probability estimate, a standard frequency-based conditional probability estimate, and variants thereof based on different smoothing methods (Foster et al., 2006).

- A 4-gram language model trained on the combined Europarl and News Commentary target-language corpora.

- A 3-gram *adapted language model*: this is trained on a mini-corpus of test-relevant target-language sentences, extracted from the training material using standard information retrieval techniques.

- A 5-gram truecasing model, trained on the combined Europarl and News Commentary target-language corpora.

2.3 Training data

Ideally, the training material for the post-editing layer of our system should consist in a corpus of text in two parallel versions: on the one hand, raw machine translation output, and on the other hand, manually post-edited versions of these translations. This is the type of data that was used in the initial study of Simard et al. (2007).

Unfortunately, this sort of training data is seldom available. Instead, we propose using training material derived directly from standard, source-target parallel corpora. The idea is to translate the source portion of the parallel corpus into the target language, using the rule-based MT component. The post-editing component can then be trained using this translation as "source" training material, and the existing target portion of the parallel corpus as "target" training material. Note how this sort of data is subtly different from the data used by Simard et al.: there, the "target" text was dependent on the "source", in the sense that it was produced by manually post-editing the machine translation; here, the two can be said to be independent, in the sense that both "source" and "target" were produced independently by man and machine (but from the same "real" source, of course). It was one of the initial motivations of the current work to verify to what extent the performance of the APE approach is affected by using two different translations (human and ma-

[1] A version of PORTAGE is made available by the NRC to Canadian universities for research and education purposes.

	en → fr	fr → en
Europarl (>32M words/language)		
SYSTRAN	23.06	20.11
PORTAGE	31.01	30.90
SYSTRAN+PORTAGE	31.11	30.61
News Commentary (1M words/language)		
SYSTRAN	24.41	18.09
PORTAGE	25.98	25.17
SYSTRAN+PORTAGE	28.80	26.79

Table 1: System performances on WMT-06 test. All figures are single-reference BLEU scores, computed on truecased, detokenized translations.

chine) instead of two versions of the same translation (raw MT versus post-edited MT).

We concentrated our efforts on the English-French language pair. For each translation direction, we prepared two systems: one for the Europarl domain, and one for the News Commentary domain. The two systems have almost identical configurations (phrase tables, log-linear model features, etc.); the only differences between the two are the *adapted language model*, which is computed based on the specific text to be translated and the parameters of the log-linear models, which are optimized using domain-specific development sets. For the Europarl domain system, we used the *dev2006* and *devtest2006* data sets, while for the News Commentary, we used the *nc-dev2007*. Typically, the optimization procedure will give higher weights to Europarl-trained phrase tables for the Europarl domain systems, and inversely for the News Commentary domain systems.

3 Experimental Results

We computed BLEU scores for all four systems on the 2006 test data (*test2006* for the Europarl domain and *nc-devtest2007* for the News Commentary). The results are presented in Table 1. As points of comparison, we also give the scores obtained by the SYSTRAN systems on their own (i.e. without a post-editing layer), and by the PORTAGE MT systems on their own (i.e. translating directly source into target).

The first observation is that, as was the case in the Simard et al. study, post-editing (*SYSTRAN+PORTAGE* lines) very significantly increases the BLEU scores of the rule-based system (*SYSTRAN* lines). This increase is more spectacular in the Europarl domain and when translating into English, but it is visible for all four systems.

For the News Commentary domain, the APE strategy (*SYSTRAN+PORTAGE* lines) clearly outperforms the direct SMT strategy (*PORTAGE* lines): translating into English, the gain exceeds 1.5 BLEU points, while for French, it is close to 3 BLEU points. In contrast, for the Europarl domain, both approaches display similar performances. Let us recall that the News Commentary corpus contains less than 50K sentence pairs, totalling a little over one million words in each language. With close to 1.3 million sentence pairs, the Europarl corpus is almost 30 times larger. Our results therefore appear to confirm one of the conjectures of the Simard et al. study: that APE is better suited for domains with limited quantities of available training data. To better understand this behavior, we trained series of APE and SMT systems on the Europarl data, using increasing amounts of training data. The resulting learning curves are presented in Figure 1.[2]

As observed in the Simard et al. study, while both the SMT and APE systems improve quite steadily with more data (note the logarithmic scale), SMT appears to improve more rapidly than APE. However, there doesn't seem to be a clear "crossover" point, as initially conjectured by Simard et al. Instead, SMT eventually catches up with APE (anywhere between 100K and 1M sentence pairs), beyond which point both approaches appear to be more or less equivalent. Again, one impressive feature of the APE strategy is how little data is actually required to improve upon the rule-based system upon which it is built: around 5000 sentence pairs for English-to-French, and 2000 for French-to-English.

4 Conclusions

We have presented a combination MT system based on a post-editing strategy, in which a statistical phrase-based system corrects the output of a rule-based translation system. Experiments confirm the

[2]The systems used for this experiment are simplified versions of those described in Section 2, using only one phrase table, a trigram language model and no rescoring; furthermore, they were optimized and tested on short sentences only.

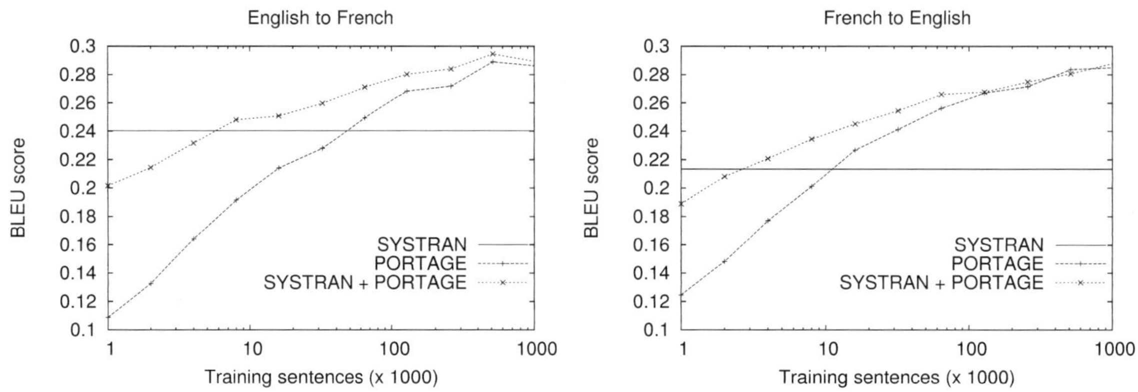

Figure 1: BLEU scores on Europarl data under increasing amounts of training data for PORTAGE SMT alone and SYSTRAN MT with PORTAGE APE.

conclusions of earlier studies: not only can phrase-based post-editing significantly improve the output of a rule-based MT system (in terms of BLEU score), but when training data is scarce, it also outperforms a direct phrase-based MT strategy. Furthermore, our results indicate that the training data for the post-editing component does not need to be manually post-edited translations, it can be generated from standard parallel corpora. Finally, our experiments show that while post-editing is most effective when little training data is available, it remains competitive with phrase-based translation even with much larger amounts of data.

This work opens the door to a number of lines of investigation. For example, it was mentioned earlier that phrase-based APE could be seen as a form of automatic domain-adaptation for rule-based methods. One thing we would like to verify is how this approach compares to the standard "lexical customization" method proposed by most rule-based MT vendors. Also, in the experiments reported here, we have used identical configurations for the APE and direct SMT systems. However, it might be possible to modify the phrase-based system so as to better adapt it to the APE task. For example, it could be useful for the APE layer to "look" at the real source-language text, in addition to the MT output it is post-editing. Finally, we have so far considered the front-end rule-based system as a "black box". But in the end, the real question is: Which part of the rule-based processing is really making things easier for the phrase-based post-editing layer? Answering this question will likely require diving into the internals of the rule-based component. These are all directions that we are currently pursuing.

Acknowledgements

This work was done as part of a collaboration with SYSTRAN S.A. Many thanks go to Jean Senellart, Jens Stephan, Dimitris Sabatakakis and all those people behind the scene at SYSTRAN.

References

L. Dugast, J. Senellart, and P. Koehn. 2007. Statistical Post-Edition on SYSTRAN Rule-Based Translation System. In *Proceedings of the Second Workshop On Statistical Machine Translation*, Prague, Czech Republic.

G. Foster, R. Kuhn, and H. Johnson. 2006. Phrasetable Smoothing for Statistical Machine Translation. In *Proceedings of EMNLP 2006*, pages 53–61, Sydney, Australia.

F. Sadat, H. Johnson, A. Agbago, G. Foster, R. Kuhn, J. Martin, and A. Tikuisis. 2005. PORTAGE: A Phrase-Based Machine Translation System. In *Proceedings of the ACL Workshop on Building and Using Parallel Texts*, pages 129–132, Ann Arbor, USA.

M. Simard, C. Goutte, and P. Isabelle. 2007. Statistical Phrase-Based Post-Editing. In *Human Language Technologies 2007: The Conference of the North American Chapter of the Association for Computational Linguistics; Proceedings of the Main Conference*, pages 508–515, Rochester, USA.

N. Ueffing, M. Simard, S. Larkin, and H. Johnson. 2007. NRC's PORTAGE system for WMT 2007. In *Proceedings of the Second Workshop On Statistical Machine Translation*, Prague, Czech Republic.

The 'noisier channel': translation from morphologically complex languages

Christopher J. Dyer
Department of Linguistics
University of Maryland
College Park, MD 20742
redpony@umd.edu

Abstract

This paper presents a new paradigm for translation from inflectionally rich languages that was used in the University of Maryland statistical machine translation system for the WMT07 Shared Task. The system is based on a hierarchical phrase-based decoder that has been augmented to translate ambiguous input given in the form of a *confusion network* (CN), a weighted finite state representation of a set of strings. By treating morphologically derived forms of the input sequence as possible, albeit more "costly" paths that the decoder may select, we find that significant gains (10% BLEU relative) can be attained when translating from Czech, a language with considerable inflectional complexity, into English.

1 Introduction

Morphological analysis occupies a tenuous position statistical machine translation systems. Conventional translation models are constructed with no consideration of the relationships between lexical items and instead treat different inflected (observed) forms of identical underlying lemmas as completely independent of one another. While the variously inflected forms of one lemma may express differences in meaning that are crucial to correct translation, the strict independence assumptions normally made exacerbate data sparseness and lead to poorly estimated models and suboptimal translations. A variety of solutions have been proposed: Niessen and Ney (2001) use of morphological information to improve word reordering before training and after decoding. Goldwater and McClosky (2005) show improvements in a Czech to English word-based translation system when inflectional endings are simplified or removed entirely. Their method can, however, actually harm performance since the discarded morphemes carry some information that may have bearing on the translation (cf. Section 3.3). To avoid this pitfall, Talbot and Osborne (2006) use a data-driven approach to cluster source-language morphological variants that are meaningless in the target language, and Yang and Kirchhoff (2006) propose the use of a *backoff model* that uses morphologically reduced forms only when the translation of the surface form is unavailable. All of these approaches have in common that the decisions about whether to use morphological information are made in either a pre- or post-processing step.

Recent work in spoken language translation suggests that allowing decisions about the use of morphological information to be made along side other translation decisions (i.e., inside the decoder), will yield better results. At least as early as Ney (1999), it has been shown that when translating the output from automatic speech regonition (ASR) systems, the quality can be improved by considering multiple (rather than only a single best) transcription hypothesis. Although state-of-the-art statistical machine translation systems have conventionally assumed unambiguous input; recent work has demonstrated the possibility of efficient decoding of am-

Proceedings of the Second Workshop on Statistical Machine Translation, pages 207–211,
Prague, June 2007. ©2007 Association for Computational Linguistics

biguous input (represented as confusion networks or word lattices) within standard phrase-based models (Bertoldi et al., to appear 2007) as well as hierarchical phrase-based models (Dyer and Resnik, 2007). These hybrid decoders search for the target language sentence $\hat{e}$ that maximizes the following probability, where $\mathcal{G}(o)$ represents the set of weighted transcription hypotheses produced by an ASR decoder:

$$\hat{e} = \arg\max_{e} \max_{f' \in \mathcal{G}(o)} P(e, f'|o) \quad (1)$$

The conditional probability $p(e, f|o)$ that is maximized is modeled directly using a log-linear model (Och and Ney, 2002), whose parameters can be tuned to optimize either the probability of a development set or some other objective (such as maximizing BLEU). In addition to the standard translation model features, the ASR system's posterior probability is another feature. The decoder thus finds a translation hypothesis $\hat{e}$ that maximizes the joint translation/transcription probability, which is not necessarily the one that corresponds to the best single transcription hypothesis.

2 Noisier channel translation

We extend the concept of translating from an ambiguous set of source hypotheses to the domain of text translation by redefining $\mathcal{G}(\cdot)$ to be a set of weighted sentences derived by applying *morphological transformations* (such as stemming, compound splitting, clitic splitting, etc.) to a given source sentence f. This model for translation extends the usual noisy channel metaphor by suggesting that an "English" source signal is first distorted into a morphologically neutral "French" and then morphological processes represent a further distortion of the signal, which can be modeled independently. Whereas in the context of an ASR transcription hypothesis, $\mathcal{G}(\cdot)$ assigns a posterior probability to each sentence, we redefine of this value to be a *backoff penalty*. This can be intuitively thought of as a measure of the "distance" that a given morphological alternative is from the observed input sentence.

The remainder of the paper is structured as follows. In Section 2, we describe the basic hierarchical translation model. In Section 3, we describe the data and tools used and present experimental results for Czech-English. Section 4 concludes.

3 Hierarchical phrase-based decoding

Chiang (2005; to appear 2007) introduced hierarchical phrase-based translation models, which are formally based on synchronous context-free grammars. These generalize phrase-based translation models by allowing phrase pairs to contain variables. Like phrase correspondences, the corresponding synchronous grammar rules can be learned automatically from aligned, but otherwise unannotated, training bitext. For details about the extraction algorithm, refer to Chiang (to appear 2007).

The rules of the induced grammar consist of pairs of strings of terminals and non-terminals in the source and target languages, as well one-to-one correspondences between non-terminals on the source and target side of each pair (shown as indexes in the examples below). Thus they encapsulate not only meaning translation (of possibly discontinuous spans), but also typical reordering patterns. For example, the following two rules were extracted from the Spanish $\leftrightarrow$ English segment of the Europarl corpus (Koehn, 2003):

$$\text{X} \rightarrow \langle \text{la X}_{\boxed{1}} \text{ de X}_{\boxed{2}}, \text{X}_{\boxed{2}} \text{ 's X}_{\boxed{1}} \rangle \quad (2)$$

$$\text{X} \rightarrow \langle \text{el X}_{\boxed{1}} \text{ verde, the green X}_{\boxed{1}} \rangle \quad (3)$$

Rule (2) expresses the fact that possessors can be expressed prior to the possessed object in English but must follow in Spanish. Rule (3) shows that the adjective *verde* follows the modified expression in Spanish whereas the corresponding English lexical item *green* precedes what it modifies. Although the rules given here correspond to syntactic constituents, this is accidental. The grammars extracted make use of only a single non-terminal category and variables are posited that may or may not correspond to linguistically meaningful spans.

Given a synchronous grammar G, the translation process is equivalent to parsing an input sentence with the source side of G and thereby inducing a target sentence. The decoder we used is based on the CKY+ algorithm, which permits the parsing of rules that are not in Chomsky normal form (Cheppalier and Rajman, 1998) and that has been adapted to admit input that is in the form of a confusion network (Dyer and Resnik, 2007). To incorporate target

Language	Tokens	Types	Singletons
Czech surface	1.2M	88037	42341
Czech lemmas	1.2M	34227	13129
Czech truncated	1.2M	37263	13093
English	1.4M	31221	10508
Spanish	1.4M	47852	20740
French	1.2M	38241	15264
German	1.4M	75885	39222

Table 1: Corpus statistics, by language, for the WMT07 training subset of the News Commentary corpus.

language model probabilities into the model, which is important for translation quality, the grammar is intersected during decoding with an m-gram language model. This process significantly increases the effective size of the grammar, and so a beam-search heuristic called *cube pruning* is used, which has been experimentally determined to be nearly as effective as an exhaustive search but far more efficient.

4 Experiments

We carried out a series of experiments using different strategies for making use of morphological information on the News Commentary Czech-English data set provided for the WMT07 Shared Task. Czech was selected because it exhibits a rich inflectional morphology, but its other morphological processes (such as compounding and cliticization) that affect multiple lemmas are relatively limited. This has the advantage that a morphologically simplified (i.e., lemmatized) form of a Czech sentence has the same number of tokens as the surface form has words, which makes representing $\mathcal{G}(f)$ as a confusion network relatively straightforward. The relative morphological complexity of Czech, as well as the potential benefits that can be realized by stemming, can be inferred from the corpus statistics given in Table 1.

4.1 Technical details

A trigram English language model with modified Kneser-Ney smoothing (Kneser and Ney, 1995) was trained using the SRI Language Modeling Toolkit (Stolcke, 2002) on the English side of the News Commentary corpus as well as portions of the GigaWord v2 English Corpus and was used for all experiments. Recasing was carried out using SRI's `disambig` tool using a trigram language model. The feature set used included bidirectional translation probabilities for rules, lexical translation probabilities, a target language model probability, and count features for target words, number of non-terminal symbols used, and finally the number of morphologically simplified forms selected in the CN. Feature weight tuning was carried out using minimum error rate training, maximizing BLEU scores on a held-out development set (Och, 2003). Translation scores are reported using case-insensitive BLEU (Papineni et al., 2002) with a single reference translation. Significance testing was done using bootstrap resampling (Koehn, 2004).

4.2 Data preparation and training

We used a Czech morphological analyzer by Hajič and Hladká (1998) to extract the lemmas from the Czech portions of the training, development, and test data (the Czech-English portion of the News Commentary corpus distributed as as part of the WMT07 Shared Task). Data sets consisting of truncated forms were also generated; using a length limit of 6, which Goldwater and McClosky (2005) experimentally determined to be optimal for translation performance. We refer to the three data sets and the models derived from them as SURFACE, LEMMA, and TRUNC. Czech→English grammars were extracted from the three training sets using the methods described in Chiang (to appear 2007). Two additional grammars were created by combining the rules from the SURFACE grammar and the LEMMA or TRUNC grammar and renormalizing the conditional probabilities, yielding the combined models SURFACE+LEMMA and SURFACE+TRUNC.

Confusion networks for the development and test sets were constructed by providing a single backoff form at each position in the sentence where the lemmatizer or truncation process yielded a different word form. The backoff form was assigned a cost of 1 and the surface form a cost of 0. Numbers and punctuation were not truncated. A "backoff" set, corresponding approximately to the method of Yang and Kirchhoff (2006) was generated by lemmatizing only unknown words. Figure 1 shows a sample surface+lemma CN from the test set.

1	2	3	4	5	6	7	8	9	10	11	12
z	amerického americký	břehu břeh	atlantiku atlantik	se s	veskerá	taková takový	odůvodnění	jeví jevit	jako	naprosto	bizarní

Figure 1: Example confusion network generated by lemmatizing the source sentence to generate alternates at each position in the sentence. The upper element in each column is the surface form and the lower element, when present, is the lemma.

Input	BLEU	Sample translation
SURFACE	22.74	From the **US side** of the Atlantic all such **odůvodnění** appears to be **a** totally bizarre.
LEMMA	22.50	From the **side** of the Atlantic **with** any such **justification** seem completely bizarre.
TRUNC (l=6)	22.07	From the **bank** of the Atlantic, all such **justification** appears to be totally bizarre.
backoff (SURFACE+LEMMA)	23.94	From the **US bank** of the Atlantic, all such **justification** appears to be totally bizarre.
CN (SURFACE+LEMMA)	**25.01**	From the **US side** of the Atlantic all such **justification** appears to be **a** totally bizarre.
CN (SURFACE+TRUNC)	23.57	From the **US** Atlantic any such **justification** appears to be **a** totally bizarre.

Table 2: Czech-English results on WMT07 Shared Task DEVTEST set. The sample translations are translations of the sentence shown in Figure 1.

4.3 Experimental results

Table 2 summarizes the performance of the six Czech→English models on the WMT07 Shared Task development set. The basic SURFACE model tends to outperform both the LEMMA and TRUNC models, although the difference is only marginally significant. This suggests that the Goldwater and McClosky (2005) results are highly dependent on the kind of translation model and quantity of data. The backoff model, a slightly modified version of the method proposed by Yang and Kirchhoff (2006),[1] does significantly better than the baseline ($p < .05$). However, the joint (SURFACE+LEMMA) model outperforms both surface and backoff baselines ($p < .01$ and $p < .05$, respectively). The SURFACE+TRUNC model is an improvement over the SURFACE model, but it performances significantly worse than the SURFACE+LEMMA model.

5 Conclusion

We presented a novel model-driven method for using morphologically reduced forms when translating from a language with complex inflectional morphology. By allowing the decoder to select among the surface form of a word or phrase and variants of morphological alternatives on the *source* side, we outperform baselines where hard decisions about what form to use are made in advance of decoding, as has typically been done in systems that make use of morphological information. This "decoder-guided" incorporation of morphology was enabled by adopting techniques for translating from ambiguous sources that were developed to address problems specific to spoken language translation. Although the results presented here were obtained using a hierarchical phrase-based system, the model generalizes to any system where the decoder can accept a weighted word graph as its input.

[1]Our backoff model has two primary differences from model described by Y&K. The first is that our model effectively creates backoff forms for *every* surface string, whereas Y&K do this only for forms that are not found in the surface string. This means that in our model, the probabilities of a larger number of surface rules have been altered by backoff discounting than would be the case in the more conservative model. Second, the joint model we used has the benefit of using morphologically simpler forms to improve alignment.

Acknowledgements

The author would like to thank David Chiang for making the Hiero decoder sources available to us and Daniel Zeman for his assistance in the preparation of the Czech data. This work was generously supported by the GALE program of the Defense Advanced Research Projects Agency, Contract No. HR0011-06-2-0001.

References

N. Bertoldi, R. Zens, and M. Federico. to appear 2007. Speech translation by confusion network decoding. In *32nd International Conference on Acoustics, Speech, and Signal Processing (ICASSP)*, Honolulu, Hawaii, April.

J. Cheppalier and M. Rajman. 1998. A generalized CYK algorithm for parsing stochastic CFG. In *Proceedings of the Workshop on Tabulation in Parsing and Deduction (TAPD98)*, pages 133–137, Paris, France.

D. Chiang. to appear 2007. Hierarchical phrase-based translation. *Computational Linguistics*, 33(2).

C. Dyer and P. Resnik. 2007. Word Lattice Parsing for Statistical Machine Translation. Technical report, University of Maryland, College Park, April.

S. Goldwater and D. McClosky. 2005. Improving statistical mt through morphological analysis. In *Proceedings of Human Language Technology Conference and Conference on Empirical Methods in Natural Language Processing*, pages 676–683, Vancouver, British Columbia.

J. Hajič and B. Hladká. 1998. Tagging inflective languages: Prediction of morphological categories for a rich, structured tagset. In *Proceedings of the COLING-ACL Conference*, pages 483–490.

R. Kneser and H. Ney. 1995. Improved backing-off for m-gram language modeling. In *Proceedings of IEEE Internation Conference on Acoustics, Speech, and Signal Processing*, pages 181–184.

P. Koehn. 2003. Europarl: A multilingual corpus for evaluation of machine translation. Draft, unpublished.

P. Koehn. 2004. Statistical signficiance tests for machine translation evluation. In *Proceedings of the 2004 Conference on Empirical Methods in Natural Language Processing (EMNLP)*, pages 388–395.

H. Ney. 1999. Speech translation: Coupling of recognition and translation. In *IEEE International Conference on Acoustic, Speech and Signal Processing*, pages 517–520, Phoenix, AR, March.

S. Niessen and H. Ney. 2001. Morpho-syntactic analysis for reordering in statistical machine translation. In *Proceedings of MT Summit VIII*, Santiago de Compostela, Galicia, Spain.

F. Och and H. Ney. 2002. Discriminitive training and maximum entropy models for statistical machine translation. In *Proceedings of the 40th Annual Meeting of the ACL*, pages 295–302.

F. Och. 2003. Minimum error rate training in statistical machine translation. In *Proceedings of the 41st Annual Meeting of the Association for Computational Linguistics (ACL)*, pages 160–167, Sapporo, Japan, July.

K. Papineni, S. Roukos, T. Ward, and W.-J. Zhu. 2002. Bleu: a method for automatic evaluation of machine translation. In *Proceedings of the 40th Annual Meeting of the ACL*, pages 311–318.

A. Stolcke. 2002. SRILM – an extensible language modeling toolkit. In *Intl. Conf. on Spoken Language Processing*.

D. Talbot and M. Osborne. 2006. Modelling lexical redundancy for machine translation. In *Proceedings of ACL 2006*, Sydney, Australia.

M. Yang and K. Kirchhoff. 2006. Phrase-based backoff models for machine translation of highly inflected languages. In *Proceedings of the EACL 2006*, pages 41–48.

UCB System Description for the WMT 2007 Shared Task

Preslav Nakov
EECS, CS division
University of California at Berkeley
Berkeley, CA 94720
nakov@cs.berkeley.edu

Marti Hearst
School of Information
University of California at Berkeley
Berkeley, CA 94720
hearst@ischool.berkeley.edu

Abstract

For the WMT 2007 shared task, the UC Berkeley team employed three techniques of interest. First, we used monolingual syntactic paraphrases to provide syntactic variety to the source training set sentences. Second, we trained two language models: a small in-domain model and a large out-of-domain model. Finally, we made use of results from prior research that shows that cognate pairs can improve word alignments. We contributed runs translating English to Spanish, French, and German using various combinations of these techniques.

1 Introduction

Modern Statistical Machine Translation (SMT) systems are trained on aligned sentences of bilingual corpora, typically from one domain. When tested on text from that same domain, such systems demonstrate state-of-the art performance; however, on out-of-domain text the results can get significantly worse. For example, on the WMT 2006 Shared Task evaluation, the French to English translation BLEU scores dropped from about 30 to about 20 for nearly all systems, when tested on *News Commentary* rather than *Europarl* (Koehn and Monz, 2006).

Therefore, this year the shared task organizers have provided 1M words of bilingual *News Commentary* training data in addition to the *Europarl* data (about 30M words), thus challenging the participants to experiment with domain adaptation.

Below we describe our domain adaptation experiments, trying to achieve better results on the *News Commentary* data. In addition to training on both data sets, we make use of monolingual syntactic paraphrases of the English side of the data.

2 Monolingual Syntactic Paraphrasing

In many cases, the testing text contains "phrases" that are equivalent, but syntactically different from the phrases learned on training, and the potential for a high-quality translation is missed. We address this problem by using nearly equivalent syntactic paraphrases of the original sentences. Each paraphrased sentence is paired with the foreign translation that is associated with the original sentence in the training data. This augmented training corpus can then be used to train an SMT system. Alternatively, we can paraphrase the test sentences making them closer to the target language syntax.

Given an English sentence, we parse it with the Stanford parser (Klein and Manning, 2003) and then generate paraphrases using the following syntactic transformations:

1. $[_{NP}\ \mathbf{NP}_1\ \mathbf{P}\ \mathbf{NP}_2] \Rightarrow [_{NP}\ \mathbf{NP}_2\ \mathbf{NP}_1]$.
   inequality in income ⇒ *income inequality*.
2. $[_{NP}\ \mathbf{NP}_1\ \textit{of}\ \mathbf{NP}_2] \Rightarrow [_{NP}\ \mathbf{NP}_2\ \mathbf{poss}\ \mathbf{NP}_1]$.
   inequality of income ⇒ *income's inequality*.
3. $\mathbf{NP}_{poss} \Rightarrow \mathbf{NP}$.
   income's inequality ⇒ *income inequality*.
4. $\mathbf{NP}_{poss} \Rightarrow \mathbf{NP}_{PP_{of}}$.
   income's inequality ⇒ *inequality of income*.
5. $\mathbf{NP}_{NC} \Rightarrow \mathbf{NP}_{poss}$.
   income inequality ⇒ *income's inequality*.
6. $\mathbf{NP}_{NC} \Rightarrow \mathbf{NP}_{PP}$.
   income inequality ⇒ *inequality in incomes*.

Proceedings of the Second Workshop on Statistical Machine Translation, pages 212–215,
Prague, June 2007.

Sharply rising income inequality has raised the stakes of the economic game .
Sharply rising *income inequality* has raised the *economic game 's stakes* .
Sharply rising *income inequality* has raised the *economic game stakes* .
Sharply rising *inequality of income* has raised the *stakes of the economic game* .
Sharply rising *inequality of income* has raised the *economic game 's stakes* .
Sharply rising *inequality of income* has raised the *economic game stakes* .
Sharply rising *inequality of incomes* has raised the *stakes of the economic game* .
Sharply rising *inequality of incomes* has raised the *economic game 's stakes* .
Sharply rising *inequality of incomes* has raised the *economic game stakes* .
Sharply rising *inequality in income* has raised the *stakes of the economic game* .
Sharply rising *inequality in income* has raised the *economic game 's stakes* .
Sharply rising *inequality in income* has raised the *economic game stakes* .
Sharply rising *inequality in incomes* has raised the *stakes of the economic game* .
Sharply rising *inequality in incomes* has raised the *economic game 's stakes* .
Sharply rising *inequality in incomes* has raised the *economic game stakes* .

Table 1: Sample sentence and automatically generated paraphrases. Paraphrased NCs are in italics.

7. **remove *that* where optional**
   I think that *he is right* ⇒ *I think he is right.*
8. **add *that* where optional**
   I think he is right ⇒ *I think* that *he is right.*

where:

poss	possessive marker: ' or 's;
P	preposition;
NP$_{PP}$	NP with internal PP-attachment;
NP$_{PP_{of}}$	NP with internal PP headed by *of*;
NP$_{poss}$	NP with internal possessive marker;
NP$_{NC}$	NP that is a Noun Compound.

While the first four and the last two transformations are purely syntactic, (5) and (6) are not. The algorithm must determine whether a possessive marker is feasible for (5) and must choose the correct preposition for (6). In either case, for noun compounds (NCs) of length 3 or more, it also needs to choose the position to modify, e.g., *inquiry's committee chairman* vs. *inquiry committee's chairman.*

In order to ensure accuracy of the paraphrases, we use statistics gathered from the Web, using a variation of the approaches presented in Lapata and Keller (2004) and Nakov and Hearst (2005). We use patterns to generate possible prepositional or copula paraphrases in the context of the preceding and the following word in the sentence, First we split the NC into two parts N_1 and N_2 in all possible ways, e.g., *beef import ban lifting* would be split as: (a) N_1="*beef*", N_2="*import ban lifting*", (b) N_1="*beef import*", N_2="*ban lifting*", and (c) N_1="*beef import ban*", N_2="*lifting*". For every split, we issue exact phrase queries to the Google search engine using the following patterns:

"`lt` N_1 `poss` N_2 `rt`"
"`lt` N_2 `prep det` N_1' `rt`"
"`lt` N_2 `that be det` N_1' `rt`"
"`lt` N_2 `that be prep det` N_1' `rt`"

where: `lt` is the word preceding N_1 in the original sentence or empty if none, `rt` is the word following N_2 in the original sentence or empty if none, `poss` is a possessive marker ('s or '), `that` is *that*, *which* or *who*, `be` is *is* or *are*, `det` is a determiner (*the*, *a*, *an*, or none), `prep` is one of the 8 prepositions used by Lauer (1995) for semantic interpretation of NCs: *about*, *at*, *for*, *from*, *in*, *of*, *on*, and *with*, and N_1' can be either N_1, or N_1 with the number of its last word changed from singular/plural to plural/singular.

For all splits, we collect the number of page hits for each instantiation of each pattern, filtering out the paraphrases whose page hit count is less than 10. We then calculate the total number of page hits H for all paraphrases (for all splits and all patterns), and retain those ones whose page hits count is at least 10% of H. Note that this allows for multiple paraphrases of an NC. If no paraphrases are retained, we repeat the above procedure with `lt` set to the empty string. If there are still no good paraphrases, we set the `rt` to the empty string. If this does not help either, we make a final attempt, by setting both `lt` and `rt` to the empty string.

Table 1 shows the paraphrases for a sample sentence. We can see that *income inequality* is paraphrased as *inequality of income*, *inequality of incomes*, *inequality in income* and *inequality in incomes*; also *economic game's stakes* becomes *economic game stakes* and *stakes of the economic game*.

3 Experiments

Table 2 shows a summary of our submissions: the official runs are marked with a $\star$. For our experiments, we used the baseline system, provided by the organizers, which we modified in different ways, as described below.

3.1 Domain Adaptation

All our systems were trained on both corpora.

- **Language models**. We used two language models (LM) – a small in-domain one (trained on *News Commentary*) and a big out-of-domain one (trained on *Europarl*). For example, for EN $\rightarrow$ ES (from English to Spanish), on the lowercased tuning data set, using in-domain LM only achieved a BLEU of 0.332910, while using both LMs yielded 0.354927, a significant effect.

- **Cognates.** Previous research has found that using cognates can help get better word alignments (and ultimately better MT results), especially in case of a small training set. We used the method described in (Kondrak et al., 2003) in order to extract cognates from the two data sets. We then added them as sentence pairs to the *News Commentary* corpus before training the word alignment models[1] for *ucb3*, *ucb4* and *ucb5*.

- **Phrases.** The *ucb5* system uses the *Europarl* data in order to learn an additional phrase table and an additional lexicalized re-ordering model.

3.2 Paraphrasing the Training Set

In two of our experiments (*ucb3*, *ucb4* and *ucb5*), we used a paraphrased version of the training *News Commentary* data, using all rules (1)-(8). We trained two separate MT systems: one on the original corpus, and another one on the paraphrased version. We then used both resulting lexicalized re-ordering models and a merged phrase table with extra parameters: if a phrase appeared in both phrase tables, it now had 9 instead of 5 parameters (4 from each table, plus a phrase penalty), and if it was in one of the phrase tables only, the 4 missing parameters were filled with 1e-40.

The *ucb5* system is also trained on *Europarl*, yielding a third lexicalized re-ordering model and adding 4 new parameters to the phrase table entries.

Unfortunately, longer sentences (up to 100 tokens, rather than 40), longer phrases (up to 10 tokens, rather than 7), two LMs (rather than just one), higher-order LMs (order 7, rather than 3), multiple higher-order lexicalized re-ordering models (up to 3), etc. all contributed to increased system's complexity, and, as a result, time limitations prevented us from performing minimum-error-rate training (MERT) (Och, 2003) for *ucb3*, *ucb4* and *ucb5*. Therefore, we used the MERT parameter values from *ucb1* instead, e.g. the first 4 phrase weights of *ucb1* were divided by two, copied twice and used in *ucb3* as the first 8 phrase-table parameters. The extra 4 parameters of *ucb5* came from training a separate MT system on the *Europarl* data (scaled accordingly).

3.3 Paraphrasing the Test Set

In some of our experiments (*ucb2* and *ucb4*), given a test sentence, we generated the single most-likely paraphrase, which makes it syntactically closer to Spanish and French. Unlike English, which makes extensive use of noun compounds, these languages strongly prefer connecting the nouns with a preposition (and less often turning a noun into an adjective). Therefore, we paraphrased all NCs using prepositions, by applying rules (4) and (6). In addition, we

[1] Following (Kondrak et al., 2003), we considered words of length 4 or more, we required the length ratio to be between $\frac{7}{10}$ and $\frac{10}{7}$, and we accepted as potential cognates all pairs for which the longest common subsequence ratio (LCSR) was 0.58 or more. We repeated 3 times the cognate pairs extracted from the *Europarl*, and 4 times the ones from *News Commentary*.

Languages	System	LM size		Paraphrasing		Cognates?	Extra phrases	MERT
		News	*Europarl*	*train?*	*test?*		*Europarl*	*finished?*
EN → ES	ucb1*	3	5					+
	ucb2	3	5		+			+
	ucb3	5	7	+		+		
	ucb4	5	7	+	+	+		
	ucb5	5	7	+		+	+	
EN → FR	ucb3	5	7	+		+		
	ucb4*	5	7	+	+	+		
EN → DE	ucb1*	5	7			+		+
	ucb2	5	7		+	+		+

Table 2: **Summary of our submissions.** All runs are for the *News Commentary* test data. The official submissions are marked with a star.

applied rule (8), since its Spanish/French equivalent *que* (as well as the German *daß*) is always obligatory. These transformations affected 927 out of the 2007 test sentences. We also used this transformed data set when translating to German (however, German uses NCs as much as English does).

3.4 Other Non-standard Settings

Below we discuss some non-standard settings that differ from the ones suggested by the organizers in their baseline system. First, following Birch et al. (2006), who found that higher-order LMs give better results[2], we used a 5-gram LM for *News Commentary*, and 7-gram LM for *Europarl* (as opposed to 3-gram, as done normally). Second, for all runs we trained our systems on all sentences of length up to 100 (rather than 40, as suggested in the baseline system). Third, we used a maximum phrase length limit of 10 (rather than 7, as typically done). Fourth, we used *both* a lexicalized and distance-based reordering models (as opposed to lexicalized only, as in the baseline system). Finally, while we did not use any resources other than the ones provided by the shared task organizers, we made use of Web frequencies when paraphrasing the training corpus, as explained above.

4 Conclusions and Future Work

We have presented various approaches to domain adaptation and their combinations. Unfortunately, computational complexity and time limitations prevented us from doing proper MERT for the interesting more complex systems. We plan to do a proper MERT training and to study the impact of the individual components in isolation.

Acknowledgements: This work supported in part by NSF DBI-0317510.

References

Alexandra Birch, Chris Callison-Burch, Miles Osborne, and Philipp Koehn. 2006. Constraining the phrase-based, joint probability statistical translation model. In *Proc. of Workshop on Statistical Machine Translation*, pages 154–157.

Dan Klein and Christopher Manning. 2003. Accurate unlexicalized parsing. In *Proceedings of ACL '03*.

Philipp Koehn and Christof Monz. 2006. Manual and automatic evaluation of machine translation between european languages. In *Proceedings on the Workshop on Statistical Machine Translation*, pages 102–121.

Grzegorz Kondrak, Daniel Marcu, and Kevin Knight. 2003. Cognates can improve statistical translation models. In *Proceedings of NAACL*, pages 46–48.

Mirella Lapata and Frank Keller. 2004. The web as a baseline: Evaluating the performance of unsupervised web-based models for a range of nlp tasks. In *Proceedings of HLT-NAACL '04*.

Mark Lauer. 1995. Corpus statistics meet the noun compound: some empirical results. In *Proceedings of ACL '95*.

Preslav Nakov and Marti Hearst. 2005. Search engine statistics beyond the n-gram: Application to noun compound bracketing. In *Proceedings of CoNLL '05*.

Franz Josef Och. 2003. Minimum error rate training in statistical machine translation. In *Proceedings of ACL*, pages 160–167.

[2]They used a 5-gram LM trained on *Europarl*, but we pushed the idea further, using a 7-gram LM with a Kneser-Ney smoothing.

The Syntax Augmented MT (SAMT) System for the Shared Task in the 2007 ACL Workshop on Statistical Machine Translation

Andreas Zollmann and **Ashish Venugopal** and **Matthias Paulik** and **Stephan Vogel**
School of Computer Science, Carnegie Mellon University, Pittsburgh
interACT Lab, University of Karlsruhe
{ashishv,zollmann,paulik,vogel+}@cs.cmu.edu

Abstract

We describe the CMU-UKA Syntax Augmented Machine Translation system 'SAMT' used for the shared task "Machine Translation for European Languages" at the ACL 2007 Workshop on Statistical Machine Translation. Following an overview of syntax augmented machine translation, we describe parameters for components in our open-source SAMT toolkit that were used to generate translation results for the Spanish to English in-domain track of the shared task and discuss relative performance against our phrase-based submission.

1 Introduction

As Chiang (2005) and Koehn et al. (2003) note, purely lexical "phrase-based" translation models suffer from sparse data effects when translating conceptual elements that span or skip across several source language words. Phrase-based models also rely on distance and lexical distortion models to represent the reordering effects across language pairs. However, such models are typically applied over limited source sentence ranges to prevent errors introduced by these models and to maintain efficient decoding (Och and Ney, 2004).

To address these concerns, hierarchically structured models as in Chiang (2005) define weighted transduction **rules**, interpretable as components of a probabilistic synchronous grammar (Aho and Ullman, 1969) that represent translation and reordering operations. In this work, we describe results from the open-source Syntax Augmented Machine Translation (SAMT) toolkit (Zollmann and Venugopal, 2006) applied to the Spanish-to-English in-domain translation task of the ACL'07 workshop on statistical machine translation.

We begin by describing the probabilistic model of translation applied by the SAMT toolkit. We then present settings for the pipeline of SAMT tools that we used in our shared task submission. Finally, we compare our translation results to the CMU-UKA phrase-based SMT system and discuss relative performance.

2 Synchronous Grammars for SMT

Probabilistic synchronous context-free grammars (PSCFGs) are defined by a source terminal set (source vocabulary) $\mathcal{T}_S$, a target terminal set (target vocabulary) $\mathcal{T}_T$, a shared nonterminal set $\mathcal{N}$ and production rules of the form

$$X \rightarrow \langle \gamma, \alpha, \sim, w \rangle$$

where following (Chiang, 2005)

- $X \in \mathcal{N}$ is a nonterminal
- $\gamma \in (\mathcal{N} \cup \mathcal{T}_S)^*$: sequence of source nonterminals and terminals
- $\alpha \in (\mathcal{N} \cup \mathcal{T}_T)^*$: sequence of target nonterminals and terminals
- the count $\#\mathrm{NT}(\gamma)$ of nonterminal tokens in γ is equal to the count $\#\mathrm{NT}(\alpha)$ of nonterminal tokens in α,
- $\sim$: $\{1, \ldots, \#\mathrm{NT}(\gamma)\} \rightarrow \{1, \ldots, \#\mathrm{NT}(\alpha)\}$ one-to-one mapping from nonterminal tokens in γ to nonterminal tokens in α
- $w \in [0, \infty)$: nonnegative real-valued weight

Chiang (2005) uses a single nonterminal category, Galley et al. (2004) use syntactic constituents for the PSCFG nonterminal set, and Zollmann and Venugopal (2006) take advantage of CCG (Combinatorial Categorical Grammar) (Steedman, 1999) inspired "slash" and "plus" categories, focusing on target (rather than source side) categories to generate well formed translations.

We now describe the identification and estimation of PSCFG rules from parallel sentence aligned corpora under the framework proposed by Zollmann and Venugopal (2006).

Proceedings of the Second Workshop on Statistical Machine Translation, pages 216–219,
Prague, June 2007.

2.1 Grammar Induction

Zollmann and Venugopal (2006) describe a process to generate a PSCFG given parallel sentence pairs $\langle f, e \rangle$, a parse tree π for each e, the maximum *a posteriori* word alignment a over $\langle f, e \rangle$, and phrase pairs $Phrases(a)$ identified by any alignment-driven phrase induction technique such as e.g. (Och and Ney, 2004).

Each phrase in $Phrases(a)$ (phrases identifiable from a) is first annotated with a syntactic category to produce initial **rules**. If the target span of the phrase does not match a constituent in π, heuristics are used to assign categories that correspond to partial rewriting of the tree. These heuristics first consider concatenation operations, forming categories like "NP+VP", and then resort to CCG style "slash" categories like "NP/NN" giving preference to categories found closer to the leaves of the tree.

To illustrate this process, consider the following French-English sentence pair and selected phrase pairs obtained by phrase induction on an automatically produced alignment a, and matching target spans with π.

$$\begin{array}{rcl} f & = & \text{il ne va pas} \\ e & = & \text{he does not go} \\ \text{PRP} & \rightarrow & \text{il, he} \\ \text{VB} & \rightarrow & \text{va, go} \\ \text{RB+VB} & \rightarrow & \text{ne va pas, not go} \\ \text{S} & \rightarrow & \text{il ne va pas, he does not go} \end{array}$$

The alignment a with the associated target side parse tree is shown in Fig. 1 in the alignment visualization style defined by Galley et al. (2004).

Following the Data-Oriented Parsing inspired rule generalization technique proposed by Chiang (2005), one can now generalize each **identified** rule (initial or already partially generalized) $N \rightarrow f_1 \ldots f_m / e_1 \ldots e_n$ for which there is an **initial** rule $M \rightarrow f_i \ldots f_u / e_j \ldots e_v$ where $1 \leq i < u \leq m$ and $1 \leq j < v \leq n$, to obtain a new rule

$$N \rightarrow f_1 \ldots f_{i-1} M_k f_{u+1} \ldots f_m / e_1 \ldots e_{j-1} M_k e_{v+1} \ldots e_n$$

where k is an index for the nonterminal M that indicates the one-to-one correspondence between the new M tokens on the two sides (it is not in the space of word indices like i, j, u, v, m, n). The initial rules listed above can be generalized to additionally extract the following rules from f, e.

$$\begin{array}{rcl} \text{S} & \rightarrow & \text{PRP}_1 \text{ ne va pas , PRP}_1 \text{ does not go} \\ \text{S} & \rightarrow & \text{il ne VB}_1 \text{ pas , he does not VB}_1 \\ \text{S} & \rightarrow & \text{il RB+VB}_1\text{, he does RB+VB}_1 \\ \text{S} & \rightarrow & \text{PRP}_1 \text{ RB+VB}_2\text{, PRP}_1 \text{ does RB+VB}_2 \\ \text{RB+VB} & \rightarrow & \text{ne VB}_1 \text{ pas , not VB}_1 \end{array}$$

Fig. 2 uses regions to identify the labeled, source and target side span for all initial rules extracted on our example sentence pair and parse. Under this representation, generalization can be viewed as a process that selects a region, and proceeds to subtract out any sub-region to form a generalized rule.

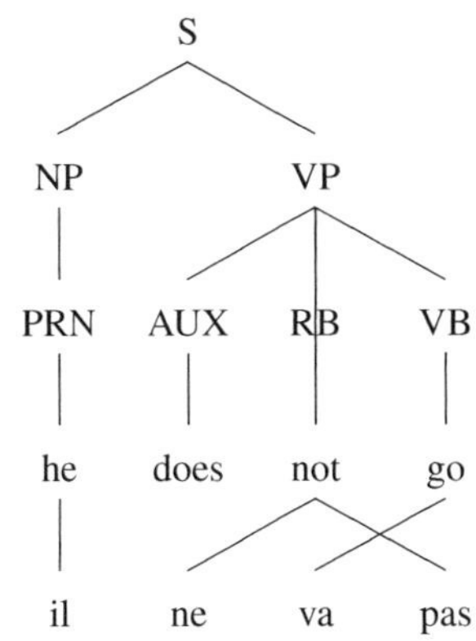

Figure 1: Alignment graph (word alignment and target parse tree) for a French-English sentence pair.

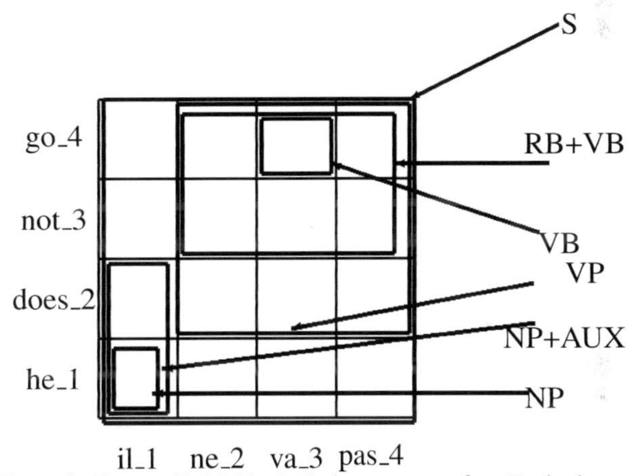

Figure 2: Spans of initial lexical phrases w.r.t. f, e. Each phrase is labeled with a category derived from the tree in Fig. 1.

2.2 Decoding

Given a source sentence f, the translation task under a PSCFG grammar can be expressed analogously to monolingual parsing with a CFG. We find the most likely derivation D with source-side f and read off the English translation from this derivation:

$$\hat{e} = \text{tgt}\left(\underset{D:\text{src}(D)=f}{\arg\max}\; p(D) \right) \tag{1}$$

where $\text{tgt}(D)$ refers to the target terminals and $\text{src}(D)$ to the source terminals generated by derivation D.

Our distribution p over derivations is defined by a log-linear model. The probability of a derivation D

is defined in terms of the rules r that are used in D:

$$p(D) = \frac{p_{LM}(\text{tgt}(D))^{\lambda_{\text{LM}}} \prod_{r \in D} \prod_i \phi_i(r)^{\lambda_i}}{Z(\lambda)} \quad (2)$$

where ϕ_i refers to features defined on each rule, p_{LM} is a language model (LM) probability applied to the target terminal symbols generated by the derivation D, and $Z(\lambda)$ is a normalization constant chosen such that the probabilities sum up to one. The computational challenges of this search task (compounded by the integration of the LM) are addressed in (Chiang, 2007; Venugopal et al., 2007). The feature weights λ_i are trained in concert with the LM weight via minimum error rate (MER) training (Och, 2003).

We now describe the parameters for the SAMT implementation of the model described above.

3 SAMT Components

SAMT provides tools to perform grammar induction ("extractrules", "filterrules"), from bilingual phrase pairs and target language parse trees, as well as translation ("FastTranslateChart") of source sentences given an induced grammar.

3.1 extractrules

extractrules is the first step of the grammar induction pipeline, where rules are identified based on the process described in section 2.1. This tool works on a per sentence basis, considering phrases extracted for the training sentence pair $\langle s_i, t_i \rangle$ and the corresponding target parse tree π_i. **extractrules** outputs identified rules for each input sentence pair, along with associated statistics that play a role in the estimation of the rule features ϕ. These statistics take the form of real-valued feature vectors for each rule as well as summary information collected over the corpus, such as the frequency of each nonterminal symbol, or unique rule source sides encountered.

For the shared task evaluation, we ran **extractrules** with the following extraction parameter settings to limit the scope and number of rules extracted. These settings produce the same initial phrase table as the CMU-UKA phrase based system. We limit the source-side length of the phrase pairs considered as initial rules to 8 (parameter `MaxSourceLength`). Further we set the maximum number of source and target terminals per rule (`MaxSource/MaxTargetWordCount`) to 5 and 8 respectively with 2 of nonterminal pairs (i.e., substitution sites) per rule (`MaxSubstititionCount`). We limit the total number of symbols in each rule to 8 (`MaxSource/TargetSymbolCount`) and require all rules to contain at least one source-side terminal symbol (`noAllowAbstractRules`, `noAllowRulesWithOnlyTargetTerminals`) since this reduces decoding time considerably. Additionally, we discard all rules that contain source word sequences that do not exist in the development and test sets provided for the shared task (parameter `-r`).

3.2 filterrules

This tool takes as input the rules identified by **extractrules**, and associates each rule with a feature vector ϕ, representing multiple criteria by which the decoding process can judge the quality of each rule and, by extension, each derivation. **filterrules** is also in charge of pruning the resulting PSCFG to ensure tractable decoding.

ϕ contains both real and Boolean valued features for each rule. The following probabilistic features are generated by **filterrules**:

- $\hat{p}(r|\,\text{lhs}(X))$: Probability of a rule given its left-hand-side ("result") nonterminal
- $\hat{p}(r|\,\text{src}(r))$: Prob. of a rule given its source side
- $\hat{p}(\text{ul}(\text{src}(r)), \text{ul}(\text{tgt}(r))|\,\text{ul}(\text{src}(r))$: Probability of the unlabeled source and target side of the rule given its unlabeled source side.

Here, the function ul removes all syntactic labels from its arguments, but retains ordering notation, producing relative frequencies similar to those used in purely hierarchical systems. As in phrase-based translation model estimation, ϕ also contains two lexical weights (Koehn et al., 2003), counters for number of target terminals generated. ϕ also boolean features that describe rule types (i.e. purely terminal vs purely nonterminal).

For the shared task submission, we pruned away rules that share the same source side based on $\hat{p}(r|\,\text{src}(r))$ (the source conditioned relative frequency). We prune away a rule if this value is less that 0.5 times the one of the best performing rule (parameters `BeamFactorLexicalRules`, `BeamFactorNonlexicalRules`).

3.3 FastTranslateChart

The **FastTranslateChart** decoder is a chart parser based on the CYK+(Chappelier and Rajman, 1998) algorithm. Translation experiments in this paper are performed with a 4-gram SRI language model trained on the target side of the corpus. **FastTranslateChart** implements both methods of handling the LM intersection described in (Venugopal et al., 2007). For this submission, we use the Cube-Pruning (Chiang, 2007) approach (the default setting). LM and rule feature parameters λ are trained with the included MER training tool. Our pruning settings allow up to 200 chart items per cell with left-hand side nonterminal '_S' (the reserved sentence spanning nonterminal), and 100 items per cell for each other nonterminal. Beam pruning based on an (LM-scaled) additive beam of neglob probability 5 is used to prune the search further. These pruning settings correspond to setting `'PruningMap=0-100-5-@_S-200-5'`.

4 Empirical Results

We trained our system on the Spanish-English in-domain training data provided for the workshop. Initial data processing and normalizing is described in the workshop paper for the CMU-UKA ISL phrase-based system. NIST-BLEU scores are reported on the 2K sentence development 'dev06' and test 'test06' corpora as per the workshop guidelines (case sensitive, de-tokenized). We compare our scores against the CMU-UKA ISL phrase-based submission, a state-of-the art phrase-based SMT system with part-of-speech (POS) based word reordering (Paulik et al., 2007).

4.1 Translation Results

The SAMT system achieves a BLEU score of 32.48% on the 'dev06' development corpus and 32.15% on the unseen 'test06' corpus. This is slightly better than the score of the CMU-UKA phrase-based system, which achieves 32.20% and 31.85% when trained and tuned under the same in-domain conditions. [1]

To understand why the syntax augmented approach has limited additional impact on the Spanish-to-English task, we consider the impact of reordering within our phrase-based system. Table 1 shows the impact of increasing reordering window length (Koehn et al., 2003) on translation quality for the 'dev06' data.[2] Increasing the reordering window past 2 has minimal impact on translation quality, implying that most of the reordering effects across Spanish and English are well modeled at the local or phrase level. The benefit of syntax-based systems to capture long-distance reordering phenomena based on syntactic structure seems to be of limited value for the Spanish to English translation task.

ReOrder	1	2	3	4	POS	**SAMT**
BLEU	31.98	32.24	32.30	32.26	32.20	**32.48**

Table 1: Impact of phrase based reordering model settings compared to SAMT on the 'dev06' corpus measured by NIST-BLEU

5 Conclusions

In this work, we briefly summarized the Syntax-augmented MT model, described how we trained and ran our implementation of that model on the MT'07 Spanish-to-English translation task. We compared SAMT translation results to a strong phrase-based system trained under the same conditions. Our system is available open-source under the GNU General Public License (GPL) and can be downloaded at `www.cs.cmu.edu/~zollmann/samt`

[1]The CMU-UKA phrase-based workshop submission was tuned on out-of-domain data as well.

[2]Variant of the CMU-UKA ISL phrase-based system without POS based reordering. With POS-based reordering turned on, additional window-based reordering even for window length 1 had no improvement in NIST-BLEU.

References

Alfred Aho and Jeffrey Ullman. 1969. Syntax directed translations and the pushdown assembler. *Journal of Computer and System Sciences*.

Jean-Cedric. Chappelier and Martin Rajman. 1998. A generalized CYK algorithm for parsing stochastic CFG. In *Proc. of Tabulation in Parsing and Deduction (TAPD'98)*, Paris, France.

David Chiang. 2005. A hierarchical phrase-based model for statistical machine translation. In *Proc. of ACL*.

David Chiang. 2007. Hierarchical phrase based translation. *Computational Linguistics*. To appear.

Michel Galley, Mark Hopkins, Kevin Knight, and Daniel Marcu. 2004. What's in a translation rule? In *Proc. of HLT/NAACL*, Boston, Massachusetts.

Philipp Koehn, Franz Josef Och, and Daniel Marcu. 2003. Statistical phrase-based translation. In *Proc. of HLT/NAACL*, Edmonton,Canada.

Franz Och and Hermann Ney. 2004. The alignment template approach to statistical machine translation. *Comput. Linguistics*.

Franz Josef Och. 2003. Minimum error rate training in statistical machine translation. In *Proc. of ACL*, Sapporo, Japan, July 6-7.

Matthias Paulik, Kay Rottmann, Jan Niehues, Silja Hildebrand, and Stephan Vogel. 2007. The ISL phrase-based MT system for the 2007 ACL workshop on statistical MT. In *Proc. of the Association of Computational Linguistics Workshop on Statistical Machine Translation*.

Mark Steedman. 1999. Alternative quantifier scope in CCG. In *Proc. of ACL*, College Park, Maryland.

Ashish Venugopal, Andreas Zollmann, and Stephan Vogel. 2007. An efficient two-pass approach to synchronous CFG driven MT. In *Proc. of HLT/NAACL*, Rochester, NY.

Andreas Zollmann and Ashish Venugopal. 2006. Syntax augmented machine translation via chart parsing. In *Proc. of the Workshop on Statistical Machine Translation, HLT/NAACL*, New York, June.

Statistical Post-Editing on SYSTRAN's Rule-Based Translation System

Loïc Dugast, Jean Senellart
SYSTRAN SA
La Grande Arche
1, Parvis de la Défense
92044 Paris La Défense Cedex
France
dugast@systran.fr
senellart@systran.fr

Philipp Koehn
School of Informatics
University of Edinburgh
2 Buccleuch Place
Edinburgh, EH8 9LW
United Kingdom
pkoehn@inf.ed.ac.uk

Abstract

This article describes the combination of a SYSTRAN system with a "statistical post-editing" (SPE) system. We document qualitative analysis on two experiments performed in the shared task of the ACL 2007 Workshop on Statistical Machine Translation. Comparative results and more integrated "hybrid" techniques are discussed.

1 Introduction

The evolution of SYSTRAN's architecture over the last years has been to « open » the system to enable interaction between the internal system's rules and the external input – see Senellart (2003), Attnas et al. (2005). Based on this architecture, several directions are explored to introduce the use of « corpus-based » approaches at several levels of the process:
- use of corpus-based tools to validate and enrich linguistic resources (detection of forbidden sequences, bilingual terminology extraction), - automatic recognition of the text domain, - use of a corpus-based decision mechanism within « word boundary » (Chinese word identification), disambiguation… - use of word sense disambiguation techniques – and the use of a language model in the generation phase to select alternative translations, prepositions, and local reordering (adjective positioning).

These tools have been presented in Senellart (2006) and most of them will be integrated in SYSTRAN version 7 systems.

Independently, two experiments were carried out for the shared task of the ACL 2007 Workshop on Statistical Machine Translation to combine a raw SYSTRAN system with a statistical post-editing (SPE) system. One experiment was run by NRC using the language pair English<>French in the context of « Automatic Post-Edition » systems using the PORTAGE system as described in Simard et al. (2007). The second experiment based on the same principle was run on the German>English and Spanish>English[1] language pairs using the Moses system (Koehn et al. 2007). The objective was to train a SMT system on a parallel corpus composed of SYSTRAN translations with the referenced source aligned with its referenced translation.

Beyond both (a) the huge (and expected) improvement of the BLEU score for the combined system compared to raw translation output (for German-English, around 10 BLEU points for the Europarl test set of WMT2007) and (b) the (expected) corresponding improvement of the translation fluency, we provide qualitative analysis on the contributions (positive and negative) of the SPE layer imposed on the SYSTRAN translation output in this paper. For this analysis we classifiy the different types of "post-editing" changes and point out the alternative isolated statistical components that could achieve the same results.

We conclude with two possible approaches: breaking down the "statistical layer" into different components/tools each specialized in a narrow and accurate area, or refining this global SPE approach in order to introduce linguistic constraints.

[1] The Moses model was trained following the recommendations for the baseline system of WMT 2007.

Proceedings of the Second Workshop on Statistical Machine Translation, pages 220–223,
Prague, June 2007.

2 The SYSTRAN System

Covering 80 language pairs for 22 different source languages, SYSTRAN powers almost all major portals (Google, Yahoo!, BabelFish, Apple, Worldlingo, ...) with machine translation services through URL translations or translation "boxes" (estimated traffic: over 40 million sentence translations and over 10 million web page translations per day).

Customized systems are used by corporate customers either within a post-editing workflow, or without post-editing for the translation of technical Knowledge Bases.

SYSTRAN engines are also available as desktop applications through "plugins" or within post-editing tools. The same engines are also available on ultra-light architectures such as for PDA devices.

The SYSTRAN system is traditionally classified as a "rule-based" system and its design – which has been in constant evolution - has, over the years, always been driven by pragmatic considerations – progressively integrating most of the available productive techniques. As such, it is difficult to classify SYSTRAN and simply describe its architecture. However, the evolution of the SYSTRAN system is governed by the following principles:

- provide a deterministic output : it is possible to easily explain the translation results for a specific sentence and change the rule
- incremental translation quality: the more important evaluation criterion for mature systems is to perform a comparative evaluation of translation output between two consecutive versions. Since it is impossible to guarantee 0 regressions in linguistic development, 8 improvements for 1 degradation defines the acceptance criterion for a linguistic patch.

Crucial components of the SYSTRAN system are the linguistic resources for each language/language pair ranging from 100k to 800k entries. Such "entries" should be understood as both simple or multiword "lexical entries" but also as customized disambiguation rules.

In this context (continuous integration of new techniques in SYSTRAN engines, adhering to determinism and incrementability), over the last three years one major evolution within SYSTRAN has been to make use of available corpora - statically through extraction/learning/validation tools such as:

- Dictionary improvement using a monolingual corpus: new terms/entities/terminology extraction (n-grams based on linguistic patterns);

and dynamically through corpus-based decision algorithms such as:

- Word sense disambiguation
- Use of a language model to select alternative translations, determiner choice, and local controlled reordering – like multiple adjective sequences.

In the following section, we present a qualitative review of the SYSTRAN+SPE output and analyze how the different contributions relate to each specific effort.

3 Experimental Results & Linguistic Evaluation

Based on the data from these two experiments: SYSTRAN+PORTAGE (En<>Fr), and SYSTRAN+Moses (De>En, Es>En), we performed linguistic evaluations on the differences between raw SYSTRAN output and SYSTRAN+SPE output. The evaluation for En<>Fr was performed on the News Commentary test 2006 corpus, while the evaluations for De>En, and Es>En were performed on the Europarl test 2007 corpus.

3.1 Impact

The first observation is the impact of the SPE on the SYSTRAN output. Table 1 displays the WCR (Word Change Rate[2]) and the ratio of sentences impacted by the statistical post-editing. It is interesting to note that the impact is quite high since almost all sentences were post-edited. On the other hand, the WCR of SYSTRAN+SPE is relatively small – as this clearly relates to post-editing and not a complete reshuffling of the translation. The same insight is reinforced when reviewing a comparator (see Table 2) – the SYSTRAN+SPE output

[2] Word Change Rate is computed similarly to the Word Error Rate, with regard to the SYSTRAN output.

is “reasonably” close to the raw SYSTRAN output, and the SPE output structure is completely based on the SYSTRAN output.

	Word Change Rate	Impact (ratio of sentences impacted)
SYSTRAN+PORTAGE En>Fr (nc devtest 2006)	0.33	98%
SYSTRAN+PORTAGE Fr>En (nc devtest 2006)	0.23	95%
SYSTRAN+Moses De>En (nc test 2007)	0.35	100%
SYSTRAN+Moses Es>En (nc test 2007)	0.31	99%

Table 1 - Impact of SPE on raw translation output

Source :En>Fr,De>En,Es>en	SYSTRAN	SYSTRAN +SPE
Monetary policy can be used to stimulate an economy just as much as fiscal policy, if not more, in election years, which politicians will always want to do.	La politique monétaire peut être employée pour stimuler une économie juste comme beaucoup que la politique fiscale, sinon plus, en années d'élection, que les politiciens voudront toujours faire.	La politique monétaire peut être utilisée pour stimuler l'économie, tout comme la politique fiscale, pour ne pas dire plus, dans les années d'élection, que les hommes politiques voudront toujours faire.
Fortschritte der 12 Bewerberländer auf dem Weg zum Beitritt	Progress of the 12 applicant countries on the way to the entry	Progress of the 12 candidate countries along the road to accession
En una perspectiva a más largo plazo, habrá una moneda única en todo el continente.	In a perspective to more long term, there will be a unique currency in all the continent.	In a more long-term perspective, there will be a single currency for the whole continent.

Table 2 - Comparison of source, SYSTRAN, and SYSTRAN+SPE: the output is “reasonably close” – and clearly preserves SYSTRAN's translation structure

3.2 Linguistic Categorization of Different Post-Editing Changes

To classify the types of “post-editing” changes brought by the SPE system, we define the following criteria:

- termchg – changes related to lexical changes.
  - termchg_nfw – word not translated by SYSTRAN generating a translation with SPE.
  - termchg_term – slight terminology change preserves part of speech and meaning. Most of the time changes improve fluency by selecting the appropriate terminology. (e.g. *politicians→politiciens* vs. the more commonly used *“hommes politiques”*).
  - termchg_loc – multiword expression/locution change (*the same is true→Le même est vrai* vs. *C'est également vrai*)
  - termchg_mean – lexical modification altering the meaning of the sentences, by changing the part of speech of the word, or by selecting a completely different meaning for a given word. (*Despite occasional grumbles→En dépit des grognements occasionnels* vs. *En dépit des maux économiser*)
- gram – changes related to grammar
  - gram_det – change in determiner (*on political commitments→sur des engagements politiques* vs. *sur les engagements politiques*)
  - gram_prep – change in preposition (*across the Atlantic→à travers l'atlantique* vs. *de l'autre côté de l'atlantique*)
  - gram_pron – change in pronoun
  - gram_tense – change in tense (*should not be hidden→ne devraient...* vs. *ne doivent...)*
  - gram_number/gram_gender – change in number/gender – often reflecting lack of agreement
  - gram_other – other grammatical changes
- punct/digit/case – change in punctuation, case, or numbers
- wordorder_local – change in local word order
- wordorder_long – change in word order (long distance)
- style – change in “style” (*justifying→justifiant* vs. *ce qui justifie*)

A detailed count of the number of improvements (*#improv*), degradations (*#degrad*) and equivalents (*#equiv*) related to each category performed for a sample corpus (100 sentences each) for En>Fr, De>En and Es>En systems, and related results are reported in the following tables[3]:

	SYSTRAN PORTAGE En>Fr	SYSTRAN Moses De>En	SYSTRAN Moses Es>En
termchg all	+22%	+46%	+46%
termchg_nfw	0%	+3%	+1%
termchg_term	**+19%**	**+42%**	**+45%**
termchg_loc	**+8%**		
termchg_mean	**-6%**		
gram all	+2%	+4%	+12%
gram_det	**14%**	+2%	+4%
gram_prep	2%	+1%	+5%
gram_pron	-1%	+1%	+4%
gram_tense	**-4%**	+1%	-0%
gram_number	0%	None	None
gram_gender	**-4%**	n/a	n/a
gram_other	**-1%**	None	None
punct/digit/case	1%	**-1%**	**-1%**
wordorder_short	-1%	+1%	+1%
wordorder_long	0%	None	+1%
style	1%	+3%	+2%

Table 3 - Relative improvements brought by the SPE system: (*#improv-#degrad*)/∑*#modif*

	#improv	*#degrad*	*#improv / #degrad*	*#equiv*
termchg all	90	32	3	33
termchg_nfw	1	0		0
termchg_term	**59**	7	**8**	29
termchg_loc	15	1	**15**	1
termchg_mean	15	**24**	1	3
gram all	44	38	1	8
gram_det	**20**	3	**7**	4
gram_prep	**12**	9	1	1
gram_pron	0	1	0	2
gram_tense	2	**8**	0	0
gram_number	4	**4**	1	0
gram_gender	2	**8**	0	0

[3] Manual evaluations for De>En and Es>En should not be compared with the results for En>Fr, as both corpus and evaluation criteria differ.

gram_other	4	**5**	1	1
punct/digit/case	8	7	1	1
wordorder_short	0	1	0	0
wordorder_long	0	0		0
style	3	1	3	1

Table 4 - Details on *#improv*, *#degrad*, *#equiv* for each category for SYSTRAN PORTAGE En>Fr

3.3 Analysis of Results

The figures from the previous section provide very useful information that requires deeper analysis, the most obvious of which follow:

- As is, this basic integration does not meet the acceptance criterion "8 improv. for 1 degrad."
- The most improved category is the "termchg" which corresponds to a local choice of word sense or alternative translation of words and locutions. In this category, the main source degradation stems from the "termchg_mean" category. This category covers changes of lexical unit parts of speech.
- In grammatical categories, productive categories are "gram_det" and "gram_prep" but the improvement/degradation ratio for this last category is very low (it shows global improvements but there are many unacceptable degradations).
- As expected, no "long-distance" restructuring is observed and local reordering is negative for En>Fr and relatively negligible for other language pairs.
- For the French target, morphology is a major issue (accounts for 25% of degradations). This was also expected since no mechanism in the SPE provides any control over the morphology.

4 Conclusions

The SYSTRAN+SPE experiments demonstrate very good results – both on automatic scoring and on linguistic analysis. Detailed comparative analysis provides directions on how to further improve these results by adding "linguistic control" mechanisms. For SPE, we would, for instance, add linguistic constraints in the decoding process, knowing that the structure/linguistic information could be made available in the translation output.

Beyond the scope of these experiments, our results set a baseline to compare with other more sophisticated/integrated "rules and statistics" combination models.

In particular, the most improved categories observed in these experiments confirm that our current development direction for integrating data-driven mechanisms within translation engines (especially for word sense disambiguation, for the selection of alternative translations or for specific local phenomena like determination) should converge on the same results while preventing associated degradations. Also, the high score reached by the "`termchg_loc`" category substantiates the need to continue exploiting phrase tables built on parallel corpora to learn new terminology.

Acknowledgments

We would like to thank Michel Simard, Roland Kuhn, George Foster and Pierre Isabelle from NRC, Canada for their collaboration on this work (Simard et al. 2007).

References

Attnäs (M.), Senellart (P.) and Senellart (J.). 2005. *Integration of SYSTRAN MT systems in an open workflow*. Machine Translation Summit, Phuket, Thailand.

Philipp Koehn & al. 2007. *Moses: Open Source Toolkit for Statistical Machine Translation*. To appear at ACL2007, Prague.

Chris Callison-Burch, Miles Osborne and Philipp Koehn, 2006. *Re-evaluating the Role of Bleu in Machine Translation Research*. In Proceedings of EACL-2006.

Simard Michel & al. 2007. *Rule-based Translation With Statistical Phrase-based Post-editing*. In Proceedings of WMT07.

Jean Senellart, & al. 2003. *XML Machine Translation*. In Proceedings of MT-Summit IX.

Jean Senellart. 2006. *Boosting linguistic rule-based MT systems with corpus-based approaches*. In Presentation. GALE PI Meeting, Boston, MA.

Experiments in Domain Adaptation for Statistical Machine Translation

Philipp Koehn and Josh Schroeder
pkoehn@inf.ed.ac.uk, j.schroeder@ed.ac.uk
School of Informatics
University of Edinburgh
2 Buccleuch Place, Edinburgh EH8 9LW
Scotland, United Kingdom

Abstract

The special challenge of the WMT 2007 shared task was domain adaptation. We took this opportunity to experiment with various ways of adapting a statistical machine translation systems to a special domain (here: news commentary), when most of the training data is from a different domain (here: European Parliament speeches). This paper also gives a description of the submission of the University of Edinburgh to the shared task.

1 Our framework: the Moses MT system

The open source Moses (Koehn et al., 2007) MT system was originally developed at the University of Edinburgh and received a major boost through a 2007 Johns Hopkins workshop. It is now used at several academic institutions as the basic infrastructure for statistical machine translation research.

The Moses system is an implementation of the phrase-based machine translation approach (Koehn et al., 2003). In this approach, an input sentence is first split into text chunks (so-called phrases), which are then mapped one-to-one to target phrases using a large phrase translation table. Phrases may be reordered, but typically a reordering limit (in our experiments a maximum movement over 6 words) is used. See Figure 1 for an illustration.

Phrase translation probabilities, reordering probabilities and language model probabilities are combined to give each possible sentence translation a score. The best-scoring translation is searched for by the decoding algorithm and outputted by the system as the best translation. The different system components h_i (phrase translation probabilities, language model, etc.) are combined in a log-linear model to obtain the score for the translation **e** for an input sentence **f**:

$$score(\mathbf{e}, \mathbf{f}) = \exp \sum_i \lambda_i \, h_i(\mathbf{e}, \mathbf{f}) \qquad (1)$$

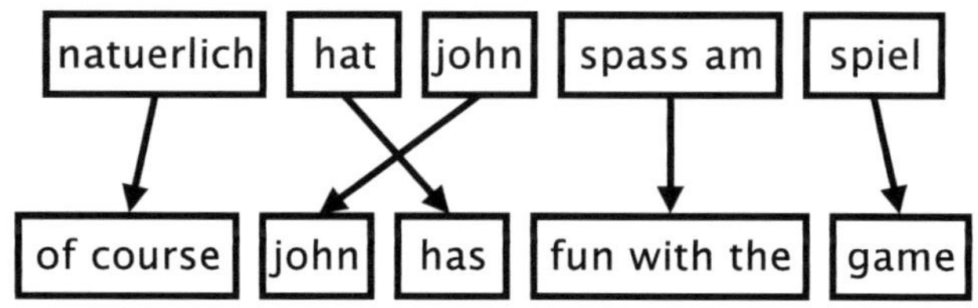

Figure 1: Phrase-based statistical machine translation model: Input is split into text chunks (phrases) which are mapped using a large phrase translation table. Phrases are mapped one-to-one, and may be reordered.

The weights of the components λ_i are set by a discriminative training method on held-out development data (Och, 2003). The basic components used in our experiments are: (a) two phrase translation probabilities (both $p(e|f)$ and $p(f|e)$), (b) two word translation probabilities (both $p(e|f)$ and $p(f|e)$), (c) phrase count, (d) output word count, (e) language model, (f) distance-based reordering model, and (g) lexicalized reordering model.

For a more detailed description of this model, please refer to (Koehn et al., 2005).

2 Domain adaption

Since training data for statistical machine translation is typically collected opportunistically from wherever it is available, the application domain for a machine translation system may be very different from the domain of the system's training data.

For the WMT 2007 shared task, the challenge was to use a large amount of out-of-domain training data

Proceedings of the Second Workshop on Statistical Machine Translation, pages 224–227,
Prague, June 2007.

(about 40 million words) combined with a much smaller amount of in-domain training data (about 1 million words) to optimize translation performance on that particular domain. We carried out these experiments on French–English.

2.1 Only out-of-domain training data

The first baseline system is trained only on the out-of-domain Europarl corpus, which has the following corpus statistics:

	French	English
Sentences	1,257,419	
Words	37,489,556	33,787,890

2.2 Only in-domain training data

The second baseline system is trained only on the in-domain NewsCommentary corpus. This corpus is much smaller:

	French	English
Sentences	42,884	
Words	1,198,041	1,018,503

2.3 Combined training data

To make use of all the training data, the straight-forward way is to simply concatenate the two training corpora and use the combined data for both translation model and language model training. In our situation, however, the out-of-domain training data overwhelms the in-domain training data due to the sheer relative size. Hence, we do not expect the best performance from this simplistic approach.

2.4 In-domain language model

One way to force a drift to the jargon of the target domain is the use of the language model. In our next setup, we used only in-domain data for training the language model. This enables the system to use all the translation knowledge from the combined corpus, but it gives a preference to word choices that are dominant in the in-domain training data.

2.5 Interpolated language model

Essentially, the goal of our subsequent approaches is to make use of all the training data, but to include a preference for the in-domain jargon by giving more weight to the in-domain training data. This and the next approach explore methods to bias the language model, while the final approach biases the translation model.

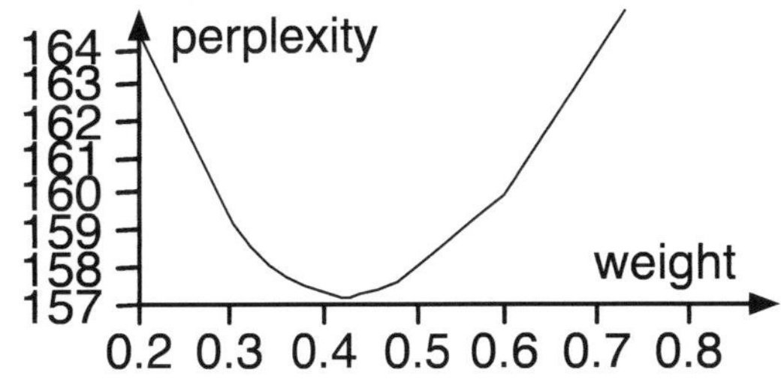

Figure 2: Interpolating in-domain and out-of-domain language models: effect of interpolation weight on perplexity of LM on development set.

We trained two language models, one for each the out-of-domain and the in-domain training data. Language modeling software such as the SRILM toolkit we used (Stolke, 2002) allows the interpolation of these language models. When interpolating, we give the out-of-domain language model a weight in respect to the in-domain language model.

Since we want to obtain a language model that gives us the best performance on the target domain, we set this weight so that the perplexity of the development set from that target domain is optimized. We searched for the optimal weight setting by simply testing a set of weights and focusing on the most promising range of weights.

Figure 2 displays all the weights we explored during this process and the corresponding perplexity of the resulting language model on the development set (nc-dev2007). The optimal weight can be picked out easily from this very smooth curve.

2.6 Two language models

The log-linear modeling approach of statistical machine translation enables a straight-forward combination of the in-domain and out-of-domain language models. We included them as two separate features, whose weights are set with minimum error rate training. The relative weight for each model is set directly by optimizing translation performance.

2.7 Two translation models

Finally, besides biasing the language model to a specific target domain, we may also bias the translation model. Here, we take advantage of a feature of the Moses decoder's factored translation model framework. In factored translation models, the representa-

Method	%BLEU
Large out-of-domain training data	25.11
Small in-domain training data	25.88
Combined training data	26.69
In-domain language model	27.46
Interpolated language model	27.12
Two language models	27.30
Two translation models	27.64

Table 1: Results of domain adaptation experiments

tion of words is extended to a vector of factors (e.g., surface form, lemma, POS, morphology).

The mapping of an input phrase to an output phrase is decomposed into several translation and generation steps, each using a different translation or generation table, respectively. Such a decomposition is called a decoding path.

A more recent feature of the factored translation model framework is the possible use of multiple alternative decoding paths. This alternate decoding path model was developed by Birch et al. (2007). For our purposes, we use two decoding paths, each consisting of only one translation step. One decoding path is the in-domain translation table, and the other decoding path is the out-of-domain translation table. Again, respective weights are set with minimum error rate training.

3 Domain adaptation results

Table 1 shows results of our domain adaptation experiments on the development test set (nc-devtest-2007). The results suggest that the language model is a useful tool for domain adaptation. While training on all the data is essential for good performance, using an in-domain language model alone already gives fairly high performance (27.46). The performance with the interpolated language model (27.12) and two language models (27.30) are similar. All perform better than the three baseline approaches.

The results also suggest that higher performance can be obtained by using two translation models through the Moses decoder's alternative decoding path framework. We saw our best results under this condition (27.64).

4 WMT 2007 shared task submissions

We participated in all categories. Given the four language pairs, with two translation directions and (except for Czech) two test domains, this required us to build 14 translation systems.

We had access to a fairly large computer cluster to carry out our experiments over the course of a few weeks. However, speed issues with the decoder and load issues on the crowded cluster caused us to take a few shortcuts. Also, a bug crept in to our English–French experiments where we used the wrong detokenizer, resulting drop of 2–3 points in %BLEU.

4.1 Tuning

Minimum error rate training is the most time-consuming aspects of the training process. Due to time constraints, we did not carry out this step for all but the Czech systems (a new language for us). For the other systems, we re-used weight settings from our last year's submission.

One of the most crucial outcomes of tuning is a proper weight setting for output length, which is especially important for the BLEU score. Since the training corpus and tokenization changed, our re-used weights are not always optimal in this respect. But only in one case we felt compelled to manually adjust the weight for the word count feature, since the original setup led to a output/reference length ratio of 0.88 on the development test set.

4.2 Domain adaptation

For the Europarl test sets, we did not use any domain adaptation techniques, but simply used either just the Europarl training data or the combined data — whatever gave the higher score on the development test set, although scores differed by only about 0.1–0.2 %BLEU.

In order to be able to re-use the old weights, we were limited to domain adaptation methods that did not change the number of components. We decided to use the interpolated language model method described in Section 2.5. For the different language pairs, optimal interpolation weights differed:

Language pair	Weight for Europarl LM
French–English	0.43
Spanish–English	0.41
German–English	0.40
English–French	0.51
English–Spanish	0.42
English–German	0.45

Language pair	Europarl			NewsCommentary		
	%BLEU	Length	NIST	%BLEU	Length	NIST
French–English	32.66	0.96	7.94	28.27	1.03	7.50
Spanish–English	33.26	1.00	7.82	34.17	1.06	8.35
German–English	28.49	0.94	7.32	25.45	1.01	7.19
Czech–English	–	–	–	22.68	0.98	6.96
English–French	26.76	1.08	6.66	24.38	1.02	6.73
English–Spanish	32.55	0.98	7.66	33.59	0.94	8.46
English–German	20.59	0.97	6.18	17.06	1.00	6.04
English–Czech	–	–	–	12.34	1.02	4.85

Table 2: Test set performance of our systems: BLEU and NIST scores, and output/reference length ratio.

4.3 Training and decoding parameters

We tried to improve performance by increasing some of the limits imposed on the training and decoding setup. During training, long sentences are removed from the training data to speed up the GIZA++ word alignment process. Traditionally, we worked with a sentence length limit of 40. We found that increasing this limit to about 80 gave better results without causing undue problems with running the word alignment (GIZA++ increasingly fails and runs much slower with long sentences).

We also tried to increase beam sizes and the limit on the number of translation options per coverage span (ttable-limit). This has shown to be successful in our experiments with Arabic–English and Chinese–English systems. Surprisingly, increasing the maximum stack size to 1000 (from 200) and ttable-limit to 100 (from 20) has barely any effect on translation performance. The %BLEU score changed only by less than 0.05, and often worsened.

4.4 German–English system

The German–English language pair is especially challenging due to the large differences in word order. Collins et al. (2005) suggest a method to reorder the German input before translating using a set of manually crafted rules. In our German–English submissions, this is done both to the training data and the input to the machine translation system.

5 Conclusions

Our submission to the WMT 2007 shared task is a fairly straight-forward use of the Moses MT system using default parameters. In a sense, we submitted a baseline performance of this system. BLEU and NIST scores for all our systems on the test sets are displayed in Table 2. Compared to other submitted systems, these are very good scores, often the best or second highest scores for these tasks.

We made a special effort in two areas: We explored domain adaptation methods for the NewsCommentary test sets and we used reordering rules for the German–English language pair.

Acknowledgments
This work was supported in part under the GALE program of the Defense Advanced Research Projects Agency, Contract No. HR0011-06-C-0022 and in part under the EuroMatrix project funded by the European Commission (6th Framework Programme).

References

Birch, A., Osborne, M., and Koehn, P. (2007). CCG supertags in factored statistical machine translation. In *Proceedings of the Workshop on Statistical Machine Translation*, Prague. Association for Computational Linguistics.

Collins, M., Koehn, P., and Kucerova, I. (2005). Clause restructuring for statistical machine translation. In *Proceedings of the 43rd Annual Meeting of the Association for Computational Linguistics (ACL'05)*, pages 531–540, Ann Arbor, Michigan. Association for Computational Linguistics.

Koehn, P., Axelrod, A., Mayne, A. B., Callison-Burch, C., Osborne, M., and Talbot, D. (2005). Edinburgh system description for the 2005 IWSLT speech translation evaluation. In *Proc. of the International Workshop on Spoken Language Translation*.

Koehn, P., Hoang, H., Birch, A., Callison-Burch, C., Federico, M., Bertoldi, N., Cowan, B., Shen, W., Moran, C., Zens, R., Dyer, C., Bojar, O., Constantin, A., and Herbst, E. (2007). Moses: Open source toolkit for statistical machine translation. In *Proceedings of the Annual Meeting of the Association for Computational Linguistics, demonstation session*.

Koehn, P., Och, F. J., and Marcu, D. (2003). Statistical phrase based translation. In *Proceedings of the Joint Conference on Human Language Technologies and the Annual Meeting of the North American Chapter of the Association of Computational Linguistics (HLT-NAACL)*.

Och, F. J. (2003). Minimum error rate training in statistical machine translation. In Hinrichs, E. and Roth, D., editors, *Proceedings of the 41st Annual Meeting of the Association for Computational Linguistics*, pages 160–167.

Stolke, A. (2002). SRILM - an extensible language modeling toolkit. In *Proceedings of the International Conference on Spoken Language Processing*.

METEOR: An Automatic Metric for MT Evaluation with High Levels of Correlation with Human Judgments

Alon Lavie and **Abhaya Agarwal**
Language Technologies Institute
Carnegie Mellon University
Pittsburgh, PA, 15213, USA
{alavie,abhayaa}@cs.cmu.edu

Abstract

METEOR is an automatic metric for Machine Translation evaluation which has been demonstrated to have high levels of correlation with human judgments of translation quality, significantly outperforming the more commonly used BLEU metric. It is one of several automatic metrics used in this year's shared task within the ACL WMT-07 workshop. This paper recaps the technical details underlying the metric and describes recent improvements in the metric. The latest release includes improved metric parameters and extends the metric to support evaluation of MT output in Spanish, French and German, in addition to English.

1 Introduction

Automatic Metrics for MT evaluation have been receiving significant attention in recent years. Evaluating an MT system using such automatic metrics is much faster, easier and cheaper compared to human evaluations, which require trained bilingual evaluators. Automatic metrics are useful for comparing the performance of different systems on a common translation task, and can be applied on a frequent and ongoing basis during MT system development. The most commonly used MT evaluation metric in recent years has been IBM's BLEU metric (Papineni et al., 2002). BLEU is fast and easy to run, and it can be used as a target function in parameter optimization training procedures that are commonly used in state-of-the-art statistical MT systems (Och, 2003). Various researchers have noted, however, various weaknesses in the metric. Most notably, BLEU does not produce very reliable sentence-level scores. METEOR , as well as several other proposed metrics such as GTM (Melamed et al., 2003), TER (Snover et al., 2006) and CDER (Leusch et al., 2006) aim to address some of these weaknesses.

METEOR , initially proposed and released in 2004 (Lavie et al., 2004) was explicitly designed to improve correlation with human judgments of MT quality at the segment level. Previous publications on METEOR (Lavie et al., 2004; Banerjee and Lavie, 2005) have described the details underlying the metric and have extensively compared its performance with BLEU and several other MT evaluation metrics. This paper recaps the technical details underlying METEOR and describes recent improvements in the metric. The latest release extends METEOR to support evaluation of MT output in Spanish, French and German, in addition to English. Furthermore, several parameters within the metric have been optimized on language-specific training data. We present experimental results that demonstrate the improvements in correlations with human judgments that result from these parameter tunings.

2 The METEOR Metric

METEOR evaluates a translation by computing a score based on explicit word-to-word matches between the translation and a given reference translation. If more than one reference translation is available, the translation is scored against each reference independently, and the best scoring pair is used. Given a pair of strings to be compared, METEOR creates a *word alignment* between the two strings. An alignment is mapping between words, such that every word in each string maps to at most *one* word in the other string. This alignment is incrementally produced by a sequence of word-mapping modules. The "exact" module maps two words if they are exactly the same. The "porter stem" module maps two words if they are the same after they are stemmed using the Porter stemmer. The "WN synonymy" module maps two words if they are considered synonyms, based on the fact that they both belong to the same "synset" in WordNet.

The word-mapping modules initially identify all

Proceedings of the Second Workshop on Statistical Machine Translation, pages 228–231,
Prague, June 2007.

possible word matches between the pair of strings. We then identify the largest subset of these word mappings such that the resulting set constitutes an alignment as defined above. If more than one maximal cardinality alignment is found, METEOR selects the alignment for which the word order in the two strings is most similar (the mapping that has the least number of "crossing" unigram mappings). The order in which the modules are run reflects word-matching preferences. The default ordering is to first apply the "exact" mapping module, followed by "porter stemming" and then "WN synonymy".

Once a final alignment has been produced between the system translation and the reference translation, the METEOR score for this pairing is computed as follows. Based on the number of mapped unigrams found between the two strings (m), the total number of unigrams in the translation (t) and the total number of unigrams in the reference (r), we calculate unigram precision $P = m/t$ and unigram recall $R = m/r$. We then compute a parameterized harmonic mean of P and R (van Rijsbergen, 1979):

$$F_{mean} = \frac{P \cdot R}{\alpha \cdot P + (1 - \alpha) \cdot R}$$

Precision, recall and Fmean are based on single-word matches. To take into account the extent to which the matched unigrams in the two strings are in the same word order, METEOR computes a penalty for a given alignment as follows. First, the sequence of matched unigrams between the two strings is divided into the fewest possible number of "chunks" such that the matched unigrams in each chunk are adjacent (in both strings) and in identical word order. The number of chunks (ch) and the number of matches (m) is then used to calculate a fragmentation fraction: $frag = ch/m$. The penalty is then computed as:

$$Pen = \gamma \cdot frag^{\beta}$$

The value of γ determines the maximum penalty ($0 \leq \gamma \leq 1$). The value of β determines the functional relation between fragmentation and the penalty. Finally, the METEOR score for the alignment between the two strings is calculated as:

$$score = (1 - Pen) \cdot F_{mean}$$

In all previous versions of METEOR , the values of the three parameters mentioned above were set to be: $\alpha = 0.9$, $\beta = 3.0$ and $\gamma = 0.5$, based on experimentation performed in early 2004. In the latest release, we tuned these parameters to optimize correlation with human judgments based on more extensive experimentation, as reported in section 4.

3 METEOR Implementations for Spanish, French and German

We have recently expanded the implementation of METEOR to support evaluation of translations in Spanish, French and German, in addition to English. Two main language-specific issues required adaptation within the metric: (1) language-specific word-matching modules; and (2) language-specific parameter tuning. The word-matching component within the English version of METEOR uses stemming and synonymy modules in constructing a word-to-word alignment between translation and reference. The resources used for stemming and synonymy detection for English are the Porter Stemmer (Porter, 2001) and English WordNet (Miller and Fellbaum, 2007). In order to construct instances of METEOR for Spanish, French and German, we created new language-specific "stemming" modules. We use the freely available *Perl* implementation packages for Porter stemmers for the three languages (Humphrey, 2007). Unfortunately, we have so far been unable to obtain freely available WordNet resources for these three languages. METEOR versions for Spanish, French and German therefore currently include only "exact" and "stemming" matching modules. We are investigating the possibility of developing new synonymy modules for the various languages based on alternative methods, which could then be used in place of WordNet. The second main language-specific issue which required adaptation is the tuning of the three parameters within METEOR , described in section 4.

4 Optimizing Metric Parameters

The original version of METEOR (Banerjee and Lavie, 2005) has instantiated values for three parameters in the metric: one for controlling the relative weight of precision and recall in computing the Fmean score (α); one governing the shape of the penalty as a function of fragmentation (β) and one for the relative weight assigned to the fragmentation penalty (γ). In all versions of METEOR to date, these parameters were instantiated with the values $\alpha = 0.9$, $\beta = 3.0$ and $\gamma = 0.5$, based on early data experimentation. We recently conducted a more thorough investigation aimed at tuning these parameters based on several available data sets, with the goal of finding parameter settings that maximize correlation with human judgments. Human judgments come in the form of "adequacy" and "fluency" quantitative scores. In our experiments, we looked at optimizing parameters for each of these human judgment types separately, as well as optimizing parameters for the sum of adequacy and fluency. Parameter adapta-

Corpus	Judgments	Systems
NIST 2003 Ara-to-Eng	3978	6
NIST 2004 Ara-to-Eng	347	5
WMT-06 Eng-to-Fre	729	4
WMT-06 Eng-to-Ger	756	5
WMT-06 Eng-to-Spa	1201	7

Table 1: Corpus Statistics for Various Languages

tion is also an issue in the newly created METEOR instances for other languages. We suspected that parameters that were optimized to maximize correlation with human judgments for English would not necessarily be optimal for other languages.

4.1 Data

For English, we used the NIST 2003 Arabic-to-English MT evaluation data for training and the NIST 2004 Arabic-to-English evaluation data for testing. For Spanish, German and French we used the evaluation data provided by the shared task at last year's WMT workshop. Sizes of various corpora are shown in Table 1. Some, but not all, of these data sets have multiple human judgments per translation hypothesis. To partially address human bias issues, we *normalize* the human judgments, which transforms the raw judgment scores so that they have similar distributions. We use the normalization method described in (Blatz et al., 2003). Multiple judgments are combined into a single number by taking their average.

4.2 Methodology

We performed a "hill climbing" search to find the parameters that achieve maximum correlation with human judgments on the training set. We use Pearson's correlation coefficient as our measure of correlation. We followed a "leave one out" training procedure in order to avoid over-fitting. When n systems were available for a particular language, we train the parameters n times, leaving one system out in each training, and pooling the segments from all other systems. The final parameter values are calculated as the mean of the n sets of trained parameters that were obtained. When evaluating a set of parameters on test data, we compute segment-level correlation with human judgments for each of the systems in the test set and then report the mean over all systems.

4.3 Results

4.3.1 Optimizing for Adequacy and Fluency

We trained parameters to obtain maximum correlation with normalized adequacy and fluency judgments separately and also trained for maximal correlation with the sum of the two. The resulting optimal parameter values on the training corpus are shown in Table 2. Pearson correlations with human judgments on the test set are shown in Table 3.

	Adequacy	Fluency	Sum
α	0.82	0.78	0.81
β	1.0	0.75	0.83
γ	0.21	0.38	0.28

Table 2: Optimal Values of Tuned Parameters for Different Criteria for English

	Adequacy	Fluency	Sum
Original	0.6123	0.4355	0.5704
Adequacy	0.6171	0.4354	0.5729
Fluency	0.6191	0.4502	0.5818
Sum	0.6191	0.4425	0.5778

Table 3: Pearson Correlation with Human Judgments on Test Data for English

The optimal parameter values found are somewhat different than our previous metric parameters (lower values for all three parameters). The new parameters result in moderate but noticeable improvements in correlation with human judgments on both training and testing data. Tests for statistical significance using bootstrap sampling indicate that the differences in correlation levels are all significant at the 95% level. Another interesting observation is that precision receives slightly more "weight" when optimizing correlation with fluency judgments (versus when optimizing correlation with adequacy). Recall, however, is still given more weight than precision. Another interesting observation is that the value of γ is higher for fluency optimization. Since the fragmentation penalty reflects word-ordering, which is closely related to fluency, these results are consistent with our expectations. When optimizing correlation with the sum of adequacy and fluency, optimal values fall in between the values found for adequacy and fluency.

4.3.2 Parameters for Other Languages

Similar to English, we trained parameters for Spanish, French and German on the available WMT-06 training data. We optimized for maximum correlation with human judgments of adequacy, fluency and for the sum of the two. Resulting parameters are shown in Table 4.3.2. For all three languages, the parameters that were found to be optimal were quite different than those that were found for English, and using the language-specific optimal parameters re-

	Adequacy	Fluency	Sum
French:α	0.86	0.74	0.76
β	0.5	0.5	0.5
γ	1.0	1.0	1.0
German:α	0.95	0.95	0.95
β	0.5	0.5	0.5
γ	0.6	0.8	0.75
Spanish:α	0.95	0.62	0.95
β	1.0	1.0	1.0
γ	0.9	1.0	0.98

Table 4: Tuned Parameters for Different Languages

sults in significant gains in Pearson correlation levels with human judgments on the training data (compared with those obtained using the English optimal parameters)[1]. Note that the training sets used for these optimizations are comparatively very small, and that we currently do not have unseen test data to evaluate the parameters for these three languages. Further validation will need to be performed once additional data becomes available.

5 Conclusions

In this paper we described newly developed language-specific instances of the METEOR metric and the process of optimizing metric parameters for different human measures of translation quality and for different languages. Our evaluations demonstrate that parameter tuning improves correlation with human judgments. The stability of the optimized parameters on different data sets remains to be investigated for languages other than English. We are currently exploring broadening the set of features used in METEOR to include syntax-based features and alternative notions of synonymy. The latest release of METEOR is freely available on our website at: `http://www.cs.cmu.edu/~alavie/METEOR/`

Acknowledgements

The work reported in this paper was supported by NSF Grant IIS-0534932.

References

Satanjeev Banerjee and Alon Lavie. 2005. METEOR: An Automatic Metric for MT Evaluation with Improved Correlation with Human Judgments. In *Proceedings of the ACL Workshop on Intrinsic and Extrinsic Evaluation Measures for Machine Translation and/or Summarization*, pages 65–72, Ann Arbor, Michigan, June.

John Blatz, Erin Fitzgerald, George Foster, Simona Gandrabur, Cyril Goutte, Alex Kulesza, Alberto Sanchis, and Nicola Ueffing. 2003. Confidence Estimation for Machine Translation. Technical Report Natural Language Engineering Workshop Final Report, Johns Hopkins University.

Marvin Humphrey. 2007. Perl Interface to Snowball Stemmers. http://search.cpan.org/ creamyg/Lingua-Stem-Snowball-0.941/lib/Lingua/Stem/Snowball.pm.

Alon Lavie, Kenji Sagae, and Shyamsundar Jayaraman. 2004. The Significance of Recall in Automatic Metrics for MT Evaluation. In *Proceedings of the 6th Conference of the Association for Machine Translation in the Americas (AMTA-2004)*, pages 134–143, Washington, DC, September.

Gregor Leusch, Nicola Ueffing, and Hermann Ney. 2006. CDER: Efficient MT Evaluation Using Block Movements. In *Proceedings of the Thirteenth Conference of the European Chapter of the Association for Computational Linguistics.*

I. Dan Melamed, Ryan Green, and Joseph Turian. 2003. Precision and Recall of Machine Translation. In *Proceedings of the HLT-NAACL 2003 Conference: Short Papers*, pages 61–63, Edmonton, Alberta.

George Miller and Christiane Fellbaum. 2007. WordNet. http://wordnet.princeton.edu/.

Franz Josef Och. 2003. Minimum Error Rate Training for Statistical Machine Translation. In *Proceedings of the 41st Annual Meeting of the Association for Computational Linguistics.*

Kishore Papineni, Salim Roukos, Todd Ward, and Wei-Jing Zhu. 2002. BLEU: a Method for Automatic Evaluation of Machine Translation. In *Proceedings of 40th Annual Meeting of the Association for Computational Linguistics (ACL)*, pages 311–318, Philadelphia, PA, July.

Martin Porter. 2001. The Porter Stemming Algorithm. http://www.tartarus.org/ martin/PorterStemmer/index.html.

Matthew Snover, Bonnie Dorr, Richard Schwartz, Linnea Micciulla, and John Makhoul. 2006. A Study of Translation Edit Rate with Targeted Human Annotation. In *Proceedings of the 7th Conference of the Association for Machine Translation in the Americas (AMTA-2006)*, pages 223–231, Cambridge, MA, August.

C. van Rijsbergen, 1979. *Information Retrieval.* Butterworths, London, UK, 2nd edition.

[1]Detailed tables are not included for lack of space.

English-to-Czech Factored Machine Translation

Ondřej Bojar
Institute of Formal and Applied Linguistics
ÚFAL MFF UK, Malostranské náměstí 25
CZ-11800 Praha, Czech Republic
bojar@ufal.mff.cuni.cz

Abstract

This paper describes experiments with English-to-Czech phrase-based machine translation. Additional annotation of input and output tokens (multiple factors) is used to explicitly model morphology. We vary the translation scenario (the setup of multiple factors) and the amount of information in the morphological tags. Experimental results demonstrate significant improvement of translation quality in terms of BLEU.

1 Introduction

Statistical phrase-based machine translation (SMT) systems currently achieve top performing results.[1] Known limitations of phrase-based SMT include worse quality when translating to morphologically rich languages as opposed to translating from them (Koehn, 2005). One of the teams at the 2006 summer engineering workshop at Johns Hopkins University[2] attempted to tackle these problems by introducing separate FACTORS in SMT input and/or output to allow explicit modelling of the underlying language structure. The support for factored translation models was incorporated into the Moses open-source SMT system[3].

In this paper, we report on experiments with English-to-Czech multi-factor translation. After a brief overview of factored SMT and our data (Sections 2 and 3), we summarize some possible translating scenarios in Section 4. Section 5 studies the level of detail useful for morphological representation and Section 6 compares the results to a setting with more data available, albeit out of domain. The second part (Section 7) is devoted to a brief analysis of MT output errors.

1.1 Motivation for Improving Morphology

Czech is a Slavic language with very rich morphology and relatively free word order. The Czech morphological system (Hajič, 2004) defines 4,000 tags in theory and 2,000 were actually seen in a big tagged corpus. (For comparison, the English Penn Treebank tagset contains just about 50 tags.) In our parallel corpus (see Section 3 below), the English vocabulary size is 35k distinct token types but more than twice as big in Czech, 83k distinct token types.

To further emphasize the importance of morphology in MT to Czech, we compare the standard BLEU (Papineni et al., 2002) of a baseline phrase-based translation with BLEU which disregards word forms (lemmatized MT output is compared to lemmatized reference translation). The theoretical margin for improving MT quality is about 9 BLEU points: the same MT output scores 12 points in standard BLEU and 21 points in lemmatized BLEU.

2 Overview of Factored SMT

In statistical MT, the goal is to translate a source (foreign) language sentence $f_1^J = f_1 \dots f_j \dots f_J$ into a target language (Czech) sentence $c_1^I = c_1 \dots c_j \dots c_I$. In phrase-based SMT, the assumption is made that the target sentence can be constructed by segmenting source sentence into phrases, translating each phrase and finally composing the

[1] http://www.nist.gov/speech/tests/mt/
[2] http://www.clsp.jhu.edu/ws2006/
[3] http://www.statmt.org/moses/

Proceedings of the Second Workshop on Statistical Machine Translation, pages 232–239,
Prague, June 2007.

target sentence from phrase translations, s_1^K denotes the segmentation of the input sentence into K phrases. Among all possible target language sentences, we choose the sentence with the highest probability,

$$\hat{e}_1^{\hat{I}} = \underset{I, c_1^I, K, s_1^K}{\operatorname{argmax}} \{Pr(c_1^I | f_1^J, s_1^K)\} \quad (1)$$

In a log-linear model, the conditional probability of c_1^I being the translation of f_1^J under the segmentation s_1^K is modelled as a combination of independent feature functions $h_1(\cdot,\cdot,\cdot) \dots h_M(\cdot,\cdot,\cdot)$ describing the relation of the source and target sentences:

$$Pr(c_1^I | f_1^J, s_1^K) = \frac{\exp(\sum_{m=1}^{M} \lambda_m h_m(c_1^I, f_1^J, s_1^K))}{\sum_{c'^{I'}_1} \exp(\sum_{m=1}^{M} \lambda_m h_m(c'^{I'}_1, f_1^J, s_1^K))} \quad (2)$$

The denominator in 2 is used as a normalization factor that depends on the source sentence f_1^J and segmentation s_1^K only and is omitted during maximization. The model scaling factors λ_1^M are trained either to the maximum entropy principle or optimized with respect to the final translation quality measure.

Most of our features are phrase-based and we require all such features to operate synchronously on the segmentation s_1^K and independently of neighbouring segments. In other words, we restrict the form of phrase-based features to:

$$h_m(c_1^I, f_1^J, s_1^K) = \sum_{k=1}^{K} \tilde{h}_m(\tilde{c}_k, \tilde{f}_k) \quad (3)$$

where $\tilde{f}_k$ represents the source phrase and $\tilde{c}$ represents the target phrase k given the segmentation s_1^K.

2.1 Decoding Steps

In factored SMT, source and target words f and c are represented as tuples of F and C FACTORS, resp., each describing a different aspect of the word, e.g. its word form, lemma, morphological tag, role in a verbal frame. The process of translation consists of DECODING steps of two types: MAPPING steps and GENERATION steps. If more steps contribute to the same output factor, they have to agree on the outcome, i.e. partial hypotheses where two decoding steps produce conflicting values in an output factor are discarded.

A MAPPING step from a subset of source factors $S \subseteq \{1 \dots F\}$ to a subset of target factors $T \subseteq \{1 \dots C\}$ is the standard phrase-based model (see e.g. (Koehn, 2004a)) and introduces a feature in the following form:

$$\tilde{h}_m^{\text{map}:S \to T}(\tilde{c}_k, \tilde{f}_k) = \log p(\tilde{f}_k^S | \tilde{c}_k^T) \quad (4)$$

The conditional probability of $\tilde{f}_k^S$, i.e. the phrase $\tilde{f}_k$ restricted to factors S, given $\tilde{c}_k^T$, i.e. the phrase $\tilde{c}_k$ restricted to factors T is estimated from relative frequencies: $p(\tilde{f}_k^S | \tilde{c}_k^T) = N(\tilde{f}^S, \tilde{c}^T)/N(\tilde{c}^T)$ where $N(\tilde{f}^S, \tilde{c}^T)$ denotes the number of co-occurrences of a phrase pair $(\tilde{f}^S, \tilde{c}^T)$ that are consistent with the word alignment. The marginal count $N(\tilde{c}^T)$ is the number of occurrences of the target phrase $\tilde{c}^T$ in the training corpus.

For each mapping step, the model is included in the log-linear combination in source-to-target and target-to-source directions: $p(\tilde{f}^T | \tilde{c}^S)$ and $p(\tilde{c}^S | \tilde{f}^T)$. In addition, statistical single word based lexica are used in both directions. They are included to smooth the relative frequencies used as estimates of the phrase probabilities.

A GENERATION step maps a subset of target factors T_1 to a disjoint subset of target factors T_2, $T_{1,2} \subset \{1 \dots C\}$. In the current implementation of Moses, generation steps are restricted to word-to-word correspondences:

$$\tilde{h}_m^{\text{gen}:T_1 \to T_2}(\tilde{c}_k, \tilde{f}_k) = \log \prod_{i=1}^{\text{length}(\tilde{c}_k)} p(\tilde{c}_{k,i}^{T_1} | \tilde{c}_{k,i}^{T_2}) \quad (5)$$

where $\tilde{c}_{k,i}^T$ is the i-th words in the k-th target phrase restricted to factors T. We estimate the conditional probability $p(\tilde{c}_{k,i}^{T_2} | \tilde{c}_{k,i}^{T_1})$ by counting over words in the target-side corpus. Again, the conditional probability is included in the log-linear combination in both directions.

In addition to features for decoding steps, we include arbitrary number of target language models over subsets of target factors, $T \subseteq \{1 \dots C\}$. Typically, we use the standard n-gram language model:

$$h^T_{\text{LM}_n}(f^J_1, c^I_1) = \log \prod_{i=1}^{I} p(c^T_i | c^T_{i-1} \dots c^T_{i-n+1}) \quad (6)$$

While generation steps are used to enforce "vertical" coherence between "hidden properties" of output words, language models are used to enforce sequential coherence of the output.

Operationally, Moses performs a stack-based beam search very similar to Pharaoh (Koehn, 2004a). Thanks to the synchronous-phrases assumption, all the decoding steps can be performed during a preparatory phase. For each span in the input sentence, all possible translation options are constructed using the mapping and generation steps in a user-specified order. Low-scoring options are pruned already during this phase. Once all translation options are constructed, Moses picks source phrases (all output factors already filled in) in arbitrary order, subject to a reordering limit, producing output in left-to-right fashion and scoring it using the specified language models exactly as Pharaoh does.

3 Data Used

The experiments reported in this paper were carried out with the News Commentary (NC) corpus as made available for the SMT workshop[4] of the ACL 2007 conference.[5]

The Czech part of the corpus was tagged and lemmatized using the tool by Hajič and Hladká (1998), the English part was tagged MXPOST (Ratnaparkhi, 1996) and lemmatized using the Morpha tool (Minnen et al., 2001). After some final cleanup, the corpus consists of 55,676 pairs of sentences (1.1M Czech tokens and 1.2M English tokens). We use the designated additional tuning and evaluation sections consisting of 1023, resp. 964 sentences.

In all experiments, word alignment was obtained using the grow-diag-final heuristic for symmetrizing GIZA++ (Och and Ney, 2003) alignments. To reduce data sparseness, the English text was lowercased and Czech was lemmatized for alignment estimation. Language models are based on the target side of the parallel corpus only, unless stated otherwise.

3.1 Evaluation Measure and MERT

We evaluate our experiments using the (lowercase, tokenized) BLEU metric and estimate the empirical confidence using the bootstrapping method described in Koehn (2004b).[6] We report the scores obtained on the test section with model parameters tuned using the tuning section for minimum error rate training (MERT, (Och, 2003)).

4 Scenarios of Factored Translation English→Czech

We experimented with the following factored translation scenarios.

The baseline scenario (labelled T for translation) is single-factored: input (English) lowercase word forms are directly translated to target (Czech) lowercase forms. A 3-gram language model (or more models based on various corpora) checks the stream of output word forms. The baseline scenario thus corresponds to a plain phrase-based SMT system:

English		Czech	
lowercase	⟶	lowercase	+LM
lemma		lemma	
morphology		morphology	

In order to check the output not only for word-level coherence but also for morphological coherence, we add a single generation step: input word forms are first translated to output word forms and each output word form then generates its morphological tag.

Two types of language models can be used simultaneously: a (3-gram) LM over word forms and a (7-gram) LM over morphological tags.

We used tags with various levels of detail, see section 5. We call this the "T+C" (translate and check) scenario:

[4] http://www.statmt.org/wmt07/

[5] Our preliminary experiments with the Prague Czech-English Dependency Treebank, PCEDT v.1.0 (Čmejrek et al., 2004), 20k sentences, gave similar results, although with a lower level of significance due to a smaller evaluation set.

[6] Given a test set of sentences, we perform 1,000 random selections with repetitions to estimate 1,000 BLEU scores on test sets of the same size. The empirical 90%-confidence upper and lower bounds are obtained after removing top and bottom 5% of scores. For conciseness, we report the average of the distance between to standard BLEU value and the empirical upper and lower bound after the "±" symbol.

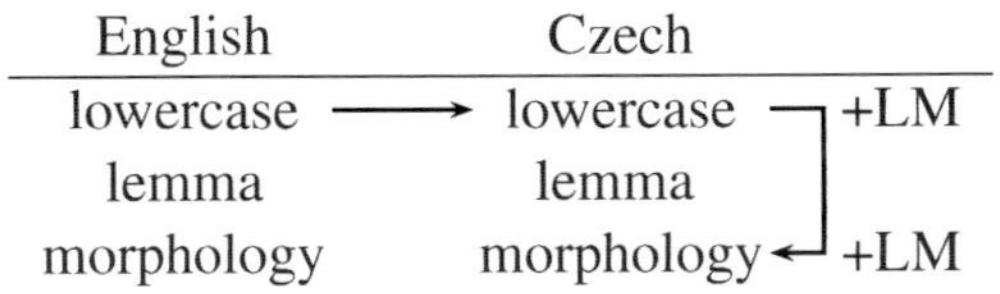

As a refinement of T+C, we also used T+T+C scenario, where the morphological output stream is constructed based on both output word forms and input morphology. This setting should reinforce correct translation of morphological features such as number of source noun phrases. To reduce the risk of early pruning, the generation step operationally precedes the morphology mapping step. Again, two types of language models can be used in this "T+T+C" scenario:

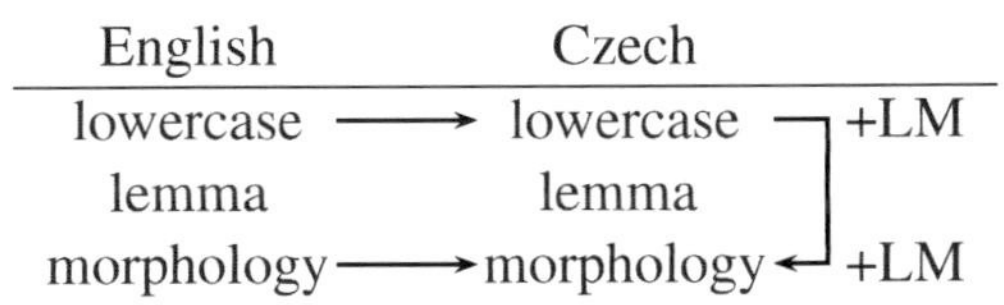

The most complex scenario we used is linguistically appealing: output lemmas (base forms) and morphological tags are generated from input in two independent translation steps and combined in a single generation step to produce output word forms. The input English text was not lemmatized so we used English word forms as the source for producing Czech lemmas.

The "T+T+G" setting allows us to use three types of language models. Trigram models are used for word forms and lemmas and 7-gram language models are used over tags:

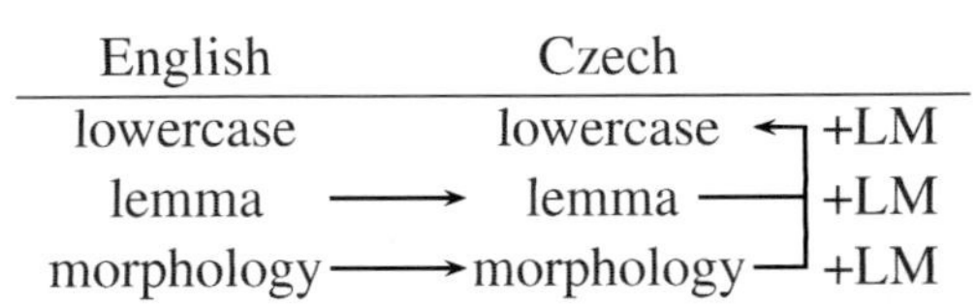

4.1 Experimental Results: Improved over T

Table 1 summarizes estimated translation quality of the various scenarios. In all cases, a 3-gram LM is used for word forms or lemmas and a 7-gram LM for morphological tags.

The good news is that multi-factored models always outperform the baseline T.

Unfortunately, the more complex multi-factored scenarios do not bring any significant improvement over T+C. Our belief is that this effect is caused by search errors: with multi-factored models, more hypotheses get similar scores and future costs of partial hypotheses might be estimated less reliably. With the limited stack size (not more than 200 hypotheses of the same number of covered input words), the decoder may more often find sub-optimal solutions. Moreover, the more steps are used, the more model weights have to be tuned in the minimum error rate training. Considerably more tuning data might be necessary to tune the weights reliably.

	BLEU
T+T+G	13.9±0.7
T+T+C	13.9±0.6
T+C	13.6±0.6
Baseline: T	12.9±0.6

Table 1: BLEU scores of various translation scenarios.

5 Granularity of Czech Part-of-Speech

As stated above, the Czech morphological tag system is very complex: in theory up to 4,000 different tags are possible. In our T+T+C scenario, we experiment with various simplifications of the system to find the best balance between richness and robustness of the statistics available in our corpus. (The more information is retained in the tags, the more severe data sparseness is.)

Full tags (1200 unique seen in the 56k corpus): Full Czech positional tags are used. A tag consists of 15 positions, each holding the value of a morphological property (e.g. number, case or gender).[7]

POS+case (184 unique seen): We simplify the tag to include only part and subpart of speech (distinguishes also partially e.g. verb tenses). For nouns, pronouns, adjectives and prepositions[8], also the case is included.

CNG01 (621 unique seen): CNG01 refines POS. For nouns, pronouns and adjectives we include not only the case but also number and gender.

[7] In principle, each of the 15 positions could be used as a separate factor. The set of necessary generation steps to encode relevant dependencies would have to be carefully determined.

[8] Some Czech prepositions select for a particular case, some are ambiguous. Although the case is never shown on surface of the preposition, the tagset includes this information and Czech taggers are able to infer the case.

CNG02 (791 unique seen): Tag for punctuation is refined: the lemma of the punctuation symbol is taken into account; previous models disregarded e.g. the distributional differences between a comma and a question mark. Case, number and gender added to nouns, pronouns, adjectives, prepositions, but also to verbs and numerals (where applicable).

CNG03 (1017 unique seen): Optimized tagset:

- Tags for nouns, adjectives, pronouns and numerals describe the case, number and gender; the Czech reflexive pronoun *se* or *si* is highlighted by a special flag.
- Tag for verbs describes subpart of speech, number, gender, tense and aspect; the tag includes a special flag if the verb was the auxiliary verb *být (to be)* in any of its forms.
- Tag for prepositions includes the case and also the lemma of the preposition.
- Lemma included for punctuation, particles and interjections.
- Tag for numbers describes the "shape" of the number (all digits are replaced by the digit *5* but number-internal punctuation is kept intact). The tag thus distinguishes between 4- or 5-digit numbers or the precision of floating point numbers.
- Part of speech and subpart of speech for all other words.

5.1 Experimental Results: CNG03 Best

Table 2 summarizes the results of T+T+C scenario with varying detail in morphological tag.

	BLEU
Baseline: T (single-factor)	12.9±0.6
T+T+C, POS+case	13.2±0.6
T+T+C, CNG01	13.4±0.6
T+T+C, CNG02	13.5±0.7
T+T+C, full tags	13.9±0.6
T+T+C, CNG03	14.2±0.7

Table 2: BLEU scores of various granularities of morphological tags in T+T+C scenario.

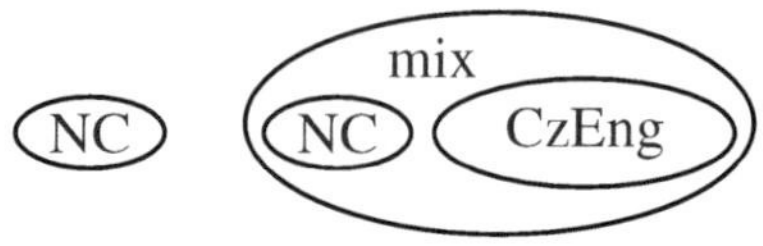

$$\text{weighted} = \alpha\text{NC} + \beta\text{mix}$$

Scenario	Phrases from	LMs	BLEU
T	NC	NC	12.9±0.6
T	mix	mix	11.8±0.6
T	mix	weighted	11.8±0.6
T+C CNG03	NC	NC	13.7±0.7
T+C CNG03	mix	mix	13.1±0.7
T+C CNG03	mix	weighted	13.7±0.7
T+C full tags	NC	NC	13.6±0.6
T+C full tags	mix	mix	13.1±0.7
T+C full tags	mix	weighted	13.8±0.7

Figure 1: The effect of additional data in T and T+C scenarios.

Our results confirm improvement over the single-factored baseline. Detailed knowledge of the morphological system also proves its utility: by choosing the most relevant features of tags and lemmas but avoiding sparseness, we can improve on BLEU score by about 0.3 absolute over T+T+C with full tags.

6 More Out-of-Domain Data in T and T+C Scenarios

In order to check if the method scales up with more parallel data available, we extend our training data using the CzEng parallel corpus (Bojar and Žabokrtský, 2006). CzEng contains sentence-aligned texts from the European Parliament (about 75%), e-books and stories (15%) and open source documentation. By "Baseline" corpus we denote NC corpus only, by "Large" we denote the combination of training sentences from NC and CzEng (1070k sentences, 13.9M Czech and 15.5 English tokens) where in-domain NC data amounts only to 5.2% sentences.

Figure 1 gives full details of our experiments with the additional data. We varied the scenario (T or T+C), the level of detail in the T+C scenario (full tags vs. CNG03) and the size of the training corpus. We extract phrases from either the in-domain corpus only (NC) or the mixed corpus (mix). We use either one LM per output factor, varying the corpus size (NC or mix), or two LMs per output factors with weights trained independently in the MERT procedure (weighted). Independent weights allow us to take domain difference into account, but we exploit this in the target LM only, not the phrases.

The only significant difference is caused by the scenario: T+C outperforms the baseline T, regardless of corpus size. Other results (insignificantly) indicate the following observations:

- Ignoring the domain difference and using only the mixed domain LM in general performs worse than allowing MERT to optimize LM weights for in-domain and generic data separately.[9]

- CNG03 outperforms full tags only in small data setting, with large data (treating the domain difference properly), full tags perform better.

7 Untreated Morphological Errors

The previous sections described improvements gained on small data sets when checking morphological agreement using T+T+C scenario (BLEU raised from 12.9% to 13.9% or up to 14.2% with manually tuned tagset, CNG03). However, the best result achieved is still far below the margin of lemmatized BLEU (21%), as mentioned in Section 1.1.

When we searched for the unexploited morphological errors, visual inspection of MT output suggested that local agreement (within 3-word span) is relatively correct but Verb-Modifier relations are often malformed causing e.g. a bad case for the Modifier. To quantify this observation we performed a micro-study of our best MT output using an intuitive metric. We checked whether Verb-Modifier relations are properly preserved during the translation of 15 sample sentences.

The *source* text of the sample sentences contained 77 Verb-Modifier pairs. Table 3 lists our observations on the two members in each Verb-Modifier pair. We see that only 56% of verbs are translated correctly and 79% of nouns are translated correctly. The system tends to skip verbs quite often (27% of cases).

[9]In our previous experiments with PCEDT as the domain-specific data, the difference was more apparent because the corpus domains were more distant. In the T scenario reported here, the weighted LMs did not bring any improvement over "mix" and even performed worse than the baseline NC. We attribute this effect to some randomness in the MERT procedure.

Translation of	**Verb**	**Modifier**
... preserves meaning	56%	79%
... is disrupted	14%	12%
... is missing	27%	1%
... is unknown (not translated)	0%	5%

Table 3: Analysis of 77 Verb-Modifier pairs in 15 sample sentences.

More importantly, our analysis has shown that even in cases where both the Verb and the Modifier are lexically correct, the relation between them in Czech is either non-grammatical or meaning-disrupted in 56% of these cases. Commented samples of such errors are given in Figure 2 below. The first sample shows that a strong language model can lead to the choice of a grammatical relation that nevertheless does not convey the original meaning. The second sample illustrates a situation where two correct options are available but the system chooses an inappropriate relation, most probably because of backing off to a generic pattern verb-noun$^{accusative}_{plural}$. This pattern is quite common for expressing the object role of many verbs (such as *vydat*, see Correct option 2 in Figure 2), but does not fit well with the verb *vyběhnout*. While the target-side data may be rich enough to learn the generalization vyběhnout–s–*instr*, no such generalization is possible with language models over word forms or morphological tags only. The target side data will be hardly ever rich enough to learn this particular structure in all correct morphological and lexical variants: *vyběhl–s–reklamou, vyběhla–s–reklamami, vyběhl–s–prohlášením, vyběhli–s–oznámením, ...* We would need a mixed model that combines verb lemmas, prepositions and case information to properly capture the relations.

Unfortunately, our preliminary experiments that made use of automatic Czech dependency parse trees to construct a factor explicitly highlighting the Verb (lexicalized) its Modifiers (case and the lemma of the preposition, if present) and boundary symbols such as punctuation or conjunctions and using a dummy token for all other words did not bring any improvement over the baseline. A possible reason is that we employed only a standard 7-gram language model to this factor. A more appropriate treatment is to disregard the dummy tokens in the language model at all and use an n-gram language model that looks at last $n-1$ non-dummy items.

8 Related Research

Class-based LMs (Brown et al., 1992) or factored LMs (Bilmes and Kirchhoff, 2003) are very similar to our T+C scenario. Given the small differences in all T+... scenarios' performance, class-based LM might bring equivalent improvement. Yang and Kirchhoff (2006) have recently documented minor BLEU improvement using factored LMs in single-factored SMT to English. The multi-factored approach to SMT of Moses is however more general.

Many researchers have tried to employ morphology in improving word alignment techniques (e.g. (Popović and Ney, 2004)) or machine translation quality (Nießen and Ney (2001), Koehn and Knight (2003), Zollmann et al. (2006), among others, for various languages; Goldwater and McClosky (2005), Bojar et al. (2006) and Talbot and Osborne (2006) for Czech), however, they focus on translating *from* the highly inflectional language.

Durgar El-Kahlout and Oflazer (2006) report preliminary experiments in English to Turkish single-factored phrase-based translation, gaining significant improvements by splitting root words and their morphemes into a sequence of tokens. In might be interesting to explore multi-factored scenarios for different Turkish morphology representation suggested the paper.

de Gispert et al. (2005) generalize over verb forms and generate phrase translations even for unseen target verb forms. The T+T+G scenario allows a similar extension if the described generation step is replaced by a (probabilistic) morphological generator.

Nguyen and Shimazu (2006) translate from English to Vietnamese but the morphological richness of Vietnamese is comparable to English. In fact the Vietnamese vocabulary size is even smaller than English vocabulary size in one of their corpora. The observed improvement due to explicit modelling of morphology might not scale up beyond small-data setting.

As an alternative option to our verb-modifier experiments, structured language models (Chelba and Jelinek, 1998) might be considered to improve clause coherence, until full-featured syntax-based MT models (Yamada and Knight (2002), Eisner (2003), Chiang (2005) among many others) are tested when translating to morphologically rich languages.

9 Conclusion

We experimented with multi-factored phrase-based translation aimed at improving morphological coherence in MT output. We varied the setup of additional factors (translation scenario) and the level of detail in morphological tags. Our results on English-to-Czech translation demonstrate significant improvement in BLEU scores by explicit modelling of morphology and using a separate morphological language model to ensure the coherence. To our knowledge, this is one of the first experiments showing the advantages of using multiple factors in MT.

Verb-modifier errors have been studied and a factor capturing verb-modifier dependencies has been proposed. Unfortunately, this factor has yet to bring any improvement.

10 Acknowledgement

The work on this project was partially supported by the grants Collegium Informaticum GAČR 201/05/H014, grants No. ME838 and GA405/06/0589 (PIRE), FP6-IST-5-034291-STP (Euromatrix), and NSF No. 0530118.

References

Jeff A. Bilmes and Katrin Kirchhoff. 2003. Factored language models and generalized parallel backoff. In *Proc. of NAACL 2003*, pages 4–6.

Ondřej Bojar and Zdeněk Žabokrtský. 2006. CzEng: Czech-English Parallel Corpus, Release version 0.5. *Prague Bulletin of Mathematical Linguistics*, 86:59–62.

Ondřej Bojar, Evgeny Matusov, and Hermann Ney. 2006. Czech-English Phrase-Based Machine Translation. In *Proc. of FinTAL 2006*, pages 214–224, Turku, Finland.

Peter F. Brown, Vincent J. Della Pietra, Peter V. deSouza, Jennifer C. Lai, and Robert L. Mercer. 1992. Class-based n-gram models of natural language. *Computational Linguistics*, 18(4):467–479.

Ciprian Chelba and Frederick Jelinek. 1998. Exploiting syntactic structure for language modeling. In *Proc. of ACL 1998*, pages 225–231, San Francisco, California.

Input:	Keep on investing.
MT output:	Pokračovalo investování. (grammar correct here!)
Gloss:	Continued investing. (Meaning: The investing continued.)
Correct:	Pokračujte v investování.

Input:	brokerage firms rushed out ads ...			
MT Output:	brokerské	firmy	vyběhl	reklamy
Gloss:	brokerage	$\text{firms}_{pl.fem}$	$\text{ran}_{sg.masc}$	$\text{ads}^{pl.voc,sg.gen}_{pl.nom,pl.acc}$
Correct option 1:	brokerské	firmy	vyběhly	s $\text{reklamami}_{pl.instr}$
Correct option 2:	brokerské	firmy	vydaly	$\text{reklamy}_{pl.acc}$

Figure 2: Two sample errors in translating Verb-Modifier relation from English to Czech.

David Chiang. 2005. A hierarchical phrase-based model for statistical machine translation. In *Proc. of ACL 2005*, pages 263–270.

Martin Čmejrek, Jan Cuřín, Jiří Havelka, Jan Hajič, and Vladislav Kuboň. 2004. Prague Czech-English Dependecy Treebank: Syntactically Annotated Resources for Machine Translation. In *Proc. of LREC 2004*, Lisbon, Portugal.

Adrià de Gispert, José B. Mariño, and Josep M. Crego. 2005. Improving statistical machine translation by classifying and generalizing inflected verb forms. In *Proc. of Eurospeech 2005*, pages 3185–3188, Lisbon, Portugal.

İlknur Durgar El-Kahlout and Kemal Oflazer. 2006. Initial Explorations in English to Turkish Statistical Machine Translation. In *Proc. of the Workshop on Statistical Machine Translation, ACL 2006*, pages 7–14, New York City.

Jason Eisner. 2003. Learning non-isomorphic tree mappings for machine translation. In *Proc. of ACL 2003, Companion Volume*, pages 205–208, Sapporo, Japan.

Sharon Goldwater and David McClosky. 2005. Improving statistical MT through morphological analysis. In *Proc. of HLT/EMNLP 2005*, pages 676–683.

Jan Hajič and Barbora Hladká. 1998. Tagging Inflective Languages: Prediction of Morphological Categories for a Rich, Structured Tagset. In *Proc. of COLING/ACL 1998*, pages 483–490, Montreal, Canada.

Jan Hajič. 2004. *Disambiguation of Rich Inflection (Computational Morphology of Czech)*. Nakladatelství Karolinum, Prague.

Philipp Koehn and Kevin Knight. 2003. Empirical methods for compound splitting. In *Proc. of EACL 2003*, pages 187–193.

Philipp Koehn. 2004a. Pharaoh: A beam search decoder for phrase-based statistical machine translation models. In *Proc. of AMTA 2004*, pages 115–124.

Philipp Koehn. 2004b. Statistical Significance Tests for Machine Translation Evaluation. In *Proc. of EMNLP 2004*, Barcelona, Spain.

Philipp Koehn. 2005. Europarl: A Parallel Corpus for Statistical Machine Translation. In *Proc. of MT Summit X*.

Guido Minnen, John Carroll, and Darren Pearce. 2001. Applied morphological processing of English. *Natural Language Engineering*, 7(3):207–223.

T.P. Nguyen and A. Shimazu. 2006. Improving Phrase-Based SMT with Morpho-Syntactic Analysis and Transformation. In *Proc. of AMTA 2006*, pages 138–147.

Sonja Nießen and Hermann Ney. 2001. Toward hierarchical models for statistical machine translation of inflected languages. In *Proc. of Workshop on Data-driven methods in machine translation, ACL 2001*, pages 1–8.

Franz Josef Och and Hermann Ney. 2003. A systematic comparison of various statistical alignment models. *Computational Linguistics*, 29(1):19–51.

Franz Josef Och. 2003. Minimum error rate training in statistical machine translation. In *Proc. of ACL 2003*, Sapporo, Japan.

Kishore Papineni, Salim Roukos, Todd Ward, and Wei-Jing Zhu. 2002. BLEU: a Method for Automatic Evaluation of Machine Translation. In *Proc. of ACL 2002*, pages 311–318.

M. Popović and H. Ney. 2004. Improving Word Alignment Quality using Morpho-Syntactic Information. In *Proc. of COLING 2004*, Geneva, Switzerland.

Adwait Ratnaparkhi. 1996. A Maximum Entropy Part-Of-Speech Tagger. In *Proc. of EMNLP 1996*, Philadelphia, USA.

David Talbot and Miles Osborne. 2006. Modelling lexical redundancy for machine translation. In *Proc. of COLING and ACL 2006*, pages 969–976, Sydney, Australia.

Kenji Yamada and Kevin Knight. 2002. A decoder for syntax-based statistical MT. In *Proc. of ACL 2002*, pages 303–310.

Mei Yang and Katrin Kirchhoff. 2006. Phrase-based backoff models for machine translation of highly inflected languages. In *Proc. of EACL 2006*.

Andreas Zollmann, Ashish Venugopal, and Stephan Vogel. 2006. Bridging the inflection morphology gap for arabic statistical machine translation. In *Proc. of HLT/NAACL*.

Sentence Level Machine Translation Evaluation as a Ranking Problem: one step aside from BLEU

Yang Ye
University of Michigan
yye@umich.edu

Ming Zhou
Microsoft Research Asia
mingzhou@microsoft.com

Chin-Yew Lin
Microsoft Research Asia
cyl@microsoft.com

Abstract

The paper proposes formulating MT evaluation as a ranking problem, as is often done in the practice of assessment by human. Under the ranking scenario, the study also investigates the relative utility of several features. The results show greater correlation with human assessment at the sentence level, even when using an n-gram match score as a baseline feature. The feature contributing the most to the rank order correlation between automatic ranking and human assessment was the dependency structure relation rather than BLEU score and reference language model feature.

1 Introduction

In recent decades, alongside the growing research on Machine Translation (MT), automatic MT evaluation has become a critical problem for MT system developers, who are interested in quick turnaround development cycles. The state-of-the-art automatic MT evaluation is an n-gram based metric represented by BLEU (Papineni et al., 2001) and its variants. Ever since its creation, the BLEU score has been the gauge of Machine Translation system evaluation. Nevertheless, the research community has been largely aware of the deficiency of the BLEU metric. BLEU captures only a single dimension of the vitality of natural languages: a candidate translation gets acknowledged only if it uses exactly the same lexicon as the reference translation. Natural languages, however, are characterized by their extremely rich mechanisms for reproduction via a large number of syntactic, lexical and semantic rewriting rules. Although BLEU has been shown to correlate positively with human assessments at the document level (Papineni et al., 2001), efforts to improve state-of-the-art MT require that human assessment be approximated at sentence level as well. Researchers report the BLEU score at document level in order to combat the sparseness of n-grams in BLEU scoring. But, ultimately, document-level MT evaluation has to be pinned down to the granularity of the sentence. Unfortunately, the correlation between human assessment and BLEU score at sentence level is extremely low (Liu et al., 2005, 2006). While acknowledging the appealing simplicity of BLEU as a way to access one perspective of an MT candidate translation's quality, we observe the following facts of n-gram based MT metrics. First, they may not reflect the mechanism of how human beings evaluate sentence translation quality. More specifically, optimizing BLEU does not guarantee the optimization of sentence quality approved by human assessors. Therefore, BLEU is likely to have a low correlation with human assessment at sentence level for most candidate translations. Second, it is conceivable that human beings are more reliable ranking the quality of multiple candidate translations than assigning a numeric value to index the quality of the candidate translation even with significant deliberation. Consequently, a more intuitive approach for automatic MT evaluation is to replicate the quality ranking ability of human assessors. Thirdly, the BLEU score is elusive and hard to interpret; for example, what can be concluded for a

Proceedings of the Second Workshop on Statistical Machine Translation, pages 240–247,
Prague, June 2007. ©2007 Association for Computational Linguistics

candidate translation's quality if the BLEU score is 0.0168, particularly when we are aware that even a human translation can receive an embarrassingly low BLEU score? In light of the discussion above, we propose an alternative scenario for MT evaluation, where, instead of assigning a numeric score to a candidate translation under evaluation, we predict its rank with regard to its peer candidate translations. This formulation of the MT evaluation task fills the gap between an automatic scoring function and human MT evaluation practice. The results from the current study will not only interest MT system evaluation moderators but will also inform the research community about which features are useful in improving the correlation between human rankings and automatic rankings.

2 Problem Formulation

2.1 Data and Human Annotation Reliability

We use two data sets for the experiments: the test data set from the LDC MTC corpus (LDC2003T17[1]) and the data set from the MT evaluation workshop at ACL05[2]. Both data sets are for Chinese-English language pairs and each has four reference translations and seven MT system translations as well as human assessments for fluency and adequacy on a scale of 1 to 5, with 5 indicating the best quality. For the LDC2003T17 data, human assessments exist for only three MT systems; for the ACL05 workshop data, there are human assessments for all seven MT systems. Table 1 summarizes the information from these two data sets.

The Kappa scores (Cohen, 1960) for the human assessment scores are negative, both for fluency and adequacy, indicating that human beings are not consistent when assigning quality scores to the candidate translations. We have much sympathy with a concern expressed in (Turian, 2003) that "Automatic MT evaluation cannot be faulted for poor correlation with the human judges, when the judges do not correlate well each other."To determine whether human assessor might be more consistent when ranking pairs of sentences, we examined the "ranking consistency score"of the human assessment data for the LDC2003T17 data. For this consistency score, we are only concerned with whether multiple judges are consistent in terms of which sentence of the two sentences is better: we are not concerned with the quantitative difference between judges. Since some sentences are judged by three judges while others are judged by only two judges, we calculated the consistency scores under both circumstances, referred to as "Consistent 2"and "Consistent 3"in the following table. For "Consistent 2", for every pair of sentences, where sentence 1 is scored higher (or lower or equal) than sentence 2 by both judges, then the two judges are deemed consistent. For "Consistent 3", the proportion of sentences that achieved the above consistency from triple judges is reported. Additionally, we also considered a consistency rate that excludes pairs for which only one judge says sentence 1 is better and the other judge(s) say(s) sentence 2 is better. We call these "Consistent 2 with tie"and "Consistent 3 with tie". From the rank consistency scores in Table 2, we observe that two annotators are more consistent with the relative rankings for sentence pairs than with the absolute quality scores. This finding further supports the task of ranking MT candidate sentences as more reliable than the one of classifying the quality labels.

2.2 Ranking Over Classification and Regression

As discussed in the previous section, it is difficult for human assessors to perform MT candidate translation evaluation with fine granularity (e.g., using real-valued numeric score). But humans' assessments are relatively reliable for judgments of quality ranking using a coarser ordinal scale, as we have seen above. Several approaches for automatically assigning quality scores to candidate sentences are available, including classification, regression or ranking, of which ranking is deemed to be a more appropriate approach. Nominalize the quality scores and formulating the task as a classification problem would result in a loss of the ordinal information encoded in the different scores. Additionally, the low Kappa scores in the human annotation reliability analysis reported above also confirms our previous speculation that a classification approach is less appropriate. Regression would be more reasonable than classification because it preserves the ordinal information in the quality labels, but it also inappropriately im-

[1] http://www.ldc.upenn.edu/Catalog/

[2] http://www.isi.edu/~ cyl/MTSE2005/

Data Index	MT Systems	References	Documents	Sentences
LDC2003T17	7	4	100	878
ACL05 Workshop	7	4	100	919

Table 1: Data Sets Information

Inter-Judge Score	Consistent 2	Consistent 3	Consistent 2 with Tie	Consistent 3 with Tie
Ranking Consistency Score	45.3%	23.4%	92.6%	87.0%

Table 2: Ranking Consisteny Scores for LDC2003T17 Data

poses interval scaling onto the quality labels. In contrast, ranking considers only the relative ranking information from human labels and does not impose any extra information onto the quality labels assigned by human beings.

The specific research question addressed in this paper is three-fold: First, in addition to investigating the correlation between automatic numeric scoring and human assessments, is ranking of peer candidate translations an alternative way of examining correlation that better suits the state of affairs of human annotation? Second, if the answer to the above question is yes, can better correlation be achieved with human assessment under the new task scenario? Finally, in addition to n-gram matching, which other knowledge sources can combat and even improve the rank order correlation? The process of ranking is a crucial technique in Information Retrieval (IR) where search engines rank web pages depending on their relevance to a query. In this work, sentence level MT evaluation is considered as a ranking problem. For all candidate translations of the same source Chinese sentence, we predict their translation quality ranks. We evaluate the ranker by Spearman's rank order correlation coefficient between human ranks and predicted ranks described by the following formula (Siegel,1956):

$$r = 1 - \left(\frac{6\sum D^2}{N(N^2-1)}\right) \quad (1)$$

where D is the difference between each pair of ranks and N is the number of candidates for ranking.

3 Related Works

Papineni et al.(2001) pioneered the automatic MT evaluation study, which scores translation quality via n-gram matching between the candidate and reference translations. Following the growing awareness of the deficiency of n-gram based automatic MT evaluation, many studies attempted to improve upon n-gram based metrics (Zhou et al., 2006; Liu, et al., 2005,2006) as well as propose ways to evaluate MT evaluation metrics (Lin, et al. 2004). Previous studies, however, have focused on MT evaluation at the document level in order to fight n-gram sparseness problem. While document level correlation provides us with a general impression of the quality of an MT system, researchers desire to get more informative diagnostic evaluation at sentence level to improve the MT system instead of just an overall score that does not provide details. Recent years have seen several studies investigating MT evaluation at the sentence level (Liu et al., 2005,2006; Quirk, 2004). The state-of-the-art sentence level correlations reported in previous work between human assessments and automatic scoring are around 0.20. Kulesza et al.(2004) applied Support Vector Machine classification learning to sentence level MT evaluation and reported improved correlation with human judgment over BLEU. However, the classification taxonomy in their work is binary, being either machine translation or human translation. Additionally, as discussed above, the inconsistency from the human annotators weakens the legitimacy of the classification approach. Gamon et al.(2005) reported a study of English to French sentence-level MT evaluation without reference translations. In order to improve on the correlation between human assessments and the perplexity score alone, they combined a perplexity score with a classification score obtained from an SVM binary classifier distinguishing machine-translated sentences from human translations. The results showed that even the combination of the above two scores cannot outperform BLEU.

To sum up, very little consideration has been taken in previous research as to which learning approach is better motivated and justified by the state of affairs of human annotation reliability. Presumably, research that endeavors to emulate human performance on tasks that demontrate good inter-judge reliability is most useful.

a learning approach that is better supported by human annotation reliability can alleviate the noise from human assessments and therefore achieve more reliable correlations.

4 Experiments and Evaluation

4.1 Ranking SVM Learning Algorithm

Ranking peer candidate sentence translations is a task in which the translation instances are classified into a number of ranks. This is a canonical ordinal regression scenario, which differs from standard classification and metric regression. For implementation, we use the Ranking SVM of SVMlight (Joachims, 2004), which was originally developed to rank the web pages returned upon a certain query in search engines. Given an instance of a candidate translation, Ranking SVM assigns it a score based on:

$$U(x) = W^{\mathrm{T}}x \qquad (2)$$

where W represents a vector of weights (Xu et al., 2005). The higher the value of U(x), the better x is as a candidate translation. In an ordinal regression, the values of U(x) are mapped into intervals corresponding to the ordinal categories. An instance falling into one interval is classified into the corresponding translation quality. In ranking experiments, we use the Ranking SVM scores to rank the candidate sentences under evaluation.

4.2 Features

We experiment with three different knowledge sources in our ranking experiments:

1. N-gram matching between the candidate translation and the reference translation, for which we use BLEU scores calculated by the NIST script with smoothing[3] to avoid undefined log probabilities for zero n-gram probabilities.

2. Dependency relation matching between the candidate translation and the reference translation.

3. The log of the perplexity score of the candidate translation, where the perplexity score is obtained from a local language model trained on all sentences in the four reference translations using CMU SLM toolkit. The n-gram order is the default trigram.

4.2.1 N-gram matching feature

N-gram matching is certainly an important criterion in some cases for evaluating the translation quality of a candidate translation. We use the BLEU score calculated by the BLEU score script from NIST for this feature.

As has been observed by many researchers, BLEU fails to capture any non n-gram based matching between the reference and candidate translations. We carried out a pair-wise experiment on four reference translations from the LDC2003T17 test data, where we took one reference sentence as the reference and the other three references as candidate translations. Presumably, since the candidate sentences are near-optimal translations, the BLEU scores obtained in such a way should be close to 1. But our analysis shows a mean BLEU of only 0.1456398, with a standard deviation of 0.1522381, which means that BLEU is not very predictive of sentence level evaluation. The BLEU score is, however, still informative in judging the average MT system's translation.

4.2.2 Dependency Structure Matching

Dependency relation information has been widely used in Machine Translation in recent years. Fox (2002) reported that dependency trees correspond better across translation pairs than constituent trees. The information summarization community has also seen successful implementation of ideas similar to the depedency structure. Zhou et al.(2005) and Hovy et al.(2005) reported using Basic Elements (BE) in text summarization and its evaluation. In the current

[3] We added an extremely small number to both matched n-grams and total number of n-grams.

paper, we match a candidate translation with a reference translation on the following five dependency structure (DS) types:

- Agent - Verb
- Verb - Patient
- Modified Noun - Modifier
- Modified Verb - Modifier
- Preposition - Object

Besides the consideration of the presence of certain lexical items, DS captures information as to how the lexical items are assembled into a good sentence. By using their dependency relation match for ranking the quality of peer translations, we assume that the dependency structure in the source language should be well preserved in the target language and that multiple translations of the same source sentence should significantly share dependency structures. Liu et al.(2005) make use of dependency structure in sentence level machine translation evaluation in the form of headword chains, which are lexicalized dependency relations. We propose that unlexicalized dependency relations can also be informative. Previous research has shown that key dependency relations tend to have a strong correspondence between Chinese and English (Zhou et al., 2001). More than 80 % of subject-verb, adjective-noun and adverb-verb dependency relations were able to be mapped, although verb-object DS mapping is weaker at a rate of 64.8%. In our paper, we considered three levels of matching for dependency relation triplets, where a triplet consists of the DS type and the two lexical items as the arguments.

We used an in-house dependency parser to extract the dependency relations from the sentences. Figure 1 illustrates how dependency relation matching can go beyond n-gram matching. We calculated 15 DS scores for each sentence correponding to the counts of match for the 5 DS types at the 3 different levels.

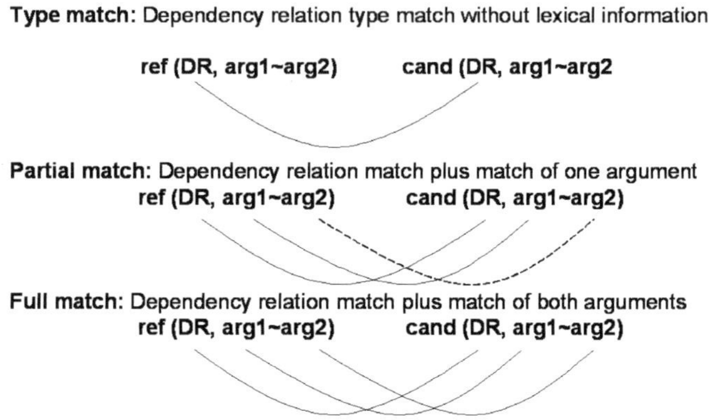

Figure 1: Dependency Relation Matching Scheme

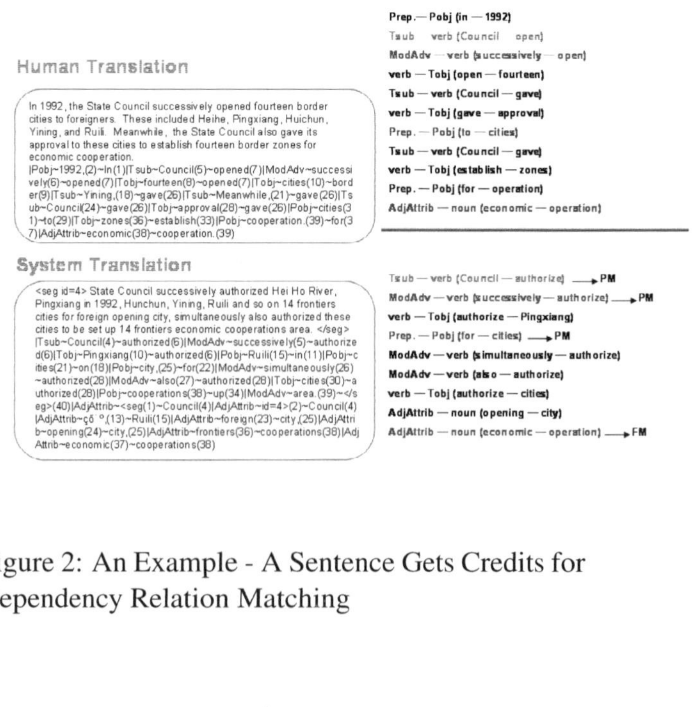

Figure 2: An Example - A Sentence Gets Credits for Dependency Relation Matching

4.2.3 Reference language model (RLM) feature

Statistical Language Modeling (SLM) is a key component in Statistical Machine Translation. The most dominant technology in SLM is n-gram models, which are typically trained on a large corpus for applications such as SMT and speech recognition. Depending on the size of the corpora used to train the language model, a language model can be tuned to reflect n-gram probabilities for both a narrowed scope as well as a general scope covering the distribution of n-gram probabilities of the whole language. In the BLEU calculation, the candidate sentence is evaluated against an extremely local language model of merely the reference sentence. We speculate that a language model that stands in between such an immediate local language model and the large general English language model could help capture the variation of lexical and even structural selections in the translations by using information beyond the scope of the local sentence. Additionally, this language model could represent the style of a certain group of translators in a certain domain on the genre of news articles. To pursue such a language model, we explore a language model that is trained on all sentences in the four references. We obtain the perplexity score of each candidate sentence based on the reference language model. The perplexity score obtained this way reflects the degree to which a candidate translation can be generated from the n-gram probability distribution of the whole collection of sentences in the four references. It adds new information to BLEU because it not only compares the candidate sentence to its corresponding reference sentence but also reaches out to other sentences in the current document and other documents on the same topics. We choose perplexity over the language model score because the perplexity score is normalized with regard to the length of the sentence; that is, it does not favor sentences of relatively shorter length.

In our ranking experiments, for training, both the seven MT translations and the four reference translations of the same source sentence are evaluated as "candidate" translations, and then each of these eleven sentences is evaluated against the four reference sentences in turn. The BLEU score of each of these sentences is calculated with multiple references. Each dependency score is the average score of the four references. For the reference language model feature, the perplexity score is used for each sentence.

Conceptually, the reference language model and dependency structure features are more relevant to the fluency of the sentence than to the adequacy. Because the candidate sentences' adequacy scores are based on arbitrary reference sentences out of the four references in the human assessment data, we decided to focus on fluency ranking for this paper. The ranking scenario and features can easily be generalized to adequacy evaluation: the full and partial match dependency structure features are relevant to adeqaucy too. The high correlation between adequacy and fluency scores from human assessments (both pearson and spearman correlations are 0.67) also indicates that the same features will achieve improvements for adequacy evaluation.

Feature Set	Mean Corr	Corr Var
BLEU	0.3590644	0.0076498
DS	0.4002753	0.0061299
PERP	0.4273000	0.0014043
BLEU+DS	0.4128991	0.0027576
BLEU+PERP	0.4288112	0.0013783
PERP+DS	0.4313611	0.0014594
All	0.4310457	0.0014494

Table 3: Training and Testing on Within-year Data (Test on 7 MT and 4 Human)

4.3 Sentence Ranking on Within-year Data

In the first experiment, we performed the ranking experiment on the ACL05 workshop data and test on the same data set. We did three-fold cross-validation on two different test scenarios. On the first scenario, we tested the ranking models on the seven MT system output sentences and the four human reference sentences. It is widely agreed upon among researchers that a good evalutation metric should rank reference translation as higher than machine translation (Lin et al., 2004). We include the four human reference sentences into the ranking to test the ranker's ability to discriminate optimal translations from poor ones. For the second scenario, we test the ranking models on only the seven MT system output sentences. Because the quality differences across the seven system translations are more subtle, we are particularly interested in the ranking quality on those sentences. Tables 3 and 4 summarize the results from both scenarios.

The experimental results in the above tables conveyed several important messages: in the ranking setup, for both the MT and human mixed output and MT only output scenarios, we have a significantly

Feature Set	Mean Corr	Corr Var
BLEU	0.2913541	0.0324386
DS	0.3058766	0.0226442
PERP	0.2921684	0.0210605
BLEU+DS	0.315106	0.0206144
BLEU+PERP	0.2954833	0.0211094
PERP+DS	0.3067157	0.0217037
All	0.305248	0.0218777

Table 4: Training and Testing on Within-year Data (Test on MT only)

Feature Set	Mean Corr	Corr Var
BLEU	0.3133257	0.1957059
DS	0.4896355	0.0727430
PERP	0.4582005	0.0542485
BLEU+DS	0.4907745	0.0678395
BLEU+PERP	0.4577449	0.0563994
PERP+DS	0.4709567	0.0549708
All	0.4707289	0.0565538

Table 5: Training and Testing on Across-year Data (test on 3 MT plus 1 human)

improved correlation between human scoring and automatic ranking at sentence level compared to the state-of-the-art sentence level correlation for fluency score of approximately 0.202 found previously (Liu et al., 2006). When the ranking task is performed on a mixture of MT sentences and human translations, dependency structure and reference language model perplexity scores sequentially improve on BLEU in increasing the correlation. When the ranking task is performed only on MT system output sentences, dependency structure still significantly outperforms BLEU in increasing the correlation, and the reference language model, even trained on a small number of sentences, demonstrates utility equal to that of BLEU. The dependency structure feature proves to have robust utility in informing fluency quality in both scenarios, even with noise from the dependency parser, likely because a dependency triplet with inaccurate arguments is still rewarded as a type match or partial match. Additionally, the feature is reward-based and not penalty-based. We only reward matches and do not penalize mismatches, such that the impact of the noise from the MT system and the dependency parser is weakened.

4.4 Sentence Ranking on Across-year Data

It is trivial to retrain the ranking model and test on a new year's data. But we speculate that a model trained from a different data set can have almost the same ranking power as a model trained on the same data set. Therefore, we conducted an experiment where we trained the ranking model on the ACL 2005 workshop data and test on the LDC2003T17 data. We do not need to retrain the ranking SVM model; we only need to retrain the reference language model on the multiple references from the new year's data to obtain the perplexity scores. Because LDC2003T17 has human assessments for only three MT systems, we test on the three system outputs plus a human translation chosen randomly from the four reference translations. The results in Table 5 show an encouraging rank order correlation with human assessments. Similar to training and testing on within-year data, both dependency structure and perplexity scores achieve higher correlation than the BLEU score. Combining BLEU and dependency structure achieves the best correlation.

4.5 Document Level Ranking Testing

Previously, most researchers working on MT evaluation studied the correlation between automatic metric and human assessment on the granularity of the document to mitigate n-gram sparseness. Presumably, good correlation at sentence level should lead to good correlation at document level but not vice versa. Table 6 reports the correlations using the model trained on the 2005 workshop data and tested on the 100 documents of the LDC 2003 data. Comparing these correlations with the correlations reported in the previous section, we see that using the same model, the document level rank order correlation is substantially higher than the sentence level correlation, with the dependency structure showing the highest utility.

5 Conclusion and Future Work

The current study proposes to formulate MT evaluation as a ranking problem. We believe that a reliable ranker can inform the improvement of BLEU for a better automatic scoring function. Ranking in-

Feature Set	Mean Corr	Corr Var
BLEU	0.543	0.0853
DS	0.685	0.0723
PERP	0.575	0.0778
BLEU+DS	0.639	0.0773
BLEU+PERP	0.567	0.0785
PERP+DS	0.597	0.0861
All	0.599	0.0849

Table 6: Document Level Ranking Testing Results

formation could also be integrated into tuning process to better inform the optimization of weights of the different factors for SMT models. Our ranking experiments show a better correlation with human assessments at sentence level for fluency score compared to the previous non-ranking scenario, even with BLEU as the baseline feature. On top of BLEU, both the dependency structure and reference language model have shown encouraging utility for different testing scenarios. Looking toward the future work, more features could be explored, e.g., a parsing-based score of each candidate sentence and better engineering for dependency triplet extraction. Additionally, the entire research community on MT evaluation would benefit from a systematic and detailed analysis of real data that can provide a quantitative breakdown of the proportions of different "operations" needed to rewrite one sentence to another. Such an effort will guide MT evaluation researchers to decide which features to focus on.

References

J. Cohen, A Coefficient of Agreement for Nominal Scales, Educational and Psychological Measurement, 20, 37-46, 1960.

G. Doddington. Automatic Evaluation of Machine Translation Quality Using N-gram Co-occurrence Statistics. HLT, pages 128–132, 2002.

H. J. Fox, Phrasal Cohesion and Statistical Machine Translation. EMNLP, 2002.

M. Gamon, et al., Sentence-level MT Evaluation without Reference Translations: Beyond Language Modeling, Proceedings of EAMT, 2005.

T. Joachims, Making Large-scale Support Vector Machine Learning Practical, in B. Scholkopf, C. Burges, A. Smola. Advances in Kernel Methods: Support Vector Machines, MIT Press, Cambridge, MA, December, 1998.

A. Kulesza and S. M. Shieber, A Learning Approach to Improving Sentence-Level MT Evaluation, 10th International Conference on Theoretical and Methodological Issues in Machine Translation, 2004.

C. Lin, et al., ORANGE: a Method for Evaluating Automatic Evaluation Metrics for Machine Translation. COLING, 2004.

C. Lin, et al., Automatic Evaluation of Machine Translation Quality Using Longest Common Subsequence and Skip-Bigram Statistics, ACL, 2004.

D. Liu, et al., Syntactic Features for Evaluation of Machine Translation, ACL Workshop on Intrinsic and Extrinsic Evaluation Measures for Machine Translation and/or Summarization, 2005.

D. Liu, et al., Stochastic Iterative Alignment for Machine Translation Evaluation, COLING/ACL Poster Session, Sydney, 2006.

C. B. Quirk, Training a Sentence-Level Machine Translation Confidence Measure, In Proceedings of LREC, 2004.

E. Hovy, et al., Evaluating DUC 2005 using Basic Elements. Document Understanding Conference (DUC-2005), 2005.

K. Papineni, et al., BLEU: a Method for Automatic Evaluation of Machine Translation, IBM research division technical report, RC22176 (W0109-022), 2001.

S. Siegel and N.J. Catellan, Non-parametric Statistics for the Behavioral Sciences, McGraw-Hill, 2nd edition, 1988.

M. Snover, et al., A Study of Translation Error Rate with Targeted Human Annotation, LAMP-TR-126, CS-TR-4755, UMIACS-TR-2005-58, University of Maryland, 2005.

J. Turian, et al., Evaluation of Machine Translation and its Evaluation, MT Summit IX, 2003.

J. Xu, et al., Ranking Definitions with Supervised Learning Method, WWW'05 industry track, 811-819, 2005.

L. Zhou, et al., A BE-based Multi-document Summarizer with Query Interpretation. Document Understanding Conference (DUC-2005), 2005.

L. Zhou, C. Lin, E-evaluating Machine Translation Results with Paraphrase Support, EMNLP, 2006.

M. Zhou, C. Huang, Approach to the Chinese dependency formalism for the tagging of corpus. Journal of Chinese Information Processing, 8(3): 35-52, 1994.

Localization of Difficult-to-Translate Phrases

Behrang Mohit[1] and **Rebecca Hwa**[1,2]
Intelligent Systems Program[1]
Department of Computer Science[2]
University of Pittsburgh
Pittsburgh, PA 15260 U.S.A.
{behrang, hwa}@cs.pitt.edu

Abstract

This paper studies the impact that difficult-to-translate source-language phrases might have on the machine translation process. We formulate the notion of difficulty as a measurable quantity; we show that a classifier can be trained to predict whether a phrase might be difficult to translate; and we develop a framework that makes use of the classifier and external resources (such as human translators) to improve the overall translation quality. Through experimental work, we verify that by isolating difficult-to-translate phrases and processing them as special cases, their negative impact on the translation of the rest of the sentences can be reduced.

1 Introduction

For translators, not all source sentences are created equal. Some are straight-forward enough to be automatically translated by a machine, while others may stump even professional human translators. Similarly, within a single sentence there may be some phrases that are more difficult to translate than others. The focus of this paper is on identifying *Difficult-to-Translate Phrases* (DTPs) within a source sentence and determining their impact on the translation process. We investigate three questions: (1) how should we formalize the notion of difficulty as a measurable quantity over an appropriately defined phrasal unit? (2) To what level of accuracy can we automatically identify DTPs? (3) To what extent do DTPs affect an MT system's performance on other (not-as-difficult) parts of the sentence? Conversely, would knowing the correct translation for the DTPs improve the system's translation for the rest of the sentence?

In this work, we model difficulty as a measurement with respect to a particular MT system. We further assume that the degree of difficulty of a phrase is directly correlated with the quality of the translation produced by the MT system, which can be approximated using an automatic evaluation metric, such as BLEU (Papineni et al., 2002). Using this formulation of difficulty, we build a framework that augments an off-the-shelf phrase-based MT system with a DTP classifier that we developed. We explore the three questions in a set of experiments, using the framework as a testbed.

In the first experiment, we verify that our proposed difficulty measurement is sensible. The second experiment evaluates the classifier's accuracy in predicting whether a source phrase is a DTP. For that, we train a binary SVM classifier via a series of lexical and system dependent features. The third is an oracle study in which the DTPs are perfectly identified and human translations are obtained. These human-translated phrases are then used to constrain the MT system as it translates the rest of the sentence. We evaluate the translation quality of the entire sentence and also the parts that are not translated by humans. Finally, the framework is evaluated as a whole. Results from our experiments suggest that improved handling of DTPs will have a positive impact the overall MT output quality. Moreover, we find the SVM-trained DTP classifier to have a promising rate of accuracy, and that the incorporation of DTP information can improve the outputs of the underlying MT system. Specifically, we achieve an improvement of translation quality for non-difficult seg-

Proceedings of the Second Workshop on Statistical Machine Translation, pages 248–255,
Prague, June 2007.

ments of a sentence when the DTPs are translated by humans.

2 Motivation

There are several reasons for investigating ways to identify DTPs. For instance, it can help to find better training examples in an active learning framework; it can be used to coordinate outputs of multiple translation systems; or it can be used as means of error analysis for MT system development. It can also be used as a pre-processing step, an alternative to post-editing. For many languages, MT output requires post-translation editing that can be cumbersome task for low quality outputs, long sentences, complicated structures and idioms. Pre-translation might be viewed as a kind of preventive medicine; that is, a system might produce an overall better output if it were not thwarted by some small portion of the input. By identifying DTPs and passing those cases off to an expensive translation resource (e.g. humans) first, we might avoid problems further down the MT pipeline. Moreover, pre-translation might not always have to be performed by humans. What is considered difficult for one system might not be difficult for another system; thus, pre-translation might also be conducted using multiple MT systems.

3 Our Approach

Figure 1 presents the overall dataflow of our system. The input is a source sentence (a_1 ... a_n), from which DTP candidates are proposed. Because the DTPs will have to be translated by humans as independent units, we limit the set of possible phrases to be syntactically meaningful units. Therefore, the framework requires a source-language syntactic parser or chunker. In this paper, we parse the source sentence with an off-the-shelf syntactic parser (Bikel, 2002). From the parse tree produced for the source sentence, every constituent whose string span is between 25% and 75% of the full sentence length is considered a DTP candidate. Additionally we have a tree node depth constraint that requires the constituent to be at least two levels above the tree's yield and two levels below the root. These two constraints ensure that the extracted phrases have balanced lengths.

We apply the classifier on each candidate and select the one labeled as difficult with the highest classification score. Depending on the underlying classifier, the score can be in various formats such as class probablity, confidence measure, etc. In our SVM based classifier, the score is the distance from the margin.

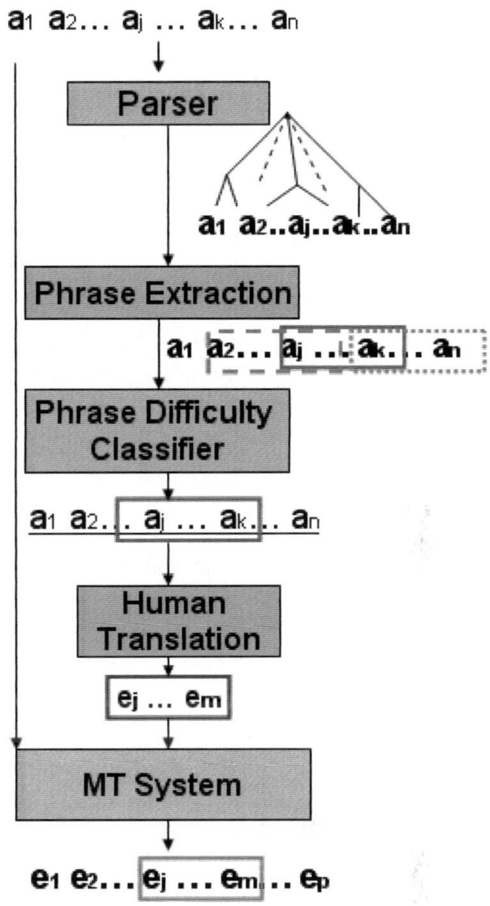

Figure 1: An overview of our translation framework.

The chosen phrase (a_j ... a_k) is translated by a human (e_i ... e_m). We constrain the underlying phrase-based MT system (Koehn, 2003) so that its decoding of the source sentence must contain the human translation for the DTP. In the following subsections, we describe how we develop the DTP classifier with machine learning techniques and how we constrain the underlying MT system with human translated DTPs.

3.1 Training the DTP Classifier

Given a phrase in the source language, the DTP classifier extracts a set of features from it and predicts whether it is *difficult* or not based on its feature values. We use an SVM classifier in this work. We train the SVM-Light implementation of the algorithm (Joachims 1999). To train the classifier, we need to tackle two challenges. First, we need to develop some appropriate training data because there is no corpus with annotated DTPs. Second, we need to determine a set of predictive features for the classifier.

Development of the Gold Standard

Unlike the typical SVM training scenario, labeled training examples of DTPs do not exist. Manual creation of such data requires deep understanding of the linguistics differences of source and target languages and also deep knowledge about the MT system and its training data. Such resources are not accessible to us. Instead, we construct the gold standard automatically. We make the strong assumption that difficulty is directly correlated to translation quality and that translation quality can be approximately measured by automatic metrics such as BLEU. We have two resource requirements – a sentence-aligned parallel corpus (different from the data used to train the underlying MT system), and a syntactic parser for the source language. The procedure for creating the gold standard data is as follows:

1. Each source sentence is parsed.
2. Phrase translations are extracted from the parallel corpus. Specifically, we generate word-alignments using GIZA++ (Och 2001) in both directions and combine them using the refined methodology (Och and Ney 2003), and then we applied Koehn's toolkit (2004) to extract parallel phrases. We have relaxed the length constraints of the toolkit to ensure the extraction of long phrases (as long as 16 words).
3. Parallel phrases whose source parts are not well-formed constituents are filtered out.
4. The source phrases are translated by the underlying MT system, and a baseline BLEU score is computed over this set of MT outputs.
5. To label each source phrase, we remove that phrase and its translation from the MT output and calculate the set's new BLEU score. If new-score is greater than the baseline score by some threshold value (a tunable parameter), we label the phrase as *difficult*, otherwise we label it as *not difficult*.

Rather than directly calculating the BLEU score for each phrase, we performed the round-robin procedure described in steps 4 and 5 because BLEU is not reliable for short phrases. BLEU is calculated as a geometric mean over n-gram matches with references, assigning a score of zero to an entire phrase if no higher-ordered n-gram matches were found against the references. However, some phrases with a score of 0 might have more matches in the lower-ordered n-grams than other phrases (and thus ought to be considered "easier"). A comparison of the relative changes in BLEU scores while holding out a phrase from the corpus gives us a more sensitive measurement than directly computing BLEU for each phrase.

Features

By analyzing the training corpus, we have found 18 features that are indicative of DTPs. Some phrase-level feature values are computed as an average of the feature values of the individual words. The following first four features use some probabilities that are collected from a parallel data and word alignments. Such a resource does not exist at the time of testing. Instead we use the history of the source words (estimated from the large parallel corpus) to predict the feature value.

(I) **Average probability of word alignment crossings**: word alignment crossings are indicative of word order differences and generally structural difference across two languages. We collect word alignment crossing statistics from the training corpus to estimate the crossing probability for each word in a new source phrase. For example the Arabic word *rhl* has 67% probability of alignment crossing (word movement across English). These probabilities are then averaged into one value for the entire phrase.

(II) **Average probability of translation ambiguity**: words that have multiple equally-likely translations contribute to translation ambiguity. For example a word that has 4 different translations with similar frequencies tends to be more ambiguous than a word that has one dominant translation. We collect statistics about the lexical translational ambiguities from the training corpus and lexical translation tables and use them to predict the ambiguity of each word in a new source phrase. The score for the phrase is the average of the scores for the individual words.

(III) **Average probability of POS tag changes**: Change of a word's POS tagging is an indication of deep structural differences between the source phrase and the target phrase. Using the POS tagging information for both sides of the training corpus, we learn the probability that each source word's POS gets changed after the translation. To overcome data sparseness, we only look at the collapsed version of POS tags on both sides of the corpus. The phrase's score is the average the individual word probabilities.

(IV) **Average probability of null alignments**: In many cases null alignments of the source words are indicative of the weakness of information about the word. This feature is similar to average ambiguity probability. The difference is that we use the probability of null alignments instead of lexical probabilities.

(V-IX) **Normalized number of unknown words, content words, numbers, punctuations:** For each of these features we normalize the count (e.g.: unknown words) with the length of the phrase. The normalization of the features helps the classifier to not have length preference for the phrases.

(X) **Number of proper nouns:** Named entities tend to create translation difficulty, due to their diversity of spellings and also domain differences. We use the number of proper nouns to estimate the occurrence of the named entities in the phrase.

(XI **Depth of the subtree**: The feature is used as a measure of syntactic complexity of the phrase. For example continuous right branching of the parse tree which adds to the depth of the subtree can be indicative of a complex or ambiguous structure that might be difficult to translate.

(XII) **Constituency type of the phrase**: We observe that the different types of constituents have varied effects on the translations of the phrase. For example prepositional phrases tend to belong to difficult phrases.

(XIII) **Constituency type of the parent phrase**

(XIV) **Constituency types of the children nodes of the phrase:** We form a set from the children nodes of the phrase (on the parse tree).

(XV) **Length of the phrase:** The feature is based on the number of the words in the phrase.

(XVI) **Proportional length of the phrase:** The proportion of the length of the phrase to the length of the sentence. As this proportion gets larger, the contextual effect on the translation of the phrase becomes less.

(XVII) **Distance from the start of the sentence and**: Phrases that are further away from the start of the sentence tend to not be translated as well due to compounding translational errors.

(XVIII) **Distance from a learned translation phrase:** The feature measure the number of words before reaching a learned phrase. In other words it s an indication of the level of error that is introduced in the early parts of the phrase translation.

3.2 Constraining the MT System

Once human translations have been obtained for the DTPs, we want the MT system to only consider output candidates that contain the human translations. The additional knowledge can be used by the phrase-based system without any code modification. Figure 2 shows the data-flow for this process. First, we append the pre-trained phrase-translation table with the DTPs and their human translations with a probability of 1.0. We also include the human translations for the DTPs as training data for the language model to ensure that the phrase vocabulary is familiar to the decoder and relax the phrase distortion parameter that the decoder can include all phrase translations with any length in the decoding. Thus, candidates that contain the human translations for the DTPs will score higher and be chosen by the decoder.

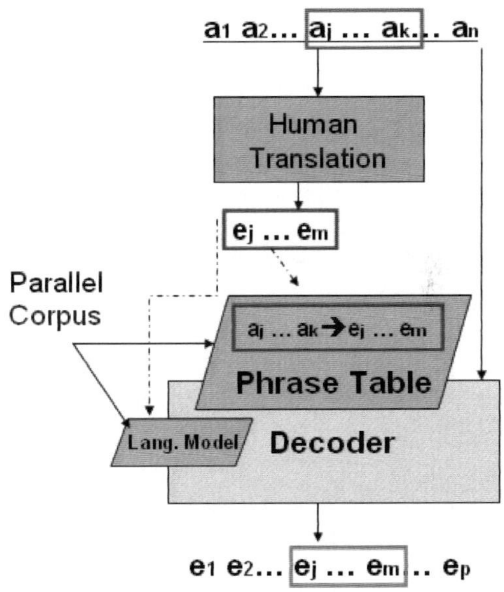

Figure 2: Human translations for the DTPs can be incorporated into the MT system's phrase table and language model.

4 Experiments

The goal of these four experiments is to gain a better understanding of the DTPs and their impact on the translation process. All our studies are conducted for Arabic-to-English MT. We formed a one-million word parallel text out of two corpora released by the Linguistic Data Consortium: Arabic News Translation Text Part 1 and Arabic English Parallel News Part 1. The majority of the data was used to train the underlying phrase-based MT system. We reserve 2000 sentences for development and experimentation. Half of these are used for the training and evaluation of the DTP classifier (Sections 4.1 and 4.2); the other half is used for translation experiments on the rest of the framework (Sections 4.3 and 4.4).

In both cases, translation phrases are extracted from the sentences and assigned "gold standard" labels according to the procedure described in Section 3.1. It is necessary to keep two separate datasets because the later experiments make use of the trained DTP classifier.

For the two translation experiments, we also face a practical obstacle: we do not have an army of human translators at our disposal to translate the identified phrases. To make the studies possible, we rely on a pre-translated parallel corpus to simulate the process of asking a human to translate a phrase. That is, we use the phrase extraction toolkit to find translation phrases corresponding to each DTP candidate (note that the data used for this experiment is separate from the main parallel corpus used to train the MT system, so the system has no knowledge about these translations).

4.1 Automatic Labeling of DTP

In this first experiment, we verify whether our method for creating positive and negative labeled examples of DTPs (as described in Section 3.1) is sound. Out of 2013 extracted phrases, we found 949 positive instances (DTPs) and 1064 negative instances. The difficult phrases have an average length of 8.8 words while the other phrases have an average length of 7.8 words[1]. We measured the BLEU scores for the MT outputs for both groups of phrases (Table 1).

Experiment	BLEU Score
DTPs	14.34
Non-DTPs	61.22

Table 1: Isolated Translation of the selected training phrases

The large gap between the translation qualities of the two phrase groups suggests that the DTPs are indeed much more "difficult" than the other phrases.

[1] Arabic words are tokenized and lemmatized by Diab's Arabic Toolset (Diab 2004).

4.2 Evaluation of the DTP Classifier

We now perform a local evaluation of the trained DTP classifier for its classification accuracy. The classifier is trained as an SVM using a linear kernel. The "gold standard" phrases from the section 4.1 are split into three groups: 2013 instances are used as training data for the classifier; 100 instances are used for development (e.g., parameter tuning and feature engineering); and 200 instances are used as test instances. The test set has an equal number of difficult and non-difficult phrases (50% baseline accuracy).

In order to optimize the accuracy of classification, we used a development set for feature engineering and trying various SVM kernels and associated parameters. For the feature engineering part, we used the all-but-one heuristic to test the contribution of each individual feature. Table 2 presents the most and least contributing four features that we used in our classification. Among various features, we observed that the syntactic features are the most contributing sources of information for our classification.

Least Useful Features	Most Useful Features
Ft1: Align Crossing	Ft 2: Lexical Ambiguity
Ft 8: Count of Nums	Ft 11: Depth of subtree
Ft:9: Count of Puncs	Ft 12: Const type of Phr
Ft 10: Count of NNPs	Ft 13: Const type of Par

Table 2: The most and least useful features

The DTP classifier achieves an average accuracy of 71.5%, using 10 fold cross validation on the test set.

4.3 Study on the effect of DTPs

This experiment concentrates on the second half of the framework: that of constraining the MT system to use human-translations for the DTPs. Our objective is to assess to what degree do the DTPs negatively impact the MT process. We compare the MT outputs of two groups of sentences. Group I is made up of 242 sentences that contain the most difficult to translate phrases in the 1000 sentences we reserved for this study. Group II is a control group made up of 242 sentences with the least difficult to translate phrases. The DTPs make up about 9% of word counts in the above 484 sentences. We follow the procedure described in Section 3.1 to identify and score all the phrases; thus, this experiment can be considered an oracle study. We compare four scenarios:

1. **Adding phrase translations for Group I**: MT system is constrained using the method described in Section 3.2 to incorporate human translations of the pre-identified DTPs in Group I.[2]
2. **Adding phrase translations for Group II**: MT system is constrained to use human translations for the identified (non-difficult) phrases in Group II.
3. **Adding translations for random phrases**: randomly replace 242 phrases from either Group I or Group II.
4. **Adding translations for classifier labeled DTPs**: human translations for phrases that our trained classifier has identified as DTPs from both Group I and Group II.

All of the above scenarios are evaluated on a combined set of 484 sentences (group 1 + group 2). This set up normalizes the relative difficulty of each grouping.

If the DTPs negatively impact the MT process, we would expect to see a greater improvement when Group I phrases are translated by humans than when Group II phrases are translated by humans.

The baseline for the comparisons is to evaluate the outputs of the MT system without using any human translations. This results in a BLEU score of 24.0. When human translations are used, the BLEU score of the dataset increases, as shown in Table 3.

Experiment	BLEU
Baseline (no human trans)	24.0
w/ translated DTPs (Group I)	39.6
w/ translated non-DTPs (Group II)	33.7
w/ translated phrases (random)	35.1
w/ translated phrases (classifier)	37.0

Table 3: A comparison of BLEU scores for the entire set of sentences under the constraints of using human translations for different types of phrases.

While it is unsurprising that the inclusion of human translations increases the overall BLEU score, this comparison shows that the boost is sharper when more DTPs are translated. This is consistent with our conjecture that pre-translating difficult phrases may be helpful.

A more interesting question is whether the human translations still provide any benefit once we factor out their direct contributions to the increase in BLEU scores. To answer this question, we compute the BLEU scores for the outputs again, this time filtering out all 484 identified phrases from the evaluation. In other words in this experiment we focus on the part of the sentence that is not labeled and does include any human translations. Table 4 presents the results.

Experiment	BLEU
Baseline (no human trans)	23.0
w/ translated DTPs (Group I)	25.4
w/ translated non-DTPs (Group II)	23.9
w/ translated phrases (random)	24.5
w/ translated phrases (classifier)	25.1

Table 4: BLEU scores for the translation outputs excluding the 484 (DTP and non-DTP) phrases.

The largest gain (2.4 BLEU increment from baseline) occurs when all and only the DTPs were translated. In contrast, replacing phrases from Group II did not improve the BLEU score very much. These results suggest that better handling of DTPs will have a positive effect on the overall MT process. We also note that using our SVM-trained classifier to identify the DTPs, the constrained MT system's outputs obtained a BLEU score that is nearly as high as if a perfect classifier was used.

4.4 Full evaluation of the framework

This final experiment evaluates the complete framework as described in Section 3. The setup of this study is similar to that of the previous section. The main difference is that now, we rely on the classifier to predict which phrase would be the most difficult to translate and use human translations for those phrases.

Out of 1000 sentences, 356 have been identified to contain DTPs (that are in the phrase extraction list). In other words, only 356 sentences hold DTPs that we can find their human translations through phrase projection. For the remaining sentences, we do not use any human translation.

[2] In this study, because the sentences are from the training parallel corpus, we can extract human translations directly from the corpus.

Table 5 presents the increase in BLEU scores when human translations for the 356 DTPs are used. As expected the BLEU score increases, but the improvement is less dramatic than in the previous experiment because most sentences are unchanged.

Experiment	BLEU
Baseline (no human trans)	24.9
w/ human translations	29.0

Table 5: Entire Corpus level evaluation (1000 sentences) when replacing DTPs in the hit list

Table 6 summarizes the experimental results on the subset of the 356 sentences. The first two rows compare the translation quality at the sentence level (similar to Table 3); the next two rows compare the translation quality of the non-DTP parts (similar to Table 4). Rows 1 and 3 are conditions when we do not use human translation; and rows 2 and 4 are conditions when we replace DTPs with their associated human translations. The improvements of the BLEU score for the hit list are similar to the results we have previously seen.

Experiment on 356 sentences	BLEU
Baseline: full sent.	25.1
w/ human translation: full sent.	37.6
Baseline: discount DTPs	26.0
w/ human translation: discount DTPs	27.8

Table 6: Evaluation of the subset of 356 sentences: both for the full sentence and for non-DTP parts, with and without human translation replacement of DTPs.

5 Related Work

Our work is related to the problem of confidence estimation for MT (Blatz et. al. 2004; Zen and Ney 2006). The confidence measure is a score for n-grams generated by a decoder[3]. The measure is based on the features like lexical probabilities (word posterior), phrase translation probabilities, N-best translation hypothesis, etc. Our DTP classification differs from the confidence measuring in several aspects: one of the main purposes of our classification of DTPs is to optimize the usage of outside resources. To do so, we focus on classification of phrases which are syntactically meaningful, because those syntactic constituent units have less dependency to the whole sentence structure and can be translated independently. Our classification relies on syntactic features that are important source of information about the MT difficulty and also are useful for further error tracking (reasons behind the difficulty). Our classification is performed as a pre-translation step, so it does not rely on the output of the MT system for a test sentence; instead, it uses a parallel training corpus and the characteristics of the underlying MT system (e.g.: phrase translations, lexical probabilities).

Confidence measures have been used for error correction and interactive MT systems. Ueffing and Ney (2005) employed confidence measures within a trans-type-style interactive MT system. In their system, the MT system iteratively generates the translation and the human translator accepts a part of the proposed translation by typing one or more prefix characters. The system regenerates a new translation based on the human prefix input and word level confidence measures. In contrast, our proposed usage of human knowledge is for translation at the phrase level. We use syntactic restrictions to make the extracted phrases meaningful and easy to translate in isolation. In other words, by the usage of our framework trans-type systems can use human knowledge at the phrase level for the most difficult segments of a sentence. Additionally by the usage of our framework, the MT system performs the decoding task only once.

The idea of isolated phrase translation has been explored successfully in MT community. Koehn and Knight (2003) used isolated translation of NP and PP phrases and merge them with the phrase based MT system to translate the complete sentence. In our work, instead of focusing on specific type of phrases (NP or PP), we focus on isolated translation of difficult phrases with an aim to improve the translation quality of non-difficult segments too.

6 Conclusion and Future Work

We have presented an MT framework that makes use of additional information about difficult-to-translate source phrases. Our framework includes an SVM-based phrase classifier that finds the segment of a sentence that is most difficult to translate. Our classifier achieves a promising 71.5% accuracy. By asking external sources (such as human translators) to pre-translate these DTPs and using them to constrain the MT process, we im-

[3] Most of the confidence estimation measures are for unigrams (word level measures).

prove the system outputs for the other parts of the sentences.

We plan to extend this work in several directions. First, our framework can be augmented to include multiple MT systems. We expect different systems will have difficulties with different constructs, and thus they may support each other, and thus reducing the need to ask human translators for help with the difficult phrases. Second, our current metric for phrasal difficulty depends on BLEU. Considering the recent debates about the shortcomings of the BLEU score (Callison-Burch et. al. 2006), we are interested in applying alternative metrics such a Meteor (Banerjee and Lavie 2005). Third, we believe that there is more room for improvement and extension of our classification features. Specifically, we believe that our syntactic analysis of source sentences can be improved by including richer parsing features. Finally, the framework can also be used to diagnose recurring problems in the MT system. We are currently developing methods for improving the translation of the difficult phrases for the phrase-based MT system used in our experiments.

Acknowledgements

This work is supported by NSF Grant IIS-0612791. We would like to thank Alon Lavie, Mihai Rotaru and the NLP group at Pitt as well as the anonymous reviewers for their valuable comments.

References

Satanjeev Banerjee, Alon Lavie. 2005. METEOR: An automatic metric for MT evaluation with improved correlation with human judgments. In *Proceedings of the ACL Workshop on Intrinsic and Extrinsic Evaluation Measures for MT and/or Summarization, pages 65–72.*

Daniel M. Bikel. 2002. Design of a multi-lingual, parallel-processing statistical parsing engine. In Proceedings of *ARPA Workshop on Human Language Technology*

John Blatz, Erin Fitzgerald, George Foster, Simona Gan drabur, Cyril Goutte, Alex Kulesza, Alberto Sanchis, and Nicola Ueffing. 2003. Confidence estimation for machine translation. Technical report, Center for Language and Speech Processing, Johns Hopkins University, Baltimore. Summer Workshop Final Report.

Chris Callison-Burch, Miles Osborne, and Philip Koehn. 2006. Re-evaluating the Role of Bleu in Machine Translation Research. In Proc. of the European Chapter of the Association for Computational Linguistics (EACL), Trento, Italy.

Mona Diab, Kadri Hacioglu, and Daniel Jurafsky. 2004. Automatic tagging of Arabic text: From raw text to base phrase chunks. *In Proceeding of NAACL-HLT 2004*. Boston, MA.

Thorsten Joachims, Making large-Scale SVM Learning Practical. Advances in Kernel Methods - Support Vector Learning, B. Schölkopf and C. Burges and A. Smola (ed.), MIT-Press, 1999.

Philipp Koehn. 2004. Pharaoh: a beam search decoder for phrase-based statistical machine translation models. *In Proceedings of the Sixth Conference of the Association for Machine Translation in the Americas*, pages 115–124

Philipp Koehn and Kevin Knight. 2003. Feature-rich statistical translation of noun phrases. In *Proceedings of 41st the Annual Meeting on Association for Computational Linguistics (ACL-2003)*, pages 311–318.

Franz Och, 2001, "Giza++: Training of statistical translation model": http://www.fjoch.com/GIZA++.html

Franz. Och and Hermann Ney. 2003. A systematic comparison of various statistical alignment models. *Computational Linguistics, 29(1):19–51.*

Kishore Papineni and Salim Roukos and Todd Ward and Wei-Jing Zhu. 2002. BLEU: a method for automatic evaluation of machine translation. In *Proceedings of the 40th Annual Meeting on Association for Computational Linguistics (ACL-2002)*, Pages 311-318, Philadelphia, PA

Nicola Ueffing and Hermann Ney. 2005. Application of word-level confidence measures in translation. In *Proceedings of the conference of the European Association of Machine Translation (EAMT 2005)* , pages 262–270, Budapest, Hungary

Richard Zens and Hermann Ney, 2006. N -Gram Posterior Probabilities for Statistical Machine Translation. In Proceedings of ACL Workshop on Statistical Machine Translation. 2006

Linguistic Features for Automatic Evaluation of Heterogenous MT Systems

Jesús Giménez and **Lluís Màrquez**
TALP Research Center, LSI Department
Universitat Politècnica de Catalunya
Jordi Girona Salgado 1–3, E-08034, Barcelona
{jgimenez,lluism}@lsi.upc.edu

Abstract

Evaluation results recently reported by Callison-Burch et al. (2006) and Koehn and Monz (2006), revealed that, in certain cases, the BLEU metric may not be a reliable MT quality indicator. This happens, for instance, when the systems under evaluation are based on different paradigms, and therefore, do not share the same lexicon. The reason is that, while MT quality aspects are diverse, BLEU limits its scope to the lexical dimension. In this work, we suggest using metrics which take into account linguistic features at more abstract levels. We provide experimental results showing that metrics based on deeper linguistic information (syntactic/shallow-semantic) are able to produce more reliable system rankings than metrics based on lexical matching alone, specially when the systems under evaluation are of a different nature.

1 Introduction

Most metrics used in the context of Automatic Machine Translation (MT) Evaluation are based on the assumption that *'acceptable'* translations tend to share the lexicon (i.e., word forms) in a predefined set of manual reference translations. This assumption works well in many cases. However, several results in recent MT evaluation campaigns have cast some doubts on its general validity. For instance, Callison-Burch et al. (2006) and Koehn and Monz (2006) reported and analyzed several cases of strong disagreement between system rankings provided by human assessors and those produced by the BLEU metric (Papineni et al., 2001). In particular, they noted that when the systems under evaluation are of a different nature (e.g., rule-based vs. statistical, human-aided vs. fully automatical, etc.) BLEU may not be a reliable MT quality indicator. The reason is that BLEU favours MT systems which share the expected reference lexicon (e.g., statistical systems), and penalizes those which use a different one.

Indeed, the underlying cause is much simpler. In general, lexical similarity is nor a sufficient neither a necessary condition so that two sentences convey the same meaning. On the contrary, natural languages are expressive and ambiguous at different levels. Consequently, the similarity between two sentences may involve different dimensions. In this work, we hypothesize that, in order to 'fairly' evaluate MT systems based on different paradigms, similarities at more abstract linguistic levels must be analyzed. For that purpose, we have compiled a rich set of metrics operating at the lexical, syntactic and shallow-semantic levels (see Section 2). We present a comparative study on the behavior of several metric representatives from each linguistic level in the context of some of the cases reported by Koehn and Monz (2006) and Callison-Burch et al. (2006) (see Section 3). We show that metrics based on deeper linguistic information (syntactic/shallow-semantic) are able to produce more reliable system rankings than those produced by metrics which limit their scope to the lexical dimension, specially when the systems under evaluation are of a different nature.

Proceedings of the Second Workshop on Statistical Machine Translation, pages 256–264,
Prague, June 2007.

2 A Heterogeneous Metric Set

For our experiments, we have compiled a representative set of metrics[1] at different linguistic levels. We have resorted to several existing metrics, and we have also developed new ones. Below, we group them according to the level at which they operate.

2.1 Lexical Similarity

Most of the current metrics operate at the lexical level. We have selected 7 representatives from different families which have been shown to obtain high levels of correlation with human assessments:

BLEU We use the default accumulated score up to the level of 4-grams (Papineni et al., 2001).

NIST We use the default accumulated score up to the level of 5-grams (Doddington, 2002).

GTM We set to 1 the value of the e parameter (Melamed et al., 2003).

METEOR We run all modules: 'exact', 'porter_stem', 'wn_stem' and 'wn_synonymy', in that order (Banerjee and Lavie, 2005).

ROUGE We used the ROUGE-S* variant (skip bigrams with no max-gap-length). Stemming is enabled (Lin and Och, 2004a).

mWER We use 1 − mWER (Nießen et al., 2000).

mPER We use 1 − mPER (Tillmann et al., 1997).

Let us note that ROUGE and METEOR may consider stemming (i.e., morphological variations). Additionally, METEOR may perform a lookup for synonyms in WordNet (Fellbaum, 1998).

2.2 Beyond Lexical Similarity

Modeling linguistic features at levels further than the lexical level requires the usage of more complex linguistic structures. We have defined what we call *'linguistic elements'* (LEs).

2.2.1 Linguistic Elements

LEs are linguistic units, structures, or relationships, such that a sentence may be partially seen as a 'bag' of LEs. Possible kinds of LEs are: word forms, parts-of-speech, dependency relationships, syntactic phrases, named entities, semantic roles, etc. Each LE may consist, in its turn, of one or more LEs, which we call 'items' inside the LE. For instance, a 'phrase' LE may consist of 'phrase' items, 'part-of-speech' (PoS) items, 'word form' items, etc. Items may be also combinations of LEs. For instance, a 'phrase' LE may be seen as a sequence of 'word-form:PoS' items.

2.2.2 Similarity Measures

We are interested in comparing linguistic structures, and linguistic units. LEs allow for comparisons at different granularity levels, and from different viewpoints. For instance, we might compare the semantic structure of two sentences (i.e., which actions, semantic arguments and adjuncts exist) or we might compare lexical units according to the semantic role they play inside the sentence. For that purpose, we use two very simple kinds of similarity measures over LEs: *'Overlapping'* and *'Matching'*. We provide a general definition:

Overlapping between items inside LEs, according to their type. Formally:

$$\text{Overlapping}(t) = \frac{\sum_{i \in items_t(hyp)} count'_{hyp}(i,t)}{\sum_{i \in items_t(ref)} count_{ref}(i,t)}$$

where t is the LE type[2], $items_t(s)$ refers to the set of items occurring inside LEs of type t in sentence s, $count_{ref}(i,t)$ denotes the number of times item i appears in the reference translation inside a LE of type t, and $count'_{hyp}(i,t)$ denotes the number of times i appears in the candidate translation inside a LE of type t, limited by the number of times i appears in the reference translation inside a LE of type t. Thus, 'Overlapping' provides a rough measure of the proportion of items inside elements of a certain type which have been 'successfully' translated. We also introduce a coarser metric, **'Overlapping(*)'**, which considers the uniformly averaged 'overlapping' over all types:

$$\text{Overlapping}(\star) = \frac{1}{|T|} \sum_{t \in T} \text{Overlapping}(t)$$

where T is the set of types.

[1] All metrics used in this work are publicly available inside the IQMT Framework (Giménez and Amigó, 2006). `http://www.lsi.upc.edu/~nlp/IQMT`

[2] LE types vary according to the specific LE class. For instance, in the case of Named Entities types may be 'PER' (i.e., person), 'LOC' (i.e., location), 'ORG' (i.e., organization), etc.

Matching between items inside LEs, according to their type. Its definition is analogous to the 'Overlapping' definition, but in this case the relative order of the items is important. All items inside the same element are considered as a single unit (i.e., a sequence in left-to-right order). In other words, we are computing the proportion of 'fully' translated elements, according to their type. We also introduce a coarser metric, **'Matching(*)'**, which considers the uniformly averaged 'Matching' over all types.

notes:

- 'Overlapping' and 'Matching' operate on the assumption of a single reference translation. The extension to the multi-reference setting is computed by assigning the maximum value attained over all human references individually.
- 'Overlapping' and 'Matching' are general metrics. We may apply them to specific scenarios by defining the class of linguistic elements and items to be used. Below, we instantiate these measures over several particular cases.

2.3 Shallow Syntactic Similarity

Metrics based on shallow parsing (*'SP'*) analyze similarities at the level of PoS-tagging, lemmatization, and base phrase chunking. Outputs and references are automatically annotated using state-of-the-art tools. PoS-tagging and lemmatization are provided by the SVM*Tool* package (Giménez and Màrquez, 2004), and base phrase chunking is provided by the P*hreco* software (Carreras et al., 2005). Tag sets for English are derived from the Penn Treebank (Marcus et al., 1993).

We instantiate 'Overlapping' over parts-of-speech and chunk types. The goal is to capture the proportion of lexical items correctly translated, according to their shallow syntactic realization:

SP-O_p-t Lexical overlapping according to the part-of-speech 't'. For instance, 'SP-O_p-NN' roughly reflects the proportion of correctly translated singular nouns. We also introduce a coarser metric, **'SP-O_p-*'** which computes average overlapping over all parts-of-speech.

SP-O_c-t Lexical overlapping according to the chunk type 't'. For instance, 'SP-O_c-NP' roughly reflects the successfully translated proportion of noun phrases. We also introduce a coarser metric, **'SP-O_c-*'** which considers the average overlapping over all chunk types.

At a more abstract level, we use the NIST metric (Doddington, 2002) to compute accumulated/individual scores over sequences of:

Lemmas – **SP-NIST(i)$_l$-n**
Parts-of-speech – **SP-NIST(i)$_p$-n**
Base phrase chunks – **SP-NIST(i)$_c$-n**

For instance, **'SP-NIST$_l$-5'** corresponds to the accumulated NIST score for lemma n-grams up to length 5, whereas 'SP-NISTi$_p$-5' corresponds to the individual NIST score for PoS 5-grams.

2.4 Syntactic Similarity

We have incorporated, with minor modifications, some of the syntactic metrics described by Liu and Gildea (2005) and Amigó et al. (2006) based on dependency and constituency parsing.

2.4.1 On Dependency Parsing (DP)

'DP' metrics capture similarities between dependency trees associated to automatic and reference translations. Dependency trees are provided by the MINIPAR dependency parser (Lin, 1998). Similarities are captured from different viewpoints:

DP-HWC(i)-l This metric corresponds to the HWC metric presented by Liu and Gildea (2005). All head-word chains are retrieved. The fraction of matching head-word chains of a given length, 'l', is computed. We have slightly modified this metric in order to distinguish three different variants according to the type of items head-word chains may consist of:

Lexical forms – **DP-HWC(i)$_w$-l**
Grammatical categories – **DP-HWC(i)$_c$-l**
Grammatical relationships – **DP-HWC(i)$_r$-l**

Average accumulated scores up to a given chain length may be used as well. For instance, 'DP-HWCi$_w$-4' retrieves the proportion of matching length-4 word-chains, whereas **'DP-HWC$_w$-4'** retrieves average accumulated proportion of matching word-chains up to length-4. Analogously, **'DP-HWC$_c$-4'**, and **'DP-HWC$_r$-4'** compute average accumulated proportion of category/relationship chains up to length-4.

DP-$O_l|O_c|O_r$ These metrics correspond exactly to the LEVEL, GRAM and TREE metrics introduced by Amigó et al. (2006).

- **DP-O_l-l** Overlapping between words hanging at level 'l', or deeper.
- **DP-O_c-t** Overlapping between words *directly hanging* from terminal nodes (i.e. grammatical categories) of type 't'.
- **DP-O_r-t** Overlapping between words ruled by non-terminal nodes (i.e. grammatical relationships) of type 't'.

Node types are determined by grammatical categories and relationships defined by MINIPAR. For instance, 'DP-O_r-s' reflects lexical overlapping between subtrees of type 's' (subject). 'DP-O_c-A' reflects lexical overlapping between terminal nodes of type 'A' (Adjective/Adverbs). 'DP-O_l-4' reflects lexical overlapping between nodes hanging at level 4 or deeper. Additionally, we consider three coarser metrics (**'DP-O_l-*'**, **'DP-O_c-*'** and **'DP-O_r-*'**) which correspond to the uniformly averaged values over all levels, categories, and relationships, respectively.

2.4.2 On Constituency Parsing (CP)

'CP' metrics capture similarities between constituency parse trees associated to automatic and reference translations. Constituency trees are provided by the Charniak-Johnson's Max-Ent reranking parser (Charniak and Johnson, 2005).

CP-STM(i)-l This metric corresponds to the STM metric presented by Liu and Gildea (2005). All syntactic subpaths in the candidate and the reference trees are retrieved. The fraction of matching subpaths of a given length, 'l', is computed. For instance, 'CP-STMi-5' retrieves the proportion of length-5 matching subpaths. Average accumulated scores may be computed as well. For instance, **'CP-STM-9'** retrieves average accumulated proportion of matching subpaths up to length-9.

2.5 Shallow-Semantic Similarity

We have designed two new families of metrics, 'NE' and 'SR', which are intended to capture similarities over Named Entities (NEs) and Semantic Roles (SRs), respectively.

2.5.1 On Named Entities (NE)

'NE' metrics analyze similarities between automatic and reference translations by comparing the NEs which occur in them. Sentences are automatically annotated using the *BIOS* package (Surdeanu et al., 2005). BIOS requires at the input shallow parsed text, which is obtained as described in Section 2.3. See the list of NE types in Table 1.

Type	Description
ORG	Organization
PER	Person
LOC	Location
MISC	Miscellaneous
O	Not-a-NE
DATE	Temporal expressions
NUM	Numerical expressions
ANGLE_QUANTITY DISTANCE_QUANTITY SIZE_QUANTITY SPEED_QUANTITY TEMPERATURE_QUANTITY WEIGHT_QUANTITY	Quantities
METHOD MONEY LANGUAGE PERCENT PROJECT SYSTEM	Other

Table 1: Named Entity types.

We define two types of metrics:

NE-O_e-t Lexical overlapping between NEs according to their type t. For instance, 'NE-O_e-PER' reflects lexical overlapping between NEs of type 'PER' (i.e., person), which provides a rough estimate of the successfully translated proportion of person names. The **'NE-O_e-*'** metric considers the average lexical overlapping over all NE types. This metric includes the NE type 'O' (i.e., Not-a-NE). We introduce another variant, **'NE-O_e-**'**, which considers only actual NEs.

NE-M_e-t Lexical matching between NEs according to their type t. For instance, 'NE-M_e-LOC' reflects the proportion of fully translated NEs of type 'LOC' (i.e., location). The **'NE-M_e-*'**

metric considers the average lexical matching over all NE types, this time excluding type 'O'.

Other authors have measured MT quality over NEs in the recent literature. In particular, the **'NE-M_e-*'** metric is similar to the **'NEE'** metric defined by Reeder et al. (2001).

2.5.2 On Semantic Roles (SR)

'SR' metrics analyze similarities between automatic and reference translations by comparing the SRs (i.e., arguments and adjuncts) which occur in them. Sentences are automatically annotated using the SwiRL package (Màrquez et al., 2005). This package requires at the input shallow parsed text enriched with NEs, which is obtained as described in Section 2.5.1. See the list of SR types in Table 2.

Type	Description
A0 A1 A2 A3 A4 A5	arguments associated with a verb predicate, defined in the PropBank Frames scheme.
AA	Causative agent
AM-ADV	Adverbial (general-purpose) adjunct
AM-CAU	Causal adjunct
AM-DIR	Directional adjunct
AM-DIS	Discourse marker
AM-EXT	Extent adjunct
AM-LOC	Locative adjunct
AM-MNR	Manner adjunct
AM-MOD	Modal adjunct
AM-NEG	Negation marker
AM-PNC	Purpose and reason adjunct
AM-PRD	Predication adjunct
AM-REC	Reciprocal adjunct
AM-TMP	Temporal adjunct

Table 2: Semantic Roles.

We define three types of metrics:

SR-O_r-t Lexical overlapping between SRs according to their type t. For instance, 'SR-O_r-A0' reflects lexical overlapping between 'A0' arguments. **'SR-O_r-*'** considers the average lexical overlapping over all SR types.

SR-M_r-t Lexical matching between SRs according to their type t. For instance, the metric 'SR-M_r-AM-MOD' reflects the proportion of fully translated modal adjuncts. The **'SR-M_r-*'** metric considers the average lexical matching over all SR types.

SR-O_r This metric reflects 'role overlapping', i.e.. overlapping between semantic roles independently from their lexical realization.

Note that in the same sentence several verbs, with their respective SRs, may co-occur. However, the metrics described above do not distinguish between SRs associated to different verbs. In order to account for such a distinction we introduce a more restrictive version of these metrics ('SR-M_{rv}-t', 'SR-O_{rv}-t', **'SR-M_{rv}-*'**, **'SR-O_{rv}-*'**, and **'SR-O_{rv}'**), which require SRs to be associated to the same verb.

3 Experimental Work

In this section, we study the behavior of some of the metrics described in Section 2, according to the linguistic level at which they operate. We have selected a set of coarse-grained metric variants (i.e., accumulated/average scores over linguistic units and structures of different kinds)[3]. We analyze some of the cases reported by Koehn and Monz (2006) and Callison-Burch et al. (2006). We distinguish different evaluation contexts. In Section 3.1, we study the case of a single reference translation being available. In principle, this scenario should diminish the reliability of metrics based on lexical matching alone, and favour metrics based on deeper linguistic features. In Section 3.2, we study the case of several reference translations available. This scenario should alleviate the deficiencies caused by the shallowness of metrics based on lexical matching. We also analyze separately the case of *'homogeneous'* systems (i.e., all systems being of the same nature), and the case of *'heterogenous'* systems (i.e., there exist systems based on different paradigms).

As to the metric meta-evaluation criterion, the two most prominent criteria are:

Human Acceptability Metrics are evaluated on the basis of correlation with human evaluators.

Human Likeness Metrics are evaluated in terms of descriptive power, i.e., their ability to distinguish between human and automatic translations (Lin and Och, 2004b; Amigó et al., 2005).

In our case, metrics are evaluated on the basis of 'Human Acceptability'. Specifically, we use Pearson correlation coefficients between metric scores

[3]When computing 'lexical' overlapping/matching, we use lemmas instead of word forms.

and the average sum of adequacy and fluency assessments at the document level. The reason is that meta-evaluation based on 'Human Likeness' requires the availability of heterogenous test beds (i.e., representative sets of automatic outputs and human references), which, unfortunately, is not the case of all the tasks under study. First, because most translation systems are statistical. Second, because in most cases only one reference translation is available.

3.1 Single-reference Scenario

We use some of the test beds corresponding to the *"NAACL 2006 Workshop on Statistical Machine Translation" (WMT 2006)* (Koehn and Monz, 2006). Since linguistic features described in Section 2 are so far implemented only for the case of English being the target language, among the 12 translation tasks available, we studied only the 6 tasks corresponding to the Foreign-to-English direction. A single reference translation is available. System outputs consist of 2000 and 1064 sentences for the 'in-domain' and 'out-of-domain' test beds, respectively. In each case, human assessments on adequacy and fluency are available for a subset of systems and sentences. Table 3 shows the number of sentences assessed in each case. Each sentence was evaluated by two different human judges. System scores have been obtained by averaging over all sentence scores.

	in	out	sys
French-to-English	2,247	1,274	11/14
German-to-English	2,401	1,535	10/12
Spanish-to-English	1,944	1,070	11/15

Table 3: WMT 2006. 'in' and 'out' columns show the number of sentences assessed for the 'in-domain' and 'out-of-domain' subtasks. The 'sys' column shows the number of systems counting on human assessments with respect to the total number of systems which presented to each task.

Evaluation of Heterogeneous Systems

In four of the six translation tasks under study, all the systems are statistical except *'Systran'*, which is rule-based. This is the case of the German/French-to-English in-domain/out-of-domain tasks. Table 4 shows correlation with human assessments for some metric representatives at different linguistic levels.

Level	Metric	fr2en in	fr2en out	de2en in	de2en out
Lexical	1-PER	0.73	0.64	0.57	0.46
	1-WER	0.73	0.73	0.32	0.38
	BLEU	0.71	0.87	0.60	0.67
	NIST	0.74	0.82	0.56	0.63
	GTM	0.84	0.86	0.12	0.70
	METEOR	**0.92**	**0.95**	**0.76**	**0.81**
	ROUGE	0.85	0.89	0.65	**0.79**
Shallow Syntactic	SP-O_p-*	**0.81**	0.88	0.64	0.71
	SP-O_c-*	**0.81**	0.89	0.65	0.75
	SP-NIST$_l$-5	0.75	0.81	0.56	0.64
	SP-NIST$_p$-5	0.75	**0.91**	**0.77**	**0.77**
	SP-NIST$_c$-5	0.73	0.88	0.71	0.54
Syntactic	DP-HWC$_w$-4	0.76	0.88	0.64	0.74
	DP-HWC$_c$-4	**0.93**	**0.97**	0.88	0.72
	DP-HWC$_r$-4	**0.92**	**0.96**	**0.91**	0.76
	DP-O_l-*	0.87	0.94	0.84	0.84
	DP-O_c-*	0.91	0.95	0.88	**0.87**
	DP-O_r-*	0.87	**0.97**	**0.91**	**0.88**
	CP-STM-9	**0.93**	0.95	**0.93**	**0.87**
Shallow Semantic	NE-M_e-*	0.80	0.79	**0.93**	0.63
	NE-O_e-*	0.79	0.76	**0.91**	0.59
	NE-O_e-**	0.81	0.87	0.63	0.70
	SR-M_r-*	0.83	**0.95**	**0.92**	0.84
	SR-O_r-*	0.89	**0.95**	0.88	0.90
	SR-O_r	**0.95**	0.85	0.80	0.75
	SR-M_{rv}-*	0.77	0.92	0.72	0.85
	SR-O_{rv}-*	0.81	0.93	0.76	**0.94**
	SR-O_{rv}	0.84	0.93	0.81	**0.92**

Table 4: WMT 2006. Evaluation of Heterogeneous Systems. French-to-English (fr2en) / German-to-English (de2en), in-domain and out-of-domain.

Although the four cases are different, we have identified several regularities. For instance, BLEU and, in general, all metrics based on lexical matching alone, except METEOR, obtain significantly lower levels of correlation than metrics based on deeper linguistic similarities. The problem with lexical metrics is that they are unable to capture the actual quality of the 'Systran' system. Interestingly, METEOR obtains a higher correlation, which, in the case of French-to-English, rivals the top-scoring metrics based on deeper linguistic features. The reason, however, does not seem to be related to its additional linguistic operations (i.e., stemming or synonymy lookup), but rather to the METEOR matching strategy itself (unigram precision/recall).

Metrics at the shallow syntactic level are in the same range of lexical metrics. At the properly syntactic level, metrics obtain in most cases high correlation coefficients. However, the 'DP-HWC$_w$-4' metric, which, although from the viewpoint of dependency relationships, still considers only lexical matching, obtains a lower level of correlation. This reinforces the idea that metrics based on rewarding long n-grams matchings may not be a reliable quality indicator in these cases.

At the level of shallow semantics, while 'NE' metrics are not equally useful in all cases, 'SR' metrics prove very effective. For instance, correlation attained by 'SR-O_r-*' reveals that it is important to translate lexical items according to the semantic role they play inside the sentence. Moreover, correlation attained by the 'SR-M_r-*' metric is a clear indication that in order to achieve a high quality, it is important to 'fully' translate 'whole' semantic structures (i.e., arguments/adjuncts). The existence of all the semantic structures ('SR-O_r'), specially associated to the same verb ('SR-O_{rv}'), is also important.

Evaluation of Homogeneous Systems

In the two remaining tasks, Spanish-to-English in-domain/out-of-domain, all the systems are statistical. Table 5 shows correlation with human assessments for some metric representatives. In this case, BLEU proves very effective, both in-domain and out-of-domain. Indeed, all metrics based on lexical matching obtain high levels of correlation with human assessments. However, still metrics based on deeper linguistic analysis attain in most cases higher correlation coefficients, although not as significantly higher as in the case of heterogeneous systems.

Level	Metric	es2en	
		in	out
Lexical	1-PER	0.82	0.78
	1-WER	0.88	0.83
	BLEU	**0.89**	**0.87**
	NIST	0.88	0.84
	GTM	0.86	0.80
	METEOR	0.84	0.81
	ROUGE	**0.89**	0.83
Shallow Syntactic	SP-O_p-*	0.88	0.80
	SP-O_c-*	**0.89**	0.84
	SP-NIST$_l$-5	0.88	0.85
	SP-NIST$_p$-5	0.85	**0.86**
	SP-NIST$_c$-5	0.84	0.83
Syntactic	DP-HWC$_w$-4	**0.94**	0.83
	DP-HWC$_c$-4	0.91	0.87
	DP-HWC$_r$-4	0.91	**0.88**
	DP-O_l-*	0.91	0.84
	DP-O_c-*	0.88	0.83
	DP-O_r-*	0.88	0.84
	CP-STM-9	0.89	0.86
Shallow Semantic	NE-M_e-*	0.75	0.76
	NE-O_e-*	0.71	0.71
	NE-O_e-**	0.88	0.80
	SR-M_r-*	0.86	0.82
	SR-O_r-*	**0.92**	**0.92**
	SR-O_r	0.91	**0.92**
	SR-M_{rv}-*	0.89	0.88
	SR-O_{rv}-*	0.91	**0.92**
	SR-O_{rv}	0.91	0.91

Table 5: WMT 2006. Evaluation of Homogeneous Systems. Spanish-to-English (es2en), in-domain and out-of-domain.

3.2 Multiple-reference Scenario

We study the case reported by Callison-Burch et al. (2006) in the context of the Arabic-to-English exercise of the *"2005 NIST MT Evaluation Campaign"*[4] (Le and Przybocki, 2005). In this case all systems are statistical but *'LinearB'*, a human-aided MT system (Callison-Burch, 2005). Five reference translations are available. System outputs consist of 1056 sentences. We obtained permission[5] to use 7 system outputs. For six of these systems we counted on a subjective manual evaluation based on adequacy and fluency for a subset of 266 sentences (i.e., 1596 sentences were assessed). Each sentence was evaluated by two different human judges. System scores have been obtained by averaging over all sentence scores.

Table 6 shows the level of correlation with human assessments for some metric representatives (see 'ALL' column). In this case, lexical metrics obtain extremely low levels of correlation. Again, the problem is that lexical metrics are unable to capture the actual quality of 'LinearB'. At the shallow syntactic level, only metrics which do not consider any lexical information ('SP-NIST$_p$-5' and 'SP-NIST$_c$-5') attain a significantly higher quality. At the properly syntactic level, all metrics attain a higher correlation. At the shallow semantic level, again, while 'NE' metrics are not specially useful, 'SR' metrics prove very effective.

On the other hand, if we remove 'LinearB' (see

[4] `http://www.nist.gov/speech/tests/summaries/2005/mt05.htm`

[5] Due to data confidentiality, we contacted each participant individually and asked for permission to use their data. A number of groups and companies responded positively: University of Southern California Information Sciences Institute (ISI), University of Maryland (UMD), Johns Hopkins University & University of Cambridge (JHU-CU), IBM, University of Edinburgh, MITRE and LinearB.

Level	Metric	ar2en	
		ALL	SMT
Lexical	1-PER	-0.35	0.75
	1-WER	-0.50	0.69
	BLEU	**0.06**	0.83
	NIST	0.04	0.81
	GTM	0.03	**0.92**
	ROUGE	-0.17	0.81
	METEOR	0.05	0.86
Shallow Syntactic	SP-O_p-*	0.05	0.84
	SP-O_c-*	0.12	0.89
	SP-NIST$_l$-5	0.04	0.82
	SP-NIST$_p$-5	0.42	0.89
	SP-NIST$_c$-5	0.44	0.68
Syntactic	DP-HWC$_w$-4	0.52	0.86
	DP-HWC$_c$-4	0.80	0.75
	DP-HWC$_r$-4	**0.88**	0.86
	DP-O_l-*	0.51	0.94
	DP-O_c-*	0.53	0.91
	DP-O_r-*	0.72	0.93
	CP-STM-9	0.74	**0.95**
Shallow Semantic	NE-M_e-*	0.33	0.78
	NE-O_e-*	0.24	0.82
	NE-O_e-**	0.04	0.81
	SR-M_r-*	**0.72**	**0.96**
	SR-O_r-*	0.61	0.87
	SR-O_r	0.66	0.75
	SR-M_{rv}-*	0.68	**0.97**
	SR-O_{rv}-*	0.47	0.84
	SR-O_{rv}	0.46	0.81

Table 6: NIST 2005. Arabic-to-English (ar2en) exercise. 'ALL' refers to the evaluation of all systems. 'SMT' refers to the evaluation of statistical systems alone (i.e., removing 'LinearB').

'SMT' column), lexical metrics attain a much higher correlation, in the same range of metrics based on deeper linguistic information. However, still metrics based on syntactic parsing, and semantic roles, exhibit a slightly higher quality.

4 Conclusions

We have presented a comparative study on the behavior of a wide set of metrics for automatic MT evaluation at different linguistic levels (lexical, shallow-syntactic, syntactic, and shallow-semantic) under different scenarios. We have shown, through empirical evidence, that linguistic features at more abstract levels may provide more reliable system rankings, specially when the systems under evaluation do not share the same lexicon.

We strongly believe that future MT evaluation campaigns should benefit from these results, by including metrics at different linguistic levels. For instance, the following set could be used:

{ *'DP-HWC$_r$-4', 'DP-O_c-*', 'DP-O_l-*', 'DP-O_r-*', 'CP-STM-9', 'SR-O_r-*', 'SR-O_{rv}'* }

All these metrics are among the top-scoring in all the translation tasks studied. However, none of these metrics provides, in isolation, a *'global'* measure of quality. Indeed, all these metrics focus on *'partial'* aspects of quality. We believe that, in order to perform *'global'* evaluations, different quality dimensions should be integrated into a single measure of quality. With that purpose, we are currently exploring several metric combination strategies. Preliminary results, based on the QUEEN measure inside the QARLA Framework (Amigó et al., 2005), indicate that metrics at different linguistic levels may be robustly combined.

Experimental results also show that metrics requiring linguistic analysis seem very robust against parsing errors committed by automatic linguistic processors, at least at the document level. That is very interesting, taking into account that, while reference translations are supposedly well formed, that is not always the case of automatic translations. However, it remains pending to test the behaviour at the sentence level, which could be very useful for error analysis. Moreover, relying on automatic processors implies two other important limitations. First, these tools are not available for all languages. Second, usually they are too slow to allow for massive evaluations, as required, for instance, in the case of system development. In the future, we plan to incorporate more accurate, and possibly faster, linguistic processors, also for languages other than English, as they become publicly available.

Acknowledgements

This research has been funded by the Spanish Ministry of Education and Science, projects OpenMT (TIN2006-15307-C03-02) and TRANGRAM (TIN2004-07925-C03-02). We are recognized as a Quality Research Group (2005 SGR-00130) by DURSI, the Research Department of the Catalan Government. Authors are thankful to the WMT organizers for providing such valuable test beds. Authors are also thankful to Audrey Le (from NIST), and to the 2005 NIST MT Evaluation Campaign participants who agreed to share their system outputs and human assessments for the purpose of this research.

References

Enrique Amigó, Julio Gonzalo, Anselmo Peñas, and Felisa Verdejo. 2005. QARLA: a Framework for the Evaluation of Automatic Sumarization. In *Proceedings of the 43th Annual Meeting of the Association for Computational Linguistics*.

Enrique Amigó, Jesús Giménez, Julio Gonzalo, and Lluís Màrquez. 2006. MT Evaluation: Human-Like vs. Human Acceptable. In *Proceedings of COLING-ACL06*.

Satanjeev Banerjee and Alon Lavie. 2005. METEOR: An Automatic Metric for MT Evaluation with Improved Correlation with Human Judgments. In *Proceedings of ACL Workshop on Intrinsic and Extrinsic Evaluation Measures for Machine Translation and/or Summarization*.

Chris Callison-Burch, Miles Osborne, and Philipp Koehn. 2006. Re-evaluating the Role of BLEU in Machine Translation Research. In *Proceedings of EACL*.

Chris Callison-Burch. 2005. Linear B system description for the 2005 NIST MT evaluation exercise. In *Proceedings of the NIST 2005 Machine Translation Evaluation Workshop*.

Xavier Carreras, Lluís Márquez, and Jorge Castro. 2005. Filtering-ranking perceptron learning for partial parsing. *Machine Learning*, 59:1–31.

Eugene Charniak and Mark Johnson. 2005. Coarse-to-fine n-best parsing and MaxEnt discriminative reranking. In *Proceedings of ACL*.

George Doddington. 2002. Automatic evaluation of machine translation quality using n-gram co-occurrence statistics. In *Proceedings of the 2nd IHLT*.

C. Fellbaum, editor. 1998. *WordNet. An Electronic Lexical Database*. The MIT Press.

Jesús Giménez and Enrique Amigó. 2006. IQMT: A Framework for Automatic Machine Translation Evaluation. In *Proceedings of the 5th LREC*.

Jesús Giménez and Lluís Màrquez. 2004. SVMTool: A general POS tagger generator based on Support Vector Machines. In *Proceedings of 4th LREC*.

Philipp Koehn and Christof Monz. 2006. Manual and Automatic Evaluation of Machine Translation between European Languages. In *Proceedings of the Workshop on Statistical Machine Translation*, pages 102–121.

Audrey Le and Mark Przybocki. 2005. NIST 2005 machine translation evaluation official results. Technical report, NIST, August.

Chin-Yew Lin and Franz Josef Och. 2004a. Automatic Evaluation of Machine Translation Quality Using Longest Common Subsequence and Skip-Bigram Statics. In *Proceedings of ACL*.

Chin-Yew Lin and Franz Josef Och. 2004b. ORANGE: a Method for Evaluating Automatic Evaluation Metrics for Machine Translation. In *Proceedings of COLING*.

Dekang Lin. 1998. Dependency-based Evaluation of MINIPAR. In *Proceedings of the Workshop on the Evaluation of Parsing Systems*.

Ding Liu and Daniel Gildea. 2005. Syntactic Features for Evaluation of Machine Translation. In *Proceedings of ACL Workshop on Intrinsic and Extrinsic Evaluation Measures for Machine Translation and/or Summarization*.

Mitchell P. Marcus, Beatrice Santorini, and Mary Ann Marcinkiewicz. 1993. Building a large annotated corpus of english: The penn treebank. *Computational Linguistics*, 19(2):313–330.

I. Dan Melamed, Ryan Green, and Joseph P. Turian. 2003. Precision and Recall of Machine Translation. In *Proceedings of HLT/NAACL*.

Lluís Màrquez, Mihai Surdeanu, Pere Comas, and Jordi Turmo. 2005. Robust Combination Strategy for Semantic Role Labeling. In *Proceedings of HLT/EMNLP*.

S. Nießen, F.J. Och, G. Leusch, and H. Ney. 2000. Evaluation Tool for Machine Translation: Fast Evaluation for MT Research. In *Proceedings of the 2nd LREC*.

Kishore Papineni, Salim Roukos, Todd Ward, and Wei-Jing Zhu. 2001. Bleu: a method for automatic evaluation of machine translation, rc22176, ibm. Technical report, IBM T.J. Watson Research Center.

Florence Reeder, Keith Miller, Jennifer Doyon, and John White. 2001. The Naming of Things and the Confusion of Tongues: an MT Metric. In *Proceedings of the Workshop on MT Evaluation "Who did what to whom?" at MT Summit VIII*, pages 55–59.

Mihai Surdeanu, Jordi Turmo, and Eli Comelles. 2005. Named Entity Recognition from Spontaneous Open-Domain Speech. In *Proceedings of the 9th International Conference on Speech Communication and Technology (Interspeech)*.

C. Tillmann, S. Vogel, H. Ney, A. Zubiaga, and H. Sawaf. 1997. Accelerated DP based Search for Statistical Translation. In *Proceedings of European Conference on Speech Communication and Technology*.

Author Index

Agarwal, Abhaya, 228
Ahrenberg, Lars, 181

Banchs, Rafael E., 96, 167
Birch, Alexandra, 9
Bojar, Ondřej, 232

Callison-Burch, Chris, 136
Casacuberta, Francisco, 56
Cettolo, Mauro, 88
Chen, Yu, 193
Civera, Jorge, 177
Crego, Josep M., 167

Dorr, Bonnie, 120
Dugast, Loïc, 220
Durgar El-Kahlout, Ilknur, 25
Dyer, Christopher J., 207

Eisele, Andreas, 193

Fazil Ayan, Necip, 120
Federico, Marcello, 88
Federmann, Christian, 193
Fordyce, Cameron, 136
Foster, George, 17, 128

Giménez, Jesús, 159, 256
González, M. Teresa, 56

Hasler, Eva, 193
He, Xiaodong, 72, 80
Hearst, Marti, 212
Hildebrand, Silja, 197
Holmqvist, Maria, 181
Hwa, Rebecca, 248

Isabelle, Pierre, 203

Jellinghaus, Michael, 193
Joanis, Eric, 17
Johnson, Howard, 185
Juan, Alfons, 177

Kashani, Mehdi M., 17
Khalilov, Maxim, 167
Koehn, Philipp, 9, 136, 220, 224
Kuhn, Roland, 17, 128, 203

Lambert, Patrik, 167
Larkin, Samuel, 185
Lavie, Alon, 228
Leusch, Gregor, 96
Liang, Huashen, 64
Lin, Chin-Yew, 240
Lin, Shouxun, 40
Liu, Qun, 40

Madnani, Nitin, 120
Mahajan, Milind, 72
Mario, José B., 167
Màrquez, Lluís, 159, 256
Menezes, Arul, 1
Mohit, Behrang, 248
Monz, Christof, 136
Moore, Robert, 112

Nakov, Preslav, 212
Ney, Hermann, 33, 48, 96
Nguyen, Patrick, 72
Niehues, Jan, 197

Oflazer, Kemal, 25
Osborne, Miles, 9
Owczarzak, Karolina, 104

Paulik, Matthias, 197, 216
Pérez, Alicia, 56
Peter, Jan-Thorsten, 33
Popovic, Maja, 48
Popowich, Fred, 17

Quirk, Chris, 1, 112

R. Costa-jussià, Marta, 167, 171
R. Fonollosa, José A., 167, 171
Resnik, Philip, 120
Rottmann, Kay, 197

Schroeder, Josh, 136, 224
Schwenk, Holger, 189
Senellart, Jean, 220
Simard, Michel, 185, 203
Stymne, Sara, 181
Sun, Jiadong, 64

Theison, Silke, 193
Torres, M. Inés, 56

Ueffing, Nicola, 185, 203

van Genabith, Josef, 104
Venugopal, Ashish, 216
Vilar, David, 33, 96
Vogel, Stephan, 197, 216

Way, Andy, 104

Xiong, Deyi, 40

Ye, Yang, 240

Zhao, Tiejun, 64
Zhou, Ming, 240
Zollmann, Andreas, 216